# PRINCIPLES

# OF

# WILLS, TRUSTS AND ESTATES

By

## William M. McGovern, Jr.
*Professor of Law*
*University of California, Los Angeles*

## Sheldon F. Kurtz
*Percy Bordwell Professor of Law and Professor of Surgery*
*University of Iowa*

## CONCISE HORNBOOK SERIES®

Mat #40302878

*Concise Hornbook Series*, *WESTLAW* and West Group are trademarks registered in the U.S. Patent and Trademark Office.

© 2005 Thomson/West
      610 Opperman Drive
      P.O. Box 64526
      St. Paul, MN 55164–0526
      1–800–328–9352

Printed in the United States of America
**ISBN** 0–314–15617–8

TEXT IS PRINTED ON 10% POST CONSUMER RECYCLED PAPER

# Preface

This book is an abridged and slightly revised version of McGovern & Kurtz, Wills, Trusts and Estates including Taxation and Future Interests (3d edition 2004). A reader of this book who seeks additional information on any topic can turn to the larger version. This is easy because the section numbers in both versions are the same.

*

# Summary of Contents

*

# Table of Contents

# PRINCIPLES
## OF
# WILLS, TRUSTS AND ESTATES

\*

# Chapter 1

# TERMINOLOGY AND CHOICE OF LAW

*Table of Sections*

## § 1.1  Terminology

This section lists alphabetically terms which recur elsewhere in the book. A brief definition of the term is given, with a reference to the section in where the term is more fully discussed.

*abatement*  The reduction of devises in a will in order to pay claims against the estate. See Section 8.2.

*ademption*  The defeat of specific devises by transfer or loss of the devised property after the will is executed. See Section 8.1.

*administrator*  Someone appointed to administer the estate of a decedent who died intestate, or whose will failed to designate effectively an executor. The rules for choosing administrators are discussed in Section 12.4.

*advancement*  A gift made by a person which is taken into account if the donor later dies intestate. See Section 2.6.

*ancillary administration*  Administration of assets outside the state where a decedent was domiciled at death. See Section 12.3.

*annuity*  A provision for periodic fixed payments to a person, usually for life. The trustee of a trust may be directed to pay such an annuity. Annuities can also be created by a contract between a company and a person who buys an annuity, either for the purchaser or for another. In this situation the annuity functions like life insurance; by promising to pay the agreed amount for the life of the

1

annuitant the company assumes the risk that the payments may total more than the original price. Insurance proceeds are often paid out in the form of an annuity after the death of the insured.

*ante-nuptial agreement*   Also known as prenuptial, an agreement between persons about to marry which may alter the respective rights of a spouse in the other's property. See Section 3.9.

*apportionment*   A rule by which a burden on an estate, such as death taxes, is shared pro rata by all the beneficiaries of the estate. See Section 8.2.

*attest, attestation*   Bear witness, especially as to a will. See Section 4.3.

*bequeath, bequest*   A somewhat antiquated name for a gift of personal property in a will. See *devise.*

*bona fide purchaser*   A person who buys property believing in good faith that the other is the owner of it. See Section 9.2, 12.8.

*bypass trust*   A trust whose assets are not included in the gross or probate estate of the person(s) designated as the life beneficiary. See Section 9.3.

*child*   Many problems arise from this simple word. Does it include an adopted child? a step child? See Section 2.10. A child born out of wedlock? See Section 2.9. A grandchild? See Section 10.1.

*class gifts*   A gift to a group, like "children", as distinguished from a gift to individuals, like "John and Mary". See Section 8.3.

*clear and convincing evidence*   A requirement of proof intermediate between a preponderance of the evidence, the ordinary rule in civil cases, and proof beyond a reasonable doubt, which is required to convict in criminal cases. The Uniform Probate Code allows wills which fail to meet the formal requirements if there is "clear and convincing evidence" that the decedent intended the document to be a will.[1]

*codicil*   A document used to modify a will. Codicils are usually shorter than wills, but they are subject to the same formal requirements. "Republication" by codicil is discussed in Section 6.2.

*common trust fund*   A fund maintained by a professional trustee for investing the funds of many trusts in order to reduce costs and facilitate diversification. See Section 12.7.

*community property*   The system of property ownership for spouses in 8 American states and many foreign countries. It affects

§ 1.1

1. Unif. Prob. Code § 2–503. See also *id.* § 6–211(b) (ownership of joint account based on contributions unless clear and convincing evidence of a different intent).

intestate succession and limits one spouse's right to devise or give away property. See Section 3.8.

*confidential relationship* The basis for a presumption that a will or gift was caused by undue influence. See Section 7.3. Also the basis for an exception to the requirement that trusts of land must be in writing. See Section 6.4.

*conservator* Under the UPC a conservator is "person appointed by a Court to manage the estate of a protected person,"[2] either a minor, or an adult who has been judged incompetent. The conservator only deals with the conservatee's property. In California, on the other hand, there may be a conservator of the *person* of an adult, and persons appointed to manage a minor's property are called "guardians of the estate" rather than conservators.[3] Both guardians and conservators are fiduciaries, and many of the rules governing trustees also apply to them, but there are also differences. See Section 9.2.

*constructive trust* Commonly distinguished from "express" trusts which are based on the intent of the settlor whereas constructive trusts are said to be imposed regardless of intent in order to prevent unjust enrichment, e.g. on a thief.[4] However, constructive trusts are often imposed to carry out an intent which was informally expressed, as in oral trusts of land. See Sections 6.1, 6.4.

*contingent remainder* A future interest which is not necessarily going to take effect, as in a gift "to A for life, then to her children who survive her." While A is alive, one cannot know whether or not she will have children who survive her. Contingent remainders are contrasted with "vested" remainders, e.g. "To A for life, then to B." Even though B cannot take possession while A is alive, if he dies before A, the property will be part of B's estate. See Section 10.1.

*corpus* Another term for the principal of a trust as distinguished from its income. See Section 9.4.

*custodian* A fiduciary designated to handle property under the Uniform Transfers to Minors Act. See Section 9.2.

*cy pres* The term is most often used to describe the modification of charitable trusts. See Section 9.7. More recently, the term has been used for modifying a private trust which violates the Rule against Perpetuities. See Section 11.4.

*death taxes* The generic term for taxes occasioned by death. The most common types are the estate tax, imposed by the United States and several states, and "inheritance" taxes imposed by some

---

**2.** *Id.,* § 1–201(8). *See also* Unif. Trust Code § 103(4).

**3.** Cal. Prob. Code § 1510, 1800.3.

**4.** *Restatement, Third, of Trusts* § 1, comm. e (2001).

states. Inheritance taxes are based on the amount passing to each successor, with different rates for different kinds of successor, *e.g.* children are taxed at a lower rate than unrelated devisees. The estate tax, on the other hand, is based on the estate as a whole, and is not affected by who gets the property, except there are deductions for gifts to spouses and charities. A survey of the federal estate tax appears in Chapter 15.3.

*deed*   Although in ordinary English, the word can refer to any act, in this book it usually means a written instrument transferring property (usually land). See Section 4.5.

*descend*   Traditionally land was said to "descend" to the heirs of a person who died intestate, whereas personal property was "distributed" to the intestate's next of kin. Vestiges of this terminology survive but the rules governing both types of property are the same nearly everywhere today. Do not confuse "descend" and "descendant." Property may "descend" to a collateral relative or spouse who is not a "descendant."

*descendant*   Synonymous with "issue," this term includes children, grandchildren, great-grandchildren, etc., but not collateral relatives; the latter are descendants of the decedent's *parents* or other ancestor. See Section 2.2.

*devise*   Originally this word was used (both as a noun and a verb) to describe a gift of *land* in a will. The proper term for a gift of personal property was "bequest" or "legacy". Today the Uniform Probate Code uses "devise" to cover both real and personal property.

*disclaimer*   A refusal to accept a gift or inheritance. Different consequences attach to disclaimers as distinguished from accepting property and then giving it away. See Section 2.8. Renunciation is sometimes used as an equivalent term.

*domicil, or domicile*   The term is significant in the choice of law, especially for personal property. See Section 1.2. It is also important for venue; under the Uniform Probate Code administration of an estate may be commenced "where the decedent had his domicile at the time of his death."[5]

*donee*   (1) The recipient of a gift, or (2) a person on whom a power of appointment is conferred. See *power of appointment*

*dower*   The common law term for a widow's rights in her husband's land; the counterpart to the widower's right to "curtesy." See Section 3.7.

*durable power*   A power of attorney which does not terminate when the principal becomes incompetent. See Section 9.2.

---

**5.** Unif.Prob.Code § 3–201.

*elective share*  The share of an estate to which the surviving spouse is entitled, even if he or she was disinherited by the decedent's will. See Section 3.7.

*entireties, tenancy by*  A peculiar form of joint tenancy between spouses, which no longer exists in many states. See Section 13.2.

*Equity*  The court which historically enforced trusts. Although today the courts of law and equity have merged, vestiges of the idea that trusts are "equitable" survive. See Section 12.8.

*ERISA*  Employee Retirement Security Act of 1974, a federal statute governing most pension plans, which subjects them to many, but not all of the rules governing trusts. See Section 13.1.

*escheat*  When a person dies without a will and without heirs, his/her property passes to the state by "escheat."[6]

*estate*  The term sometimes refers only to the "probate" estate, the assets which pass by will or intestacy under the jurisdiction of the probate court. Much property today passes "outside probate." See Section 9.1 Most of this property is subject to the federal estate tax, which is based on the "gross" estate. See Section 15.3.

*exculpatory provision*  A provision under which a fiduciary is not held liable for a loss even if the fiduciary was at fault. The effectiveness of such provisions is limited. See Section 12.8.

*execute*  Doing what is necessary to make an instrument formally valid, typically signing a will or deed. The place where an instrument was executed and the time of execution may be important for various purposes. See Sections 1.2, 1.3.

*executor*  A person or persons designated in a will to "execute", *i.e.* carry out the testator's wishes. The executor may be either an individual or a bank which has a trust department. The term "executrix" for female executors was once common but is rarely used today. Executors have no power to act until they are appointed by the court, which usually happens when the will is probated. See Section 12.4. Their compensation is one of the costs of probate. See Section 12.5.

*executory interest*  A type of future interest distinguishable from a remainder on technical grounds. The distinction was once important but is virtually obsolete today. See Section 11.1.

*expectancy*  A hope of acquiring property, *e.g.* by inheritance from a parent who is still alive. *Property* can be transferred without

---

**6.** Historically, escheat occurred when land reverted to the lord of the fee, either for lack of qualified heirs or as a forfeiture. 2 W. BLACKSTONE, COMMENTARIES *244.

consideration, but an *expectancy* cannot. The distinction between the two is thin in borderline cases. See Section 4.5.

*express trust* A term used in contradistinction to resulting and constructive trusts.[7]

*family allowance* An amount paid to members of a decedent's family (particularly the surviving spouse) for support while the estate is administered. See Section 3.5.

*fee simple, fee tail* A fee tail, in contrast to a fee simple, ceased when the holder died without issue. A serious clog on alienation at one time, the fee tail has been abolished or severely restricted today. See Section 10.2.

*fiduciary* Derived from the Latin *fiducia*, trust or confidence, the term covers a wide spectrum of persons who are entrusted with property which belongs to another. The Uniform Probate Code defines the term to include personal representatives, guardians, conservators and trustees. Custodians and agents are also fiduciaries. The relationship between clients and lawyers is often described as fiduciary.

*fraud* A knowing misrepresentation, which may be the basis for denying probate to a will. See Section 6.1. The term is also used to describe a promise made without intent to perform, which may cause the imposition of a constructive trust even if the promise was oral. See Section 6.5. Fraud is also sometimes used to get around various defenses, such as statutes of limitations and res judicata. See Section 12.8.

*fraudulent conveyance* A gift which is subject to attack by the donor's creditors, *e.g.* because the donor was insolvent when the gift was made. See Section 13.1.

*future interest* An interest in property which does not allow present possession or enjoyment, a generic term for remainders, executory interests, reversions.

*general devise* Contrasted with specific and with residuary devises for purposes of ademption and abatement. See Sections 8.1–8.2.

*general power* See *power of appointment*

*gift causa mortis* A concept borrowed from Roman law which applied special rules to gifts made by persons who were contemplating death at the time. See Section 5.5.

*guardian* See *conservator*

---

**7.** *Restatement, Third, of Trusts* § 2, comm a (2001).

*guardian ad litem*   A person appointed to represent a minor or other incompetent person in litigation. See Section 12.8. A guardian ad litem's role is limited to litigation, unlike other guardians.

*heir*   From the Latin *heres*, but a Latin *heres* was often a person designated in a will to whom the testator was not related, whereas in English such persons are "devisees" but not heirs. In correct English usage heirs are the person(s) designated by the law of intestacy to take from a decedent. However, the term is sometimes used by ill-informed testators to mean devisees or children. See Section 2.4

When a person dies intestate without issue, the estate passes to collateral relatives, such as brothers and sisters. Section 2.2. They can be heirs, but "heirs *of the body*" connotes only issue and so collateral relatives would not qualify.

Sometimes the word "heirs" is used as a "word of limitation" as in a deed "to *A* and his heirs." In this case *A*'s heirs acquire no interest at all; the word simply means *A* gets a fee simple. See Section 10.2.

*holographic*   A will written entirely in the testator's handwriting. In many states they are valid even though the will is unwitnessed. See Section 4.4.

*homestead*   A certain amount of property, usually a residence, which is exempt from creditors. There are typically restrictions on voluntary transfer of homestead by the owner. See Section 3.4.

*honorary trust*   A name sometimes given to trusts for non-charitable purposes without a definite human beneficiary, like a trust for a pet. See Section 9.7.

*immoveable property*   The distinction between moveable and immoveable property corresponds roughly with that between real and personal property. It is important in the choice of law. See Section 1.2.

*independent administration*   The system which allows personal representatives to perform acts of administration without court approval. Section 12.6.

*intangible*   Property such as securities, bank accounts, patents, which cannot be touched, in contrast to furniture, cattle, etc. Even securities which are represented by a certificate are considered intangibles. The formal requirements for gifts are somewhat different for tangible and intangible property. Section 4.5.

*in terrorem*   A clause designed to deter someone from contesting a will by providing that any devise to him in the will is forfeited by such a contest. See Section 12.1.

*inter vivos*   Latin "between the living," contrasted with a testamentary gift or trust which is made by a will. "Living" trust is a common synonym for inter vivos. Section 4.6.

*intestate*   Without a will; the rules governing intestate succession are described in Chapter 2.

*issue*   See *descendants*

*joint tenancy*   A form of co-ownership in which property passes to the surviving owner(s) when a tenant dies. Contrasted with tenancy in common, under which the decedent's interest passes to his/her estate. See Section 4.8.

*joint will*   A will signed by two persons, usually husband and wife, purporting to dispose of the property of both. See Section 4.9.

*laches*   A defense to a claim based on delay in asserting it. See Section 12.8.

*lapse*   Failure of a devise, usually because the devisee predeceased the testator. Most states have "anti-lapse" statutes to deal with this situation. See Section 8.3.

*legacy, legatee*   See *devise*

*legal interest, title*   An interest which historically was enforced in the law courts, as distinguished from equitable interests, which were recognized only in the courts of equity. In a trust, the trustee has legal title, while the interests of the beneficiaries are equitable.

*legal list*   Lists of the types of investment which are authorized for fiduciaries by statute in some states. See Section 12.7.

*letters*   An official certification of the appointment of a fiduciary by a court establishing his or her authority to act on behalf of an estate. It includes letters testamentary (given to an executor), letters of administration (given to an administrator), letters of guardianship and letters of conservatorship.

*living will*   "A relatively short instrument saying * * * that the life of the person signing is not to be artificially prolonged by extraordinary medical measures when there is no reasonable expectation of recovery."[8] See Section 14.5.

*marital deduction*   A deduction permitted under the federal estate and gift taxes for transfers from one spouse to another. See Section 15.3.

*marital property*   Roughly the equivalent of community property. A Uniform Marital Property Act has been adopted only in Wisconsin, but the term is used in many other states to categorize property for division upon a divorce. Section 3.8.

---

**8.**   Mellinkoff, Dictionary of American Legal Usage 572 (1992).

*Medicaid Qualifying Trust*   A trust that causes property to be attributed to a beneficiary as an available resource for determining eligibility for Medicaid. See Section 9.5.

*mistake*   The law distinguishes between mistake of fact and mistake in execution. If I sign a "will" not realizing it is a will, it may be denied probate, but if my will disinherits my son because I erroneously think he is a drug addict, the will is valid. See Section 6.1.

*Model Code of Professional Responsibility, Model Rules of Professional Conduct*   Two sets of provisions governing proper conduct by lawyers. Nearly all states have adopted one or the other. See Section 7.4.

*mortmain*   Statutes which restrict gifts to charity by will. In nearly all states they have been repealed or held unconstitutional. See Section 3.10.

*mutual wills*   Wills executed by two persons, usually spouses, with reciprocal provisions, *e.g.* *H* leaves his estate to *W* if she survives, *W* leaves her estate to *H* if he survives. See Section 4.9.

*non-claim statutes*   Statutes which requiring claims against an estate to be filed within a limited period. See Section 13.3.

*notary public*   "A person authorized by law to administer oaths, [and] authenticate signatures and documents." Do not confuse the American notary with "the far more significant role and status of notaries public in civil law jurisdictions."[9] See Sections 4.3, 4.5.

*nuncupative will*   An oral will, allowed in some states in limited circumstances. See Section 4.4.

*pecuniary devise*   See general devise.

*per capita, per stirpes*   Alternative ways to divide property among heirs or devisees. See Section 2.2.

*personal representative*   The generic term which covers both executors and administrators. See Section 12.4.

*possibility of reverter*   A type of future interest reserved in a grant. The technical distinctions between these and rights of entry are discussed in Section 11.6.

*posthumous child*   One born after the death of the father. See Section 10.3.

*pourover (also pour-over)*   A will which leaves property to a trust created by another document. See Section 6.2.

---

**9.** Id, at 428.

*power*   Authority conferred on a fiduciary to act, e.g. to sell property of an estate. It may be conferred by the terms of the instrument or implied by law. Section 12.6.

*power of appointment*   Authority given to a person (called the donee) to direct where property shall pass. Powers are either testamentary or presently exercisable. The law also distinguishes between general and special powers. See Section 10.4.

*power of attorney*   Instrument authorizing an "attorney in fact" to act on behalf of the principal. Attorneys in fact are usually not members of the legal profession. See also *durable power*.

*precatory*   Words in an instrument which are not intended to impose any enforceable obligation. See Section 4.6.

*presumption*   This "slipperiest of the family of legal terms" is often used in this area of the law, *e.g.*, if a will is lost, "it is *presumed* that the testator destroyed the will with the intent to revoke it."[10] If the issue is decided by a jury, a presumption means that a verdict must be directed for the party claiming revocation when the basic fact is proved (that the will is lost) unless the proponents of the will produce evidence to the contrary.[11] If such contrary evidence is produced (e.g. indicating that the will was lost by accident), there is disagreement as to whether the presumption should be mentioned to the jury.

*pretermitted*   A child or other heir who is omitted from a will by oversight. See Section 3.5.

*principal*   The distinction between "principal" and "income" of a trust is discussed in Section 9.4. The relationship between a "principal" and an agent is discussed at Section 7.2. Neither word should be confused with "principle."

*private trust*   Used in contrast to charitable trusts which are governed by special rules. See Section 9.7.

*probate*   The term often refers to the process of proving that a will is valid. A will which the court finds valid is "admitted to probate." The court which performs this function is usually called the probate court. Section 12.1. The term "probate" is often loosely used to include administration of the estate, but the two concepts are not identical. See Section 12.2. Probate courts traditionally had limited jurisdiction, but in recent years there has been a trend to expand their competence.

---

**10.**   Cal.Prob.Code § 6124. A similar presumption exists at common law. See Section 5.2.

**11.**   In this respect a presumption differs from a "permissible inference" which would *allow* the jury to find that the will was revoked, but not compel them to do so.

*prudent man/person rule*    In states which do not have a *legal list* of proper investments for fiduciaries, the governing standard allows them to make those investments that a prudent man (person) would make. See Section 12.7. This standard has been extended to other aspects of fiduciary conduct.

*publication*    An oral statement by the testator that a document is his/her will. See Section 4.3. The term is also used to refer to a notice published in a newspaper, *e.g.* to creditors of an estate. See Section 13.3.

*putative spouse*    A person not legally married, but who is treated as a spouse because he/she in good faith thought there was a valid marriage. See Section 2.11.

*quasi community property*    Property treated as if it were community property even though it is not, acquired by someone while living in a separate property state who later moved to a community property state. See Section 3.8.

*reformation*    Correcting a writing to make it conform to what the signer intended. See Sections 6.1, 6.4. Also used for modifying a trust to avoid a violation of the Rule against Perpetuities. See Section 11.4.

*representation*    The concept whereby more remote relatives take a share of a decedent's property in place of a parent or other ancestor who is dead. See Section 2.2. The term is also used when a judgment binds someone who was a minor or unborn on the ground that his/her interests were represented by another. See Section 12.8.

*res*    From the Latin *res*, thing. A somewhat antiquated term for the property held in a trust.

*residue, residuary estate*    The property remaining in an estate after the payment of claims, specific and general devises. See Sections 8.1, 8.2.

*Restatement*    Two of the many Restatements are particularly important in this area. The *Restatement, Second, of Trusts* was promulgated in 1959. Portions of a third version have been issued. The *Restatement, Second, of Property (Donative Transfers)* was issued between 1981 and 1990, and already a Third Restatement on the subject is being drafted.

*restraint on alienation*    A rule designed to prevent property from becoming inalienable, different from, but associated with, the Rule against Perpetuities. See Section 11.8.

*resulting trust*    When a trust fails there is a "resulting trust" for the settlor. It is the equitable counterpart to a reversion. The term "purchase money resulting trust" is used when one person pays for property which is transferred to another. See Section 6.4.

*reversion*   A future interest reserved the grantor, expressly or by implication. When *A* gives *B* a life estate, and the deed says nothing about what happens when *B* dies, the land will "revert" to *A*.

*revival*   When a will which revoked a prior will is later revoked, this may "revive" the first will. See Section 5.3.

*Rule against Perpetuities*   A rule designed to prevent property from being tied up by the dead hand for too long. Discussed at length in Chapter 11.

*Rule in Shelley's case*   A virtually obsolete rule dealing with a remainder to the "heirs" of a life tenant. See Section 10.2.

*separate property*   Contrasted with *community property.*

*settlor*   A person who creates a trust. "Trustor" and "grantor" are also used occasionally.

*sever, severance*   The term for turning a joint tenancy into a tenancy in common. See Section 5.5.

*situs*   From the Latin *situs*, location. The situs of property is often important for choice of law. See Section 1.2. It is also important for venue; an estate can be administered where property of the decedent was located even if the decedent was not domiciled in the state.

*special power*   See *power of appointment*

*specific devise*   A devise of specific property, such as "my house" or "my furniture," contrasted with a general or residuary devise. See Section 8.1.

*spendthrift trust*   A trust which restricts a beneficiary from alienating his/her interest and prevents creditors of the beneficiary from reaching it. See Section 13.1.

*Statute of Frauds*   Most parts of the original English statute of 1676 have become law in most American states. It (a) prescribed formal requirements for wills (later superseded in England by the Wills Act of 1837), (b) required a signed writing to convey land, to create a trust of land, and for certain contracts. See Sections 4.1, 4.5, and 4.9.

*substituted judgment*   The standard employed by courts in authorizing conservators (guardians) to make gifts of the conservatee's (ward's) property. See Section 7.2.

*testamentary/ testator*   From the Latin word for will, *testamentum*. In modern English, "will" has largely replaced testament, but the adjective "testamentary" is still current, *e.g.* a trust created by will is a testamentary trust, in contradistinction to a "living" trust. The person who executes a will is a testator.

*Totten trust*    Trusts of a bank account, named after a leading case which held them valid. See Section 4.6. They have little in common with ordinary trusts, since they terminate when the settlor dies.

*trust*    Certain uses of this multi-purpose word have nothing to do with the subject of this book, such as business trusts, and "trust deeds," a security device like a mortgage. The primary purposes of trusts covered in this book are described in Section 9.1.

*undue influence*    A basis for invalidating a will or other transfer, often linked with a claim that the maker was incapacitated. See Section 7.3.

*Uniform Acts (Codes)*    Many Uniform Acts relate to the subject matter of this book. The word "uniform" is a misnomer. Almost none of them have been universally adopted and many states which have adopted them have departed from the version as promulgated by the Commissioners on Uniform State Laws.

*Uniform Principal and Income Act*    A version promulgated in 1931 has 1 adoption today. A revision in 1962 lists 15 adoptions. The 1997 revision has 29 adoptions. Discussed in Section 9.4.

*Uniform Probate Code*    Promulgated in 1969 and adopted in 15 states. A revised version of Article VI appeared in 1989, of Article II in 1990, and Article V was revised in 1998. The UPC incorporated certain existing Uniform acts, and parts of it appear in free-standing versions, some of which have been more widely adopted than the UPC as a whole.

*Uniform Prudent Investor Act*    Approved in 1994 and adopted in over half the states. Discussed in Section 12.7.

*Uniform Simultaneous Death Act*    Promulgated in 1940 and almost universally adopted. The UPC incorporates a revision made in 1991. Discussed in Section 8.3.

*Uniform Statutory Rule against Perpetuities*    Promulgated in 1986 26 adoptions. Discussed in Section 11.4.

*Uniform Statutory Will Act.*    Drafted by knowledgeable estate planners as a model for lawyers who are less experienced in the field, it is often cited as a model of what good drafters can do to avoid problems treated in the book.

*Uniform Testamentary Additions to Trusts Act*    Promulgated in 1960. 39 adoptions listed. Discussed in Section 6.2.

*Uniform Transfers to Minors Act*    A revision of the Uniform Gifts to Minors Act, promulgated in 1983 and adopted in nearly all states. Discussed in Section 9.2.

*Uniform Trustees' Powers Act* Promulgated in 1964 and adopted in 16 states. Discussed in Chapter 12.

*Uniform Trust Code* Not to be confused with the Uniform Trusts Act, which is much less comprehensive. Approved in 2000, the Code "mostly restates familiar principles."[12] The Code is intended to replace the Uniform Trustees Powers and Uniform Trusts Acts.

*vested remainder* See *contingent remainder.*

*wait and see* A reform of the common-law Rule against Perpetuities based on waiting to see if the interest vests in time. See Section 11.4.

*ward* A person for whom a guardian has been appointed. Equivalent to a conservatee.

*waste* Misuse or neglect of property by a legal life tenant which may be actionable by the remainderman. See Section 9.3.

*will contest* A proceeding brought to have a will declared invalid, e.g. for incapacity or undue influence. In many states a contest can be instituted even after the will is admitted to probate. See Section 12.1.

*will substitutes* A general name for various devices whereby property passes at death which are free from the formal requirements for wills, including probate and administration. A recurring question is whether such devices should be subject to the rules governing wills themselves.

*worthier title* An almost obsolete doctrine which held that a gift to the "heirs" of a grantor or testator gave them no interest in the property conveyed. See Section 10.2.

*wrongful death* Statutes abrogating the common law rule that death of an injured person abated any claim for the injury. They are discussed in Section 2.5.

## § 1.2   Conflict of Laws

The law of wills is largely statutory. Although the laws of the American states agree on most basic points, they differ in many details. Thus it is often necessary to decide which law applies to a case. A whole Restatement is devoted to the subject. Various factors have been used to determine the governing law.

*Designation by transferor* A statement in a will that "this will shall be governed by the law of [for example] Virginia" is usually controlling. Allowing the transferor to choose the applicable law makes good sense insofar as the law seeks to effectuate intention.

---

**12.** Langbein, *The Uniform Trust Code: Codification of the Law of Trusts* *in the United States,* 15 Trust Law International 66 (2001).

But this is not always the case. A testator's designation of New York law in a will did not bar his spouse from claiming greater rights under the law of Virginia where the spouses were domiciled.[1]

Can a testator (or other transferor) designate the law of a state which has no connection to the testator, the property or the beneficiaries? One court refused to respect a designation of Georgia law in a trust because Georgia had no such tie.[2] However, this is not a stated requirement in the UPC or the Restatement.[3]

To say "the law of X shall govern" may include X's rules on the choice of law, which may point to another state's substantive rules. Under this, a concept, commonly known as renvoi, a trust provision that Massachusetts law should govern was held to include the Massachusetts rule that the legitimacy of a child was governed by the law of his domicile, which in this case was New Hampshire.[4]

*Situs*    The situs of land often determines the choice of law. When a woman domiciled in Germany died owning land in Florida, the court applied Florida law to determine her heirs as to her land there.[5] Many state statutes, and the Restatement, agree,[6] but the rule has been questioned. A person who leaves property in several states probably considers the estate as a unit, but the situs rule may impose different laws on the various parts of the estate. The situs rule can protect legitimate interests. It allows prospective purchasers of land to consult the law with which they are most familiar. In other situations the interest of the situs is more doubtful, for example, disputes between members of a family who all reside in another state.

The situs rule in the case of land is easy to apply. The leading alternative is to look to the law of the owner's domicile, which, as we shall see, is often hard to determine.

Generally the situs rule is confined to land. This raises the question, what is land and what is personal property? If I own a company which owns land, should one focus on the stock which represents my interest (personal property) or the underlying asset, the land?

**§ 1.2**

**1.** Estate of Clark, 236 N.E.2d 152 (N.Y.1968). *See also Restatement, Second, of Conflict of Laws* § 270, comm. b (1971). *But see* Matter of Estate of Wright, 637 A.2d 106 (Me.1994) (designation of Maine law bars child's claim under Swiss law).

**2.** First National Bank v. Daggett, 497 N.W.2d 358 (Neb.1993).

**3.** *Restatement, Second, of Conflict of Laws* §§ 224, comm. e, 264, comm. e, 268, comm. b. But if the question is the validity of the trust, the designated state must have "a substantial relation to the trust." *Id.* § 270, comm. b.

**4.** Powers v. Steele, 475 N.E.2d 395 (Mass.1985).

**5.** In re Estate of Salathe, 703 So.2d 1167 (Fla.App.1997).

**6.** Cal. Civil Code § 755 (land within California governed by California law); *Restatement, Second, of Conflict of Laws* §§ 223 (conveyance of land), 277–78 (trust of land).

In some cases the law of the situs governs personal property. When an Illinois resident died intestate without heirs, owning a bank account in Washington, the account escheated to Washington.[7]

*Domicile*   The law of the owner's domicile usually governs personal property, or "movables," the term commonly used in conflicts literature. When a man domiciled in New York died owning property in Louisiana, his wife invoked Louisiana law to claim a share as community property. Her claim was allowed as to land, but not as to the personal property; Louisiana was said to have no interest "in protecting and regulating the rights of married persons residing and domiciled in New York."[8]

Since many persons own property in more than one jurisdiction but have a single domicile, reference to the law of the domicile has the advantage of treating the owner's property as a unit. The Uniform Probate Code uses domicile to determine the elective share of a surviving spouse as to *all* the decedent's property, including land.[9] Some courts refer to the law of the testator's domicile when construing a will even when land is involved.[10]

Domicile may also be important in questions of status, which in turn may control inheritance. Thus when a man claimed to inherit a share of his "wife's" estate, the court applied German law to determine the validity of their marriage, because they were domiciled there.[11]

Domicile is often hard to determine. Although the words domicile and residence are often used interchangeably, they are not the same. A person may have several residences, but only one domicile. When a man died in a nursing home where he had lived for 8 years, the court held he was not domiciled there. "A change of domicile requires 'an actual moving with an intent to go to a given place and remain there.' "[12] Conversely, a residence of only a few days may constitute a change of domicile when there was an intent to make the new residence home.[13]

---

**7.**  O'Keefe v. State, Department of Revenue, 488 P.2d 754 (Wash.1971). *But see* Delaware v. New York, 507 U.S. 490, 498 (1993) ("since a debt is property of the creditor . . . the debt should be accorded to the State of the creditor's last known address").

**8.**  Estate of Crichton, 228 N.E.2d 799 (N.Y.1967).

**9.**  Uniform Probate Code § 2–202(d). But In Banks v. Junk, 264 So.2d 387 (Miss.1972), the court refused to apply Mississippi law to land in Louisiana owned by a Mississippi domiciliary.

**10.**  Beauchamp v. Beauchamp, 574 So.2d 18, 20–21 (Miss.1990); *Restatement, Second, of Conflict of Laws* § 224, illus. 1 (1971).

**11.**  In re Estate of Salathe, 703 So.2d 1167 (Fla.App.1997).

**12.**  Matter of Estate of Brown, 587 N.E.2d 686, 689 (Ind.App.1992). *See also* Matter of Estate of Marcos, 963 P.2d 1124 (Haw.1998) (Marcos not domiciled in Hawaii although he spent the last 3 1/2 years of his life there).

**13.**  In re Estate of Elson, 458 N.E.2d 637 (Ill.App.1983).

Courts may reach conflicting decisions as to where a person was domiciled, but under the Uniform Probate Code "the determination of domicile in the proceeding first commenced must be accepted as determinative" in all cases.[14]

Reference to the law of the domicile usually means that of the decedent at the time of death, but not always. According to the Restatement, courts "usually construe a given word or phrase [in a will] in accordance with the usage prevailing in the state where the testator was domiciled at the time the will was executed."[15] In some cases, courts look to the domicile of the survivors rather than that of the decedent. When a question arose as to the rights to insurance proceeds on a policy on the life of a man who lived in Arkansas, the court looked to Oklahoma law because all of the claimants lived there.[16]

*Forum*  Sometimes the forum simply applies its own law, e.g., "a court usually applies its own local rules prescribing how litigation shall be conducted."[17] An Oregon court refused to apply a Washington statute which would have barred an insured's widow from testifying, even though Washington substantive law governed the case.[18] It is not always clear whether a question should be characterized as substantive or procedural for choice of law. Succession to the property of a mother and daughter turned on which one survived; the rules for resolving this question in England (the forum) and Germany (the decedents' domicile) differed. The court treated the question one of substantive law and applied German law.[19]

In the absence of satisfactory proof of contrary applicable foreign law, the law of the forum is applied. [20]

A choice-of-law rule which looks to the law of another jurisdiction may be ignored if that law is inconsistent with a fundamental

**14.** Uniform Probate Code § 3–202; *cf.* Southern v. Glenn, 568 So.2d 281, 287 (Miss.1990) (Texas finding that couple was domiciled in Mississippi relitigated in Mississippi).

**15.** *Restatement, Second, of Conflict of Laws* § 264, comm. f (1971). But in Gellerstedt v. United Missouri Bank, 865 S.W.2d 707 (Mo.App.1993), even though the testator was domiciled in Kansas when she executed her will, the court held that if she had moved to Missouri before she died, Missouri law should control.

**16.** Whirlpool Corp. v. Ritter, 929 F.2d 1318, 1321 (8th Cir.1991). *See also* Matter of Estate of Gilmore, 946 P.2d 1130, 1138 (N.M.App.1997) (interest of state of decedent's domicile is "slight" as against the domicile of the potential beneficiaries of a wrongful death claim).

**17.** *Restatement, Second, of Conflict of Laws* § 122 (1971).

**18.** Equitable Life Assurance Society v. McKay, 760 P.2d 871 (Or.1988), following *Restatement, Second, of Conflict of Laws* § 138 (1971).

**19.** In re Cohn, [1945] Ch 5 (1944).

**20.** *Restatement, Second, of Conflict of Laws* § 136, comm. f (1971); Razzaghe–Ashrafi v. Razzaghe–Ashrafi, 558 So.2d 1368, 1370 (La.App.1990) (N.Y. assumed to have community property since no evidence to the contrary produced!)

policy of the forum. This restriction is construed narrowly, since otherwise the forum would never apply a foreign law which differed from its own.[21]

*Interests*   The Restatement, while restating the traditional rules described above on many issues, says that for inter vivos trusts where the governing law is not designated by the settlor, the court should look to "the local law of the state with which, as to the matter at issue, the trust has its most significant relationship."[22] This permits consideration of several factors, including the place of execution of the trust, the situs of the assets, and the domicile of the settlor and of the beneficiaries. In a case involving a contract to devise property, the court applied Massachusetts law, even though the promissor died domiciled in New Hampshire, because Massachusetts "has the most significant relationship to the transaction," since the contract was negotiated and executed and the beneficiaries resided there.[23]

*Favoring validity*   A recurring theme in choice of law is fulfilling the expectations of the transferor (testator, settlor, etc.). Under the Uniform Probate Code a will is valid if it complies with the Code *or* with the law of the place where the will was executed *or* where the testator was domiciled, the purpose being "to provide a wide opportunity for validation of expectations of testators."[24] Some courts reach this result even without a statute. Thus when a will attested by interested witnesses was executed in Florida, which allowed this, it could be probated in Ohio, where the testator was domiciled at death, even though Ohio invalidated devises to interested witnesses.[25]

The choice of law rules on marriage reflect a similar desire to sustain validity. Generally a marriage which satisfies the requirements of the state where it took place will be recognized in other states.[26]

*Drafting*   One who undertakes to draft a will or trust should be familiar with choice of law issues, since the client may have property in another jurisdiction either now or later, or may die

---

**21.** In re Portnoy, 201 B.R. 685, 700 (S.D.N.Y. 1996) (choice of law provision in a trust disregarded as contrary to public policy); *cf.* Allen v. Storer, 600 N.E.2d 1263 (Ill.App.1992) (error to reject claim of common-law marriage as against public policy of Illinois).

**22.** *Restatement, Second, of Conflict of Laws* § 270(2) (1971). *See also* Uniform Trust Code § 107(2).

**23.** Nile v. Nile, 734 N.E.2d 1153, 1161 (Mass.2000).

**24.** Unif.Prob.Code § 2–506, comment. *See also* Unif.Trust Code § 403; *Restatement, Third, of Property (Wills and Other Donative Transfers)* § 3.1, comm. e (1998) (favoring rule "as a principle of decisional law" where no statute).

**25.** Hairelson v. Estate of Franks, 720 N.E.2d 989 (Ohio App.1998).

**26.** Estate of Loughmiller, 629 P.2d 156 (Kan.1981) (marriage between first cousins valid because celebrated in state which allowed it).

domiciled in another state or country. A provision in the instrument which specifies the governing law may avoid undesirable rules or uncertainty as to the governing law. Clients should also be advised to make their domicile clear. A recital in a will as to the testator's domicile is helpful, since domicile is largely a question of intent, but not conclusive, since the testator may have changed domicile after signing the will.[27]

## § 1.3　Change in the Law

Although the law of property has a reputation for being conservative, it has been subject to many changes over time, so questions as to when a change in the law becomes effective often arise. The answer may depend on whether the change comes about by a judicial decision or by a statute. Because of the somewhat fictitious notion that judges "discover" the law but do not make it, they ordinarily do not hesitate to apply their rulings to cases which arose earlier. Despite this comforting rationalization, judges hesitate to overrule precedents on which parties may have relied, and may prefer to leave a questionable rule unchanged.

*Prospective Overruling*　Judges sometimes overrule precedents prospectively. In 1984 a court announced that "for the future we shall no longer follow the rule announced" in an earlier case, but since "the bar has been entitled reasonably to rely on that rule in advising clients" the new rule would apply only in future cases.[1] Prospective overruling is rather rare, however. One court has said that it "should be limited to a case in which the hardship on a party who has relied on the old rule outweighs the hardship on the party denied the benefit of the new rule; and there are few cases where such rigorous demonstrations can be made."[2]

*Retroactive Legislation*　When change in law comes through legislation, the effective date usually depends on the terms of the statute. The Uniform Trust Code alters the common law by making trusts presumptively revocable, but this rule is expressly inapplicable to trusts created before the Code becomes effective.[3] On the other hand, a statute passed in 1997 was applied to a conveyance made in 1996 because the court accepted the legislature's claim that the statute was "intended as a clarification of existing law and not as a new enactment."[4]

---

**27.** Lotz v. Atamaniuk, 304 S.E.2d 20 (W.Va.1983) (finding of Ohio domicile erroneous even though the will recited it).

**§ 1.3**

**1.** Sullivan v. Burkin, 460 N.E.2d 572, 576–77 (Mass.1984).

**2.** Decker v. Meriwether, 708 S.W.2d 390, 394–95 (Tenn.App.1985).

**3.** Unif.Trust Code § 602(a).

**4.** Premier Property Management, Inc. v. Chavez, 728 N.E.2d 476, 480 (Ill. 2000).

Statutes which do not make clear when they become applicable are usually presumed to be prospective. Even when a statute is clearly stated to apply retrospectively, a court may hold that this is unconstitutional.[5] On the other hand, constitutional attacks on retroactive legislation often failed. A statute which restricted gifts to lawyers in instruments which they drafted was applied to a revocable trust drafted before the statute was enacted; this did not violate due process because the lawyer "did not have a vested right" under the trust so long as it was revocable.[6]

Today there is less reluctance to make changes in the law retroactive than formerly. For example, the first Uniform Principal and Income Act (1931) did not apply to trusts in existence when the Act was adopted, but the second version (1962) did, and has been held constitutional.[7] The recently promulgated Uniform Trust Code applies to all trusts, whenever created, being "intended to have the widest possible effect within constitutional limitations."[8]

There are two arguments in favor of making changes retroactive. First, presumably the new rule is better than the old one or it would not have been made. If the new rule is better, why postpone its applicability? Secondly, having the new rule and the old one operate simultaneously makes the law more complicated. Trustees, for example, would have to keep track of different rules applicable to different trusts depending upon the date of their creation.

On the other hand, it may be unfair to parties who have relied on existing law when a change is made retroactive. Sometimes this argument focuses on the transferor (testator, settlor, etc.), sometimes on other persons, such as the transferee, or a fiduciary who has acted in reliance on the old rule. Even though Illinois now includes adopted children in class gifts, regardless of when a will was executed, a trustee who made a distribution under the old law which excluded adopted children cannot be held liable therefor.[9]

"Retroactivity" is a general term, and courts do not always use it consistently. Several points in time may be deemed relevant.

*Date of Execution*    Some statutes by their terms apply only to instruments executed thereafter.[10] However, the more common effective date for laws affecting wills is the date of the testator's

**5.** In re Marriage of Buol, 705 P.2d 354 (Cal.1985).

**6.** Bank of America v. Angel View, 85 Cal.Rptr.2d 117, 121 (App.1999).

**7.** Bogert, *The Revised Uniform Principal and Income Act,* 38 N.D.Law 50, 52 (1962). However, one part of the 1962 Act and its counterpart in the 1997 version (§ 411(d)) are made prospective due to "concerns about the constitution-ality" of retroactivity. See Comment to § 411.

**8.** Unif.Trust Code § 1106, comment.

**9.** 755 ILCS § 5/2–4(g); *But see* note 3, *supra* Chicago Title and Trust Co. v. Steinitz, 681 N.E.2d 669 (Ill.App.1997).

**10.** Cal.Prob.Code § 246(b) (construction of the term "per stirpes").

death. When a change occurs after a will was executed but before the testator dies, he/she can change the will if the change in the law does not reflect the testator's desires. This is also true for revocable trusts. However, for *irrevocable* instruments the date of execution is more significant.[11]

For some purposes, the UPC looks to the date of execution even for wills. A will is valid if it complies "with the law at the time of execution" even if it does not comply with more stringent formalities imposed thereafter. However, if formal requirements are *relaxed* after the will is executed, this may validate a defective will.[12] On the same principle, statutes imposing formal requirements on contracts to make wills do not apply to contracts previously made.[13]

*Date of Death*   For most purposes the date of death determines the governing law. When changes in status, such as adoption, marriage and divorce affect the distribution of property at death, courts generally look to the law as of the date of death rather than the law in effect when the adoption, marriage or divorce occurred.[14]

Even when a change in the law occurs shortly after a decedent's death, before the estate has been distributed, courts usually apply the law as of the date of death. A woman was killed in April 1972. In July, the state adopted the Uniform Probate Code which altered the rule of succession. Although by its terms the Code applies to proceedings which are still pending when the Code takes effect, any "accrued right" is protected, and the court held that this included the shares determined under prior law. [15]

If the law in effect at the date of death is unconstitutional, however, it may not control.[16] When a father died children born out of wedlock could not inherit under Texas law. A few months later the United States Supreme Court held a similar statute unconstitutional. Texas could not apply its statute to bar a child because the administration of the father's estate was still in progress, but "after an estate has been finally distributed, the interest in finality may provide [a] * * * valid justification for barring the belated assertion of claims."[17]

**11.** Ohio Citizens Bank v. Mills, 543 N.E.2d 1206 (Ohio 1989) (law as of date of execution of trust applied in determining to exclude adoptees).

**12.** Uniform Probate Code § 2–506, comment.

**13.** Cal.Prob.Code § 21700(c).

**14.** Dye v. Battles, 112 Cal.Rptr.2d 362 (App. 2001). *But see* In re Estate of Crohn, 494 P.2d 258 (Or.App.1972) (applying statute in effect at date of divorce).

**15.** Hogan v. Hermann, 623 P.2d 900 (Idaho 1980).

**16.** So also, if a retroactive statute replaces an unconstitutional one, its retroactive application is likely to be upheld. In re Marriage of Bouquet, 546 P.2d 1371 (Cal.1976) (statute providing equal treatment for wives and husbands could be applied retroactively).

**17.** Reed v. Campbell, 476 U.S. 852, 855 (1986).

The probable reliance of persons who receive distributions is protected. An even stronger claim for protection is presented by bona fide purchasers for value and fiduciaries who have made prior distributions. When a will made a gift of income to the testator's "descendants," a statutory presumption excluding children born out of wedlock was held unconstitutional, but the court refused to hold that a child born out of wedlock was entitled to income from the beginning, since this would "ignore the countervailing interests of the beneficiaries [born in wedlock who had been getting all the income] and the trustee." The child only received income which the trustee had held in reserve pending resolution of the dispute.[18]

*Future Interests*    Suppose a will gives an interest to A for life, and a remainder to A's "issue." Under the law in effect when the testator died, an adopted child of A would not have taken. After the testator dies but during A's life, the law changes. Does the new rule apply? The many decisions on this issue are inconsistent. Many cases hold the new law inapplicable on the theory that the testator relied on the law in effect at his/her death. But many question whether the testator in this situation actually relied on the old rule. Some courts have applied the new rules on the ground that the testator intended to have whatever law was in effect at the time of final distribution of the trust control.[19]

*Vested Interests*    Sometimes the discussion focuses on the interests of the devisees rather than the testator's intentions. Once property has been distributed, it will not be taken back from the distributee on the ground that the law has changed. On the other hand, rights which have not yet irrevocably vested may be defeated by a change in the law.[20] Courts often say that "vested" interests are entitled to protection, but this word is variously interpreted. In some opinions the term becomes circular. "A reviewing court applies the law as it exists at the time of the appeal unless doing so would interfere with a vested right. * * * A vested right is * * * 'an expectation that cannot be taken away by legislation.' "[21]

*Fiduciary Administration*    Many trusts go on for years, during which time questions of allocations between principal and income arise. The Uniform Principal and Income Act of 1962, unlike its predecessor, applied to trusts created prior to its adoption, but only to "any receipt or expense received or incurred after the effective date" of the Act.[22] A similar approach is taken to investments by

**18.** Estate of Dulles, 431 A.2d 208 (Pa.1981).

**19.** Annan v. Wilmington Trust Co., 559 A.2d 1289 (Del.1989) (inclusion of children born out of wedlock).

**20.** In re Estate of Antonopoulos, 993 P.2d 637, 644 (Kan.1999).

**21.** Premier Property Management, Inc. v. Chavez, 728 N.E.2d 476, 481 (Ill. 2000).

**22.** Unif.Prin. & Inc.Act (1962) § 14.

trustees. "Whether an investment is proper is determined by the terms of the statute in force at the time when the investment is made" regardless when the trust was created.[23]

*Procedural Changes* Courts sometimes say that legislatures are "free to apply changes in rules of evidence or procedure retroactively,"[24] but the Uniform Probate Code says that it may be appropriate to defer the effectiveness of procedural changes "in the interest of justice."[25] When a will contest was pending when the legislature abolished trial by jury in such proceedings, the court applied the new law despite a similar savings clause.[26]

**23.** *Restatement, Second, of Trusts* § 227, comm. p (1959).

**24.** In re Marriage of Buol, 705 P.2d 354, 358 (Cal.1985).

**25.** Uniform Probate Code § 8–101(b)(2). *See also* Unif.Trust Code § 1106(a)(3).

**26.** Estate of Gardner, 2 Cal.Rptr.2d 664 (App.1991).

# Chapter 2

# INTESTATE SUCCESSION

*Table of Sections*

## § 2.1   The Surviving Spouse's Share

What happens to the property of a person who dies without a will? Although Blackstone in the 18th century devoted considerable discussion to the common law "canons of descent,"[1] today in every state intestate succession is controlled by a statute. In all states a share, sometimes the whole estate, passes to the decedent's surviving spouse if any.[2]

*History*   The spouse was never an heir to land at common law. Widows and widowers were relegated to lifetime enjoyment of the marital estates of dower and curtesy. Dower for widows was limited to one third of the husband's land. Curtesy for widowers extended to all of the wife's land, but was dependent on issue being born of the marriage.[3] Limiting spouses to a life interest stemmed from a

---

**§ 2.1**
**1.** W. Blackstone, *Commentaries* Bk 2, Chap. 14. These applied only to land; even in Blackstone's day succession to personal property was governed by a Statute of Distributions.

**2.** As to who is a "spouse" *see* Section 2.11.

**3.** A. Simpson, *An Introduction to the History of Land Law* 66 (1961).

fear that if the spouse inherited land in fee it would be permanently removed from the decedent's family. But the marital life estates in land hindered marketability; land is hard to sell when ownership is divided between a life tenant and remaindermen.

Personal property was subject to different rules. Under the Statute of Distribution of 1670, a widow took one-third of her husband's personalty if he left surviving issue and one-half if he did not.[4] Intestacy provisions for widowers were unnecessary because a husband acquired all his wife's personal property upon marriage.

Most American jurisdictions today give a spouse an outright (fee simple) share of the decedent's property. Distinctions between widows and widowers have disappeared, and would be of doubtful constitutionality. Spouses receive a larger share than was provided by common-law dower and curtesy or the Statute of Distributions. Empirical data suggests that most people want a larger share to pass to the spouse than the former rules provided.[5] Also, most surviving spouses are "beyond working years" and a large percent of them are "either poor or near poor, * * * having income no more than two times the poverty level," when the decedent died intestate.[6]

*Division Between Spouse and Issue*   When a decedent leaves both surviving spouse and issue, arguably the entire estate should go to the spouse. If the issue include minor children, giving them a share would require a guardianship for managing the property.[7] If the spouse is the children's other parent, awarding the estate to the spouse may actually be a better way to provide for the children. If the decedent's children are adults (as is most commonly true today because of increased life expectancy), they are usually capable of providing for themselves. For these reasons the Uniform Probate Code gives the entire estate to the spouse in intestacy "if all the decedent's surviving descendants are also descendants of the surviving spouse and there is no other [surviving] descendant of the surviving spouse."[8] The comment points out that that "testators in smaller estates (which intestate estates overwhelmingly tend to be) tend to devise their entire estates to their surviving spouses, even when the couple has children."

Today decedents are often survived by children of a prior marriage, or their spouse has children by another marriage (or

---

**4.**   22 & 23 Car. 2, c. 10, § 5.

**5.**   *E.g.*, Waggoner, *The Multiple Marriage Society and Spousal Rights under the Revised Uniform Probate Code*, 76 Iowa L. Rev. 223, 230–31 (1991). The use of surveys to shape the intestacy rules is discussed at 2.3.

**6.**   Waggoner, *Marital Property Rights in Transition*, 59 Mo.L.Rev. 21, 31–33 (1994).

**7.**   As to the disadvantages of guardianship for managing property see Section 9.2.

**8.**   Uniform Probate Code § 2–102.

children born out of wedlock). In this situation the spouse is less likely to provide for the decedent's children, so the Uniform Probate Code reduces the spouse's share as do many other (but not all) statutes.[9]

Arguably the spouse's share ought to depend upon the length of the marriage. The length of the marriage is an important factor in community property states where the spouse typically receives all the community property and only a fraction of the decedent's separate property upon intestacy.[10] Since community property is generally limited to property acquired during the marriage, there is usually little or no community property accumulated during a brief marriage.[11]

Some states make the spouse's share depend on how many children the intestate has, *e.g.*, the spouse gets one-half if there is only one child (or the issue of one child), but only one-third if more than one child (or child's issue) survives.[12]

In some states the fraction received by the spouse depends on the size of the estate. Under the Uniform Probate Code even a spouse who has children by a prior marriage receives $150,000 and one half of the balance of the estate, *i.e.* all of a small estate, but only a fraction of a larger one.[13] A spouse may need a larger share of a smaller estate for support, whereas a fraction of a larger estate may suffice.

*Spouse's Share in the Absence of Issue*   Modern statutes generally increase the spouse's share if the decedent has no surviving issue. Many give all to the surviving spouse if no issue survive,[14] but under some, the decedent's parents share with the surviving spouse.[15] If no parents survive, the surviving spouse takes the entire intestate estate under the UPC, but in some states the spouse must share with the decedent's siblings and their issue.[16]

---

**9.** New Hampshire Rev. Stat. Ann. 561:1; Vernon's Tex. Prob. Code Ann. § 45 (community property). These special rules do not cover the case where the spouse remarries and has children by another person after the decedent dies. Cf. La.Civ.Code art. 890 (spouse gets usufruct of decedent's share of community property *terminable upon remarriage*).

**10.** Cal.Prob.Code § 6401 says the spouse gets "the one half of the community property that belongs to the decedent;" the other half already belongs to the spouse. The spouse's share of separate property is 1/2 or 1/3 depending on the number of children.

**11.** A more complete discussion of community property appears in Section 3.8.

**12.** Cal.Prob.Code § 6401(c) (separate property); Ohio Rev.Code § 2105.06.

**13.** Uniform Probate Code § 2–102(2).

**14.** Ariz.Rev.Stat. § 14–2102(1) (separate property); Colo.Rev.Stat. § 15–11–102(1)(a).

**15.** Uniform Probate Code § 2–102(2).

**16.** Cal.Prob.Code § 6401 (separate property equally divided between spouse and parents or issue of parents).

When a decedent has no issue the property of both spouses may pass ultimately to the relatives of the survivor. California seeks to avoid this result by giving the relatives of the predeceasing spouse a share of the surviving spouse's estate if the latter dies intestate.[17] The English Administration of Estates Act puts the bulk of an intestate estate in trust for the surviving spouse for life if there are no issue, with a remainder to the intestate's collateral relatives.[18] A similar pattern is found in many American wills.[19]

## § 2.2   Relatives

Normally whatever does not pass to the surviving spouse on intestacy goes to the decedent's blood relatives. Spouses of relatives (e.g. sons-in-law, daughters-in-law) get no share, although such relatives by affinity may ultimately take property of the decedent as heirs or devisees of their spouse. The issue of a decedent are the first takers. Issue (or descendants—the two terms are synonymous) include children, grandchildren, great-grandchildren, etc. Only if there are no surviving issue do collateral relatives (such as brothers, sisters, nieces, nephews, etc.) or ancestors (parents, grandparents, etc.) inherit. This is true in all states.

*Exclusion of Issue of Living Ancestors*   Grandchildren and more remote relatives who have a living ancestor in a generation closer to the decedent do not take. Thus, if the intestate is survived by all her children and by grandchildren, the latter do not get a share.

*Representation*   A child who predeceases the decedent does not get a share; only persons who survive the intestate can be heirs. However, an heir does not have to survive until the decedent's estate is distributed; the share of an heir who survives the decedent but dies prior to distribution passes to the heir's estate.

Children of a relative who would have been an heir but who failed to survive the decedent receive the share the relative would have taken if he or she had survived. These children are said to "represent" their parent, but their share is not subject to the parent's will or claims of the parent's creditors.[1]

All states today allow representation. The common law governing land allowed it without limit, but the Statute of Distributions of 1670, which governed personal property, did not allow representation among collateral relatives except in the case of brothers' and

---

17. Cal.Prob.Code § 6402.5.

18. Administration of Estates Act, c. 23, § 46 (1925). So also under the French Code Civil art 767 the spouse, except in the absence of close blood relatives, gets only a life interest (*usufruit*).

19. Such "by-pass" trusts will be discussed in Section 9.3.

### § 2.2

1. Uniform Probate Code § 2–110.

sisters' children (the decedent's nephews and nieces).[2] Some American statutes today also bar representation among collaterals after a certain point, *e.g.* children of a deceased aunt or uncle, will not share in an estate if the decedent had surviving aunts or uncles.[3] The Uniform Probate Code, on the other hand, does not limit representation and would give the cousins a share.[4]

*Computation of Shares* Suppose that Mary has three children, Alice, Andrew and Arthur. Alice predeceases her, but Andrew and Arthur and Alice's three children Bob, Bill, and Betsy survive. All states agree that Bob, Bill and Betsy would split Alice's one-third and so each takes one-ninth of Mary's estate by representation. Division among grandchildren when there are no surviving children is more controversial. Suppose all of Mary's children predecease her and that, in addition to Alice's three children, Andrew had one child, Ben, and Arthur two, Burt and Barbara. In many states each of the grandchildren would take an equal (1/6) share.[5] The common law, on the other hand, adopted a method of division often called per stirpes, "according to the roots; since all the branches [of a family] inherit the same share that their root, whom they represent, would have done."[6] Under this system, Ben takes his father's 1/3, while Burt and Barbara divide their father's 1/3, each getting 1/6. Alice's three children each take 1/9. Some states still follow this approach.[7]

The same issue can arise when inheritance goes to collateral relatives (because the intestate died without issue). If Mary had no issue, parents, or spouse, and her siblings were all dead, her estate would go to their children (Mary's nieces and nephews), equally in some states,[8] per stirpes in others.[9]

In some cases there are surviving children and grandchildren by two or more deceased children, *e.g.,* Alice and Andrew predecease Mary but Arthur survives her. In many states, Bob, Bill, and Betsy will divide Alice's share, each receiving one-ninth of Mary's estate, and Ben will take Andrew's one-third share.[10] Thus persons

**2.** Statute of Distributions, 22 & 23 Car. 2, c. 10, § 7 (1670).

**3.** Dahood v. Frankovich, 746 P.2d 115 (Mont.1987).

**4.** Uniform Probate Code § 2–103(4).

**5.** Cal.Prob.Code § 6402(a); Uniform Probate Code § 2–103, comment; Brice v. Seebeck, 595 P.2d 441 (Okl.1979) (division among nieces and nephews).

**6.** 2 W. Blackstone, *Commentaries* *217 (1766).

**7.** 755 ILCS § 5/2–1(a); Kentucky Rev. Stat. § 391.040.

**8.** Matter of Estate of Kendall, 968 P.2d 364 (Okla.Civ.App.1998) (estate divided equally among 12 nieces and nephews, children of 3 deceased siblings).

**9.** The answer is not necessarily the same for collaterals and descendants. *See* Ga.Code Ann. § 53–2–1(b)(1) (among descendants distribution is per stirpes), § 53–2–1(b)(5) (distribution among nieces and nephews is per capita).

**10.** Calif.Prob.Code § 240.

in the same generation get unequal shares. Professor Waggoner argued that persons of the same degree should always take equally.[11] The UPC has now adopted his system,[12] sometimes called "per capita with representation," which would give Arthur one-third, but the remaining two-thirds would drop down to the next generation and be equally divided, so the children of Alice and Andrew would each receive one-sixth of Mary's estate.

When there are no surviving children and an estate is to be divided among grandchildren and great-grandchildren, where does the initial division occur? A trust created by the founder of the Hastings Law School, raised this question; Hastings' living issue were four grandchildren and two great-grandchildren, children of deceased grandchildren.[13] The court divided the estate initially at the level of Hastings' children even though they were all dead. As a consequence, claimants in the same degree received unequal shares and a great-grandchild received more than three of the grandchildren. The Restatement calls this method of division "strict per stirpes."[14] Under the Uniform Probate Code, on the other hand, the estate would have been initially divided at the closest level to the intestate where there were living claimants; Hastings' children would be ignored because they were all dead.[15]

*Interpretation of Wills* The question how to compute shares also arises under wills. If a will devises property to "my grandchildren" courts usually require an equal distribution, without regard to the number of children from which the claimants stem.[16]

If a devise is to "issue" or to "heirs" the UPC follows the rules of intestacy in determining the shares,[17] but additional language may change the result, since the testator's intent controls. There has been much litigation about words like "equally" or "share and share alike." For example, a will left land to the testator's son's "heirs, share and share alike." By the law of intestacy, the son's estate would go half to his daughter and half to the children of his deceased son, but the court held that "share and share alike"

---

**11.** Waggoner, *A Proposed Alternative to the Uniform Probate Code's System for Intestate Distribution Among Descendants,* 66 Nw.U.L.Rev. 626, 628 (1972).

**12.** Uniform Probate Code § 2–106.

**13.** Maud v. Catherwood, 155 P.2d 111 (Cal.App.1945).

**14.** *Restatement, Third, of Property (Wills and Other Donative Transfers)* § 2.3, comm. d (1998). The same method was followed in Boston Safe Deposit and Trust Co. v. Goodwin, 795 N.E.2d 581 (Mass.App.Ct.2003).

**15.** Uniform Probate Code § 2–106. *See also* Hockman v. Estate of Lowe, 624 S.W.2d 719 (Tex.App.1981) (when intestate had nine nieces and nephews, each living one gets 1/8 and the ninth share divided between the children of a dead nephew).

**16.** *Restatement, Second, of Property (Donative Transfers)* § 28.1 (1987).

**17.** Uniform Probate Code §§ 2–708, 2–711.

required that each heir take one third.[18] Other courts, however, have held that " 'equally,' referring to a multi-generational class, normally means per stirpes,"[19] *i.e.* each stirps gets an equal share, but not each taker.

"Per stirpes" is ambiguous unless defined. When a will gives property "per stirpes to my grand nieces and the issue of any deceased grandnieces" should the basis of division be the testator's nieces and nephews or the next generation?[20] One court held that the grandnieces and grandnephews were the roots, but on similar facts other courts have disagreed.[21] Drafters who use words like "per stirpes" or "by representation" should define them.[22]

*Parents and their Issue* If a decedent leaves no surviving issue, parents or siblings are next in line. Most American jurisdictions today prefer the decedent's parents (or surviving parent) over brothers and sisters,[23] but in some states siblings share with parents under various formulas.[24]

*More Remote Relatives* Some intestacy statutes name no specific takers after the issue of parents; they simply give the inheritance to the decedent's "next of kin."[25] Collateral relatives share a common ancestor with the decedent. The degree of kinship between a decedent and a collateral relative is computed by adding the number of generations from the decedent to the common ancestor and then down to the relative; a brother is in the second degree, a nephew is in the third degree, the common ancestors being the decedent's parents. First cousins are related in the fourth degree.

Issue of a nearer ancestor are preferred to issue of a more remote ancestor even if they are not as close in degree. A nephew, even though he is in the third degree of kinship, takes ahead of grandparents who are in the second degree because the nephew is issue of a closer ancestor (the decedent's parents). The Uniform Probate Code designates as heirs first the issue of the decedent (§ 2–103(1)), then the decedent's parents and their issue (§ 2–103(2)(3)), then the grandparents and their issue (§ 2–103(4)).

Everyone has two sets of grandparents, maternal and paternal. The UPC divides the estate into maternal and paternal halves, and then subdivides each half. Thus if the only surviving relatives were

---

**18.**  Black v. Unknown Creditors, 155 N.W.2d 784 (S.D.1968).

**19.**  Dewire v. Haveles, 534 N.E.2d 782, 786 (Mass.1989).

**20.**  Estate of Edwards, 250 Cal.Rptr. 779 (App.1988).

**21.**  *Restatement, Second, of Property (Donative Transfers)* § 28.2, comm. b (1987).

**22.**  For clear language see Uniform Statutory Will Act § 1(5).

**23.**  Uniform Probate Code § 2–103(2); Conn.Gen.Stat.Ann. § 45a–439(a)(1).

**24.**  755 ILCS § 5/2–1(d) (equal division among parents and siblings); Tex. Prob.Code Ann. § 38(a) (all to parents but if one dead 1/2 to siblings).

**25.**  Conn.Gen.Stat. § 45a–439.

a paternal aunt (father's sister) and three maternal uncles (mother's brothers), the paternal aunt would take one-half of the estate and the maternal uncles would take one-sixth each.[26] Some states would give one-fourth to each of the aunts and uncles in this situation.[27]

*Ancestral Property*  Historically, land returned to the branch of the family from which it came.[28] If a woman had inherited Blackacre from her paternal grandfather and died without surviving issue of herself or her parents, her paternal collaterals (uncles, aunts, cousins) would take Blackacre to the exclusion of her maternal collaterals. This doctrine never applied to personalty. The ancestral property idea creates administrative difficulties because it requires tracing the source of land. It has been discarded by most jurisdictions today, but a few states retain vestiges of it.[29]

*Half-blood*  Half-bloods are related to each other through only one common ancestor rather than two. If Arthur and Andrew have the same father but different mothers, Arthur being a child of his father's prior marriage, Arthur and Andrew are half-brothers. A son of Andrew would be Arthur's half-nephew. Historically, half-blood relatives could not inherit land from each other, but as to personal property, half-bloods always shared equally with whole-blood relatives.[30] Most modern statutes make no distinction between whole-bloods and half-bloods.[31] A few states give the half-blood only half as much as a whole-blood of the same degree.[32] A devise of property "to my brothers and sisters" is presumed to include half-brothers and half-sisters.[33]

*"Laughing Heirs" and Escheat*  If a person is survived by neither spouse nor close blood relatives, should the decedent's property escheat to the state or be distributed to remote relatives? The latter are sometimes called "laughing heirs" because they are personally unaffected by the decedent's death and so (supposedly) laugh all the way to the bank. The Uniform Probate Code excludes such remote relatives, limiting inheritance to issue of grandparents.[34] However, most statutes permit inheritance by distant blood

---

**26.**  Uniform Probate Code § 2–103(1), (4).

**27.**  Cal.Prob.Code § 6402(d).

**28.**  2 W. Blackstone, *Commentaries* *220 (1765).

**29.**  Ky.Rev.Stat. § 391.020. *See Restatement, Third, of Property (Wills and Other Donative Transfers)* § 2.4, comm. d (1998).

**30.**  2 W. Blackstone, *Commentaries* 224, 505 (1765).

**31.**  Uniform Probate Code § 2–107; Calif.Prob.Code § 6406.

**32.**  Fla.Stat.Ann. § 732.105; Curry v. Williman, 834 S.W.2d 443 (Tex.App. 1992) (full brother gets 20% of estate, 3 half brothers get 10% each).

**33.**  *Restatement, Second, of Property (Donative Transfers)* § 25.8, comment d (1987); Uniform Probate Code § 2–705(a).

**34.**  Uniform Probate Code § 2–103.

relatives rather than let the property escheat to the state.[35] Some states allow persons related to the decedent's spouse but not to the decedent to inherit if the decedent has no surviving relatives.[36]

A person who feels no affection for remote heirs can disinherit them by will, but heirs can contest a will, *e.g.* for incapacity or undue influence, and in most states they must be notified when a will is offered for probate.[37] As a result, an heir-tracing industry has evolved. Most firms charge a percentage of the estate to the estate or to the heirs. In a large estate these fees can be quite substantial.

*Aliens* At common law an alien could not hold land in England. This rule has been invoked in modern cases, but the right to inherit may be conferred on aliens by treaty or statute.[38] Under Restatement of Property, unless a statute otherwise provides, non-citizens can acquire and transmit property.[39]

## § 2.3  General Aspects of Intestacy: Statutory Wills

*Empirical Studies* Intestate succession statutes purport to distribute estates along the lines that the average person would prefer. However, studies of public preferences regarding the disposition of wealth at death suggest that some common statutory provisions are out of line with today's attitudes. These studies are of two types. The first examines probate court records of decedents' wills. Such studies influenced the Uniform Probate Code.[1] The second type relies on interviews with living persons who say how they would want their property to pass on death in various hypothetical situations. Both types of study have deficiencies. The examination of wills may be misleading as to the average person's desires because "willmakers tend to be wealthier, better educated, and engaged in higher status occupations than those who die without a will."[2] Also wills usually reflect the influence of lawyers who draft them. But lawyers' advice often brings up factors which the client had not previously considered. If the law should be modeled on the *informed* wishes of citizens, studies based on interviews with the public may mislead as to what people *really* want.

**35.** Estate of McGuigan, 99 Cal. Rptr.2d 887, 890 (App.2000).

**36.** Cal.Prob.Code § 6402(e).

**37.** As to notice and standing to contest wills see Section 12.1.

**38.** In re Estate of Constan, 384 A.2d 495 (N.H.1978).

**39.** *Restatement, Third, of Property (Wills and Other Donative Transfers)* § 1.3 (1998). A Statutory Note appended to this section lists many relevant statutes.

**§ 2.3**

**1.** See Comment to Part 1, § 2–102, comment.

**2.** Beckstrom, *Sociobiology and Intestate Wealth Transfers,* 76 Nw. U.L.Rev. 216, 217–19 (1981).

*Why Not Die Intestate?*　Attorneys may be asked why a client needs a will. One reason is that state intestacy laws only meet the needs of a 'normal' family and may not fit the client's situation. The spouse of a year is generally treated the same as the spouse of a long time; a wealthy or unloving child is treated the same as a needy and devoted one. Unrelated persons are excluded even if they have enjoyed the same kind of relationship with the decedent as a child. Remote relatives may take an estate which the owner would prefer to leave to a charity or friends.[3]

When a client has minor children intestacy is particularly undesirable because a guardian of the minor's property may have to be appointed to manage the minor's property. Many states impose strict court supervision over guardians. These restrictions are cumbersome and generally antithetical to the child's interest in earning a fair return on the property and reducing costs.[4] Moreover, guardianship ends when a child ceases to be a minor, and many children who are 18 (or sometimes much older) should have property managed for them. The best method for accomplishing this is a trust. Many testators with minor children avoid guardianship by leaving everything to their spouse in the expectation that the spouse will take care of the children, but this solution may be unsatisfactory if the surviving spouse is not the parent of the decedent's children, or has other children by a prior marriage. Here too a trust can provide a better solution than the intestacy statutes.

Even if a person wants all her property to pass to the heirs designated by the intestacy laws, a will can designate an executor to administer the estate and can give the executor powers beyond those conferred by law. Administration of an estate is more efficient when the executor has such powers.[5]

*Statutory Wills*　Despite the advantages of wills, many persons do not have them. According to one study, only 20% of the decedents in the area studied had a will.[6] To some extent this is due to the availability of nonprobate methods of transfer at death.[7] To some extent it is based on reluctance to hire lawyers.

Some states have promulgated statutory wills which lay persons can use at a very modest cost. Many of the disadvantages of dying intestate can be avoided by using the California Statutory Will, for example. It allows a testator to leave all the estate to the

---

**3.** In Estate of Griswold, 24 P.3d 1191 (Cal.2001) half siblings with whom decedent had had no contact and who were unaware of his existence inherited from him.

**4.** For further discussion of alternatives to guardianship see Section 9.2.

**5.** A general discussion of administration appears in Chapter 12.

**6.** Schoenblum, *Will Contests—An Empirical Study*, 22 Real Prop. Prob. and Trust J. 607 (1987).

**7.** For a discussion of the advantages of avoiding probate see Section 9.1.

spouse by signing the appropriate box.[8] The testator can also designate a custodian for his/her children, which avoids many of the disadvantages of guardianship.[9] The form allows designation of an executor, and confers powers on the executor which are more extensive than those given to an administrator without a will.[10]

A Uniform Statutory Will Act allows testators to create a trust for a spouse for life, and a trust for a child who "cannot effectively manage * * * property by reason of mental illness * * * or other cause."[11] Few lay persons are aware of this Act; its object is "to provide attorneys a simple will * * * at minimum cost to the client."[12] Lawyers who have little experience or training in probate are well advised to consult the Act before drafting a will. Although adopted in only a few states, the Act can be incorporated by reference by a drafter in any state.

## § 2.4   Gifts to "Heirs"

Although lawyers advise clients not to die intestate, they often use the intestacy laws in drafting wills by including a gift to the "heirs" of the testator. This term is normally interpreted to incorporate by reference the laws of intestate succession.

*Equivalent Words*   Occasionally an instrument uses the word "next of kin" rather than heirs. Historically this term was used to describe persons who took personal property while the heirs inherited the land, but the differences between the two have almost universally disappeared. The Uniform Probate Code uses "heirs" for all takers by intestacy, and calls for interpreting the word "next of kin" as a gift to the same persons.[1] The Uniform Probate Code also construes words of more uncertain import, like "relatives" and "family" to mean the takers under intestacy statutes.[2]

*Other Meanings of "Heirs:" Devisees*   The word "heirs" does not always refer to the intestacy statutes. Its Latin root, *heres,* was used in Roman law to mean either a person designated by will or someone who took upon intestacy.[3] This usage still survives in

**8.** Cal. Prob. Code § 6240, par. 5, Choice One.

**9.** Custodianships are discussed at Section 9.2

**10.** Cal.Prob.Code § 6241.

**11.** Unif.Stat.Will Act § 6 (trust for spouse), § 9 (trust for disabled individual).

**12.** *Id.*, Prefatory Note.

### § 2.4

**1.** Uniform Probate Code § 1–201(21), 2–711.

**2.** Id., § 2–711. *See also Restatement, Second, of Property (Donative Transfers)* § 29.1, comm. b (1987) ("relatives"); Boston Safe Deposit & Trust Co. v. Wilbur, 728 N.E.2d 264, 268 (Mass.2000).

**3.** Justinian, *Institutes* 2.20.34 (the main purpose of a will is to designate the heir).

Louisiana.[4] In the common law tradition, however, heirs ordinarily means only persons designated by law to take upon intestacy.[5] But the context may show that the testator used the word "heirs" to mean devisees.[6]

*Spouses* Most courts construe gifts to "heirs" to include a spouse because most modern intestacy statutes give spouses a share on intestacy.[7] The Uniform Probate Code agrees unless the spouse has remarried when the disposition takes effect.[8]

Some testators use the word "heirs" to mean "children" or "issue." When a testator left land to his grandson's heirs, "and if he should die without heirs to my other Grandchildren," the court construed "heirs" to mean "issue," since the "other Grandchildren" would *be* the grandson's heirs if he had no issue, and a gift to a person's heirs if he dies without heirs is nonsense.[9]

*Choice of Law* A drafter who decides to use a gift to "heirs" should make clear *which* intestacy statute should control. For example, a trust provided that a grandson's widow "shall receive such portion of the trust estate as she would be entitled to had her husband died intestate." This portion was greater under Maryland law, where the trust was created and administered, than under the law of Texas, where the grandson was domiciled. The court held that Maryland law governed,[10] but the Uniform Probate Code would have looked to Texas, the "law of the designated individual's domicile."[11] The Restatement of Property would also have looked to the law of Texas including its choice of law rules, which might in turn lead to the situs of any real property involved.[12] A well drafted will can avoid controversy by specifying the relevant law, *e.g.* "the individuals who would be entitled to receive the estate as if the property were located in this state and [the ancestor] had then died intestate domiciled in this state."[13]

Since the governing intestacy statute may change between the time the testator executes the will and the time the property is

---

**4.** Succession of Dinwiddie, 263 So.2d 739 (La.App.1972).

**5.** PNC Bank, Ohio, N.A. v. Stanton, 662 N.E.2d 875 (Ohio App.1995).

**6.** Evans v. Cass, 256 N.E.2d 738 (Ohio Prob.1970); *Restatement, Second, of Property (Donative Transfers)* § 29.1, comm. g (1987).

**7.** *Id.* § 29.1, comm. j; Estate of Calden, 712 A.2d 522 (Me.1998). *But see Restatement, Second, of Property (Donative Transfers)* § 29.3, comm. a (1987) (spouse is not an heir where governing law allows only dower). As to the spouse's share on intestacy see Section 2.1.

**8.** Uniform Probate Code § 2–711. *See also* Cal.Prob.Code § 21114.

**9.** Cheuvront v. Haley, 444 S.W.2d 734 (Ky.1969). *See also Restatement, Second, of Property (Donative Transfers)* § 29.1, comm. f (1987).

**10.** Lansburgh v. Lansburgh, 632 A.2d 221 (Md.App.1993).

**11.** Uniform Probate Code § 2–711.

**12.** *Restatement, Second, of Property (Donative Transfers)* § 29.2 (1987).

**13.** Uniform Statutory Will Act § 6(3).

distributed, the will should also specify the time for applying the controlling law.

*Planning* Objections can be raised to using the word "heirs" in drafting. Most testators do not know what the intestacy statutes provide; some whose wills left property to "heirs" understood this to mean something different from what the law provides.[14] Nevertheless, the word "heirs" is useful because the intestacy statutes cover a wide variety of situations. Many wills specify a distribution for the situations most likely to prevail, but use a devise to "heirs" as an "end limitation" to cover remote contingencies.[15] This is simpler than spelling out all possible contingencies in the will. But a gift to "heirs" may require a costly search for remote relatives or even escheat, so some testators might prefer an end limitation to charity.

## § 2.5  Recovery for Wrongful Death

Many decedents who have accumulated little or no property leave their families with a valuable claim against a tortfeasor who was responsible for their death. At common law tort claims died with the person, but all states now allow wrongful death actions. The law on this subject is not generally considered part of the law of wills. Although wrongful death actions are typically brought by the decedent's personal representative who is appointed by the probate court, the recovery is not subject to the decedent's will.

Many statutes refer to the intestacy laws in designating the beneficiaries of a wrongful death. In California the action is brought on behalf of the "decedent's surviving spouse, children, and issue of deceased children, or, if none, the persons who would be entitled to the property of the decedent by intestate succession."[1] But the beneficiaries of wrongful death actions are not always the same persons who take on intestacy. A statute which designated "the heir or heirs of the deceased" was interpreted to include only descendants of the decedent and not collateral relatives who might inherit, because the purpose of the statute was "to compensate those who suffer pecuniary loss by reason of the death" and this would not be generally true of the latter.[2] In some states, certain heirs, such as the surviving spouse and children, are presumed to have been damaged by the death, whereas others are

---

**14.** Brunson v. Citizens Bank and Trust Co., 752 S.W.2d 316 (Ky.App. 1988) (testator apparently thought his "heirs" included his sisters even though he had a daughter).

**15.** Uniform Statutory Will Act § 7(a)(2) (devise to heirs if testator dies without issue).

**§ 2.5**

**1.** Cal.Code Civ.Proc. § 377.60.

**2.** Ablin v. Richard O'Brien Plastering Co., 885 P.2d 289 (Colo.App.1994) (siblings cannot sue even though they are literally "heirs").

eligible to claim, but must prove that they were damaged.[3] Conversely, dependent relatives of the decedent have been allowed to recover for wrongful death even though they could not inherit.[4]

Even if the decedent's heirs and the statutory wrongful death beneficiaries are the same persons, the fixed shares prescribed by the intestacy statutes do not always control the allocation of a wrongful death recovery.[5] Under the typical intestacy statute, parents inherit equally, but they often are awarded unequal amounts for wrongful death based on their relationship with the child.[6] In California the court allocates the recovery among the eligible claimants.[7] The statute does not say how this discretion is to be exercised. In Ohio the court makes the allocation "having due regard for the injury and loss to each beneficiary * * * and for the age and condition of the beneficiaries."[8]

*Survival Statutes* Most states allow the decedent's estate to recover for some losses, and *this* recovery can be controlled by the decedent's will. Under the Model Act, for example, damages which "accrued to [the decedent] before his death* * * become part of the decedent's estate and are distributable in the same manner as other assets of the estate."[9] These damages usually include medical expenses or pain and suffering by the decedent before death.[10] Thus a death may produce two types of recovery, one going to the decedent's estate and the other to the statutory beneficiaries. Both claims are usually enforced by the decedent's personal representative, and the Model Act allows them to be combined in a single action.[11] It is sometimes hard to allocate a recovery between them.

# § 2.6 Advancements

If Mary has three children, Alice, Arthur and Andrew, in all states they would share equally if Mary died intestate. Suppose that Mary while she was alive gave $10,000 to Alice. If this $10,000 is not taken into account in dividing Mary's estate, Alice will get more

---

**3.** Miller v. Allstate Ins. Co., 676 N.E.2d 943 (Ohio App.1996) (sister of decedent can claim but does not benefit from the statutory presumption of damage).

**4.** Luider v. Skaggs, 693 N.E.2d 593 (Ind.App.1998).

**5.** In some states, however, the intestacy statutes control the allocation. Pogue v. Pogue, 434 So.2d 262 (Ala.Civ. App.1983) (recovery equally divided between mother and father who had failed to support the child because intestacy statute controlled).

**6.** Jones v. Jones, 641 N.E.2d 98 (Ind.App.1994) (proper to award 65% to the mother who had custody of the child).

**7.** Cal.Code Civ.Proc. § 377.61.

**8.** Ohio Rev. Code § 2125.03(A)(1); *cf.* Booker v. Lal, 726 N.E.2d 638, 641 (Ill.App.2000) (allocation on basis of "percentage of dependency").

**9.** Model Survival and Death Act § 2(b). *See also* Cal. Code Civ. Proc. § 377.34.

**10.** In re Thornton, 481 N.W.2d 828 (Mich.App.1992) (pain and suffering).

**11.** Model Survival and Death Act § 4. *See also* Cal.Code Civ. Proc. § 377.62.

of Mary's property than her brothers, contrary to the general assumption that parents want their children to share equally. Many states today have statutes dealing with such "advancements" on an inheritance.

*Proof of Intent*   Under the Uniform Probate Code a lifetime gift is treated as an advancement against the donee's share of the donor's intestate estate "only if the decedent declared in a contemporaneous writing or the heir acknowledged in writing that the gift is an advancement."[1] The fact that a gift is in writing (*e.g.* a check or a deed) does not suffice unless the writing describes the gift as an advancement. Under such a statute few advancements will be legally recognized because persons who die intestate do not usually consult lawyers and are not likely to know about the writing requirement.[2] Some have praised the Code because it eliminates "wasteful litigation" about the decedent's intention which is often "either nonexistent or obscure."[3]

Many states do not require a writing to prove that a gift was intended as an advancement. If there is no evidence at all as to the donor's intent, some states presume that gifts are not advancements,[4] but some make the opposite presumption.[5]

The intention that a gift be an advancement must have existed when the gift was made; the donor cannot later convert an absolute gift into an advancement; hence the requirement in the UPC of a "contemporaneous writing."[6] However, a change of heart by the donor which is *beneficial* to the recipient is allowed; a provision in a will that loans previously made to a child shall be treated only as advancements was given effect.[7] Conversely, the *recipient* can acknowledge that a prior gift should be treated as an advancement; the word "contemporaneous" does not apply to such a writing.

*Computation of Shares*   A comment to the Uniform Probate Code illustrates how shares are computed when there is an advancement.[8] Suppose a decedent with a wife (*W*) and three children, *A*, to whom he had advanced $50,000, *B*, who had received $10,000, and *C*. The father dies intestate with an estate of $190,000. The

---

**§ 2.6**

**1.** Uniform Probate Code § 2–109. *See also* N.Y.EPTL § 2–1.5(b).

**2.** Fellows, *Concealing Legislative Reform in the Common–Law Tradition*, 37 Vand.L.Rev. 671, 678 (1984).

**3.** Chaffin, *A Reappraisal of the Wealth Transmission Process*, 10 Ga. L.Rev. 447, 497, 499 (1976). In Matter of Martinez' Estate, 633 P.2d 727 (N.M.App.1981), the court rejected the claim of an advancement based on "self-serving testimony in 1980 [by another heir] to a conversation with [the decedent] in 1953 to prove [his] intent in 1941."

**4.** Iowa Code § 633.224.

**5.** La.Civ.Code § 1230.

**6.** Uniform Probate Code § 2–109(a).

**7.** O'Brien v. O'Brien, 526 S.E.2d 1 (Va.2000).

**8.** Uniform Probate Code § 2–109, comment.

advancements are figuratively added back into the estate, bringing it up to $250,000. This increases W's share under the UPC, but in some states advancements only affect descendants of the donor.[9] The balance passing to the three children would be $75,000, or $25,000 each. A, who has already received more than his share, is not required to refund the excess, but he gets no more of the decedent's estate.[10] A's advancement and his share are now disregarded, and new calculations are made for a $200,000 estate ($190,-000 plus the $10,000 advancement to B). After W takes her share, $50,000 is left to be divided between B and C. B has already received $10,000, so he gets $15,000 more, and $25,000 goes to C.

What if B predeceases the decedent and B's children take by representation? Their share would not be affected by the advancement under the UPC, "unless the decedent's contemporaneous writing provides otherwise,"[11] but some states take advancements into account in computing the shares of descendants of the recipient.[12]

If the advancement is in the form of property, any subsequent appreciation or depreciation of the property is ignored; the Uniform Probate Code follows the generally accepted principle that "the property advanced is valued as of the time the heir came into possession or enjoyment of the property or as of the time of the death of the decedent, whichever first occurs."[13]

*Satisfaction of Devises*    The rules on advancements apply only to intestate succession. If a will leaves an estate "to my children equally," any gifts received from the testator before the will was executed are disregarded; the law assumes that the testator has taken them into account.[14] Should a gift by a testator *after* the will was executed be treated as a partial or total satisfaction of a devise?[15] The Uniform Probate Code provision on this issue paral-

---

**9.** Md. Estates and Trusts Code § 3–106(d). In the UPC hypothetical, W is not the mother of the decedent's children. In some situations the spouse would get the entire estate even had there been no advancement. Uniform Probate Code § 2–102.

**10.** O'Brien v. O'Brien, 526 S.E.2d 1 (Va.2000) (child to whom advancement made cannot be sued for the excess). However, if the $50,000 which A received was a *loan*, it would be set off against his share, and he would have to refund the difference. Uniform Probate Code § 3–903

**11.** *Id.,* § 2–109. On the other hand, a gift to a grandchild may be an advancement even though the recipient was not a prospective heir at the time of

the gift, if the grandchild later turns out to be an heir.

**12.** Md. Estates and Trusts Code § 3–106(c); La.Civ.Code § 1240.

**13.** Uniform Probate Code § 2–109(b).

**14.** In Louisiana, "collation" is required both in testate and intestate succession. La. Civil Code § 1228.

**15.** N.Y. EPTL § 2–1.5(a) uses the term "advancement" to include gifts to the "beneficiary under an existing will of the donor," but the more common term is "satisfaction" or "ademption by satisfaction" of the prior devise. A specific devise can be adeemed by extinction when the testator gives the devised

lels its rule on advancements; lifetime gifts are not taken into account unless the will (or some other writing) so provides.[16] The writing requirement does not apply to loans.[17]

Some states allow oral evidence of intent in all cases.[18] Similarities between the devise and the gift may show an intent to substitute one for the other, *e.g.* when a will left $5,000 to a home in memory of the testator's wife and the testator later gave the same amount to the home for the same purpose.[19]

The Uniform Probate Code rules on valuation of gifts in satisfaction of devises are the same as for advancements, but the effect on the issue of a recipient who predeceases the donor differs: a donor-testator is presumed to have intended that the share of the donee-devisee's issue be reduced or eliminated in this situation.[20]

*Planning* An attorney drafting a will should ask the testator about any prior gifts. The testator may wish to reduce the share of for a child or spouse who has already received substantial gifts. The law assumes that testators have taken prior gifts into account, and drafters should make sure that this assumption is correct.

## § 2.7  Homicide

If a wife murders her husband can she inherit from him? There are no reported decisions on this question before the end of the nineteenth century. When the argument that a murderer should not be allowed to inherit began to appear, many courts rejected it, saying that any change in the intestacy statute must come from legislation.[1] In 1897 Dean Ames suggested that courts should impose a constructive trust on the murderer.[2] The Restatement of Restitution and some courts adopted this suggestion,[3] but many courts reject the constructive trust approach as "somewhat fictitious."[4]

property to the devisee or someone else. See Section 8.1.

**16.** Uniform Probate Code § 2–609.

**17.** In Matter of Estate of Button, 830 P.2d 1216 (Kan.App.1992).

**18.** Ky. Rev. Stat. § 394.370.

**19.** In re Kreitman's Estate, 386 N.E.2d 650 (Ill.App.1979).

**20.** Uniform Probate Code § 2–609.

### § 2.7

**1.** McGovern, *Homicide and Succession to Property*, 68 Mich.L.Rev. 65–57 (1968).

**2.** Ames, *Can a Murderer Acquire Title by His Crime and Keep It?*, 36 Am.Law Reg. (n.s.) 225, 228–29 (1897).

[This essay was republished in J. Ames, *Lectures on Legal History* 310 (1913).]

**3.** *Restatement of Restitution* § 187 (1937); Sikora v. Sikora, 499 P.2d 808 (Mont.1972).

**4.** In re Estate of Thomann, 649 N.W.2d 1, 8 (Iowa 2002) (court will not "substitute its judgment for that of the legislature by imposing a constructive trust on the murderer's proportional share").

*Statutes*   Most states now have statutes which bar a murderer from inheriting from the victim. Some of these statutes are incomplete. One says that a devisee or heir, if convicted of intentionally killing a decedent, forfeits his share of the decedent's estate.[5] The statute does not cover nonprobate transfers, *e.g.* an insurance policy beneficiary who murders the insured. The cases interpreting such incomplete statutes are hard to reconcile. One court allowed a person convicted of manslaughter to inherit because the governing statute only covered "murder,"[6] but another barred a person convicted of manslaughter on the theory that the statute did not "completely supplant the common law principle * * * that one should not be allowed to profit by his own wrong."[7]

The Uniform Probate Code provision on this subject covers a broad range of cases and adds a catchall: "A wrongful acquisition of property or interest by the killer not covered by this section must be treated in accordance with the principle that a killer cannot profit from his [or her] wrong."[8] This principle was applied to someone who killed his grandmother, whose heir died a few months later leaving the killer as her heir. "An intervening estate should not * * * thwart the intent of the legislature that the murderer not profit by his wrong."[9]

*Degree of Crime*   The killer's motives are immaterial,[10] but some courts have allowed one to take if the killing did not amount to murder.[11] Louisiana, on the other hand, bars an insurance beneficiary from collecting the proceeds if he is "criminally responsible" for the death of the insured; this includes even an unintentional killing.[12] The Uniform Probate Code bars anyone who "feloniously and intentionally" kills the decedent.[13] This formula encompasses voluntary manslaughter as well as murder, but not involuntary manslaughter. A killer who is guilty of no criminal offense at all, *e.g.,* one who kills in self-defense or by accident, is not disqualified,[14] nor is a killer who was insane.[15]

---

**5.**  14 Vt.Stat. § 551(6).

**6.**  Nable v. Godfrey's Estate, 403 So.2d 1038 (Fla.App.1981).

**7.**  Quick v. United Benefit Life Ins. Co., 213 S.E.2d 563 (N.C.1975).

**8.**  Uniform Probate Code § 2–803(f). A similar provision appeared in a statute proposed in 1936 which a few states have adopted. Wade, *Acquisition of Property by Willfully Killing Another—A Statutory Solution,* 49 Harv.L.Rev. 715, 750–51 (1936).

**9.**  In re Estate of Vallerius, 629 N.E.2d 1185, 1189 (Ill.App.1994). *See also Restatement, Second, of Property (Donative Transfers)* § 34.8, illus. 2 (1992) (son who kills sibling cannot thereby increase his share of his mother's estate).

**10.**  Francis v. Marshall, 841 S.W.2d 51 (Tex.App.1992). *Compare* Sherman, *Mercy Killing and the Right to Inherit,* 61 U.Cinn.L.Rev. 803 (1993) (mercy killer should be allowed to inherit).

**11.**  Aranda v. Camacho, 931 P.2d 757 (N.M.App.1997).

**12.**  In re Hamilton, 446 So.2d 463 (La.App.1984).

**13.**  Uniform Probate Code § 2–803(b).

**14.**  State Farm Life Ins. Co. v. Smith, 363 N.E.2d 785 (Ill.1977); Huff v. Union Fidelity Life Ins. Co., 470 N.E.2d 236 (Ohio App.1984) (killing in defense of another).

**15.**  Estate of Artz v. Artz, 487 A.2d 1294 (N.J.Super.A.D.1985). *Contra,* Ind. Code § 29–1–2–12.1.

*Proof of Crime*   Often the alleged killer has not been tried, e.g. because he committed suicide after the crime. Courts operating under a statute which bars one "convicted" of murder have held that the murder can be established only by a criminal conviction,[16] but most courts conclude that the absence of a criminal conviction does not prevent them from determining guilt.[17] Even when the accused has been acquitted, most courts admit evidence that the accused was in fact guilty[18] on the ground that an acquittal may mean merely failure to meet the higher standard of proof required in criminal proceedings. Under the Uniform Probate Code, "in the absence of a conviction, the court * * * must determine whether, under the preponderance of evidence standard, the individual would be found criminally accountable."[19]

If the killer has been convicted, the Uniform Probate Code makes a conviction conclusive in determining the right to succession,[20] but some statutes simply make the conviction admissible evidence.[21]

*Avoiding Forfeiture*   The law no longer imposes forfeiture of property for crime. Barring a murderer from inheriting is distinguishable because it does "not deprive the murderer of any property rights, but [only] prevent(s) his acquisition of *additional* rights."[22] The distinction between depriving someone of what he already owns and barring the "acquisition of additional rights" can be fuzzy. Suppose *A* and *B* own land in joint tenancy, and *A* murders *B*. Most authorities would allow *A* to keep his share of income from the property since he did not acquire that interest by his crime.[23] When *A* dies, some courts would award all the land to *B*'s estate on the theory that but for the murder, *B* might have

**16.**  Holliday v. McMullen, 756 P.2d 1179 (Nev.1988).

**17.**  Bernstein v. Rosenthal, 671 P.2d 979 (Colo.App.1983).

**18.**  Matter of Congdon's Estate, 309 N.W.2d 261 (Minn.1981). *But see* Turner v. Estate of Turner, 454 N.E.2d 1247 (Ind.App.1983).

**19.**  Uniform Probate Code § 2–803(g). In Federal Kemper Life Assur. v. Eichwedel, 639 N.E.2d 246 (Ill.App. 1994), a confession which was inadmissible in criminal proceedings was used to bar the killer from collecting insurance.

**20.**  Uniform Probate Code § 2–803(g). Under the UPC, the conviction is

conclusive only "after all right of appeal has been exhausted." But some courts treat a conviction as conclusive even if an appeal is pending. Angleton v. Estate of Angleton, 671 N.E.2d 921 (Ind.App. 1996).

**21.**  20 Pa.Stat. § 8814;  Rev.Code Wash. § 11.84.130.

**22.**  Sundin v. Klein, 269 S.E.2d 787 (Va.1980) (emphasis added). *See also* In re Estate of Fiore, 476 N.E.2d 1093, 1097 (Ohio App.1984).

**23.**  In re Hawkins' Estate, 213 N.Y.S.2d 188 (1961). *But see* First Kentucky Trust Co. v. United States, 737

taken as surviving joint tenant.[24] But most courts divide the property equally between the estates of A and B[25] on the theory that no one knows who would have survived but for the killing. Joint bank accounts are treated differently from land. Ownership of joint bank accounts is deemed proportional to contributions, so if A contributed all the money in a joint account, the account is "his" during his lifetime, even if B is also designated as a party.[26] A could therefore keep the account if he killed B, but if B killed A, the whole account would be awarded to A's estate.[27] A donee who murders the donor would not forfeit the property which had been previously given to him.[28]

The beneficiary of an insurance policy on A's life will not collect the proceeds if he kills A. The insurance company is not bound to pay *anyone* when the beneficiary took out the policy with the intent to kill the insured, because the policy is voidable for fraud.[29]

*Alternate Takers*  If a killer is disqualified, who does take? In most situations, the victim's property is distributed as if the killer predeceased the victim.[30] This principle may allow the children of the killer to take.[31] Wills and insurance policies often designate alternate beneficiaries if a devisee or primary beneficiary fails to survive. Usually the fiction that the killer died before the victim is also applied in this situation, and the alternate beneficiary takes.[32]

F.2d 557 (6th Cir.1984) (killer forfeits all interest in joint tenancy).

**24.** Hargrove v. Taylor, 389 P.2d 36 (Or.1964).

**25.** In re Estates of Covert, 761 N.E.2d 571, 576 (N.Y. 2001); *Restatement, Second, of Property, Donative Transfers*, § 34.8, comment c (1992). Courts have reached the same result as to community property; the killer spouse retains his or her half interest. Armstrong v. Bray, 826 P.2d 706 (Wash.App. 1992).

**26.** Uniform Probate Code § 6–211(b).

**27.** Uniform Probate Code § 2–803, comment In In re Estate of Fiore, 476 N.E.2d 1093 (Ohio App.1984), where both parties had contributed but the proportions were unclear, the whole account was awarded to the victim's estate.

**28.** The rule is otherwise under the civil law which allows gifts to be revoked for "ingratitude" by the donee. See Section 5.5.

**29.** Federal Kemper Life Assur. v. Eichwedel, 639 N.E.2d 246 (Ill.App. 1994).

**30.** *Restatement, Second, of Property (Donative Transfers)* § 34.8, comment b (1992). Uniform Probate Code § 2–803 uses the expression "as if the killer disclaimed," but this amounts to the same thing, since under § 2–1106(b)(3)(A) property disclaimed normally devolves as if the disclaimant had died.

This provision does not control the killer's own property; the victim's estate takes from the killer's when both are deceased only if the victim actually survived. In re Estate of Miller, 840 So.2d 703 (Miss.2003).

**31.** Matter of Estate of Van Der Veen, 935 P.2d 1042 (Kan.1997). Heinzman v. Mason, 694 N.E.2d 1164.

**32.** Hulett v. First Nat. Bank and Trust Co., 956 P.2d 879 (Okl.1998); In re Estates of Covert, 761 N.E.2d 571, 576 (N.Y. 2001). If no alternate beneficiary is designated, insurance proceeds may go to the insured's probate estate. Estate of Chiesi v. First Citizens Bank, 613 N.E.2d 14 (Ind.1993).

*Protection of Third Parties* Sometimes a crime is discovered after a person has acted in reliance on the normal devolution of property, *e.g.* by buying property from the killer. The Uniform Probate Code does not apply its killer-disqualification rules to anyone who "purchases property for value and without notice" and "payors" (such as insurance companies) are not liable for payments made before they receive "written notice of a claimed forfeiture."[33]

*Other Misconduct* Courts have refused to bar persons guilty of misconduct other than homicide. A mother was allowed to inherit from her 15 year old child although for most of his life she had "failed to provide any financial support to, maintain any interest in, or display any love and affection for" him.[34] The Uniform Probate Code, however, bars a parent from inheriting from a child unless the parent "has openly treated the child as his [or hers], and has not refused to support the child."[35] The Third Restatement of Property states a similar principle as common law[36] (although there is little case law support for it), but does not apply the principle to other heirs, such as children who abuse their parents. The effect of misconduct by one spouse toward the other will be treated in Section 2.11.

## § 2.8 Disclaimers

*Tax Consequences* Suppose that a man dies survived by his wife and a son who would share his property by intestate succession or by his will. The widow may have ample resources and prefer that her share pass to their son. She could give her share of her husband's estate to the son, but this might require payment of a gift tax. She can avoid a gift tax by making a "qualified disclaimer" under the Internal Revenue Code.[1] A disclaimer *by the son* may have advantageous tax consequences for the father's estate by increasing the size of the widow's share and thus the marital deduction.[2]

These results occur because disclaimers "relate back" to the time of the testator's or intestate's death, so the share goes directly to the person who takes as a result of the disclaimer. Disclaimers allow "post-mortem estate planning." Without them there would be

**33.** Uniform Probate Code § 2–803(h), (i)(1).
**34.** Hotarek v. Benson, 557 A.2d 1259, 1263 (Conn.1989).
**35.** Uniform Probate Code § 2–114(c).
**36.** *Restatement, Third, of Property (Wills and Other Donative Transfers)* § 2.5(5) (1999).

**§ 2.8**
**1.** Int.Rev.Code § 2518.
**2.** DePaoli v. C.I.R., 62 F.3d 1259 (10th Cir.1995). The estate tax charitable deduction can also under some circumstances be augmented by a disclaimer. Treas.Reg. § 20.2055–2 (c).

"an unwarranted and unrealistic demand for wills to be perfected and updated before a testator's death."[3]

Before 1977 a disclaimer was a taxable gift unless it was "effective under the local law," and state disclaimer laws varied considerably. Many states liberalized their rules on disclaimer in order to maximize the potential tax savings for their residents. A Uniform Disclaimer of Property Interests Act along these lines is incorporated into the Uniform Probate Code. The 1999 version has a catch-all provision designed to assure that all tax-effective disclaimers are also valid for state law purposes.[4]

Congress attempted to avoid unequal treatment of citizens of different states in 1976 by enacting Section 2518 of the Internal Revenue Code which sets forth uniform requirements for a "qualified disclaimer." Even a disclaimer which are not recognized under state law may escape gift tax if they meet the requirements of the Code.[5]

Lawyers who fail to advise clients about the tax advantages of disclaimers are subject to suit for malpractice.[6]

*Creditors' Rights* Sometimes a person wishes to disclaim because she is insolvent; her creditors would take her share if she accepted it. Some states treat disclaimers made to avoid creditors' claims as fraudulent conveyances,[7] but most states adopt the "relation-back" idea in this context also; disclaimed shares pass directly to the new takers, free from the disclaimant's creditors.[8] However, a disclaimer made by a person who is in bankruptcy is voidable.[9] Some courts treat disclaimers as an assignment which may disqualify the disclaimant for welfare benefits under need-based programs.[10]

*Requirements for Disclaimer* Disclaimers, when properly made, are irrevocable. Unlike the assignment of an expectancy

---

**3.** Halbach, *Curing Deficiencies in Tax and Property Law*, 65 Minn.L.Rev. 89, 120 (1980). See also Grassi, *Drafting Flexibility Into Trusts Helps Cope With Uncertainty*, 29 Est. Plann. 347, 350–51 (2002).

**4.** UDPIA § 14.

**5.** Internal Revenue Code § 2518(c)(3).

**6.** Kinney v. Shinholser, 663 So.2d 643 (Fla.App.1995).

**7.** Stein v. Brown, 480 N.E.2d 1121 (Ohio 1985); Matter of Reed's Estate, 566 P.2d 587 (Wyo.1977).

**8.** In re Atchison, 925 F.2d 209 (7th Cir.1991); Frances Slocum Bank and Trust Co. v. Martin, 666 N.E.2d 411 (Ind.App.1996).A good discussion of the policy issues appears in Hirsch, *The Problem of the Insolvent Heir*, 74 Corn. L.Rev 587 (1989).

**9.** In re Detlefsen, 610 F.2d 512 (8th Cir.1979). A disclaimer made on the eve of bankruptcy, on the other hand, is not voidable unless it constitutes a fraudulent conveyance under state law. Matter of Simpson, 36 F.3d 450 (5th Cir.1994).

**10.** Troy v. Hart, 697 A.2d 113 (Md. App.1997); Hoesly v. State, Dept. of Social Services, 498 N.W.2d 571 (Neb. 1993).

which requires consideration,[11] a disclaimer can be gratuitous. There is less risk of an improvident disclaimer than in the case of an expectancy, because disclaimers occur after the original transferor is dead.

Under the Uniform Probate Code a disclaimer must be signed by the disclaimant.[12] The Internal Revenue Code requires them to be in writing. Some statutes require them to be filed in court,[13] but Internal Revenue Code § 2518 merely requires that they be "received by" the legal representative of the transferor.

Once a person has accepted property, it is too late to disclaim it. Mere failure to act for an extended period may amount to acceptance. The Internal Revenue Code allows 9 months from the date of the decedent's death.[14]

Some state laws allow future interests to be disclaimed for up to 9 months after they become possessory.[15] This may occur long after the will which created them took effect, *e.g.* if a will creates a trust for "Mary for life, at her death, to her then living issue." However, the nine months allowed by the Internal Revenue Code starts to run when "the transfer creating the interest * * * is made," *i.e.* at the testator's death. Thus a disclaimer by a child of Mary at her death may be effective under state law, but would be a gift for tax purposes.[16]

Under Section 2518 the time allowed to a minor to disclaim does not begin to run until the child reaches age 21,[17] presumably because a minor is not competent to disclaim. Most states deal with this problem by allowing a guardian to disclaim on behalf of a minor.

*Disclaimers by Fiduciaries* Disclaimers by the conservator of a disabled person or guardian of a minor require court approval, which depends "on the decision the protected person would have made, to the extent that [this] can be ascertained."[18] Normally guardians have a duty to conserve a minor's property so a court refused to allow the guardian of minor children to disclaim their

**11.** See Section 4.5.

**12.** Uniform Probate Code § 2–1105(c), defined to include an electronic signature.

**13.** Matter of Estate of Griffin, 812 P.2d 1256 (Mont.1991).

**14.** Internal Revenue Code § 2518(b). In State ex. rel Counsel for Disc. v. Mills, 671 N.W.2d 765 (Neb. 2003), a lawyer who backdated a disclaimer in order to have it qualify for tax purposes was suspended from practice for 2 years.

**15.** Cal. Prob. Code § 279(e).

**16.** Internal Revenue Code § 2518(b)(2)(A); United States v. Irvine, 511 U.S. 224 (1994) (disclaimer in 1979 of a future interest created in 1917 was a taxable transfer).

**17.** Internal Revenue Code § 2518(b)(2)(B). Although virtually all states have reduced the age of majority from 21 to 18, the Code does not take this change into account.

**18.** Unif.Prob.Code § 5–411(c).

share in their father's estate in order to get the maximum marital deduction for the estate because the children would lose by it.[19] However, a court acting under the Uniform Probate Code might have approved the disclaimer, since the children's mother, who would benefit from the disclaimer, would probably use the funds (augmented by the tax savings) for their support.

Uniform Probate Code also allows disclaimers by an agent acting under a power of attorney. However, if the power of attorney does not authorizes disclaimers expressly, some courts would hesitate to infer that an attorney is empowered to diminish the principal's estate.[20]

If an heir or devisee dies shortly after the decedent, the Uniform Probate Code allows the executor of the heir or devisee to disclaim but here too fiduciary duties may be an obstacle. One court refused to allow an executor to disclaim over an objection from one of the devisee's creditors.[21] But another court allowed a trustee to disclaim on behalf of trust beneficiaries when the decision was "made in good faith with the best interests of the trust's beneficiaries in mind."[22]

*Interests Disclaimable*    Historically, heirs taking by intestacy could not disclaim but devisees under a will could. Most states have abolished this distinction. The Uniform Probate Code expressly allows a disclaimer of "any interest in * * * property."[23]

A donee can disclaim an inter-vivos gift. In this case the time starts to run "when there is a completed gift for Federal gift-tax purposes."[24] If a person creates a revocable living trust, the time within which the beneficiaries must disclaim only starts to run when the settlor's power to revoke expires (normally at the settlor's death).

*Effect of Disclaimer*    If property is effectively disclaimed, the "disclaimed interest passes as if the disclaimant had died immediately before the time of distribution."[25] The effect of this depends on the circumstances. In the hypothetical described at the beginning of this section, if the son was the decedent's only issue and the

---

**19.** In re Estate of De Domenico, 418 N.Y.S.2d 1012 (Surr.1979).

**20.** Cal.Prob.Code § 4264(d)(agent cannot disclaim unless expressly authorized without court approved). As to gifts under a power of attorney see Section 7.2.

**21.** In re Estate of Heater, 640 N.E.2d 654 (Ill.App.1994). This is hard to reconcile with the general rule that a live debtor can disclaim to defeat his creditors.

**22.** McClintock v. Scahill, 530 N.E.2d 164 (Mass.1988). *But see* Rev.

Rul. 90–110, 1990–2 C.B. 209 (trustee's disclaimer of power to invade corpus for a grandchild is ineffective without grandchild's consent).

**23.** Uniform Probate Code § 2–1105(a).

**24.** Treas.Reg. § 25.2518–2(b)(3). As to when a gift is complete for tax purposes see Section 15.2.

**25.** Uniform Probate Code § 2–1106(c)(3)(A).

decedent died intestate and if the local intestacy statute gave the surviving spouse everything in the absence of issue, the son's disclaimer would cause his share to go to the widow. But if the son had children, they would take his share by representation,[26] so the son could not increase the marital deduction in his father's estate,[27] unless *both* he *and* his children disclaimed.[28]

Estate planners sometimes draft wills in anticipation of a possible disclaimer. If a will devises property "to my wife Mary, but if she predeceases me, to Andrew," Andrew would take if Mary survived the testator but disclaimed.[29] If Mary needs property for her support, but wishes to reduce estate taxes at her death, the best solution may be to have the property pass to a trust in which she gets the income for life. A testator who is uncertain whether or not his estate will be large enough to warrant such a trust may leave it to his widow outright with a provision that any property which she disclaims shall go into a trust for her for life.

*Agreements Among Successors*   Heirs and devisees can also alter the devolution of an estate by agreement. An agreement can provide for whatever distribution the parties desire. A child can agree that his share should go to his mother, even though a disclaimer would give his share to his children. Unlike disclaimers, such agreements constitute transfers subject to the rights of creditors and to taxes.[30] Even when an agreement increases the surviving spouse's share, the marital deduction will not be increased, since in order to qualify for the marital deduction the property must pass from one spouse to the other.[31]

The Uniform Probate Code refers to a "written" agreement, and this has been interpreted to make an oral agreement among successors unenforceable.[32] But a letter which repudiates an agree-

**26.**  Estate of Bryant, 196 Cal.Rptr. 856 (App.1983); Estate of Burmeister, 594 P.2d 226 (Kan.1979).

**27.**  Webb v. Webb, 301 S.E.2d 570 (W.Va.1983) (disclaimant intended to benefit his mother but property goes to his children).

**28.**  McInnis v. McInnis, 560 S.E.2d 632 (S.C.App. 2002) (disclaimer by children and grandchildren causes property to pass to decedent's widow).

**29.**  Matter of Estate of Bruce, 877 P.2d 999 (Mont.1994) (secondary beneficiaries of IRA account take when primary beneficiary disclaims). When a life interest is disclaimed, the remainder is accelerated so as to take effect immediately. Uniform Probate Code § 2–1106(b)(4); Pate v. Ford, 376 S.E.2d 775 (S.C.1989).

**30.**  Uniform Probate Code § 3–912, allows such agreements "subject to the rights of creditors and taxing authorities." When a child who owed his ex-wife money agreed to give his share of his mother's estate to his sibling, the ex-wife had the agreement set aside. Matter of Estate of Haggerty, 805 P.2d 1338 (Mont.1990).

**31.**  Jeschke v. United States, 814 F.2d 568 (10th Cir.1987). The result is different if the agreement is made to settle a bona-fide contest. Reg. § 20.2056(c)–2(d).

**32.**  Matter of Estate of Leathers, 876 P.2d 619 (Kan.App.1994). *But cf.* In re Estate of Flake, 71 P.3d 589, 598 (Utah 2003) (oral agreement involving distribution under a *trust* is effective, since UPC speaks only of *wills*).

ment while acknowledging its existence may suffice.[33] In some states no writing is necessary.[34]

A person who agrees to take less than her share is making a gift, which requires no consideration.[35] Sometimes heirs make an agreement with an "heir-hunting" firm which locates the heir and informs him of his interest in return for a large percentage of his share. In California, a court may refuse to distribute a share of an estate to an assignee if the consideration for the assignment was "grossly unreasonable."[36]

## § 2.9  Children Born Out of Wedlock

*History and Policy*   One in every three American babies is now born out of wedlock.[1] The legal right to succession of such children has dramatically improved in recent years. In the 12th century, Glanville said "no bastard born outside a lawful marriage can be an heir,"[2] and this remained the law in England until 1969.[3] In America, the Uniform Probate Code provides that for purposes of succession "an individual is the child of his [or her] natural parents, regardless of their marital status."[4] Some American statutes are less favorable to children born out of wedlock, but courts beginning in 1968 have held many such statutes unconstitutional.[5] Today, the term "illegitimate" (and *a fortiori* "bastard") is considered offensive and replaced in legal terminology by "born out of wedlock" or "non-marital child."

*Proof of Paternity*   The problem of proving paternity clearly influenced the common-law rules on inheritance. Science has recently made great progress in making accurate paternity determinations.[6] This has undercut the difficulty-of-proof argument against

**33.**  Matter of Estate of Cruse, 710 P.2d 733 (N.M.1985); *Restatement, Second, of Contracts* § 133, comm. c (1979).

**34.**  Gregory v. Rice, 678 S.W.2d 603 (Tex.App.1984).

**35.**  As to the requirements for making a gift, see Section 4.5.

**36.**  Cal.Prob.Code § 11604. But in other states, courts have upheld agreements which gave the firm a large percent of the heir's share. Nelson v. McGoldrick, 896 P.2d 1258 (Wash.1995) (50% fee was not unconscionable as a matter of law).

### § 2.9

**1.**  Statistical Abstract of the United States: 2002, No. 74 (for year 2000).

**2.**  R. Glanville, *Tractatus de Legibus* 87 (G. Hall ed. 1965).

**3.**  Family Law Reform Act, § 14 (1969).

**4.**  UPC § 2–114(a). *See also* Cal. Prob.Code § 6450; *Restatement, Third, of Property (Wills and Other Donative Transfers)* § 2.5 (1998).

**5.**  Levy v. Louisiana, 391 U.S. 68 (1968) (a wrongful death action). In Trimble v. Gordon, 430 U.S. 762 (1977), the Court first held unconstitutional an intestacy statute which restricted inheritance by children born out of wedlock.

**6.**  *E.g.* Nwabara v. Willacy, 733 N.E.2d 267, 274 (Ohio App.1999) (DNA test identifies father with 99.95% probability. Such proof may be available even after the father is dead). Alexander v. Alexander, 537 N.E.2d 1310 (Ohio Prob. 1988) (proper to order body exhumed for DNA testing to establish paternity).

inheritance by non-marital children. Proof of biological paternity is not always determinative of the parent/child relationship, however. According to the Restatement of Property, children produced by assisted reproductive technologies "should be treated as part of the family of * * * parents who treat the child as their own" even though "one or both of them might not be the child's genetic parent."[7] Conversely, claims by biological fathers to parental rights have sometimes been rejected in order to protect a family unit when the mother is married to someone else.[8] The Uniform Probate Code bars a parent or a relative of a parent from inheriting if the parent has not "openly treated the child as his [or hers]" or has "refused to support the child."[9]

*Inheritance from Mother* Proof of maternity is rarely an issue. As early as 1827 several American statutes allowed children born out of wedlock to inherit from their mother; by 1934 this rule was virtually universal.[10] The Uniform Parentage Act has some rather complex rules on proving paternity, but motherhood is simply established "by proof of her having given birth to the child."[11]

When children born out of wedlock seek to inherit *through* the mother from her relatives, the decedent's intent is more doubtful. If John's daughter has a son out of wedlock, even if the daughter would want him to inherit her property, John might not want him to share in *his* estate. Nevertheless, most statutes would allow the son to inherit from John by representation as well as from his mother.[12]

*Inheritance from Father* Claims to inherit by, from and through the father present the major area of uncertainty today. Some states do not distinguish between fathers and mothers; "paternity is a fact to be proved as any other fact, *i.e.,* by a preponderance of the evidence."[13] Some states, however, impose an extra burden on non-marital children who seek to inherit from a father, *e.g.,* the child must establish paternity by "clear and convincing" evidence.[14] Some states require a written acknowledgement of pa-

**7.** *Restatement, Third, of Property (Wills and Other Donative Transfers)* § 2.5, comm. l (1998).

**8.** Dawn D. v. Superior Court (Jerry K.), 952 P.2d 1139 (Cal.1998).

**9.** Section 2–114(c). *See also Restatement, Third, of Property (Wills and Other Donative Transfers)* § 2.5(5) (1998).

**10.** Vernier & Churchill, *Inheritance By and From Bastards*, 20 Iowa L.Rev. 216 (1934).

**11.** Uniform Parentage Act § 3(1) (1973). The matter is more complicated under the counterpart to this provision in the UPA of 2000 which refers to Article 8 dealing with surrogate mothers. Unif. Parentage Act § 201(a) (2000)

**12.** Uniform Probate Code § 2–114(a). *See also* Cal.Prob.Code § 6450(a).

**13.** Matter of Estate of Cook, 698 P.2d 1076 (Wash.App.1985).

**14.** Matter of Estate of King, 837 P.2d 463 (Okl.1990) (claim denied because proof of paternity not clear).

ternity.[15] The Supreme Court upheld against a constitutional challenge a New York statute which allowed children born out of wedlock to inherit from their father only if a court order had established paternity during the father's life reasoning that "fraudulent assertions of paternity will be much less likely to succeed * * * where proof is put before a court of law at a time when the putative father is available to respond."[16] But as a dissenting justice observed, the statute could exclude the *most* meritorious cases; a father who voluntarily supports a child would probably want the child to inherit, but the child, having no reason to bring paternity proceedings, would not qualify under the statute.[17] The New York statute was later amended to abolish the requirement of adjudication of paternity during the father's lifetime, and most states today agree.[18]

*Presumptions of Paternity* The question of paternity may be resolved by a presumption. The Uniform Parentage Act of 1973, to which the Uniform Probate Code refers, creates five such presumptions.[19] First, if the mother is married and the child is born during the marriage, or within 300 days after it is terminated, the mother's husband is presumed to be the father. This presumption was virtually irrebuttable at common law, but under the Act, it can be rebutted by "clear and convincing evidence,"[20] but only by the child, the mother, or a man who is presumed to be the father under other provisions of the Act. Thus a sister of the decedent who would inherit in the absence of issue would not be permitted to prove that a child born to her brother's wife was not in fact his.[21]

Second, a presumption of paternity also arises if the mother and man "attempted to marry each other by a marriage solemnized in apparent compliance with law, although the marriage is or could be declared invalid."[22] At common law a child was illegitimate if the marriage of the father and mother was invalid, e.g. bigamous. But the Supreme Court has held it unconstitutional to deny inheritance

---

**15.** Wis. Stat. § 852.05(1) (adjudication, or acknowledgement in court or written); In re Estate of Geller, 980 P.2d 665 (Okl.Civ.App.1999) (statute requires either written acknowledgement or taking into the home).

**16.** Lalli v. Lalli, 439 U.S. 259 (1978).

**17.** 439 U.S. at 278.

**18.** N.Y. EPTL § 4–1.2(a)(2); Wood v. Wingfield, 816 S.W.2d 899 (Ky.1991) (can prove paternity after death of the father).

**19.** Uniform Probate Code § 2–114(a): The presumptions appear in Uniform Parentage Act § 4. A child without a presumed father under Section 4 can sue to establish paternity under Section 6.

**20.** Uniform Parentage Act § 4(b). *See also* Green v. Estate of Green, 724 N.E.2d 260, 265 (Ind.App.2000) (child proved that he was not the son of his mother's husband).

**21.** Uniform Parentage Act § 6(a); *cf.* Unif. Parentage Act § 602 (2000).

**22.** Uniform Parentage Act § 4(b)(2) (1973), § 204(3) (2000)

when the parents went through a marriage ceremony even though one of them was already married.[23]

Historically, a child born during a valid marriage was legitimate regardless of when the child was *conceived*, but a marriage of the parents after a child was *born* did not make the child legitimate until 1926.[24] Under the Uniform Parentage Act a man who marries the mother after the child is born is presumed to be the father if "with his consent, he is named as the child's father on the child's birth certificate," or is obligated to support the child by a "written voluntary promise or by court order."[25]

Even a man who never married or attempted to marry the mother is presumed to be the father under the 1973 Parentage Act if "he receives the child into his home and openly holds out the child as his" while the child is a minor.[26] This presumption is eliminated in the 2000 Act on the ground that "genetic testing is a far better means of determining paternity."

All these presumptions are rebuttable, but an attempt to rebut may be barred by failure to act promptly. Under the 2000 Parentage Act a presumed father must commence proceedings with 2 years of the child's birth, unless he did not cohabit or have sexual intercourse with the mother during the time of conception and never openly treated the child as his own.[27]

Time limits are also imposed on claims of paternity. The 1973 Uniform Parentage Act allows a child with no presumed father to sue to establish paternity up to three "years after the child reaches the age of majority."[28] Some courts have allowed children who failed to establish paternity judicially after they reached majority to claim an inheritance on the theory that they had no reason sue to establish the decedent's paternity during his life when he acknowledged it.[29]

**23.** Reed v. Campbell, 476 U.S. 852 (1986).

**24.** Legitimacy Act, § 1 (1926).

**25.** Section 4. (1973); *cf.* § 204(4) (2000) (husband is the father if "he voluntarily asserted his paternity"). *See also* Green v. Estate of Green, 724 N.E.2d 260 (Ind.App.2000) (person who married mother after child was born and acknowledged child held to be the father). *But see* Garrison v. Smith, 561 N.E.2d 1041 (Ohio App.1988) (man who later married the mother but did not acknowledge the child as his is not the child's father for inheritance purposes). A step-child relationship between a husband and his wife's children may allow inheritance, in rare situations. See Section 2.10.

**26.** Section 4.

**27.** § 607 (2000). Cf. 1973 Act § 6(a)(2) ("within a reasonable time after obtaining knowledge of relevant facts, but in no event later than" 5 years after birth).

**28.** Section 7.

**29.** In re Estate of Palmer, 647 N.W.2d 13 (Minn.App. 2002). *But see* Matter of Estate of Foley, 925 P.2d 449 (Kan.App.1996) (claim to inherit rejected because 3 year statute had run).

*Inheritance by Parents*    The common law deemed a child born out of wedlock to be the child of no one, so that such a child who had no spouse or issue had no heirs.[30] Today, however, most statutes allow parents of a child born out of wedlock and their relatives to inherit from the child,[31] but parents who challenge a statute which bars them from inheriting have a less appealing case than a child who seeks to inherit from a parent, since the child's status is involuntary, whereas the parents are responsible for their situation.[32] Nevertheless, the Supreme Court held unconstitutional a statute which did not permit a mother to sue for the wrongful death of her child born out of wedlock.[33] A state court struck down a statute which allowed mothers but not fathers to inherit from children born out of wedlock as sex discrimination.[34]

*Claims not Based on Intent*    Claims of children born out of wedlock for wrongful death or other benefits over which the decedent has no control seem particularly strong. Refusal to allow children to inherit may reflect the decedent's intent; if it does not, the decedent can provide for the child by will. But a will cannot dispose of wrongful death claims or Social Security benefits. The "burdens of illegitimacy" seem particularly unfair "when neither parent nor child can legally lighten them."[35] Also, the problem of proof is less acute when statutes require claimants to be a dependent of the decedent, since spurious "children" would not qualify.

*Wills*    Claims to take under a will turn on the testator's intent. If the will gives no clue to the intent, courts traditionally presumed the testator intended to exclude children born out of wedlock in a devise to "children" or the like. This presumption could be overcome by showing "a contrary intent * * * from additional language or circumstances," such as the fact that the only possible takers under the devise were illegitimate.[36]

The law today is more favorable to children born out of wedlock. Under the Uniform Probate Code, unless a will provides otherwise "individuals born out of wedlock and their respective descendants * * * are included in class gifts in accordance with the rules for intestate succession."[37] Even without a similar statute,

---

**30.** Glanville, *supra* note 2, at 88; 1 W. Blackstone, *Commentaries* * 459 (1765).

**31.** Uniform Probate Code § 2–114. *See also Restatement, Third, of Property (Wills and Other Donative Transfers)* § 2.5 (1998).

**32.** Parham v. Hughes, 441 U.S. 347 (1979) (upholding a statute barring a father who had not legitimated a child from suing for child's wrongful death).

**33.** Glona v. American Guarantee & Liability Ins. Co., 391 U.S. 73 (1968).

**34.** Estate of Hicks, 675 N.E.2d 89 (Ill.1996).

**35.** Weber v. Aetna Casualty & Surety Co., 406 U.S. 164, 173 (1972).

**36.** *Restatement    of    Property* § 286(1)(a) (1940) .

**37.** Uniform Probate Code § 2–705. The comparable provision in the pre–1990 UPC applied only to wills, but the

intestacy statutes are often cited as evidence of probable intent in construction issues,[38] and several courts have presumed that class gifts in wills included children born out of wedlock.[39] Circumstances or language in the will may show a contrary intent, however. A gift to "the children of John" would not include a child who John claimed (albeit erroneously) was not his.[40] Giving effect to a testator's intent to exclude children born out of wedlock does not violate the constitution, since this does not involve "state action."[41]

*Planning* An attorney who drafts a will should ascertain the testator's intent and make it clear in the will. Some persons would wish children born out of wedlock to share in their estates and some would not. Even if there are no such children presently in the testator's family, the question cannot be ignored since many wills provide for issue who are as yet unborn. Most testators would probably wish to include children who are "technically" illegitimate, e.g. because a divorce predating the marriage of their parents was invalid. At the other extreme, they would not want someone who falsely claimed to be a child to share in the estate. Naming the testator's children in a will (or reciting lack of children) does not always preclude a child from proving paternity.[42]

The effect of a provision for "lawful" descendants is not clear. Since most states no longer use the term "illegitimate" to describe children born out of wedlock, they might be included in a gift to "lawful" children.[43] The language of the Uniform Statutory Will Act probably reflects the views of most testators: "an individual born out of wedlock is not the child of the father unless the individual is openly and notoriously so treated by the father."[44]

## 2.10  Adoption

Although well known in the civil law, the common law did not recognize adoption. But adoption today has become to a common occurrence; Americans adopt more than 130,000 children annually.[1]

---

present provision covers all "governing instruments." Uniform Probate Code § 2–701.

**38.** *Restatement, Second, of Property (Donative Transfers)* § 25.2, comment a (1988). If the will gives property to "heirs," the intestacy statute is particularly persuasive as to intent. *Id.* § 29.1; Section 2.4.

**39.** Matter of Estate of Best, 485 N.E.2d 1010 (N.Y.1985).

**40.** *Restatement, Second, of Property (Donative Transfers)* § 25.2, comment e, illus. 6, § 25.8, illus. 2 (1988).

**41.** Harris Trust and Sav. Bank v. Donovan, 582 N.E.2d 120 (Ill.1991).

**42.** Matter of Padilla's Estate, 641 P.2d 539 (N.M.App.1982).

**43.** *Restatement, Second, of Property (Donative Transfers)* § 25.2, illus. 1 (1985) ("lawful" includes child born out of wedlock but legitimated). *But see* Continental Bank, N.A. v. Herguth, 617 N.E.2d 852 (Ill.App.1993) ("lawful" excludes children born out of wedlock).

**44.** Uniform Statutory Will Act § 1(1).

### § 2.10

**1.** Prefatory Note, Uniform Adoption Act (1994).

Adoption raises questions both as to intestate succession and the construction of instruments.

*Intestate Succession*    When a person adopts another several types of question can arise regarding intestate succession. Can the adoptee inherit from the adopter? from the adopter's relatives, *e.g.* if the adopter predeceases his parents? Can the adoptee's children inherit from the adopter or his relatives? Can the adopter or his relatives inherit from the adoptee? Uniform Probate Code § 2–114 answers yes to all these questions and most states agree. A court recently held unconstitutional a state statute which did not allow an adopted child to inherit from a half-sister by adoption.[2]

Some states allow adoptees to inherit both from their birth parents and their adoptive parents.[3] If the adoptee is a minor (as is usually the case), arguably the child should not be prejudiced by losing a right of inheritance she would otherwise have. But maintaining inheritance ties between an adoptee and the biological family conflicts with the policy of strengthening the new family unit. The Uniform Probate Code severs the tie in most cases,[4] but in many adoptions the birth parents continue to associate with the child, especially when children are adopted by step parents or relatives.[5] If a man adopts his wife's children by a prior marriage, for example, Uniform Probate Code § 2–114(b) would allow the children to inherit not only from him and his relatives but also from their genetic father and his relatives. The genetic father and his relatives would not inherit from the adopted child however.[6] The Restatement favors retaining the tie to genetic relatives when the adoption is by a relative of either parent or the spouse of a relative. For example, when after the death of both parents, a child is adopted by a maternal aunt, the child could inherit from relatives of both genetic parents.[7] Some states, however, cut the tie between an adoptee and the genetic parents in all cases.[8]

Some courts have even allowed a child adopted by a family member to inherit twice from the same decedent, once as an adopted child and once, by representation, through his biological

---

**2.** MacCallum v. Seymour, 686 A.2d 935 (Vt.1996). *But see* Nunnally v. Trust Co. Bank, 261 S.E.2d 621 (Ga.1979).

**3.** Matter of Estate of Van Der Veen, 935 P.2d 1042 (Kan.1997) .

**4.** Uniform Probate Code § 2–114(b). *See also Restatement, Third, of Property (Wills and Other Donative Transfers)* § 2.5, comm. e (1998).

**5.** Prefatory Note, Uniform Adoption Act (1994).

**6.** The Restatement allows inheritance both ways in this situation. *Restatement, Third, of Property (Wills and Other Donative Transfers)* § 2.5(2)(C) (1998).

**7.** *Id.*, comm. f.

**8.** Buchea v. United States, 154 F.3d 1114 (9th Cir.1998) (under Alaska law, child adopted by grandparents cannot recover for wrongful death of biological father).

parents.[9] The Uniform Probate Code, however, only gives the child a single share in this situation.[10]

*Class Gifts*  If a will makes a class gift to someone's "children," or the like, can someone who enters the designated class by adoption share? Conversely, does a child of John who has been adopted by someone else still count as John's "child" in construing a devise? This depends on the testator's intent. Courts often treat the intestacy statutes as evidence of the average person's intent, but not always. Construction of the word "heirs" is more closely tied to the intestacy rules.[11]Under the Uniform Probate Code, the same rules generally determine the effect of adoption for intestate succession and the construction of class gifts, both for wills and other instruments, such as living trusts and deeds.[12] Often class gifts appear in instruments which were executed many years earlier, when the prevailing construction excluded "strangers to the adoption," *i.e.*, if John adopted Mary, she would be his "child" in construing his will, but she would not be John's "child" in construing the will of another person who left property to the "children" of John. This was the presumed meaning under the first Restatement of Property[13], but the second Restatement, like the UPC and most states, has abandoned it.[14]

What evidence is sufficient to show an intent contrary to the presumption? According to the Restatement, a gift to "blood descendants" or "natural-born children" manifests an intent to exclude children by adoption.[15] But most cases hold that the word "body" (as in "heirs of his body") does *not* exclude adoptees.[16] The fact that the exclusion of a child would make a gift meaningless may show an intent to include, since words in an instrument are presumably intended to mean something. If a trust provides for the settlor's "children," and his only children have been adopted by his sister, under the Uniform Probate Code, these children would be

---

**9.** In re Estate of Cregar, 333 N.E.2d 540 (Ill.App.1975) (children adopted by an aunt can inherit from another aunt in both capacities).

**10.** Uniform Probate Code § 2–113. *See also Restatement, Third, of Property (Wills and Other Donative Transfers)* § 2.5, comm. i (1998).

**11.** Boston Safe Deposit & Trust Co. v. Wilbur, 728 N.E.2d 264, 270 (Mass. 2000) (adopted child takes since gift was to "representatives"-construed to mean heirs).

**12.** Section 2–705.

**13.** Section 287. The exclusion of strangers to the adoption was only a presumption. For example, in In re

Bankers Trust Co., 291 N.E.2d 137 (N.Y. 1972), the court found that as testator intended to include an adoptee even under the old rules.

**14.** *Restatement, Second, of Property (Donative Transfers)* § 25.4 (1988).

**15.** *Ibid.*, comm. c. *See also* Matter of Will of Paats, 589 N.Y.S.2d 147 (Surr.1992) ("natural children born of the marriage").

**16.** Hagaman v. Morgan, 886 S.W.2d 398 (Tex.App.1994). *But see* Schroeder v. Danielson, 640 N.E.2d 495 (Mass.App. Ct.1994).

presumptively disqualified,[17] but since no one else qualifies as a "chiid" of the settlor, they should be included.[18]

*Adult Adoptions*  The adoption of adults poses special problems. Most states permit such adoptions with simpler procedures than for child adoptions. No home investigation is made and consent of the adoptee's parents is not required.[19] Parental support obligations involved in the adoption of a minor do not apply. The adoptee often does not change his name, live with the adopter or change his life. Nevertheless, the inheritance rules for an adopted adult are the same as for minors.[20] In construing class gifts, however, many courts have refused to allow persons adopted as adults to take as "children" of the adopter.[21] However, in other cases adult adoptees have been held to qualify under class gifts.[22]

A few courts have questioned the motive for the adoption of an adult, but this is hard to determine. The Uniform Probate Code provides a limitation that is easier to apply: in construing class gifts "an adopted individual is not considered the child of the adopting parent unless the adopted individual lived while a minor * * * as a regular member of the household of the adopting parent."[23] This is a not uncommon occurrence, e.g., a step-parent wishes to adopt stepchildren but cannot do it so long as the children are minors, because their other parent refuses to consent.[24]

Adoptions which affect succession to property are sometimes challenged by persons adversely affected. When a remainder was devised to the issue of the testator's two sons, Leo and Roy, and Leo adopted his stepchildren, Roy's children tried to challenge the adoption, but the court held they had no standing to do so. Moreover, a statute required any challenge to an adoption to be brought within one year of the decree and this had long since expired.[25] Another court, however, set aside an adoption for "fraud" when challenged by the adopter's heir, despite the running of a six-month statute of limitations.[26]

---

**17.**  Uniform Probate Code §§ 2–114, 2–705.

**18.**  *Restatement, Second, Property (Donative Transfers)* § 25.2, illus. 1 (1988).

**19.**  Wadlington, *Adoption of Adults: A Family Law Anomaly,* 54 Cornell L.Rev. 566, 571–73 (1969).

**20.**  Uniform Probate Code § 2–114(b). *See also* In re Estate of Brittin, 664 N.E.2d 687 (Ill.App.1996) (children of person adopted at age 46 inherit from adopter).

**21.**  Matter of Trust Created by Belgard, 829 P.2d 457 (Colo.App.1991) (wife who was adopted by her husband not

one of his "issue" under his parent's trust).

**22.**  Solomon v. Central Trust Co., 584 N.E.2d 1185 (Ohio 1992) (adoptee had lived with adopter from age 9, even though adopted as an adult).

**23.**  Uniform Probate Code § 2–705(c). This limitation applies only when the donor or testator is a stranger to the adoption.

**24.**  Uniform Adoption Act § 5–101, comment.

**25.**  Hurt v. Noble, 817 P.2d 744 (Okl.App.1991).

**26.**  In re Estate of Reid, 825 So.2d 1, 7 (Miss. 2002).

Normally an adoption in one state will be given effect in other jurisdictions,[27] but a state may refuse to recognize a foreign adoption as being "repugnant to its policies."[28] The law of the state of adoption does not always control its effect in another state. Thus an adoption in Louisiana did not bar inheritance from the birth father under Mississippi law even though it would have had that effect in Louisiana.[29]

*Equitable Adoption* A person who was raised from infancy by another does not become the latter's "child" for purposes of intestacy if there was no adoption. However, some children who have never been formally adopted have been treated as if they had been under the theory of equitable adoption. The usual rationale is that the child is the beneficiary of a promise made to adopt him.[30] Even when a child has been raised from infancy, most courts will not find an equitable adoption unless there was a contract to adopt the child,[31] but such a contract is often inferred from conduct.[32]

An equitable adoption has limited effect. It does not usually allow the child to take *through* the adoptive parents, unlike a formal adoption,[33] or allow the parents to take from the child,[34] or cut off inheritance by the child from birth relatives or their right to inherit from the child.[35] Some courts refuse to give any effect to alleged equitable adoptions.[36]

*Stepchildren* Unadopted stepchildren (children of a spouse) are not heirs in most states, although a few states allow them to inherit if an intestate has no close blood relatives.[37] A devise "to

**27.** *Restatement, Second, of Conflict of Laws* § 290 (1971).

**28.** Kupec v. Cooper, 593 So.2d 1176, 1178 (Fla.App.1992). Also, the state which granted the adoption must have had jurisdiction to do so. 1 J. Schoenblum, *Multistate and Multinational Estate Planning* § 12.05 (2d ed.1999).

**29.** Estate of Jones v. Howell, 687 So.2d 1171, 1177 (Miss.1996).

**30.** Board of Education v. Browning, 635 A.2d 373, 376–77 (Md.1994).

**31.** O'Neal v. Wilkes, 439 S.E.2d 490 (Ga.1994) (contract made by unauthorized relative and so did not create equitable adoption).

**32.** *Restatement, Third, of Property (Wills and Other Donative Transfers)* § 2.5, comm. k (1998).

**33.** Board of Education v. Browning, 635 A.2d 373 (Md.1994) (claim to inherit

from adopter's sister). But in Wheeling Dollar Saving & Trust Co. v. Singer, 250 S.E.2d 369 (W.Va.1978), the court allowed an equitably adopted child to take under the will of a relative of the adopter.

**34.** Reynolds v. City of Los Angeles, 222 Cal.Rptr. 517 (App.1986) (parents of equitably adopted child cannot sue for wrongful death of child). *Contra*, Lawson v. Atwood, 536 N.E.2d 1167 (Ohio 1989).

**35.** Gardner v. Hancock, 924 S.W.2d 857 (Mo.App.1996) (equitably adopted child can inherit from birth father).

**36.** Matter of Estate of Robbins, 738 P.2d 458 (Kan.1987).

**37.** Md.Estates and Trusts Code § 3–104(e); Fla.Stat. § 732.103(5) (kindred of deceased spouse).

children" normally does not include stepchildren,[38] but courts sometimes infer from the circumstances that a testator intended otherwise. A will which left property to "my children" was held to include stepchildren whom the testator had raised from infancy and habitually referred to as her children, since she had only one natural child and the will referred to "children."[39]

Stepchildren may also be included in a gift to "the family" of a stepparent.[40] They have been awarded damages for the death of a stepparent under a statute allowing recovery to "dependents,"[41] and are covered under many workers' compensation statutes.[42]

*Planning*  Many standard forms used in drafting wills assume that the testator intends to include adopted children in class gifts. Unless qualified, such language includes all adoptees,[43] but some suggested forms expressly exclude persons adopted as adults.[44] The Uniform Statutory Will, like the Uniform Probate Code, treats an adoptee as "the child of the adopting parents and not of the natural parents" except when the adopter is a natural parent's spouse.[45] Some testators may not want an adoption to break the tie to genetic relatives in other cases if the adoptee lived with them for a significant period or continued to associate with them.[46]

## § 2.11  Spouses

For many purposes it becomes necessary to determine whether a person was a decedent's spouse. A "surviving spouse" receives share of an intestate estate, a right to elect against a will, a family allowance, and priority in appointment as a decedent's personal representative.[1] A will or other instrument frequently designates a spouse as beneficiary. If the instrument also names the spouse, it is immaterial whether or not the person named is actually a lawful spouse. The validity of a marriage is less commonly an issue in construing instruments than the question who is a "child" within

---

**38.** *Restatement, Second, of Property (Donative Transfers)* § 25.6 (1987); National Home Life Assur. Co. v. Patterson, 746 P.2d 696 (Okl.App.1987) (insurance beneficiary designation).

**39.** In re Gehl's Estate, 159 N.W.2d 72 (Wis.1968). *See also Restatement, Second, of Property (Donative Transfers)* § 25.6, illus. 1 (1987).

**40.** *Id.,* § 25.10, illus. 5.

**41.** Greer Tank & Welding, Inc. v. Boettger, 609 P.2d 548 (Alaska 1980); Cal.Code Civ.Proc. § 377.60(b).

**42.** Code of Ala. § 25–5–1(2); Ind. Code § 22–3–3–19(b).

**43.** Diemer v. Diemer, 717 S.W.2d 160 (Tex.App.1986).

**44.** Martin, *The Draftsman Views Wills for a Young Family,* 54 N.C.L.Rev. 277, 307 (1976).

**45.** Uniform Statutory Will Act § 1(1).

**46.** Halbach, *Issues About Issue: Some Recurrent Class Gift Problems,* 48 Mo.L.Rev. 333, 348 (1983).

### § 2.11

**1.** Uniform Probate Code §§ 2–102, 2–202, 2–404, 3–203(a).

the meaning of a class gift, because "children" are often not named in a will whereas spouses usually are.[2]

A number of objections can be raised to a person's claim to be a spouse, but choice of law rules helps to sustain the validity of a marriage if possible. Also, challenges to a marriage are often not allowed after the death of one of the parties, the time when the issue of the validity of a marriage becomes relevant in probate cases. For example, a claim that the purported marriage is void as incestuous can under the Uniform Marriage and Divorce Act be made only while both spouses are alive.[3]

Since marriage is a contract, it is subject to the standard grounds for avoiding contracts, such as fraud, duress and incapacity.[4] Some states bar such challenges after one of the spouses has died,[5] but others do not. One court declared a marriage invalid for "fraud of the grossest kind" when the deceased "spouse" had been married while she was incapacitated and terminally ill.[6]

Two challenges to a marriage are especially common and usually survive death: (1) bigamy and (2) lack of a marriage ceremony.

*Bigamy* Suppose John marries Frances, abandons her without a valid divorce, and then marries Sally who is unaware of the prior marriage, or believes that it has been legally dissolved. When John dies, who is his wife? Sally can invoke a number of theories to support her claim. A presumption that a marriage is valid may lead a court to assume that John had divorced Frances before he married Sally, or that his marriage to Frances was invalid and thus no bar.[7] Sally might have also have rights as a "putative spouse." The Louisiana Civil Code says that a void marriage "nevertheless produces civil effects in favor of a party who contracted it in good faith."[8] "Good faith" includes reasonable errors of law as well as mistakes of fact.[9] The "civil effects" enjoyed by a putative "spouse"

---

**2.** But if an instrument simply designates a "spouse" without adding a name, only a lawful spouse qualifies. Serradell v. Hartford Acc. and Indem. Co., 843 P.2d 639 (Alaska 1992).

**3.** Uniform Marriage and Divorce Act § 208(c). This is not true under Alternative B, but the comment suggests disapproval of this alternative.

**4.** In re Marriage of Davis, 576 N.E.2d 972 (Ill.App.1991) (suit by spouse's guardian to avoid marriage for incapacity); Uniform Marriage and Divorce Act § 208(a)(1) (marriage can be voided for fraud or incapacity).

**5.** Uniform Marriage and Divorce Act § 208(b); Matter of Estate of Fuller,

862 P.2d 1037 (Colo.App.1993) (children cannot challenge their father's marriage for incapacity after his death).

**6.** Matter of Estate of Lint, 957 P.2d 755 (Wash.1998).

**7.** Chandler v. Central Oil Corp., 853 P.2d 649 (Kan.1993).

**8.** La.Civ.Code, art. 96. This is based on (French) Code Civil art. 201.

**9.** Jones v. Equitable Life Assur. Soc., 173 So.2d 373 (La.App.1965). *But see* Estate of Depasse, 118 Cal.Rptr.2d 143, 156 (App.2002) (party to an unlicensed marriage who knew of license requirement cannot be a putative spouse).

include the right to inherit, sue for wrongful death, and take under an insurance policy payable by its terms to the insured's "widow."[10]

The common law did not recognize "putative" spouses, but the idea is spreading. The Uniform Marriage and Divorce Act gives putative spouses all the rights of a legal spouse.[11] The Social Security Act gives benefits to applicants who "in good faith went through a marriage ceremony" which "but for a legal impediment not known to the applicant * * * would have been a valid marriage."[12] If the lawful wife is entitled to social security benefits, the putative spouse gets none,[13] but the Uniform Marriage and Divorce Act authorizes courts to "apportion property * * * among the claimants as appropriate in the circumstances and in the interests of justice."[14]

*Separation and Divorce*   Some states bar even lawful spouses from rights in the other spouse's estate under certain circumstances. In Pennsylvania a spouse who has "willfully and maliciously" deserted or "willfully neglected or refused" to support the other spouse for a year or more cannot share in the spouse's estate.[15] Modern counterparts appear in some states to the Statute of Westminster of 1285 which barred an adulterous wife from claiming dower.[16] Under the Uniform Probate Code, however, a separation, absent a divorce, does not affect succession rights unless a separation agreement waived claims to share in the other's estate.[17] Many spouses have successfully asserted claims to share in a decedent spouse's estate even though divorce proceedings between them were pending when the decedent died,[18] but some courts only allow a surviving spouse in this situation an equitable share of the marital property as in a divorce.[19]

A legal spouse who contracts a bigamous marriage may be barred from asserting rights under the first marriage "if, under the circumstances, it would be inequitable for him to do so."[20] The

**10.** King v. Cancienne, 316 So.2d 366 (La.1975); Succession of Choyce, 183 So.2d 457 (La.App.1966).

**11.** Uniform Marriage and Divorce Act § 209; Estate of Whyte v. Whyte, 614 N.E.2d 372 (Ill.App.1993).

**12.** 42 U.S.C.A. § 416(h)(1)(B).

**13.** Martin v. Harris, 653 F.2d 428 (10th Cir.1981).

**14.** Uniform Marriage and Divorce Act § 209. *See also Restatement, Third, of Property (Wills and Other Donative Transfers)* § 1.2, comm. e (1998).

**15.** 20 Pa.C.S. § 2106(a). Or.Rev. Stat. § 114.135 gives courts discretion to deny or reduce a spouse's elective share if the couple was separated at death.

**16.** In Oliver v. Estate of Oliver, 554 N.E.2d 8 (Ind.App.1990), such a statute was used to bar a husband from claiming a devise under his wife's will.

**17.** Uniform Probate Code § 2–802, comment; In re Estate of Salathe, 703 So.2d 1167 (Fla.App.1997) (husband gets a share of wife's estate despite separation agreement).

**18.** McClinton v. Sullivan, 430 S.E.2d 794 (Ga.App.1993).

**19.** Carr v. Carr, 576 A.2d 872 (N.J. 1990).

**20.** Kosak v. MacKechnie, 505 N.E.2d 579 (Mass.App.Ct.1987). *See also* Matter of Estate of Warner, 687 S.W.2d 686 (Mo.App.1985) (husband estopped to

Uniform Probate Code denies spousal status to persons who have obtained or consented to an invalid divorce, or who have remarried after such a divorce.[21] A *valid* divorce terminates a marriage without resort to the idea of estoppel, but in community property states rights to community property of the former marriage survive if they were not disposed of at the time of the divorce.[22]

*No Ceremonial Marriage*  Some states do not require a ceremony for a valid marriage. Canon law, which governed the law of marriage throughout the Middle Ages, held that consent alone was necessary. In England, no marriage ceremony was legally required until a statute of 1753.[23] Today a few states still permit non-ceremonial "common-law" marriages, but their number is declining.[24] Nevertheless, all states recognize a common-law marriage if it was valid where contracted.[25]

How is a "common-law" marriage proved? Some courts require a specific agreement concerning marriage,[26] but others infer a marriage contract when a couple live together and hold themselves out as man and wife.[27] Even when a contract of marriage exists, some courts hold that cohabitation and reputation as husband and wife are also necessary.[28]

Even if the relevant law does not recognize common-law marriages, the dramatic increase in recent years of cohabitation by unmarried couples may bring about a change in the law comparable to the expansion of the rights of children born out of wedlock. From 1970 to 1993 alone, the number of unmarried couple households in the U.S. increased from 523,00 to 3,510,000.[29]

challenge validity of Mexican divorce so as to claim property as tenant by the entirety).

**21.** Uniform Probate Code § 2–802(b). *But see* Matter of Estate of Kueber, 390 N.W.2d 22 (Minn.App.1986) (a deserted wife who had remarried can claim rights as her legal husband's widow).

**22.** In re Marriage of Moore and Ferrie, 18 Cal.Rptr.2d 543, 547 (App.1993).

**23.** 1 W. Blackstone, *Commentaries* 439 (1765); Statute, 26 Geo. 2, c. 33 (1753).

**24.** Younger, *Marital Regimes,* 67 Cornell L.Review 45, 75 (1981). Idaho abolished common law marriage effective Jan. 1, 1996, Matter of Estate of Wagner, 893 P.2d 211 (Idaho 1995), but Utah adopted it in 1987, Whyte v. Blair, 885 P.2d 791 (Utah 1994).

**25.** Varoz v. Estate of Shepard, 585 N.E.2d 31 (Ind.App.1992) (Indiana must

recognize Colorado judgment declaring plaintiff to be decedent's common-law wife).

**26.** Gonzalez v. Satrustegui, 870 P.2d 1188 (Ariz.App.1993).

**27.** Brown v. Carr, 402 S.E.2d 296 (Ga.App.1991). *But see* Estate of Wires, 765 P.2d 618 (Colo.App.1988) (no marriage where couple cohabited for years but chose not to marry so W would not lose her Social Security).

**28.** Matter of Estate of Vandenhook, 855 P.2d 518 (Mont.1993) (no marriage if parties do not cohabit or hold selves out as spouses).

**29.** Salzman v. Bachrach, 996 P.2d 1263, 1267 (Colo.2000). By 2000 the number of "unmarried partner households" had climbed to 5.475 million. Cohen, *Estate Planning Needs of Unmarried Partners,* 30 Est.Plann. 188 (2003). However, such cohabitation is for most a temporary status; "the parties either

So far protection for unmarried cohabitants has been limited. The Restatement calls the right of a "domestic partner" to be treated as a spouse a "developing question," as to which it takes no position.[30] In New Hampshire, "Persons cohabiting and acknowledging each other as husband and wife, and generally reputed to be such, for the period of three years, and until the decease of one of them, shall thereafter be deemed to have been legally married."[31] But most states have no such legislation and the equal protection clause in the Constitution, which has protected children born out of wedlock, does not help unmarried cohabitants.[32] The problem of proving paternity is outweighed by the unfairness of penalizing children for a difficulty which they did not create; unmarried cohabitants cannot make this argument.[33]

*Contract* Unmarried cohabitants sometimes assert rights under a contract with their partner, usually while both parties are alive. "Claims arising at death are less common because, if the parties remain devoted to one another, the surviving partner is probably provided for in the decedent's will or other parts of the estate plan."[34] The argument that such contracts violate public policy because they involve illicit sex is generally rejected on the ground that sex plays only an incidental role in the relationship.[35] But express contracts concerning the arrangement are rather unusual; the significant issue is whether courts will infer a contract between cohabitants.

Some critics contend that recognizing an implied contract between cohabitants conflicts with the legislative decision to abolish common-law marriage,[36] but there are differences between the two. Historically, common-law marriages might make a later formal marriage invalid as bigamous,[37] but courts can imply a contract which does not eliminate the rights of a lawful spouse.[38] However, a

break up or get married fairly quickly." Waggoner, *Marital Property Rights in Transition*, 59 Mo.L.Rev. 21, 63 (1994).

**30.** *Restatement, Third, of Property (Wills and Other Donative Transfers)* § 2.2, comm. g (1998).

**31.** N.H.Rev.Stat. § 457.39.

**32.** Califano v. Boles, 443 U.S. 282, 289 (1979). The protection given by the Social Security Act to putative spouses is limited to those who go through a marriage ceremony. Thomas v. Sullivan, 922 F.2d 132 (2d Cir.1990).

**33.** Sykes v. Propane Power Corp., 541 A.2d 271 (N.J.Super.A.D.1988) (justifying refusal to allow unmarried cohabitant to sue for wrongful death).

**34.** Waggoner, *supra* note 29, at 65.

**35.** Marvin v. Marvin, 557 P.2d 106 (Cal.1976); Morone v. Morone, 413 N.E.2d 1154 (N.Y.1980). *But see* Hewitt v. Hewitt, 394 N.E.2d 1204 (Ill.1979).

**36.** Clark, *The New Marriage*, 12 Will.L.J. 441, 449 (1976); In re Estate of Alexander, 445 So.2d 836 (Miss.1984).

**37.** Richard III claimed the throne of England on the basis of an earlier unsolemnized marriage by his brother which made the brother's children illegitimate. P. Kendall, *Richard the Third* 257 (1955).

**38.** "Enforcement of the contract between plaintiff and defendant * * * will not impair any right of" Marvin's wife. Marvin v. Marvin, 557 P.2d 106, 115 (Cal.1976).

line must be drawn between casual cohabitation and a stable relationship.

Assuming a court implies a contract, what will be its terms? One theory would compensate the plaintiff for services performed during the relationship, less any benefits received, but courts often reject such claims on the ground that the services were rendered without any expectation of payment.[39] A cohabitant who contributes to the acquisition of property in ways other than performing domestic services has more chance of success.[40] Courts sometimes infer an agreement to divide all property acquired during a relationship equally.[41]

Professor Blumberg maintains that the law should "assimilate cohabitants to married persons" for all purposes, since "most cohabitants feel there is no difference between marriage and cohabitation,"[42] but others argue that this would defeat expectations, since cohabitants refrain from marriage because they wish to avoid its legal incidents.[43] Waggoner's proposed statute would give cohabitants "a substantially smaller intestate share than a spouse would take under the UPC" and no right to an elective share.[44]

*Same Sex Marriages*  Even more problematic are the claims of homosexual cohabitants, who, according to one estimate, number over 3 million.[45] A court allowed a homosexual lover to sue on an express promise of a share of the defendant's property,[46] but another rejected a partner's claim to a spouse's share of an estate, saying that the statutory limitation of marriage to persons of the opposite sex was constitutional.[47] But in Hawaii when a court questioned the constitutionality of the limitation,[48] the legislature responded with a statute which gives "reciprocal beneficiaries" the same rights as

**39.** Osborne v. Boatmen's Nat. Bank, 732 S.W.2d 242 (Mo.App.1987) (disregarding claimant's "self-serving" testimony to the contrary); Neumann v. Rogstad, 757 P.2d 761 (Mont.1988) (rejecting a claim by a husband for compensation for services to his wife).

**40.** Adams v. Jankouskas, 452 A.2d 148 (Del.1982).

**41.** Western States Construction v. Michoff, 840 P.2d 1220 (Nev.1992); Wilkinson v. Higgins, 844 P.2d 266 (Or.App. 1992).

**42.** Blumberg, *Cohabitation Without Marriage*, 28 UCLA L.Rev. 1125, 1166–67 (1981).

**43.** Connell v. Francisco, 898 P.2d 831, 836 (Wash.1995).

**44.** Waggoner, *supra* note 29, at 80.

**45.** Spitko, *The Expressive Function of Succession Law and the Merits of Non–Marital Inclusion*, 41 Ariz.L.Rev. 1063, 1071 (1999). The author advocates giving "same-sex committed partners" rights to inherit on intestacy.

**46.** Whorton v. Dillingham, 248 Cal. Rptr. 405 (App.1988).

**47.** Matter of Cooper, 592 N.Y.S.2d 797 (App.Div.1993). *See also* In re Estate of Hall, 707 N.E.2d 201 (Ill.App. 1998) (surviving partner has no standing to challenge constitutionality of bar to single-sex marriage).

**48.** Baehr v. Lewin, 852 P.2d 44 (Haw.1993). *See also* Baker v. State, 744 A.2d 864 (Vt.1999); Goodridge v. Department of Public Health, 798 N.E.2d 941 (Mass.2003).

spouses, *e.g.* to an intestate or elective share.[49] This status is open to unmarried adults who are legally prohibited from marrying one another and who file a notarized statement of intent.[50] A Vermont statute allows persons of the same sex to enter into a "civil union" which gives them similar benefits.[51] Because of other states might be forced to recognize marriages between persons of the same sex under the general rule which recognizes marriages as valid if valid in the state where they took place, the 1996 Defense of Marriage Act provides that states are not "required to give effect" to laws of other states "respecting a relationship between persons of the same sex that is treated as a marriage."[52]

*Planning* Many of the problems discussed in this section can be avoided by careful drafting. The Uniform Statutory Will Act defines the term "surviving spouse" of the testator to exclude a person from whom the testator was separated under a decree of separation or a written separation agreement, or divorced even if the divorce is not recognized in the state. Conversely, a person to whom the testator is not legally married because the termination of a previous marriage was not valid is deemed to be the testator's spouse.[53] A testator who after executing the will divorces the spouse should review the will and make appropriate changes, although the law makes default provisions to cover this situation.[54]

Although the legal rights of unmarried partners are limited in most states, a client who wishes to provide for a partner can designate him or her in a will or will substitute. Although the marital deduction is not available to avoid transfer taxes on gifts or devises to the non-spouse partner, other tax-reducing methods can help.[55]

**49.** Haw.Rev.Stat. §§ 560:2–102, 560:2–202.

**50.** Haw.Rev.Stat. § 572C–5.

**51.** 15 Vt.Stat.Ann § 1204. *See also* Cal.Fam.Code § 297.5(c).

**52.** 28 U.S.C. § 1738C.

**53.** Unif. Statutory Will Act § 1(7).

**54.** See Section 5.4.

**55.** Cohen, supra note 29, at 190–91.

# Chapter 3

# LIMITS ON TESTAMENTARY POWER

*Table of Sections*

## § 3.1  Policy Considerations

This chapter discusses the question how much freedom an owner should have to dispose of property. One reason for limiting this freedom arises from the duty of parents to support their children and their spouse. Blackstone said the duty of parents to support their children was "a principle of natural law," and parents should be obligated to leave their children "at least a necessary subsistence,"[1] but this does not represent the law in most American states.

*Spouses v. Children*  Spouses receive more protection against disinheritance than children in most of the United States.[2] In a way

---

§ 3.1

**1.**  1 W. Blackstone, *Commentaries** 447, 449–50 (1765).

**2.**  Only Georgia permits a spouse to be disinherited. Kwestel & Seplowitz, *Testamentary Substitutes—A Time for Statutory Clarification*, 23 Real Prop.

P.T.J. 467, 468 (1988). As to the elective share see Section 3.7. The spouse's claim to half the community property is its counterpart in a number of states. See Section 3.8.

this is surprising since young children cannot support themselves, whereas many spouses can.[3] But the duty to support children usually applies only to minors, and since minors are incapable of managing property, any property which they get must be managed by a guardian. Guardianship is inconvenient and expensive, and many parents seek to avoid it by leaving all their property to the other spouse in the expectation that he or she will use it for the children. A will which leaves all the estate to the testator's spouse technically disinherits the testator's children, but why should the law upset this sensible estate plan?[4]

Spouses have another basis for claiming a share of the decedent's estate; usually both spouses contribute to the accumulation of property during a marriage whereas children normally make no such contribution.[5]

If the surviving spouse is the other parent of the decedent's children, the claims of spouse children usually coincide. But with the increase in multiple marriages, the surviving spouse often is not the children's parent and there may be hostility between them. Most litigation today about the spouse's forced share arises in this context.

*Arguments for Free Disposition*    Arguments against the claims of spouses and children to a forced share in a decedent's estate have been made for centuries. Bracton in the 13th century asserted that men would have no incentive to work and save if they were compelled to leave their property at death to their widows and children.[6] Similar arguments have been made in modern times. However, the law compels living persons to support dependents even though this may also deter work or saving. A person's duty to pay debts survives death, so should not the duty to support survive as well?

Bracton also argued that freedom of testation gave wives and children an incentive to treat the testator well. Some parents use their testamentary freedom to control the lives of their children in an unappealing way, for example, disinheriting a child who adopts a religion or marries a person of whom the parent disapproves. Arguably the law should allow a will to disinherit a child or spouse only for certain misconduct.[7]

---

**3.** Rein, *A More Rational System for the Protection of Family Members from Disinheritance*, 15 Gonz.L.Rev. 11, 47 (1979).

**4.** Chaffin, *A Reappraisal of the Wealth Transmission Process*, 10 Ga. L.Rev. 447, 475 (1976).

**5.** A child who has helped a parent in a business or provided care may have an enforceable claim against the estate if the parent agreed in return to leave property to the child at death. See Section 4.9.

**6.** 2 Bracton, *De Legibus et Consuetudinibus Angliae* 181 (Thorne ed. 1968).

**7.** Thus BGB (German Civil Code) §§ 2333–35 specify grounds for which a spouse, parent or descendant may be deprived of the forced share.

A better argument for testamentary freedom is that it permits more intelligent estate planning than the rigid rules of intestate succession: A will may depart from the equal treatment of children mandated by the intestacy laws in order to take account of their differing needs. Or, a testator who has provided for one child by gifts during lifetime may leave this child less than the others; the law of advancements[8] is a crude alternative for reflecting this desire. Or a testator may wish to provide for children equally, but in different ways, for example, by leaving a family business to one child and equivalent assets to the others. Or, a testator may wish to leave property in trust for a child or spouse who is unable to handle property. Why should the law allow a child or spouse to upset reasonable wills like these?

*Fixed-Share v. Discretionary Restraints*  Restraints on testamentary freedom, where they exist, are of two types: (1) fixed share and (2) discretionary. The most important limitation on testamentary freedom in the United States today, the spouse's elective or community property share, is generally a fraction of the estate which imperfectly fits the duty-of-support rationale. "The fraction of the estate to which the surviving spouse is entitled does not vary with the size of the estate. * * * One-third of an estate of $1,000,000 may enable a spouse to live in the accustomed style, but one-third of an estate of $200,000 may not."[9] Some states reduce the surviving spouse's share by gifts received from the decedent or by the spouse's other resources, however acquired. Even these statutes correlate only imperfectly with the need for support because they ignore the spouse's earning capacity. Also support needs can change over time, and yet virtually all American statutes give the spouse a lump sum and take no account of later changes in circumstances.[10]

These objections do not apply to recognition of the spouse's contributions to the estate. A spouse who helped to build up an estate should not be denied a share in it on the ground that the spouse is self-supporting. However, if the spouse's contribution to the accumulation of property justifies the forced share, the share ought to depend upon the length of the marriage. If a marriage has lasted only a few weeks, the surviving spouse would have contributed very little, but would receive a large portion of the estate under most elective share statutes.

Discretionary statutes avoid many of the traditional objections to limiting testamentary freedom. They do *not* disrupt intelligent estate plans by imposing an "inflexible blanket rule" modeled on

---

**8.** Section 2.6.

**9.** E. Halbach ed., *Death, Taxes and Family Property* 111–12 (1977).

**10.** The family allowance provides a relatively unimportant exception to this statement. See Section 3.4.

the laws of intestate succession. Some object that discretionary statutes would promote litigation because courts would be "without guideposts or rules,"[11] but American courts regularly make similar discretionary determinations when they fix alimony and child support or divide property in divorce proceedings.

Since wills which disinherit children or spouses are much rarer than divorce,[12] there would be few occasions to litigate.[13] A statute protecting disinherited children might not actually increase the incidence of litigation because disinherited children often contest wills today on the ground that the testator was incapacitated or subject to undue influence.[14] Nevertheless, the drafters of the Uniform Probate Code refused to model the spouse's elective share on divorce law. "Although all or most all states now follow the so-called equitable-distribution system upon divorce, there is considerable division among the states in the details," and so the system was not compatible "with a uniform laws project striving to achieve uniformity within the probate system." Uniformity was important "in order to prevent a spouse bent on disinheritance from domicile shopping by relocating property to a state with fewer safeguards against this sort of behavior." [15]

*Inter-vivos Transfers* If either spouses or children or both should be able to upset a will should they also be allowed to attack transfers which the decedent made while alive? One might distinguish between transfers made for consideration and gifts. To upset sales would impede commerce and be unfair to purchasers who paid value. Moreover, the assets available for support of the seller's dependents are not depleted by a sale, since the sale proceeds take the place of the property sold. But community property states often allow one spouse to attack even sales of community real property made by the other. On the other hand, a person with a claim for support should not be allowed to dictate which assets are used to fulfill that duty. Thus the Uniform Probate Code allows spouses to attack only lifetime transfers for which the decedent did not receive adequate consideration.[16]

Perhaps even donees should be protected; they may be unfairly prejudiced if they are forced to return property which was given to them years earlier. Many states, therefore, only allow surviving

---

**11.** Chaffin, *supra* note 4 at 462.

**12.** Browder, *Recent Patterns of Testate Succession in the United States and England,* 67 Mich.L.Rev. 1303, 1305–08 (1969).

**13.** Plager, *The Spouse's Nonbarrable Share: A Solution in Search of a Problem,* 33 U.Chi.L.Rev. 681, 715 (1966).

**14.** As to incapacity and undue influence see Sections 7.1, 7.3.

**15.** Waggoner, *The Multiple Marriage Society,* 76 Iowa L.Rev. 223, 242–44 (1991).

**16.** Uniform Probate Code § 2–208(a).

spouses a share of the property which the decedent owned at death. But the line between transfers during life and those which take effect at death is often blurred. How should one classify a gift made by a husband two days before he died? Or a trust created by a wife under which she reserved the income for her life and a power to revoke the trust until she died? In recent years "will substitutes," which purport to be present gifts but which have virtually no effect until death, have become increasingly popular. Many American states now allow spouses to reach them.

## § 3.2  History and Comparative Law

*Land*  Wills of land and personal property followed different paths historically. Land could not be devised by will until the Statute of Wills of 1540. Blackstone attributes this rule to feudalism, "a branch of the feodal doctrine of non-alienation without the consent of the lord. * * * The reason of conferring the feud being the personal abilities of the feudatory to serve in war, it was not fit that he should be at liberty to transfer this gift * * * to others who might prove less able."[1] A feudal lord's concern with the personal abilities of tenants would apply to all transfers of land, but from 1290 on tenants could alienate their land inter vivos without the lord's permission.[2] Feudal opposition to wills in the later Middle Ages focused not on concern with the "personal abilities" of the tenant, but on the feudal incidents such as wardship which gave lords the profits of land when it descended to a minor heir. If tenants could make wills they could avoid wardship.

The prohibition against wills was a logical consequence of the requirement that land be transferred by delivery, or livery of seisin. Juries originally were made up of neighbors who relied on their own knowledge in rendering verdicts rather than the testimony of witnesses. If possession of land was not delivered, the neighbors would not learn of the gift.[3] Only the church courts, which did not employ juries, could probate wills. But the common law would not allow church courts to deal with *land*.[4]

*Uses*  The prohibition on devises was evaded in the 15th century by uses. If John wanted to devise land to Arthur, he would deliver seisin to Tom and Dick "to the use" of John's last will and declare his will that the land should pass to Arthur when John died. If Tom and Dick failed to carry out John's will, the Chancellor would compel them to do so at the suit of the intended devisee. The inadequacy of juries to try wills was irrelevant because the Chancellor did not use them; he examined witnesses under oath to ascer-

---

§ 3.2

1.  2 W. Blackstone, *Commentaries* 57,373 (1765).

2.  18 Edw. 1, c. 1 (1290).

3.  Plucknett, *A Concise History of the Common Law* 736 (5th ed.1956).

4.  2 Bracton, *De Legibus* 70, 149; Plucknett, *supra* note 3, at 737.

tain the testator's intent. The fact that uses, the ancestor of modern trusts, were originally enforced by the Chancellor in Equity still affects the enforcement of trusts today, where trial is not usually by jury. [5]

In the 16th century, Henry VIII tried to end uses in order to maximize his revenue as a feudal lord by persuading Parliament to enact the Statute of Uses which provided that when land was held in use legal title should pass to the beneficiary.[6] This made it impossible to evade the common-law prohibition on wills.

The abolition of wills produced a popular outcry, so Henry VIII had to consent to the Statute of Wills of 1540 which allowed wills, but partially protected the interests of feudal lords. Person holding land by knight service could only dispose of two-thirds of it; as to the other third, the lord's right to wardship and other feudal incidents was expressly preserved.[7] This limitation became obsolete in 1660 when the feudal incidents were abolished.[8]

*Personal Property* Feudal considerations did not apply to personal property. The common law conceded jurisdiction over testaments of personal property to the church courts, which did not employ jury trial, and allowed wills. There were, however, limitations on a testator's right to disinherit his wife[9] and children. In the 12th century a decedent's movables were divided into three equal parts, one for his children, one for his wife, and a third "over which he has free power of disposition." If the testator died without a wife he could dispose of half of his personalty.[10] In the later Middle Ages, however, freedom of testation became the general rule: widows or children who sought a forced share had to allege a local custom. The differing rules in different localities allowed local restrictions to be evaded.[11] These local customs were all ultimately eliminated by statutes in the late 17th and early 18th centuries.[12] Similarly in the United States today, state restrictions on disinheritance may simply encourage a flight of property to jurisdictions where testamentary freedom is unimpaired.

*British and Civil Law*   In the British Commonwealth, instead of the medieval fixed share, modern legislatures, beginning with

---

**5.** Juries today are often used to try will contests, see Section 12.1, but today juries' knowledge of the facts depends on evidence produced in court rather than their own knowledge.

**6.** Statute of Uses, 27 Hen. 8, c. 10, § 9 (1536).

**7.** Statute of Wills, 32 Henry 8, c. 1, § 4 (1540).

**8.** Statute, 12 Car. 2, c. 24, § 1 (1660).

**9.** At common law a husband acquired title to his wife's personal property upon marriage, 2 W. Blackstone, *Commentaries* *433 (1765). Therefore there was no occasion to consider the wife's right to disinherit her husband.

**10.** R. Glanville, *Tractatus de Legibus* 80 (G.Hall ed. 1965).

**11.** Statute, 11 Geo. 1, c. 18, § 1 (1724).

**12.** 2 W. Blackstone, *Commentaries* *492–93 (1765).

New Zealand in 1900 have established discretionary controls to protect spouses and children. The present English statute includes step-children who were "treated by the deceased as a child," former spouses, and any other person who was "being maintained" by the decedent.[13]

The fixed share for children which prevailed in medieval England still exists throughout much of the world. The French Civil Code of 1804 prescribed fixed shares in order to prevent parents from leaving all their property to the eldest son; the leaders of the French Revolution considered this repugnant to their egalitarian ideals.[14] The share reserved for children, the *legitime,* varies with the number of children: a parent with one child can dispose of half his estate, but if there are three children the disposable share is only one fourth.[15] Even if a testator has no children, a share is reserved for any surviving ascendants (parents, grandparents, etc.). The *legitime* is protected against *inter vivos* gifts as well as wills.[16] Louisiana once had similar rules, but they have been watered down considerably in recent years. Since 1995, only children who are under age 24 or "who, because of mental incapacity or physical infirmity, are incapable of taking care of" themselves, are protected.[17]

Since forced heirship is common in most of the world, American courts have had to deal with choice of law. The will of a French domiciliary disinheriting her son, provided that it should be "regulated by the laws of the State of New York." A New York court denied the son's claim to a *legitime,* saying it was "counter to our local policy."[18] Courts in Europe look less favorably on such attempts to evade the forced share.[19]

# § 3.3   Survival of Claims for Support

The issue whether a father's duty to support a child survives his death rarely arises when the father is married to the child's

---

**13.** Inheritance (Provision for Family and Dependants) Act, 1975, § 1(1).

**14.** H. Maine, *Ancient Law* 187 (World Classics ed. 1931).

**15.** French Code Civil art. 913. A larger share can be left to the testator's spouse for life. *Id.* art. 1094–1.

**16.** *Id.,* art. 914, 922–23.

**17.** An earlier attempt by the legislature to limit forced heirship to such children was held unconstitutional in Succession of Lauga, 624 So.2d 1156 (La. 1993). The constitutional protection of forced heirship was thereafter limited in 1995. La. Const. Art. 12, § 5.

**18.** Estate of Renard, 439 N.E.2d 341 (N.Y.1982). *See also* Matter of Estate of Wright, 637 A.2d 106 (Me.1994) (claim under Swiss law rejected where will said Maine law should govern). However, American courts have recognized claims by children to a forced share under civil law. Nahar v. Nahar, 656 So.2d 225 (Fla.App.1995) (applying Dutch law to a Florida bank account because the owner was domiciled in the Netherlands Antilles).

**19.** J–P. Béraudo, *Les Trusts Anglo-Saxons et le Droit Francais* 210–11 (1992); H. Flick & D. Piltz, *Der Internationale Erbfall* 37–38 (1999).

mother. Usually the father leaves all or most of his estate to the mother, who will use the property she receives (plus her own property) to support the child, since mothers are also obligated to support their children.[1] But if parents are divorced when the father dies, or if they were never married, the mother is not a "surviving spouse" entitled to a share of his estate. Fathers' wills often do not provide for children by a former marriage or born out of wedlock. Normally at the time of a divorce, the father is ordered or agrees to make payments for the child's support. Does this obligation survive the father's death? This may depend on the terms of the agreement or divorce decree; if it is silent, the obligation to make future payments expires at death in some states, but not in all.

Many of the traditional justifications for freedom of testation do not apply in this situation. The disinheritance of children here is not merely the "technical" one which occurs when a spouse leaves everything to the other parent of the decedent's children. The disadvantage of guardianship for minors is irrelevant since support payments typically go to the mother for the benefit of the children, so a guardianship is not needed.[2] Reluctance to confer discretion on courts is not a valid objection to enforcing a duty of support which was fixed at the time of the divorce or in a paternity action. But adjustment of a prior support order may be called for by the changed circumstances produced by the parent's death. Life insurance proceeds or Social Security benefits may render continuation of the support payments no longer necessary.[3] If a father has remarried and incurred obligations to a new family, enforcing his duty to support his children by the prior marriage might deplete his estate at the expense of his new dependents.

*Alimony*  The duty to pay alimony to a former spouse usually ceases when the payer dies,[4] but an agreement may provide otherwise, either expressly or by implication.[5] For example, an agreement to pay annual support until a wife remarried or died was held

**§ 3.3**

**1.** H. Clark, *The Law of Domestic Relations* § 6.2 (1968); Cal.Family Code § 3900 (father and mother have equal responsibility to support their child).

**2.** H. Clark, *The Law of Domestic Relations* § 15.1, at 490 (1968); L.W.K v. E.R.C., 735 N.E.2d 359, 362 (Mass. 2000).

**3.** In re Marriage of Bertrand, 39 Cal.Rptr.2d 151 (App.1995) (support order modified to take account of Social Security payments accruing to child at father's death); *cf.* In re Marriage of Meek, 669 P.2d 628 (Colo.App.1983)

(proper to terminate support obligation because of Social Security benefits); *cf.* Matter of Marriage of Perry, 68 Cal. Rptr.2d 445 (App.1997) (child support order revised upward to reflect the end of the father's personal needs with his death).

**4.** Hendricks v. Hendricks, 817 P.2d 1339 (Or.App.1991); Barron v. Puzo, 610 N.E.2d 973 (Mass.1993).

**5.** In re Estate of Dahlstrom, 992 P.2d 1256 (Kan.App.1999); In re Last Will and Testament of Sheppard, 757 So.2d 173 (Miss.2000).

to create a claim against the husband's estate, since the explicit criteria for termination did not include the husband's death.[6]

*Planning*  Lawyers who negotiate divorce settlements which provide for support should anticipate that the payer may die while the children or spouse still need support. A provision for continuation of payments from the obligor's estate is not an adequate solution, because the estate may be insufficient—even if the obligor currently earns a high income, that income will cease at death. Also, it is generally undesirable to keep an estate open to continue periodic payments. Many divorce settlements require a parent to maintain life insurance for the benefit of children whom the divorcing parent is obligated to support. The California Family Code provides that unless otherwise agreed, obligations to support a spouse terminate "upon the death of either party",[7] but a court may order payment of an amount "sufficient to purchase an annuity * * * or to maintain insurance for the benefit of the supported spouse on the life of the spouse required to make the payment of support" or to establish a trust for support.[8] Such a provision can provide security that the claim will be paid,[9] and avoid having to keep a decedent's estate open.

## § 3.4  Family Allowance and Homestead

*Family Allowance*  A decedent's assets are frozen for a substantial period while the estate is administered. During this period claims against the estate are ascertained and paid. The decedent's family cannot be left to starve during administration, so the law provides a family allowance for them. Some statutes give the allowance only to minor children, but the Uniform Probate Code covers "minor children whom the decedent was obligated to support and children who were in fact being supported by him."[1] The allowance is paid to the surviving spouse "for the use of" the children, but if a child is not living with the spouse, "the allowance

---

**6.**  Lipe v. Lipe, 728 P.2d 1124 (Wyo. 1986). *See also* Cohan v. Feuer, 789 N.E.2d 157 (Mass.App.Ct.2003). *But see* Matter of Riconda, 688 N.E.2d 248 (N.Y. 1997).

**7.**  Cal. Family Code § 4337. Uniform Marriage and Divorce Act § 316 distinguishes between "maintenance" of a spouse, which terminates on the death of either party, and "support" for a child, which is "terminated by the emancipation of the child but not by the death of the parent."

**8.**  Cal.Family Code § 4360; cf. Benson v. Benson, 977 P.2d 88, 94–5 (Alaska 1999) (proper to order father who had

been dilatory in making support payments to create a trust to satisfy them).

**9.**  But if the father who is obligated to keep insurance in force allows the policy to lapse, it may be necessary to enforce the claim against his probate estate. For further discussion of this issue see Section 13.2.

**§ 3.4**

**1.**  Uniform Probate Code § 2–404; *cf.* In re Estate of Degner, 518 N.E.2d 400 (Ill.App.1987) ("dependent" includes a child unable to support herself even though decedent had not been supporting her).

may be made partially to the child or his guardian or other person having his care and custody."[2]

The Uniform Probate Code provides for "a reasonable allowance," in which "account should be taken of the previous standard of living."[3] This can be very substantial if the claimants were accustomed to "the finer things of life,"[4] but "account should be taken of * * * the nature of other resources available to the family."[5] Some courts hold that a spouse's independent means do not bar an award but benefits derived from the decedent do.[6] Some courts also consider a spouse's earning capacity. A spouse's remarriage precludes receiving an award in some states.[7]

Some statutes fix the amount of the family allowance, leaving nothing to the court's discretion,[8] and others provide for a minimum award.[9] Where statutes designate a specific amount, inflation may make it unrealistic as time goes by if it is not revised.

The American family allowance resembles family maintenance legislation in the British Commonwealth, but the American allowance provides support only "during the period of administration" of the estate.[10]

Many statutes, including the Uniform Probate Code, provide that the allowance may be paid in installments. Payments cease if a recipient dies before all the installments are paid according to the UPC.[11]

The family allowance takes precedence over nearly all claims against the estate, but it may be limited if an estate is insolvent. The family allowance is payable only out of assets which the

**2.** Uniform Probate Code § 2–404. *Cf.* 755 ILCS 5/15–2(a) (award to child not residing with spouse goes to "such person as the court directs").

**3.** Uniform Prob.Code § 2–404.

**4.** William Randolph Hearst's widow received an allowance of $10,000 per month. T. Atkinson, *Handbook of the Law of Wills* 134 (2d ed. 1953). Compare Matter of Estate of Hamilton, 869 P.2d 971 (Utah App.1994) ($1,000 a month for 24 months); Matter of Estate of Lettengarver, 813 P.2d 468 (Mont.1991) ($6,000 award).

**5.** Uniform Probate Code § 2–404, comment. *Cf.* In re Estate of Wentworth, 452 N.W.2d 714 (Minn.App.1990) (proper to deny allowance to spouse with other means of support).

**6.** Matter of Estate of Caffrey, 458 N.E.2d 1147 (Ill.App.1983). In Matter of Estate of Parkhill, 548 N.E.2d 821 (Ill.

App.1989), a widower was given the minimum allowance because he had received over $249,000 from assets held in joint tenancy with the decedent.

**7.** *Id.* § 53–3–2(a).

**8.** Md.Estates and Trusts Code § 3–201 ($5,000 for spouse and $2,500 for each minor child); Ohio Code § 2106.13(A) ($40,000); Ind.Code § 29–1–4–1 ($25,000).

**9.** 755 ILCS 5/15–1(a) ($10,000 to spouse plus $5,000 for each eligible child).

**10.** Uniform Probate Code § 2–404. *See also* Cal.Prob.Code § 6543(a) (allowance terminates when estate is distributed). This is not true in Maine. *See* Me. Rev.Stat. tit. 18–A, § 2–403.

**11.** Uniform Probate Code § 2–404(b). *But see* 755 ILCS 5/15–1(a) (unpaid family allowance passes to the spouse's estate).

decedent owned, and if the decedent's property was mortgaged or held in trust, the rights of the mortgagee or trust beneficiary are superior.[12] Although the family allowance is usually payable only out of the probate estate, the Uniform Probate Code allows many non-probate assets (*e.g.* joint bank accounts) to be reached if the probate estate is insolvent,[13] but other non-probate assets such as life insurance are not reachable to satisfy the family allowance.[14]

The family of a decedent can get an allowance even if they are disinherited by the decedent's will. If the will provides for them, they can take under the will and claim an allowance too, unless the will expressly requires them to elect between the two.[15]

*Homestead; Exempt Property*  The Uniform Probate Code has two other provisions for spouses and children, a "homestead allowance" and one for "exempt property," which, like the family allowance, take precedence over claims of creditors and any will of the decedent.[16] The amounts involved are relatively small. The UPC homestead allowance gives the spouse $15,000, and exempt property is only $10,000.[17] However, these amounts are not dependent upon need,[18] and are not affected by other provisions made for the claimant by the decedent.

In some states, homestead is more substantial. The Arkansas Constitution provides a homestead of up to one-quarter acre of land in cities and 80 acres elsewhere without regard to value, but widows only get a life estate and children only a right to the income until they are 21.[19] Moreover, homestead is available in many states only if the decedent owned a residence.[20] The homestead and exempt property allowance under the Uniform Probate Code, how-

**12.**  Parson v. Parson, 56 Cal.Rptr.2d 686 (App.1996); Matter of Estate of Epstein, 561 N.W.2d 82, 87 (Iowa App. 1996).

**13.**  Uniform Probate Code § 6–102; Matter of Estate of Wagley, 760 P.2d 316 (Utah 1988).

**14.**  In re Estate of Agans, 998 P.2d 449 (Ariz.App.1999).

**15.**  Uniform Prob.Code § 2–404(b); *cf.* In re Estate of Reddick, 657 N.E.2d 531 (Ohio App.1995) (will put spouse to an election).

**16.**  Uniform Prob.Code §§ 2–402, 2–403. However, a constructive trust can be imposed on homestead property which was wrongfully acquired. Kostelnik v. Roberts, 680 S.W.2d 532 (Tex. App.1984).

**17.**  Uniform Probate Code § 2–403. Before 1990, it was only $3,500. This amount goes, in the absence of a spouse,

to the "children"—it is not restricted to minors and dependent children.

**18.**  In re Estate of Wentworth, 452 N.W.2d 714 (Minn.App.1990) (proper to deny family allowance but not homestead and exempt property claim on basis that spouse had sufficient resources of her own).

**19.**  Ark.Const. art. 9, §§ 4–6. In contrast, under the UPC if a wife dies before receiving her homestead allowance her executor can claim it. Matter of Estate of Merkel's, 618 P.2d 872 (Mont. 1980).

**20.**  Brantley & Effland, *Inheritance, the Share of the Surviving Spouse, and Wills: Arkansas Law and the Uniform Probate Code Compared,* 3 U.Ark. at Little Rock L.J. 361, 388 (1980).

ever, do not depend on the type of property in the decedent's estate.[21]

Some homestead laws protect children, but under the UPC homestead and exempt property all go to the surviving spouse; children benefit only if no spouse survives.[22]

Even though homestead and the exemption take precedence over claims of creditors, they may provide less protection than the elective share as to property not in the probate estate.[23] But some states protect homestead against inter-vivos conveyances by one spouse without the other's consent.[24]

## § 3.5　Pretermitted Heirs

Most American states today have "pretermitted" or "omitted heir"[1] statutes, based on the idea that failure to mention a child in a will was an oversight, so the omitted child should get a share of the estate in order to fulfill the testator's true intent. The common law held that if a testator married *and* had a child after executing a will, the will was revoked.[2] American pretermitted heir statutes, which began in the 18th century, do not depend on the testator's marrying subsequent to the will.

*Variations in the Statutes*　Modern pretermitted heir statutes differ on several points.

1.　*Are all children*[3] *covered, or only those born or adopted after the will was executed?* Many statutes cover only children who were born after the will was executed.[4] Others are not so limited.[5] It is

---

**21.** *Restatement, Third, of Property (Wills and Other Donative Transfers)* § 1.1, comm. j (1998); Uniform Probate Code § 2–402.

**22.** *Cf.* In re Estate of Garwood, 38 P.3d 362 (Wash.App. 2002) (when surviving spouse, to whom the decedent's estate was devised, did not petition for homestead, adult child by a prior marriage could not).

**23.** Estate of Overmire v. American Nat. Red Cross, 794 P.2d 518 (Wash. App.1990) (no award in lieu of homestead out of revocable trust).

**24.** Fla.Const. art. 10, § 4(c); Sims v. Cox, 611 So.2d 339 (Ala.1992) (deed of homestead to daughter not signed by wife is voidable).

### § 3.5

**1.** Although from the Latin *praeter*, the prefix is commonly spelled *preter* in modern English. Uniform Probate Code § 2–302 uses the term "omitted."

**2.** 2 W. Blackstone, *Commentaries* 502–03 (1765). In England today, however, marriage alone, but not the birth of children, revokes a will. Wills Act, 1837, §§ 18–19.

**3.** "Children" are defined in the same way as for intestate succession. Uniform Probate Code § 1–201(5). Thus, a child adopted by another may not qualify as a pretermitted heir of the natural parents. Matter of Estate of Couch, 726 P.2d 1007 (Wash.App.1986), and a child born out of wedlock takes under the statute only if he qualifies as an heir. In re Sanders, 3 Cal.Rptr.2d 536 (App.1992).

**4.** Uniform Probate Code § 2–302; Tex.Probate Code § 67(c).

**5.** Mass.Gen.Laws c. 191, § 20; In re Estate of Richardson, 50 P.3d 584 (Okl. App.2002).

questionable whether statutes which include all children are consistent with the testator's probable intent. "Forgetting about the existence of a child one already has is * * * not very likely."[6] Providing a share for an omitted, existing child may be consistent with intent, however, if the testator mistakenly believed that the child was dead. The Uniform Probate Code also covers such children.[7]

The date of the child's birth, not conception, is controlling; even when a testator was five months pregnant when she executed her will, her child qualified as after-born under a pretermitted heir statute.[8] For an adopted child, the date of adoption rather than the date of birth controls.[9]

When, after the execution of a will and the subsequent birth of a child, a testator executes a codicil to the earlier will, the child is no longer regarded as after-born. The execution of a codicil is said to "republish" the will as of the date of the codicil.[10]

2. *Is the statute limited to children, or are more remote descendants included?* The Uniform Probate Code and many other statutes only protect omitted children,[11] but some statutes also cover issue of a deceased child.[12] The limitation to "children" in the Uniform Probate Code is hard to understand since the Code allows grandchildren of a decedent to take by representation if a decedent dies intestate.

3. *What evidence is admissible to show that the disinheritance was intentional?* Some courts admit any evidence of the testator's actual intent. Thus a claim by three daughters was rejected on the basis of testimony that the testator had had no contact with them and had represented himself to the world as a single man.[13] But under many statutes evidence of an intent to disinherit the child must appear in the will itself. The Uniform Probate Code says that it must appear *"from the will* that the omission was intentional," unless "the testator provided for the child by transfer outside the will" which was intended to "be in lieu of a testamentary provi-

---

**6.** Rein, *A More Rational System for the Protection of Family Members Against Disinheritance*, 15 Gonz.L.Rev. 11, 24–25 (1979).

**7.** Uniform Probate Code § 2–302(c). *See also* Cal.Prob.Code § 21622.

**8.** DeCoste v. Superior Court, 470 P.2d 457 (Ariz.1970).

**9.** Uniform Probate Code § 2–302; N.Y. EPTL § 5–3.2.

**10.** Azcunce v. Estate of Azcunce, 586 So.2d 1216 (Fla.App.1991). *But see Restatement, Third, of Property (Wills and Other Donative Transfers)* § 3.4, il-

lus. 3 (1998) (disapproving the result in Azunce).

**11.** Uniform Probate Code § 2–302; Cal.Prob.Code § 21620.

**12.** Mass.Gen.Laws c. 191, § 20; Ohio Rev.Code § 2107.34.

**13.** In re Estate of Blank, 219 N.W.2d 815 (N.D.1974). According to *Restatement, Second, of Property (Donative Transfers)* § 34.2(2), comment f (1990) "evidence outside the will as to the testator's intent should be admissible" unless the statute provides otherwise.

sion." This intent can be "shown by the testator's statements or * * * inferred from the amount of the transfer or other evidence."[14] The Code also bars claims by omitted children when the will devises "all or substantially all the estate to the other parent of the omitted child,"[15] presumably on the theory that the devisee will use the property for the children, so they are not really disinherited.

Language in the will can also bar claims by a pretermitted heir. Some wills make nominal devises to persons whom the testator wishes to disinherit, but a statement in a will that "I do not wish to provide for my son Arthur" is sufficient.

There has been much litigation about what language is sufficient to bar heirs who are not mentioned by name in the will. Courts are reluctant to treat "boilerplate" provisions as showing an intent to disinherit children, for example, a statement that "all other persons are excluded from receiving anything from my estate."[16] But when a will provides for the testator's "descendants," a child who is not mentioned by name is not pretermitted, e.g., "to my wife, Mary, if she survives me, otherwise to my descendants." If Mary survives, the descendants take nothing, but they were not overlooked.[17]

Even a substantial devise in a will to a person whom the testator later adopts does not bar a pretermitted-heir claim by the devisee; courts assume that the testator's failure to change the will to give the devisee more after the adoption was an oversight.[18]

4. *What does a pretermitted heir take?* In a few states the birth of a child to the testator revokes a previous will, but in most states, pretermitted heirs receive their intestate share, while the rest of the will remains intact.[19] A pretermitted heir's share may amount to the whole estate, but this depends on the facts. In community property states where all community property usually passes to the spouse on intestacy the share of a pretermitted child may be zero.

Giving pretermitted heirs a full intestate share sometimes produces a questionable result. Suppose that a will leaves $3,000 each to the testator's two children, A and B, and the rest of the

**14.** Uniform Probate Code § 2–302(b). See also Cal.Prob.Code § 21621. But see In re Estate of Came, 529 A.2d 962 (N.H.1987) (beneficiary of $500,000 trust also takes as pretermitted heir).

**15.** Uniform Probate Code § 2–302(a)(1); cf. Cal.Prob.Code § 21621(b) (applicable only when testator had some children when the will was executed).

**16.** Matter of Estate of Woodward, 807 P.2d 262 (Okl.1991).

**17.** Matter of Estate of Broughton, 828 P.2d 443 (Okl.App.1991). But see Robinson v. Mays, 610 S.W.2d 885 (Ark. 1981).

**18.** Brown v. Crawford, 699 P.2d 162 (Okl.App.1984).

**19.** Cal.Prob.Code § 21620; 755 ILCS 5/4–10.

large estate to charity. A daughter C is born later. C's intestate share would give her more than her older siblings, but it is doubtful that testator would have wanted this. The Uniform Probate Code would only give C a share equal to that of her siblings, whose shares would abate ratably to make up C's share, so each child would get $2,000.[20]

5. *Non-probate property* A man had insurance on his life which designated his "children, Robert and Tamara" as the beneficiaries. He later had a third child who claimed a share of the insurance proceeds. This situation fits within the rationale but is not covered by the pretermitted heir statutes, which refer only to *wills*.[21] But the Restatement of Property states that the policy of the statute "should be applied by analogy to the omitted issue" in a will substitute.[22]

*Planning* Although pretermitted heir statutes are designed to carry out the testator's probable intent, they often fail to do so. Lawyers whose negligence caused a will to be upset by a pretermitted heir's claim may be liable to the devisees for malpractice.[23] They can usually guard against unintended omission of an after-born child by using class gifts. If a will leaves the estate "to my issue"[24] instead of "to Arthur and Andrew," an after-born child would not have to (and could not) invoke a pretermitted heir statute.

## § 3.6   Omitted Spouse

In England the Wills Act of 1837 provided that marriage revoked any existing will.[1] This rule prevails in some states today,[2] but in others a will is revoked only if the testator later marries *and* has a child.[3]

Many statutes give an intestate share to an omitted spouse like an omitted child. This is not the same as revoking the will, even when the spouse's intestate share amounts to the entire estate,

---

**20.** Uniform Probate Code § 2–302(a)(2). *See also* N.Y. EPTL § 5–3.2(a)(1)(B).

**21.** Penn Mutual Life Ins. Co. v. Abramson, 530 A.2d 1202 (D.C.App. 1987).

**22.** *Restatement, Second, of Property (Donative Transfers)* § 34.2(2) (1990). According to Comment g, this policy does not apply to a "one-item substitute for a will, such as a joint bank account." Cal.Prob.Code § 21620 applies to revocable living trusts as well as wills.

**23.** Leak–Gilbert v. Fahle, 55 P.3d 1054 (Okl.2002).

**24.** As to the extent to which after-borns are included in a class gift, see Section 10.3.

**§ 3.6**

**1.** Wills Act, 1 Vict. c. 26, § 18 (1837).

**2.** R.I.Gen.Laws § 33–5–9 (unless will made in contemplation of marriage). This statute applies even though the spouse predeceases the testator, Lessard v. Lessard, 273 A.2d 307 (R.I.1971), but under Ore.Rev.Stat. § 112.305, a subsequent marriage revokes the will only if the spouse survives the testator.

**3.** Kan.Stat. § 59–610; Md.Estates and Trusts Code § 4–105(3).

since administrative provisions in the will remain effective. Also, any omitted spouse claim disappears if the new spouse predeceases the testator or they are divorced before the testator dies.

Uniform Probate Code § 2–301, giving an intestate share to a spouse who marries the testator after a will is executed, resembles § 2–302, protecting after-born children, but there are curious differences between the two. A spouse who is omitted from a will because the testator mistakenly believes he/she is dead is not covered by the Code, but a child in the same situation is. The Code does not give the spouse a share if "the will was made in contemplation of the testator's marriage,"[4] but there is no comparable bar on claims by children whose birth was contemplated when the will was executed.

Since the underlying theory in the provisions for omitted spouses and children is the correction of an oversight, both rules are subject to evidence that the omission was in fact intentional. Both sections use virtually identical language covering a "transfer outside the will" intended to "be in lieu of a testamentary provision."[5] Under this proviso a widow who had received a $230,000 gift from the testator was held not to be an omitted spouse.[6]

An intent not to provide for the spouse may also be manifested in the will itself. (Such an express disinheritance would not preclude a claim to an *elective share*. See the next Section). General language disinheriting heirs is not sufficient. Many wills provide for a friend whom the testator later marries. Most courts have held that such devises do not bar an omitted spouse claim unless the will was made in contemplation of the marriage,[7] but there are also contrary decisions.[8] The comment to Uniform Probate Code § 2–301 says the section should apply even "if the person the decedent later married was a devisee in his or her premarital will," but "the value of any such devise * * * must be counted toward and not be in addition to the ultimate share" which the spouse receives.

The UPC also bars an omitted spouse from taking property which the testator's will leaves to children of a prior marriage, on

**4.** Uniform Probate Code § 2–301(a)(1). In Estate of Dennis, 714 S.W.2d 661 (Mo.App.1986), the court rejected a claim by an omitted spouse when the will was executed on the same day as the marriage. *But see* Matter of Estate of Wagley, 760 P.2d 316 (Utah 1988) (claim allowed where marriage took place 5 days after will executed).

**5.** Uniform Probate Code §§ 2–301(a)(3), 2–302(b)(2).

**6.** Matter of Estate of Bartell, 776 P.2d 885 (Utah 1989).

**7.** Miles v. Miles, 440 S.E.2d 882 (S.C.1994); In re Estate of Deoneseus, 906 P.2d 922 (Wash.1995).

**8.** Matter of Estate of Keeven, 716 P.2d 1224 (Idaho 1986); Porter v. Porter, 726 P.2d 459 (Wash.1986).

the theory that the failure to provide for the spouse in this situation is not likely to be an oversight.[9]

In several states a testator's marriage has no effect on a will. Arguably spouses need no other protection than the elective share. But the elective share is usually smaller than the intestate share which an omitted spouse receives.[10] However, most omitted spouse statutes only give a share of the decedent's *probate* estate, and do not apply to property held in a living trust, for example,[11] whereas non-probate transfers are often included computing the elective share.

Omitted spouse statutes have been the basis for malpractice actions against a lawyer who drafted a will which failed to include a provision as to the testator's impending marriage.[12] All testators should be advised to review the will if they should later marry. A competent drafter can provide for after-born children by a class gift, but an intelligent provision for an unknown, possible future spouse of the testator is hard to imagine.

## § 3.7  Elective Share

*History*  At common law the rights of surviving spouses depended on their sex. A widow received *dower,* a life estate in one-third of lands which her husband owned. A widower received *curtesy,* a life estate in *all* the lands which his wife owned, but only if issue were born of the marriage.[1] Today distinctions between the sexes have been eliminated. Some states still retain the name "dower," but the husband and wife usually receive equivalent shares by that name.[2]

Dower did not adequately protect spouses. It attached only to land, but today the chief or only form of wealth in many families is personal property. Because dower attached to all land which the husband owned at any time during marriage, it gave the wife a "veto * * * over all her husband's transactions involving his real

**9.**  Waggoner, *The Multiple Marriage Society,* 76 Iowa L.Rev. 223, 254 (1991).

**10.**  Uniform Probate Code §§ 2–102, 2–102A. In Hellums v. Reinhardt, 567 So.2d 274 (Ala.1990), an omitted spouse took the entire estate. Under Cal.Prob. Code § 21610, however, an omitted spouse gets no more than one half of the decedent's separate property even if on a true intestacy all would go to the spouse.

**11.**  Estate of Heggstad, 20 Cal. Rptr.2d 433 (App.1993) (revocable trust not covered by omitted spouse claim); Riccelli v. Forcinito, 595 A.2d 1322 (Pa.Super.1991) (joint tenancy). However, the California statute was subsequently amended to include revocable trusts. Cal.Prob.Code § 21601, 21610.

**12.**  Heyer v. Flaig, 449 P.2d 161 (Cal.1969).

**§ 3.7**

**1.**  2 W. Blackstone, *Commentaries* *126, 129 (1765).

**2.**  Mass.Gen.Laws c. 189 § 1 (1/3 of land held at death by deceased spouse for life).

property."[3] Since dower was only a life estate, widows could not sell the land without the consent of the persons who would succeed to it after her death. For these reasons modern statutes usually give a surviving spouse (husband or wife) a fee interest instead of a life estate,[4] but only in property which the decedent owned at death. Many statutes explicitly abolish dower and curtesy and replace it with an "elective share."[5]

*Size of Elective Share* The elective share is computed in various ways in different states. Sometimes it equals the spouse's intestate share, or is a fraction thereof, but in the Uniform Probate Code the two are computed differently. The size of a spouse's intestate share depends on whether the decedent was survived by issue. This is irrelevant in the UPC[6] elective share which is based primarily on the length of the marriage, rising from 3% for a marriage which lasted less than 2 years to 50% for marriages of 15 years or more.[7] In the elective share, unlike intestacy, the surviving spouse's own assets are taken into account. Thus even in a long marriage, if the surviving spouse is wealthier than the decedent, the elective share may amount to nothing.[8]

The UPC elective share is similar in many ways to the community property system which we will discuss in the next Section. It is the same for real and personal property. This is consistent with the trend to eliminate distinctions between the two, but they survive in a few states. Unlike the family allowance, the spouse's elective share is subject to claims against the decedent's estate.[9]

*Non-probate Assets* Unlike common-law dower, many modern elective share statutes only include assets owned by the decedent at death, the so-called "probate" estate. This has allowed spouses to evade the elective share by using will substitutes or inter-vivos gifts to deplete the estate before they die.[10] Lawyers drafting instru-

**3.** Sterling v. Wilson, 621 N.E.2d 767 (Ohio App.1993) (contract to sell land unenforceable because seller's wife refused to release dower)

**4.** *But see* R.I.Gen.Laws § 33–25–2 (surviving spouse gets life estate in land).

**5.** Uniform Probate Code § 2–112; Md. Estates and Trusts Code § 3–202; 755 ILCS § 5/2–9.

**6.** But many states give a larger elective share if the decedent has no issue. Ohio Rev.Code § 2106.01(c); 755 ILCS § 5/2–8(a).

**7.** Uniform Probate Code § 2–202(a). If the marriage last less than a year, the spouse can elect only the minimum amount.

**8.** In re Estate of Karnen, 607 N.W.2d 32 (S.D.2000) (H's elective share in 50 year marriage was 0 because he had substantial assets of his own).

**9.** Uniform Prob.Code § 2–204; 755 ILCS § 5/ 2–8(a) (after payment of all just claims). As to estate taxes compare In re Estate of Pericles, 641 N.E.2d 10, 13 (Ill.App.1994) (elective share computed after payment of taxes) with Uniform Probate Code § 3–916(e)(2) (marital deduction inures to spouse's benefit in apportioning tax liability).

**10.** Dalia v. Lawrence, 627 A.2d 392 (Conn.1993); Soltis v. First of America Bank, 513 N.W.2d 148 (Mich.App.1994).

ments for a married client should be aware of the possibility of the estate plan being upset by a spousal election and consider possible steps to avoid this; otherwise they are subject to suit for malpractice.[11]

Some courts subject property which the decedent transferred before death to the elective share on the theory that the transfer was "illusory." Revocable living trusts are frequently so characterized.[12] The Restatements of Property and Trusts both allow spouses to reach the assets of any revocable trust created by the decedent.[13]

A second approach to non-probate transfers focuses on "fraud." A Tennessee statute makes voidable "any conveyances made fraudulently * * * with an intent to defeat the surviving spouse of his * * * elective share."[14] "Fraud" suggests the idea of fraudulent conveyances which creditors can set aside if they render the transferor insolvent[15]. But the elective share is a percentage of the estate, so if a husband reduces his estate by transfers, his estate can still literally satisfy the elective share, so the analogy to a fraudulent conveyance is hard to apply. Some courts interpret the "fraud" test to allow "reasonable" transfers which do not "substantially" deplete the probate estate.[16]

The Uniform Probate Code gives spouses a share of the "augmented estate," which includes the probate estate and property transferred by the decedent within two years of death,[17] and property transferred at any time if the decedent reserved the right to revoke or the income for life,[18] and joint tenancies, to the extent of the "decedent's fractional interest" therein.[19] The fractional inter-

---

**11.** Johnson v. Sandler, Weinstein, P.C., 958 S.W.2d 42 (Mo.App.1997).

**12.** Johnson v. Farmers & Merchants Bank, 379 S.E.2d 752 (W.Va. 1989); Seifert v. Southern Nat. Bank, 409 S.E.2d 337 (S.C.1991).

**13.** *Restatement, Second, of Property (Donative Transfers)* § 34.1(3) (1990); *Restatement, Third, of Trusts* § 25, Comment d (2001).

**14.** Tenn.Code § 31–105. *See also* Wis.Stat. § 861.17; 755 ILCS § 25/1.

**15.** See Section 13.1.

**16.** Warren v. Compton, 626 S.W.2d 12, 18 (Tenn.App.1981) ("the amount of the transfers in relation to the total estate is not so great as to infer fraudulent intent").

**17.** Uniform Probate Code § 2–205(3). *See also Restatement, Second, of Property (Donative Transfers)* § 34.1(2)

(1990) (transfers in contemplation of the imminent death of the donor).

**18.** Uniform Probate Code § 2–205(2). In Bongaards v. Millen, 793 N.E.2d 335, 348 (Mass.2003), the court accepted a similar judicially created rule, but refused to extend it to a trust created by decedent's mother even though decedent had a power to terminate it, rejecting *Restatement, Third, of Property (Wills and Other Donative Transfers)* § 9.1(c) (2001).

**19.** Uniform Probate Code § 2–205(1)(ii). *Restatement, Third, of Property (Wills and Other Donative Transfers)* § 9.1(c) (2001) purports to restate similar rules as part of the common law, but courts do not generally allow a surviving spouse to reach property held in joint tenancy by the decedent and another. In re Estate of Mocny, 630 N.E.2d 87 (Ill. App.1993); Smith v. McCall, 477 S.E.2d 475 (S.C.App.1996).

est is presumptively based on the number of joint tenants[20], but if the surviving party contributed all the funds in a joint account, the decedent would have no fractional interest for purposes of computing the augmented estate.[21]

The UPC list is modeled on the Internal Revenue Code which includes such life-time transfers in a decedent's "gross" estate for tax purposes. Before 1990 the Probate Code exempted life insurance and pensions from the augmented estate,[22] but now insurance on the decedent's life is expressly included if the decedent owned the policy.[23] Most pensions are subject to federal law (ERISA) which requires that they be taken in the form of an annuity which benefits the employee's surviving spouse.[24]

The Uniform Probate Code formerly included in the augmented estate only property which was transferred "during marriage,"[25] but the present version also includes assets subject to the decedent's control at the time of death, regardless of when they were transferred.[26]

The Uniform Probate Code augmented estate excludes property transferred "to the extent that the decedent received adequate and full consideration in money or money's worth."[27] Thus, unlike common-law dower and community property (in some states), the elective share is not an obstacle to sales by a spouse.

*Other Benefits conferred on Spouse*  If a husband's will leaves Blackacre to his wife, what effect will this have on her elective share? The law might allow her to take *both* her elective share *and* Blackacre unless the will provided otherwise. This is rule for the family allowance, homestead, and Social Security benefits. [28]

Some states require the wife to elect between the will and her statutory share, hence the term *elective* share.[29] The Uniform

**20.** In re Estate of Hart, 801 A.2d 599 (Pa.Super. 2002) (W can reach H's half interest in land given by his parents to H and his son as joint tenants)

**21.** Uniform Probate Code § 2–205, Comment, Examples 4, 6–7; In re Estate of Antonopoulos, 993 P.2d 637 (Kan. 1999) (remand to consider contributions of surviving joint tenant, a child of the decedent by a prior marriage).

**22.** Uniform Probate Code § 2–202(1) (pre–1990). Insurance is excluded from the New York and Pennsylvania statutes N.Y. EPTL § 5–1.1(b)(2); 20 Pa. Stat. § 2203(b)(2).

**23.** Uniform Probate Code § 2–205(1)(iv).

**24.** 29 U.S.C. § 1055(a); Matter of Estate of Harrison, 967 P.2d 1091 (Kan. App.1998).

**25.** Uniform Probate Code § 2–202(1) (pre–1990). *See also* Estate of Kotz, 406 A.2d 524 (Pa.1979) (spouse can't attack a joint tenancy created 8 years prior to marriage).

**26.** Uniform Probate Code § 2–205(1); In re Estate of Antonopoulos, 993 P.2d 637 (Kan.1999) (property put in joint tenancy prior to marriage included in augmented estate).

**27.** Uniform Probate Code § 2–208(a).

**28.** Uniform Probate Code §§ 2–206, 2–402, 2–404(b).

**29.** Matter of Estate of Spurgeon, 572 N.W.2d 595 (Iowa 1998) (wife's elec-

Probate Code, however, simply reduces the statutory share by the value of any devise to the spouse.[30] Many wills create a trust which gives the spouse the income for life with a remainder to others. Valuation of the spouse's interest in this case is problematic, since no one knows how long the spouse will live. Since 1993, the Code has allowed spouses to avoid this problem by disclaiming any devises; they are not charged with devises which they disclaim.[31]

If the husband instead of *devising* Blackacre to his wife had put it into joint tenancy with her, some states would ignore such nonprobate transfers to the spouse[32], but the Uniform Probate Code includes all property owned by the surviving spouse in the calculating the elective share.[33] The second Restatement of Property only considers assets that the spouse acquired from the decedent; if the spouse can show that an asset was his or her own acquisition, it is not considered.[34]

*Making the Election* Spouses have a limited time in which to choose whether to take the elective share.[35] A spouse who fails to act in time usually only gets the benefits provided in the decedent's will,[36] but courts have given relief to spouses who made an unwise election in ignorance of relevant facts, such as the size of the decedent's estate.[37] A lawyer can help a surviving spouse choose intelligently whether or not to claim the elective share, but if the lawyer drafted the decedent's will, an ethical problem is raised by Rule 1.9 of the Model Rules of Professional Conduct: "a lawyer who has formerly represented a client in a matter shall not thereafter (a) represent another person in the same or a substantially related matter in which the other person's interests are materially adverse to the interests of the former client." It may be advisable for the surviving spouse to have independent counsel, since the attorney for the estate may feel an obligation to preserve the testator's estate plan. If the spouse does not have independent counsel, the attorney for the estate should observe Model Rule 4.3: "in dealing on behalf of a client with a person who is not represented by

tion bars her from taking devise under will); 755 ILCS § 5/2–8(a) ("if a will is renounced" spouse gets a share).

**30.** Uniform Probate Code § 2–209(a).

**31.** Uniform Probate Code § 2–209, Comment. Not all UPC states have adopted this change. In re Estate of Karnen, 607 N.W.2d 32, 37 (S.D.2000).

**32.** Gallagher v. Evert, 577 S.E.2d 217, 221 (S.C.App.2002).

**33.** Uniform Probate Code §§ 2–207, 2–209(2).

**34.** In re Estate of Ziegenbein, 519 N.W.2d 5 (Neb.App.1994) (joint account excluded from calculation because widower was the sole contributor).

**35.** Uniform Probate Code § 2–211. Compare the time allowed for disclaimers. Section 2.8.

**36.** In re Estate of Delaney, 819 A.2d 968, 984 (D.C.2003).

**37.** Matter of Estate of Epstein, 561 N.W.2d 82, 85 (Iowa App.1996).

counsel, a lawyer shall not state or imply that the lawyer is disinterested.''

What factors should the spouse (and the lawyer) consider? A simple comparison between the size of the elective share and the benefits given to the spouse by the will is not always determinative. If the decedent's will creates a bypass trust which gives a widow the income for her life, and the widow has enough property to generate an estate tax when she dies, she may not want an elective share because any additional money would be taxed in her estate. Failure to take an elective share, like a disclaimer, does not constitute a taxable transfer.[38] On the other hand, if the decedent husband's estate is large and his will does not qualify for the marital deduction,[39] the widow may wish to elect against the will in order to reduce the taxes on her husband's estate.

A widow's decision may also be affected by the form of the devise in her husband's will. If it creates a trust for her, is she happy with the designated trustee, or would she prefer to manage the assets herself? When the marriage was childless and/or the spouses have children by prior marriages, the surviving spouse may wish to elect against the will in order to reduce the assets passing to the decedent's devisees.

*Election by Conservator* If the surviving spouse is legally incompetent, a conservator (guardian) must decide on the spouse's behalf. Agents under a durable power of attorney previously executed by the spouse have also been allowed to make the election for the spouse.[40] A conservator's decision to claim an elective share requires court approval, which may be withheld if the conservatee does not need the additional money for support.[41] But in some states conservators must elect against a will whenever this is in the conservatee's "best interests."[42] The Uniform Probate Code allows conservators to claim the share, but the funds go into a trust for the spouse's support, and when the spouse dies, they pass under the decedent's will.[43] This removes any incentive to claim an elective share in order to benefit the spouse's relatives or children by a prior marriage.

In most states if a spouse dies before making the election, the right to elect disappears and cannot be exercised by the spouse's

---

**38.** As to disclaimers see Section 2.8. As we shall see in the next section, the rule is otherwise with respect to the surviving spouse's share of community property.

**39.** As to the marital deduction see Section 15.3.

**40.** In re Estate of Reifsneider, 610 A.2d 958 (Pa.1992); Uniform Probate

Code § 2–212(a). As to durable powers see Section 7.2.

**41.** In re Estate of Wentworth, 452 N.W.2d 714 (Minn.App.1990); Uniform Probate Code § 2–203 (pre–1990) (for the present UPC solution see *infra*).

**42.** McElroy v. Taylor, 977 S.W.2d 929, 932 (Ky.1998).

**43.** Uniform Probate Code § 2–212.

personal representative.[44] The right of election cannot be asserted by a creditor of the spouse,[45] but it may render the spouse ineligible for state welfare benefits based on need.[46]

*Choice of Law*   Different laws may apply to a single estate when land is governed by the law of its situs and personal property by the law of the decedent's domicile,[47] but the Uniform Probate Code provides that the latter governs all a decedent's property.[48] However, if ancillary proceedings in another state are necessary, that state may not agree that the law of the decedent's domicile controls.[49]

## § 3.8  Community Property

*Significance of Community Property*   In eight states, Arizona, California, Idaho, Louisiana, Nevada, New Mexico, Texas, and Washington, the community property system provides a counterpart to the elective share. Community property *may* provide a more generous portion than the elective share but this depends on how a couple's property is classified, since a spouse in a community property state usually has no rights in the other spouse's separate property if the other spouse devises or gives it to a third person.[1]

The classification of a spouse's property as either community or separate is relevant for several purposes. The rules of intestate succession distinguish between community and separate property. In most community property states, the surviving spouse gets both halves of their community property if the decedent left no will; the spouse's intestate share of the decedent's separate property is normally smaller.[2]

Community property states restrict inter-vivos transfers as well as devises of community property. Even if a testator leaves all his or her property to the other spouse, it may make a difference whether this property was separate or community. Since one-half of the community property already belongs to each spouse, there is no taxable transfer of this half. If either spouse earns income during

**44.** Kirkeby v. Covenant House, 970 P.2d 241, 248 (Or.App.1998).

**45.** Matter of Savage's Estate, 650 S.W.2d 346 (Mo.App.1983).

**46.** Tannler v. DHSS, 564 N.W.2d 735 (Wis.1997) (medical assistance); Estate of Wyinegar, 711 A.2d 492 (Pa.Super.1998) (guardian of incompetent spouse must elect since otherwise he would be ineligible for benefits).

**47.** In re Estate of Pericles, 641 N.E.2d 10, 13 (Ill.App.1994) (out of state land excluded in computing elective share under law of domicile).

**48.** Uniform Probate Code § 2–202(a)(d).

**49.** De Werthein v. Gotlib, 594 N.Y.S.2d 230 (App.Div.1993) (applying New York law to defeat claims of widow of Argentinian).

**§ 3.8**

**1.** Cal.Fam.Code § 752. However, a surviving spouse receives a substantial share of the decedent's separate property if the decedent died intestate.

**2.** Calif.Prob.Code § 6401; Uniform Prob.Code § 2–102A.

the marriage, one-half of it is attributed to the other for income tax purposes. Some litigation involving community property concerns taxes.[3] However, the marital deduction very often produces the same tax result for separate property.

The classification of a couple's property as community or separate can affect its allocation in a divorce.[4] Since divorce is more common today than disinheritance of a spouse by will, most classification cases arise in this context. The classification of property may also affect the rights of creditors of either spouse.[5]

*History and Rationale* Community property today exists in many countries of Europe,[6] but it never took hold in England for reasons which are not clear.[7] The American states which were once under Spanish rule chose to adopt community property even though they rejected everything else in the civil law tradition (except for Louisiana), because they considered the common law rules, which then held that a wife's property belonged to her husband, unfair.[8]

American courts originally treated the wife's interest in community property as only an expectancy until her husband died, but this changed when the tax advantages of the Spanish system were recognized. "If the community was equally owned by the spouses, then only one-half the community would be includible in the decedent spouse's estate. * * * To the extent that state law regarded the spouses as equal owners, the spouses could divide the community [income] for tax purposes, each separately reporting one half. This allowed the use of a considerably lower tax rate."[9]

From this history one might infer that community property is a "tax gimmick" which is no longer useful since the marital deduction confers similar advantages in separate property states. However, community property continues to flourish. In fact, there is a trend in all states toward the community property approach in

**3.** Keller v. Department of Revenue, 642 P.2d 284 (Or.1982) (half of H's income attributed to W for tax purposes, since it was community property); Estate of Cavenaugh v. Commissioner, 51 F.3d 597 (5th Cir.1995) (error to include all insurance proceeds in H's taxable estate, since W had a CP interest).

**4.** Hatcher v. Hatcher, 933 P.2d 1222 (Ariz.App.1996) (division of property in divorce reversed due to erroneous classification of property as separate). However, the division of community property at divorce varies in different states. *Compare* Calif.Fam.Code § 2550 (CP divided equally) *with* Ariz.Rev.Stat. § 25–318 (CP divided "equitably")

**5.** Nichols Hills Bank v. McCool, 701 P.2d 1114 (Wash.1985) (contract creditor of H cannot reach his share of community property).

**6.** Rheinstein, *Division of Marital Property*, 12 Wil.L.J. 413, 419–20 (1976).

**7.** Donahue, *What Causes Fundamental Legal Ideas*, 78 Mich.L.Rev. 59 (1979).

**8.** Prager, *The Persistence of Separate Property Concepts in California's Community Property System, 1849–1975*, 24 UCLA L.Rev. 1, 6, 10 (1976).

**9.** *Id.*, at 60.

dividing marital assets at divorce.[10] Many states give special treatment to "marital property," which is much like community property.[11] Community property thinking inspired the provisions of the Uniform Probate Code governing the elective share.

The community property system recognizes the contributions to marital wealth of a spouse who does not earn wages, such as a housewife. When a couple has little community property, the spouse has few rights, but arguably this is as it should be. Property which "was not acquired because of the performance of marital duties * * * should not be available for the survivor to share."[12] However, some have criticized the community property system for failing to give a needy surviving spouse any rights in the decedent's separate property.[13] The community property system has also been criticized because it raises difficult factual questions as to the classification of property. The Uniform Probate Code, while adopting the basic rationale of community property, uses an approximation system which only considers the length of the marriage without having "to identify which of the couple's property was earned during the marriage and which was acquired prior to the marriage or acquired during the marriage by gift or inheritance."

*Classification of Property* In some European countries all the assets of both spouses are community property, but the Spanish system, which is the basis of the rules in American community property states, limits community property to acquisitions due to the gainful activity of either spouse during marriage. What a spouse owned prior to marriage, or acquired during marriage by inheritance or donation remains separate property.[14] This principle is common to all American community property systems, but answers to many specific questions vary in different states.

Assume a wife owns land as separate property and leases it to a tenant while she is married. Spanish law would treat the rent she receives as community property and so would some American states,[15] but in others income from separate property is separate.[16] If the land rises in value during marriage, the appreciation will be separate property in all states, unless it was due to the expenditure

**10.** Reppy, *Community Property in the U.S. Supreme Court,* 10 Comm.Prop. L.J. 93, 119 (1983).

**11.** Uniform Marital Property Act, Prefatory Note; In re Marriage of Smith, 405 N.E.2d 884 (Ill.App.1980) (citing cases from community property states in defining "marital property.")

**12.** Greene, *Comparison of the Property Aspects of the Community and Common Law Marital Property Systems,* 13 Creighton L.Rev. 71, 110 (1979).

**13.** Niles, *Probate Reform in California,* 31 Hast.L.J. 185, 193 (1979).

**14.** Calif.Fam.Code §§ 760, 770; Idaho Code § 32–903, 32–906.

**15.** Alsenz v. Alsenz, 101 S.W.3d 648, 654 (Tex.App.2003) (royalties from H's patent granted prior to marriage).

**16.** Bayer v. Bayer, 800 P.2d 216, 222 (N.M.App.1990) (contrasting Arizona and New Mexico rules).

of community funds or labor on improvements. When a wife owned land prior to marriage, and $20,000 in community funds were used to build a home on the land which enhanced its value by $54,000, the community was awarded an interest measured by this enhancement in value.[17] But other courts hold that simple reimbursement of expenditures is the appropriate measure.[18] In the converse case when separate funds are used to improve community property, California law reimburses the spouse whose funds were used "without interest or adjustment for change in monetary values."[19]

If a spouse's separate property is subject to a mortgage at the time of the marriage and community funds are used to reduce the mortgage, some states simply reimburse the community for the amount paid,[20] but others give the community an interest in the property proportional to its contribution to the total price paid.[21]

Sometimes a spouse owns a business at the beginning of a marriage and works for it during the marriage. If the spouse was not adequately compensated by the business for the services, and they increased the value of the business, the community acquires a share of the business according to some courts.[22] Others only reimburse the community for the value of the services.[23]

Classification issues also arise when a spouse owned life insurance prior to marriage and premiums were paid during the marriage. Many courts hold that the proceeds "will be separate property or community property in proportion to the percentage of total premiums which have been paid with separate or community funds,"[24] but in Texas the community is only reimbursed for the premiums paid with community funds.[25]

If a couple separate but do not divorce, how are their earnings during separation classified? In California they are separate property,[26] but in Texas the community continues until a divorce.[27]

**17.** Anderson v. Gilliland, 684 S.W.2d 673 (Tex.1985).

**18.** In In re Marriage of Wolfe, 110 Cal.Rptr.2d 921 (App.2001), where there was no "claim to the enhanced value of a separate asset attributable to a community-funded improvement nor . . . a claim that the improvement is without value," the wife was awarded one half of the amount of community funds expended in improving the husband's separate property.

**19.** Cal.Fam.Code § 2640. This provision applies only in dividing property at divorce.

**20.** Pringle v. Pringle, 712 P.2d 727 (Idaho App.1985).

**21.** Malmquist v. Malmquist, 792 P.2d 372 (Nev.1990).

**22.** Lindemann v. Lindemann, 960 P.2d 966 (Wash.App.1998) (increase in value of husband's separate business attributable to his labor during marriage divided upon separation); cf. Josephson v. Josephson, 772 P.2d 1236 (Idaho App. 1989) (community has no interest in business where husband was paid an adequate salary for his services).

**23.** Jensen v. Jensen, 665 S.W.2d 107 (Tex.1984).

**24.** Porter v. Porter, 726 P.2d 459 (Wash.1986).

**25.** Rev. Rul. 80–242, 1980–2 Cum. Bull 799.

**26.** Cal.Fam.Code § 771.

**27.** Seizer v. Sessions, 940 P.2d 261 (Wash.1997).

If a spouse recovers damages for personal injury, compensation for pain and suffering is regarded as separate property, but amounts given to replace lost earnings during the marriage are community property.[28]

Questions of fact in classifying property may be resolved by a presumption that everything acquired during a marriage is community property,[29] even though title is in the name of only one spouse.[30] But a spouse can establish that property is separate by tracing its source.[31]

Classification may be altered by agreement between the spouses, a couple may "transmute separate property of either spouse to community property" or vice versa.[32] Such an agreement may be inferred from conduct. If a husband, for example, uses his separate property to buy a house and takes title in the names of both spouses, many courts would infer that he intended the house to be community property.[33]

*Non-probate Transfers* Because each spouse has a present interest in community property, transfers by one spouse may be voidable by the other.[34] This gives more protection to spouses than the elective share. Many separate property states exclude insurance proceeds from the elective share, but if an insurance policy was purchased with community funds a spouse can get half the proceeds even if the insured designated someone else as beneficiary.[35]

Third persons who deal in good faith, e.g. an insurance company which pays a beneficiary designated by an insured spouse, may be free from claims by the other spouse.[36] Purchasers of community

**28.** In Brown v. Brown, 675 P.2d 1207 (Wash.1984), an action for personal injury was pending when a couple divorced. The court said that "allocation of the damages should proceed upon special interrogatories" to the jury.

**29.** Gagan v. Gouyd, 86 Cal.Rptr.2d 733, 738 (App.1999). In Estate of Hull v. Williams, 885 P.2d 1153 (Idaho App. 1994), the court applied this presumption even though the marriage had lasted only 8 years and the date of acquisition of the property was unclear.

**30.** Matter of Estate of Mundell, 857 P.2d 631 (Idaho 1993) (H owns half interest in IRA accounts listed in W's name).

**31.** Cooper v. Cooper, 635 P.2d 850 (Ariz.1981); Cal.Prob.Code § 5305 (bank accounts).

**32.** Cal.Fam.Code §§ 850, 852. *See also* Bosone v. Bosone, 768 P.2d 1022

(Wash.App.1989) (separate property converted to community by agreement).

**33.** In re Estate of Hansen, 892 P.2d 764 (Wash.App.1995); Schmanski v. Schmanski, 984 P.2d 752, 755 (Nev. 1999) (separate property put into a joint brokerage account).

**34.** Bosone v. Bosone, 768 P.2d 1022 (Wash.App.1989); Ackel v. Ackel, 595 So.2d 739 (La.App.1992) (gift of stock voidable by non-consenting spouse).

**35.** Emard v. Hughes Aircraft Co., 153 F.3d 949, 955 (9th Cir.1998); Aetna Life Ins. Co. v. Boober, 784 P.2d 186 (Wash.App.1990).

**36.** Cal.Fam.Code § 755 (payment under an employee retirement plan discharges payer who has received no written notice of community property rights).

real property held in the name of one spouse are protected if they bought "in good faith without knowledge of the marital relation."[37]

A transfer may also be deemed a legitimate exercise of the transferor-spouse's managerial powers. Thus a court rejected a husband's challenge of his wife's selection of a payment option under her pension plan which increased payments during her lifetime but gave nothing to the husband when she died.[38] Some states even permit gifts of community property by one spouse if they are not "excessive."[39]

*Differences Between Community Property and Elective Share* All community property states give each spouse one-half of the community property, regardless of whether or not the decedent spouse had surviving children.

In separate property states the right to an elective is lost if the spouse dies before exercising it. Community property rights, on the other hand, do not turn on survival; the estate of a wife who predeceased her husband was entitled one half of her husband's retirement benefits because they were community property.[40]

If a will devises property to a spouse, in separate property jurisdictions the spouse must usually renounce the devise in order to get the elective share but in community property states, normally the spouse can keep half of the community property and get the devise too. If a will simply leaves "one half my estate to my wife," courts assume that the testator "intended only to dispose of his own interest (his separate property and one-half of the community property), and no election is necessary." However, the spouse *is* put to an election, "if the testator purported to dispose of both his and his spouse's share of the community property." [41]

If a testator owns community property, the will should make clear whether or not the spouse must elect. Some testators want to put both halves of the community into a trust, either because they do not think the spouse can manage property, or because they want to have a unified management of all the community property, or in order to save probate costs when the spouse dies. Although a testator cannot dispose of more than one half of the community property against the other spouse's wishes, the other spouse often

**37.** *Id.,* § 1102.

**38.** O'Hara v. State ex rel. Public Employees Retirement Board, 764 P.2d 489 (Nev.1988).

**39.** Street v. Skipper, 887 S.W.2d 78 (Tex.App.1994) (designation of estate as beneficiary of insurance upheld because not "unfair" to the spouse); La.Civ.Code art 2349 (allowing a "customary gift of a value commensurate with the economic position of the spouses").

**40.** In re Estate of MacDonald, 794 P.2d 911 (Cal.1990). However, this result is precluded by federal law as to plans governed by ERISA. Boggs v. Boggs, 520 U.S. 833 (1997).

**41.** Burch v. George, 866 P.2d 92 (Cal.1994).

does not object, particularly if he or she was used to letting the decedent manage their property and does not wish to undertake the burdens of management now.[42] Moreover, benefits to the surviving spouse from taking under the will may exceed the spouse's community property rights. Unless a widow is quite old, the income from all the community property for life (as a typical trust provides) may be worth more than her half of the community property.

*Choice of Law*   The traditional rule is that the law of the situs governs land, but there is a trend to have domicile control even land. California defines community property as "all property, real or personal, *wherever situated*, acquired by a married person during the marriage *while domiciled in this state*."[43] If a non-domiciliary buys land in California, the law of the owner's domicile governs the rights of the owner's surviving spouse.[44]

Couples often change domicile during marriage. In America domicile at the time property is acquired determines whether it is community or separate.[45] Thus if a spouse buys stock while living in a separate property state, it remains separate property if the couple later move to a community property state.[46] This rule may leave a spouse unprotected because the elective share of the separate property state is unavailable if the decedent was domiciled elsewhere and the community property system of the new domicile is of no use if all the decedent's assets are separate property. California and Idaho solve this dilemma by the concept of "quasi-community" property: property acquired in another state is treated "as if" the decedent acquirer had been domiciled in the community property state.[47] As with community property the surviving spouse is entitled to half of the quasi-community property despite the decedent's will, and inherits all of it if the decedent had no will.[48]

What about a move in the other direction, i.e. from a community property to a separate property state? Stock while domiciled in a community property state continues to be community property if the owners move to a separate property state.[49] Can a surviving

**42.** Kahn & Gallo, *The Widow's Election,* 24 Stan.L.Rev. 531, 536–38 (1972).

**43.** Cal.Fam.Code § 760. For a more general discussion of domicile v. status as determining choice of law see Section 1.2.

**44.** Calif.Prob.Code § 120. *See also* Uniform Prob. Code § 2–201.

**45.** Matter of Unanue, 710 A.2d 1036, 1039 (N.J.Super.A.D.1998) (even though couple married in Puerto Rico, property acquired while domiciled in N.J. was not community).

**46.** *Restatement, Second, of Conflict of Laws* §§ 258, 259 (1969); In re Mar-

riage of Moore and Ferrie, 18 Cal. Rptr.2d 543, 547 (App.1993).

**47.** Calif.Prob.Code § 66; Idaho Code § 15–2–201; *cf.* In re Succession of Hubbard, 803 So.2d 1074 (La.App. 2001)(stock acquired while domiciled in Florida is CP for purposes of intestate succession when owner died in Louisiana).

**48.** Cal.Prob.Code §§ 101, 6401(b).

**49.** In re Marriage of Moore and Ferrie, 18 Cal.Rptr.2d 543, 547 (App.1993).

spouse also claim an elective share in the decedent's half of the community? A Uniform Disposition of Community Property Rights at Death Act would bar such a claim.[50]

Community property interests may be preempted by federal law. The United States Supreme Court has dealt with the problem in several cases, but the underlying principles remain unclear. When a husband used community funds to purchase United States Savings Bonds payable on death to his brother, this did not deprive the widow of her rights under state law.[51] But the Court rejected a claim by an Army officer's widow to half the proceeds of a National Service Life Insurance Policy purchased with community funds; a federal statute which said the proceeds went to the named beneficiary was held to supersede state community property law.[52] ERISA has also been held to supersede community property claims in undistributed pension benefits.[53]

## § 3.9  Waivers

Agreements between spouses to limit the survivor's claim to an elective share are increasingly common as more persons enter into second marriages and wish to protect the inheritance of children of a prior marriage from the new spouse. Lawyers who draft wills for spouses which are later upset by claims to an elective share have been held liable for malpractice on the ground that the other spouse could have been persuaded to sign a valid waiver if asked to do so.[1]

*Time of Waiver*  Such agreements are sometimes made prior to marriage, sometimes after the couple are married. The rules in the two situations may differ. ERISA allows the "spouse" of a participant to waive rights to an annuity,[2] and one court has held that an antenuptial waiver of ERISA rights is ineffectual because a fiancée is not a spouse.[3]

Many states have adopted a Uniform Premarital Agreement Act. It does not cover postnuptial agreements,[4] but the standards in

---

**50.** Uniform Disposition of Community Property Rights at Death Act § 3.

**51.** Yiatchos v. Yiatchos, 376 U.S. 306 (1964).

**52.** Wissner v. Wissner, 338 U.S. 655 (1950). The California Supreme Court was able to perceive a distinction between this and a very similar insurance program for civilian employees of the federal government in Carlson v. Carlson, 521 P.2d 1114 (Cal.1974).

**53.** Boggs v. Boggs, 520 U.S. 833 (1997).

**§ 3.9**

**1.** Estate of Gaspar v. Vogt, Brown & Merry, 670 N.W.2d 918 (S.D.2003)

**2.** 29 U.S.C. § 1055(c)(2).

**3.** Hurwitz v. Sher, 789 F.Supp. 134 (S.D.N.Y.1992). For suggestions how to get around this problem see Belcher & Pomeroy, *A Practitioner's Guide to Negotiating, Drafting, and Enforcing Premarital Agreements*, 37 Real Prop., Prob. & T.J. 1, 21–23 (2002).

**4.** Uniform Premarital Agreement Act § 1.

the Act are incorporated in the Uniform Probate Code, which applies to agreements made "before or after marriage."[5] California, on the other hand, has adopted both the Uniform Premarital Agreement Act[6] and somewhat different provisions governing postnuptial agreements.[7]

The California Family Code expresses an idea which can also be found in many judicial opinions: spouses occupy "confidential relations with each other * * * and neither shall take unfair advantage of the other."[8] The situation of parties who are not yet married, is arguably different.[9] Agreements made after a couple has separated and are anticipating divorce are also less likely to be affected by undue confidence in the other spouse.[10]

A surviving spouse may also waive rights in the estate after the other spouse has died. Although not covered by any statute, such waivers can be voided for abuses of confidence, e.g., when the executor, the testator's child by a prior marriage, "failed to disclose the facts which would enable [the widow] to make a free and understanding consent."[11]

*Formal Requirements*   Oral or unsigned waivers are in most states unenforceable under the Statute of Frauds,[12] or under a special provision like Uniform Probate Code § 2–213.[13] ERISA requires that a spouse's waiver of rights in a pension be "witnessed by a plan representative or a notary public."[14] Comparable agreements must be executed before a notary in Europe,[15] where the notaries are members of the legal profession and play a more important role than in the United States.

Uniform Probate Code § 2–208 excludes from the elective share property which the decedent transferred "with the written joinder of" the surviving spouse. This section says nothing about a signature but presumably such a consent can be avoided for fraud

---

**5.** Uniform Probate Code § 2–213. *See also Restatement, Third, of Property (Wills and Other Donative Transfers)* § 9.4 (2001); Day v. Vitus, 792 P.2d 1240 (Or.App.1990), applying the Act by analogy to a postnuptial agreement.

**6.** Cal.Fam.Code §§ 1600 *et seq.*

**7.** Cal.Prob.Code §§ 140–47; In re Estate of Gagnier, 26 Cal.Rptr.2d 128 (App.1993) (different rules apply to pre- and postnuptial agreements).

**8.** Cal.Fam.Code § 721(b).

**9.** In re Marriage of Bonds, 5 P.3d 815, 831 (Cal.2000).

**10.** Estate of Gibson, 269 Cal.Rptr. 48 (App.1990).

**11.** Matter of Estate of Hessenflow, 909 P.2d 662, 672 (Kan.App.1995).

**12.** *Restatement, Second, of Contracts* § 124, illus. 3 (1979).

**13.** *See also* Unif. Premarital Agreement Act § 2 (agreement must be signed by both parties); Estate of Calcutt v. Calcutt, 576 N.E.2d 1288 (Ind.App.1991) (oral waiver unenforceable).

**14.** 29 U.S.C. § 1055(c)(2)(A).

**15.** BGB (German Civil Code) § 1410 (marriage contract affecting property rights must be executed before a notary), § 2348 (same for disclaimer of the right to a forced share). In France premarital agreements must be notarized. Code Civil art. 1394.

or undue influence, since "the principles of law and equity supplement its provisions."[16]

*Disclosure*  A common theme in both statutes and case law is the need for disclosure. The Uniform Premarital Agreement Act and UPC say that an agreement which is "unconscionable" is valid only if the party challenging it was "provided a fair and reasonable disclosure of the property or financial obligations of the other party" or waived such disclosure or otherwise had or could have had adequate knowledge thereof.[17] Many judicial opinions also suggest that disclosure is necessary only if the agreement is unfair.[18]

Sometimes a party attacks an agreement which recites such disclosure, denying that it actually occurred. The drafter can deal with this problem by attaching a schedule of assets to the agreement itself; this should be effective even if the spouse signing the waiver failed to read it,[19] and even if the value of the listed assets is not given.[20] However, the parties should discuss a premarital agreement well in advance of the wedding, since "wedding eve ultimatums" are often held voidable.[21]

In community property states, a spouse's knowledge about the other spouse's separate property seems irrelevant, since spouses have no rights in it anyway. In all states, one may question whether a spouse's knowledge of the other spouse's wealth should matter unless the spouse understands his or her rights in it. Some courts stress the business experience (or lack thereof) of the party who challenges it.[22] Arguably the waiving party must have received legal advice. Some courts question waivers prepared by a lawyer for one spouse when the other has no lawyer.[23] A lawyer who advised his stepmother to waive her right to take against her husband's will was held to have violated the Rules of Professional Conduct, because his interest as a beneficiary of his father's will "jeopardized his ability to provide objective legal advice."[24] The California Su-

**16.**  Uniform Probate Code § 1–103.

**17.**  Unif. Premarital Agreement Act § 6. Uniform Probate Code § 2–213 is similar. *But see* Estate of Brown, 955 S.W.2d 940 (Mo.App.1997).

**18.**  In re Estate of Geyer, 533 A.2d 423, 427 (Pa.1987). *See also* Sasarak v. Sasarak, 586 N.E.2d 172 (Ohio App. 1990) (even though amount received was "disproportionate" to widow's rights, valid because of full disclosure).

**19.**  Wiley v. Iverson, 985 P.2d 1176 (Mo.1999); *Restatement, Third, of Property (Wills and Other Donative Transfers)* § 9.4, comm. h (2001).

**20.**  Matter of Marriage of Yager, 963 P.2d 137 (Or.App.1998).

**21.**  Belcher & Pomeroy, supra note 3 , at 11.

**22.**  *Compare* Wiley v. Iverson, 985 P.2d 1176, 1181 (Mont.1999) (wife was "a relatively experienced businesswoman, well educated") *with* In re Estate of Grassman, 158 N.W.2d 673, 675 (Neb. 1968) (husband "inexperienced in business and legal affairs").

**23.**  Rowland v. Rowland, 599 N.E.2d 315 (Ohio App.1991).

**24.**  Matter of Taylor, 693 N.E.2d 526, 528 (Ind.1998).

preme Court, however, recently rejected a claim that "a premarital agreement in which one party is not represented by independent counsel should be subjected to strict scrutiny" where the lawyer for the prospective husband had suggested to fiancee that she get her own counsel but she declined to do so. The lawyer then explained to her that she was giving up her community property rights under the agreement. The court held that the rule "prohibiting counsel for one party from giving legal advice to an opposing party who is unrepresented" did not preclude enforcing the contract.[25]

Most spouses in deciding whether or not to waive their rights would want to know who will benefit thereby; a wife may be willing to allow her husband to leave property to his children, but not to his mistress. In California a spouse's consent to a nonprobate transfer of community property is revoked if the other spouse later changes the beneficiary.[26]

*Fairness* According to the Uniform Premarital Agreement Act, an agreement requires no "consideration" but may be unenforceable if it was "unconscionable," absent adequate disclosure.[27] Courts often say that the marriage itself provides consideration for the waiver in premarital agreements.[28] Even in postnuptial agreements, courts usually have no difficulty in finding consideration, but they sometimes refuse to enforce agreements which they consider "unfair." This may mean an agreement which gives the spouse substantially less than his or her share of property under the law.[29] But many agreements which do just this are sustained, particularly when they protect the decedent's children,[30] especially when the legal rights of a spouse seem unduly great, *e.g.* a large share of an estate after a short marriage. One court found unenforceable a wife's waiver of all rights "by virtue of the expenditure of community funds or community labor" on her husband's separate property,[31] but another upheld one which allowed a husband to put his wife's half of the community into a trust which made

---

**25.** In re Marriage of Bonds, 5 P.3d 815, 827, 833 (Cal.2000).

**26.** Cal.Prob.Code § 5023. *See also* 26 U.S.C. § 417(a)(2) (pension plan)

**27.** Uniform Premarital Agreement Act §§ 2, 6.

**28.** Beatty v. Beatty, 555 N.E.2d 184 (Ind.App.1990).

**29.** Estate of Mader, 89 Cal.Rptr. 787, 792 (App.1970) (presumption of undue influence when agreement gives wife "less than what she would receive by way of her community property

rights"). But in Davis v. Miller, 7 P.3d 1223 (Kan.2000), the court upheld a settlement which gave the wife over $1 million, without discussing what she might have received without the agreement.

**30.** Matter of Baggerley's Estate, 635 P.2d 1333 (Okl.App.1981) ("the antenuptial pact was aimed at achieving a natural and entirely appropriate end— the protection of the inheritance rights of his daughter").

**31.** Matter of Marriage of Foran, 834 P.2d 1081, 1086 (Wash.App.1992).

"ample provision" for her even though she had no independent counsel.[32]

Although the Uniform Probate Code says that an "unconscionable" waiver, absent disclosure, is "not enforceable," the California counterpart allows courts to modify an agreement; courts are not limited to either enforcing or invalidating it altogether.[33]

*Construction*   An enforceable agreement may raise problems of construction. An agreement that "all property owned by each party at the time of the marriage would remain the separate property of each" did not bar the husband from a statutory surviving spouse's allowance.[34] The Uniform Probate Code, however, presumes that "a waiver of 'all rights,' or equivalent language, in the property or estate of a present or prospective spouse" covers the family allowance, an elective or intestate share or any devise under a will executed before the waiver.[35] It does not, however, preclude a spouse from receiving gifts made by the other spouse after the waiver.[36]

## § 3.10   Negative Limitations

We have heretofore discussed rights of a disinherited spouse or child to take part of an estate. A few rules invalidate particular types of devises and may operate in favor of all heirs.

*Mortmain*   Several American states until recently had "mortmain" statutes invalidating wills made to charity shortly before the testator died. The purpose was to prevent wills made under undue influence. A traditional way to circumvent the statutes was to use will substitutes, since they generally covered only wills. Revocable trusts and even death-bed gifts were immune.[1] The statutes operated arbitrarily, and most have now been repealed or held unconstitutional. When a daughter invoked a mortmain statute to attack her mother's will leaving property to a hospital, the court held that the statute violated the state constitution, because it "does not protect against overreaching by unscrupulous lawyers, doctors, nurses, housekeepers, companions or others with a greater opportunity to influence a testator* * * Nor is it rational to apply the statute in

---

**32.**  Whitney v. Seattle–First Nat. Bank, 579 P.2d 937 (Wash.1978).

**33.**  Calif.Prob.Code § 144(b); *cf.* Uniform Commercial Code § 2–302.

**34.**  Estate of Calcutt v. Calcutt, 576 N.E.2d 1288 (Ind.App.1991). *See also* Matter of Estate of Zimmerman, 579 N.W.2d 591 (N.D.1998) (elective share).

**35.**  Uniform Probate Code § 2–213(d).

**36.**  Bowen v. Bowen, 575 S.E.2d 553 (S.C. 2003).

### § 3.10

**1.**  In re Estate of Katz, 528 So.2d 422 (Fla.App.1988); Matter of Estate of Kirk, 907 P.2d 794 (Idaho 1995). *Contra, Restatement, Third, of Trusts* § 25, comment d (2001).

cases where the testator dies suddenly due to an accident during the six-month period after making a charitable bequest ."[2]

*Negative Wills* A "testator cannot disinherit his heirs by words alone, but in order to do so, the property must be given to somebody else."[3] The Uniform Probate Code, however, specifically authorizes "so-called negative wills."[4] Under the Code, the disinherited heirs' shares pass as if they had disclaimed, i.e., they are deemed to have predeceased the testator.[5] Even without a statute like the UPC, some courts give effect to disinheritance clauses by construing them as implied gifts to another person, e.g., a will saying "I leave nothing to my husband" was held to be an implied devise to the testator's children.[6]

*Conditions Relating to Marriage or Divorce* Some testators try to control the lives of the devisees, e.g. a devise the testator's fiancée "so long as she remains unmarried."[7] The Restatement of Property invalidates restrictions which are "designed to prevent the acquisition or retention of" property "in the event of any first marriage of the transferee" because "we are reluctant to brook any interference with the marriage choice of the parties to the marriage." But such conditions are valid if "the dominant motive of the transferor is to provide support until marriage" rather than to induce the transferee to remain unmarried. Any evidence as to motive is admissible, and a recital in the instrument itself is not conclusive.[8] The Restatement of Trusts says such provisions may be "judicially reformed to accomplish the permissible objectives * * * while removing or minimizing socially undesirable effects," for example, by replacing a condition with a provision allowing a trustee to exercise discretion to provide for needs.[9]

Devises conditioned on the testator's spouse remaining unmarried are allowed.[10] But the Restatement says that the only legitimate justification for such a condition is to preserve property for the testator's children, and so the rule "may come to be applied" only if the testator is survived by issue.[11]

---

**2.** Shriners Hospitals v. Zrillic, 563 So.2d 64, 69–70 (Fla.1990). *See also* Shriners' Hospital for Crippled Children v. Hester, 492 N.E.2d 153 (Ohio 1986).

**3.** Estate of Baxter, 827 P.2d 184, 187 (Okl.App.1992). *See also* Cook v. Estate of Seeman, 858 S.W.2d 114 (Ark. 1993).

**4.** Uniform Probate Code § 2–101, Comment.

**5.** *Id.,* § 2–801(d).

**6.** In re Thomas, (1984) 1 W.L.R. 237 (1983).

**7.** Matter of Estate of Romero, 847 P.2d 319 (N.M.App.1993).

**8.** *Restatement, Second, of Property (Donative Transfers)* § 6.1 (1981).

**9.** *Restatement, Third, of Trusts* § 29, comm. j (2001).

**10.** *Id.,* illus. 1; *Restatement, Second, of Property (Donative Transfers)* § 6.3 (1981); Matter of 1942 Gerald H. Lewis Trust, 652 P.2d 1106 (Colo.App.1982).

**11.** *Restatement, Second, of Property (Donative Transfers)* 6.3, comment c, e (1981). In Estate of Guidotti, 109 Cal. Rptr.2d 674 (App.2001) a provision whereby the testator's wife lost her benefits under a trust if she remarried was

The Restatement also allows partial restraints, *i.e.* those which restrict "some, but not all, first marriages" of the devisee so long as they do not "unreasonably limit" freedom to marry. Under this theory a court allowed a devise to the testator's son "only if he is married * * * to a Jewish girl."[12] Restrictions which impose difficult problems of interpretation on the courts may be rejected, such as a requirement that a daughter marry "her social equal."[13]

Conditions designed to induce divorce or separation are also invalid, unless the "dominant motive * * * is to provide support in the event of separation or divorce."[14] Today's more liberal rules for divorce do not "indicate an abandonment of the policy of preventing outsiders from inducing the break-up of a marriage by offers of wealth."[15] But recent cases suggest that courts are willing to allow just that if it seems appropriate; a court sustained a trust under which the settlor's daughter got nothing until she reached 65 or her husband died or they were divorced. The court noted that the daughter's husband "had tricked [the settlor] into investing $10,000 in a worthless venture" and his "financial affairs were under Federal investigation."[16]

Conditions which do not depend upon the beneficiary's conduct after the testator's death are permitted. A devise to a daughter to take effect only if "at the time of my death, she is married to and living with her husband" was upheld, since "public policy regarding restraints on marriage should only be concerned with continuing inducements" whereas in this case the "rights become absolutely fixed at [the testator's] death."[17]

The Restatement of Property allows conditions designed to affect other types of conduct, such as religious practices, choice of education or career, unless they are too indefinite.[18] The Third Restatement of Trusts, however, suggests that the "risk of excessive influence on a serious and fundamentally personal decision"

---

held to be invalid. Otherwise it would have disqualified the trust for the marital deduction.

**12.** Shapira v. Union Nat. Bank, 315 N.E.2d 825 (Ohio Com.Pl.1974). *But see Restatement, Second, of Property ( Donative Transfers)* § 6.2, illus. 3 (restraint invalid when child unlikely to marry someone of the designated religion) (1981); *Restatement Third, of Trusts* § 29, illus. 3 (2001).

**13.** *Restatement, Second, of Property (Donative Transfers)* § 6.2, illus. 4 (1981).

**14.** *Id.,* § 7.1; In re Gerbing's Estate, 337 N.E.2d 29 (Ill.1975) (to son if he divorces his wife).

**15.** *Restatement, Second, Property (Donative Transfers)* § 7.1, Comment b (1981).

**16.** Matter of Estate of Donner, 623 A.2d 307 (N.J.Super.A.D.1993). See also *Restatement, Third, of Trusts* § 29, comment j (2001).

**17.** In re Estate of Heller, 159 N.W.2d 82, 85 (Wis.1968). *See also Restatement, Second, Property (Donative Transfers)* § 6.1, comment c (1981); *Restatement, Third, of Trusts* § 29, comment i(2) (2001).

**18.** *Restatement, Second, Property (Donative Transfers)* §§ 8.1–8.3 (1981).

may justify a policy restraint. The Uniform Trust Code requires that all trust terms "must be for the benefit of the beneficiaries."[19] Recent cases on this issue are too infrequent to derive firm conclusions. It is also hard to derive from the cases a clear rule as to what happens in the event that a condition is invalid; does the devisee get the property whether or not she complies with the condition or does the gift fail altogether?[20]

*Destruction of Property* Virgil's will directed his executors to destroy his poem, the Aeneid. They refused to do so, and it has become a classic of world literature.[21] "A settlor may destroy his own Rembrandt. But he cannot establish a trust and order his trustees to destroy it."[22] Such restraints on ownership rights are not needed for the living who have a natural desire to preserve what they own, but the law must impose checks on a *decedent's* "extravagance and eccentricity."[23]

Provisions in a will restricting a devisee's use of land may be enforced only if they "are confined within reasonable bounds;" otherwise, courts "may refashion the restrictions so that they are reasonable."[24]

---

**19.** Unif.Trust Code § 404.

**20.** The various possibilities are discussed in Sherman, *Posthumous Meddling,* 1999 U.Ill.L.Rev. 1273, 1322–26.

**21.** Zabel, *The Wills of Literary Figures,* 128 Trusts and Estates, Sept. 1989, p. 59. Franz Kafka's novel, *Der Process* (The Trial) was also published posthumously against the express wishes of the author.

**22.** E. Halbach ed., *Death, Taxes, and Family Property* 126 (1977).

**23.** Eyerman v. Mercantile Trust Co., N.A., 524 S.W.2d 210, 215, 217 (Mo. App.1975).

**24.** Crowell v. Shelton, 948 P.2d 313 (Okl.1997) (restriction that land "never be used for residential or commercial purposes"). As to restraints on alienation see Section 11.8.

# Chapter 4

# FORMALITIES

## § 4.1　History and Policy

Over the course of history wills have been subjected to an increasing number of formal requirements but in recent years a contrary trend has emerged. The Statute of Frauds of 1677 required that devises of land be signed by the testator and subscribed by witnesses. Wills of personal property had to be in writing, but unsigned and unwitnessed wills were allowed.[1] The Wills Act of 1837 imposed the same requirements for both types of property, and added a few new ones, the signature must be at the "end" of the will, and the witnesses must be present at the same time.[2] The Statute of Frauds and the 1837 Wills Act have been the models for many American statutes, but an important American development is the authorization of unwitnessed holographic wills.[3]

*Function of Formalities*　The most obvious function of formal requirements is evidentiary. If wills did not have to be in writing, witnesses might either misremember or deliberately lie about alleged statements of intention by the testator. The weakness of oral testimony is "especially serious" in the case of wills, as distin-

---

**§ 4.1**

**1.**　2 W. Blackstone, *Commentaries* *501–2 (1766).

**2.**　Wills Act, 1 Vict. c. 26, § 9 (1837).

**3.**　See Section 4.4.

guished from contracts, because the testator is "unavailable to testify, or to clarify or contradict other evidence" concerning intention.[4]

Even if the testator actually said (or wrote) particular words, they may not have been intended to effectuate a disposition. "Even if the witnesses are entirely truthful and accurate, what is a court to conclude from testimony showing only that a father once stated that he wanted to give certain bonds to his son John? * * * Dispositive effect should not be given to statements which were not intended to have that effect. The formalities of transfer therefore generally require the performance of some ceremonial."[5] A ceremonial makes the testator realize the seriousness of the enterprise, and allows courts to determine whether words were uttered or written with testamentary intent. That this function is more important than the evidentiary one is shown by the fact that courts accept proof of lost wills.

*Liberalizing Trend* Many today believe that the traditional requirements for wills are too strict, that they emanate from a time when most wills were made on the testator's deathbed and are no longer needed because wills today are usually made "in the prime of life and in the presence of attorneys."[6] Also, today when form-free will substitutes like joint tenancy are widely used to pass property at death, to impose more rigorous formalities for wills seems "incongruous and indefensible."[7] The advent of the computer and tape recorder has raised questions about the need for a writing, but the Uniform Electronic Transactions Act, which says that an electronic record satisfies any writing requirement, expressly excludes wills from its operation.[8]

Some requirements, like the one that witnesses be disinterested,[9] probably do more harm than good in that they "are employed more frequently against innocent parties who have accidentally transgressed the requirement than against deliberate wrong-doers."[10]

Many recent statutes have reduced the formal requirements for wills. The Uniform Probate Code dropped the requirements that

**4.** Gulliver & Tilson, *Classification of Gratuitous Transfers,* 51 Yale L.J. 1, 4 (1941).

**5.** *Id,* at 3–4.

**6.** Langbein, *Substantial Compliance with the Wills Act,* 88 Harv.L.Rev. 489, 497 (1975). *See* Stein & Fierstein, *The Demography of Probate Distribution,* 15 U.Balt.L.Rev. 54, 86 (1985) (average testator executes a will 5 to 7 years prior to death).

**7.** Langbein, *supra* note 6, at 504; *Restatement, Second, of Property ( Donative Transfers)* § 33.1, comm. g (1990). The formal requirements for various will substitutes are discussed in Sections 4.5–4.8.

**8.** Uniform Electronic Transactions Act §§ 3(b)(1), 7.

**9.** See Section 4.3.

**10.** Gulliver & Tilson, *supra* note 4, at 12.

the witnesses sign in the testator's presence, or that the testator sign the will at the end.[11] Some recent cases have overruled earlier decisions which had rejected wills due to formal defects.[12]

*Substantial Compliance* In 1975 Professor John Langbein proposed a rule of "substantial compliance" whereby a noncomplying document which sufficiently approximated the prescribed formalities to fulfill their underlying purposes should be admitted to probate.[13] The Uniform Probate Code now allows probate of any document if the proponent "establishes by clear and convincing evidence that the decedent intended" it to be a will.[14] The Restatement of Property prescribes a similar approach for courts "in the absence of a legislative corrective" such as that provided by the UPC.[15] It remains to be seen how far courts will accept this idea. One commentator has suggested that American courts have given the "substantial compliance" idea a "cool reception" despite nearly "uniform support" from academic commentators.[16]

A comment to the Uniform Probate Code suggests that some statutory requirements are more important than others in assessing substantial compliance. Under similar legislation in Australia and Israel, courts "lightly excuse breaches of the attestation requirements, [but] they have never excused noncompliance with the requirement that a will be in writing."[17] Courts are not likely to treat an unsigned will as being in substantial compliance with the requirements.[18]

Advocates of admitting defectively executed wills do not deny that cautionary procedures for wills are desirable, but they argue that the sanction of invalidating noncomplying wills is often inappropriate. Professor Lindgren contends that "supervising a will execution * * * without using witnesses could subject the lawyer or other professional to a fine" or damages, "but the will itself would not be invalidated by the drafter's ignorance or carelessness."[19]

---

**11.** Uniform Probate Code § 2–502.

**12.** Estate of Black, 641 P.2d 754 (Cal.1982); Waldrep v. Goodwin, 195 S.E.2d 432 (Ga.1973).

**13.** Langbein, *supra* note 6, at 489. For earlier expressions of this idea in some judicial opinions see Bonfield, *Reforming the Requirements for Due Execution of Wills: Some Guidance from the Past,* 70 Tul.L.Rev. 1893, 1900–01 (1996).

**14.** Uniform Probate Code § 2–502.

**15.** *Restatement, Second, of Property ( Donative Transfers)* § 33.1, comm. g (1990); *Restatement, Third, of Property (Wills and Other Donative Transfers)* § 3.3 (1998).

**16.** Bonfield, *supra* note 13, at 1906.

**17.** Uniform Probate Code § 2–503, comment. *See also Restatement, Third, of Property (Wills and Other Donative Transfers)* § 3.3, comm. b (1998).

**18.** BankAmerica Pension Plan v. McMath, 206 F.3d 821, 831 (9th Cir. 2000) (unsigned beneficiary designation "did not substantially comply with" requirements of pension plan); Allen v. Dalk, 826 So.2d 245 (Fla. 2002) (court refuses to give effect to an unsigned will via a constructive trust).

**19.** Lindgren, *The Fall of Formalism,* 55 Alb.L.Rev. 1009, 1026–7 (1992). *Compare* BGB (German Civil Code) § 2247 (will should state time and place

The second Restatement of Property recommends a check list to follow in executing a will that goes beyond the minimum formalities prescribed by any statute.[20] Such precautionary measures are particularly desirable for wills which may have to be probated in several states, some of which have stricter requirements than others. However, many states allow wills to be probated if they were executed in compliance with the law at the time and place of execution.[21]

## § 4.2  Signature

The requirement that wills be signed is found today in all states. The signature helps to identify the will with the testator and serves to show finality; the distinction between tentative scribblings and a consummated product is symbolized by the act of signing. The second function is more significant than the first, since all statutes allow someone else to sign for the testator.[1] When another person signs the testator's name, the signature itself does not show that the testator approved the will, but if the signer acted at the testator's request, the testator considered the will to be complete.

A partial signature, even initials or an "X" suffices,[2] since they can indicate the will was complete, whereas the testator's full name on pre-printed stationery does not.[3]

*Place of Signature*  Most of the controversy regarding the signature centers on its place in the will. The Statute of Frauds was silent on this point. Courts held that the testator's name at the beginning of a will ("I, John Smith ... ") was a valid signature.[4] This was a dubious rule if the signature is designed to indicate finality, so the 1837 Wills Act required wills to be signed at the end.[5] This gives rise to a host of problems if taken literally, *e.g.*, is a will signed at the end if any blank space appears between the writing and the testator's signature? In 1982 England eliminated the requirement altogether; now it suffices "that the testator intended by his signature to give effect to the will."[6]

of execution, but failure to do so does not necessarily cause invalidity).

**20.** *Restatement, Second, of Property (Donative Transfers)* § 33.1, comm. c (1990).

**21.** See Section 1.2.

**§ 4.2**

**1.** Uniform Probate Code § 2–502. *See also Restatement, Third, of Property (Wills and Other Donative Transfers)* § 3.1, comm. n (1998).

**2.** Orozco v. Orozco, 917 S.W.2d 70 (Tex.App.1996) (X); Trim v. Daniels, 862 S.W.2d 8 (Tex.App.1992) (initials); Uniform Probate Code § 2–502, Comment.

**3.** Matter of Reed's Estate, 625 P.2d 447, 452 (Kan.1981).

**4.** 2 W. Blackstone, *Commentaries** 376 (1765).

**5.** Wills Act, 1 Vict. c. 26, § 9 (1837).

**6.** Administration of Justice Act, 1982, § 17.

Some American statutes still require that wills be signed at the end but others do not specify where the signature must appear.[7] Differences in the governing statutes are not always determinative. Courts have upheld wills which were not literally signed "at the end" even when these words appeared in the controlling statute.[8] On the other hand, even under the Uniform Probate Code the testator's putting his or her name on a will is not necessarily a sufficient signature.[9]

Many wills contain several pages. American courts routinely uphold wills which are signed only on the last page, but careful lawyers have the testator sign (or at least initial) each page.[10] At the least, a connection between the signature and the preceding pages should be shown by numbering the pages, attaching them with staples, or run-over sentences.[11] Otherwise unsigned pages may be denied probate.[12]

Most wills contain an attestation clause at the end, designed for the witnesses' signature. If the testator signs below the attestation clause, the signature, though removed from the body of the will proper, is usually held sufficient.[13]

## § 4.3  Witnesses

*Number and Competency*   The Statute of Frauds required that wills be attested by "three or four credible" witnesses, but most American states today require only two.[1] If a will is signed by 2 witnesses, it can be probated even if only one (or none) of them is available to testify when the will is offered for probate.[2] Nevertheless, it is advisable to use as witnesses persons who are likely to survive the testator and be able to testify if the will is contested.

The Uniform Probate Code says that "any person generally competent to be a witness may act as a witness to a will."[3] A few

---

**7.** Uniform Probate Code § 2–502; Cal.Prob.Code § 6110.

**8.** In re Powell's Will, 395 N.Y.S.2d 334 (Surr.1977) (page following the signature "constructively inserted" above it).

**9.** Matter of Estate of Erickson, 806 P.2d 1186, 1189–90 (Utah 1991).

**10.** *Restatement, Second, of Property ( Donative Transfers)* § 33.1, comm. c (1990).

**11.** *Restatement, Third, of Property (Wills and Other Donative Transfers)* § 3.5, comm. b and c (1998).

**12.** In Matter of Estate of Rigsby, 843 P.2d 856 (Okl.App.1992), two pages were found folded together after the tes-

tator's death. Because they did not refer to each other, only the signed page was probated.

**13.** In re Estate of Milward, 73 P.3d 155, 159 (Kan.App.2003); Hickox v. Wilson, 496 S.E.2d 711 (Ga.1998). *But see* Orrell v. Cochran, 695 S.W.2d 552 (Tex. 1985) (signature on self-proving affidavit does not suffice).

**§ 4.3**

**1.** *E.g.,* Uniform Probate Code § 2–502; Cal.Prob.Code § 6110.

**2.** Uniform Probate Code § 3–406(a); In re Will of McCauley, 565 S.E.2d 88, 92 (N.C.2002).

**3.** Uniform Probate Code § 2–505(a).

states have minimum age requirements for witnesses.[4] At common law someone who had been convicted of an infamous crime could not be a witness, but the modern trend is to remove such disabilities.[5]

In Europe wills executed before notaries are difficult to challenge.[6] An American counterpart is the "international will," which requires two witnesses and an "authorized person," which, under the Uniform Probate Code means a lawyer who is "in good standing" as an active practitioner.[7] Witnesses to ordinary wills need no special qualifications.

Most litigation concerning witnesses involves witnesses who benefit from the will. Many American statutes render void devises to witnesses of wills,[8] even though the general common law bar against interested witnesses in litigation has disappeared. Some statutes apply to a devisee's spouse as well as the devisee,[9] but other relatives or friends of the devisee are not disqualified.[10] Persons designated in a will as executor or trustee can act as witnesses on the theory that they earn their fee, unlike devisees who receive an unearned benefit.[11]

If a witness is both a devisee and an heir of the testator and the devise exceeds what the witness would take by intestacy only the excess is void.[12] Many statutes also except supernumerary (extra) witnesses, i.e., if three persons witness a will which leaves property to one of them, and the statute requires only two witnesses, the devise to the witness is valid.[13]

Many commentators have criticized these statutes as an outmoded vestige of the old rules against interested witnesses. Testators can get disinterested persons to witness a will, but most

**4.** Tex.Prob.Code § 59(a) (witness must be over 14); Norton v. Hinson, 989 S.W.2d 535 (Ark.1999) (will witnessed by a 14 year old is invalid under a like statute).

**5.** McGarvey v. McGarvey, 405 A.2d 250 (Md.1979) (witness convicted of perjury is competent).

**6.** Bonfield, *Reforming the Requirements for Due Execution of Wills*, 70 Tul.L.Rev. 1893, 1918 (1996) ("by requiring written wills to be drafted by notaries, continental Europeans essentially eliminated the will contest").

**7.** Uniform Probate Code §§ 2–1003, 2–1009. Such wills can be probated in any country which has signed a convention which established this procedure.

**8.** *E.g.,* 755 ILCS § 5/4–6(a); Tex. Prob.Code § 61; Ohio Rev.Code § 2107.15.

**9.** Conn.Gen.Stat. § 45a–258; Matter of Estate of Webster, 574 N.E.2d 245 (Ill.App.1991). However, in Matter of Estate of Harrison, 738 P.2d 964 (Okl. App.1987), the court refused to invalidate a devise to a witness's spouse.

**10.** Succession of Harvey, 573 So.2d 1304, 1308 (La.App.1991) (granddaughter of devisee can serve as witness);. In re Estate of Farr, 49 P.3d 415, 425 (Kan. 2002) (friends of devisees were competent witnesses).

**11.** Wis.Stat. § 853.07(3)(a); *Restatement, Third, of Trusts* § 32, comm. a (2001).

**12.** Wis.Stat. § 853.07(2)(b); Tex. Prob.Code § 61.

**13.** N.Y. EPTL § 3–3.2(a)(1); Brickhouse v. Brickhouse, 407 S.E.2d 607 (N.C.App.1991).

laymen and not a few lawyers are unaware of the rule and so many "accidental" infringements occur. The deterrent effect of the rule is questionable; "in most cases of fraud or undue influence, the wrongdoer would be careful not to sign as a witness" but would find an apparently "disinterested" witness, who might be bribed without this appearing on the face of the will.[14] The Uniform Probate Code breaks with tradition by providing that "the signing of a will by an interested witness does not invalidate the will or any provision of it."[15] Of course, if the will is contested, testimony from a disinterested witness will carry more weight.

*Must Witnesses See Testator Sign?* Normally the testator signs the will in the presence of the witnesses, but the will may be valid even if the testator signed before the witnesses appeared, if he or she acknowledges the signature before them. The 1837 Wills Act required that the testator's signature "shall be made or acknowledged by the Testator in the Presence of Two or more Witnesses *present at the same Time*," and some American statutes also so provide.[16]

*Publication and Request* A testator might sign a paper in the presence of witnesses without realizing that it was a will. Some American statutes require that the testator "declare to each of the attesting witnesses that the instrument * * * is his will" and request them to sign.[17] In all states lawyers supervising a will execution should ask the testator questions to remove any doubts about testamentary intent. The law does not generally require wills to be read aloud or orally explained to the testator,[18] since many testators want the contents of the will to be kept secret until they die.[19]

*Signing in Testator's Presence* The Statute of Frauds required wills of land to be "subscribed [by the witnesses] in the presence of" the testator and most modern statutes impose a similar requirement for all wills.[20] The requirement is supposed "to prevent a fraud's being perpetrated * * * by substituting another

---

**14.** Gulliver & Tilson, *Classification of Gratuitous Transfers,* 51 Yale L.J. 1, 12–13 (1941); Uniform Prob.Code § 2–505, comment.

**15.** Uniform Probate Code § 2–505(b).

**16.** Wills Act, 1 Vict. c. 26, § 9 (1837). *See also* Calif.Prob.Code § 6110; Va.Code § 64.1–49.

**17.** N.Y. EPTL § 3–2.1(a)(3), (4).

**18.** *Restatement, Third, of Property (Wills and Other Donative Transfers)* § 3.1, comm. h (1998). *But see* La.Civ. Code art. 1579; In re Succession of Gra-

ham, 803 So.2d 195 (La.App. 2001) (will rejected because not read to illiterate testator).

**19.** In France wills by "public act" are dictated to the notaries by the testator, but the Code also allows "mystic" wills which the testator delivers under seal to the notary (if the testator is literate). Code Civil art. 972, 976.

**20.** 29 Car. 2, c. 3, § 5 (1676); Ohio Rev.Code § 2107.03; Md.Estates and Trusts Code § 4–102.

for the true will,"[21] but dishonest witnesses could falsely swear they signed a spurious will in the testator's presence, so many commentators have attacked the "presence" requirement.[22] If a witness takes the will into another room to sign, some courts uphold the will if the testator was aware that the witness was signing the will.[23] The Uniform Probate Code dispenses with the presence requirement altogether; it does not matter where the witnesses are when they sign the will.[24] Several courts have rejected wills which the witnesses signed only after the testator died,[25] but the UPC would allow this so long as the signing occurs "within a reasonable time."[26]

*Attestation Clauses and Affidavits* Even though the wills acts are based on distrust of oral testimony, a will which appears regular on its face may be denied probate if the witnesses testify that it was not duly executed.[27] The standard way to deal with this problem is to append an attestation clause reciting that all the formalities were duly performed. No state requires such a clause, but everyone recommends its use. The clause is not conclusive, but many wills have been sustained on the basis of one even though the witnesses' testimony contradicted it.[28]

If the witnesses sign an affidavit, in many states the will can be probated without producing the witnesses in court.[29] This streamlines probate proceedings.

## § 4.4 Holographic and Oral Wills

Holographic wills are wholly handwritten by the testator. Because they provide a more generous sample of the testator's handwriting than just a signature, there is less risk of an undetected

**21.** Glenn v. Mann, 214 S.E.2d 911 (Ga.1975).

**22.** O'Connell & Effland, *Intestate Succession and Wills*, 14 Ariz.L.Rev. 205, 240 (1972).

**23.** In re Politowicz' Estate, 304 A.2d 569 (N.J.Super.A.D.1973). This is sometimes referred to as "conscious presence," a term used in Uniform Probate Code § 2–502(a)(2) with respect to someone who signs in place of the testator.

**24.** Uniform Prob.Code § 2–502.

**25.** Matter of Estate of Royal, 826 P.2d 1236 (Colo.1992); Gonzalez v. Satrustegui, 870 P.2d 1188 (Ariz.App. 1993). In Disciplinary Counsel v. Bandy, 690 N.E.2d 1280 (Ohio 1998) a lawyer who induced a witness to sign a will after the testator died was suspended from practice.

**26.** Uniform Probate Code § 2–502(a)(3), Comment; *cf.* In Matter of Estate of McGrew, 906 S.W.2d 53 (Tex. App.1995) (will allowed even though 2 years elapsed between the testator's and the witnesses' signing).

**27.** Burns v. Adamson, 854 S.W.2d 723 (Ark.1993); Pool v. Estate of Shelby, 821 P.2d 361 (Okl.1991).

**28.** In re Estate of Rosen, 737 N.Y.S.2d 656 (App.Div.2002); *Restatement, Third, of Property (Wills and Other Donative Transfers)* § 3.1, comm. q (1999) (clause raises a "rebuttable presumption of the truth of the recitals").

**29.** Uniform Probate Code § 2–504 suggests a form of affidavit suitable for this purpose.

forgery. Therefore, no witnesses are needed for them in many states[1] but not all.[2] Litigation about holographic wills has centered on three points: (1) a requirement in many states that holographic wills be dated; (2) the requirement in many states that they be "entirely" in the testator's handwriting; and (3) testamentary intent.

*Date*　It may be necessary to ascertain the date of a will (1) to determine which of several inconsistent wills was the testator's last, and (2) to establish that the will was made while the testator was competent. In theory, the witnesses to an attested will can establish the date of its execution, but since holographic wills have no witnesses, many states require that they be dated.[3] Holographic wills have been rejected for lack of a date even though the date was irrelevant in the particular case or was otherwise known. The Uniform Probate Code does not require that holographic wills be dated.[4] California has also eliminated the requirement, but an undated will may be invalid if the date is important and cannot be established by other proof.[5]

*Printed Matter*　Often a testator writes a holographic will on a sheet of paper containing printed or typewritten words, such as preprinted stationery or a will form with filled-in blanks. Even if the governing statute requires that the will be "entirely" in the testator's handwriting, some cases have overlooked other writing on the page as "surplusage."[6] Other courts reject the will if the testator intended the nonholographic material to be part of it.[7]

It is hard to see what purpose is served by rejecting such wills. A substantial sample of the testator's handwriting provides a safeguard against forgery whether or not other words appear on the same page. The Uniform Probate Code only requires that the "signature and material portions" of the will be in the testator's handwriting.[8] This may permit a printed will form with handwritten insertions to be probated as a holograph.[9]

### § 4.4

1.　Pennsylvania is unique in allowing unwitnessed wills which are *not* in the testator's handwriting. 20 Pa.Stat. § 2502.

2.　A similar discrepancy exists in foreign countries. H. Flick & D. Piltz, *Der Internationale Erbfall* 268 (1999) (holographic will allowed in Quebec but not in England).

3.　*E.g.,* La.Civ.Code art. 1575.

4.　Uniform Probate Code § 2–502.

5.　Calif.Prob.Code § 6111(b). In Matter of Estate of Harrington, 850 P.2d 158 (Colo.App.1993), an undated

holograph was rejected where an attested will revoked all prior wills.

6.　Charleston Nat. Bank v. Thru the Bible, 507 S.E.2d 708, 712 (W.Va.1998).

7.　Matter of Estate of Dobson, 708 P.2d 422 (Wyo.1985); Matter of Estate of Krueger, 529 N.W.2d 151 (N.D.1995) (will invalid when the name of one devisee was not in testator's handwriting).

8.　Uniform Probate Code § 2–502(b).

9.　Matter of Estate of Muder, 765 P.2d 997 (Ariz.1988); *Restatement, Third, of Property (Wills and Other Donative Transfers)* § 3.2, illus. 4 (1998).

*Testamentary Intent*  The absence of attestation may create doubt whether a writing was intended to be a will. Writings which appears to be notes for a contemplated will rather than a will itself have been denied probate.[10] However, a court probated a letter written to the testator's attorney, saying that "even if decedent intended that the attorney draft a formal will for execution, she would also have intended that her property pass in accordance with her recorded wishes if she died before execution of a formal will."[11]

Some courts insist that the document offered for probate show testamentary intent without resort to extrinsic evidence,[12] but the Uniform Probate Code and many courts allow testamentary intent to be proved by extrinsic evidence.[13] The place where the paper is found may be relevant. A North Carolina statute requires that holographic wills be found among the testator's "valuable papers" or in the custody of someone with whom it was "deposited * * * for safekeeping."[14] The fact that the testator once executed an attested will arguably shows that an unattested paper was not written with testamentary intent,[15] but not always.[16]

A question as to testamentary intent also arises when a will is expressed in conditional terms. For example, a holographic will started with the words "If anything should happen to me on this trip to Rapid City." The testator survived the trip but died later. The court probated the will, in part because of extrinsic evidence. "The reference to her Rapid City trip was not a condition but * * * represented the motivation behind the drafting of the will. * * * [The testator's] comments to several disinterested individuals * * * demonstrate that [she] intended her writing to be an effective disposition of her property."[17]

*Are Holographic Wills Desirable?*  The difficulty of determining testamentary intent is an argument against allowing holographic wills. "If a document has been executed with the usual testamentary formalities, a court can be reasonably certain that * * * it was

**10.**  Matter of Will of Smith, 528 A.2d 918 (N.J.1987) (instructions to attorney for preparing will); Matter of Estate of Erickson, 806 P.2d 1186 (Utah 1991) (note cards intended as a draft).

**11.**  Will of Smith, 507 A.2d 748, 750 (N.J.Super.A.D.1986); In re Estate of Kuralt, 15 P.3d 931 (Mont.2000).

**12.**  Mallory v. Mallory, 862 S.W.2d 879 (Ky.1993); Wolfe v. Wolfe, 448 S.E.2d 408 (Va.1994).

**13.**  Uniform Probate Code § 2–502(c). *See also* Cal.Prob.Code § 6111.5; *Restatement, Third, of Property (Wills and Other Donative Transfers)* § 3.2, comm c (1998).

**14.**  N.C.Gen.Stat.    § 31–3.4(a)(3). The statute has been rather liberally interpreted. *E.g.,* Matter of Will of Church, 466 S.E.2d 297 (N.C.App.1996) (will found in pocketbook).

**15.**  *Cf.* Williams v. Springfield Marine Bank, 475 N.E.2d 1122 (Ill.App. 1985) (fact that decedent executed a will on the same day indicates another paper was written without testamentary intent).

**16.**  In re Laurin's Estate, 424 A.2d 1290 (Pa.1981).

**17.**  In re Estate of Martin, 635 N.W.2d 473, 477 (S.D. 2001).

seriously intended as a will," whereas a holograph leaves this question "open to doubt."[18]

Few lawyers would advise clients to write a holographic will, since the costs of attestation are slight and it reduces the risk of contest. Since holographic wills are primarily the work of lay persons, they are often ill-considered and ambiguous. However, to deny effect to holographic wills appears "to force the public to rely on lawyers," and hurts the image of the profession.[19]

*Oral Wills* The Statute of Frauds of 1676 permitted nuncupative (oral) wills when made "in the time of the last sickness of the deceased" when there might be no time to draft and execute a written will. The testator must "bid the persons present * * * bear witness that such was his will."[20] Blackstone says that the requisites for oral wills were "so numerous" that they had "fallen into disuse."[21] The Wills Act of 1837 abolished them but with a proviso that "any Soldier being in actual Military Service, or any Mariner or Seaman being at Sea, may dispose of his Personal Estate" as permitted under prior law.[22] Some American states have provisions for oral wills modeled on the Statute of Frauds,[23] while others have special rules for wills of soldiers and seamen.[24] Neither provision is often used. Courts require the evidence of an oral will to be of the "clearest and most convincing character."[25] The Uniform Probate Code does not allow oral wills, and its liberal choice-of-law rule only applies to "written" wills.[26]

## § 4.5  Formalities for Gifts

*History (1) First Stage: Delivery of Property Required* The history of the formal requirements for gifts is marked by four stages. Originally, an effective transfer required delivery of the property. A writing purporting to transfer property was ineffective if the transferor stayed in possession, even if the writing was delivered. A transferor who stayed in possession of property might later sell it to *B* who would be unaware of the prior transfer. The

**18.** Estate of Brown, 218 Cal.Rptr. 108, 110 (App.1985). Getting witnesses to subscribe a document does not preclude claims that there was no testamentary intent, however. Williams v. Springfield Marine Bank, 475 N.E.2d 1122 (Ill.App.1985).

**19.** Wellman, *Arkansas and the Uniform Probate Code,* 2 U.Ark.L.R.L.J. 1, 15 (1979).

**20.** Statute of Frauds, 29 Car. 2, c. 3, § 19 (1676).

**21.** W. Blackstone, *Commentaries* 501 (1765).

**22.** Wills Act, 1 Vict. c. 26, §§ 9, 11 (1837).

**23.** Ohio Rev.Code § 2107.60; Tex. Prob.Code § 65; Miss.Code § 91–5–15.

**24.** Va.Code § 64.1–53; N.Y. EPTL 3–2.2(b) (holographic and nuncupative will allowed if testator in armed services).

**25.** Dabney v. Thomas, 596 S.W.2d 561, 563 (Tex.Civ.App.1980).

**26.** Uniform Probate Code § 2–506.

delivery requirement protected *B* by making the prior transfer invalid.

*(2) Second Stage: Deed as a Substitute for Delivery*  By the 15th century goods could be transferred without delivery; the buyer in a sale of personal property got title even before the goods were delivered. This idea was later extended to land in Equity. When land was sold, the buyer acquired the use (*i.e.* became the equitable owner) by virtue of the deed of bargain and sale.[1] The expansion of literacy contributed to this change. "In the days when few people could write, * * * livery of seisin was necessary to transfer ownership of real estate. As writing became more common, deeds * * * were found to be more reliable in demonstrating the intentions of the parties."[2]

*(3) Third Stage: Writing Required for All Transfers of Land*  The Statute of Frauds of 1676 provided that livery of seisin of land conveyed only an estate at will absent a signed writing.[3] Thus a writing, which was originally ineffective to transfer land, became the *only* effective method of transfer. Nearly all American states today have legislation based on the Statute of Frauds. The writing must be signed by the donor or an authorized agent; in many states an agent must be authorized in writing to act. These statutes do not apply to personal property, for which an oral statement of donative intent plus delivery still suffices.[4] This leads to some technical distinctions, e.g., the owner of a condominium has an interest in land, whereas a cooperative apartment represented by shares of stock can be transferred orally.[5]

Despite the Statute of Frauds, courts give effect to oral gifts of land if the donee has taken possession and made valuable improvements.[6] Nor does the Statute of Frauds bar giving effect to a lost deed, if there is clear proof that it once existed.[7]

*(4) Modern Recording Statutes*  American states today all have recording statutes under which unrecorded deeds are ineffective against later bona fide purchasers from the transferor,[8] but are

**§ 4.5**

**1.** Y.B.Hil. 21 Hen. 7, f. 18, pl. 30 (1505).

**2.** Lewis v. Burke, 226 N.E.2d 332, 335 (Ind.1967).

**3.** Statute of Frauds, 29 Car. 2, c. 3, § 1 (1676).

**4.** However, many contracts for the *sale* of personal property are also subject to a writing requirement. *See* Uniform Commercial Code § 2–201; *Restatement, Second, of Contracts* §§ 110, 125 et seq. (1979).

**5.** *Restatement, Second, of Property (Donative Transfers)* § 31.4, comm. f.

**6.** Conradi v. Perkins, 941 P.2d 1083 (Or.App.1997); *Restatement, Second, of Contracts* § 129, illus. 4 (1979).

**7.** *Id.,* § 137; Cole v. Guy, 539 N.E.2d 436 (Ill.App.1989).

**8.** The statutes differ as to who exactly is protected against an unrecorded deed. Cal.Civ.Code § 1214 (unrecorded deed is "void as against any subsequent purchaser or mortgagee ... in good faith and for a valuable consideration, whose conveyance is first duly recorded,

still valid between the parties. Even third parties are usually not protected if they had notice of the unrecorded prior conveyance.[9] Most statutes require special formalities in addition to the transferor's signature in order to have a deed recorded; for example, in California deeds must be "duly acknowledged" before a notary public or other official before they can be recorded.[10]

*Personal Property: Tangibles*   A person can give away tangible personal property either by delivering the property itself,[11] or by executing and delivering a written instrument of gift.[12]

*Intangibles*   Most wealth today is in the form of intangible property, like bank accounts, shares of stock and bonds. Gifts of such property can be made in several ways. If they are represented by a paper like a stock certificate or a passbook, the donor may simply deliver it to the donee.[13] However, intangibles usually represent a claim against an institution and the rules of the institution may require that it receive notice of the transfer. When a woman delivered United States Savings Bonds to her granddaughters her intent to give the bonds failed because she did not have the bonds reissued in the donees' names as required by Treasury regulations.[14] But some courts hold that such rules only protect the institution from liability if it pays without notice of the transfer, and should not control who owns the claim.[15]

Second, a donor may give intangibles by having them re-registered in the donee's name, even if nothing is delivered, and the donee is not aware of the gift.[16]

Third, the donor may sign a writing indicating an intent to give stock (for example), and deliver the writing but retain the stock certificate.[17]

and as against any judgment affecting the title"); Siegel Mobile Home Group, Inc. v. Bowen, 757 P.2d 1250 (Idaho App.1988) (unrecorded deed effective against judgment creditor of donor).

**9.**   Calhoun v. Higgins, 797 P.2d 404 (Or.App.1990).

**10.**   Cal.Civ.Code §§ 1170, 1181.

**11.**   In re Estate of Kremer, 546 N.E.2d 1047 (Ill.App.1989) (cameras); *Restatement, Second, of Property ( Donative Transfers)* § 31.1 (1990).

**12.**   Gruen v. Gruen, 496 N.E.2d 869 (N.Y.1986) (letter describing painting which was retained by donor effective as gift); *Restatement, Second, of Contracts* § 332, comment b (1981); *Restatement, Second, of Property (Donative Transfers)* §§ 32.1–.2 (1990).

**13.**   Mashburn v. Wright, 420 S.E.2d 379 (Ga.App.1992) (certificate of depos-

it); Rogers v. Rogers, 319 A.2d 119 (Md. 1974) (stock); *Restatement, Second, of Property (Donative Transfers)* § 31.1, comm. a (1990).

**14.**   United States v. Chandler, 410 U.S. 257 (1973).

**15.**   *Restatement, Second, of Property (Donative Transfers)* § 31.1, comm. b (1990); Abney v. Western Res. Mut. Cas. Co., 602 N.E.2d 348 (Ohio App.1991) (gift of boat effective despite failure to get new title certificate).

**16.**   Uniform Transfers to Minors Act § 9(a)(1)(i). *See also* Barham v. Jones, 647 P.2d 397, 399 (N.M.1982) (trailer registered in donee's name).

**17.**   Estate of Davenport v. C.I.R., 184 F.3d 1176, 1186 (10th Cir.1999); *Restatement, Second, of Property (Donative Transfers)* § 32.2, illus. 4 (1990).

Signing and delivering a check to a donee is not effective as an assignment of the drawer's funds in the bank.[18] A payee who cashes the check before the drawer dies can keep the money, but if the drawer dies before the check is paid, the check is not enforceable against the drawer's estate.[19]

*Delivery* The idea of delivery often recurs in the law of gifts. A person can convey land while retaining possession of it, but the donor must deliver a *deed* to the donee; an undelivered deed is ineffective.[20] If a deed has been recorded, delivery is presumed, but the presumption can be rebutted.[21] Similarly a gift of personal property may fail for lack of delivery. Thus when the owner of a company endorsed stock certificates intending to give them to certain employees but died before they were delivered, the stock was held to belong to his estate.[22]

Delivery, like the formal requirements for wills, forces the donor to consider the effects of the gift. It also has evidentiary value in that a donee's possession supports the claim of gift. Nevertheless the delivery requirement has been questioned. The second Restatement of Property suggests that the law should recognize gifts of personal property "without a delivery by proof of the donor's manifested intention to make a gift."[23] Courts often uphold gifts on the basis of a "constructive" delivery.[24] Even this fiction is occasionally dispensed with: some cases say there is no reason to insist on delivery when donative intent is clear.[25] Sometimes "delivery" seems to describe a result reached on other grounds, *i.e.* a finding of "no delivery" simply reflects a belief that no gift was intended.

Courts tend to excuse delivery in situations where it was impossible or very difficult. A woman two days before she died told the donee that he was to have certain securities which were not in her possession; because she was "physically incapable of" deliver-

---

**18.** Uniform Commercial Code § 3–408; Hieber v. Uptown Nat. Bank, 557 N.E.2d 408 (Ill.App.1990).

**19.** In re Estate of Heyn, 47 P.3d 724 (Colo.App. 2002); Creekmore v. Creekmore, 485 S.E.2d 68 (N.C.App. 1997). *But see Restatement, Third, of Property (Wills and Other Donative Transfers)* § 6.2, comm. n (2001) (delivery of a "certified or cashier's check" can be a gift, and even an ordinary check given to a charity may represent an enforceable promise).

**20.** Julian v. Petersen, 966 P.2d 878 (Utah App.1998).

**21.** Johnson v. Ramsey, 817 S.W.2d 200 (Ark.1991). However, under Uni-

form Transfers to Minors Act § 9(a)(5), recording alone is sufficient.

**22.** Lauerman v. Destocki, 622 N.E.2d 1122 (Ohio App.1993).

**23.** *Restatement, Second, of Property (Donative Transfers)* § 31.1, comm. k (1990).

**24.** Whisnant v. Whisnant, 928 P.2d 999 (Or.App.1996) (instructions to broker); *Restatement, Second, of Property (Donative Transfers)* § 31.1, comm. b (1990).

**25.** Hengst v. Hengst, 420 A.2d 370 (Pa.1980); Estate of O'Brien v. Robinson, 749 P.2d 154 (Wash.1988).

ing the property, the court found "constructive delivery."[26] Even if delivery is possible, it may be inconvenient to leave the donee in possession. Sometimes a donor delivers a deed to the donee who returns it to the donee "to hold for her," *e.g.* because the donee has no safe-deposit box. This is deemed delivery.[27] If the donee is already in possession of the property, *e.g.* as a custodian or borrower, the law dispenses with delivery.[28] A similar exception is made when donor and donee live in the same household, *e.g.* a husband gives his wife a piano in their living room.[29]

Delivery can be made to someone other than the donee,[30] but not if the person to whom delivery was made is deemed to be the donor's agent and the donor dies before the donee gets possession, since the agent's authority to complete the transfer expires when the donor dies.[31]

*Testamentary Transfers* When gifts are challenged after the donor's death, the problems of proving intent resemble those which arise in wills. Some gifts are held to be "testamentary" and subject to the requirements for a will.[32] On the other hand, deeds have been held valid even though they had the practical effects of a will because the donor reserved a life estate, or a power to revoke.[33]

The manifestation of intention by a signed writing provides almost as much protection against fraud as an attested will. A comment to the Uniform Probate Code observes that "the benign experience with such familiar will substitutes as the revocable inter-vivos trust * * * demonstrated that the evils envisioned if the statute of wills were not rigidly enforced simply do not materialize. Because these provisions often are part of a business transaction and are evidenced by a writing, the danger of fraud is largely eliminated."[34]

*Clear and Convincing Evidence* The Uniform Probate Code allows probate of defectively executed wills only if there is "clear

**26.** McCarton v. Estate of Watson, 693 P.2d 192 (Wash.App.1984).

**27.** Fontaine v. Colt's Mfg. Co., Inc., 814 A.2d 433, 436 (Conn.App.2003) (constructive delivery when revolver "presented" but then taken back to make improvements).

**28.** Justinian, *Institutes* 2.1.44; *Restatement, Second, of Contracts* § 332, comment e (1981); *Restatement, Second, of Property ( Donative Transfers)* § 31.1, illus. 1 (1990); Little City Foundation v. Capsonic Group, 596 N.E.2d 146 (Ill. App.1992).

**29.** *Restatement, Third, of Property (Wills and Other Donative Transfers)* § 6.2, comm. e (2001).

**30.** Matter of Estate of Ashe, 753 P.2d 281 (Idaho App.1988). *See also Restatement, Second, of Property (Donative Transfers)* § 31.1 (1990).

**31.** Huskins v. Huskins, 517 S.E.2d 146 (N.C.App.1999) (mailing letter to third party, donor dies before letter received); *Restatement, Second, of Trusts* § 57, comm. b (1959).

**32.** Matter of Estate of Dittus, 497 N.W.2d 415 (N.D.1993).

**33.** Hamilton v. Caplan, 518 A.2d 1087 (Md.App.1987).

**34.** Uniform Probate Code § 6–101, Comment. Many non-UPC states have adopted a similar provision. *E.g.*, Cal. Prob.Code § 5000.

and convincing evidence" that they represent the decedent's intent.[35] Courts use similar language when examining claims that a decedent had made a gift prior to death,[36] but in some cases gifts have been proved by the donee's own testimony.[37] It is difficult to ascertain what "clear and convincing evidence" really means, since appellate courts usually defer to trial courts' findings. Conflicting evidence does not preclude a finding that a gift was made.[38]

*Distinction Between Gifts and Promises*   The need for "consideration" in conveyances by deed has disappeared in modern law, although consideration is customarily recited.[39] Promises, on the other hand, must be supported by consideration. A note promising to pay money, even if delivered, is unenforceable by the payee, unless (in some states) the note is under seal, or unless action in reliance makes it enforceable by promissory estoppel.[40]

The law normally refuses to enforce donative *promises* because delivery and a signed writing are not *enough* protection against rash promises since persons tend to be less cautious about future commitments.[41] A person cannot give property which she expects to inherit; transfers of an "expectancy" are effective only if supported by adequate consideration.[42] This guards against improvident transfers, like Esau who, according to the Bible, sold his inheritance for beans.[43] The line between "expectancies" and "property" has wavered over time. Contingent remainders were once regarded as expectancies, but in modern law they are considered property.[44] The distinction is arbitrary; the expectation of inheriting from a parent can be less uncertain than many contingent remainders, *e.g.,* "to Clara if Alice (who has seven healthy children) dies without issue."

## § 4.6   Trusts

A settlor can create a trust in one of two ways. First, she can declare herself trustee of property; in this case the same person is

**35.**  Uniform Probate Code § 2–503.

**36.**  Smith v. Shafer, 623 N.E.2d 1261, 1263 (Ohio App.1993).

**37.**  Estate of Lennon v. Lennon, 29 P.3d 1258, 1266 (Wash.App. 2001).

**38.**  Rogers v. Rogers, 319 A.2d 119, 121 (Md.1974).

**39.**  In re Conservatorship of Moran, 821 So.2d 903, 907 (Miss.2002) ("love and affection" sufficient consideration to support a deed).

**40.**  *Restatement, Second, of Contracts* §§ 90, 95 (1981). Courts tend to expand the notion of consideration or ignore it when promises to charity are

involved. *Id.,* § 90(2); King v. Trustees of Boston University, 647 N.E.2d 1196 (Mass.1995).

**41.**  Eisenberg, *Donative Promises,* 47 U.Chi.L.Rev. 1, 5 (1979).

**42.**  Johnson By and Through Lackey v. Schick, 882 P.2d 1059 (Okl.1994) (expected inheritance assigned to satisfy assignor's debts); *Restatement, Third, of Property (Wills and Other Donative Transfers)* § 2.6, comm. j (1998).

**43.**  *Id.* comment b; Genesis 25:29–34.

**44.**  *Compare* Calif.Civ.Code § 1044 *with* 2 W. Blackstone, *Commentaries* *290 (1765).

both settlor and trustee. Second, the settlor can transfer the property to a another person (or corporation) as trustee. If the settlor does this by a will, the trust is a "testamentary" trust. If the settlor transfers the property to the trustee during life, or declares herself trustee, the trust is an *inter-vivos* or "living" trust. Generally speaking every trust has one or more beneficiaries[1] as well as a settlor(s) and trustee(s).

*Consideration and Delivery* A declaration of trust, like an outright gift, requires no consideration.[2] Delivery is not required for a declaration of trust.[3] Nor does the law require "formal change in ownership records or documents of title," such as recording a deed or re-registration of stock certificates, assuming no rights of third parties are affected.[4] Why is delivery unnecessary for declarations of trust? Courts of equity did not use juries, and the delivery requirement was associated with jury trial. A feeling that juries are less sophisticated fact finders than judges is reflected in other rules, such as the parol evidence rule, which does not apply to equitable proceedings. Gulliver and Tilson suggest a second reason for the absence of a delivery requirement for trusts: "laymen would not normally think of using a declaration of trust" so the words "I declare myself trustee of this property" perform a channeling function similar to delivery.[5] But the Restatement of Trusts says that a "property arrangement may constitute a trust * * * even though such terms as 'trust' or 'trustee' are not used."[6]

*Transfer to Trustee* A settlor who wishes to use another person as trustee must effectively transfer the property to the trustee. If "title does not pass to the intended trustee for want of delivery of the property or the deed, no trust is created." For this purpose the rules governing transfer of legal title control.[7] The delivery requirement has been watered down in this context just as in non-trust cases. A "symbolic delivery" may suffice.[8] Delivery of a

---

**§ 4.6**

**1.** For the exceptional case of trusts for a purpose without a beneficiary see Section 9.7.

**2.** *Restatement, Third, of Trusts* § 15 (2001).

**3.** Estate of Heggstad, 20 Cal. Rptr.2d 433 (App.1993); Taliaferro v. Taliaferro, 921 P.2d 803 (Kan.1996).

**4.** *Restatement, Third, of Trusts* § 10, comm. e (2001). Unif.Trust Code § 401, comment, agrees but *recommends* that assets comprising the trust be re-registered in the settlor's name as trustee.

**5.** Gulliver & Tilson, *Classification of Gratuitous Transfers,* 51 Yale L.J. 1, 16–17 (1941).

**6.** *Restatement, Third, of Trusts* § 5, comm. a (2001). *See also* Marshall v. Grauberger, 796 P.2d 34 (Colo.App. 1990). However, an unsuccessful attempt to make an outright gift as distinguished from a trust "will not be given effect by treating it as a declaration of trust." *Restatement, Third, of Trusts* § 16(2) (2001).

**7.** *Id.,* § 14, comm. d.

**8.** Edinburg v. Edinburg, 492 N.E.2d 1164, 1169 (Mass.App.Ct.1986). *Restatement, Third, of Trusts* § 16, comm. b (2001) (delivery may be "constructive or symbolic").

deed of land to a trustee is effective even though the settlor retains possession of the land itself.

In a testamentary trust, the trust property is transferred to the trustee by the will; no delivery is necessary but the formal requirements for wills apply. Failure to designate a trustee in a testamentary trust, or a refusal to serve by the designated trustee do not cause the trust to fail; normally a (new) trustee will be appointed to do the job.[9]

*Words of Futurity; Expectancies* A declaration that the settlor "will" create a trust is not sufficient without consideration or some recognized substitute.[10] A man cannot create a trust of property which he does not yet own, any more than he can make an outright gift of an expectancy. A trust of an expectancy, or a promise to create a future trust, is binding only if supported by consideration.[11]

Sometimes the only asset put into a trust is an insurance policy on the settlor's life. The policy may have little present value so long as the settlor is alive, but courts routinely uphold such "insurance trusts," and many state statutes confirm their validity.[12]

*Is the Revocable Trust Testamentary?* Many living trusts are the functional equivalent of wills; the settlor retains the right to control and enjoy the property for life, and the beneficiary's interest becomes meaningful only when the settlor dies. Some older cases and the first Restatement of Trusts held such trusts were testamentary and invalid unless executed with the formalities prescribed for wills,[13] but any claim that a trust is invalid as "testamentary" is unlikely to succeed today.[14] Why should a transfer which has so many characteristics of a will not be treated like one? Because normally in a living trust "a formal instrument will be prepared and delivered even though it is not doctrinally essential to do so. As a result, the main objectives of the statute of wills seem to be satisfied,"[15] particularly in a trust drafted by an attorney and signed by the settlor and an independent trustee. More questionable is a declaration of trust like a "Dacey" trust, so called after the author of *How to Avoid Probate,* a phenomenally successful book of the 60's, which contains tear-out trust forms. But Dacey trusts

**9.** *Id.* § 31.

**10.** *Id,* § 15, comm. b (2001).

**11.** Bemis v. Estate of Bemis, 967 P.2d 437 (Nev.1998) (promise to create a trust for children in divorce settlement). As to outright gifts of expectancies see Section 4.5.

**12.** Barrientos v. Nava, 94 S.W.3d 270, 281 (Tex.App.2002); N.Y. EPTL § 13–3.3(a).

**13.** *Restatement of Trusts* § 57(2) (1935). *See also* Osborn v. Osborn, 226 N.E.2d 814, 822–25 (Ohio Com.Pl.1966).

**14.** Zuckerman v. Alter, 615 So.2d 661 (Fla.1993); Matter of Estate of Groesbeck, 935 P.2d 1255 (Utah 1997).

**15.** Gulliver & Tilson, note 7 *supra,* at 24. *See also* Roberts v. Roberts, 646 N.E.2d 1061, 1065 (Mass.1995). No "delivery," however, is customary for a declaration of trust.

have been upheld, perhaps because they are hard to distinguish from printed forms which can be probated as holographic wills in many states.[16]

Many persons open bank accounts as "trustee" for another. These are often called "Totten" trusts after a leading case decided a century ago.[17] Use of the word "trustee" indicates that the depositor meant to create a trust but there is often little other evidence of intent. The trustee's duties and the beneficiary's rights are not specified. Nevertheless, courts hold that such accounts pass to the designated beneficiary when the trustee dies.[18] Bank account trusts are "widely used," and so the expectations of many settlors would be defeated if courts were to hold them invalid. But because they are so much like wills, they are treated like wills for many purposes other than formal requirements, such as the rights of the settlor's spouse and creditors[19].

*Need for a Writing* A living trust does not have to be executed like a will, but Section 7 of the Statute of Frauds of 1676 required that "all declarations or creations of trust * * * of any lands * * * shall be manifested and proved by some writing signed by the party who is by law enabled to declare such trust." Section 8 excepted trusts which "arise or result by the implication or construction of law." Most American states have similar provisions. The writing requirement arises in two contexts. First, a person may declare herself trustee of land for another. Such oral declarations are not enforceable[20] unless the beneficiary improves the land, or otherwise changes his position in reliance on the trust.[21] Second, the settlor may convey land to another by a deed which does not indicate that the grantee was intended to hold the land in trust for another. Such a deed, although in writing and signed, does not satisfy the Statute since it does not refer to the trust.[22] But the transferee, if allowed to keep land intended for another, would be unjustly enriched, so courts frequently impose a constructive trust in order to avoid this.[23]

In order to satisfy Section 7 of the Statute of Frauds, a writing must indicate the terms of the trust. A deed which simply conveys

**16.** Wilkerson v. McClary, 647 S.W.2d 79 (Tex.App.1983).

**17.** In re Totten, 71 N.E. 748 (N.Y. 1904).

**18.** Sanchez v. Sanchez De Davila, 547 So.2d 943 (Fla.App.1989); *Restatement, Third, of Trusts* § 26 (2001). This arrangement has also been recognized for forms of property other than bank accounts. In re Estate of Zukerman, 578 N.E.2d 248 (Ill.App.1991) (bond); Tom-linson v. Tomlinson, 960 S.W.2d 337 (Tex.App.1997) (pension benefits).

**19.** See Sections 3.8, 13.1.

**20.** French v. French, 606 P.2d 830 (Ariz.App.1980).

**21.** *Restatement, Third, of Trusts* § 24, comm. c (2001).

**22.** Id., § 22(1).

**23.** See Section 6.4.

land "to $T$ as trustee" is not enough.[24] The writing may be signed by either the settlor or by the trustee, depending upon the circumstances. If $S$'s deed to $T$ sets forth the terms of the trust, $T$ is bound even though she did not sign it, but $S$ cannot impose a trust by signing a writing after title to the land has passed to $T$.[25] $T$, on the other hand, can satisfy the Statute by signing a writing either prior or subsequent to the transfer.[26] The writing need not have *created* the trust; a later written acknowledgement of the trust is sufficient.

The Statute of Frauds applies only to trusts of land.[27] In most states oral trusts of personal property are valid,[28] but they are rarely encountered. Even in informal bank-account trusts the settlor usually signs a card indicating that the account is held in trust. The Uniform Trust Code says that "the creation of an oral trust * * * may only be established by clear and convincing evidence."[29]

*Precatory Language*  Wills which contain language suggesting that a devisee should use property for someone else raise the question whether the testator intended to create a trust or whether the words were precatory, *i.e.*, intended to impose only a moral obligation, or to explain the motive for the devise, e.g., "to enable him to bring up his children." Vagueness as to the beneficiaries and their interests "tends to suggest that the transferor did not intend to create a trust."[30] "Wish," "hope," and "desire" are usually construed as precatory,[31] but not always[32] Courts sometimes compare different parts of the will in construing ambiguous language, e.g., the word "request" was held not to create a trust when other provisions in the same will showed that the testator "was aware of how to leave assets in trust."[33] The financial situation of the parties may also be relevant. A devise of the testator's estate to his wife with a "request that she use whatever of it she thinks necessary for the support and care of my brother," imposes a duty upon her "as

---

**24.**  Gammarino v. Hamilton Cty. Bd. of Revision, 702 N.E.2d 415, 418 (Ohio 1998); *Restatement, Third, of Trusts* § 22 (2001). However, a *devise* to "X, as trustee" may be the basis for imposing a *constructive* trust if there is extrinsic evidence of the trust terms. See Section 6.1.

**25.**  *Restatement, Third, of Trusts* § 23(1) (2001).

**26.**  Id., § 23(2)(b); Schaneman v. Wright, 470 N.W.2d 566 (Neb.1991).

**27.**  However, in some states it also covers the assignment of an interest in any trust. *Id.*, § 53, comm. a. As to what is "land" for this purpose see *id.*, § 22, comm. b.

**28.**  Snuggs v. Snuggs, 571 S.E.2d 800 (Ga. 2002).

**29.**  Unif.Trust Code § 407; *cf.* Calif.Prob.Code § 15207.

**30.**  *Restatement, Third, Trusts* § 13, comm. d (2001).

**31.**  Dwyer v. Allyn, 596 N.E.2d 903 (Ind.App.1992); *Restatement, Third, of Trusts* § 13, illus. 5–7 (2001).

**32.**  Gillespie v. Davis, 410 S.E.2d 613 (Va.1991).

**33.**  Estate of Lowry, 418 N.E.2d 10, 12 (Ill.App.1981).

trustee to make reasonable provision for *B*'s support and care" if he is needy and the wife is independently wealthy. [34]

*Condition* Some instruments are construed to impose a condition rather than a trust. Many years after land was conveyed to a town "in trust for" a library, the town closed the library. Had this been a trust, the land might have been applied to a related purpose under the *cy pres* doctrine.[35] But the court held that the land should return to the grantors' heirs (the grantors having died in the interim), because the town held "subject to a condition subsequent" rather than in trust.[36]

On the other hand, the word "condition" is not always read literally, especially when this would frustrate the transferor's intent to benefit a third person. When a testator left his estate to his son Barnard "on the condition" that he support his brother, James, the court refused to construe this as a condition, since Barnard's failure to support James would cause the estate to pass by intestacy to the testator's disinherited children, and this would "make less of the assets of the estate available for the support of James" contrary to the testator's wishes.[37]

## § 4.7　Payable-on-Death Contracts

A payable-on-death (POD) account is created when a person deposits money in a bank under an agreement which provides that upon the depositor's death the account will be paid to another. The policy reasons for upholding Totten trusts,—the convenience of avoiding probate, the small amounts usually involved, widespread popular use, and the lack of serious doubt as to the decedent's intent when manifested in a written instrument—apply equally to P.O.D. accounts. Though at one time POD accounts were sometimes rejected as "testamentary", they are valid under the Uniform Probate Code and many other state statutes,[1] although some statutes govern only one type of financial institution, banks, for example, but not savings and loan associations.[2]

Insurance contracts have obvious testamentary aspects—benefits payable at death with power to revoke until then, but they have

---

**34.** *Restatement, Third, of Trusts* § 13, illus. 8 (2001).

**35.** State v. Rand, 366 A.2d 183 (Me. 1976); Section 9.7.

**36.** Walton v. City of Red Bluff, 3 Cal.Rptr.2d 275 (App.1991).

**37.** Whicher v. Abbott, 449 A.2d 353, 355 (Me.1982).

**§ 4.7**

**1.** Uniform Probate Code §§ 6–212(b), 6–214; Cal.Prob.Code §§ 5302(b), 5304. The prefatory note to

Article VI of the UPC says that this part of the Code "is one of the most broadly accepted, having been adopted ... by over half the states."

**2.** The Uniform Probate Code, on the other hand covers all accounts at financial institutions. These terms are broadly defined in § 6–201.

long been upheld. In insurance beneficiary designations, as in POD bank accounts, evidence of the decedent's (insured's) intention appears in the written records of a disinterested institution, the insurer.

In 1989 the Uniform Probate Code extended the P.O.D. concept to securities. The drafters noted that any distinction between bank accounts and securities made little sense.[3] As to securities the Code uses the term TOD or "transfer on death" rather than POD in order to avoid the implication that "the investment is to be sold or redeemed at the owner's death."[4]

In addition, the more general terms of Uniform Probate Code § 6–101 allow nonprobate transfers on death in a "deed of gift * * * or other written instrument of a similar nature."

Some statutes require that the beneficiary designation in a nonprobate transfer be in writing and subscribed by the owner.[5] However, the Uniform Probate Code by its terms requires a signed writing to *change* an account, but not to establish one,[6] and oral designations of a beneficiary have been upheld.[7]

## § 4.8  Joint Tenancy

Like the trust, joint tenancy has roots in medieval law. In the 15th century, Littleton stated rules for joint tenancy substantially in their modern form. "The nature of joint tenancy is that the one who survives will have the whole tenancy." This applied to both land and personal property, but not where two or more persons held as tenants in common.[1] In modern times joint tenancy has become a popular way to avoid probate, particularly for bank accounts and land.

*Differences Between Historical and Modern Joint Tenancy* Historically, if *A* wished to put property into joint tenancy with *B*, he had to deliver it to a third person who would reconvey the property to *A* and *B*, but modern statutes allow persons to create a joint tenancy without any such conveyance to a straw man.[2] Some courts say that joint bank accounts are created by a contract between the depositor and the bank, and so the requirements for gifts do not apply.[3]

---

**3.** Uniform Probate Code Art. VI, Prefatory Note.

**4.** Uniform Probate Code § 6–305, comment.

**5.** Mo.Stat. § 461.062. *See also* N.Y. EPTL § 13–3.2(e) (designation of beneficiary of pension or insurance).

**6.** Uniform Probate Code § 6–213.

**7.** Union Nat. Bank v. Ornelas–Gutierrez, 772 F.Supp. 962 (S.D.Tex.1991).

**§ 4.8**

**1.** T. Littleton, *Tenures* §§ 280–82.

**2.** Neb.Rev.Stat. § 76–118; Helmholz, *Realism and Formalism in the Severance of Joint Tenancies*, 77 Neb.L.Rev. 1, 5 (1998).

**3.** Malek v. Patten, 678 P.2d 201, 205 (Mont.1984).

A frequently litigated issue concerns the language needed to create a joint tenancy. Historically, a joint tenancy was created whenever property was conveyed "to A and B" without more, but many statutes today reverse the common-law presumption in favor of joint tenancy. For example, in Missouri "every interest in real estate granted or devised to two or more persons * * * shall be a tenancy in common unless expressly declared, in such grant or devise, to be in joint tenancy."[4] These statutes differ in their terms and have led to some curious distinctions which in many cases do not reflect the parties' understanding, since joint tenancies are typically created without legal advice.

The Uniform Probate Code provides that bank accounts which are payable to two or more parties pass to the survivor "whether or not a right of survivorship is mentioned" unless "the terms of the account" negate a right of survivorship.[5] The Code also provides model forms, which, if used intelligently, provide better evidence of the parties' wishes than phrases like "joint tenancy," the meaning of which is not clear to many persons. The Code provisions dealing with securities or brokerage accounts provide only for TOD registration which the drafters preferred to the "frequently troublesome joint tenancy form of title."[6] Nor does the Code apply to deeds of land; thus interpretation of the words "to A and B" in a deed may differ from that given to the same words in a bank account.[7]

*Safe Deposit Boxes* Deposit of articles in a jointly leased safe-deposit box usually has no effect on the contents of the box; the joint-tenancy language in the lease is generally construed to apply only to use of the box.[8] A safe-deposit box differs from a bank account in that it usually contains most of the lessee's title documents. If a surviving joint tenant could claim the contents of a box, this might conflict with the form of registered securities in the box.

*Intent* Although the *validity* of joint tenancy is rarely challenged today, claims are frequently made that a purported joint tenancy was not *intended* to give the other party a beneficial interest, but only to allow him or her to make deposits and withdrawals on behalf of the depositor.[9] A person who has only this purpose in mind should use a power-of-attorney instead.

**4.** Mo.Stat. § 442.450. *See also* Kan. Stat. § 58–501; 765 ILCS § 1005/1.

**5.** Uniform Probate Code § 6–201(5), 6–212.

**6.** Uniform Probate Code, Prefatory Note to Article VI.

**7.** Calif.Prob.Code §§ 5130, 5302 (as to bank accounts, like the UPC); Cal.

Civ.Code § 683(a)(presumption of tenancy in common).

**8.** In re Estate of Silver, 1 P.3d 358, 362 (Mont.2000). Calif.Civ.Code § 683.1

**9.** Litigation on this issue is further treated at Section 6.3.

*Writing*　A few states require a signed writing to create a joint account,[10] but most do not.[11] The Uniform Probate Code allows joint accounts to be opened orally but requires a signed writing to alter the form of the account thereafter.[12]

## § 4.9　Contracts to Make Wills

Contracts to devise property appear often in litigation. Sometimes they are made in return for services to be performed by the promisee, but more commonly the contract is for the benefit of a third party, for example, spouses promise each other that the survivor will leave their property to relatives of both spouses.

*Joint and Mutual Wills*　Some courts infer the existence of a contract when two spouses execute a "joint" will. For example, a husband and wife executed a joint will which said "It is our intention that this Will shall be binding." The husband survived the wife and executed a new will leaving his estate to one of their two children. The other child successfully claimed that the new will was a breach of contract.[1] Many courts, however, have refused to infer the existence of a contract from joint wills with somewhat different wording.[2] The Uniform Probate Code provides that "the execution of a joint will * * * does not create a presumption of a contract not to revoke the will."[3]

More common than joint wills are "mutual" wills, separate wills executed by spouses at the same time with reciprocal provisions. Most courts say that mere execution of mutual wills does not indicate a contract, but courts have found on the basis of extrinsic evidence that mutual wills were in fact made pursuant to a contract.[4]

*Statute of Frauds*　Many states today have provisions which deal with contracts to make wills. The Uniform Probate Code requires either "(i) provisions of a will stating the material provisions of the contract, (ii) an express reference in a will to a contract and extrinsic evidence proving the terms of the contract, or (iii) a

---

**10.**　Rynn v. Owens, 536 N.E.2d 959 (Ill.App.1989) (right of survivorship exists only between persons who sign); Tex.Prob.Code §§ 46, 439(a).

**11.**　Morris v. Cullipher, 816 S.W.2d 878 (Ark.1991) (applying Arkansas law which does not require a writing rather than Texas law which does).

**12.**　Uniform Probate Code § 6–213.

**§ 4.9**

**1.**　Adkins v. Oppio, 769 P.2d 62, 64 (Nev.1989).

**2.**　Long v. Waggoner, 558 S.E.2d 380 (Ga. 2002).

**3.**　Uniform Probate Code § 2–514. *See also* Calif.Prob.Code § 21700(b).

**4.**　Todd v. Cartwright, 684 S.W.2d 154 (Tex.App.1984); In re Dale, [1994] Ch. 31 (1993).

writing signed by the decedent evidencing the contract."[5] Simply signing a will does not satisfy the statute unless the will refers to or states the terms of the contract.

Refusal to enforce a contract after one party has performed it allows unjust enrichment. Courts sometimes avoid this by granting restitutionary relief.[6] Courts have used the value of the promisor's estate which was promised to the plaintiff as evidence of the value of the services performed, so that the result is nearly equivalent to enforcing the contract.[7]

Many courts hold that a promisee's part performance satisfies or excuses a statutory writing requirement,[8] but others have taken the statutory proof requirements more seriously, saying that "application of the equitable principle of part performance * * * would nullify the purpose of the statute."[9]

A promise which was made without intent to perform it, has been held to be actionable as fraud without a writing.[10] A lost or destroyed writing can satisfy the statute.[11]

*Clear and Convincing Evidence* Even if a statutory writing requirement is not a bar, claims under a contract often fail because the plaintiff's evidence is not clear and convincing. Even evidence in writing may not suffice if the terms are vague.[12]

*Executory Contracts* Parties who have agreed that a will shall be irrevocable may agree to rescind the contract. Most authorities also allow either party to repudiate the contract *unilaterally* before there has been any performance. "While * * * the parties to such an agreement are yet alive, any party may recede therefrom, * * * on giving proper notice to the other party."[13]

*Fairness* Contracts to make a will must be supported by consideration. Past consideration is not enough; a promise to devise in return for services previously rendered by the promisee is not enforceable.[14] Plaintiffs usually seek what amounts to specific per-

**5.** Uniform Probate Code § 2–514.

**6.** *Restatement, Second, of Contracts* § 373 (1979).

**7.** Slawsby v. Slawsby, 601 N.E.2d 478 (Mass.App.Ct.1992). *See also Restatement, Second, of Contracts* § 375 (1979).

**8.** Estate of Von Wendesse, 618 N.E.2d 1332 (Ind.App.1993); *Restatement, Second, of Contracts* § 129, illus. 10 (1979).

**9.** Rieck v. Rieck, 724 P.2d 674, 676 (Colo.App.1986).

**10.** Brody v. Bock, 897 P.2d 769 (Colo.1995).

**11.** Murphy v. Glenn, 964 P.2d 581, 585 (Colo.App.1998).

**12.** Olesen v. Manty, 438 N.W.2d 404, 407 (Minn.App.1989).

**13.** Boyle v. Schmitt, 602 So.2d 665, 667 (Fla.App.1992). *But see In re Estate of Johnson, 781 S.W.2d 390 (Tex.App. 1989) (refusing to allow unilateral rescission).

**14.** In re Estate of Casey, 583 N.E.2d 83 (Ill.App.1991); *cf. Restatement, Second, of Contracts* § 86 (1979) (promises made in recognition of benefit previously received are "binding to the extent necessary to prevent injustice").

formance, and this brings into play equity's traditional reluctance to enforce unfair contracts.[15] Nevertheless, many contracts have been enforced despite an unequal exchange.[16] The value of a party's performance may be hard to measure in monetary terms, for example, the promisee's "emigration to this country and the consequent disruption this caused to both himself and his family."[17]

*Inter–Vivos Transfers*    Sometimes a promisor while still living seeks to undercut the contract by conveying property to others. The beneficiaries of the contract may succeed in setting aside such conveyances on the theory that the contract confined the promisor to a life estate in his or her property with a remainder in the beneficiaries of the contract,[18] or the agreement not to change a will "carried with it an implicit agreement * * * to make no disposition of that estate property inconsistent with that intent."[19] However, a husband's promise to leave his estate to his children was held to give them no claim to assets he put in joint tenancy, since the contract did not require that he "have property at the time of his demise."[20] Some courts apply a rule of reason the contract "does not prohibit the [promisor] from using her property for the necessities and comforts of life * * * from changing the form of the property and * * * from making reasonable gifts of estate property to third parties."[21]

*Third Parties*    The promisor is usually dead when an action to enforce the contract is brought, and the action is brought either against the promisor's estate or against a third party. Courts may impress a trust upon the promisor's property in favor of the contract beneficiaries.[22] A bona fide purchaser of property prevails over the equitable claims of the contract beneficiaries,[23] but the beneficiaries can recover property in the hands of donees and devisees from the promisor.[24]

Some courts have rejected a claim by the promisor's spouse to an elective share on the ground that it only applies to the decedent's estate after payment of claims, which include the contract.[25]

---

**15.** *Restatement, Second, of Contracts* § 364 (1979).

**16.** Kitchen v. Estate of Blue, 498 N.E.2d 41, 45 (Ind.App.1986) (promisor's receipt of his wife's $300 estate was sufficient consideration for his promise to dispose of $130,000 estate).

**17.** In re Beeruk's Estate, 241 A.2d 755, 759 (Pa.1968).

**18.** Young v. Young, 569 N.E.2d 1, 5 (Ill.App.1991).

**19.** Robison v. Graham, 799 P.2d 610, 615 (Okl.1990).

**20.** Duran v. Komyatte, 490 N.E.2d 388 (Ind.App.1986). *See also* Blackmon v. Estate of Battcock, 587 N.E.2d 280 (N.Y.1991) (revocable trust).

**21.** Powell v. American Charter Fed. S. & L., 514 N.W.2d 326, 334 (Neb. 1994).

**22.** Robison v. Graham, 799 P.2d 610 (Okl.1990).

**23.** Olive v. Biggs, 173 S.E.2d 301 (N.C.1970). See also Section 12.8.

**24.** Musselman v. Mitchell, 611 P.2d 675 (Or.App.1980).

**25.** Johnson v. Girtman, 542 So.2d 1033 (Fla.App.1989).

But in other cases a promisor's spouse prevails over the contract beneficiaries because of "the public policy surrounding the marriage relationship."[26] Some courts reach intermediate solutions, considering several factors, "including whether the surviving spouse had notice of the contract prior to the marriage, * * * the length of the marriage and * * * whether the surviving spouse would be deprived of the entire estate by enforcement of the contract."[27] The spouse's contribution to the accumulation of the decedent's property is also relevant; the spouse should get half of any community property of the marriage.[28]

After-born children of the promisor may also be protected if full enforcement of a contract would deprive them of any share of their father's estate.[29]

*Remedies*   Because probate courts traditionally had no jurisdiction to enforce contracts, a will executed in breach of a contract is often admitted to probate, and the contract beneficiary's only remedy is in a court of general jurisdiction.[30] Since admitting a will to probate in one court and denying it effect in another seems inefficient, more recent cases have refused to probate wills made in breach of contract.[31]

Actions to enforce contracts to make wills are usually classified as equitable, which means there is no right to jury trial.[32] The statute of limitations starts to run only when the promisor dies, so cases often come to trial many years after the alleged contract was made.[33]

Suit is sometimes brought against a promisor who repudiated the contract while still alive. In this situation courts have enjoined the promisor from transferring the property, vacated conveyances previously made, and even appointed a trustee to take charge of the property.[34]

*Planning*   Contracts to make wills are common, but they are a bad idea. "If a young husband and wife sign a [contractual] will when they are about twenty-five years of age and then one of them dies, the survivor is bound (even if he or she lives another fifty

**26.** Shimp v. Huff, 556 A.2d 252, 263 (Md.1989).

**27.** Id., at 259.

**28.** Porter v. Porter, 726 P.2d 459 (Wash.1986).

**29.** Matter of Estate of Sherry, 698 P.2d 94 (Wash.App.1985).

**30.** Perino v. Eldert, 577 N.E.2d 807 (Ill.App.1991).

**31.** Estate of McKusick, 629 A.2d 41 (Me.1993); In re Estate of Gibson, 893 S.W.2d 749 (Tex.App.1995).

**32.** Walton v. Walton, 36 Cal.Rptr.2d 901 (App.1995). *But see* Wilkison v. Wiederkehr, 124 Cal.Rptr.2d 631 (App. 2002) (equitable relief denied because damages provided an adequate remedy).

**33.** Taylor v. Abernethy, 560 S.E.2d 233, 240 (N.C.App.2002) (action filed in 1998 on contract made in 1978 is timely because promisor died in 1998).

**34.** Lawrence v. Ashba, 59 N.E.2d 568 (Ind.App.1945); Turley v. Adams, 484 P.2d 668 (Ariz.App.1971).

years) [to] leave all of his or her property exactly as required by the joint will. * * * The vicissitudes of life are such that * * * we ought not to presume such an intent."[35]

There is no objective sought by a contractual will which could not be better accomplished by a trust. An independent, financially responsible trustee provides more security that the plan will be carried out. Trust beneficiaries are not subject to claims of the trustee's spouse or creditors.[36] A discretionary trust provides flexibility so the plan is not "set in concrete."

Because of the risk of false claims that mutual wills were made pursuant to a contract, wills which spouses execute at the same time should expressly state that they are not being executed pursuant to a contract.

---

**35.** In re Hoeppner's Estate, 145 N.W.2d 754, 760 (Wis.1966) (concurring opinion).

**36.** Section 13.1.

# Chapter 5

# REVOCATION

---

## § 5.1  Subsequent Instrument

A will can be revoked even if a power of revocation is not expressly reserved, but all states impose formal requirements for revocation. Wills can be revoked (1) by a subsequent instrument, (2) by a physical act, (3) by a change of circumstances.

The Uniform Probate Code is typical. "A will or any part thereof is revoked (1) by a subsequent will which revokes the prior will or part expressly or by inconsistency."[1] A "will" can revoke prior wills even though it contains no other provisions and so the testator dies intestate.[2] The subsequent instrument must be executed with the formalities prescribed for wills. However, a lost will, if duly proved, may revoke an earlier will.[3]

In jurisdictions which allow holographic wills, a holographic will may revoke an attested one,[4] but handwritten changes by the testator on a typewritten will have been disallowed.[5] However, the Restatement would allow testators to make handwritten changes in

---

**§ 5.1**

**1.** Uniform Probate Code § 2–507(a)(1). *See also* Calif.Prob.Code § 6120.

**2.** Uniform Probate Code § 1–201(56).

**3.** In re Will of McCauley, 565 S.E.2d 88, 93 (N.C. 2002).

**4.** Cason v. Taylor, 51 S.W.3d 397 (Tex.App. 2001) (even though statute required revocation by a "subsequent will . . . executed with like formalities").

**5.** In re Estate of Foxley, 575 N.W.2d 150 (Neb.1998).

a will if the statute allows holographic wills; changes in an attested will must be signed, but not alterations in a holograph.[6] Oral wills, even in states which allow them, are ineffective to revoke a written one.[7]

*Inconsistency*  Most wills contain a clause or phrase expressly revoking prior wills. Even if a will does not have such language, an implied revocation may occur if a later will contains provisions which are inconsistent with an earlier will. Courts are reluctant to find such revocation by inconsistency, however. Under the Uniform Probate Code a testator is presumed to have intended a subsequent will to replace rather than supplement a previous will if the subsequent will makes a complete disposition of the testator's estate, but the presumption is reversed when the later document does not purport to dispose of all the estate.[8] The reluctance to find revocation by inconsistency is particularly strong when the subsequent instrument is labelled a "codicil," since this word suggests a supplement to a prior will rather than an abrogation of it. Drafters should make the relationship between a codicil and an earlier will clear.

## § 5.2  Physical Act

*Nature of Act*  The Statute of Frauds allowed devises to be revoked "by burning, cancelling, tearing or obliterating the same."[1] American states today have similar provisions. A will can be effectively revoked by physical act even though it remains legible,[2] but throwing a will in the trash is not enough to revoke it.[3] According to some courts, is it not enough to make marks on a will which do not touch any words,[4] but the Uniform Probate Code provides otherwise if the intent to revoke is clear.[5] The revocatory act must

---

**6.** *Restatement, Third, of Property (Wills and Other Donative Transfers)* § 3.2, comm. f and g (1998). *See also* Estate of Nielson, 165 Cal.Rptr. 319 (App.1980) (will effectively changed by crossing out devisees and inserting others when changes initialed by testator). In Hancock v. Krause, 757 S.W.2d 117 (Tex.App.1988), the court gave effect to similar changes on the theory that the testator "adopted" his prior signature when he made them.

**7.** In re Estate of Mantalis, 671 N.E.2d 1062 (Ohio App.1996).

**8.** Uniform Probate Code § 2–507.

### § 5.2

**1.** Statute of Frauds, 29 Car. 2, c. 3, § 6 (1676). The Statute of Wills used the terms "burning, tearing or otherwise destroying." 1 Vict., c. 26, § 20 (1837).

**2.** Matter of Estate of Ausley, 818 P.2d 1226 (Okl.1991) (VOID written over parts of will).

**3.** SouthTrust Bank v. Winter, 689 So.2d 69 (Ala.Civ.App.1996).

**4.** Kronauge v. Stoecklein, 293 N.E.2d 320 (Ohio App.1972).

**5.** Uniform Probate Code § 2–507(a)(2). *See also* Kroll v. Nehmer, 705 A.2d 716, 717 (Md.1998) (will revoked by writing VOID on the back).

be done with the intent to revoke; an accidental destruction does not revoke a will.

The act upon the will must be done "by either (1) the testator or (2) another person in the testator's presence and by the testator's direction."[6] A testator's clear intent to revoke may be frustrated if her directions to destroy a will are carried out in another place,[7] but the Uniform Probate Code requires only the "testator's conscious presence" which "need not be * * * in the testator's line of sight."[8]

Sometimes a testator's directions to destroy a will are not carried out, e.g. his wife pretended to tear up the will according to his instructions, but produced it unharmed after the testator died. The court probated the will, but said that a constructive trust might be imposed on the widow.[9]

*Partial Revocation*  Cases in which a testator intends to revoke only part of a will have given courts much trouble. The Uniform Probate Code allows a will "or any part thereof" to be revoked, but a testator cannot make a new will without a signed writing. The line between revocation and making a new will is hazy. When a will left the estate to the testator's sons, Michael and Edward, and he later crossed out Edward's name, the court refused to give this effect "because this amounted to an enlargement of the bequest to Michael."[10] But another court gave effect to the cancellation of a pecuniary devise even though the effect was to increase the residuary devise.[11]

A testator cannot add words to a will without re-executing it, but alterations made in a will *prior* to its execution are valid. Correcting typographical errors in a will by hand is risky, since someone may argue that the change was made after the will was executed.

*Presumption of Revocation*  When a will which was in the testator's possession cannot be found, or is found in a mutilated condition, after the testator dies, courts presume that the testator intended to revoke the will.[12] Proponents of the will usually offer evidence to rebut the presumption, and courts often find no intent to revoke even though the original will cannot be found, e.g., when

**6.**  Calif.Prob.Code § 6120(b); Estate of DeWald v. Whittenburg, 925 P.2d 903 (Okl.App.1996) (cancellation by a friend of testator at his direction).

**7.**  In re Haugk's Estate, 280 N.W.2d 684 (Wis.1979).

**8.**  Uniform Probate Code § 2–507(a)(2), comment.

**9.**  Morris v. Morris, 642 S.W.2d 448 (Tex.1982). *See also Restatement, Third,*

*of Property (Wills and Other Donative Transfers)* § 8.3, comm. l (2001).

**10.**  In re Estate of Eastman, 812 P.2d 521 (Wash.App.1991).

**11.**  Patrick v. Patrick, 649 A.2d 1204 (Md.App.1994).

**12.**  *Restatement, Third, of Property (Wills and Other Donative Transfers)* § 4.1, comm. j (1998).

persons other than the testator had access to the will.[13] Some courts have inferred from a testator's sloppy habits that the will was simply lost in the mess. Courts admit even oral declarations by the testator indicating that the lost will reflected her wishes or continued affection for the devisees or hostility toward persons disinherited by the will.[14]

The presumption of revocation is sometimes overcome by the preservation of a duplicate,[15] but courts have found a will was revoked despite the production of a duplicate, particularly when the duplicate was not in the testator's possession.[16] Conversely, the presumption of revocation applies only when the missing will was once in the testator's possession.[17]

The loss or preservation of an *unexecuted* copy of the will has no significance in determining whether there was a revocation. Presumably this applies also to photocopies of an executed original. Many lawyers advise testators to sign only one copy of a will in order to reduce the risk that accidental loss of an executed copy will be misunderstood. The lawyer can keep the executed will, but this may be regarded as an unethical attempt to give the drafter an edge in being hired to handle the testator's estate.[18]

*Lost Wills* Normally when a will cannot be found and the fact-finder determines that it was not revoked, a copy of the will is probated or other proof is used to establish its contents.[19] Some lost wills cannot be probated even though there is no evidence that the testator wished to revoke them, simply because the contents cannot be satisfactorily proved. An alleged lost will of Howard Hughes was denied probate because a statute required proof of lost wills by two witnesses and the proponents produced only one.[20]

*Planning* No lawyer should advise a client to revoke a will by tearing it up since this act, even though legally effective, can be misinterpreted. If the testator keeps the will, the lawyer should warn the testator to keep it in a safe place and not to try to change the will without professional assistance. The location of the original

---

**13.** Lonergan v. Estate of Budahazi, 669 So.2d 1062 (Fla.App.1996). Destruction of a will without the testator's permission may constitute a criminal offense. E.g., 18 Pa.C.S.A. § 4103.

**14.** Succession of Altazan, 682 So.2d 1320 (La.App.1996).

**15.** Matter of Estate of Shaw, 572 P.2d 229 (Okl.1977).

**16.** Estate of Fowler v. Perry, 681 N.E.2d 739 (Ind.App.1997).

**17.** Golini v. Bolton, 482 S.E.2d 784 (S.C.App.1997).

**18.** State v. Gulbankian, 196 N.W.2d 733 (Wis.1972).

**19.** *Restatement, Third, of Property (Wills and Other Donative Transfers)* § 4.1, comm. k (1998).

**20.** Howard Hughes Medical Institute v. Gavin, 621 P.2d 489 (Nev.1980). In In re Will of McCauley, 565 S.E.2d 88, 95 (N.C. 2002), a single witness' testimony was held sufficient to prove a lost will, but only if the evidence was "clear, strong and convincing."

should be noted on the copies, one of which should be retained by the drafter.

## § 5.3   Revival and Dependent Relative Revocation

*Dependent Relative Revocation*   Even an intentional destruction may not revoke the will if the circumstances indicate that the testator would not want this, as when the destruction of a will is linked with an abortive attempt to make a new will. When a marked-up will was found together with an unsigned will of a later date, the court probated the marked-up will under the doctrine of dependent relative revocation, sometimes called conditional revocation. The testator "would have preferred * * * the earlier will over the only other alternative—intestacy."[1] This is a reasonable inference if the dispositive provisions of the two wills are similar, but if they are not, the court may infer that the testator would have preferred to die intestate.[2]

Dependent relative revocation is sometimes applied to partial revocations. A will devised 12 shares (out of 100) to the testator's mother and 7 each to his sisters and brother. The testator later crossed out the number 12 in the bequest to his mother and put "24" in its place. The court, finding that the cancellations "were made with conditional revocatory intent," admitted the original provision for 12 shares to probate.[3]

Dependent relative revocation has also been applied to revocation by subsequent instrument, for example when a devise in the revoking will was invalid under the Rule against Perpetuities[4] or the rule invalidating devises to a witness of the will.[5]

*Revival*   When a testator executes two wills and then revokes the second, is the first one revived or does the testator die intestate? This question is typically governed by a statute. For example, a will left the residuary estate to one child. A subsequent will left it to three children equally. The testator later destroyed the second will. She was held to have died intestate since a statute provided that a "revoked will * * * shall not be revived except by reexecution of by a duly executed codicil expressing an intention to revive

**§ 5.3**

**1.**   Carter v. First United Methodist Church, 271 S.E.2d 493 (Ga.1980).

**2.**   *Restatement, Third, of Property (Wills and Other Donative Transfers)* § 4.3, comm. c (1998); Kroll v. Nehmer, 705 A.2d 716, 723 (Md.1998).

**3.**   Estate of Uhl, 81 Cal.Rptr. 436 (App.1969). The changes might have

been effective if the testator had initialed them, since California allows holographic wills.

**4.**   In re Jones' Estate, 352 So.2d 1182 (Fla.App.1977); *Restatement, Third, of Property (Wills and Other Donative Transfers)* § 4.3, illus. 17 (1998).

**5.**   Re Finnemore, [1991] 1 W.L.R. 793 (Ch.D).

it."[6] The Uniform Probate Code, on the other hand, allows the testator's intent to revive an earlier will to be given effect: revocation of a second will by physical act revives the first if "it is evident from the circumstances of the revocation of the subsequent will or from testator's contemporary or subsequent declarations that the testator intended" this.[7] Presumably even testimony by interested witnesses would be admissible, *i.e.,* the beneficiaries of the first will could testify that the testator told them she wished to revive it, but the Restatement of Property requires "clear and convincing" evidence of the intent to revive.[8]

The Code presumes against an intent to revive, so if there is *no* evidence as to intent, the testator dies intestate. However, the presumption is reversed when the second instrument only partially revoked the first. Thus if a codicil alters a will and then the codicil is destroyed, the provisions of the original will which the codicil revised are reinstated, unless there is evidence that the testator did not so intend.[9]

## § 5.4  Divorce

A change of circumstances after a will is executed may create doubt whether the will still reflects the testator's wishes. The Uniform Probate Code provides that a divorce or annulment of a marriage revokes any disposition of property "made by a divorced individual to his [or her] former spouse."[1] Although this was not the rule at common law,[2] many states have similar statutes. In a few states a divorce revokes the whole will, but more commonly only the provisions relating to the former spouse are affected.

Under the Uniform Probate Code, extrinsic evidence of a contrary intent is generally irrelevant;[3] the provisions for the spouse are revived if the testator remarries the former spouse,[4] but not if they merely cohabit. [5]

Divorce only revokes a devise to the *testator's* spouse, not devises to an in-law. Thus when a will left property to the testator's

---

**6.** Matter of Estate of Lagreca, 687 A.2d 783, 785 (N.J.Super.A.D.1997). This situation is to be distinguished from one in which the later will is ineffective because of faulty execution or incapacity. Here the earlier will is never revoked.

**7.** Uniform Probate Code § 2–509(a).

**8.** *Restatement, Third, of Property (Wills and Other Donative Transfers)* § 4.2, comm. i (1998). *See also* White v. Wilbanks, 393 S.E.2d 182 (S.C.1990).

**9.** Uniform Probate Code § 2–509(b).

**§ 5.4**

**1.** Uniform Probate Code § 2–804(b).

**2.** Hinders v. Hinders, 828 So.2d 1235 (Miss.2002).

**3.** Uniform Probate Code § 2–804(b) allows only for a contrary express provision in the will or "a court order, or a contract relating to the division of the marital estate made between the divorced individuals."

**4.** Id., § 2–804(e). *See also* N.Y.EPTL § 5–1.4; Calif.Prob.Code § 6122(b).

**5.** Estate of Reeves, 284 Cal.Rptr. 650 (App.1991); Pekol v. Estate of Pekol, 499 N.E.2d 88 (Ill.App.1986).

nephew and "his wife Shirley," Shirley took even though she had divorced the nephew.[6]

The Uniform Probate Code also revokes devises to a relative of the former spouse. Statutes without such provision have been construed to leave devises to the testator's step-children or former in-laws in effect despite a divorce between the testator and the spouse.[7]

Under the Code the disqualified spouse or relatives are deemed to have disclaimed the devise, which generally produces the same result as if the former spouse (relative) were dead. [8]

*Separation*  A separation that does not terminate the status of husband and wife does not revoke a devise to the spouse,[9] but a separation agreement may by its terms bar a spouse from claiming under the other spouse's will. This depends on how the agreement is drafted and construed. An agreement releasing "all claims or rights * * * by reason of the marriage between the parties with respect to any property" belonging to each other was held not to preclude the wife from taking under a will which the husband had previously executed.[10] The Uniform Probate Code, however, presumes that "a waiver of 'all rights' " in the other spouse's property in a settlement entered into "after or in anticipation of separation or divorce" renounces any provisions of a prior will of the other spouse.[11]

*Other Change of Circumstances*  The Uniform Probate Code and many other statutes provide that apart from divorce "no change in circumstances * * * revokes a will,"[12] but an after-born child or later spouse of the testator may have rights even if not mentioned in the will.[13]

## § 5.5  Gifts and Will Substitutes

*Power to Revoke Gifts*  A testator can revoke a will even though it contains no express power to revoke. Inter-vivos gifts, on the other hand, are irrevocable. Lawyers should make sure that clients understand this and discourage them from making gifts that could jeopardize their economic independence. There is an exception for gifts made in expectation of imminent death[1] that comes

---

**6.**  Estate of Kelly v. Stambaugh, 724 N.E.2d 1285, 1287 (Ill.App.2000).

**7.**  Bloom v. Selfon, 555 A.2d 75 (Pa. 1989) (substitute devise to testator's ex-husband's uncle).

**8.**  Uniform Probate Code § 2–804(d). As to the effect of a disclaimer see Section 2.8.

**9.**  Uniform Probate Code § 2–804(a)(1).

**10.**  Matter of Estate of Maruccia, 429 N.E.2d 751 (N.Y.1981).

**11.**  Uniform Probate Code § 2–213(d).

**12.**  *Id.,* § 2–804(f).

**13.**  Sections 3.5 and 3.6.

### § 5.5

**1.**  Welton v. Gallagher, 630 P.2d 1077 (Haw.App.1981) (bonds given to

from Roman law which allowed gifts "causa mortis" to be revoked because they were so much like wills.[2]

A donor who repents of a gift may have it set aside if the donor lacked capacity, or was the victim of the undue influence or fraud; these possibilities will be discussed later. Courts also allow gifts to be revoked on the basis of an unsatisfied condition. Such a condition is implied for gifts connected with a contemplated marriage. The Restatement of Property allows a donor to recover an engagement ring if the donee breaks the engagement, or the donor does so for a justified reason.[3] Many courts allow the donor to recover regardless of which party refused to go through with the marriage and the reason.[4] Some courts have allowed recovery of other forms of property given in contemplation of a marriage which never took place.[5] Parents sometimes give property to a child on the understanding that the donee will support and care for them. If the child fails to do this, the donor can get the property back even if the deed of gift was not expressly conditional.[6] Usually, however, a condition in a gift must be expressed when the gift is made.[7]

*Trusts* The Second Restatement of Trusts stated that living trusts could not be revoked unless the trust instrument reserved a power to revoke, but the Third Restatement presumes that a trust is revocable if the settlor "has retained a beneficial interest in the trust" on the ground that this may "protect the settlor from unanticipated, adverse tax consequences."[8] Some state statutes say that all trusts are revocable unless they otherwise provide.[9] Since many trusts are created for tax reasons, and the tax consequences are different for revocable and irrevocable trusts, most instruments make clear whether or not the trust was intended to be revocable.

Trusts created by two or more settlors, *e.g.* a husband and wife, trusts raise the question whether *one of* the settlors can revoke. In

defendant cannot be recovered where gift was not in contemplation of death); *Restatement, Second, of Contracts* § 332(1) (1981) (gratuitous assignment is irrevocable).

**2.** Justinian, *Institutes* 2.7.1–2; Cal. Prob.Code § 5704. In Louisiana gifts can be revoked for "ingratitude," but this is narrowly defined, *e.g.* "cruel treatment, crimes or grievous injuries." La.Civ. Code art. 1559–60.

**3.** *Restatement, Second, Property (Donative Transfers)* § 31.2, illus. 5–8 (1990).

**4.** Meyer v. Mitnick, 625 N.W.2d 136 (Mich.App. 2001).

**5.** Boydstun v. Loveless, 890 P.2d 267 (Colo.App.1995) (land put in joint

tenancy with "wife"). *Contra*, Cooper v. Smith, 800 N.E.2d 372 (Ohio App.2003) (recovery limited to engagement ring).

**6.** Trout v. Parker, 595 N.E.2d 1015 (Ohio App.1991).

**7.** Courts v. Annie Penn Memorial Hospital, 431 S.E.2d 864 (N.C.App. 1993)

**8.** *See Restatement, Third, of Trusts* § 63, comment c (2001). Compare *Restatement, Second, Trusts* § 330 (1959). Revocation. with the consent of all the beneficiaries is discussed in Section 9.6. Reformation (discussed at Section 6.4) may allow a power of revocation which was omitted by mistake to be enforced.

**9.** Cal.Prob.Code § 15400; Uniform Trust Code § 602.

California "if a trust is created by more than one settlor, each settlor may revoke the trust as to the portion of the trust contributed by that settlor."[10] Trusts created by married couples often expressly limit the power of the surviving settlor to revoke, usually for tax reasons.

A power to revoke may be exercised by the settlor only if he/she has capacity, but it may be exercised on the settlor's behalf by a conservator or agent under a durable power.[11]

In order to revoke a trust the settlor must comply with any method of revocation specified in the trust instrument, but under the Uniform Trust Code, "substantial compliance" with the prescribed method of revocation is sufficient.[12] If no method is specified, a power to revoke (assuming one is implied) "can be exercised in any manner which sufficiently manifests the intention of the settlor."[13] Oral revocations have occasionally been recognized, but California requires a writing signed by the settlor and delivered to the trustee.[14]

*Insurance* Most modern policies expressly give the insured (the person on whose life the policy is based) the right to change the beneficiary. The right to designate the beneficiary is an incident of ownership of the policy, so an insured who assigns the ownership can no longer change the beneficiary but the new owner can.[15] However, if the policy was simply assigned as security for a loan, the beneficiaries designated by the insured are entitled to any surplus after the loan is paid.[16]

Policies typically require that written notice be received by the insurer if the beneficiary is changed. This protects the company from liability for paying the wrong person. "Substantial compliance" with this requirement is enough, e.g., when an insured signed a form to change the beneficiary, but died suddenly before delivering the form, the change was held effective.[17] Insurers some-

---

**10.** Cal.Prob.Code § 15401(b); cf. Unif.Trust Code § 602(b); *Restatement, Third, of Trusts* § 63, comment k (2001).

**11.** *Restatement, Third, of Trusts* § 63, comment l (2001).

**12.** Uniform Trust Code § 602(c)(1). See also Matter of Trust Estate of Daoang, 953 P.2d 959 (Haw.App.1998) (informal letter signed by settlor satisfied requirement of "another instrument" to amend trust).

**13.** *Restatement, Third, of Trusts* § 63, comment h (2001).

**14.** Cal.Prob.Code § 15401(a)(2); *cf.* Unif.Trust Code § 602(c)(B) (any meth-

od manifesting clear and convincing evidence of intent).

**15.** American Western Life Ins. Co. v. Hooker, 622 P.2d 775 (Utah 1980). For the tax advantages of such a transfer of ownership of life insurance see Section 15.3.

**16.** Prudential Ins. Co. of America v. Glass, 959 P.2d 586 (Okl.1998).

**17.** Connecticut Gen. Life Ins. Co. v. Gulley, 668 F.2d 325 (7th Cir.1982). *But see* Eschler v. Eschler, 849 P.2d 196 (Mont.1993) (merely requesting change-of-beneficiary forms is not enough).

times interplead competing claimants to the proceeds of a policy, and this may be deemed a "waiver" of strict compliance with policy terms.[18] Similar rules apply to the designation of beneficiaries under pension plans, but here ERISA, the federal statute which governs most pensions, supersedes state law.[19]

*Joint Tenancy: Land*   A person who puts land into joint tenancy cannot get it back, but a joint tenant can destroy the *right of survivorship* and convert the property into a tenancy in common under which each tenant's share passes to his or her estate at death.[20] Historically joint tenants had to convey their interest to a third party in order to effectuate such a "severance," but modern courts have eliminated this requirement, so a joint tenant's deed purporting "to dissolve any and all rights of survivorship" was held effective after her death.[21] In California, however, a severance deed must be recorded. This is to avoid the risk that a tenant might execute such a deed, keep it secret, and then destroy it if he turned out to be the surviving joint tenant.[22]

Some states do not allow one spouse to sever when two spouses hold land jointly; they hold as "tenants by the entirety" and "being considered as one person in law * * * neither the husband nor the wife can dispose of any part without the assent of the other but the whole must remain to the other."[23] This form of tenancy can exist only between spouses and some states no longer recognize it.[24]

A joint tenant's right to sever may be barred by the terms of the document which created the joint tenancy.[25]

*Joint Tenancy: Personal Property*   Courts generally regard joint tenancy in personal property as a will substitute rather than an irrevocable gift. The Uniform Probate Code says that joint bank accounts belong to the party who contributed the funds while the parties are alive "unless there is clear and convincing evidence of a different intent."[26] The contributing party while still alive can

**18.** Burkett v. Mott, 733 P.2d 673 (Ariz.App.1986). *Contra*, McCarthy v. Aetna Life Ins. Co., 704 N.E.2d 557, 561 (N.Y.1998).

**19.** BankAmerica Pension Plan v. McMath, 206 F.3d 821, 830 (9th Cir. 2000).

**20.** *Restatement, Second, Property (Donative Transfers)* § 31.1, illus. 16 (1990).

**21.** Minonk State Bank v. Grassman, 447 N.E.2d 822 (Ill.1983).

**22.** Cal.Civ.Code § 683.2; Fetters, *An Invitation to Commit Fraud: Secret Destruction of Joint Tenant Survivorship Rights*, 55 Ford.L.Rev. 173 (1986).

**23.** 2 W. Blackstone, *Commentaries* *182 (1765); Shwachman v. Meagher, 699 N.E.2d 16 (Mass.App.Ct.1998).

**24.** Schimke v. Karlstad, 208 N.W.2d 710 (S.D.1973).

**25.** Albro v. Allen, 454 N.W.2d 85 (Mich.1990) (no severance possible when deed expressly refers to right of survivorship); Hilterbrand v. Carter, 27 P.3d 1086 (Or.App. 2001) (mother's putting land in joint tenancy with two children and their spouses created "cross-contingent remainders" which could not be destroyed).

**26.** Uniform Probate Code § 6-211(b).

withdraw the funds or change the form of the account, but withdrawals by a noncontributing party can be recovered by the contributing party or his estate. Changes in the form of an account require a signed written notice "received by the financial institution during the party's lifetime."[27]

The rules governing joint tenancy in personal property other than bank accounts are unclear. Some courts have treated brokerage accounts like bank accounts,[28] but the common claim that a joint bank account was created simply for convenience in making deposits and withdrawals without donative intent seems less apposite for other types of property.

*Divorce*　In most states provisions in a will in favor of the testator's spouse are revoked if they later divorce. The assumption as to intent which underlies this rule applies also to will substitutes like insurance, but courts do not treat them the same way. An ex-wife who had been named as beneficiary of her husband's POD account during the marriage was awarded the account after he died despite the fact that they had been divorced.[29] Claims by ex-spouses have been defeated on the basis of a waiver executed at the time of the divorce, but not if the language in the divorce settlement was too general.[30] The Uniform Probate Court calls for a broad construction of a waiver of "all rights" in a separation agreement, but this does not apply to benefits to the former spouse in a living trust as distinguished from a will.[31]

In many states divorce ends the right of survivorship between spouses who own property jointly.[32] In others the result may turn on the terms of the decree; some courts have found an agreement to sever therein.[33]

Some statutes extend the divorce rule for wills to will substitutes. Under the Uniform Probate Code, a divorce "severs the interests of the former spouses in property held by them" as joint tenants, and revokes any revocable disposition made by one spouse to the other in a "governing instrument" which is defined to include trusts, insurance policies, POD accounts, and pension bene-

---

**27.** Uniform Probate Code § 6–213. Many banks impose similar rules by contract.

**28.** Lebitz–Freeman v. Lebitz, 803 A.2d 156 (N.J.Super.A.D. 2002). *But see* In re Marriage of Orlando, 577 N.E.2d 1334 (Ill.App.1991) (wife's putting stock into joint tenancy creates a presumption of a gift which could be rebutted only by clear proof).

**29.** Matter of Estate of Leone, 860 P.2d 973 (Utah App.1993).

**30.** Eredics v. Chase Manhattan Bank, 790 N.E.2d 1166 (N.Y. 2003) (Totten trust).

**31.** Matter of Estate of Groesbeck, 935 P.2d 1255 (Utah 1997).

**32.** Goldman v. Goldman, 733 N.E.2d 200 (N.Y.2000) (divorce turns tenancy by the entirety into tenancy in common); 28 Pa.Stat. § 3507.

**33.** Fitts v. Stokes, 841 So.2d 229, 232 (Ala.2002).

fits as well as wills.[34] This presumption is not rebuttable by oral evidence of contrary intent.[35] As to pension benefits, ERISA preempts state statutes[36] but some courts have reached the same result as a matter of federal common law.[37] Some courts in states without a statutes like the UPC have applied statutes governing wills to will substitutes by analogy.[38]

*Wills* Will provisions which purport to deal with property covered by a will substitute may not be effective. A purported devise of property held in joint tenancy is void, "for no testament takes effect till after the death of the testator and by such death the right of the survivor is already vested."[39] This rule, though ancient, seems questionable.

The Restatement of Trusts allows settlors of bank account trusts to revoke them by will,[40] but general language in a will does not suffice, e.g., a devise of all the estate "of whatsoever nature" did not revoke the testator's bank account trusts.[41] Even a clear intent to revoke a living trust may be rejected for failure to satisfy a requirement in the trust that amendments be delivered to the trustee during the settlor's lifetime.[42]

The Uniform Probate Code does not allow beneficiary designations in a P.O.D. account or a right of survivorship in a joint account to be altered by will.[43] A will has also been held ineffective to change the beneficiary designation in an insurance policy.[44] This rule allows banks and insurers to pay funds promptly after a depositor/insured's death without worrying about a possible will. This concern could be better addressed by simply protecting any bank or insurer which makes payment without notice of the will. The Third Restatement of Property protects payors who pay the beneficiary of record, but if they receive prior notice of the change of beneficiary designation in the will, they must comply with it.[45]

**34.** Uniform Probate Code §§ 1–201(19), 2–804(b).

**35.** Mearns v. Scharbach, 12 P.3d 1048 (Wash.App.2000). Contrast the rules of construction in part 7 which apply "in the absence of a finding of a contrary intention." Uniform Probate Code § 2–701.

**36.** Egelhoff v. Egelhoff, 532 U.S. 141 (2001) .

**37.** Weaver v. Keen, 43 S.W.3d 537, 545 (Tex.App. 2001).

**38.** Clymer v. Mayo, 473 N.E.2d 1084 (Mass.1985).

**39.** 2 W. Blackstone, *Commentaries* *186 (1765). *See also* Matter of Estate of Kokjohn, 531 N.W.2d 99 (Iowa 1995) (joint account).

**40.** *Restatement, Third, of Trusts* § 26, comm. c (2001).

**41.** Eredics v. Chase Manhattan Bank, 790 N.E.2d 1166 (N.Y.2003).

**42.** One Valley Bank, Nat. Ass'n v. Hunt, 516 S.E.2d 516 (W.Va. 1999).

**43.** Uniform Probate Code § 6–213(b). *See also* Calif.Prob.Code § 5302(e). *But see* Wash.Stat. § 11.11.020 ("any nonprobate asset specifically referred to in the owner's will" can be controlled by the will).

**44.** McCarthy v. Aetna Life Ins. Co., 704 N.E.2d 557 (N.Y.1998).

**45.** *Restatement, Third, of Property (Wills and Other Donative Transfers)* § 7.2, comm. e (2001).

*Planning*   Lawyers who draft wills should ascertain what gifts or will substitutes the testator has made. The testator cannot revoke irrevocable gifts, but joint tenancies can be severed, revocable trusts revoked and insurance beneficiaries changed. This requires more than a duly executed will. If the testator does *not* wish to disturb non-probate arrangements express confirmation of them in the will may be advisable.

# Chapter 6

# EXTRINSIC EVIDENCE

## § 6.1   Wills: Mistake and Ambiguity

*Policy*  If a will leaves property "to *A*," and *B* attempts to show by evidence extrinsic to the will that the testator intended that *she* should get the property, there are two possible bases for denying her claim. The first is the parol evidence rule which applies to wills and other written documents. The statute of wills provides another theoretical basis for excluding any evidence of the testator's intent that is not in writing, signed, and attested. Courts admit oral evidence to correct mistakes in written contracts, even those which the Statute of Frauds requires to be in writing and signed, but in the case of wills, the best evidence of the testator's intent, the testator, is dead when the will is probated. Therefore, courts have been especially reluctant to allow extrinsic evidence in interpreting wills.

*Mistake*  Nevertheless, courts admit extrinsic evidence of a testator's intent in some situations. The typical wills act says that wills must be in writing and signed, but it does not bar courts from refusing to probate a will which was signed by mistake, or a part of a will which was included by mistake.[1] Thus words inserted in a will by mistake may be struck out but words omitted by mistake

---

§ 6.1

1.  In re Estate of Herbert, 979 P.2d 39, 51–52 (Haw.1999).

may not be added, e.g, if a will leaves property "to my brothers and sisters," and the word "brothers" was included by mistake, a court can delete it,[2] but if a devise to the testator's son was left out, the court can not add it.[3] The distinction between adding and deleting words can be explained by the wording of the wills act, but the policy considerations in both cases are the same. Whether words are added or deleted, the same threat exists of untrustworthy evidence, unrebuttable by the testator. Moreover, in some cases striking words may have the same practical effect as adding them.[4]

Some courts refuse to probate a will when extrinsic evidence shows that it was not actually meant to operate as a will. According to the Restatement of Property, a clear expression of testamentary intent in a document "raises a strong presumption" of testamentary intent, but can be rebutted by clear contrary evidence.[5] But one court refused to admit evidence from a contestant that the testator "didn't really mean it; he was merely bluffing."[6]

*Ambiguity* The rule which bars adding words omitted from a will is sometimes displaced by a rule allowing courts to use extrinsic evidence to resolve "latent ambiguities." A will which purports to devise property which the testator does not own may be deemed "ambiguous," e.g., a testator who devised "all of the lots that I own on Suber Street" owned no such land but owned other land known as "the Suber property." This "latent ambiguity" was resolved on the basis of extrinsic evidence.[7] Similar mistakes often arise in a will's designation of a devisee.

"Latent" ambiguities are not apparent until one looks outside the will and discovers that two devisees (or properties) (or none) fit the description in the will. Some courts refuse to consider extrinsic evidence when the ambiguity is "patent", *i.e.* apparent on the face of the will. But the distinction between latent and patent ambiguities seems irrelevant to the policy issues involved, and many courts reject it.[8]

The mere fact that parties disagree on the proper interpretation does not necessarily make a will "ambiguous." Courts sometimes reject extrinsic evidence, asserting that the will is unambigu-

---

**2.**   In re Fenwick, [1972] V.R. 646.

**3.**   Knupp v. District of Columbia, 578 A.2d 702 (D.C.App.1990) (name of residuary devisee omitted by mistake).

**4.**   Breckheimer v. Kraft, 273 N.E.2d 468 (Ill.App.1971).

**5.**   *Restatement, Third, of Property (Wills and Other Donative Transfers)* § 3.1, comm. g (1998). *See also* Cal.Prob. Code § 6111.5 ("extrinsic evidence is admissible to determine whether a document constitutes a will").

**6.**   Matter of Estate of Duemeland, 528 N.W.2d 369 (N.D.1995).

**7.**   Fenzel v. Floyd, 347 S.E.2d 105 (S.C.App.1986). *But see* Matter of Estate of Greenfield, 757 P.2d 1297 (Mont. 1988) (devise of property which did not exist held unambiguous).

**8.**   In re Gibson's Estate, 312 N.E.2d 1, 3 (Ill.App.1974).

ous, e.g. when a will left property to the "blood heirs" of the testator, the court excluded evidence that the testator thought that his heirs were his sisters and his child, saying "there was no ambiguity in the will."[9] The law has created rules of construction to deal with certain questions like whether "children" includes adopted children, etc. Do such rules render language unambiguous, or can extrinsic evidence be used to show that the testator intended something contrary to the rule of construction? The many cases raising this issue are hard to reconcile. Statutory language may make a difference. In some, the construction rules govern where a contrary "intention of the transferor is not indicated by the instrument,"[10] but the Uniform Probate Code simply says the rules apply "in the absence of a finding of a contrary intention."[11]

Even if a will is ambiguous, extrinsic evidence showing an intent totally at odds with the language of the will may be rejected, e.g., a will left paintings "to the New York Museum of Fine Arts" which does not exist. Evidence indicating that the testator meant the Boston Museum of Fine Arts was admitted, but other evidence indicating that she wanted her cousin to have the paintings was not, since the will showed a devise to a museum, not a person.[12]

The Second Restatement of Property adopts a more liberal position as to extrinsic evidence; a "drafting error in carrying out * * * a testator's intention" can be reformed.[13] This goes farther than most case law today, but there are signs of a trend in this direction which is followed in the Uniform Trust Code.[14] Reformation of living trusts and deeds has long been accepted, and with the increasing use of will-substitutes, there has been a trend to assimilate the rules governing both.[15] The risk of false testimony can be reduced by requiring clear and convincing evidence.[16] Also, since reformation of mistakes is an equitable matter, the question is tried by the court rather than a jury.

**9.** Brunson v. Citizens Bank and Trust Co., 752 S.W.2d 316 (Ky.App. 1988). As to the meaning of "heirs" see Section 2.4.

**10.** Last Will and Testament of Lawson v. Lambert, 792 So.2d 977, 981 (Miss. 2001) (extrinsic evidence inadmissible when statute provides for apportionment of taxes unless "the decedent's will directs" otherwise).

**11.** Uniform Probate Code § 2–601.

**12.** Phipps v. Barbera, 498 N.E.2d 411 (Mass.App.Ct.1986). See also Estate of Kaila, 114 Cal.Rptr.2d 865, 874 (App. 2001) (extrinsic evidence must "show a meaning to which the language is reasonably susceptible").

**13.** Restatement, Second, of Property (Donative Transfers) § 34.7, Comment d (1990).

**14.** Uniform Trust Code § 415. See also Restatement, Third, of Trusts § 62 (2001); In re Estate of Herceg, 747 N.Y.S.2d 901 (Surr.2002) (inserting name of devisee omitted by mistake).

**15.** As to reformation in deeds and living trusts see Section 6.3,, Section 6.4.

**16.** Langbein & Waggoner, Reformation of Wills on the Ground of Mistake, 130 U.Pa.L.Rev. 521, 579 (1982). See also Uniform Trust Code § 414; cf. Phipps v. Barbera, 498 N.E.2d 411 (Mass.App.Ct.1986) (preponderance of evidence suffices when resolving a latent ambiguity).

*Nature of the Evidence.* Although the question posed is whether extrinsic evidence is "admissible," the trial court usually hears it, and the strength of the evidence may determine the outcome. In some cases the evidence of a mistake is overwhelming, as when a husband and wife, executing wills at the same time each signed the other's will. The court reformed the wills, saying that what had occurred was "so obvious, and what was intended so clear" that there was "absolutely no danger of fraud."[17]

Many courts distinguish between evidence of the circumstances and alleged declarations of the testator. In a will which created a trust to support the testator's wife, the question arose whether the trustee should consider the wife's own resources. Testimony that according to the testator's instructions the will should have contained the phrase "having in mind [the wife's] separate income" was excluded, but it was proper to consider the amount which the testator had contributed to his wife's support while he was alive.[18]

The identity of the drafter may affect the construction of technical words. If a will was drafted by a non-lawyer, a devise of "all my money" may include all the testator's assets,[19] whereas a testator who worked in a county recording office could not have meant to include real estate in a bequest of "personal effects."[20]

Evidence of the circumstances, *e.g.* the age of the testator's children when he executed his will, is hard to manufacture. From this circumstance, one may infer that the testator must have meant "youngest" when a will referred to the time when his "oldest" child should reach 30, because his oldest child was already 30 when the will was signed.[21]

In some cases even when the circumstantial evidence is uncontroverted, its bearing on intent is not clear. Circumstantial evidence may show that one construction of a will treats all the testator's children equally, but some testators do not want this. Courts in recent years have been willing to construe or reform wills to achieve tax reductions which (it is assumed) the testator would want.[22] But some courts have refused to make such changes, doubting whether the testator was so focused on tax savings.[23]

---

**17.** Matter of Snide, 418 N.E.2d 656, 658 (N.Y.1981).

**18.** Estate of Utterback, 521 A.2d 1184 (Me.1987).

**19.** *Restatement of Property* § 242, comm. f (1940). *See also* Transamerica Occidental Life Ins. Co. v. Burke, 368 S.E.2d 301 (W.Va.1988) ("children" includes stepchildren when will is not drawn by a lawyer).

**20.** Kaufhold v. McIver, 682 S.W.2d 660 (Tex.App.1984). *See also* In re Estate of Goodwin, 739 N.Y.S.2d 239, 247 (Surr.2002) (emphasizing that drafter was a "meticulous and careful scrivener").

**21.** Matter of Ikuta's Estate, 639 P.2d 400 (Haw.1981).

**22.** In re Substitute Indenture of Trust, 789 N.E.2d 1051 (Mass.2003); Uniform Trust Code § 415 (court may modify trust in order to achieve settlor's tax objectives).

**23.** Estate of Heim v. Commissioner, 914 F.2d 1322 (9th Cir.1990).

Some evidence of intent is more reliable than other. In remanding a case for consideration of extrinsic evidence, one court said that "self-serving statements by [devisees] as to their understanding of the testator's intent would not be admissible."[24] On the other hand, courts often rely on testimony by the attorney who drafted a will. Written extrinsic evidence seems more reliable than oral. But even a genuine written expression of a testator's wishes may have been intended as precatory rather than legally binding when it is not included in the will.

*Malpractice*  Malpractice suits have added a new dimension to the extrinsic evidence problem. Disappointed devisees have successfully sued attorneys for drafting wills which allegedly omitted a devise which the testator intended for them. The intended devisee is not required to seek reformation of the will since generally "the doctrine of reformation is not applicable to wills," but the court could use evidence outside the will to establish the testator's intent in a malpractice action.[25] However, other courts have refused to hold a drafter liable on the basis of evidence of the testator's intent which would be inadmissible in probate proceedings.[26]

*Mistake of Fact*  American courts do not usually correct a will allegedly made under a mistake of fact, such as the paternity of a child.[27] Materiality is the great difficulty; when a testator is mistaken as to a fact, it is often unclear what she would have desired had she known the truth.

Under the Uniform Probate Code, if a testator fails to provide in a will "for a living child solely because he believes the child to be dead," the child gets an intestate share.[28] This is a strong case for believing that a mistake was material. According to the second Restatement of Property, a donative transfer, including a will, should be set aside if it was caused by a mistake of fact, but the illustrations to this provision suggest that it will be hard to prove causation when the mistake is one of fact, as distinguished from a mistake in the terms of the will.[29] If a mistake amounts to an "insane delusion" the rule is different; this will be discussed in treating incapacity.

**24.** District of Columbia v. Estate of Parsons, 590 A.2d 133, 138 (D.C.App. 1991).

**25.** Hamilton v. Needham, 519 A.2d 172 (D.C.App.1986).

**26.** Mieras v. DeBona, 550 N.W.2d 202 (Mich.1996).

**27.** In re Estate of Angier, 552 A.2d 1121 (Pa.Super.1989).

**28.** Uniform Probate Code § 2–302(c). *See* *also* Calif.Prob.Code § 21622.

**29.** *Restatement, Second, of Property (Donative Transfers)* § 34.7, comm. e, illus. 9 (no rescission of gift to stepson when donor was unaware that his marriage was invalid).

*Fraud*   Courts are more receptive to claims of fraud than mistake. Here too it is necessary to show that the fraud induced the devise, but someone who misrepresents a fact to a testator probably considered the fact was material and it is not implausible to assume he was right. Thus a will leaving the testator's property to her daughters was set aside because they had falsely told her that their father had left all his property to his sons.[30] Even nondisclosure may amount to fraud if there is a confidential relationship between the testator and another.[31] Claims of fraud are usually linked with undue influence, which will be discussed in Section 7.3.

*Constructive Trusts*   The bar against adding words to a will does not apply where wrongful conduct was involved, e.g., a testator expressed a desire to make a new will leaving property to *A*, but *B*, the beneficiary of her existing will, prevented her from doing so by false representations and physical force. A devisee who "prevents the testator by fraud, duress, or undue influence from revoking the will and executing a new will in favor of another * * * holds the property thus acquired for the intended legatee."[32]

Constructive trusts (like other trusts) were historically enforced in equity and thus there is no right to trial by jury. This may explain why courts allow oral evidence of a decedent's intent in such suits; hostility to such evidence is partly based on the fear that inexperienced juries cannot assess it adequately. However, the Restatement of Torts allows a tort suit against anyone who "by fraud, duress or other tortious means intentionally prevents another from receiving from a third person an inheritance or gift that he would otherwise receive."[33]

*Promises*   Constructive trusts are also imposed on devisees who promised the testator that they would give the devised property to another person, e.g., a mother with an incompetent child, Mary, left half her estate to Mary's sister, Emily, who agreed to look after Mary. When Emily refused to do so, the court imposed a constructive trust on her. The promise, on which the constructive trust is based, can be inferred from the devisee's silence when the testator expressed her intent.[34] The trustee's promise need not be connected with making a will. If a decedent leaves a will unchanged in reliance on a devisee's promise, or makes no will at all, relying

---

**30.** Matter of Estate of Vick, 557 So.2d 760, 768–69 (Miss.1989).

**31.** Rood v. Newberg, 718 N.E.2d 886, 893 (Mass.App.Ct.1999) (because of confidential relationship daughter had a duty to disclose to testator that she was mistaken in believing son had stolen from her).

**32.** Latham v. Father Divine, 85 N.E.2d 168 (N.Y.1949). *See also Restatement, Third, of Property (Wills and Other Donative Transfers)* § 8.3, comm. 1 (2001).

**33.** *Restatement, Second, of Torts* § 774B (1979).

**34.** Kauzlarich v. Landrum, 274 N.E.2d 915 (Ill.App.1971).

on an heir's promise to give property to another, courts will impose a trust.[35] But the wishes decedent's must have been communicated to the devisee or heir during the decedent's lifetime.[36] This restriction seems odd, since a devisee would seem to be unjustly enriched by taking property which was intended for another, even if she learned of this intent only after the decedent's death.[37]

Courts impose a high standard of proof for a constructive trust. "The agreement to hold property in trust must be shown by clear and convincing evidence * * * because the proof must * * * substitute for the normal statutory requirements of the Wills Act."[38]

*Semi-secret Trusts* Some wills show on their face that a devisee was intended to give the devise to others but the intended beneficiaries are not identified in the will. These are called "semi-secret" trusts as contrasted with "secret" trusts in which the will gives no clue that any trust was intended. The Restatement of Trusts makes semi-secret trusts enforceable, and dispenses with the higher burden of proof required for constructive trusts in this situation.[39] But some courts refuse to enforce semi-secret trusts, e.g., when a will directed the executor to distribute the estate "in accordance with the verbal guidelines last given by me," the court held this was invalid, since the "guidelines" were not "in writing and attested in conformity with the statute of wills." Refusal to enforce a semi-secret trust does not leave the devisee unjustly enriched because he does not get to keep the property.[40] But the result leaves the *testator's heirs* unjustly enriched, since they will get property which was not intended for them.[41]

## § 6.2   Incorporation by Reference, Facts of Independent Significance and Pour–Over Wills

Multi-page wills can probated even though only the last page is signed. The earlier pages are "integrated" into the will if they were present when the will was executed. Writings which were not present at the time of execution can also be probated if they were incorporated in a will by reference.[1] Attempts to incorporate by

**35.** *Restatement, Third, of Trusts* § 18(2) (2001).

**36.** *Id.,* comm. f.

**37.** Hirsch, *Inheritance Law, Legal Contraptions, and the Problem of Doctrinal Change*, 79 Or.L.Rev. 527, 558n (2000).

**38.** *Restatement, Third, of Trusts* § 18, comm. h (2001).

**39.** *Id.,* comm. c, h (2001).

**40.** Matter or Reiman's Estate, 450 N.E.2d 928 (Ill.App.1983).

**41.** *Restatement, Third, of Trusts* § 18, comm. a (2001).

**§ 6.2**

**1.** Clark v. Greenhalge, 582 N.E.2d 949 (Mass.1991); Matter of Estate of Sneed, 953 P.2d 1111 (Okl.1998). New York does not recognize incorporation by reference. In re Philip, 192 A.D.2d 610 (N.Y.A.D.1993). *But cf.* In re Estate of Schmidt, 619 N.Y.S.2d 245 (Surr.1994) (statutory exception for published fee schedules).

reference fail if the identification in the will is not sufficiently precise, e.g., an attempt to have an unexecuted will incorporated by reference in a duly executed codicil failed because no reference in the codicil itself clearly designated the will.[2] But some courts permit incorporation if extrinsic evidence shows that the document in question was the one mentioned in the will.[3]

*Republication by Codicil*　A codicil which refers to an earlier will is said to "republish" it. This has the effect of incorporation by reference, allowing probate of an unexecuted will.[4] Incorporation of a typewritten document into a holographic codicil does not destroy its holographic character.[5]

*Future Documents*　An important limitation on incorporation by reference prevents testators from changing their wills informally. Any document to be incorporated must have been in existence when the will was executed. When a will left property to a friend to distribute "to the persons named in a letter or memorandum of instructions which I shall leave addressed to her," the letter could not be admitted.[6] It is not enough that the document *might have been* in existence before the will; its prior existence must be proved,[7] but according to the Restatement of Property this is presumed.[8] Courts sometimes say that the incorporated document must also *be referred to in the will* as an existing document,[9] but the Uniform Probate Code does not require this.[10]

When a codicil "republishes" an earlier will, a document produced between the time of execution of the will and the codicil can be incorporated.[11]

*Lists of Tangible Personalty*　The Uniform Probate Code allows wills to refer to a "written statement or list to dispose of items of tangible personal property" if the list is signed by the testator, even if it was prepared or altered after the execution of the will.[12] The restriction to tangible personal property reflects the idea that

**2.** Matter of Estate of Norton, 410 S.E.2d 484, 488 (N.C.1991).

**3.** In re Estate of McGahee, 550 So.2d 83 (Fla.App.1989) (paper clipped to the will).

**4.** *Restatement, Third, of Property (Wills and Other Donative Transfers)* § 3.6, comm. d (1998).

**5.** In re Foxworth's Estate, 50 Cal. Rptr. 237 (App.1966); *Restatement, Third, of Property (Wills and Other Donative Transfers)* § 3.6, comm. f (1998).

**6.** Hastings v. Bridge, 166 A. 273 (N.H.1933).

**7.** Tierce v. Macedonia United Meth. Church, 519 So.2d 451, 456 (Ala.1987).

**8.** *Restatement, Third, of Property (Wills and Other Donative Transfers)* § 3.6, comm. b (1998).

**9.** Estate of Sweet, 519 A.2d 1260 (Me.1987) (the "will must describe the extrinsic writing as an existing document"); *Restatement (Second) of Trusts* § 54, comm. c (1959).

**10.** Uniform Probate Code § 2–510, comment; *Restatement, Third, of Property (Wills and Other Donative Transfers)* § 3.6, comm. a (1998).

**11.** Clark v. Greenhalge, 582 N.E.2d 949 (Mass.1991).

**12.** Uniform Probate Code § 2–513.

less formality should be required for property of relatively small value, as tangible personalty is in most estates.[13] The requirement that the list be signed by the testator distinguishes this from incorporation by reference, since wills can incorporate writings by someone other than the testator. The Uniform Statutory Wills Act, for example, is designed to be incorporated by reference in wills.[14]

*Facts of Independent Significance*    If a will leaves property "to my wife" without naming her, a court must resort to evidence outside the will in order to identify the wife. The Uniform Probate Code, like the common law, allows wills to "dispose of property by reference to acts and events that have significance apart from their effect upon the dispositions made by the will, whether they occur before or after the execution of the will."[15] The rationale is that such facts are not likely to be seriously disputed. Courts have allowed devises even of the contents of a house or of a safe-deposit box under this theory.[16]

*Pour–Over Wills*    Both incorporation by reference and facts of independent significance have been used to validate a modern estate planning device, the "pour-over" will. A couple who had created a revocable trust later executed wills which left property to the trustees of the trust to be held pursuant to its terms. The ultimate beneficiaries of the will could only be ascertained by looking at the trust. The couple amended the trust after executing their wills. Could property passing under their wills be governed by the subsequent amendment of the trust? Earlier cases had refused to allow this, based on the restrictions against incorporating future documents. But this court upheld the pour-over devise by treating the trust as a fact of independent significance, since the trust contained assets other than those which the will poured into it.[17] This theory presents problems if the assets in the trust have only nominal value prior to the pour-over.[18]

The difficulties posed by the incorporation-by-reference and facts-of-independent-significance ideas have led most states to adopt statutes which expressly authorize pour-over wills. The Uniform Probate Code allows them "regardless of the existence, size,

---

**13.** Compare the exemption of sales of goods for less than $500 from the Statute of Frauds. Uniform Commercial Code § 2–201. *Cf.* Matter of Estate of Harrington, 850 P.2d 158 (Colo.App. 1993) (note attempting to devise $25,000 not covered).

**14.** Uniform Statutory Wills Act § 3.

**15.** Uniform Probate Code § 2–512. *See also Restatement, Second, of Trusts* § 54(c) (1959).

**16.** Matter of Estate of Nelson, 419 N.W.2d 915 (N.D.1988) ("personal items used in connection with my farm"); *Restatement, Third, of Property (Wills and Other Donative Transfers)* § 3.7, comm. c, e (1998).

**17.** Second Bank–State Street Trust Co. v. Pinion, 170 N.E.2d 350 (Mass. 1960).

**18.** *Restatement, Third, of Trusts* § 19, comm. h (2001).

or character of the corpus of the trust."[19] The UPC requires that
the trust terms be "set forth in a written instrument," but the
trust can be amended after the pour-over will is executed.[20]

Pour-over devises perform a useful function, allowing various
parts of an estate plan to be consolidated. Many persons wish to put
some of their assets into a living trust and have other assets pass to
a trust for the same beneficiaries when they die. Or spouses may
wish to put their respective assets into a trust for their common
children. Or a parent may wish to add property to a trust created
by a child for the parent's grandchildren. Administrative costs can
be reduced by consolidating trusts.

If a settlor revokes the receptacle trust before dying, the
Uniform Probate Code provides that the pour-over devise lapses
unless the will otherwise provides.[21] In Illinois, however, the devise
takes effect "according to the terms * * * of the trust as they
existed at the time of the termination."[22]

*Pour-up Trusts*    The parts of an estate plan can also be
merged by going in the other direction, *i.e.* by making an insurance
policy or death benefit under a pension plan payable to the trustee
under a will.[23] This technique has the advantage of not having to
draft two documents, a will and a trust; the drafter and testator
can focus their attention on the terms of the will which controls all
the testator's assets.

## § 6.3  Will Substitutes

*Comparison with Wills*    In cases involving wills, extrinsic evidence is generally excluded because the testator is unable to contradict possibly perjured testimony about his or her intent. Will
substitutes present a similar problem, but a more liberal admission
of extrinsic evidence may be appropriate for them. Most wills are
made to order for the testator, but the terms of multiple party
accounts (joint, trust or P.O.D.) usually appear on printed forms
drafted primarily to protect the bank rather than to express the
depositor's intention.[1]

**19.** Uniform Probate Code § 2–511.
In Tyson v. Henry, 514 S.E.2d 564
(N.C.App.1999) the terms of a trust
were given effect as having been incorporated by reference in a pour-over will
even though no property had been transferred to the trust.

**20.** Uniform Probate Code § 2–
511(a).

**21.** *Id.,* § 2–511(c).

**22.** In re Estate of Stern, 636 N.E.2d
939 (Ill.App.1994).

**23.** *Restatement, Third, of Trusts*
§ 19, comm. a(2) (2001); *Restatement,
Third, of Property (Wills and Other Donative Transfers)* § 3.8, comm. f (1998).

**§ 6.3**

**1.** Anderson v. Baker, 641 P.2d 1035,
1039 (Mont.1982). When handwritten
words conflict with the printed portion
of a form, the handwritten words control. Isbell v. Williams, 738 S.W.2d 20
(Tex.App.1987).

Nevertheless, some statutes exclude extrinsic evidence of intent,[2] or courts do so on the basis of the parol evidence rule.[3] Many persons open joint accounts simply for the convenience of having another party who can make deposits and withdrawals for them, without any intent that the other party succeed to the account when the depositor dies. Opinions often distinguish between "gift" and "convenience," e.g., "if the intent to transfer a present interest to the named survivors * * * is lacking, it will reduce the account to one of convenience only, and no survivorship right will be found."[4] This is an oversimplification; many persons who create joint accounts want the other party to make deposits and withdrawals for them *and also* receive the balance in the account when they die.

Courts sometimes use a constructive trust rationale to effectuate a decedent's intent to benefit persons not named in an account. When a father with six children put property into joint tenancy with one daughter, a court imposed a trust on the daughter since her father had intended to benefit all his children and she had "accepted title on that basis."[5]

Courts are more likely to reject extrinsic evidence of intent in construing a "custom-made" trust rather than a printed form. Although the statute of wills does not apply to inter-vivos transfers, the parol evidence rule does.[6] But trusts, like contracts, can be reformed to correct mistakes in the writing.[7] Thus a court reformed a trust, saying even though "wills cannot be reformed," living trusts "may be reformed after the death of the settlor for a unilateral[8] drafting mistake."[9]

*Type of Evidence* Trusts can be reformed only if there is " 'full, clear, and decisive proof' of mistake."[10] Similarly, evidence of an intent inconsistent with the form of a bank account must be

**2.** Baker v. Leonard, 843 P.2d 1050 (Wash.1993).

**3.** Cooper v. Crabb, 587 So.2d 236 (Miss.1991).

**4.** Offret v. DiDomenico, 623 N.E.2d 128, 130 (Ohio App. 1993).

**5.** Winsor v. Powell, 497 P.2d 292 (Kan.1972). *See also* Section 6.1.

**6.** First Nat. Bank v. Anthony, 557 A.2d 957, 960 (Me.1989). In the case of "Totten" trusts, however, written evidence of intent is so sketchy that extrinsic evidence is admissible to rebut the inferences of intent made by the law. *Restatement, Third, of Trusts* § 26, comm. a (2001).

**7.** *Restatement, Second, of Trusts* § 333 (1959); *Restatement, Second, of Contracts* § 155 (1981); Unif.Trust Code § 415.

**8.** In contracts, the mistake must usually be "mutual," i.e., shared by both parties, *Restatement, Second, of Contracts* § 155 (1981). Donative transfers are different. See Section 6.4.

**9.** In re Estate of Robinson, 720 So.2d 540, 541, 543 (Fla.App.1998). As to extending the reformation idea to wills see Section 6.1.

**10.** Loeser v. Talbot, 589 N.E.2d 301, 304 (Mass.1992).

"clear and convincing."[11] Courts tend to view extrinsic evidence offered by an interested party with suspicion. [12]

Declarations of intention by the decedent are admissible, but courts usually give especial weight to the circumstances. The fact that a written disposition appears unnatural may indicate that the decedent intended something else, e.g., when a father put one child's name on a bank account which amounted to over two-thirds of the father's assets, the account was awarded to the father's estate, since "no reason is shown why he would make such a sizeable gift" to one child.[13]

Some courts focus exclusively on evidence of a depositor's intent when the account was created. Subsequent evidence of a settlor's intent has been held inadmissible because this "would allow a settlor to revoke or modify a trust at his pleasure."[14] But most courts are not so strict. "The critical question is the intent of the alleged donor at the time the account was created * * * but subsequent events may be considered as having a bearing on" this.[15]

*Protection of Third Parties*   When extrinsic evidence of intent contradicts a writing, third parties who have reasonably relied on the writing are protected. Thus a bank is not liable if it pays sums in a multiple party account according to its terms, even if they do not reflect the decedent's intention, unless the bank has previously received written notice not to do so.[16]

## § 6.4   Deeds of Land: Reformation, Constructive and Resulting Trusts

If *A* executes a deed which conveys land to *B*, can *A* or a third person show by evidence outside the deed that *B* was not intended to keep the land? The parol evidence rule may bar such evidence,[1] but there are theories to get around the rule. Parol evidence can be used to show that a deed was not intended to operate, e.g., a mother who had deeded land to her daughter was allowed to cancel the deed on the ground that she had signed the deed only to avoid

---

**11.** Calif.Prob.Code § 5302; Matter of Estate of Martin, 559 N.E.2d 1112, 1114 (Ill.App.1990).

**12.** Sawyer v. Lancaster, 719 S.W.2d 346, 350 (Tex.App.1986). *See also* In re Estate of Lambert, 785 N.E.2d 1129 (Ind.App.2003) (interested testimony barred by Dead Man statute).

**13.** Estate of Stanley v. Sandiford, 337 S.E.2d 248, 251 (S.C.App.1985).

**14.** Bonney v. Granger, 356 S.E.2d 138 (S.C.App.1987).

**15.** In re Estate of Blom, 600 N.E.2d 427, 429 (Ill.App.1992).

**16.** Uniform Probate Code § 6–226. *See also Restatement, Second, of Contracts* § 155, comm. f (1981).

**§ 6.4**

**1.** Rubenstein v. Sela, 672 P.2d 492 (Ariz.App.1983). Parol evidence may be admissible, however, to resolve an ambiguity in the deed. Bledsoe v. Hill, 747 P.2d 10 (Colo.App.1987).

probate with no intent to give the daughter a present interest.[2] Parol evidence can also show that a deed was conditional on a promise of supporting the grantor. Someone who was induced by fraud to sign a paper which he did not realize was a deed can have it set aside.

*Reformation*   Another well-settled exception to the parol evidence rule allows mistakes in a deed to be reformed, e.g. when a deed was intended for a husband alone but was made out by mistake to the husband and his wife.[3] Relief may be denied if the mistake was the product of "supine negligence;" a person cannot claim "he did not understand what he was signing when there was nothing to prevent him from merely reading the deed to discover its contents."[4] But grantors who had "great difficulty in communicating in the English language and did not understand the legal implications of the term "life estate" were able to have a deed reformed.[5]

Opinions differ as to whether the mistake must be mutual. The Restatement of Contracts generally gives relief only when *"both* parties as to" a writing are mistaken.[6] When a husband put a house in joint tenancy with his wife, his executor could not recover the house on proof that he had not intended to create a joint tenancy; his "hidden intention," undisclosed to his wife was irrelevant.[7] However, some courts allow reformation of unilateral mistakes in a gratuitous transfer if the donee has not changed position in reliance upon the transfer.[8]

Reformation is equitable relief and "equity will not ordinarily aid a volunteer," i.e., the recipient of a gift may be barred from seeking reformation.[9] But nominal consideration accompanied by 'love and affection' has been held sufficient to allow reformation.[10] Also, a donee has been permitted to sue the donor's heirs for reformation if the donor himself would not have opposed it.[11]

---

**2.** Myers v. Weems, 876 P.2d 861 (Or.App.1994).

**3.** Geissel v. Galbraith, 695 P.2d 1316 (Nev.1985). As to the extension of the idea of reformation to wills see Section 6.1.

**4.** Yohe v. Yohe, 353 A.2d 417, 420 (Pa.1976). *See also* Wright v. Blevins, 705 P.2d 113 (Mont.1985) (no relief to party who signs a deed without reading it).

**5.** Yano v. Yano, 697 P.2d 1132, 1134–35 (Ariz.App.1985).

**6.** *Restatement, Second, of Contracts* § 155 (1981).

**7.** Estate of Levine, 178 Cal.Rptr. 275 (App.1981).

**8.** Yohe v. Yohe, 353 A.2d 417, 424 (Pa.1976) (concurring opinion). *See also Restatement, Second, of Contracts* § 155, comm. b (1981).

**9.** *Restatement, Second, of Contracts* § 155, comm. d (1981).

**10.** Snyder v. Peterson, 814 P.2d 1204 (Wash.App.1991).

**11.** Zabolotny v. Fedorenko, 315 N.W.2d 668 (N.D.1982).

Courts distinguish between mistakes as to the contents of a deed and mistakes of fact; they refuse to upset deeds just because the grantor acted under an erroneous factual supposition, e.g. when a father gave his son land under which gas was later discovered.[12] However, the second Restatement of Property says a mistake of fact may be significant enough to justify setting aside or reforming a transfer.[13]

*Constructive Trusts*  Constructive trusts are imposed on devisees who promised the testator to give the property to another person. A similar rule applies to inter-vivos transfers where the transferee at the time of the transfer[14] promised to hold the land for the transferor or for a third person. The Restatement of Trusts distinguishes between inter-vivos and testamentary transfers. A devisee or heir always "holds the property upon a constructive trust for the person for whom he agreed to hold it,"[15] but a constructive trust is imposed on inter-vivos transferees only in certain circumstances. However, the categories of cases in which constructive trusts are imposed on transfers by deed are so broad that the distinction between deeds and wills has little practical significance. First, a constructive trust will be imposed on a grantee who was guilty of fraud.[16] Fraud includes promises which were made without intent to perform; this can be inferred from refusal to perform a promise.[17] A grantee who intended to perform and later changed his mind is not guilty of fraud,[18] but some cases impose a trust on the basis of "constructive fraud."[19]

A constructive trust is also imposed if the grantor and grantee were in a "confidential relationship."[20] For some courts a confidential relationship always exists among family members, but not for others.[21] A confidential relationship can exist between unrelated friends.[22] Some opinions suggest that "confidential relationship"

---

**12.** Thomas v. Reid, 608 P.2d 1123, 1124 (N.M.1980).

**13.** *Restatement, Second, of Property (Donative Transfers)* § 34.7, comm. d (1990). *See also* Berger v. United States, 487 F.Supp. 49 (W.D.Pa.1980) (settlor can rescind a trust created under the mistaken belief he was going to obtain a government position).

**14.** A promise made *after* the transfer does not give rise to a constructive trust, Walsh v. Walsh, 841 P.2d 831 (Wyo.1992), but a declaration of trust, if in writing, may be enforceable.

**15.** *Restatement, Second, of Trusts* § 55 (1959). A transfer made in contemplation of death is treated like a will for this purpose. *Id.* § 45(1)(c).

**16.** *Restatement, Third, of Trusts* § 24(2)(a) (2001).

**17.** March v. Gerstenschlager, 436 S.W.2d 6 (Mo.1969).

**18.** *Restatement, Third, of Trusts* § 24, comm. e (2001) (refusal to perform promise is "some but not conclusive evidence of" fraud).

**19.** Baizley v. Baizley, 734 A.2d 1117, 1118 (Me.1999).

**20.** *Restatement, Third, of Trusts* § 24(2)(b) (2001).

**21.** Rudow v. Fogel, 426 N.E.2d 155, 157 (Mass.App.Ct.1981). A confidential relationship is commonly found between spouses. Rajanna v. KRR Investments, Inc., 810 S.W.2d 548 (Mo.App.1991).

**22.** David v. Russo, 415 N.E.2d 531 (Ill.App.1980).

means an unequal one.[23] This seems to confuse undue influence (where the idea of a "confidential relationship" also plays an important role) with the question whether oral promises should be enforced. One court held that while there was no confidential relationship between a father and daughter to support a claim of undue influence, "for the purpose of imposing a constructive trust, a confidential relationship can be based on an agreement."[24] A confidential relationship makes it plausible that the parties made an agreement without reducing it to writing.[25]

Oral trusts are also enforced on an "estoppel" theory when a beneficiary has relied on the trust, e.g. after a father deeded a farm to his two oldest children to hold it for all his children, the younger children who had worked to improve the farm could enforce the trust.[26]

Section 7 of the Statute of Frauds which requires that trusts of land "shall be manifested and proved" by a signed writing poses a problem to the enforcement of oral trusts. Most American jurisdictions have adopted this along with Section 8 which excepts trusts which "arise or result by the implication or construction of law." Courts have made such extensive use of the exception in Section 8 for "resulting" and "constructive" trusts that the rule of section 7 has become almost, but not quite meaningless.

The Uniform Trusts Act provides that if a trust is unenforceable on account of the Statute of Frauds, a trustee who fails to perform the trust must "convey the property to the settlor or his successor in interest."[27] This prevents the trustee from being unjustly enriched but does not effectuate the settlor's intent if the intent was to benefit a third party. The Third Restatement of Trusts adopts a modified form of this rule.[28]

*Resulting Trusts*  When an express trust fails to provide for a certain situation, there may be a resulting trust for the settlor. In this section we focus on what is commonly called the "purchase money" resulting trust. "Where the property is purchased and the title is taken in the name of one person, but the purchase price is paid by another, * * * [the person] who furnished the consideration money is presumed to intend to acquire a corresponding beneficial interest in the lands purchased."[29] The Restatement

---

**23.** Estates of Kalwitz v. Kalwitz, 717 N.E.2d 904, 913 (Ind.App.1999) (confidential relationship arises "where one party dominates a weaker party").

**24.** Heck v. Archer, 927 P.2d 495, 502 (Kan.App.1996).

**25.** Thompson v. Nesheim, 159 N.W.2d 910, 918 (Minn.1968).

**26.** Potucek v. Potucek, 719 P.2d 14, 18 (Kan.App.1986).

**27.** Uniform Trusts Act § 16.

**28.** *Restatement, Third, of Trusts* § 24, comm. h (2001).

**29.** Browder v. Hite, 602 S.W.2d 489, 492 (Tenn.App.1980). *See also Restatement, Third, of Trusts* § 9 (2001). When

requires fraud or a confidential relation to enforce a constructive trust but not for a resulting trust.[30] Perhaps the distinction is based on the fact that a deed normally means what it says and the signer should understand this. But when a buyer of land instructs the seller to put title in the name of a third person, this instruction is often not reflected in a signed writing; the grantor signs the deed but not the person who pays the price. In any event, the differing legal treatment of resulting and constructive trusts is not of great practical significance; if a gratuitous conveyance was intended to create a trust, the beneficiary can usually prove "fraud" or a "confidential relation." Conversely, the presumption of a purchase-money resulting trust can be rebutted by evidence that the payer intended to give the land to the person in whose name title was placed.[31]

When the person who pays for land and the transferee named in the deed are related by blood or marriage, courts presume that the payer intended a gift to the transferee rather than a trust.[32] The gift-presumption has been applied to a mother-in-law who paid for a house which was conveyed to her son-in-law,[33] but not an aunt who bought a home for her nephew.[34] Such distinctions seem arbitrary, but they are not very important because evidence of the parties' actual intent is always admissible.

A purchase money resulting trust can arise from a sale on credit, e.g. when a mother and son agreed that a house would be deeded to the son in order to qualify for a veteran's loan, but the mother would make all the payments and own the house.[35] However, if there is no such agreement before title passes, a resulting trust does not arise in favor of someone who furnishes funds to the owner subsequent to the purchase.[36] If someone pays part of the price of land, the resulting trust presumption arises only as to part,[37] but the land is not beneficially owned in proportion to contributions if the parties intended otherwise.[38]

*Nature of Proof* Before granting reformation or imposing a constructive or resulting trust courts require evidence that is

the parties intend to give a beneficial interest to a person other than the payer, this is treated as a constructive trust. *Id.*, comm. c.

**30.** *Compare Restatement, Third, of Trusts* § 9 *with id.* § 24 (2001).

**31.** *Id.*, § 9(1)(a) (2001); Thor v. McDearmid, 817 P.2d 1380 (Wash.App. 1991).

**32.** *Restatement, Third, of Trusts* § 9(2) (2001); Durward v. Nelson, 481 N.W.2d 586 (N.D.1992) (parents pay for land deeded to their son and his wife).

**33.** Matter of Estate of Hock's, 655 P.2d 1111 (Utah 1982).

**34.** Peterson v. Kabrich, 691 P.2d 1360 (Mont.1984).

**35.** Watkins v. Watkins, 351 S.E.2d 331, 334 (N.C.App.1986).

**36.** Leicht v. Quirin, 558 N.E.2d 715 (Ill.App.1990).

**37.** *Restatement, Third, of Trusts* § 9, comm. c (2001).

**38.** Bassett v. Bassett, 798 P.2d 160, 168 (N.M.1990).

"clear, convincing, unequivocal, and unmistakable."[39] Proof sometimes falls short of the clear and convincing standard, not because the testimony is conflicting but because the parties' intentions were indefinite or vague.[40]

Proof may be circumstantial, e.g., a grantor's staying in possession is evidence that he intended to retain a beneficial interest in property.[41] Statements of intent are also admissible if they relate to the time when the property was transferred. A person who conveys land with the intent that the grantee own it beneficially cannot later declare that the grantee holds in trust.[42] But statements of intent after a deed was executed may be admitted "to show intention at the time of the transaction."[43]

Litigation concerning oral trusts sometimes arises long after the trust was created, because the statute of limitations starts to run only when the transferee discloses his intention not to perform the trust.[44]

*Clean Hands*   Courts of equity may deny relief to plaintiffs who have "unclean hands." Constructive and resulting trusts often involve attempts to disguise ownership. A man who had land put in his brother's name in order to avoid attachments under outstanding judgments was not allowed to enforce a resulting trust.[45] Many courts reject the clean-hands defense, however, sometimes on the ground that even if the settlor intended to defraud creditors, none were actually harmed by the transaction,[46] or because harm to third persons such as creditors is irrelevant to a suit against the trustee.[47] Others reject the defense on the ground that the defendants' fault was greater than the plaintiff's,[48] *e.g.,* because the defendant suggested the transfer,[49] or there was "great inequality of condition" between the parties.[50] Since acceptance or rejection of the clean-hands defense is a discretionary matter, the result in a given case is hard to predict.

**39.** In re Estate of McCormick, 634 N.E.2d 341, 345 (Ill.App.1994).

**40.** Engel v. Breske, 681 P.2d 263 (Wash.App.1984) (intent was "very loose, very indefinite").

**41.** In re Estate of Koch, 697 N.E.2d 931 (Ill.App.1998) (husband's continued management of property put in wife's name shows no gift intended).

**42.** Fowler v. Montgomery, 326 S.E.2d 765, 766–67 (Ga.1985).

**43.** Ashbaugh v. Ashbaugh, 152 S.E.2d 888, 892 (Ga.1966).

**44.** Estates of Kalwitz v. Kalwitz, 717 N.E.2d 904, 914 (Ind.App.1999).

**45.** American Nat. Bank and Trust v. Vinson, 653 N.E.2d 13, 15 (Ill.App. 1995).

**46.** Hilliard v. Hilliard, 844 P.2d 54 (Mont.1992).

**47.** Beelman v. Beelman, 460 N.E.2d 55, 58 (Ill.App.1984).

**48.** Locken v. Locken, 650 P.2d 803, 805 (Nev.1982).

**49.** Samuelson v. Ingraham, 77 Cal. Rptr. 750, 753 (App.1969).

**50.** Hinson v. Hinson, 343 S.E.2d 266, 274 (N.C.App.1986).

*Third Parties* The law protects third persons who have relied on a deed which does not reflect the intention of the parties. Reformation of deeds is not granted if "rights of third parties, such as good faith purchasers for value will be unfairly affected."[51] However, when because of fraud, the grantor did not understand that the document was a deed, it is void and even a bona fide purchaser from the grantee does not acquire title to the land.[52]

If *A* conveys property to *B*, or pays for land which is put in *B*'s name, even if they intended that *B* hold it in trust, if *B* sells the property, a bona fide purchaser for value takes free of the beneficiary's claims,[53] although the beneficiary can impress a trust on the sale proceeds, or hold the trustee personally liable.[54] The trust can be enforced against transferees who had notice of the trust, including "constructive notice" arising from possession of the property.[55] Even a person who acquires property from the trustee without notice is not protected unless he paid value for the purchase.[56]

Creditors of a trustee who relied on the trustee's apparent ownership may be allowed to satisfy their claims out of the trust property. "The actual owner of trust property will be estopped from claiming a resulting trust in the property where the record owner obtained credit upon the strength of ownership,"[57] but some say this applies only if the beneficiary of the trust knew of the creditors' action in reliance.[58] If a trustee becomes bankrupt, the trustee in bankruptcy has powers of avoidance equivalent to those of a bona fide purchaser which may defeat the rights of the beneficiaries.[59]

*Personal Property* The rather complex rules discussed in this section involve only land. When the beneficial ownership of personal property is at stake, it is easier to show that the form of title is not conclusive, because the Statute of Frauds does not apply.[60]

**51.** *Restatement, Second, of Contracts* § 155 (1979).

**52.** Pedersen v. Bibioff, 828 P.2d 1113 (Wash.App.1992).

**53.** *Restatement, Second, of Trusts* § 284 (1959).

**54.** McMahon v. McMahon, 422 N.E.2d 1150, 1153 (Ill.App.1981).

**55.** American Nat. Bank and Trust v. Vinson, 653 N.E.2d 13, 16 (Ill.App. 1995).

**56.** Granado v. Granado, 760 P.2d 148 (N.M.1988).

**57.** Gary–Wheaton Bank v. Meyer, 473 N.E.2d 548, 555 (Ill.App.1984).

**58.** John Deere Indus. Equipment Co. v. Gentile, 459 N.E.2d 611 (Ohio App.1983).

**59.** 11 U.S.C. §§ 541(d), 544

**60.** Estate of Davenport v. C.I.R., 184 F.3d 1176, 1184 (10th Cir.1999).

# Chapter 7

# INCAPACITY AND UNDUE INFLUENCE

*Table of Sections*

## § 7.1  Incapacity

*Age Requirements* Modern American statutes typically require that a testator be at least 18 years old in order to execute a valid will.[1] The same limitation applies to inter vivos gifts, but if a minor fails to disaffirm a gift within a reasonable time after reaching majority, it becomes valid through ratification.[2]

*Mental Capacity* Most American statutes do not define testamentary capacity for adults; they simply say that the testator must be of "sound mind."[3] However, the California Probate Code defines incapacity in words which reflect the common law: either "(1) The individual does not have sufficient mental capacity to be able to (A) understand the nature of the testamentary act, (B) understand and recollect the nature of the individual's property[4], or (C) remember and understand the individual's relations to living descendants, spouse, and parents, and those whose interests are affected by the

---

### § 7.1

**1.** Uniform Probate Code § 2–501; Calif.Prob.Code § 6100.

**2.** *Restatement, Second, of Property (Donative Transfers)* § 34.4, comm. b (1990).

**3.** Uniform Probate Code § 2–501. Although the provision refers to "making" a will, the same standard applies to

revoking one. Wood v. Bettis, 880 P.2d 961 (Or.App.1994) (destruction of will by testator who lacked capacity did not revoke it).

**4.** *Cf.* Wood v. Smith, [1993] Ch. 90, 114 (finding incapacity when testator thought his estate was much smaller than it actually was).

will;" or "(2) The individual suffers from a mental disorder with symptoms including delusions or hallucinations, which delusions and hallucinations result in the individual's devising property in a way which, except for the existence of the delusions or hallucinations, the individual would not have done."[5]

*Insane Delusion* A testator with an otherwise high degree of intelligence may suffer from the second type of incapacity mentioned in the statute, generally referred to as "insane delusion." A testator's mistaken belief is not an "insane delusion" if there was some rational basis for it.[6] In order for the challenge to succeed the will must be the product of the delusion. Thus a will, allegedly motivated by an insane delusion that contestant intended to harm the testator, was probated when the court found that the testator had other reasons for the will.[7] An insane delusion sometimes invalidates only part of a will.

*General Incapacity* Far more often wills are rejected for general mental incapacity. Medical evidence is often used to determine capacity. Experts who never saw the testator can render opinions based on the testator's medical records, but testimony by doctors who treated the testator is more common. Medical testimony may be either rejected or discounted because the doctor's contact with the patient was too far removed from the time when the will was executed, e.g., a psychiatrist's testimony that the testator had "degenerative dementia" several weeks after the will's execution was outweighed by witnesses to the will who testified affirmatively as to the testator's capacity.[8]

Subscribing witnesses, even if they are not experts, can offer an opinion about the testator's capacity. The force of their testimony is enhanced if they knew the testator well, or at least had a substantial conversation with the testator when the will was signed. An attestation clause may undercut subscribing witnesses who testify that the testator *lacked* capacity.[9] Some lawyers make a tape recording of the execution to show that the testator was "making sense" at the relevant time.[10]

*Naturalness of Will* Some have suggested that our rules on capacity represent a veiled limitation on testamentary freedom. Juries are thought to reject wills which they find unfair,[11] but

---

**5.** Cal.Prob.Code § 6100.5(a).

**6.** Akers v. Hodel, 871 F.2d 924, 935 (10th Cir.1989). As to a simple mistaken belief by the testator, see Section 6.1.

**7.** Matter of Yett's Estate, 606 P.2d 1174 (Or.App.1980).

**8.** Bishop v. Kenny, 466 S.E.2d 581 (Ga.1996).

**9.** In re Estate of Chlebos, 550 N.E.2d 1069 (Ill.App.1990). See Section 4.3.

**10.** In re Estate of Smith, 827 So.2d 673, 676 (Miss. 2002) (court relies on videotape of execution in finding capacity).

**11.** Schoenblum, *Will Contests: An Empirical Study*, 22 Real Prop. Prob. and Trust J. 607, 626 (1987) (jury finds

"unnaturalness" as evidence of incapacity is also mentioned in judicial opinions. For example, a devise to a non-relative "was unexpected and unnatural. * * * The fact that the decedent made such an unlikely disposition of his one-third share of the family farm may be given significant weight by the factfinder."[12]

A will which on its face seems unnatural may be upheld when a reason for the disposition appears, e.g., a will which disinherited the testator's grandchildren was probated after her attorney testified that the testator wanted to leave everything to her sister-in-law "because [she] had been good to her."[13] Some lawyers favor stating the reasons for an unusual disposition in the will itself.

Sudden changes in a testator's wishes are viewed with suspicion. Thus a deed and will which altered an "estate plan of long standing" were voided for incapacity as "unnatural."[14] Conversely, the fact that a disputed will is similar to prior wills helps to refute claims of incapacity.[15]

## § 7.2  Conservatorship and Durable Powers of Attorney

All states have procedures for appointing a conservator or guardian for someone who is unable to manage property. A petition to have a conservator appointed typically must allege "the inability of the proposed conservatee to substantially manage his or her own financial resources, or to resist fraud or undue influence."[1] In virtually all states someone for whom a conservator has been appointed can make a will.[2] Conversely, the fact that proceedings to appoint a conservator for a testator were dismissed because he was found competent is not conclusive as to his testamentary capacity.[3]

When the question of capacity arises as to an inter vivos gift, on the other hand, a conservatorship is in many states conclusive, and any gift thereafter made is voidable.[4] Under the Uniform

for contestants more often than judges do). Jury verdicts may be avoided or controlled by summary judgment or judgment n.o.v. Quarterman v. Quarterman, 493 S.E.2d 146 (Ga.1997) (summary judgment).

**12.** Estate of Record, 534 A.2d 1319, 1322–23 (Me.1987).

**13.** Doyle v. Schott, 582 N.E.2d 1057, 1060 (Ohio App.1989).

**14.** Matter of Guardianship & Conserv. of Estate of Tennant, 714 P.2d 122, 129 (Mont.1986).

**15.** *In re* Estate of Camin's, 323 N.W.2d 827, 836 (Neb.1982).

**§ 7.2**

**1.** Cal.Prob.Code § 1821(a)(5). Cf. Uniform Probate Code § 5–401(2).

**2.** Conservatorship of Bookasta, 265 Cal.Rptr. 1, 3 (App.1989). In Oklahoma, however, a will of a person under guardianship must be signed in the presence of a judge. Myers v. Maxey, 915 P.2d 940 (Okl.App.1995).

**3.** In re Estate of Wagner, 522 N.W.2d 159 (Neb.1994).

**4.** O'Brien v. Dudenhoeffer, 19 Cal. Rptr.2d 826 (App.1993). *Restatement, Third, of Property (Wills and Other Donative Transfers)* § 8.1, comm. h (2001) speaks only of a "rebuttable presumption" of incapacity.

Probate Code appointment of a conservator "vests title in the conservator as trustee to all property of the protected person," and the conservatee's interest therein "is not assignable or transferable."[5]

The distinction between wills and gifts raises the question of will substitutes. Many courts have equated will substitutes with wills for this purpose; changing the beneficiaries of a P.O.D. accounts, for example, was "in effect, a testamentary disposition" and so the guardianship was "only prima facie evidence" of incapacity.[6]

The question of incapacity may also arise when the settlor seeks to revoke a revocable trust. Some trusts provide a mechanism for determining capacity. A settlor's attempt to amend a trust after she had moved into a nursing home was ineffective because the trust said that this would render her incompetent to revoke the trust.[7]

*Gifts Without a Conservatorship* Even when no conservatorship has been created, a gift may be set aside if a donor is incapacitated at the time of the gift, either by a conservator later appointed for the donor, or by the donor's personal representative if the donor has died.[8] Such a suit is barred, however, if the donor later recovered capacity and ratified the gift.

The Restatement of Trusts suggests that "a standard slightly higher than that for a will" is appropriate for irrevocable gifts and trusts; as to the latter, the donor or settlor must be able to "understand the effects the disposition may have on the future financial security of the settlor/donor" and his or her dependents.[9] A gift which renders the donor a pauper is likely to appear unnatural. This is not an issue in transfers which take effect at death.

A long time may elapse between the making of an inter vivos gift and a determination of the donor's capacity. During this interval the donee may transfer the property to others, or change position in reliance on the gift. If the donee sells the property to a bona fide purchaser for value, the latter is protected.[10] But persons

**5.** Uniform Probate Code §§ 5–421–2. An order for a *limited* conservatorship may specify that only part of the conservatee's property passes to the conservator.

**6.** Witt v. Ward, 573 N.E.2d 201 (Ohio App.1989).

**7.** Manning v. Glens Falls Nat. Bank, 697 N.Y.S.2d 203 (App.Div.1999).

**8.** Howe v. Johnston, 660 N.E.2d 380 (Mass.App.Ct.1996). In Olson v. Toy, 54 Cal.Rptr.2d 29 (App.1996), the devisees of the settlor of a living trust were allowed to bring suit to set aside the trust.

**9.** *Restatement, Third, of Trusts* § 11, comments b and c (2001).

**10.** First Interstate Bank v. First Wyo. Bank, 762 P.2d 379 (Wyo.1988) (mortgagee from buyer of land protected even though sale was voidable for incapacity).

to whom the donee had given the property are subject to suit.[11] And if a transfer occurs after the transferor has been adjudicated incompetent, the judgment may constitute constructive notice.[12]

*Transfers by Conservators* Some persons cannot meet even the relatively low standard which the law sets for testamentary capacity. Distribution of their property under the intestacy laws may produce an unsatisfactory solution. Can a conservator make a will for such a person? The answer in nearly all jurisdictions has traditionally been no,[13] but there is now a trend the other way.[14] Conservators have been authorized to create revocable trusts, which are the functional equivalent of wills. [15]

Many states allow conservators to make gifts of a conservatee's property. Irrevocable gifts can save income taxes and transfer taxes as well. Many statutes expressly mention tax savings as a justification for such gifts,[16] but these are not the only ones. A conservator may create a trust for the conservatee and her incompetent spouse who would otherwise take outright when the conservatee died.[17] The basic test is "the likelihood from all the circumstances that the conservatee as a reasonably prudent person would take the proposed action if the conservatee had the capacity to do so."[18] The relationship of the proposed donees to the donor is relevant; dependent family members have a strong claim, but others may also be included if the conservatee while competent had made gifts to them or they are named in the conservatee's will.[19] Such gifts should be authorized only if they leave enough property for the conservatee's prospective needs.

Some courts have held that the power to revoke a trust is "personal to the settlor" and cannot be exercised by a conservator,[20] but the Uniform Probate Code expressly authorizes conservators (with court authorization) to exercise a power to revoke.[21]

---

**11.** Robertson v. Robertson, 654 P.2d 600 (Okl.1982).

**12.** Huntington Nat. Bank v. Toland, 594 N.E.2d 1103 (Ohio App.1991).

**13.** *Restatement, Second, of Property (Donative Transfers)* § 34.5, comm. b (1990); *cf.* In re Estate of Garrett, 100 S.W.3d 72, 76 (Ark.App.2003) (making a will is too "personal" to be performed by an agent).

**14.** Cal.Prob.Code § 2580(b)(13); Unif.Prob.Code § 5–411(a)(7).

**15.** *Restatement, Third, of Trusts* § 11, comm. f (2001).

**16.** Conn.Gen.Stat. § 45a–655(e)(C).

**17.** *Restatement, Third, of Trusts* § 11 illus. 3 (2001).

**18.** Cal.Prob.Code § 2583 (k).

**19.** Cal.Prob.Code § 2583; *Restatement, Second, of Property (Donative Transfers)* § 34.5, illus. 5 (1990) (gift to nephew of ward whom ward had supported in the past).

**20.** In re Guardianship of Lee, 982 P.2d 539, 541 (Okl.Civ.App.1999).

**21.** Uniform Probate Code § 5–411(a)(4). Cal.Prob.Code § 2580(b)(11) also allows conservators to exercise a power to revoke unless the trust shows an intent to reserve the right exclusively to the settlor.

*Durable Powers of Attorney* Most statutes require prior court approval for gifts or other transfers by conservators of a conservatee's property. Because court proceedings are expensive and embarrassing to family members when they involve proof of a relative's incapacity, people have started to use durable powers of attorney to have their affairs managed.[22] Agents under a power of attorney, like conservators, are fiduciaries, but they are created and usually function without court proceedings. An "attorney" under such a power is not necessarily or even usually a lawyer.

Traditionally the powers of an agent/attorney ceased whenever the principal became incompetent. This rule made agency useless as a device for managing an incompetent's property, and so it was changed by a Uniform Durable Power of Attorney Act which has been adopted (with variations) in most states. A power of attorney is durable when it states that it "shall not be affected by the subsequent disability or incapacity of the principal" or words to that effect. Some persons prefer a "springing" power, which only comes into effect when the signer becomes incompetent.[23] A durable power is effective only if it is executed while the principal is legally competent; someone who is already incompetent can not confer a power.

Conservators have such powers as are conferred by statute, sometimes modified by the terms of the court order appointing them. The powers conferred by a power of attorney, on the other hand, depend on its terms. Traditionally powers have been strictly construed. They are often interpreted not to allow the attorney to make gifts,[24] especially when the power is held by a family member who wishes to make gifts to himself or his family, because of the general prohibition against fiduciaries engaging in transactions in which they have a conflict of interest.[25] But some more recent opinions have allowed them, e.g., children under a power of attorney conferred by their mother could make gifts to themselves and their families.[26]

Attorneys often prepare durable powers so their clients can avoid conservatorship in case they become incompetent. The plan-

**22.** McGovern, *Trusts, Custodianships and Durable Powers of Attorney*, 27 Real Prop. Prob. and Trust J. 1 (1992). Durable powers for health care will be discussed in Section 14.5.

**23.** Uniform Probate Code § 5–501, Comment. *See also* Cal.Prob.Code § 4129.

**24.** Estate of Lennon v. Lennon, 29 P.3d 1258, 1267 (Wash.App. 2001).

**25.** Kunewa v. Joshua, 924 P.2d 559 (Haw.App.1996). As to the general pro-hibition against self-dealing by fiduciaries see Section 12.9.

**26.** LeCraw v. LeCraw, 401 S.E.2d 697, 699 (Ga.1991). In In re Estate of Naumoff, 754 N.Y.S.2d 70 (App.Div. 2003), the court held invalid most of the gifts to herself made by a child under a power of attorney, but not those which were accompanied by similar gifts to her sibling.

ner should consider authorizing the attorney to use the power to transfer property to a trust. in order to take advantage of the implied powers of trustees.

## § 7.3   Undue Influence

Wills and inter-vivos transfers are often challenged as being the product of undue influence. The standards applied to the two types of transfers are generally the same.[1] Sometimes only a particular provision is challenged. A devise of $100,000 was found invalid because of the devisee's undue influence over the testator, but the rest of the will was probated because the tainted devise was "severable."[2]

Undue influence may also invalidate the revocation of a will. When it prevents the making of a will or gift the intended beneficiaries have a tort action against the person whose influence frustrated the gift or will.[3]

Claims of undue influence and incapacity are commonly combined. The same evidence may be relevant to both issues, since findings of undue influence are often predicated on the mental weakness of the testator/donor. Conversely, the fact that a testator was strong minded and intelligent is often cited in finding no undue influence.[4] Expert testimony is occasionally heard, although this is less common in undue influence than in incapacity challenges. The testimony of the subscribing witnesses to a will is also less important in claims of undue influence, since the witnesses might be unaware of influence exerted on the testator at times other than the moment of the will's execution.[5]

As in claims of incapacity, courts often stress the naturalness or unnaturalness of the disposition, e.g., "the substantial bequest to [the devisee] is * * * suspicious," since "he was no more than a casual acquaintance" of the testator.[6] Conversely, in rejecting a claim of undue influence "the will's terms were reasonable and

**§ 7.3**

**1.** McPeak v. McPeak, 593 N.W.2d 180, 186 (Mich.App. 1999) (rejecting claim that instruction given in an action regarding change of insurance beneficiaries was appropriate only for will contests) Compare the test(s) for incapacity. Section 7.2.

**2.** Estate of Lane, 492 So.2d 395 (Fla.App.1986).

**3.** *Restatement, Second, of Torts* § 774B (1977); Allen v. Hall, 974 P.2d 199 (Or.1999) (decedent's intent to devise property to plaintiff blocked by de-

fendant's misrepresentations). Compare the cases imposing a constructive trust in this situation. Section 6.1.

**4.** Pascale v. Pascale, 549 A.2d 782 (N.J.1988) (donor was a shrewd businessman). *But see* In re Estate of Miller, 778 N.E.2d 262, 267 (Ill.App. 2002) (undue influence found even though decedent was legally competent).

**5.** Succession of Hamiter, 519 So.2d 341, 347 (La.App.1988).

**6.** Matter of Estate of Dankbar, 430 N.W.2d 124, 131 (Iowa 1988).

natural.''[7] One observer has suggested that contests based on undue influence act "as a form of forced heirship" requiring that property be left to a spouse or blood relatives.[8] But relatively few wills are successfully challenged. According to one survey only about one in a hundred wills are contested at all, and of those which are, the proponent has a "statistically overwhelming likelihood of success.''[9]

Some courts focus on the impropriety of the influencer's conduct, e.g., "improper devices" were used to sway the testator, such as taking advantage of her belief in the supernatural by transmitting purported advice from dead relatives.[10] Claims of undue influence often involve misrepresentations made to the testator. Courts distinguish between undue influence and "reasonable persuasion," e.g., upholding a will which the testator's sons had helped her to change.[11] Duress, an extreme form of undue influence, requires an "unlawful" threat. When a husband induced his wife to give him property by threatening to leave her, she could not avoid the deed for duress because he had not threatened to do an unlawful act.[12]

The person exerting undue influence need not be a beneficiary. When a husband induced his wife to deed land to his sisters, the wife could avoid the deed without proving that the sisters had been involved. [13]

*Presumption of Undue Influence* The burden of proving undue influence is on the contestants, but they can rely on a presumption of undue influence if a person in a "confidential relationship" with the testator participated in preparing the will.[14] Some courts talk more generally about "suspicious circumstances" as the second ingredient in creating the presumption.

The "normal relationship between a mentally competent parent and an adult child is not *per se* a confidential relationship,''[15] which usually means an unequal relationship in which one party dominates the other.[16] Some relationships are confidential *per se*,

**7.** In re Estate of Shumway, 3 P.3d 977, 983 (Ariz.App.1999).

**8.** Madoff, *Unmasking Undue Influence*, 81 Minn.L.Rev. 571, 611 (1997).

**9.** Schoenblum, *Will Contests: An Empirical Study*, 22 Real Prop.Prob. and Trust J. 607, 625, 655 (1987). However, when the devise was to nonrelatives, the chances of a contestant's success were greater. *Id.* at 634, 659.

**10.** Estate of Baker, 182 Cal.Rptr. 550 (App.1982).

**11.** Carter v. Carter, 526 So.2d 141, 143 (Fla.App.1988).

**12.** Rubenstein v. Sela, 672 P.2d 492 (Ariz.App.1983).

**13.** Bedree v. Bedree, 528 N.E.2d 1128, 1130 (Ind.App.1988).

**14.** This presumption has also been applied to transfers other than wills. Doughty v. Morris, 871 P.2d 380 (N.M.App.1994) (joint bank accounts).

**15.** In re Estate of Elam, 738 S.W.2d 169, 173 (Tenn.1987).

**16.** *Restatement, Second, of Contracts* § 177 (1979) (a person "under the domination of another *or* [one who] is justified, by virtue of his relation with

such as guardian and ward, doctor and patient, and pastor and parishioner.[17] Powers of attorney have been held to establish a confidential relationship between the parties.[18] In other cases the existence of a confidential relationship is a question of fact.

In California "a husband and wife are subject to the general rules governing fiduciary relationships,"[19] and courts sometimes use similar language, but such a presumption "must be applied with caution as to marital relationships, because of the unique relationship between spouses."[20] Very few of the many wills which leave a large share of the estate to the testator's spouse are challenged, let alone set aside for undue influence.[21]

A presumption of undue influence allows contestants to escape summary judgment or a directed verdict. The presumption can be rebutted, but some say that the fact finder must find undue influence unless the proponent produces contrary evidence,[22] while others assert that the presumption merely "makes a case which must be submitted to the jury," but does not "*compel* a finding for the contestant."[23] In close cases appellate courts defer to the findings of the lower court or jury.[24]

## § 7.4 Role of Lawyers

*Lawyer as Witness* Decisions in will contests upholding wills often rely on the testimony of the lawyer who drafted the will. This creates a problem when the drafting attorney represents the estate in a will contest. DR 5–102 of the Code of Professional Responsibility provides that "(A) If after undertaking employment in contemplated or pending litigation, a lawyer learns * * * that he * * *

another in assuming that the other will not act inconsistently with his welfare").

**17.** Matter of Estate of Maheras, 897 P.2d 268 (Okl.1995) (devise to pastor's church). Gifts and devises to lawyers are discussed in Section 7.4.

**18.** Estate of Hamilton v. Morris, 67 S.W.3d 786, 793 (Tenn.App. 2001) (devise to attorney rejected) . *But see* In re Estate of Farr, 49 P.3d 415, 431 (Kan. 2002) (power of attorney is only "a persuasive fact in evaluating whether a confidential relationship existed").

**19.** Cal.Fam.Code § 721(b); In re Marriage of Haines, 39 Cal.Rptr.2d 673 (App.1995) (deed from W to H subject to presumption of undue influence).

**20.** In re Estate of Glogovsek, 618 N.E.2d 1231, 1237 (Ill.App.1993). *See also* In re Estate of Karmey, 658 N.W.2d 796, 799 (Mich.2003) (no presumption of undue influence from marital relationship).

**21.** In Matter of Estate of Montgomery, 881 S.W.2d 750, 756 (Tex.App. 1994), a will favoring a wife was upheld, the court noting that this was "not unusual." Occasionally, however, gifts or devises to a spouse, especially a second spouse, are found invalid for undue influence. McPeak v. McPeak, 593 N.W.2d 180 (Mich.App.1999).

**22.** Estate of Hamilton v. Morris, 67 S.W.3d 786, 795 (Tenn.App. 2001) (summary judgment based on unrebutted presumption of undue influence).

**23.** Watson v. Warren, 751 S.W.2d 406, 410 (Mo.App.1988).

**24.** In re Conservatorship of Estate of Davidson, 6 Cal.Rptr.3d 702, 722 (App.2003). Verdicts can be directed, however, if the evidence of undue influence is deemed insufficient. In re Estate of Karmey, 658 N.W.2d 796 (Mich.2003).

ought to be called as a witness on behalf of his client, he shall withdraw from the conduct of the trial."[1] The rationale for the rule is that combining the disparate functions of witness and advocate may confuse the fact finder. It does not preclude the drafting attorney from representing the estate in administration after the contest is over.[2]

*Undue Influence* A factor often mentioned when wills are contested for undue influence is whether the testator had "independent advice." The independent advisor most often mentioned is the lawyer who drafted the will. Lawyers unfortunately also often appear in a *negative* light in undue influence cases. In many rejected wills, the drafting lawyer was selected by the devisee rather than the testator, e.g., the devisees "met with an attorney of their choice, not [the testator's], and discussed the planning of his estate." The drafter did not speak with the testator until the will was signed.[3] A devisee's paying a lawyer to draft a will for the testator potentially violates the rules of the profession which in general prohibit lawyers from accepting compensation from someone other than the client.[4]

Sometimes a devisee is a client of the lawyer who drafts a will. In one such case the court rejected the contestants' argument that this created "a strong presumption of undue influence," saying that since the drafting lawyer "had known [the testator] for a number of years," she was "clearly the client."[5]

Lawyers encounter ethical issues when drafting wills for two spouses. A firm which had done this later learned that the husband had a child out of wedlock. The firm wished to disclose to the wife "that the husband's illegitimate child may ultimately inherit her property."[6] The husband objected to the disclosure on the basis of Rule 1.6(a), which says that "a lawyer shall not reveal information relating to the representation of a client unless the client consents," but the court allowed it, citing a local exception to the rule when a lawyer reasonably believes disclosure is needed "to rectify the consequences of the client's * * * fraudulent act in furtherance

**§ 7.4**

**1.** Model Rules of Professional Conduct 3.7 is similar.

**2.** Link, *Developments Regarding the Professional Responsibility of the Estate Administration Lawyer: The Effect of the Model Rules of Professional Conduct*, 26 Real Prop.Prob. and Trust L.J. 1, 98 (1991).

**3.** Matter of Estate of Bolinder, 864 P.2d 228, 232 (Kan.App.1993).

**4.** Model Rules of Professional Conduct 1.8(f). *See also* Estate of Gillespie, 903 P.2d 590 (Ariz.1995) rejecting a will where the lawyer was selected and paid by the principal devisee.

**5.** Matter of Estate of Koch, 849 P.2d 977, 996 (Kan.App.1993) *See also* In re Estate of Holcomb, 63 P.3d 9 (Okl. 2002) (will drawn by lawyer who also represented principal devisee upheld).

**6.** A. v. B., 726 A.2d 924, 926 (N.J. 1999).

of which the lawyer's services had been used."[7] The court also relied on a waiver signed by the couple when they engaged the firm, which said that "information provided by one client could become available to the other." However, the court noted decisions by Professional Ethics Committees of the New York and Florida bars which prohibited disclosure in similar situations.

Particularly troubling are wills which benefit the drafting lawyer. Here a presumption of undue influence arises because of the confidential relationship between attorney and client plus the lawyer's activity in preparing the will. Nevertheless, the presumption is rebuttable.[8]

*Rules of the Profession* The rules of conduct governing the legal profession are an important factor in this situation. The Model Rules of Professional Conduct Rule 1.8(c) says: "a lawyer shall not prepare an instrument giving the lawyer or a person related to the lawyer as parent, child, sibling, or spouse any substantial gift from a client, including a testamentary gift, except where the client is related to the donee."[9] This rule was the basis for suspending a lawyer who drafted a codicil by which a company in which the drafter's mother was a large shareholder received an option to buy stock.[10]

Ethical rules have been cited in undue influence cases to show that a lawyer's conduct was "undue."[11] Model Rule 1.8(c) was the model for a provision in the California Probate Code that "no provision * * * of any instrument shall be valid to make any donative transfer to * * * the person who drafted the instrument" with exceptions.[12] The California provision applies only to drafting instruments, but other gifts from clients to lawyers have been challenged for undue influence.[13] The Restatement of Law Governing Lawyers expressly bans (with exceptions) both preparing any instrument effecting a gift or devise to the lawyer and merely accepting such a gift.[14]

**7.** This provision differed from the relevant Model Rule in other states which provided for "narrower disclosure."

**8.** McGovern, *Undue Influence and Professional Responsibility*, 28 Real Property, Probate and Trust J. 643, 645 (1994); Section 7.3.

**9.** In 2002 this provision was amended to include soliciting a gift, whether or not the preparation of an instrument was involved. The exception where "the client is related to the donee" was expanded to define "related" to "include a spouse, child, grandchild, parent, grandparent or other relative or individual with whom the lawyer or the client maintains a close, familial relationship."

**10.** In re Watson, 733 N.E.2d 934, 937 (Ind.2000).

**11.** Krischbaum v. Dillon, 567 N.E.2d 1291 (Ohio 1991); *cf.* In re Succession of Parham, 755 So.2d 265 (La. App.1999) (will ipso facto valid because of lawyer's violation of Rule).

**12.** Cal.Prob.Code § 21350.

**13.** In re Estate of Mapes, 738 S.W.2d 853 (Mo.1987) (joint bank account).

**14.** *Restatement, Third, of Law Governing Lawyers* § 127 (2000). See also note 9.

Under the exception in the Model Rule "except where the client is related to the lawyer," may a relative draft an instrument giving the drafter more than his or her intestate share? The Restatement only allows such gifts if "not significantly disproportionate to those given to donees similarly related to the donor."[15] Friends are *not* covered by the exception for relatives, but some courts have devises to the drafter who was a close friend of the testator.[16]

Both the Model Rule and the California statute bar devises to certain persons connected with the drafter, such as a spouse or child, but the terms differ.[17] Benefits to family members of the drafting attorney have been held to raise a presumption of undue influence at common law.[18]

Neither the Model Rule nor the California statute cover instruments which designate the drafter as executor or trustee. This is not a "gift" or "donative transfer," since such fiduciaries are compensated for services rendered.[19] But in California the drafter of a trust instrument who is designated as sole trustee is subject to removal unless the court finds no undue influence.[20]

Some lawyers while refusing to draft a will from which they would benefit, have been involved in the preparation of such a will by another. In a case in which the client found another lawyer who "prepared the will based principally upon [the first lawyer's] memo and a brief meeting" with the client, the court held that it was error to dismiss the contestants' challenge to the will, because "it could be inferred that [the testator] did not receive the benefit of counselling by an independent attorney."[21]

Because of the perceived injury to the image of the bar when a lawyer benefits from a client's generosity, some courts conduct hearings over such wills even if no heir challenges them. Lawyers may be disciplined for violating the rules of the profession, regardless of the result of any probate proceedings.[22]

**15.** *Ibid.*

**16.** In re Conservatorship of Estate of Davidson, 6 Cal.Rptr.3d 702 (App. 2003). See also *Restatement, Third, of Law Governing Lawyers* § 127(1) (2000).

**17.** Compare revised Model Rule 1.8(c) with Cal.Prob.Code § 21350(a)(2). *Restatement, Third, of Law Governing Lawyers* § 127, comm. d (2000) says only that the lawyer "may not improperly induce the gift to the lawyer or to a spouse, child, or similar beneficiary of the lawyer." It also allows a lawyer to recommend a charity favored by the lawyer.

**18.** Zachary v. Mills, 660 N.E.2d 1301, 1308 (Ill.App.1996).

**19.** Burke v. Kehr, 876 S.W.2d 718, 722 (Mo.App.1994) (directed verdict for proponents of will which named drafter as executor); *Restatement, Third, of Law Governing Lawyers* § 127, comm. d (2000) (suggestion that client employ the lawyer is not solicitation of a gift).

**20.** Cal.Prob.Code § 15642(b)(6).

**21.** Matter of Henderson, 605 N.E.2d 323, 326 (N.Y.1992).

**22.** Attorney Grievance Comm'n v. Brooke, 821 A.2d 414 (Md.2003); *Restatement, Third, of Law Governing Lawyers* § 127, comm. a (2000).

*Malpractice* It has been suggested that lawyers should not prepare a will for a client whom they think is incapacitated, but no such rule appears in the Model Rules. Courts have rejected malpractice claims by heirs against lawyers who drafted a will for allegedly incapacitated testators on the ground that this would subject attorneys to "potentially conflicting duties to the client and to potential beneficiaries."[23] But lawyers who do sloppy work in *guarding against claims* of incapacity and undue influence can be liable for malpractice.[24]

**23.** Moore v. Anderson Zeigler, 135 Cal.Rptr.2d 888, 896 (App.2003).

**24.** Rathblott v. Levin, 697 F.Supp. 817 (D.N.J.1988).

# Chapter 8

# ADEMPTION, ABATEMENT
# AND LAPSE

*Table of Sections*

## § 8.1 Ademption

Sometimes after a will is executed but before the testator dies a change occurs which makes distribution of the estate problematic, e.g., a will leaves "my IBM stock to my sister, Elizabeth," and the testator sells her IBM stock. When this happens the devise of the stock is usually held to be "adeemed" so Elizabeth gets nothing.[1] Why? The testator's executor could buy equivalent IBM stock for Elizabeth with the money in the estate, but in the 18th century it was held that the devise of a bond was adeemed when it was paid off before the testator died, because "there is nothing upon which the bequest may operate. And I do not think that the question * * * turns on the intention of the testator."[2] Similar statements can be found in modern opinions, but they are misleading. "Courts purportedly following the identity theory frequently manipulate doctrine to effectuate intent."[3]

---

§ 8.1

1. Such "ademption by extinction" is sometimes contrasted with "ademption by satisfaction" when a testator gives something to a devisee, intending thereby to satisfy the devise. The latter problem is discussed in Section 2.6. Sales of property by an executor after the testator's death are discussed in Section 12.6.

2. Stanley v. Potter, 30 Eng.Rep. 83 (1789) *See also* In re Estate of Warman, 682 N.E.2d 557 (Ind.App.1997).

3. *Restatement, Third, of Property (Wills and Other Donative Transfers)* § 5.2, comm. b (1998). In some more recent courts explicitly state that ademption turns on intention. *E.g.* In re Estate of Poach, 600 N.W.2d 172, 177 (Neb.1999).

The Uniform Probate Code attempts to avoid the "harsh results" of ademption where (in the view of the drafters) it would frustrate the testator's intent. Among other things, the Code gives a specific devisee any property which the testator "acquired as a replacement for" a specifically devised asset.[4]

*Classification of Devises*    Only "specific" devises are subject to ademption. If a devise of stock is deemed "general," the executor buys shares for the devisee if the testator does not own them at death. Some devises of stock can only be classified as specific, *e.g.*, "all my IBM stock," but a devise of a designated number of shares is ambiguous. A devise of "my 147 shares of the stock of Wales Brothers" was held to be specific.[5] Even without the word "my," since the testator owned exactly 147 shares when she executed her will, some courts would classify the devise as specific.[6]

A third type of legacy, called "demonstrative," is not subject to ademption. When a will left devises totalling $500,000 to eight individuals, designating a stock fund as the source of payment, the fund had only $46,000 in it when the testator died, but the designated individuals were paid in full, because the devise was demonstrative, i.e., one which designates a particular source but may be satisfied by other sources if the identified source is insufficient.[7]

*Change in Form*    Courts sometimes avoid ademption on the ground that what occurred was a mere "change in form." A devise of "my interest in the investment plan with the United States National Bank" was not adeemed when the interest was distributed to the testator in the form of cash and stock, since this was a change "of form and not of substance."[8] One basis for the decision was the fact that the distribution "was an event over which [the testator] had no control."[9] The Uniform Probate Code gives specific devisees of stock any securities which the testator later acquires "by reason of action initiated by the organization" and any securities acquired in another company by reason of a merger.[10]

Usually to constitute a mere "change in form" the substitute for the devised property must be identifiable in the testator's estate. Even under the UPC, a specific devisee does not get a distribution of *cash*, as distinguished from securities, resulting from

---

**4.** Uniform Probate Code § 2–606(a)(5).

**5.** Estate of Wales, 727 P.2d 536, 537 (Mont.1986).

**6.** Matthews v. Matthews, 477 So.2d 391 (Ala.1985).

**7.** In re Estate of Lung, 692 A.2d 1349 (D.C.App.1997). *But see* Estate of Norwood, 443 N.W.2d 798 (Mich.App. 1989) (bequest of $6,000 from life insur-

ance fails when no insurance in the estate).

**8.** Stenkamp v. Stenkamp, 723 P.2d 336, 338 (Or.App.1986).

**9.** *Restatement, Third, of Property (Wills and Other Donative Transfers)* § 5.2, comm. d (1998).

**10.** Uniform Prob.Code § 2–605.

a merger, but it gives specific devisees any balance of the purchase price which is still owing from a purchaser at the time of the testator's death by reason of a sale of the devised property.[11]

Even when a will specifies a number of shares, the devisee may receive more as the result of a stock split. A devisee of "200 shares Exxon" was awarded an additional 200 shares which the testator subsequently received in a stock split.[12] Dividends paid in stock also go a devisee of securities but not *cash* dividends paid to the testator during life.

*Involuntary Transfers* If specifically devised assets are disposed of by a conservator after the testator has become incompetent, the Uniform Probate Code gives the specific devisee "a general pecuniary devise equal to the net sale price" of the asset sold on the theory that an incapacitated testator could not have intended to adeem.[13] Some courts reach this result without a statute, but others only give the specific devisee whatever remains of the sales proceeds when the testator dies.[14]

The Uniform Probate Code provision applies only to wills, but a similar rule has been applied to will substitutes. A court held that a conservator had exceeded his authority in closing joint accounts that the conservatee had established; "the conservator's duty is to manage the estate during the conservatee's lifetime. It is not his function * * * to control disposition after death."[15]

Today many persons use durable powers of attorney to avoid conservatorship.[16] The Uniform Probate Code applies the rule for transfers by conservators to agents with a durable power acting for an incapacitated principal.[17] The rule applies only if the testator was incompetent at the time of the sale, but acts of an agent under a durable power are "presumed to be for an incapacitated principal."[18]

Involuntary loss may also arise from accident. When a specifically devised house was damaged by fire after the will was executed, the devisee was awarded the proceeds of insurance on the house.[19] Even if a loss was uninsured, or the insurance has been paid and

---

**11.** *Id.,* § 2–606(a)(1).

**12.** Shriners Hosp. for Crippled Children v. Coltrane, 465 So.2d 1073 (Miss. 1985).

**13.** Uniform Probate Code § 2–606(b).

**14.** Matter of Estate of Swoyer, 439 N.W.2d 823 (S.D.1989).

**15.** Matter of Estate of Briley, 825 P.2d 1181, 1183–84 (Kan.App.1992). *But see* In re Conservatorship of Gobernatz, 603 N.W.2d 357, 360 (Minn.App.1999) (conservator properly terminated joint account of conservatee).

**16.** See Section 7.2.

**17.** Uniform Probate Code § 2–606(b).

**18.** *Id.,* § 2–606(e); *cf.* Chapman v. Chapman, 577 A.2d 775 (Me.1990) (finding ademption when there was no proof that the testator was incompetent when property was sold by an agent).

**19.** White v. White, 251 A.2d 470, 473 (N.J.Super.A.D.1969).

dissipated, the UPC gives the devisee the value of the missing property unless the circumstances indicate that the testator intended an ademption.[20] The examples in the comment distinguish between property stolen by a burglar (no ademption) and property given away by the testator (devise is adeemed). The Code thus reflects an overall "mild presumption against ademption."

*Other Factors*   Even a testator who voluntarily disposes of a specifically devised asset may not intend to adeem the devise. Shifting money from a savings account to a certificate of deposit in order to get a higher interest rate probably shows an intent to get more money, not to adeem. But ademption, recognizes that ademption sometimes reflects the testator's intent. The reason for a specific devise may disappear when property is disposed of, e.g., when a business is devised to employees in the hope that they will carry it on, and the testator later sells the business.[21] Ademption avoids administrative problems, such as determining the value of property which is no longer in the estate or the net sale price of property which the testator sold many years before.

Drafters can avoid such problems by a using a different type of devise. There is usually no good reason why a testator would want someone to get her IBM stock, for example, rather than an equivalent amount of money or a fraction of the estate.

*Income and Appreciation During Administration*   The classification of devises also affects the allocation of income received and appreciation or depreciation that occurs during the administration of an estate. The Uniform Principal and Income Acts give specific devisees any income from the property devised which accrues during administration in addition to the property itself.[22] General or pecuniary devises, on the other hand, do not share in the income earned by an estate during administration, but rather get interest, normally specified in a statute.[23] Income of an estate which is not attributable to specifically devised property is divided among the residuary devisees and the trustee of any pecuniary devise in trust in proportion to their respective shares of the estate.[24]

*Other Constructional Problems*   When wills devise a house and "its contents," claims have been made, generally unsuccessful, that

**20.**   Uniform Probate Code § 2–606.

**21.**   Matter of Morrissey, 684 S.W.2d 876 (Mo.App.1984).

**22.**   Unif.Prin. and Inc. Act (1962) § 5(b)(1); (1997 Act) § 201(1); (1931 Act) § 3–A(3)(a). As to the treatment of dividends, rent and interest in computing income for this purpose see Section 9.4.

**23.**   Uniform Probate Code § 3–904.

**24.**   Unif.Prin. and Inc.Act § 210(4) (1997), § 5(b)(2) (1962 Act). The question as to how a devise should be classified sometimes arises in this context. Hanna v. Hanna, 619 S.W.2d 655 (Ark. 1981) (devise of "assets which will equal one-half of my adjusted gross estate" classified as pecuniary (i.e. general)).

this includes cash and securities found in the house.[25] But such a phrase was construed to include valuable paintings in the house of an artist.[26]

The words "personal property" normally encompass intangibles such as securities, but when they appeared following "household furniture and furnishings, books, pictures, silverware, my automobiles," etc., they were given a restricted construction under "the rule of eiusdem generis," *i.e.*, "general words following the enumeration of specific meaning are not to be construed in their widest extent but only as applying to things of the same kind."[27]

It is not usual in modern wills to describe each item of a testator's property, but objects of great value should be specifically mentioned, since they may be construed not to pass under general references to "household furnishings" or "personal effects."[28]

## § 8.2    Abatement

Sometimes there are insufficient assets in an estate to carry out all the testator's directions. Suppose a will leaves (1) "my IBM stock to my sister Elizabeth," (2) "$10,000 to the First Presbyterian Church" and (3) "the residue of my estate to my issue." When the testator dies her estate contains the IBM stock (hence there is no ademption problem), but the rest of her assets are worth only $8,000. Or her assets, apart from the IBM stock, are worth $48,000 but the claims against the estate amount to $40,000. Which of the devises should be abated?

*Hierarchy of Devises*    The Uniform Probate Code provides that "shares of distributees abate * * * in the following order: (1) property not disposed of by will; (2) residuary devises; (3) general devises; (4) specific devises."[1] This hierarchy of devises (specific, general and residuary) comes from the common law.[2] Usually the will disposes of the entire estate by virtue of a residuary devise, and so there is no property in the first category, and the property which passes under the residuary clause is first used to pay claims. In the foregoing hypothetical the testator's issue would get nothing, the $10,000 general devise to the Presbyterian Church would be par-

**25.** Matter of Clark, 417 S.E.2d 856 (S.C.1992) (cash).

**26.** In re Estate of Rothko, 352 N.Y.S.2d 574 (Surr.1974).

**27.** Breckner v. Prestwood, 600 S.W.2d 52, 57 (Mo.App.1980).

**28.** *Cf.* Matter of Brecklein's Estate, 637 P.2d 444 (Kan.App.1981) (gold coins not included in "belongings"); Griffin v. Gould, 432 N.E.2d 1031 (Ill.App.1982) (extrinsic evidence admissible to deter-

mine whether valuable statues were included as "articles of household ornament").

**§ 8.2**

**1.** Uniform Probate Code § 3–902. *See also Restatement, Third, of Property (Wills and Other Donative Transfers)* § 1.1, comm. f (1998).

**2.** 2 W. Blackstone, *Commentaries* *512–13 (1765)

tially abated, and Elizabeth's specific devise would be unaffected. Abatement among devises within each category is pro-rata.[3] Thus if the will had made two general devises[4], of $10,000 and $6,000, and only $8,000 was available to pay them, each devisee would receive half of the amount designated.

Property which does not pass through probate, such as a house or bank account in joint tenancy, is not subject to claims of creditors at all in some states. Under the Uniform Probate Code it is, but only if other assets of the estate are insufficient.[5]

Usually the residuary devisees are the persons closest to the testator's heart, e.g., the testator's spouse and issue, while pecuniary or specific devises are often made to friends, collateral relatives or charities. But to abate residuary devises last, or abate all devises pro-rata, would present administrative problems. Often property which is specifically devised can not readily be sold, or the testator does not want it to be sold. If specific devisees had to contribute to the payment of claims against the estate, they might be forced to sell the property. The residuary estate, on the other hand, usually contains liquid assets more suitable for sale.

*Apportionment* In most estates claims, general and specific devises are small enough that even when all claims are charged to the residue plenty remains for the residuary devisees. The spouse's elective share, on the other hand, may seriously deplete the residue if liability is not apportioned. Therefore under the Uniform Probate Code the spouse's claim is "equitably apportioned" among all the recipients of the estate, including non-probate transferees.[6] Some states nevertheless follow the normal abatement rules in this situation.[7]

Liability for the federal estate tax is often apportioned among beneficiaries of an estate.[8] Failure to do this in cases where a considerable portion of the estate passes outside the residue might cause the residue to be completely abated. On this issue also, the testator's intent controls.[9]

*Classification* The classification of devises for purposes of abatement is sometimes problematic, e.g., a will left $15,000 to the

---

**3.** Uniform Probate Code § 3–902(a).

**4.** Such gifts are often referred to as "pecuniary" devises (or bequests), but they are not necessarily satisfied in money. Section 12.10.

**5.** See Section 13.2

**6.** Uniform Probate Code § 2–207. An exception is made for property irrevocably transferred by the decedent within two years of death. This is included in the calculation of the spouse's

share under § 2–205(3), but postponed in the apportionment under § 2–207(b).

**7.** In re Estate of Brinkman, 326 N.E.2d 167 (Ill.App.1975); Iowa Code § 633.436.

**8.** See Uniform Probate Code § 3–916(b).

**9.** In re Estate of Kuralt, 68 P.3d 662 (Mont.2003) (taxes imposed on residue per provision in will despite apportionment statute).

testator's son, and "all the rest of the my property, including the rights to receive royalty distributions from the American Society of Composers, Authors and Publishers," to his wife. The only asset in the estate was the testator's right to royalties. The wife claimed that her devise was specific, but the court classified it as residuary so the son's devise was preserved.[10]

*Contrary Intent*　　The specific/general/residuary order of abatement does not always reflect the testator's intent. It can be overcome by an express provision, or by showing that it would defeat "the testamentary plan or the express or implied purpose of the devise."[11]

Determining the testator's intent may be difficult. A will left a farm to the testator's son, and "a portion of my estate equal in value to the value of the property passing to my son" to the testator's daughter. The son's devise was specific and the daughter's general, and because the assets were insufficient the son ended up with more than his sister.[12] Perhaps because of the testator's "implied purpose" to treat his children equally the court should have ignored the preference for specific devises, but this is not obvious.

*Other Factors*　　Factors other than the type of devise may affect the order of abatement. Historically, personal property of a decedent was exhausted before real estate in paying claims, but today most states treat both types of property the same way.[13]

Some states favor certain devisees in abatement. In Iowa, for example, gifts to the testator's spouse abate last; even a specific devise to a daughter abates before a residuary devise to a wife.[14] No such preference appears in the text of the Uniform Probate Code, but the comment to § 3–902 states that "it is commonly held, even in the absence of a statute, that general legacies to a wife, or to persons with respect to which the testator is in loco parentis, are to be preferred to other legacies *in the same class* because this accords with the probable purpose of the legacies."[15]

*Exoneration*　　At common law if specifically devised property was subject to a mortgage, the devisee could insist that the mortgage be paid from the assets in the residuary estate.[16] The Uniform

---

**10.** Matter of Deutsch's Estate, 644 P.2d 768 (Wyo.1982).

**11.** Uniform Probate Code § 3–902(b); *cf.* Matter of Estate of Routh, 524 N.E.2d 46 (Ind.App.1988) (extrinsic evidence to show contrary intent is inadmissible).

**12.** Matter of Estate of Hale, 704 S.W.2d 725 (Tenn.App.1985).

**13.** Uniform Probate Code § 3–902.

**14.** Iowa Code § 633.436. *But see* In re Estate of Kraft, 186 N.W.2d 628 (Iowa 1971) (contrary intent shown).

**15.** Emphasis added. Compare Cal. Prob.Code § 21402 (preference for relatives within specific and general devises).

**16.** Martin v. Johnson, 512 A.2d 1017 (D.C.App.1986). However, this could be altered by a contrary direction

Probate Code, however, provides that "a specific devise passes subject to any mortgage," absent evidence of a different intent.[17] A direction in the will to "pay all my debts" does not show an intent to exonerate specific devises.[18]

## § 8.3  Lapse

If a will leaves Blackacre "to Alice" and Alice dies before the testator, who will get Blackacre? Several solutions are possible.

*Vested Interest*  If Alice is dead, she can not literally enjoy the devise, but the property might "vest" in her estate and pass to her devisees (if she died testate) or her heirs (if she died intestate). A vested construction is not uncommon in the case of inter-vivos instruments, e.g., when a man had a bond registered in his name "as trustee for Audrey" who later predeceased him, the bond was held to pass to Audrey's estate.[1] But the common law refused to hold that devises vested before the testator died. If a devisee predeceased the testator, the devise lapsed.[2]

*Anti–Lapse Statutes*  All states today have "anti-lapse" statutes, most of which provide that if a devisee predeceases the testator the devised property passes to any issue of the devisee who survive the testator.[3] Issue of the devisee more remote than children take only by representation.[4] Suppose that Alice, the devisee, has three children, Barbara, Ben, and Bill, each of whom has two children, and Alice and Bill predecease the testator. Under the typical anti-lapse statute, property devised to Alice would pass one third to Barbara, one third to Ben and one sixth to each of Bill's children. All would take directly from the testator, and so the devise would not be taxed in Alice's estate or be subject to claims of her spouse or creditors.[5]

Most anti-lapse statutes do not apply if the deceased devisee has no issue who survive the testator. Some statutes apply only to devisees who are descendants of the testator,[6] but others include

in the will. Gaymon v. Gaymon, 519 S.E.2d 142, 146 (Va.1999) (devise "subject to encumbrances").

**17.**  Uniform Probate Code § 2–608.

**18.**  *Id.,* § 2–609.

**§ 8.3**

**1.**  In re Estate of Zukerman, 578 N.E.2d 248 (Ill.App.1991).

**2.**  2 W. Blackstone, *Commentaries** 513 (1765); *Restatement, Third, of Property (Wills and Other Donative Transfers)* § 1.2 (1998).

**3.**  *E.g.,* Uniform Probate Code § 2–603. A list of the anti-lapse statutes ap-

pears in a Statutory Note to *Restatement, Second, of Property (Donative Transfers)* § 27.1 (1990).

**4.**  See Section 2.2.

**5.**  *Restatement, Second, of Property (Donative Transfers)* § 27.1, comm. e (1987). However, if Alice owed money to the testator, some authorities would allow the executor to set off this debt against the share which passes to her issue under the statute.

**6.**  Matter of Estate of Ross, 604 N.E.2d 982 (Ill.App.1992) (devise to siblings not covered).

devises to collateral relatives. The Uniform Probate Code version applies to devises to "a grandparent or a lineal descendant of a grandparent, or a stepchild" of the testator.[7] Some statutes cover all devises.[8]

*Non-probate Property* Some courts have applied anti-lapse statutes to living trusts by analogy.[9] But others hold that a beneficiary of a revocable trust who fails to survive the settlor has a vested interest, while others imply a condition of survival with no substitutional gift to the beneficiary's issue.[10] The Uniform Probate Code implies a condition of survival to the time of distribution in any future interest in a trust, whether or not the trust is revocable,[11] together with a substitutional gift to the issue of a beneficiary who fails to meet a condition of survival if the beneficiary is in the group protected by the anti-lapse statute, viz. "a grandparent, a descendant of a grandparent, or a stepchild of the decedent." This also applies to life insurance policies, pension plans, and POD or TOD registrations, but not joint tenancies or joint bank accounts.[12]

*Contrary Intent* Anti-lapse statutes do not apply if the will (or other governing instrument) shows that the testator (transferor) intended a different result. If a will says "to Alice if she survives me, otherwise to Arthur," Arthur takes rather than Alice's issue, if Alice predeceases the testator.[13] If the will simply says "to Alice if she survives me," many courts would interpret this to mean the testator did not want the anti-lapse statute to apply,[14] but the Uniform Probate Code disagrees[15] and so have some courts, at least where refusal to apply the anti-lapse statute would cause a devise to fail. For example, when a will left property "to my two brothers, or the survivor," and both brothers predeceased the testator, survived by issue, the court awarded the property to the issue of both brothers.[16]

**7.** Uniform Probate Code § 2–603.

**8.** Tenn.Code § 32–3–105; Ky.Rev. Stat. § 394.400.

**9.** Dollar Savings & Trust Co. v. Turner, 529 N.E.2d 1261 (Ohio 1988). See also *Restatement, Second, of Property (Donative Transfers)* § 27.1, comm. e (1987).

**10.** In re Estate of Mendelson, 697 N.E.2d 1210 (Ill.App.1998) (land trust).

**11.** Uniform Probate Code § 2–707(b).

**12.** *Id.,* § 2–706. The statutory language is far from clear on this question. See McGovern, *Nonprobate Transfers Under the Revised Uniform Probate Code*, 55 Alb.L.Rev. 1329, 1340 (1992).

**13.** *Restatement, Third, of Property (Wills and Other Donative Transfers)* § 5.5, illus. 4 (1998). However, if Arthur also predeceases the testator, the statute may apply. *See id.*, comm. g.

**14.** Erlenbach v. Estate of Thompson, 954 P.2d 350 (Wash.App.1998); *Restatement, Second, of Property (Donative Transfers)* § 27.1, illus. 6 (1987).

**15.** Uniform Probate Code §§ 2–603(b)(3), 2–706(b)(3).

**16.** Early v. Bowen, 447 S.E.2d 167, 172 (N.C.App.1994). *But cf.* Matter of Estate of Simpson, 423 N.W.2d 28 (Iowa App.1988) (statute inapplicable in devise to siblings or the survivor of them when all predecease the testator).

Some courts have held that the words "per capita" in a devise to a class show an intent not to apply the statute, but others disagree.[17] Courts often say that in order to overcome the anti-lapse statute, a will must use "clear and plain language" to this effect.[18]

*Class Gifts* A class gift, e.g. "to my daughters," implies a right of survivorship: if any daughter dies without issue before the testator, her share will go to the others. But if the deceased daughter had issue, they take her share under most anti-lapse statutes. Even when the statutes are not clear, most courts apply them to class gifts, but some do not.[19]

If a class member was already dead when the testator signed the will, some statutes and cases do not give her share to her issue, on the theory that if the testator had intended to include them, the will would have said so; a devisee's death *after* the will is executed is distinguishable because the testator may not have contemplated this when signing the will.[20] But under the Uniform Probate Code, even the shares of class members who were already dead when the will was signed go to their issue.[21]

*Substitute Gifts* If the anti-lapse statute does not apply, either because a devisee is not within the group of persons encompassed by it (*e.g.* was not related to the testator), or because the devisee had no surviving issue, the property may pass under a substitute gift in the will. A devise "to Alice or her issue" is usually interpreted as a gift to Alice's issue if she fails to survive the testator. A devise "to Alice *and* her *heirs*," on the other hand, is usually held to mean that Alice takes the property if she survives the testator, but her heirs take nothing if she does not.[22] But this language has occasionally been construed to create a substitutional gift to the devisee's heirs.[23]

It is often unclear whether a devise *is* a "class gift." A gift to a group like "children" or "issue" is, but a gift to named persons, e.g. "to Alice and Arthur," is probably not, but it *may* create a joint tenancy. If so, there is a right of survivorship more extensive than in an ordinary class gift. If two joint tenants survive the testator and one dies later, the other takes her share, whereas the right of

**17.** *Compare* Matter of Estate of Wetsel, 546 N.Y.S.2d 243 (App.Div. 1989), *with* Rowe v. Rowe, 720 A.2d 1225 (Md.App.1998).

**18.** In re Estate of Kuruzovich, 78 S.W.3d 226, 227–8 (Mo.App. 2002).

**19.** Matter of Kalouse's Estate, 282 N.W.2d 98 (Iowa 1979).

**20.** Haynes v. Williams, 686 S.W.2d 870 (Mo.App.1985); N.Y. EPTL § 3–3.3(a)(3).

**21.** Uniform Probate Code § 2–603(a)(4). *See also* N.J.Stat. § 3B:3–35.

**22.** Estate of Straube v. Barber, 990 S.W.2d 40 (Mo.App.1999).

**23.** Estate of Calden, 712 A.2d 522 (Me.1998) (devise to stepson "and his heirs" passed to stepson's widow when he predeceased testator).

survivorship in a class gift lasts only until the gift takes effect; the share of a class member who dies thereafter passes to her estate. Under the Uniform Probate Code, a P.O.D. account for "Alice and Arthur" is treated like a class gift; if only Alice survives the creator of the account (Arthur having died without issue), Alice will take it all, but if both survive the creator and one dies thereafter there is no right of survivorship.[24]

A devise "to my children, Alice and Arthur" is ambiguous: "children" suggests a class gift, but the use of names suggests otherwise. The second Restatement of Property says that the result depends upon "the facts and circumstances."[25] A devise "to Arthur and the children of Alice" is usually held to be a class gift, Arthur being a member of the class, even though he is not a child of Alice.[26] Even without names, a devise which states the number of recipients, *e.g.*, "to my *two* children," or designates the shares, *e.g,* "one-half to each," has been held to show no intent to make a class gift,[27] but not always.[28]

Courts sometimes deduce the testator's intention by comparing different parts of the will: a devise to two named persons "or to the survivor of them should either predecease me" was used to show that in another devise the testator did not intend a class gift.[29]

*Residuary Clause*    Suppose a will devises Blackacre "to Alice, Arthur, and Andrew." Alice predeceases the testator and has no issue, or is not in the group covered by the anti-lapse statute, and this language is not construed to create a class gift or a joint tenancy. Alice's share will pass under the residuary clause of the will.

If the devise was itself in the residuary clause, even though not expressed as a class gift, Arthur and Andrew would take Alice's share under the Uniform Probate Code.[30] Many courts have reached the same result without a statute.[31] The dispute over whether

**24.** Uniform Probate Code § 6–212(b)(2). *See also* King v. William M. King Family Ent., Inc., 515 So.2d 1241 (Ala.1987) (devise to children creates a tenancy in common among those who survived the testator).

**25.** *Restatement, Second, of Property (Donative Transfers)* § 27.1, comm. b (1987).

**26.** Matter of Kalouse's Estate, 282 N.W.2d 98 (Iowa 1979) ("to my first cousins and to Frank").

**27.** Henderson v. Parker, 728 S.W.2d 768 (Tex.1987) ("our three sons"); Dawson v. Yucus, 239 N.E.2d 305 (Ill.App. 1968) ("one-half to Stewart, a nephew, and one half to Gene, a nephew").

**28.** Estate of Frailey, 625 S.W.2d 241, 243 (Mo.App.1981).

**29.** Dawson v. Yucus, 239 N.E.2d 305, 310 (Ill.App.1968). *See also* Estate of Straube v. Barber, 990 S.W.2d 40, 46 (Mo.App.1999) (devise "to H and her heirs" not a substitutional gift to heirs; other devises showed that testator "knew how to address the possibility that a legatee would predecease her").

**30.** Uniform Probate Code § 2–604(b).

**31.** Matter of Estate of Winslow, 934 P.2d 1001 (Kan.App.1997); In re Leavy's Estate, 442 A.2d 588 (N.H.1982). *But see* In re Estate of Kugler, 190 N.W.2d 883 (Wis.1971).

particular language creates a "class gift" thus becomes irrelevant in a residuary clause.

*Intestacy*  Some courts give a lapsed residuary devise to the testator's heirs rather than the surviving residuary devisees.[32] Even under the Uniform Probate Code, the heirs take if *all* the residuary devisees die without issue prior to the testator.

In the case of an insurance beneficiary designation, if the designated beneficiary fails to meet a condition of survival and no anti-lapse provision or substitutional gift applies, the property falls into the insured's probate estate and ultimately passes to the heirs or devisees of the insured.[33]

*Other Causes of Lapse*  A devise may fail for reasons other than the death of the devisee before the testator. A devise to a witness to the will may be void;[34] a devisee who disclaims or who divorces or murders the testator may be disqualified.[35] In such cases a substitute gift in case a devisee predeceases the testator may be held to apply, even though the disqualified devisee actually survived,[36] but some courts hold that a substitutional gift "if A predeceases me" does not apply if the gift fails for another reason.[37]

*Planning*  A devise "to my issue who survive me, by representation" duplicates the result of most anti-lapse statutes when a devise is made to children of the testator; the descendants of any child who predeceases the testator will take the child's share.[38] Even a bequest "to my issue," may lapse if they all predecease the testator. A substitute gift to charity should be added if the testator does not wish to provide for the (sometimes very remote) relatives who would inherit in an intestacy.

*Simultaneous Death*  When spouses die in the same plane crash or automobile collision, for example, it may be necessary to determine which one lived the longest. This is often difficult. The result in such cases may be simplified by the Uniform Probate Code provision that a person who is required to survive must survive by 120 hours. For joint tenancies the property is split equally between

---

**32.**  Betts By and Through Parker v. Parrish, 320 S.E.2d 662 (N.C.1984).

**33.**  *Restatement, Third, of Trusts* § 8, comm. a (2001); Uniform Probate Code §§ 6–212(b)(2), 6–307.

**34.**  Dorfman v. Allen, 434 N.E.2d 1012 (Mass.1982); Section 4.3.

**35.**  See Sections 2.7 (homicide), 2.8 (disclaimer), 5.4 (divorce).

**36.**  Bloom v. Selfon, 555 A.2d 75, 78 (Pa.1989).

**37.**  Ray v. Tate, 252 S.E.2d 568 (S.C. 1979).

**38.**  *Cf.* Uniform Statutory Will Act § 7(a)(1). Representation should be defined to make clear what proportion each person takes. *Id.* § 1(5). More remote issue do not share under this language if the testator's children survive. Section 2.2. This language can be adapted for the will of testator who has no issue and wishes to provide for collateral relatives, *e.g.*, "to the issue of my parents."

the estates of the joint tenants in cases of virtually simultaneous death.[39]

*Provisions in Instrument*   Provisions on simultaneous death in a will can supersede the statute. Under the Uniform Statutory Will any devisee who does not survive by 30 days or more is deemed to have predeceased the testator.[40] A longer period might delay distribution by creating uncertainty as to who should take, but estates are hardly ever distributed within 30 days of the decedent's death. Wills that require devisees to survive until the property is distributed to them raise problems of interpretation, e.g. whether an estate *should have been* distributed earlier.[41]

The Uniform Probate Code's 120 hour survival requirement "avoids multiple administrations and in some instances prevents property from passing to persons not desired by the decedent,"[42] e.g., when a will leaves property to the testator's spouse who survives briefly and leaves his or her property to children by a prior marriage or collateral relatives.[43]

*Definition of Death; Disappearance*   Some cases raise the question when death actually occurred.[44] The death certificate is only prima facie evidence of this.[45]

The time of death presents a problem when a person disappears. Under the Uniform Probate Code a person who has not been heard from for five years and whose absence "is not explained after diligent search or inquiry" is presumed to have died at the end of the 5 year period.[46] A similar common-law presumption operates only after 7 years.[47]

---

**39.**   Uniform Probate Code § 2–702.

**40.**   Uniform Statutory Will Act § 11.

**41.**   Estate of Justesen, 91 Cal. Rptr.2d 574 (App.1999).

**42.**   Uniform Probate Code § 2–104, Comment.

**43.**   Matter of Estate of Villwock, 418 N.W.2d 1 (Wis.App.1987) (wife survived husband by a few minutes, so all property passed to members of her family).

**44.**   Estate of Sewart, 602 N.E.2d 1277, 1279 (Ill.App.1991). According to Uniform Probate Code § 1–107(1) death occurs when a person has sustained "irreversible cessation of all functions of the entire brain." See also Uniform Determination of Death Act § 1.

**45.**   Uniform Probate Code § 1–107(2); Uniform Simultaneous Death Act § 5(2); In re Estate of Price, 587 N.E.2d 995 (Ohio Com.Pl.1990) (deaths treated as simultaneous despite death certificates showing they were 27 minutes apart).

**46.**   Uniform Probate Code § 1–107(5).

**47.**   In re Estate of King, 710 N.E.2d 1249 (Ill.App.1999).

# Chapter 9

# TRUSTS

*Table of Sections*

## § 9.1   Uses of the Trust: Avoiding Probate

The word "trust" is used for many property arrangements which have little in common with each other apart from the fact that they were historically enforced by the court of Equity. For example, courts impose "constructive trusts" to avoid unjust enrichment when a person would otherwise profit from wrongful conduct. The trusts to be discussed in this chapter, on the other hand, are deliberately created by a person called the settlor.

Trusts are a form of transfer, usually gratuitous,[1] either *inter vivos* (from the Latin: "between the living"), or testamentary if created by will. People can make gifts without using a trust, but in many situations trusts provide important advantages. The Restatement mentions five common reasons for using trusts: "[1] the avoidance of probate, [2] providing property management for those who cannot, ought not or wish not to manage for themselves, [3] providing for the limited and successive enjoyment of property over several generations, * * * [4] the saving of taxes and [5] the

---

**§ 9.1**

**1.**   Trusts are also used as devices for conducting business or investment activities, but this book does not deal with such trusts. They are also excluded from the Restatement of Trusts. *Restatement, Third, of Trusts* § 1, comm. b (2001).

insulation of the trust property from the claims of the beneficiaries' creditors."[2] This Section discusses the first of these reasons.

*Avoiding Probate*    Many lawyers use living trusts more often than wills in estate planning. For many persons of modest means who do not use lawyers, most of their wealth passes through nonprobate channels. Why this concern for "avoiding probate?"

Living trusts do not have to be executed with all of the formalities prescribed for wills,[3] but this is not a significant advantage since compliance with these formalities is not burdensome.

Living trusts may be challenged for incapacity or undue influence just like wills, and the standards are similar. However, many states require that heirs be notified before a will is admitted to probate, whereas no such notice is given to persons adversely affected by a living trust. In many states will contests are tried by jury, and juries may be prone to reject wills which they find "unnatural." Trusts may be "more resistant to capacity challenges" than wills because they "belong to the jury-free realm of equity law."[4] However, successful contests of either wills or living trusts are rare.

When wills are probated after the testator dies they become open to inspection by all.[5] To a publicity-shy family this can cause concern. However, publicity is not a concern in most families, and the public is rarely interested in ascertaining the average citizen's estate plan.

Probate may be costlier than nonprobate transfers. In some states the fees of executors and their attorneys are based on the size of the "probate" estate, and thus can be reduced by nonprobate transfers. But there is a growing trend against basing fees simply on the size of the probate estate.[6] A living trust often requires additional work by lawyers, such as transferring title of assets to the trust, and the fees for this work may offset any savings in probate costs.[7]

The delay involved while property of a decedent is being administered is a source of popular dissatisfaction with probate, but its significance should not be exaggerated. An estate in administration continues to earn income. The needs of the beneficiaries of the

**2.** *Restatement, Third, of Trusts* § 27, comm. b(1) (2001). Creditors' rights with respect to trusts are discussed in Section 13.1.

**3.** See Section 4.6. A *testamentary* trust, on the other hand, is not valid if the will which purports to create it cannot be probated.

**4.** Langbein, *Living Probate: the Conservatorship Model*, 77 Mich.L.Rev.

63, 67 (1978). As to trial by jury in will contests see Section 12.1.

**5.** During the testator's lifetime, the will in America is a secret document, unless the testator chooses to reveal its contents.

**6.** See Section 12.5.

**7.** Weinstock, *Planning an Estate* § 6.7 (4th ed. 1995).

estate during the administration can be met by the family allowance[8] and by partial distributions.

Living trusts are occasionally used to escape limitations on
testamentary freedom imposed by the spouse's elective share. However, many states allow spouses to claim a share of assets in a
revocable trust as well as the probate estate.[9] Creditors of a testator
can reach the probate estate to satisfy their claims. In some states
creditors of the settlor of a revocable trust have no comparable
right to reach the trust, but this is no longer true in many
jurisdictions. In any event creditors are not a major consideration
in the vast majority of estates which are solvent.[10]

The reasons for avoiding probate are stronger in some states
than in others. They depend on the client's objectives and situation.
One should *not* assume that avoiding probate for all assets of all
clients is desirable.

Many persons wish to have some assets pass by nonprobate
transfer and others pass under their will. Pourover wills can be
used to coordinate the various parts of the estate plan.[11]

*Saving Taxes* Revocable living trusts, generally speaking,
have no tax advantages. If the settlor retains the power to revoke
the trust the trust income continues to be taxed to the settlor, and
the trust property is taxed in the settlor's gross estate at death.[12]
Irrevocable transfers, on the other hand, can save both income and
transfer taxes. These savings do not require the use of a trust; an
outright gift has the same effect.

*Other Ways to Avoid Probate* Living trusts are not the only
device available to avoid probate. Joint tenancy is often used for the
same reason, but most estate planners warn against its use. Joint
bank accounts are often created or alleged to have been created
only for convenience, with no intent that the survivor own the
account after the depositor dies. This has caused courts much
difficulty. Revocable trusts are less open to such disputes.

The often expressed idea that joint tenancy gives a "present
interest" to both (all) parties creates additional problems. If the
parties have a falling out, the ability of the creator of the joint
tenancy to revoke it is unclear, whereas the power to a settlor to
revoke a trust is usually expressly reserved (or negated) in the trust
instrument.

**8.** See Section 3.4.

**9.** See Section 3.7.

**10.** As to the rights of creditors
against probate and non-probate assets
see Sections 13.1–13.3.

**11.** See Section 6.2.

**12.** See Chapter 15.3.

TOD registration of securities, POD bank accounts, and the designation of beneficiaries of insurance policies and death benefits under pension plans allow nonprobate transfer without a trust or the disadvantages of joint tenancy.[13] Nevertheless, securities, bank accounts, and insurance benefits are often put into a trust in order to accomplish objectives other than avoiding probate. Many planners designate a living trust as the beneficiary of an insurance policy.[14]

## § 9.2  Management of Property

Trusts are frequently used to manage property for persons who are legally incompetent, either minors or adults who have been adjudicated incompetent, or for persons who are legally competent but unable (in the settlor's opinion) to handle property well. Many parents want property held in trust for children until they reach an age well beyond eighteen, the age of majority today. Even for fully competent family members, a trust can provide unified management of a family business. A living trust can also help persons who are concerned about their own possible future incompetence. In this case someone other than the settlor must be designated as trustee, either initially or upon defined circumstances, such as whenever a physician certifies that the settlor is no longer capable. This can avoid the expense and embarrassment of judicial proceedings to have the settlor declared incompetent.[1]

Knowledgeable estate planners prefer trusts to guardianship or conservatorship for minors or incompetent adults.[2] Guardians/conservators typically must file a bond, periodically account to a court, and obtain court approval for sales, investments and distributions.[3] Trustees are generally freer from court control. A settlor can choose to take risks with property which he puts into a trust, e.g., by waiving bond,[4] whereas restrictions on guardians cannot generally be waived.

Guardianship for minors has the additional disadvantage that it terminates when the child reaches the age of majority even though an 18–year–old may not be mature enough to manage a

---

**13.** As to these forms see Section 4.7.

**14.** As to the validity of such insurance trusts see Section 4.6.

### § 9.2

**1.** McGovern, *Trusts, Custodianships, and Durable Powers of Attorney,* 27 Real Prop., Prob. and Trust J. 1, 4 (1992).

**2.** Even if all a testator's property is left in trust, a guardian *of the person* of any minor children may be necessary if both parents die while the children are minors. For the duties of a guardian of the person (basically a surrogate parent) see Unif. Prob.Code § 5–209. A parent can appoint such a guardian by a will or other writing signed and attested by 2 witnesses. *Id.,* § 5–202.

**3.** The Uniform Probate Code reduces the differences between trusts and conservatorships. *E.g.,* § 5–425(a) (conservator has "all of the powers ... conferred by law on trustees").

**4.** As to bond see Section 12.5.

substantial amount of property. Trusts can, generally speaking, continue for as long as the settlor wishes.

*Custodianships* The Uniform Transfers (Gifts) to Minors Act provides another way to have property managed for minors. Under this Act, the donor designates a "custodian" for a minor to whom the property is given. A custodian "has all the rights, powers, and authority over the custodial property that unmarried adult owners have over their own property," to be held, however, in a fiduciary capacity.[5] Custodians are not required to give a bond or make periodic court accountings.[6] The Uniform Transfers to Minors Act is not limited to gifts. A person can create a custodianship by a will.[7] The Act allows money due to a minor to be paid to a custodian, e.g., if an insurance beneficiary is a minor when the policy matures, or if a minor has a tort claim. A personal representative or trustee can distribute to a custodian; thus an administrator of an intestate decedent could distribute the share of a minor heir to a custodian and thereby avoid the need for a guardian.

Custodians operate very much like trustees.[8] Custodianships are useful for smaller amounts of money or property because they can be established without drafting a trust instrument. A father, for example, can simply have stock registered in the name of custodian (who can be himself or another adult) "as custodian for [name of child] under the [state] Uniform Transfers to Minors Act."[9] This incorporates by reference the provisions of the Act.[10]

A custodianship can be created only for one person,[11] whereas a settlor can create a trust for a group of persons and give the trustee discretion to make unequal distributions among them on the basis of differing need, conduct or other factors.[12]

Custodianships normally end when the beneficiary reaches age 21.[13] For parents who wish to postpone distribution until their children are older, a trust is necessary. If a minor dies during a custodianship, the property passes to the minor's estate, whereas a trust can provide for distribution to others when a beneficiary

**5.** Uniform Transfers to Minors Act § 13(a).

**6.** *Id.,* §§ 15(c), 19. As to accountings by other fiduciaries see Section 12.10.

**7.** *Id.* § 5.

**8.** The Restatement of Trusts says that custodians "are subject to the rules of trust law" except where the statute otherwise provides. *Restatement, Third, of Trusts* § 5, comm. a(1) (2001)

**9.** Uniform Transfers to Minors Act § 9.

**10.** *Id.* § 11(c).

**11.** *Id.* § 10.

**12.** Discretionary trusts are further discussed in Section 9.5.

**13.** Termination may occur at 18 in some circumstances. Uniform Transfers to Minors Act § 20. The California version allows extension to age 25 in some circumstances. Cal.Prob.Code § 3920.5.

dies—indeed one purpose of many trusts is to keep the trust assets out of the beneficiary's estate at death.[14]

*Durable Powers of Attorney*    Children are legally incompetent until the age of majority. Legal incompetence at the other end of life is increasingly frequent as people live longer. Many persons use living trusts to provide a better way than conservatorship for handling their property in case they become incompetent before they die. Another alternative is to designate an agent. Traditionally an agent's powers ceased when the principal became incompetent. This made agency useless for managing property for an incompetent, so a Uniform Durable Power of Attorney Act was promulgated in 1979. The term "attorney" in this context is equivalent to agent, and has nothing to do with being a "attorney at law."[15] Its provisions have been adopted (with variations) in most states. They provide "a form of senility insurance comparable to that available to relatively wealthy persons who use funded, revocable trusts."[16]

A durable power of attorney states that it "shall not be affected by the subsequent disability or incapacity of the principal."[17] Some persons want the agent's powers to begin *only if* they become incompetent.[18] Such "springing powers" should state that "this power of attorney shall become effective upon the disability or incapacity of the principal," and should provide a method for determining when this has happened so as to avoid the legal proceedings required to determine capacity.[19]

A durable power must have been executed while the principal was legally competent; a person who is already incapacitated can not confer a power.[20]

Agents are like trustees in many respects; they manage property on behalf of the principal just as trustees manage property for the beneficiary(ies). But trustees (like custodians) have many powers implied by law,[21] whereas "most statutes authorizing durable powers confer no power on the agent. Instead [they] simply state

14. See Section 9.3.

15. " 'Attorney-in-fact' means a person granted authority to act for the principal in a power of attorney, regardless of whether the person is known as an attorney-in-fact or agent." Cal.Prob. Code § 4014(a).

16. Uniform Durable Powers of Attorney Act (Uniform Probate Code, Part 5), Prefatory Note.

17. These words are quoted from Uniform Probate Code § 5–501 which indicates that "similar words" will suffice but they must be "in writing." Without such language in most states the power terminates upon the principal's incompetence. Matter of Ciervo, 507 N.Y.S.2d 868 (App.Div.1986).

18. Unless otherwise provided a durable power is effective even while the principal is competent. Geren v. Geren, 29 P.3d 448, 452 (Kan.App. 2001).

19. Uniform Probate Code § 5–501, Comment.

20. Hagan v. Shore, 915 P.2d 435 (Or.App.1996). As to capacity in general see Section 7.1.

21. Trustees' powers of sale, investment, etc. are discussed in Sections 12.6 and 12.7.

that powers possessed by the agent are not lost when the principal becomes incapacitated. Therefore, to determine the scope of the agent's authority, one must look to the terms of the power and to the law of agency. * * * Agency law only sparingly implies powers and strictly construes express powers."[22] Courts are particularly hesitant to construe powers to allow agents to make gifts of the principal's property even though these may produce substantial tax benefits.[23] In order to simplify the problem of drafting a comprehensive list of powers, a Uniform Statutory Form Power of Attorney Act has been promulgated, but the statutory forms "are so prolix that they intimidate anyone who tries to read them," and "leave important issues unresolved."[24]

Because of the tradition of strict construction of agency powers, third persons such as banks and transfer agents have been reluctant to recognize the authority of agents to act. The Uniform Probate Code seeks to encourage them to do so by protecting them from liability if they erroneously but in good faith recognize a power in specified circumstances.[25] The protection of third parties and the absence of court supervision over agents create risks for persons using powers.[26]

Even a "durable" power of attorney terminates when the principal dies, although acts of an agent without actual knowledge of the principal's death may be binding.[27] Since trusts continue to operate after the settlor dies, they also function as will substitutes, but a power of attorney cannot. On the other hand, an agent can act under a power of attorney without the principal having to first transfer property to the agent; whereas a living trust may fail if the trustee does not obtain title to the property.[28] The respective advantages of trusts and agency can be combined by a power authorizing the attorney to transfer the principal's assets into a trust.

## § 9.3 Bypass Trusts

Many persons create a trust for a spouse, not because they lack confidence in the spouse's ability to manage property, but because

**22.** McGovern, supra note 1, at 32–33. *See also* Amcore Bank v. Hahnaman–Albrecht, Inc., 759 N.E.2d 174 (Ill. App.2001) (broad catch-all provision did not authorize attorney to sign a guaranty binding principal).

**23.** See Section 7.2.

**24.** McGovern, *supra* note 1, at 34.

**25.** Uniform Probate Code §§ 5–504, 5–505.

**26.** Johnson v. Edwardsville Nat. Bank & Trust Co., 594 N.E.2d 342 (Ill.

App.1992) (bank protected by statute even if principal incompetent when power executed, but not if power was forged and bank was negligent). As to the latter point, the statute was later amended to protect third parties who relied in good faith on a forged power. Amcore Bank v. Hahnaman–Albrecht, Inc., 759 N.E.2d 174, 185 (Ill.App.2001)

**27.** Uniform Prob.Code § 5–504.

**28.** See Section 4.6.

they do not wish the property to be taxable or subject to probate costs when the spouse dies. A person may also want to confine a spouse to a life interest, particularly if the couple has no children, or if either spouse has children by another marriage, in order to avoid property passing to unrelated persons. Similar reasons may induce parents to provide a trust for children: fear that if a child gets it outright, it may pass to the child's spouse or others outside the family. Tax motives may also operate here, *e.g.* keeping property out of the child's taxable estate at death.[1] Trusts for the life of a child are less common than trusts for the life of a spouse; since children have a longer life expectancy when their parent dies, the costs of a trust for their lifetime may outweigh the benefits if the children are capable of managing their inheritance.

Settlors cannot create a bypass trust for themselves with the same tax advantages, since if a person *retains* a life interest in a trust the assets are taxable in the settlor's estate. The assets of such a trust are also subject to the elective share of the settlor's spouse in many states,[2] whereas a bypass trust created for another can avoid claims of a spouse or creditors of the income beneficiary to a large extent.[3]

*Legal Life Estates*    One can create a life interest without using a trust. Many use legal life estates, but knowledgeable estate planners do not generally recommend them. If legal life tenants allow property to deteriorate they can be sued for waste.[4] In some circumstances they may be required to post a bond.[5] Nevertheless, financially responsible trustees protect remainder beneficiaries better than legal life tenants, but professional trustees cost money. The testator may wish to avoid the expense of trustee's fees, particularly in smaller estates or for property which does not require the management skills of a professional trustee, such as a residence, either by a legal life estate or by using a family member as trustee. Designating a person as trustee has the advantage that it incorporates by reference a body of trust law that deals with problems that recur when property is divided between present and

---

**§ 9.3**

**1.** However, in this case one may incur a generation-skipping tax. See Section 15.4

**2.** Section 3.7.

**3.** Spendthrift trusts and the extent of creditor protection which they provide are discussed in Section 13.1. As to the elective share see Bongaards v. Millen, 793 N.E.2d 335 (Mass.2003), distinguishing between a trust created by decedent's mother from one created by the decedent herself.

**4.** Moore v. Phillips, 627 P.2d 831 (Kan.App.1981).

**5.** *Cf.* Matter of Estate of Jud, 710 P.2d 1241, 1248 (Kan.1985) (rejecting a demand for a bond "in the absence of a showing of danger of loss or waste"). Compare the obligation of trustees to provide a bond. Section 12.5.

future interests. The law governing legal life estates is less well developed.[6]

Life tenants and remaindermen "may deal only with their own respective interests" in the property.[7] If a third party injures property, life tenants may only recover for the damage to their interest, leaving the remaindermen with a separate claim. A trustee, on the other hand, can sue on behalf of all the beneficiaries.[8] Life tenants cannot commit "waste" but they have no duty to take out insurance to cover the remainder interests,[9] whereas trustees are bound to insure the property for the benefit of all.[10]

Remedies against life tenants who commit waste are problematic when the succeeding interests are contingent as they often are. For example, parents left land to their daughter for life, with a remainder to her surviving issue. When the daughter sold timber standing on the property, her grandson sought relief. The court refused to give him damages since his interest was uncertain. An injunction against cutting the timber would avoid the problem of ascertaining damages, but it might also prevent the property being exploited advantageously. Hence, courts refuse to grant an injunction to persons who have only a remote chance of succeeding to the property.[11]

While the remedies available to remainder interests are restricted, life tenants' ability to exploit land is also limited. The best use of land may require a long-term lease. Trustees can execute leases extending beyond the term of the trust,[12] but life tenants can convey only what they have; if they die during the term of a lease, the remaindermen can expel the lessee.[13] Legal life estates "shackled much of the land in England" in the 19th century, leading to the enactment of legislation giving broad powers to life tenants.[14]

American law has followed a similar path, but not so far. Many statutes allow courts to authorize life tenants to sell property it appears "necessary or expedient" to the court. Court proceedings are expensive, however. They can be avoided if the instrument that creates the life estate gives the life tenant a power of sale, but a narrowly drafted power may be insufficient, because such powers are strictly construed.[15] On the other hand, broadly drafted powers

**6.** Casner, *Legal Life Estates*, 45 Neb.L.Rev. 342, 346 (1966).

**7.** *Restatement, Third, of Trusts* § 5, comm. b (2001).

**8.** *Restatement, Second, of Trusts* § 280 (1959).

**9.** Ellerbusch v. Myers, 683 N.E.2d 1352 (Ind.App.1997) (life tenant who insures property can keep all the proceeds when property is destroyed by fire).

**10.** *Restatement, Second, of Trusts* § 176, comment b (1959).

**11.** Pedro v. January, 494 P.2d 868, 875 (Or.1972).

**12.** *See* Section 12.6.

**13.** *Restatement of Property* § 124 (1936).

**14.** J. Baker, *An Introduction to English Legal History* 247 (2d ed. 1979).

**15.** Matter of Estate of Hookom, 764 P.2d 1001, 1005 (Wash.App.1988).

may allow the tenant to destroy the remainder. A tenant with "full and unrestricted power to sell, convey, dispose of, or expend all or any part of said property" can give the property away.[16]

Trustees, on the other hand, usually have power to sell trust property, but they cannot give it away without adequate consideration. When property in a trust is sold, the proceeds are retained in the trust. Legal life tenants with a power of sale, unlike trustees, are not obligated to keep the sale proceeds separate from their own property, and if the proceeds cannot be identified when the life tenant dies, the remainder fails.[17]

Since trusts and legal life estates perform a similar function, an instrument which creates a life estate may be construed to create a trust.[18] English legislation converts all life estates to trusts.[19]

*Trust Purposes*  Trusts may serve more than one objective. A drafter must understand the reason for a trust in order to draft it intelligently. Who should be trustee? If the trust is being used because of doubts about the beneficiary's capacity to handle property, the beneficiary should not be the trustee. But the beneficiary may be an ideal trustee for a by-pass trust. How long should the trust continue? This depends on whether a trust is designed to manage property until the beneficiaries are mature, or to keep property in the family or avoid estate taxes for as long as possible.

## § 9.4  Principal and Income

Suppose that a woman creates a trust which provides the trustee shall pay the income to her husband for life, and upon his death, convey the principal to her issue. The trustee may receive dividends, interest, rent, proceeds of property sold, etc. Are these receipts income to be distributed to the husband, or principal to be retained in trust for the issue? When the trust incurs expenses, such as trustee's fees or taxes, which account is charged with them? These problems arise repeatedly in the administration of trusts. Trustees need a clear answer. In most states a statute answers most questions. There are no less than three Uniform Principal and Income Acts. The first was promulgated in 1931, the second in 1962 and a third in 1997. Restatement of Trusts also has provisions on the subject.

**16.** Kelly v. Lansford, 572 S.W.2d 369 (Tex.Civ.App.1978).

**17.** South Side T. & S. Bank v. South Side T. & S. Bank, 284 N.E.2d 61 (Ill.App.1972). However, traceable property in life tenant's estate goes to the remaindermen. Caldwell v. Walraven, 490 S.E.2d 384 (Ga.1997).

**18.** Perfect U. Lodge v. Interfirst Bank, 748 S.W.2d 218 (Tex.1988).

**19.** Maudsley, *Escaping the Tyranny of Common Law Estates,* 42 Mo.L.Rev. 355 (1977).

*General Principles* The law of principal and income consists of many detailed rules. A few general principles underlie them. First, the settlor's intent controls. All the Acts expressly state that their provisions are subject to contrary directions in the trust.[1] However, it is sometimes not clear whether a testator or settlor actually intended to depart from the established rules.[2] Some wills give the trustee discretion to make allocations between principal and income. The 1997 Act says that a fiduciary may exercise such a discretionary power "even if the exercise of the power produces a result different from" the one dictated by the Act,.[3] but it is not always clear how far such discretion extends.[4]

The definition of income for other purposes influences the allocation of trust receipts.[5] However, capital gains are treated as "income" for tax purposes but are allocated to principal in trust accounting.[6]

A common theme is that receipts should be allocated so that the value of the principal is preserved and everything else is income. For example, the Restatement of Trusts allocates receipts from oil and gas "in such a way as will preserve the value of the principal."[7] However, unrealized appreciation of trust assets is not income,[8] except for charitable trusts under the Uniform Management of Institutional Funds Act.[9]

Courts sometimes suggest that doubtful allocation questions should be resolved in favor of the income beneficiaries because they are "the primary objects of [the settlor's] bounty,"[10] but the 1997 Act provides that in cases for which no rule is provided receipts shall be added to principal, since this serves the long-term interest of all beneficiaries because additions to principal will produce more income in the future.[11]

Administrative convenience is an important factor; an easily applicable rule is desirable. The 1962 Act adopted "an arbitrary allocation" of 27 1/2% of the gross receipts from natural resources to principal because apportioning them on the basis of the ratio of

§ 9.4

**1.** 1931 Act § 2; 1962 Act § 2; 1997 Act § 103(a)(1).

**2.** *See* Gaymon v. Gaymon, 519 S.E.2d 142, 146 (Va.1999); Venables v. Seattle–First Nat. Bank, 808 P.2d 769 (Wash.App.1991).

**3.** 1997 Act § 103(a)(2).

**4.** *Compare* Englund v. First Nat. Bank, 381 So.2d 8, 11 (Ala.1980) *with* duPont v. Southern Nat. Bank, 771 F.2d 874, 887 (5th Cir.1985).

**5.** 1962 Act § 8 ("generally accepted accounting principles" used in determining income of unincorporated business).

**6.** *Id.* § 3(b)(1); 1931 Act § 3(2); 1997 Act § 404(2); *Restatement, Second, of Trusts* § 233, comm. b (1959).

**7.** *Restatement, Second, of Trusts* § 239, comm. g (1959).

**8.** *Id.,* § 236, comm. y.

**9.** Unif.Man.Inst.Funds Act § 2.

**10.** Matter of Kuehn, 308 N.W.2d 398, 400 (S.D.1981).

**11.** 1997 Act § 103(a)(4), comment.

minerals extracted to minerals remaining in the ground was too difficult.[12] The 1997 Act allows trustees to rely on statements by a corporation as to the character of the distribution which it makes.[13]

Another underlying concept is the desirability of a relatively steady stream of "income," rather than wide fluctuations from year to year. The 1997 Act allocates to principal any corporate distributions amounting to more than 20% of the company's gross assets, and charges "ordinary repairs" and "regularly recurring" property taxes to income, whereas "disbursements relating to environmental matters" are charged against principal "on the assumption that they will usually be extraordinary in nature."[14]

*Specific Rules: Proceeds of Sale* When property is sold the proceeds are allocated to principal, including capital gains even though they are taxed as income. However, part of the proceeds of a sale may be treated as income in trust accounting if the property had not been producing adequate income before it was sold.[15] The 1997 Act rejects such special treatment for underproductive assets.[16] Instead it empowers trustees to make adjustments between principal and income in order to be "fair and reasonable to all beneficiaries." A trustee may invest entirely in growth stocks that produce little dividend income and at the same time transfer (an unspecified amount of) cash from principal to income in order to provide the income beneficiary "the degree of beneficial enjoyment normally accorded a person who is the income beneficiary of a trust."[17] This provision leaves much to the trustee's discretion, but has the advantage that income beneficiaries do not have to wait until unproductive property is sold in order to get their "fair share."

*Corporate Distributions* The Uniform Acts and the Restatement of Trusts have similar but not identical rules for allocating corporate distributions, including dividends, stock splits, liquidations, etc.[18] Generally speaking, cash dividends are income and other distributions including stock dividends are principal, but there are exceptions. The 1962 and 1997 Acts allocate cash dividends paid from capital gains by mutual funds to principal.[19]

A distribution made on total liquidation of a corporation is usually principal even if paid in cash.[20] Under the 1997 Act all

**12.** 1962 Act, Prefatory Note.

**13.** 1997 Act § 401(f).

**14.** 1997 Act §§ 401(d)(2), 501(3), 502(a)(7), comment.

**15.** Matter of Kuehn, 308 N.W.2d 398 (S.D.1981). *See also* 1962 Act § 12(a).

**16.** 1997 Act § 413, comment.

**17.** 1997 Act § 104, comment, Example 3.

**18.** 1962 Act § 6; 1931 Act § 5; *Restatement, Second, of Trusts* § 236 (1959).

**19.** 1962 Act § 6(c); 1997 Act § 401(b)(4).

**20.** 1962 Act § 6(b)(3); 1997 Act § 401(c)(3); 1931 Act § 5(3).

distributions in "property other than money" are principal, and also those in money which exceed 20% of the distributor's assets.[21]

The 1997 Act gives trustees holding an unincorporated business leeway to decide the extent to which receipts should be allocated to income, "just as the board of directors of a corporation owned entirely by the trust would decide the amount of annual dividends to be paid to the trust."[22] This discretion is not unlimited. When a trust holds a controlling interest in a corporation, courts can "pierce the corporate veil" and treat corporate earnings as trust income even though they have not been declared as dividends.[23]

Interest paid on bonds is income. Proceeds received on redemption are principal. The 1962 Act makes a special provision for United States Series E bonds, which nominally pay no interest but provide for redemption at a fixed schedule of appreciation in excess of the price at which the bond was issued: this appreciation is treated as income.[24]

*Wasting Assets* The counterpart to under-or unproductive property are "wasting assets," which lose value over time. Oil wells, for example, eventually run dry. If all the receipts were classified as income, principal would not be preserved. Nevertheless at common-law, "if mines were opened prior to the creation of the estates the life tenant is entitled to continue to work the mines and to take the proceeds as his own without deduction for depletion. On the other hand, where no mines were opened prior to the creation of the estates * * * the proceeds will be treated as principal" if mines are opened thereafter.[25] The 1962 Uniform Act, on the other hand, apportions oil royalties: 27 1/2% go to principal as an allowance for depletion, and the remainder is income.[26] The 1997 Act replaces this with a 90% allocation of receipts to principal.[27]

Can trustees establish a reserve for depreciation for buildings? Must they? The 1962 Uniform Act requires trustees to set up "a reasonable allowance for depreciation * * * under generally accepted accounting principles."[28] The 1997 Act, on the other hand,

**21.** 1997 Act § 401.

**22.** *Id.,* § 403, comment.

**23.** Matter of Estate of Butterfield, 341 N.W.2d 453, 462 (Mich.1983).

**24.** 1962 Act § 7(b). The 1997 Act eliminates this provision, except for bonds which mature within one year of their purchase. 1997 Act § 406(b)

**25.** First Wyoming Bank v. First Nat. Bank, 628 P.2d 1355, 1365 (Wyo. 1981). *See also Restatement, Second, of Trusts* § 239, comm. g (1959).

**26.** 1962 Act § 9(a)(3). The figure in the 1962 Act was derived from the rule then used for computing income for tax purposes.

**27.** 1997 Act § 411.

**28.** 1962 Act § 13(a)(2). There are many local variations in adopting states on this issue. New York for example did not adopt the depreciation provision of the 1962 Act. Matter of Will of Diamond, 519 N.Y.S.2d 788 (Surr.1987).

simply permits trustees to create a reserve for depreciation. The comment notes that such a reserve "has been resisted by many trustees" because it is "not needed to protect the remainder beneficiaries if the value of the land is increasing."[29]

*Apportionment Over Time* Items like interest and rent are clearly income but they may be partially allocated to principal if the income beneficiary dies between payments. Under the 1962 and 1931 Uniform Acts, unless the instrument provides otherwise, periodic payments like rent and interest are "accrued from day to day" and the estate of a deceased income beneficiary gets a share when they are ultimately paid.[30] Under the 1997 Act, on the other hand, the income beneficiary's estate receives no accrued interest, but does get income which the trustee had received but not distributed prior to the beneficiary's death.[31]

Apportionment problems also arise at the beginning of a trust. An income beneficiary of a testamentary trust is entitled to income from the date of the testator's death,[32] but this income may not actually be distributed until administration of the estate is completed. Suppose that a testator whose will creates a trust holds stock on which a dividend is declared before she dies, but paid after her death; does the dividend go to the income beneficiary? This depends upon the "record date," the date fixed by the company for determining who is entitled to receive the dividend "or, if no date is fixed, on the declaration date of the dividend." If the relevant date occurred prior to the testator's death, the dividend is assigned to principal.[33]

*Planning* Trusts can be drafted so that distributions do not depend on classification of items as income or principal. Most trusts allow invasion of principal to meet the needs of the "income" beneficiaries. A settlor may wish to have *all* distributions based on need, but, as we shall see, controversies about "need" may be harder to resolve than questions about what is "income." On the other hand, making distributions depend on "income" may distort investment decisions. Trustees traditionally could not invest in wasting property because of their duty to preserve the principal, even though "wasting property may produce such high income that its net return—income less depreciation—is comparatively sound."[34] The 1997 Act attempts to avoid this problem by empower-

**29.** 1997 Act § 503. A reserve for depreciation is not even allowed in the case of a residence held for the enjoyment of a beneficiary.

**30.** 1962 Act § 4(d); 1931 Act § 4.

**31.** 1997 Act § 303(b), comment. Under *Restatement, Second, of Trusts* § 235 (1959) interest is apportioned but not rent.

**32.** 1997 Act § 301. See also *Restatement, Second, of Trusts* § 234 (1959).

**33.** 1997 Act § 302(c). See also *Restatement, Second, of Trusts* § 236, comm. i (1959).

**34.** Comment, 50 Texas L.Rev. 747, 763–64 (1972).

ing trustees to make the necessary adjustments between principal and income "if the trustee manages trust assets as a prudent investor."[35]

It is possible draft a trust so that benefits are allocated without regard to either income or need. "[A] constant percentage rule allocates all receipts to principal, and on each payment date distributes as income a fixed percentage of the value of the principal. The annuity rule pays out a fixed dollar amount [which can be] corrected for changes in purchasing power."[36] Trusts *must* use one of these two formulas, commonly called "unitrust" and "annuity," if a charitable remainder is to qualify for a federal income, estate or gift tax deduction. The untirust has become increasingly popular among estate planners, and several states have legislation which authorizes trustees to convert "income" trusts to unitrusts.[37] Unitrusts can achieve the same goal as the discretion accorded trustees under the 1997 UPIA to make adjustments between principal and income without giving trustees such open-ended discretion. Some estate planners are more skeptical, pointing out the problems in applying the percentage when a trust contains assets which are hard to value. Also when a trust holds assets which produce little or no income, the trustee may have to sell assets in order to make the mandated distributions.

## § 9.5  Discretionary Trusts

*Advantages*  A major advantage of trusts over guardianship is that trustees can be given discretion to make distributions from time to time to different beneficiaries. Many trusts are designed to last for an extended period, and they may be unable to meet the beneficiaries' changing needs unless the trustee is allowed flexibility. A power to distribute principal (sometimes called corpus) to an income beneficiary is very common. Powers to accumulate income and add it to principal, or to "sprinkle" income and principal among a group of beneficiaries are also used with increasing frequency. When the beneficiaries of a trust are minors, it is usually advisable that any income in excess of their current needs be accumulated and reinvested by the trustee, since otherwise the excess income would have to be distributed to the beneficiary's guardian.

The financial needs of children vary as they grow up. One who is entering college usually needs more than siblings who are living at home attending public schools. Parents typically consider such

**35.**  1997 Act § 104(a). *See also* the Prefatory Note.

**36.**  Note, 33 U.Chi.L.Rev. 783, 789 (1966).

**37.**  *See, e.g.* In re Estate of Ives, 745 N.Y.S.2d 904 (Surr.2002) (income trust converted to a 4% unitrust under NY EPTL § 11–2.4).

differences in need in allocating their resources. If the parents die before their children are grown, a trustee can do the same.

Discretionary trusts offer income tax advantages. Since income of a trust is normally taxed to the person who receives it, trustees can reduce the total taxes paid by a family by distributing income to family members who are in lower tax brackets—children instead of their parents, for example, if the children are still in school and the parents have well-paying jobs.

Giving trustees discretion over distributions of income is not usually advisable, however, when a beneficiary is likely to need all the trust income, since disputes may arise between the beneficiaries and trustee as to how this discretion is exercised. But careful drafting can reduce the risk of such litigation.

*Judicial Review of Trustee's Discretion* Judicial review of trustees' decisions takes several forms. Sometimes a remainderman seeks to enjoin a trustee from distributing corpus to an income beneficiary, or to surcharge the trustee for distributions previously made.[1] Conversely, a beneficiary may complain of a trustee's refusal to make distributions. Courts may order trustees to make distributions, including payments to the estate of a beneficiary who has since died.[2]

Reported cases involving claims by beneficiaries that trustees were too stingy or overly generous in exercising discretion are relatively uncommon, because courts rarely overrule trustees' decisions. "A trustee's exercise of discretion should not be overruled by a court unless the trustee has clearly abused the discretion granted him under the trust instrument or acted arbitrarily."[3] However, courts do occasionally overturn trustees' decisions, even if the trust instrument gives the trustee "sole discretion." For example, a trustee was ordered to increase payments to a beneficiary because the trust instrument referred to the beneficiary's "comfortable maintenance and support," which showed that the "trustee's discretion was not intended to be absolute" despite the words "sole discretion."[4] Trustees must act impartially toward the beneficiaries; this does not mean that all beneficiaries must receive equal amounts, but the trustee must investigate the needs of them all.[5]

**§ 9.5**

**1.** Austin v. U.S. Bank of Washington, 869 P.2d 404 (Wash.App.1994).

**2.** Marsman v. Nasca, 573 N.E.2d 1025 (Mass.App.Ct.1991).

**3.** NationsBank of Virginia v. Estate of Grandy, 450 S.E.2d 140, 143 (Va. 1994). *See also Restatement, Third, of Trusts* § 50 (2001).

**4.** Kolodney v. Kolodney, 503 A.2d 625, 627 (Conn.App.1986). *See also* Unif. Trust Code § 814(a) (despite "absolute" discretion, trustee must act "in good faith and with regard to the purposes of the trust").

**5.** *Restatement, Third, of Trusts* § 79, comm.c (Prel.Dft.2003).

*Language of Instrument* In reviewing a trustee's action, the language of the trust instrument is important, *i.e.,* the "existence or non-existence, the definiteness or indefiniteness, of an external standard by which the reasonableness of the trustee's conduct can be judged."[6] If an instrument directs a trustee to pay whatever amount it "deems necessary for the support" of a beneficiary, the trustee will be ordered to increase payments which were inadequate for support, but if the instrument says that trustees are to make distributions as they "deem best," judicial review is very limited.[7]

The word "support" is defined by reference to station in life; the trustee is bound to maintain the beneficiary "in accordance with the standard of living which was normal for him before he became a beneficiary of the trust."[8] The size of the trust is also relevant. Where a beneficiary over time comes to enjoy a higher standard of living, this "may become the appropriate standard of support *if consistent with the trust's level of productivity.*" Conversely, "a lower level of distributions may be justifiable if the trust estate is modest relative to the probable future needs of the beneficiary."[9]

It is not clear how much weight references to the beneficiary's "comfort" or "happiness" carry. The word "comfort," when "part of a clause referencing the support, maintenance and education of the beneficiary" may mean only what was "reasonably necessary to maintain the beneficiary in his accustomed manner of living."[10]

Review of trustees' discretionary decisions sometimes reflects assumptions that the settlor preferred certain beneficiaries. Denial of a payment requested by the settlor's widow was upheld when the settlor's "children were his primary concern and any provision for his wife * * * was clearly secondary,"[11] whereas invasion of principal for a widow was approved where "the testator was concerned primarily with his wife's comfort and any residue to others was secondary."[12]

Courts often distinguish between income and principal even when the trust instrument gives the trustee the same powers over both. A trustee who was directed to "distribute to my spouse* * * as much of the income and principal * * * as the trustee believes desirable" for his support, was surcharged for excessive distributions of principal whereas the payments from income were not

---

**6.** *Restatement, Second, of Trusts* § 187, comment d (1959).

**7.** American Cancer Soc. v. Hammerstein, 631 S.W.2d 858 (Mo.App.1981).

**8.** Marsman v. Nasca, 573 N.E.2d 1025, 1030 (Mass.App.Ct.1991).

**9.** *Restatement, Third, of Trusts,* § 50, comm. e (emphasis added).

**10.** Estate of Vissering v. C.I.R., 990 F.2d 578, 581 (10th Cir.1993).

**11.** In re Flyer's Will, 245 N.E.2d 718, 720 (N.Y.1969).

**12.** Hart v. Connors, 228 N.E.2d 273, 275 (Ill.App.1967).

considered unreasonable.[13] Conversely, a trustee under a similar clause was rebuked for "niggardliness" when it accumulated much of the trust income.[14]

If a trust names a beneficiary as trustee, the resultant conflict of interest may affect judicial review of trustees' decisions. A trustee who refused to make payments to the settlor's spouse was held to have "acted with improper motives and with a clear conflict of interest * * * by seeking to preserve the trust funds for himself and his heirs as remaindermen."[15] Some jurisdictions even prohibit trustees from participating in decisions in which they have such a conflict of interest.[16] But most courts defer to the judgment of the settlor who created the conflict of interest, and approve exercise of discretionary powers from which the trustee benefits if it is deemed reasonable.[17]

*Other Resources of Beneficiary* If a trust provides for the support of a person who needs $50,000 a year and has a job which pays $35,000 a year, should the trustee take the beneficiary's earnings into account? income from assets which the beneficiary owns outside the trust? Should the trustee require the beneficiary to sell such assets before resorting to the trust?

The judicial opinions which discuss this issue are hard to reconcile, because the language of the governing instrument and the circumstances vary in every case. The Restatement of Trust presumes that the trustee "is to consider other resources but has some discretion in the matter."[18] A trustee who distributed principal to a beneficiary without determining what other funds she might have was held to have shown "reckless disregard" for the rights of the remaindermen.[19]

Some courts distinguish between income and principal; a trustee should consider the beneficiary's income from all sources but the beneficiary's own principal need not be depleted before resorting to the trust.[20] It is undesirable to force beneficiaries to sell assets which are not readily marketable to raise needed funds. Yet

**13.** Dunkley v. Peoples Bank & Trust Co., 728 F.Supp. 547, 564 (W.D.Ark.1989).

**14.** Old Colony Trust Company v. Rodd, 254 N.E.2d 886, 890 (Mass.1970).

**15.** Matter of Estate of McCart, 847 P.2d 184, 186 (Colo.App.1992). *See also Restatement, Third, of Trusts* § 79, comm. b (Prel.Dft.2003) ("trustee-beneficiary's conduct is to be closely scrutinized for abuse").

**16.** Matter of Estate of Seidman, 395 N.Y.S.2d 674 (App.Div.1977); First Union Nat. Bank v. Cisa, 361 S.E.2d 615 (S.C.1987).

**17.** *E.g.* Bracken v. Block, 561 N.E.2d 1273 (Ill.App.1990); *Restatement, Third, of Trusts* § 50, illus. 1 (2001).

**18.** *Restatement, Third, of Trusts* § 50, comm. e (2001).

**19.** Feibelman v. Worthen Nat. Bank, N.A., 20 F.3d 835 (8th Cir.1994).

**20.** Barnett Banks Trust Co. v. Herr, 546 So.2d 755 (Fla.App.1989).

sometimes it is the trust which holds illiquid assets which would have to be sold to satisfy a request for a distribution of principal.

Should trustees consider a beneficiary's right to support from a parent or spouse? The Restatement presumes that "the trustee is to take account of a parental duty to support a youthful beneficiary" since "only the parents would be likely to be benefited if the trustee provides what the child is entitled to in any event."[21]

*Welfare Eligibility* A frequently litigated issue is the effect of a discretionary trust on a beneficiary's eligibility for governmental welfare benefits. For example, the mother of a man who was receiving health care from a state agency created a trust for him. The agency terminated his benefits, saying that the trust rendered him ineligible. The court disagreed, because this was a "discretionary" trust. "Courts usually conclude that a support trust is an available asset, while a discretionary trust is not."[22] The distinction between "discretionary" and "support" trusts is often repeated, but is not really workable, since all trusts which provide "support" for a beneficiary give the trustee some discretion in determining how much the beneficiary should get.

Some courts have considered trust assets in determining welfare eligibility because "public assistance funds are ever in short supply, and public policy demands they be restricted to those without resources of their own."[23] Other courts disagree, e.g., the settlor was under no "obligation to provide for the support of his adult child. * * * [He] intended to provide his daughter with a source of supplemental support that would not jeopardize her access to basic assistance from Medicaid."[24]

Cases where the beneficiary of a discretionary trust is also the settlor are special. A federal statute deals with "medicaid qualifying trusts," trusts created "by an individual (or an individual's spouse) under which the individual may be the beneficiary of * * * payments from the trust" in the trustee's discretion, "whether or not the discretion * * * is actually exercised."[25] In such an MQT "whatever is the most the beneficiary might receive in the full

**21.** *Restatement, Third, of Trusts* § 50, comm. e (2001). *But see* McElrath v. Citizens & Southern Nat. Bank, 189 S.E.2d 49 (Ga.1972).

**22.** Matter of Leona Carlisle Trust, 498 N.W.2d 260, 264 (Minn.App.1993).

**23.** State ex rel. Sec'y of SRS v. Jackson, 822 P.2d 1033, 1040 (Kan. 1991).

**24.** Young v. Ohio Dept. of Human Serv., 668 N.E.2d 908, 911–12 (Ohio 1996).

**25.** 42 U.S.C. § 1396a(k). However, the statute allows "supplemental needs" trusts which are not counted in determining medicaid eligibility "if the State will receive all amounts remaining in the trust upon the death of" the beneficiary to the extent the beneficiary has received medical assistance from the state. *Id.,* § 1396p(d)(4)(A). *See also* Department of Social Serv. v. Saunders, 724 A.2d 1093 (Conn.1999) (authorizing the use of settlement proceeds to create such a trust on behalf of an incompetent claimant)

exercise of [the trustee's] discretion is * * * counted as available for Medicaid eligibility."[26]

The statute sometimes gives rise to the question who was the settlor of a trust. When a man settled a claim arising from a disabling injury and the settlement proceeds were placed in a discretionary trust, this was held to be a MQT. "The fact that the trust * * * was established * * * by a probate court, as settlor, is inconsequential. * * * The trust property already belonged to the beneficiary."[27] A discretionary trust established by the beneficiary's spouse is also a MQT—for this purpose the old treatment of spouses as one person governs.[28]

*Drafting* The drafter of a discretionary trust ought to deal with the question of outside resources, e.g. allow the trustee to consider "to the extent the trustee deems advisable, any income or other resources of that beneficiary known to the trustee and reasonably available."[29]

A clause which authorizes a trustee to use funds for a number of persons, such as the settlor's children, should make clear that (1) not every member of the group must receive a distribution,[30] and (2) the income need not all be distributed, assuming that the settlor wishes to provide maximum flexibility.[31]

Some commentators suggest that professional trustees tend to be overly conservative in making discretionary distributions. If the settlor is concerned about this, a beneficiary can be made a co-trustee, or be given power to remove the trustee and appoint another. Another alternative is to give the *beneficiary* a power to invade principal, assuming the settlor has confidence in the beneficiary's judgment. The tax rules should be carefully studied, to make sure that the beneficiary's power does not defeat the tax objective.[32]

*Factors Other than Need* Discretion usually involves an assessment of beneficiaries' needs, but the settlor may want other factors considered as well. A beneficiary who has no need for support may nevertheless wish distributions to allow her to reduce her taxable estate by making gifts.[33] Even if all the beneficiaries have enough income for support, it may be desirable to distribute

**26.** Cohen v. Commissioner of Div. of Med. Asst., 668 N.E.2d 769, 777 (Mass. 1996).

**27.** Barham by Barham v. Rubin, 816 P.2d 965, 967 (Haw.1991).

**28.** Prior v. Ohio Dept. of Human Serv., 704 N.E.2d 296 (Ohio App.1997).

**29.** Uniform Statutory Will Act § 6(2).

**30.** As to the distinction between "exclusive" and "non-exclusive" powers see Section 10.4.

**31.** For a model see Uniform Statutory Will Act § 8(b).

**32.** A beneficiary's power may also give creditors of the beneficiary rights to reach the interest. See Section 13.1.

**33.** In re McGuire Marital Trust, 660 N.W.2d 308, 312 (Wis.App.2003).

trust income to one who is in a lower income-tax bracket than the others.

Settlors may also wish a trustee to consider the beneficiary's ability to handle funds. Many trusts provide for distribution when a beneficiary attains a certain age. Since settlors can rarely predict when beneficiaries will achieve maturity, it may be better to let the trustee decide when a beneficiary is mature enough to receive the principal.[34]

*Single versus Separate Trusts* Related to the question of discretionary versus fixed-benefit trusts is the question *how many* trusts should be created. Is it better to create a single trust for all the testator/settlor's children, for example, or separate trusts for each? This depends on whether the settlor wants the children to receive equal benefits, or prefers to allow the trustee to give more to one child than to another. This choice often depends upon the ages of the children and on the size of the trust estate. If a modest fund is being used to provide for young children, since one child may have greater need in a particular year, a single trust with discretion in the trustee is usually desirable. At the other extreme is a large estate held in trust for children of full age. Most parents want their children to receive equal shares in this situation, so separate trusts for each child are more suitable. They allow the trustee to satisfy reasonable requests by one child for distribution without affecting the shares of the child's siblings.

*Indefinite Beneficiaries* A trust sometimes fails because the trustee has *too much* discretion in choosing beneficiaries on the theory that a trust must have ascertainable beneficiaries to enforce it. A will that directed the residuary estate "be divided among my close friends in such a way * * * as my trustee in her discretion should determine" failed because the words "close friends * * * are too uncertain."[35]

Courts have resorted to various techniques to save trusts like this. When a will directed trustees to distribute to "worthy charities, institutions and individuals," the court held that "the word 'worthy' was meant to refer only to institutions falling within the legal definition of charity.[36] The term 'relatives' or 'family' may be construed to mean heirs in order to avoid uncertainty.[37] Invalidity can also be avoided if the troublesome language is construed as an outright devise with precatory suggestions rather than a trust.

---

**34.** Uniform Statutory Will Act § 9.

**35.** Re Connor, 10 Dom.L.R.3d 5, 11 (Alberta 1970).

**36.** Newick v. Mason, 581 A.2d 1269 (Me.1990). *But see* Klassen v. Klassen, [1986] 5 W.W.R. 746 (Sask.Q.B.) (devise to "persons and/or charitable organization" determined by executors fails).

**37.** *Restatement, Third, of Trusts* § 45, comm. d (2001); McLendon v. Priest, 376 S.E.2d 679 (Ga.1989) (contract to leave property to spouse's "family" construed to mean heirs); Unif.Probate Code § 2–711.

When a will left the estate to a woman 'to divide and disperse as she sees fit,' " the court held that she took the property outright.[38]

*Trusts* must have definite beneficiaries but no such requirement exists for *powers of appointment*.[39] The Restatement of Trusts avoids invalidating trusts with no definite beneficiaries by deeming that a direction to A to distribute property among an indefinite group gives A "power but no duty to distribute the property" to the person(s) A may select.[40] The settlor's heirs can compel A to convey the property to them if A does not make distribution within a reasonable period.

Trusts (or powers) for an uncertain group of beneficiaries raise other problems, however. The person named by the settlor may fail to act, *e.g.*, predecease the settlor. When a designated trustee fails to act, courts usually appoint a successor with all the same powers, but a settlor who gives a close relative or friend a broad power to choose beneficiaries may not want some other person to make the selection.[41]

Another question is whether the person with power to choose can choose him or herself. When conflicts of interest exist in trusts with definite beneficiaries, courts can assume that the settlor was aware of them and believed that the trustee would nevertheless act fairly in making distributions. But where a person is authorized to distribute property among the testator's "friends" and chooses herself, one wonders whether the settlor actually contemplated this.[42]

## § 9.6  Modification and Termination of Trusts

Most trusts are set up to last for a considerable period after the settlor has died. Circumstances may change, and the trust terms may no longer reflect the new situation. Courts can allow deviations from the terms of a charitable trust when this occurs under the *cy pres* doctrine,[1] but they have been more hesitant to do so with private trusts. "When the intention of a settlor is plainly expressed * * * the Court will not go outside the instrument in an attempt to give effect to what it conceives to have been the actual intent or motive of the settlor."[2]

**38.** Tucker v. Bradford, 599 So.2d 611 (Ala.1992). *See also Restatement, Third, of Trusts* § 13, illus. 5–7 (2001).

**39.** For a general discussion of powers of appointment see Section 10.4.

**40.** *Restatement, Third, of Trusts* § 46 (2001).

**41.** *Id.*, comm. d (2001). For a more general discussion of whether a trustee's powers are "personal" see Section 12.4.

**42.** *See Restatement, Second, of Property (Donative Transfers)* § 12.1, illus. 10–11 (1984).

**§ 9.6**

1. See Section 9.7.

2. Taylor v. Hutchinson, 497 P.2d 527, 530 (Ariz.App.1972). *See also* Appeal of Harrell, 801 P.2d 852 (Or.App. 1990) (refusal to extend duration of a trust for a retarded child).

Some deviations in a trust do not affect the interests of remaindermen, e.g., a trust calls for distributing principal to a person at a specified age, and the person needs support before reaching the designated age. The Restatement allows the use of trust assets for support of a needy beneficiary prematurely "if the interest of no other beneficiary of the trust is impaired thereby."[3]

*Administrative Provisions* The Restatement also allows trustees to deviate from *administrative* provisions of a trust, if owing to circumstances unanticipated by the settlor, compliance with the trust terms "would defeat or substantially impair the accomplishment of the purposes of the trust."[4] Some trusts prohibit sale of the trust assets, or of a particular asset by the trustee. Although such a restriction is valid, courts may overrule it when the circumstances change.[5] Strong evidence is required to do this. The conservative attitude of courts is illustrated by a case in which the instrument required the approval of the settlor's wife before the trustee could sell property. When the wife turned out to be "impossible to work with," the court held that it was proper to remove her from the position of advisor, but not to eliminate the requirement of an advisor's consent since this would go "beyond what is necessary to correct the circumstances which threaten the purpose of the trust."[6]

Courts may remove restrictions on trust investments if circumstances change after the trust was created. A trust created in 1977 limited investments to interest-bearing bank accounts and certificates of deposit. Twenty years later a court removed this limitation, because "current economic conditions are far different from the unusual conditions that prevailed in 1977. Bank account investments now yield radically lower returns."[7] Courts do not remove such restrictions "merely because [it] would be more advantageous to the beneficiaries."[8]

When a professional trustee is used, the costs of a trust can outweigh the advantages when only a small amount is left in the

**3.** *Restatement, Second, of Trusts* § 168 (1959). A number of statutes allow a invasion of a fund being accumulated for a person who has become "destitute." Ala. Code § 35–4–253.

**4.** *Restatement, Second, of Trusts* § 167 (1959). *Restatement, Third, of Trusts* § 66 (2001) confers a broader power, not limited to administrative provisions.

**5.** Ex parte Guaranty Bank & Trust Co., 177 S.E.2d 358, 360 (S.C.1970).

**6.** Papiernik v. Papiernik, 544 N.E.2d 664, 672 (Ohio 1989).

**7.** Matter of Siegel, 665 N.Y.S.2d 813, 815 (Surr.1997).

**8.** *Restatement, Second, of Trusts* § 167, comm. b (1959). *See also* Matter of Estate of Murdock, 884 P.2d 749, 754 (Kan.App.1994) (refusing to remove investment restrictions in charitable trust "in the absence of compelling evidence to indicate that [they were] 'obsolete' ")

trust. Several statutes allow premature termination of trusts whose continued operation has become uneconomical.[9]

Another type of deviation is the consolidation of separate trusts or, conversely, the division of a trust into separate trusts. California authorizes courts to permit this "for good cause" when the change "will not defeat or substantially impair * * * the interests of the beneficiaries."[10]

The Uniform Trust Code has an open-ended provision which allows courts to modify the administrative *or dispositive* provisions of a trust when this "will further the purposes of the trust" due to "circumstances not anticipated by the settlor."[11] The few reported cases under similar legislation in some states suggest that courts will not often utilize it.[12]

*Consent of All Beneficiaries*  Sometimes trust beneficiaries agree that a trust should be modified or terminated, but most trusts have minor, unborn or unascertained beneficiaries whose existence makes unanimous consent impossible. Various legal doctrines may help to overcome this problem.

Some courts accept proof negating the possibility of future children. For example, a trust provided for termination when all of the settlor's grandchildren were 30. The beneficiaries sought to terminate the trust when the settlor's existing grandchildren were over 30 and her only children were daughters aged 65 and 70. The trustee resisted termination, citing the possibility of later grandchildren under a "presumption that the birth of a child is possible throughout the life of a woman." The court, however, said that the presumption "had its origin at a time when medical knowledge was meager" and should be rebuttable today.[13] This modern view is widely though not universally followed, but it rarely suffices to allow trusts to be modified. If a trust gives a remainder to "the issue of A," even if A is incapable of bearing further children and the possibility of adoption is disregarded, if A has children, *their* children are potential trust beneficiaries whose consent is needed in order to modify the trust.

Some trusts provide for the "heirs" of the settlor or another person. A person's heirs can only be determined at his or her death. California allows potential heirs who have only a remote possibility

---

**9.** Cal.Prob.Code § 15408(a); Uniform Trust Code § 414.

**10.** Cal.Prob.Code § 15411 (combination), 15412 (division). *See also* Uniform Trust Code § 417; Matter of Estate of Branigan, 609 A.2d 431 (N.J.1992).

**11.** Uniform Trust Code § 412(a).

**12.** Ivey v. Ivey, 465 S.E.2d 434 (Ga. 1996); Wils v. Robinson, 934 S.W.2d 774 (Tex.App.1996).

**13.** Korten v. Chicago City Bank and Trust Co., 533 N.E.2d 102, 103 (Ill.App. 1988).

of taking (e.g. collateral relatives of a person with a spouse and children) to be disregarded.[14]

Future interests can sometimes be limited by acceleration. When property is held "to S for life, remainder to S's children," and S "makes a qualified disclaimer of his life interest, * * * the remainder to S's children is accelerated, [and] * * * any child of S that is conceived or adopted" thereafter is excluded,[15] unless the court finds that this would defeat the settlor's intent.[16]

A guardian ad litem appointed to represent minor, unborn or unascertained trust beneficiaries may approve a modification of the trust terms,[17] but a guardian's duties to the persons he or she represents may preclude such approval. A court refused to allow a trust to be modified despite a guardian's "pro forma consent," since the modification "would not sufficiently protect the unborn contingent beneficiaries' interests."[18] Some statutes authorize guardians to consent on the basis of "general family benefit accruing to living members of the beneficiary's family" without focusing solely on the immediate interests of the persons they represent.[19]

Lack of consent by a beneficiary is no bar to a modification that will have no effect on the non-consenting beneficiary. Thus when all the beneficiaries except one annuitant sought to terminate a trust, the court directed the trustee to retain enough funds to pay the annuity and distribute the rest of the trust assets.[20]

*Purposes of the Settlor* Even if all the beneficiaries consent, termination is not allowed "if the continuance of the trust is necessary to carry out a material purpose of the trust."[21] This limitation does not exist in England but most American jurisdictions follow the leading case, Claflin v. Claflin,[22] which involved a testamentary trust for the settlor's son who was to get the corpus

**14.** Cal.Prob.Code § 15404(c). See also the discussion of the Doctrine of Worthier Title in Section 10.2.

**15.** *Restatement, Second, of Property (Donative Transfers)* § 26.1, comm. j (1987). *See also* Pate v. Ford, 376 S.E.2d 775 (S.C.1989); Uniform Prob.Code § 2–1106(b)(4). As to the requirements of a "qualified disclaimer" see Section 2.8.

**16.** Linkous v. Candler, 508 S.E.2d 657 (Ga.1998).

**17.** Matter of Edwards Irrevocable Trust, 966 P.2d 810 (Okla.Civ.App.1998) (error not to allow termination of trust with consent of GAL for remainderman); *Restatement, Third, of Trusts* § 65, comment b (2001).

**18.** Friedman v. Teplis, 492 S.E.2d 885, 887 (Ga.1997). *Compare* Appeal of Gannon, 631 A.2d 176, 187 (Pa.Super.1993) where a GAL approved a settlement because "his wards had only remote and contingent interest with little likelihood of vesting."

**19.** Cal.Prob.Code § 15405; Wis. Stat.§ 701.12(2); Unif.Trust Code § 305(c).

**20.** Matter of Boright, 377 N.W.2d 9, 13 (Minn.1985). *See also Restatement, Third, of Trusts* § 65, comment c (2001).

**21.** *Restatement, Second, of Trusts* § 337(2) (1959). *But see now Restatement, Third, of Trusts* § 65 (2001).

**22.** 20 N.E. 454 (Mass.1889). Even where the *Claflin* doctrine is accepted, it does not apply after the trust has endured for the period allowed by the Rule against Perpetuities. See Section 11.1.

at age 30. The son sought to get the trust assets when he was only 24. The court refused even though he was the sole beneficiary, because "the purposes of the trust have not been accomplished."

The dominant idea of *Claflin* is that the settlor's wishes should be followed. If circumstances not contemplated by the settlor arise, courts recognize that the settlor's intent might best be carried out by departing from the terms of the trust.[23] Some judges, however, *Claflin* rather strictly and refuse to "speculate on what the settlor might have done" under changed circumstances.[24]

The result depends on the "purposes of the trust." A trust may have multiple purposes, and, at least in some states, their relative importance must be weighed; the beneficiaries can compel a modification unless it "would frustrate a material purpose of the trust *and* the reasons for modification are outweighed by such material purpose."[25] Usually the trust purposes are not explicitly stated and so must be inferred from the beneficial interests created by the trust.[26]

If a trust calls for distribution when a beneficiary reaches a specified age, the settlor's purpose was probably to postpone distribution until the beneficiary was mature enough (in the settlor's opinion) to handle the money.[27] In a bypass trust, *e.g.* "to A for life, remainder to her children," even if the beneficiaries can be ascertained and are sui juris, a spendthrift provision is often held to bar early termination, because of "the testator's obvious purpose to protect the [beneficiary] against his own improvidence."[28]

If a purpose of the trust was to protect against a beneficiary's improvidence, can the beneficiary show that the settlor was mistaken about this? According to the Restatement, if a trust was created "solely on account of a physical or mental disability of the beneficiary," removal of the disability warrants termination of the trust.[29] Many drafters routinely insert spendthrift provisions without real consideration of the abilities of the beneficiaries, who are often infants or unborn when the trust is drafted. Therefore, to make

**23.** In re Bayley Trust, 250 A.2d 516 (Vt.1969).

**24.** Trabits v. First Nat. Bank, 345 So.2d 1347 (Ala.1977).

**25.** In re Mark K. Eggebrecht Irrevocable Trust, 4 P.3d 1207, 1210 (Mont. 2000); Cal.Prob.Code § 15403(b).

**26.** *Restatement, Third, of Trusts* Ch. 6, Int. Note (2001). However, extrinsic evidence may also be used to determine the trust purposes. *Restatement, Second, of Trusts* § 337, comment e (1959).

**27.** Collins v. First Nat. Bank, 251 N.E.2d 610 (Ohio App.1969); *Restate-*

*ment, Third, of Trusts* § 65, illus. 5 (2001). Even in this case, however, an earlier distribution may be ordered if the beneficiary needs the funds.

**28.** In re Estate of Davis, 297 A.2d 451, 455 (Pa.1972). *See also* Fleisch v. First American Bank, 710 N.E.2d 1281 (Ill.App.1999) (termination denied where it would "defeat the spendthrift provisions of the trust"). For spendthrift provisions see Section 13.1.

**29.** *Restatement, Second, Trusts* § 337, comm. h (1959).

spendthrift provisions a litmus test of trust purposes is unfortunate. The California Probate Code makes them "a factor" but not conclusive in deciding whether to modify or terminate a trust.[30]

Sometimes a will creates a trust for an heir who contests the will, alleging, for example, that the testator lacked capacity. If the interested parties agree on a settlement by which the contestant will receive property free of trust, the settlement may be approved despite *Claflin*.[31] A spendthrift clause does not bar a timely disclaimer by the beneficiary.[32] The Uniform Probate Code allows courts to approve settlements "even though [they] may affect a trust or an inalienable interest."[33] However, some courts deny requests for early termination of trusts even in this situation.[34]

*Settlor Consents* If the settlor of a living trust consents to early termination, the fact that a "material purpose" of the trust remains unaccomplished is no bar.[35] Thus even an "irrevocable" trust may be revoked by the settlor, if the settlor is the sole beneficiary or if the other beneficiaries agree. The consent of the trustee is not necessary.[36]

*Standing* The trustee's interest in continuing a trust in order to earn more fees is not a legitimate reason for refusing to terminate it. But if a court orders termination, the trustee has standing to appeal pursuant to its duty to see that the settlor's intent is carried out.[37]

A trustee who accedes to a request for termination by some beneficiaries can be surcharged by other beneficiaries for a wrongful distribution, but the recipient(s) of the distribution (if not legally incapacitated) cannot claim that the earlier distribution was improper, even if they were spendthrifts and dissipated the funds.[38]

*Planning* Cases in which beneficiaries seek to terminate trusts are often a result of bad planning. When a court terminates a trust because its purposes have ceased, better drafting might have created a more flexible trust which could have been terminated without costly litigation. Thoughtless insertion of a spendthrift

**30.** Cal.Prob.Code § 15409(b). *See also* Uniform Trust Code § 411(c).

**31.** Budin v. Levy, 180 N.E.2d 74 (Mass.1962).

**32.** *Restatement, Third, of Trusts* § 58, comm. c (2001); Uniform Probate Code § 2–801(a).

**33.** Uniform Probate Code § 3–1101.

**34.** St. Louis Union Trust Co. v. Conant, 499 S.W.2d 761 (Mo.1973); *cf.* Fleisch v. First American Bank, 710 N.E.2d 1281 (Ill.App.1999) (denying termination based on a settlement in the absence of "a *bona fide* family dispute").

**35.** Matter of Edwards Irrevocable Trust, 966 P.2d 810 (Okl.Civ.App.1998); Uniform Trust Code § 411(a).

**36.** Hein v. Hein, 543 N.W.2d 19, 20 (Mich.App.1995).

**37.** American National Bank v. Miller, 899 P.2d 1337 (Wyo.1995).

**38.** Hagerty v. Clement, 196 So. 330 (La.1940); *Restatement, Second, of Trusts* § 342 (1959). One who distributes to a minor, however, may have to pay again if the minor squanders the money. See Section 12.10.

provision may cause a trust to be needlessly prolonged. Perhaps courts should be more liberal in authorizing trusts to be modified, but whenever changed circumstances arise for which the trust instrument fails to provide, the settlor's intention is inevitably open to doubt.

## § 9.7  Charitable Trusts

Charitable trusts are an exception to the general rule that trusts must have definite beneficiaries. Identifiable beneficiaries are not needed to enforce charitable trusts because a public official, the attorney general, does this. Charitable trusts are allowed to go on forever, despite the Rule against Perpetuities.[1] Since terms laid down by the settlor often become out of date over the centuries, courts authorize deviations from the terms of charitable trusts under a power known as *cy pres,* the old French spelling of *si près,* "as near." Such modifications are supposed to stay "as near" to the trust terms as possible under the changed circumstances. Charitable trusts are very important in estate planning because of their tax advantages. This subject is only touched on briefly in this book.

*Definition of Charitable*  Because of the peculiar rules governing charitable trusts, courts sometimes must decide whether a particular trust is charitable. According to the Restatement a trust is charitable "if its accomplishment is of such social interest to the community as to justify permitting the property to be devoted to the [designated] purpose in perpetuity."[2] Alternatively, charity is defined by a list of purposes recognized as charitable; "(a) the relief of poverty; (b) the advancement of education; (c) the advancement of religion; (d) the promotion of health; (e) governmental or municipal purposes; (f) other purposes the accomplishment of which is beneficial to the community."[3]

An English court refused to hold charitable a trust under George Bernard Shaw's will to reform the alphabet to make spelling phonetic, saying it was like those "which advocate a change in the law."[4] American courts define charity more broadly and have upheld trusts to promote change in the law, such as one to promote the Equal Rights Amendment.[5] The definition of "charity" for private law purposes is broader than the tax definition.

**§ 9.7**

**1.** *Restatement, Third, of Trusts* § 28, comm. d (2001); Section 11.6.

**2.** *Restatement, Second, of Trusts,* § 368, comm. b (1959).

**3.** *Id.,* § 368. *See also* Uniform Trust Code § 405(a)

**4.** Re Shaw, [1957] 1 All E.R. 745, 752 (Ch.). The holding in this case is contrary to *Restatement, Third, of Trusts* § 28, comment h, illus. 5 (2001).

**5.** Estate of Breeden, 256 Cal.Rptr. 813 (App.1989).

There are limits to how far even American courts will go in finding trusts charitable, however. A trust to distribute the income to children in the first three grades of a school to further their education was held not to be charitable, since the "admonition to the children" to use the money for education "would be wholly impotent" in the light of "childhood impulses."[6] Nor could the trust be regarded as one for the relief of poverty because distributions were not limited to needy children. The social benefit in the scheme was not sufficient "to justify its existence in perpetuity as a charitable trust."

A trust is not charitable if the class of potential recipients is too narrow, *e.g.,* a trust "for the education of my descendants."[7] But a settlor can select a favored group, such as a small community.[8] Even payment to one individual may involve enough social benefit to make the trust charitable, as in a prize for an individual who has done something useful.[9]

A trust to maintain the tomb of the testator or his family is not charitable, but the perpetual upkeep of a *public* cemetery or a monument to a "notable person" is.[10] A trust to provide for the settlor's pets is not charitable, but one for the prevention of cruelty to animals in general is.[11]

Devises which are restricted to charitable purposes can be quite open-ended, e.g., "to charity" or "to such charitable organizations as my trustee shall select."[12] Even if a will fails to name a trustee, or if the designated trustee fails to act, the court normally appoints a trustee.[13]

*Racial, Gender and Religious Limitations*   The will of Stephen Girard in 1831 created a college for "poor white male orphans," naming the city of Philadelphia as trustee. The Supreme Court held that the racial restriction was state action forbidden by the 14th Amendment's equal protection clause.[14] Arguably, the state's in-

**6.** Shenandoah Valley Nat. Bank v. Taylor, 63 S.E.2d 786, 791 (Va.1951).

**7.** *Restatement, Second, of Trusts* § 375 (1959). *But cf.* Runser v. Lippi, 664 N.E.2d 1355 (Ohio App.1995) (trust for scholarships for needy persons, with preference given to settlor's nieces and nephews).

**8.** *Restatement, Third, of Trusts* § 28, comment f (2001).

**9.** *Ibid.;* Estate of Bunch v. Heirs of Bunch, 485 So.2d 284 (Miss.1986).

**10.** *Restatement, Second, of Trusts* § 374, comm. h (1959). The language of *Restatement, Third, of Trusts* § 28, comment 1 (2001) is more permissive with regard to trusts for tombs.

**11.** *Restatement, Third, of Trusts* § 28, comment 1 (2001). Trusts for the care of an animal or a grave may be sustained as "honorary." See *infra.*

**12.** Lancaster v. Merchants Nat. Bank, 961 F.2d 713 (Ark.1992).

**13.** Morton v. Potts, 781 N.E.2d 43 (Mass.App.Ct. 2003) (trust for "charitable organizations designated by the Donor" is effective even though she failed to designate any).

**14.** Commonwealth of Pennsylvania v. Board of Directors, 353 U.S. 230 (1957). *See also* Evans v. Newton, 382 U.S. 296, 301 (1966) (park for whites unconstitutional even though city resigned as trustee).

volvement in enforcing charitable trusts should subject them all to the 14th Amendment. No court has yet so held, but they have been quick to find unconstitutional state action in racially restrictive trusts.[15] Absent state action, racially discriminatory charities are charitable for purposes of trust law,[16] but they are rare because they do not qualify for federal tax benefits[17] and most charitable giving today is tax-motivated. A trust which provides benefits only for blacks can be upheld by analogy to state affirmative action programs.[18]

The Restatement of Trusts allows beneficiaries of a charitable trust to be "limited to the inhabitants of a particular place" or "to persons of a particular sex or religion."[19] The result may be different, however, where state action is involved, e.g. when school officials participate in the selection of scholarship recipients.[20]

Gender limitations have been removed under cy pres when they caused a dearth of eligible claimants,[21] but judicial hostility toward sex discrimination is not so marked as in the case of racial discrimination. When a scholarship fund was created for boys graduating from high schools in Hartford County who were "members of the Caucasian race and * * * professed * * * to be of the Protestant Congregational Faith," the court removed the racial restriction, but upheld the religious restriction as an exercise of the settlor's First Amendment rights.[22] It also held the sex restriction should be maintained if the desired increase in the number of applicants could be achieved by broadening the geographical base beyond Hartford County.

*Honorary Trusts*　A trust for a non-charitable purpose is sometimes sustained as an "honorary trust." When a testator left money to be applied "towards the promotion and furthering of fox-hunting," the court held that this purpose was not charitable, but it had been "defined with sufficient clearness" and should be given effect. If the devisee failed to apply the money to promote fox-hunting, the residuary devisees, to whom the money would otherwise pass, could

**15.** Trammell v. Elliott, 199 S.E.2d 194 (Ga.1973).

**16.** Swanson, *Discriminatory Charitable Trusts: Time for a Legislative Solution,* 48 U.Pitt.L.Rev. 153, 158 (1986).

**17.** Bob Jones University v. United States, 461 U.S. 574 (1983).

**18.** Trustees of the University of Delaware v. Gebelein, 420 A.2d 1191 (Del. Ch.1980). *See also Restatement, Third, of Trusts* § 28, comment f (2001) (only "invidious" discrimination is against public policy, no objection to "affirmative action").

**19.** *Restatement, Third, of Trusts* § 28, comm. f (2001).

**20.** In re Certain Scholarship Funds, 575 A.2d 1325 (N.H.1990); Luria, *Prying Loose the Dead Hand of the Past,* 21 U.S.F.L.Rev. 41, 48 (1986) (gender restriction in Girard College removed).

**21.** Wesley United Methodist Church v. Harvard College, 316 N.E.2d 620 (Mass.1974).

**22.** Lockwood v. Killian, 375 A.2d 998 (Conn.1977).

sue.[23] The term "honorary trust" refers to the fact that there is no beneficiary who can compel the trustee to perform its terms,[24] but the Uniform Probate Code allows such trusts to be enforced by an individual designated for this purpose in the trust instrument, or by a court.[25]

How long can such a trust go on? The Restatement allows "a reasonable period of time, normally not to exceed 21 years."[26] The purpose must not be "capricious" and the amount of the property devoted to it must not be "unreasonably large."[27] Reported cases on these questions are rare, perhaps because of the liberal definition of "charitable" purposes by American courts.

Probably the most common example of a trust for a specific noncharitable purpose is one for the care of a cemetery plot. These are governed in many states by specific statutes, most of which impose limitations on them.[28]

*Standing to Enforce Charitable Trusts*   The Attorney General's standing to enforce charitable trusts existed at common law has been confirmed by statute in many states.[29] The Attorney General has standing even when charitable organizations are named beneficiaries.[30] A suit by the Attorney General may not be precluded by a prior judgment approving the conduct of a charitable trustee if the Attorney General was not a party.[31]

The standing of persons other than the Attorney General to enforce charitable trusts is restricted. A suit by residents and taxpayers of San Francisco alleging breaches of trust by the trustees of the city's fine arts museums was dismissed. "Because the beneficiaries of charitable trusts * * * are ordinarily indefinite, the Attorney General generally is the proper party to enforce them. * * * This limitation on standing arises from the need to protect the trustee from vexatious litigation."[32]

**23.** In re Thompson [1934] 1 Ch. 342.

**24.** *Restatement, Second, of Trusts* § 124, comment c (1959).

**25.** Uniform Probate Code § 2–907(c)(4); *cf.* Unif.Trust Code § 408.

**26.** *Restatement, Third, of Trusts* § 47 (1999); *cf.* Unif.Trust Code § 409(1) (trust may not be enforced for more than 21 years)

**27.** *Restatement, Third, of Trusts* § 47, comm.e (2001).

**28.** Foshee v. Republic Nat. Bank of Dallas, 617 S.W.2d 675 (Tex. 1981) (devise for upkeep failed to meet statutory requirements); Wis.Stat. § 701.11(2)(3) (trust for perpetual care of tomb is valid unless "capricious").

**29.** *Restatement, Second, of Trusts* § 391 (1959); Wis.Stat. § 701.10(3).

**30.** In re Estate of Cappetta, 733 N.E.2d 426, 433 (Ill.App.2000) (both AG and charities have standing in case involving devise to named charities).

**31.** In re Los Angeles County Pioneer Soc'y, 257 P.2d 1 (Cal.1953). *But see* Loring v. Marshall, 484 N.E.2d 1315 (Mass.1985) (adverse will construction binding on charities even though Attorney General not a party).

**32.** Hardman v. Feinstein, 240 Cal. Rptr. 483, 485 (App.1987). See also Russell v. Yale University, 737 A.2d 941 (Conn.App.1999) (donors and students have no standing).

Even settlors have traditionally been denied standing to enforce charitable trusts, but there is now contrary authority both in the cases and in some statutes, motivated in part by the demonstrated inability of state Attorneys–General to monitor compliance with restrictions in charitable gifts.[33] The settlor, or the settlor's successors, may recover trust property if the trust terminates.[34]

The Restatement allows beneficiaries with a "special interest" in a charitable trust to sue.[35] Where a trust instrument "suggested" that trust funds be allocated to certain charities, one which had been rejected by the trustee was held to have such a "special interest;" the plaintiff was "entitled to some kind of minimal review" as to whether the trustee had abused its discretion.[36]

When there are several trustees, charitable trustees can act by a majority vote, but the minority can sue for a breach of trust, even when the Attorney General has refused to act.[37]

Some courts are liberal in conferring standing on the ground that otherwise breaches of trust may go unremedied.[38] One way to deal with the problem of over-worked Attorneys General without opening the door to a flood of litigation is to allow individuals to sue "on the relation of" the Attorney General with the latter's permission, or to bring a petition for mandamus to require the AG's office to perform its duty.[39]

*Restricted Gifts to Charitable Entities*    Many charitable gifts to established organizations impose restrictions on the use of the money or property. Even if the gift is not called a trust, a donee who "is directed by the terms of the gift to devote the property to a particular one of its purposes is under a duty, enforceable at the suit of the Attorney General" to do so.[40] However, courts are

---

**33.** Uniform Trust Code § 405(c); Wis.Stat. § 701.10(3); Smithers v. St. Luke's-Roosevelt Hosp. Center, 723 N.Y.S.2d 426 (App.Div.2001) (settlor's widow and personal representative allowed to sue, the court noting the lack of diligence in the Attorney–General's oversight in this case).

**34.** *Restatement, Second, Trusts* § 391, comm. f (1959); Evans v. Abney, 396 U.S. 435 (1970).

**35.** *Restatement, Second, of Trusts* § 391 (1959).

**36.** St. John's–St. Luke Evangelical Church v. National Bank of Detroit, 283 N.W.2d 852 (Mich.App.1979).

**37.** Holt v. College of Osteopathic Physicians & Surgeons, 394 P.2d 932 (Cal.1964).

**38.** Jones v. Grant, 344 So.2d 1210, 1212 (Ala.1977). *See also* Kapiolani Park

Pres. Soc. v. Honolulu, 751 P.2d 1022 (Haw.1988) (attorney general "actively joined" in supporting the breach of trust).

**39.** The court suggested these alternatives in rejecting a petition brought by an individual to have a successor trustee appointed for a charitable trust in Arman v. Bank of America, N.T., S.A., 88 Cal.Rptr.2d 410, 416 (App.1999). *See also Restatement, Second, of Trusts* § 391, comment a (1959). Some courts act *sua sponte*. In re Will of Crabtree, 795 N.E.2d 1157, 1169 (Mass.2003).

**40.** *Restatement, Second, of Trusts* § 348, comm. f (1959). *Cf. Restatement, Third, of Trusts* § 28, comm. a (2001) (restricted purpose gift "creates a trust of which the institution is the trustee").

reluctant to find that a donor intended to restrict the use of property especially when considerable time has elapsed since the date of the gift. Land was given in 1827 to a church "on condition that the same * * * shall be used for * * * the erection and maintenance thereon of a house of public worship." A century and a half later a court held that the donee was no longer subject to the condition "because a reasonable time has passed."[41]

*Removing Restrictions Under Cy Pres Power* Courts often remove restrictions under *cy pres*. A will probated in 1899 left property for a home for "orphans between the ages of 6 and 10, an orphan being defined as one whose father is dead." Seventy years later a court expanded the trust to include children between the ages of 6 and 18 who had been deprived of parental care for any reason because the number of applicants who qualified under the terms of the will had been declining.[42] A trust for "defraying the cost of hospitalization" was modified to allow use "for broader health care purposes" because "today, third-party payment of hospitalization costs is nearly universal."[43] Although courts are more willing to deviate from the terms of an old gift,[44] more recent ones are also modified on occasion.[45]

Cy pres is used in a variety of situations. When a will left money to Amherst for scholarships for "Protestant, Gentile" boys, the restriction was eliminated because Amherst refused to accept the gift otherwise.[46] Courts have also used *cy pres* to accommodate trusts to changes in the tax laws. [47]

When trust funds exceed what is necessary for the stated purpose the excess can be applied *cy pres,* as when a will left money for two annual scholarships and the fund produced enough income for more.[48] Conversely if funds are insufficient for the project designated by the settlor, they may be applied for a more modest purpose.[49]

**41.** Independent Congregational Soc. v. Davenport, 381 A.2d 1137 (Me.1978).

**42.** Dunbar v. Board of Trust. of George W. Clayton Col., 461 P.2d 28, 31 (Colo.1969).

**43.** Matter of Estate of Vallery, 883 P.2d 24, 29 (Colo.App.1993).

**44.** *Restatement, Third, of Trusts* § 67, comm. d (2001); *cf.* In re Estes' Estate, 523 N.W.2d 863, 869 (Mich.App. 1994) (rejecting *cy pres*, noting that only 21 years had elapsed since testator died); Unif.Trust Code § 413(b) (distinguishing trusts in existence for over 21 years from others).

**45.** Matter of Estate of Crawshaw, 819 P.2d 613 (Kan.1991) (when college

named as devisee closed a few months after testator's death, devise awarded *cy pres*).

**46.** Howard Savings Inst. v. Peep, 170 A.2d 39 (N.J.1961).

**47.** Unif.Trust Code § 416. *See also* Cal.Prob.Code § 17200(a)(15) (courts can amend trust "in the manner required to qualify a decedent's estate for the charitable estate tax deduction").

**48.** Estate of Puckett, 168 Cal.Rptr. 311 (App.1980); *Restatement, Third, of Trusts* § 67, comment c (2001).

**49.** Matter of Estate of Craig, 848 P.2d 313, 317, 322 (Ariz.App.1992).

*Cy pres* has also been invoked when money is left to an entity, such as the "Cancer Research Fund," which does not exist. Since the testator intended to benefit cancer research, the money was given to the American Cancer Society.[50] *Cy pres* has also been applied when a charitable corporation goes out of existence,[51] but when a charity is dissolved in a merger, the funds may simply pass to the successor organization.[52]

Judges are reluctant to modify a charitable trust simply because they disagree with its terms. The *cy pres* power is exercised "sparingly," because "a settlor must have assurance that his instructions will not be subject to the whim or suggested expediency of others after his death."[53]

Simes thought that courts were too hesitant to apply *cy pres*, citing the history of Benjamin Franklin's trust which was established in 1790 and lasted for 200 years. The funds were to be "loaned out to such young married artificers under the age of twenty-five years as have served an apprenticeship." The rate of interest, security and maximum loan were specified. Because of the restrictions, the funds were not always loaned out, and courts authorized modifications from time to time, but only when "the original purpose and plan was demonstrably impossible or impracticable. Moreover, when modification was made, the adherence as nearly as possible to the original purpose resulted in failure of the modification."[54] Simes proposed that after thirty years courts should have an enlarged *cy pres* power to modify charitable trusts "not only if the original purpose was found impracticable but also if * * * the amount to be expended is out of all proportion to its value to society." The Third Restatement of Trusts and the Uniform Trust Code allow the use of *cy pres* simply because a trust purpose is "wasteful."[55]

*Cy pres* is used only if the settlor had a "general charitable intent"; if not, the trust property reverts to the settlor, or the settlor's successors. Money which was raised for a bone marrow transplant for a victim of leukemia who died before the operation could be performed was returned to the donors, since the solicitation for donations "was solely directed to * * * one operative

---

**50.** In re Tomlinson's Estate, 359 N.E.2d 109 (Ill.1976).

**51.** In re Connolly's Estate, 121 Cal. Rptr. 325 (App.1975); Alexander v. Georgia Baptist Foundation, Inc., 266 S.E.2d 165 (Ga.1980); *Restatement, Third, of Trusts* § 67, comm. e (2001).

**52.** Washington Hospital v. Riggs Nat. Bank, 575 A.2d 719 (D.C.App. 1990). *But see* In re Estate of Beck, 649 N.E.2d 1011 (Ill.App.1995) (devise to or-

phanage fails when it conveys its assets to an organization which provides foster care, counseling and adoption services).

**53.** First Nat. Bank v. Brimmer, 504 P.2d 1367, 1371 (Wyo.1973).

**54.** L. Simes, *Public Policy and the Dead Hand* 131–32 (1959).

**55.** Unif.Trust Code § 413(a); *Restatement, Third, of Trusts* § 67 (2001).

procedure for one specified beneficiary."[56] This result was reached despite the "administrative difficulties in locating the present whereabouts of some contributors," many of whom were anonymous.[57]

The question whether a settlor had a "general charitable intent" is hard to answer because the settlor did not contemplate the circumstances which have come to pass. The Uniform Trust Code directs the use of *cy pres* unless the trust explicitly provides to the contrary.[58]

The presumption against intestacy is sometimes used to support *cy pres*. This argument is inapplicable when the failure of a charitable gift causes the property to go to another devisee under the will. If the substituted legatee is a charity the argument against *cy pres* is even stronger, since the public will benefit in any event. [59]

Most courts admit extrinsic evidence as to the settlor's intent in *cy pres* cases. When a will left money to Amherst for a scholarship with religious restrictions which Amherst rejected, the court removed the restrictions rather than have the money pass intestate because the testator's heirs were distant relatives with whom he had little contact, he regularly contributed to Amherst and attended reunions, and was not actively interested in any church.[60] Conversely, a donor's long-term association with Syracuse Medical College was held to show he intended the property to revert rather than go to another school when the college went out of existence.[61]

The degree of deviation requested also makes a difference. The Restatement distinguishes between *cy pres* and "deviation" from the terms of a trust with respect to administration.[62] Even in private trusts courts authorize deviations with respect to administrative provisions when unanticipated circumstances arise,[63] and they are even readier to do so in charitable trusts.[64]

**56.** Matter of Gonzalez, 621 A.2d 94, 96–97 (N.J.Super.A.D.1992).

**57.** Compare the English Charities Act, 1960, § 14 (even property given for specific purpose can be applied *cy pres* if donor cannot be found); N.Y.E.P.T.L. § 8–1.1(j) (if more than 1,000 contributors, unexpended funds after 5 years shall be applied *cy pres*).

**58.** Unif.Trust Code § 413(b). *See also Restatement, Third, of Trusts* § 67, comm. b (2001).

**59.** Home for Incurables v. University of Maryland Medical System Corp., 797 A.2d 746 (Md.2002).

**60.** Howard Savings Inst. v. Peep, 170 A.2d 39, 46 (N.J.1961).

**61.** Application of Syracuse University, 148 N.E.2d 671 (N.Y.1958). *See also Restatement, Third, of Trusts* § 67, comm. d (2001): court should consider settlor's "social or religious affiliations, personal background, charitable-giving history and the like."

**62.** *Restatement, Second, of Trusts* §§ 381, 399 (1959).

**63.** Section 9.6.

**64.** Matter of Estate of Murdock, 884 P.2d 749, 752 (Kan.App.1994).

Courts can usually modify a trust under *cy pres* without the donor's consent, but a few statutes provide otherwise.[65] A settlor's consent to a change is sufficient to remove "minor restrictions."[66]

Trustees are not supposed to deviate from trust terms without obtaining court approval,[67] but courts sometimes ratify deviations which have already occurred.[68]

*Planning*   A trust may not be the best vehicle for a charitable gift. The gift may be too small to justify the cost of a professional trustee. Trustees may be subject to burdensome restrictions which do not apply to not-for-profit corporations.[69] On the other hand, some states require state approval to create a corporation, or otherwise subject charitable corporations to restrictions from which trusts are exempt, such as limits on land holdings.[70] If the donor's purpose does not qualify as charitable, a not-for-profit corporation may be better than a trust.[71]

If the donor intends to impose an enforceable restriction, the instrument should make this clear so as to avoid the traditional strict construction of such restrictions. However, restrictions may hamper the fulfillment of charitable objectives, perhaps necessitating court proceedings to remove them.

**65.** *Restatement, Second, of Trusts* § 399, comm. g (1959); N.Y.E.P.T,L. § 8–1.1(c)(2) (consent of donor required).

**66.** *Restatement, Second, of Trusts* § 367, comm. c (1959). The Uniform Management of Institutional Funds Act Section 7 makes it sufficient to remove any restriction.

**67.** *Restatement, Second, of Trusts* § 399, comm. e (1959).

**68.** Wigglesworth v. Cowles, 648 N.E.2d 1289 (Mass.App.Ct.1995); *Re-statement, Third. of Trusts* § 67, comm. d (2001).

**69.** *Restatement, Second, of Trusts* § 348, comm. f (1959).

**70.** Fisch, *Choosing the Charitable Entity*, 114 Trusts and Estates 875 (1975).

**71.** Fratcher, *Bequests for Purposes,* 56 Iowa L.Rev. 773, 798 (1971).

# Chapter 10

# FUTURE INTERESTS

*Table of Sections*

## § 10.1  Conditions of Survival

Many wills and trusts create future interests, such as "to my spouse for life, remainder to our children." If a child fails to survive the testator, a question of lapse arises (see Section 8.3). This Section discusses what happens if a remainderman survives the testator or settlor but dies during the life of the life beneficiary, or prior to some other time fixed for distribution, such as "when she reaches age 25." If the interest is "vested", it passes to the remainderman's estate to be disposed of by his or her will[1] or to the heirs of a remainderman who died intestate. But a court may infer a condition that remaindermen must survive the life beneficiary in order to take. If so, the court must decide what happens to the share of a remainderman who fails to survive. Most anti-lapse statutes apply only to devisees who predecease the testator and so are irrelevant in this situation. A remainder "to our children" is a class gift so any children who survived would take the shares of children who did not. If no class member survives, or if the remainder was an individual who failed to survive, the remainder might go to the (other) residuary devisees under the testator's will or by intestacy to the testator's heirs if no residuary devisee

---

**§ 10.1**

1. It is also possible, but rare, for remainders to be transferred inter-vivos, assuming that there is no spendthrift restraint in the trust. *Restatement, Third, of Trusts* § 51 (2001); Section 13.1.

qualified.[2] If a remainder created by a living trust fails, a resulting trust for the settlor, or the settlor's successors may arise.[3]

*Vested or Contingent* The question whether a remainderman must survive the life interest is often posed as "was the remainder vested or contingent?" This terminology is convenient, but misleading, because (1) even vested remainders may be conditioned on survival, and (2) not all contingent remainders are conditioned on survival. As to the first point, if a will provides "remainder to my children, but if any child dies before my spouse, his or her share shall go to his or her children," the children's remainder is not *contingent* on survival, but *vested subject to divestment* for failure to survive.[4] In contrast, a remainder "to our then living children," is *contingent.* In the first case the condition of survival is *subsequent;* in the second, the condition is *precedent.* The distinction between precedent and subsequent conditions has little practical significance except in (the few) jurisdictions which still prohibit the transfer of contingent remainders.[5]

Contingent remainders are not necessarily conditioned on survival. In a devise to *A* for life, remainder to her issue if she has any, and if not, then to *B*, *B's* remainder is subject to a condition (*A's* death without issue) which renders it contingent, but it is not subject to a further condition that *B* survive the termination of *A's* life estate.[6]

*Preference for Early Vesting* According to a commonly cited rule the law favors the early vesting of estates.[7] Some states have codified the preference for a vested construction, but several writers have attacked it, and courts have begun to question it.[8] The Uniform Probate Code rejects it and presumes that "a future interest under the terms of a trust is contingent on the beneficiary's surviving to the distribution date."[9]

*(1) Taxes* One argument for implying a requirement of survival is that a vested remainder is subject to an estate tax when the remainderman dies before the life beneficiary,[10] whereas no such

---

**2.** As to anti-lapse statutes, as to what constitutes a "class gift", and whether a failed residuary gift passes intestate or to other residuary devisees, see Section 8.3.

**3.** *Restatement, Third, of Trusts* § 7, illus. 1 (2001).

**4.** National City Bank v. Beyer, 729 N.E.2d 711, 716 (Ohio 2000). *But see* Webb v. Underhill, 882 P.2d 127, 130 (Or.App.1994).

**5.** Goodwine State Bank v. Mullins, 625 N.E.2d 1056, 1074 (Ill.App.1993).

**6.** Temple Beth Israel v. Feiss, 2 P.3d 388, 390–91 (Or.App.2000).

**7.** Summers v. Summers, 699 N.E.2d 958, 962 (Ohio App.1997); McGovern, *Facts and Rules in the Construction of Wills*, 26 UCLA L.Rev. 285 (1978).

**8.** Harris Trust and Savings Bank v. Beach, 513 N.E.2d 833, 840 (Ill.1987).

**9.** Uniform Probate Code § 2–707(b). This and all other rules of construction in the Code are subject to "a finding of contrary intention." *Id.*, § 2–701,

**10.** Huggins v. United States, 684 F.2d 417 (6th Cir.1982).

tax is incurred in the estate of a contingent remainderman who dies without satisfying a condition of survival.[11] Postponing vesting does not always produce tax advantages. Many estates are too small to incur any estate tax; in others, avoiding an estate tax may be offset by incurring a generation-skipping tax at a higher rate.[12] Also, any estate tax cost of including a remainder in an estate may be outweighed by income tax savings, since the assets will get a step up in basis to their date-of-death value.[13]

*(2) Keeping Property in the Bloodline* Many rules of law are based on an assumption that persons want their property to go to blood relatives. Courts sometimes refer to this in construing instruments. The fact that a vested remainder may pass to a spouse or other devisees of the remainderman who are unrelated to the testator provides an argument for construing remainders as contingent.[14]

This reasoning has been challenged. Even if a remainder is contingent on survival, a remainderman who *does* survive can give or devise the property to a person unrelated to the testator. Testators who are disturbed by this possibility can limit the remainderman's interest to a life estate. Furthermore, the preference for blood relatives is questionable today when (1) the law usually allows adopted children to inherit from their adoptive but not their blood relatives, and (2) intestacy laws give the surviving spouse a fee simple even though this often causes property to end up in the hands of non-relatives.

*Arguments Supporting Vested Construction: (1) Promoting Alienability.* An argument *in favor of* a vested construction is that it "enables property to be freely transferred at the earliest possible date."[15] However, the question whether a remainder was contingent on survival usually arises after the life tenant has died, at which time the property is alienable whichever construction is chosen. Even before the life estate expires, the ability to transfer property burdened with a remainder does not often turn on whether the remainder is vested or contingent. Nearly all jurisdictions allow contingent as well as vested remainders to be assigned. However, when remainders are contingent on survival, other persons take if

**11.** Browning v. Sacrison, 518 P.2d 656, 658 (Or.1974). *See also Restatement, Second, of Property (Donative Transfers) §* 27.3, Reporter's Tax Note (1987); Halbach & Waggoner, *The UPC's New Survivorship and Anti–Lapse Provisions,* 55 Alb.L.Rev. 1091, 1133 (1992).

**12.** Garvey, *Drafting Wills and Trusts: Anticipating the Birth and Death of Possible Beneficiaries,* 71 Or.L.Rev.

47, 62 (1991). As to the generation-skipping tax see Section 15.4

**13.** See Section 15.1.

**14.** Lamb v. Nationsbank, N.A., 507 S.E.2d 457, 460 (Ga.1998); National City Bank v. Beyer, 729 N.E.2d 711, 716 (Ohio 2000) (testator wanted property to "remain in the family").

**15.** In re Krooss, 99 N.E.2d 222, 224 (N.Y.1951).

the remaindermen do not survive, and this increases the number of persons with potential interests making property harder to sell.[16]

Most future interests today are beneficial interests in a trust, under which the trustee has power to sell the trust assets. Although courts have traditionally applied the preference for early vesting to trusts as well as legal remainders, the Uniform Probate Code implies a condition of survivorship only for future interests in a trust, because "the ability of the parties to sell the land would be impaired if not destroyed" if legal remainders were contingent.[17] Even as to trusts, however, construing an interest as indefeasibly vested reduces the number of beneficiaries whose consent is needed to modify or terminate the trust.[18]

*(2) Avoiding Intestacy* Courts sometimes hold remainders vested in order to avoid an intestacy. If a remainder to "children" in the residuary clause of a will is contingent on surviving the life beneficiary, the property will pass to the testator's heirs by intestacy if all the children predecease the life tenant unless a substitutional devise is added.[19]

If a particular construction leads to an intestacy, is this a bad thing? Intestate succession statutes represent reasonable surmises of how decedents want their property distributed and are often used to infer probable intent in construing wills.[20] In some cases, however, intestacy may distort an estate plan. Suppose a testator has three children, Alice, Andrew and Arthur. Arthur dies survived by two children, Burt and Barbara. The testator's will creates a remainder "one third to Alice, one third to Andrew, and one sixth each to Burt and Barbara," intending to treat the three branches of the family equally. If Burt predeceases the life beneficiary, and his share passes as intestate property, Alice and Andrew will take more than the 2/3 share allotted to them under the will. The equal division which the testator intended can be effectuated by treating Burt's interest as vested.[21]

Intestacy may also give property to an heir whom the testator wished to disinherit. One court construed a remainder as vested

---

**16.** *Restatement of Property* § 243, comm. i.

**17.** Uniform Probate Code § 2–707, Comment.

**18.** In re Trust of Lane, 592 A.2d 492, 496–97 (Md.1991). Further discussion of the problem of obtaining consent of all beneficiaries in order to terminate a trust is found in Section 9.6.

**19.** In re Estate of Cruikshank, 746 N.Y.S.2d 769, 775 (Surr.2002) (citing presumption against intestacy in holding a remainder vested). However, if the remainder is in a pre-residuary devise, its

failure may simply cause the property to pass under the residuary clause of the will. Temple Beth Israel v. Feiss, 2 P.3d 388, 395 (Or.App.2000); Section 8.3.

**20.** Cal.Prob.Code § 21115(a); Uniform Probate Code § 2–705(a).

**21.** An intestacy can also be avoided in this situation by treating the gift to the brothers as a class gift, despite the use of names, but this would cut out any issue of Burt. Abrams v. Templeton, 465 S.E.2d 117, 121 (S.C.App.1995).

when an intestacy would have frustrated "the testator's expressed intention that his three daughters should each receive \$1 'and no more.' "[22]

*(3) Protecting Remoter Issue* A vested has one virtue in that it "tends to prevent unintended disinheritance of the issue of a deceased remainderman. Suppose that *T* devises Blackacre to his wife W for life, remainder to his son *S.* Suppose further that *S* dies after T but before *W,* leaving a daughter *GD* who survives W. * * * Probably *T* would want *GD* to take Blackacre if her father predeceased *W.* Vesting Blackacre at *T*'s death serves a useful purpose in materially increasing the likelihood that *GD* will eventually enjoy it."[23]

Our intestacy laws and anti-lapse statutes assume that decedents want the children of a deceased relative to take in their place. A vested construction may produce the same result, but the deceased remainderman may leave his estate to someone else, or the estate may be diminished by claims of creditors, a spouse, and death taxes. A remainderman's children can be better protected by a direct substitutional gift to them in the manner of the anti-lapse statutes. The Uniform Probate Code provides such a substitutional gift.[24]

Courts sometimes achieve the same result by construing the word "children" in a will or trust to include the children of a deceased child.[25] But courts usually follow "normal usage" under which "the term 'children' does not include grandchildren or more remote descendants."[26] A gift to "issue," on the other hand, encompasses descendants of all generations, children, grandchildren, etc. Courts have traditionally construed remainders to "issue" or "descendants," in contrast to one-generation classes like "children," as conditioned on survival of the preceding interests, since in this situation this construction does *not* disinherit descendants of deceased class members.[27]

*Drafting Errors* Most future interest cases arise because the will or trust did not deal adequately with the problem of survival. Gifts of future interests typically are expressed in words which look to the future like "then." Such words are not of themselves usually

**22.** In re Ferry's Estate, 361 P.2d 900, 905–06 (Cal.1961).

**23.** Rabin, *The Law Favors the Vesting of Estates. Why?* 65 Colum.L.Rev. 467, 483–84. In Usry v. Fair, 553 S.E.2d 789 (Ga. 2001), a vested construction preserved the interest of great-grandchildren of the testator whose father predeceased the last life tenant.

**24.** Uniform Probate Code § 2–707(b)(2).

**25.** Cox v. Forristall, 640 P.2d 878 (Kan.App.1982).

**26.** *Restatement, Second, of Property (Donative Transfers)* § 25.1, comm. a (1987).

**27.** *Id.,* § 28.2; In re Estate of Cruikshank, 746 N.Y.S.2d 769, 772 (Surr.2002).

construed to postpone vesting, e.g. in a will which gave the testator's son a life estate and "at his death the remainder shall vest in his children," the phrase about vesting at the son's death was said to refer only to the date when the remainder would be distributed.[28]

*"To Alice at 30"*  Many trusts provide for distribution of the trust assets to a beneficiary when he or she reaches a specified age such as 30. What if the beneficiary dies before reaching 30? A famous 17th century case said that if money was "to be paid" to the beneficiary at age 30 her interest was vested, but a bequest to her "at age 30" was not.[29] This subtle distinction has little to recommend it, but it appears in the Restatement of Property.[30]

*"Surviving"*  Many wills use words like "surviving" in a remainder. The word is ambiguous, since every person who is born alive survives *someone*. *Whom* must the remaindermen survive? Some cases interpret "surviving" to refer to the time of the testator's death,[31] but the Uniform Probate Code "codifies the predominant * * * position that survival relates to the distribution date."[32] A well drafted instrument avoids ambiguity by using the term "then living," which refers back to the specified date of distribution. Thus "on the death of the surviving spouse, the principal must be paid, to the children of the testator in equal shares if all the children are *then living*, otherwise to the *then living* issue of the testator"[33]

*Gifts on Death Without Children or Issue*  References to "death" in a will, like "surviving," often fail to make clear the time to which they refer. The problem arises in three kinds of cases.

(1) *Remainderman dies before life tenant.* A will left a remainder "to my sister, and in case of her predecease, to her son." The sister survived the testator but not the life tenant. The court held that sister's remainder failed and most courts would agree.[34]

(2) *Remainderman dies after life tenant.* A will left a remainder to the testator's stepsons and "in the event that any of them should die without issue," his share should go "to the survivors." One stepson survived the life tenant and died without issue years later. The court held that his share was not divested but rather passed under his will.[35] Some courts have reached the opposite result on

**28.**  Rudy v. Wagner, 198 N.W.2d 75, 79 (Neb.1972).

**29.**  Clobberie's Case, 86 Eng.Rep. 476 (Ch. 1677).

**30.**  *Restatement, Second, of Property (Donative Transfers)* § 27.3, comm. f (1987).

**31.**  Swanson v. Swanson, 514 S.E.2d 822, 825 (Ga.1999).

**32.**  Uniform Probate Code § 2–707, Comment.

**33.**  Uniform Statutory Will Act § 6(3).

**34.**  Mueller v. Forsyth, 235 N.E.2d 645 (Ill.App.1968). *See also* Canoy v. Canoy, 520 S.E.2d 128 (N.C.App.1999).

**35.**  Stanley v. Brietz, 612 S.W.2d 699, 701 (Tex.Civ.App.1981).

the ground that if the testator wanted the substitutional gift to apply only if the remainderman predeceased the life tenant, the will would have said so.[36]

(3) *Immediate devise.* A woman devised a farm to her son Alvin, but if "Alvin should die without leaving children, I devise the farm to my two daughters." Alvin died without issue after the testator. The court held that the gift over applied only if Alvin predeceased the testator,[37] but the Restatement of Property would construe it to apply whenever Alvin died.[38]

Historically, gifts over upon a devisee's death without issue were deemed to apply if the devisee *or any descendant of his* ever died without issue. This "indefinite failure of issue" construction is generally rejected in modern law in favor of the "definite" construction under which "death" refers only to the named devisee and not to his descendants.[39]

Other ambiguities lurk in the apparently simple phrase "if Alvin should die without leaving children." What if Alvin is survived by a *grandchild* but not a child? In *this* context most courts read "children" to mean "issue."[40] If Alvin has children who predecease him, has he died "died without leaving children?" Most courts, but not all, would say yes; the gift over applies unless Alvin has issue who survive him.[41]

Sometimes the devise of a life estate is followed only by a gift over "if the life tenant dies without issue." If the life tenant is survived by issue, most courts imply a gift to the issue in order to avoid an intestacy.[42]

*"To A or His Children (Heirs)"* A remainder given to "my children, or their issue (or heirs)," is usually construed to give the share of any child who fails to survive the life beneficiary to his or her issue (or heirs).[43] Such language should not be confused with devises "to A *and* his heirs" or "to A *and* his children."[44]

Some wills provide a substitutional gift to the children of a remainderman who fails to survive the life tenant, but do not say what should happen if a remainderman dies *without* children. Many

---

**36.** Adams v. Vidal, 60 So.2d 545, 548 (Fla.1952).

**37.** Lones v. Winzer, 486 S.W.2d 758 (Tenn.App.1971).

**38.** *Restatement of Property* § 267 (1940). *See also* Neb.Rev.Stat. § 76–111; Minn.Stat. § 500.14(1); Kan.Stat. § 58–504.

**39.** Minn.Stat. § 500.14(1); Kan. Stat. § 58–504.

**40.** *Restatement of Property* § 243, illus. 1 (1940).

**41.** Calif.Prob.Code § 21112; N.Y. EPTL § 6–5.6; Clark v. Strother, 385 S.E.2d 578, 582 (Va.1989).

**42.** *Restatement of Property* § 272.

**43.** Rowett v. McFarland, 394 N.W.2d 298 (S.D.1986).

**44.** As to "A and his heirs" see the next Section. As to "A and his children" see Section 10.3. As to present interests devised "to A or his children (heirs)" see Section 8.3.

courts hold that in this situation the interest of the remainderman is vested,[45] but the second Restatement of Property says that the remainder should go to the other members of the class.[46]

Some wills impose a requirement of survival on the primary remainderman but not on the designated substitute takers, e.g. a remainder to the descendants of the testator's nephew, or to "the other beneficiaries of the will if no such descendants are then living." The express condition of survival imposed on the nephew's descendants was deemed to show an intent to impose the same requirement on the other beneficiaries as well,[47] but other courts have drawn the opposite inference.[48]

*Planning* One court has suggested that "a pervasive cloud of uncertainty" surrounds the law of future interests, and courts "determine an equitable distribution and thereafter fill in the blanks with appropriate bits and pieces of the law * * * in order to reach the desirable result."[49] But what is a "desirable result" may not be clear, *e.g.* if a vested construction would increases taxes but avoid disinheriting a relative. Drafters can avoid such dilemmas. The Uniform Statutory Will Act postpones vesting of the remainder without excluding any children of a deceased child. Although the remaindermen will be uncertain while the income beneficiary is alive, the property will not be inalienable because the trustee is given a power of sale.[50] If testators prefer to let any remaindermen who predecease the life beneficiary "decide how best to provide for their own family," they can accomplish this by giving them a special power of appointment over their share.[51]

Lawyers should use formulas like the Uniform Act in preparing wills and trusts with future interests. It is inefficient and risky to draft wills "from scratch;" the future interest cases strewn though the reports demonstrate the many chances for error.

*Income Interests* Similar construction problems arise when income is payable to several beneficiaries and one of them dies before the trust terminates. What should the trustee do with the income the deceased beneficiary had been receiving? "Some courts have ordered the income to be paid to the surviving income beneficiaries under the doctrine of implication of cross remainders, as a

---

**45.** Matter of Estate of Sprinchorn, 546 N.Y.S.2d 256 (App.Div.1989) (remainder to niece and her daughter or the survivor vests in their estates when both predecease life beneficiary).

**46.** *Restatement, Second, of Property (Donative Transfers)* § 27.3, comm. e, illus. 1 (1987).

**47.** Irish v. Profitt, 330 N.E.2d 861, 871–72 (Ill.App.1975).

**48.** Mueller v. Forsyth, 235 N.E.2d 645, 649 (Ill.App.1968).

**49.** Warren–Boynton State Bank v. Wallbaum, 528 N.E.2d 640, 643 (Ill. 1988).

**50.** Uniform Statutory Will Act § 13.

**51.** As to powers of appointment see Section 10.4.

gift to a class, or as an implied joint tenancy. Other courts have ordered the income paid to the deceased beneficiary's estate until the death of the last income beneficiary. Other courts have ordered the income to be paid to the remaindermen. Finally, some courts have ordered the income to be accumulated until the death of the last income beneficiary."[52] The third Restatement of Trusts presumes that "the settlor intended the income share to be paid to the issue (if any) of the deceased income beneficiary,"[53] a solution like that of the Uniform Probate Code for future interests.

The best *drafting* solution is to allow the trustee to sprinkle income among the beneficiaries. The Uniform Statutory Will Act, for example, allows the trustee to pay income to "one or more of the issue of the testator" as needed for their support.[54] This allows the trustee to give the income directly to the decedent's children or the decedent's siblings, or accumulate it in the trustee's discretion.

## § 10.2  Gifts to Heirs

A well-drafted instrument which creates future interests contingent on survival should leave no gaps in case the designated remaindermen fail to survive. Many drafters use the intestacy statutes for this purpose. The Uniform Statutory Will Act provides that if the remainder to the testator's issue fails, the property passes "to the individuals who would be entitled to receive the estate as if the * * * the testator had then died intestate."[1] In many wills a simple gift to the "heirs" of the testator or of another person plays the same role, but this language raises construction problems which we will discuss in this section.

Intestacy statutes incorporate a requirement of survival of the ancestor,[2] with representation of deceased relatives by their issue. Thus, if a will leaves property "to Alice for life, remainder to her heirs," a child of Alice who predeceased her would get no share, but any children of the deceased child would take the share by representation.[3]

*Time of Determination*   Often wills and trusts create a remainder to the heirs of an ancestor who dies before the life tenant, e.g.,

---

**52.** Trust Agreement of Westervelt v. First Interstate Bank, 551 N.E.2d 1180, 1185 (Ind.App.1990).

**53.** *Restatement, Third, of Trusts* § 49, comm. c(3) (2001). This differs from *Restatement, Second, of Trusts* § 143(2) (1959), which gave the income to the other beneficiaries as an implied cross remainder.

**54.** Uniform Statutory Will Act § 8(b).

**§ 10.2**

**1.** Uniform Statutory Will Act § 6(3).

**2.** It is customary to refer to the person whose heirs are designated as the "ancestor," even though "heirs" can include collateral relatives as well as descendants.

**3.** Dempsey v. Dempsey, 795 N.E.2d 996 (Ill.App.2003).

a remainder was given "to the heirs of my children" and the children died before the trust terminated. The remainder was held to have vested in each child's heirs when the child died.[4] The second Restatement of Property agrees: the intestacy statute is applied as of the ancestor's death unless a contrary intent is found in "additional language and circumstances."[5] The third Restatement, however, and the Uniform Probate Code say that the "heirs" should be determined as if the ancestor "died when the disposition is to take effect in possession and enjoyment."[6]

The arguments on this question are like those about early vesting. An early date for determining heirs makes property alienable sooner. When land was devised to the testator's daughter, Doris, with a gift "to my other heirs" if Doris died without issue, Doris was able to sell the land with the consent of the testator's other children and widow.[7] But if the heirs had been determined as of Doris' death, the possible rights of persons yet unborn would have hindered a sale.

The desire to keep property in the bloodline, a standard argument for postponing vesting, is also invoked in deciding the time for determining heirs.[8] When a remainder is given to "children," the keep-property-in-the-bloodline argument may be outweighed if a contingent construction would eliminate issue of a deceased child. When a remainder is given to "heirs," however, remoter issue take by representation. In this respect gifts to "heirs" are like gifts to "issue," which are generally held to be contingent on survival.[9]

A particular will can show an intent to postpone the determination of heirs, as in a devise to "the individuals who *would be* entitled to receive the estate *as if* * * * the testator had *then* died intestate."[10] A frequently asserted argument for *inferring* such an intent is the "incongruity" which would result if the heirs were determined when the ancestor died and an heir is given a life interest in the same property. A woman conveyed land to her daughter, Annis, for life, remainder, if Annis died without issue, to her siblings if then living, if none "to my heirs." Annis died without issue and her siblings predeceased her. The donor's heirs at the time of her death were her children. Determining the heirs at her death would create the "salient incongruity" of (1) giving Annis

**4.** Matter of Dodge Testamentary Trust, 330 N.W.2d 72, 81 (Mich.App. 1982).

**5.** *Restatement, Second, of Property (Donative Transfers)* § 29.4 (1987).

**6.** Uniform Probate Code § 2–711; *Restatement, Third, of Property (Wills and Other Donative Transfers)* § 16.1 (Prel.Dft.2003).

**7.** Cole v. Plant, 440 So.2d 1054 (Ala. 1983).

**8.** Sutton v. Milburn, 711 S.W.2d 808, 813 (Ark.1986).

**9.** Section 10.1.

**10.** Uniform Statutory Will Act § 6(3).

part of the remainder even though the deed gave her only a life estate, and (2) giving her siblings an interest even though they did not survive Annis. Therefore the court determined the heirs as of Annis' death.[11]

A devise of a remainder to the "then living" heirs postpones the time of determining heirs. Although these words might be construed to mean that the heirs should be determined when the ancestor dies but they must survive the life tenant, this would make the gift a nullity if all the heirs died before the life tenant but if the determination of heirs is postponed there will usually be eligible takers.[12]

An immediate devise "to the heirs of Alice" can also raise the question when they should be determined. If Alice predeceased the testator, courts usually determine her "heirs" as of the time of the testator's death.[13] If Alice survives the testator, courts usually give the property to those persons who *would be* Alice's heirs if she were dead; otherwise distribution would have to be postponed until Alice died.[14]

*Change in Law* Since statutes governing intestate succession vary, an undefined reference to "heirs" raises the question which statute should control, e.g., when a will left a remainder to the "heirs of my children," the relevant state law did not give husbands an intestate share of their wife's land when the testator died, but it did when the testator's daughter later died. The court found the testator intended to apply the intestacy laws in effect when each child died.[15] But another court, construing a trust created in 1929 which gave a remainder to the heirs of the settlor's grandson, determined heirs as of the grandson's death but used the law in effect in 1929.[16]

*Heirs as a Word of Limitation* Historically, one had to use the word "heirs" in order to convey a fee simple; a conveyance "to John in fee simple" gave him only a life estate. This is no longer true, but many drafters still use "heirs" to indicate that a donee or devisee should get a fee simple. In this case "heirs" is a word of

---

**11.** Wells Fargo Bank v. Title Ins. & Trust Co., 99 Cal.Rptr. 464 (App.1971). The second Restatement of Property adopts the incongruity argument only when the ancestor's *sole* heir receives a prior interest under the same will. *Restatement, Second, of Property (Donative Transfers)* § 29.4 comm. f (1987).

**12.** *Restatement, Second, of Property (Donative Transfers)* § 29.4, comm. h (1987); Matter of Evans' Estate, 334 N.E.2d 850, 853 (Ill.App.1975).

**13.** *Restatement, Second, of Property (Donative Transfers)* § 29.4, comm. g (1987); Uniform Probate Code § 2–711.

**14.** *Restatement, Second, of Property (Donative Transfers)* § 29.4, comm. c (1987).

**15.** Matter of Dodge Testamentary Trust, 330 N.W.2d 72, 83 (Mich.App. 1982). *See also Restatement, Second, of Property (Donative Transfers)* § 29.3 (1987).

**16.** National City Bank v. Ford, 299 N.E.2d 310, 314 (Ohio Com.Pl.1973).

"limitation" because it limits (*i.e.*, defines) John's estate. Heirs acquire an interest under an instrument only if "heirs" is used as a "word of purchase."[17]

In a gift "to John and his heirs" John's heirs get no interest,[18] but a devise to the testator's grandson "and *at his death* to his heirs" was held to give the grandson a life estate with a remainder in his children.[19] A devise "to A and his heirs" is sometimes construed as a substitutional gift to the heirs if A predeceases the testator; *a fortiori* if the will says "to A *or* his heirs."[20]

Construing "heirs" as a word of limitation facilitates alienation of property, since one need not wait until the ancestor dies to determine the interested parties. However, courts today usually construe heirs as a word of purchase if they think it was intended as such, even though this may impede a transfer of property.

*Fee Tail* The tension between the law's desire to promote alienability and the desire of donors to keep property in the family surfaced in the 13th century with limitations of the type "to A and the heirs of his (her) body." The courts construed such words as giving A a fee simple conditional on having issue; if A had no issue, the land would revert to the donor (or pass to a remainderman if one was designated), but if A had issue s/he could transfer the property.[21] The statute *De Donis Conditionalibus* of 1285 rejected this construction as contrary to the donor's intention, and allowed A's issue to recover the land if A alienated it. The interest created by limitations "to A and the heirs of his (her) body" became known as a "fee tail." Courts eventually allowed fee tails to be conveyed by a complex legal proceeding.[22]

Most American states have adopted a statutory solution to the problem of gifts "to A and the heirs of his/her body."[23] These statutes in general allow alienation to be restrained, if at all, for only one generation, e.g., a devise to the testator's daughter "and

---

17. *Restatement, Second, of Property (Donative Transfers)* Introductory Note preceding Chapter 29 (1987). Purchase in this context does not mean "acquire for money." Even if land is given to "heirs," they are "purchasers" if they were intended to get an interest.

18. Estate of Straube v. Barber, 990 S.W.2d 40, 45 (Mo.App.1999).

19. Cheuvront v. Haley, 444 S.W.2d 734 (Ky.1969).

20. Rowett v. McFarland, 394 N.W.2d 298 (S.D.1986). *See also* Section 8.3.

21. 2 Bracton, *De Legibus* 68 (Woodbine ed.). In Prichard v. Department of Revenue, 164 N.W.2d 113 (Iowa 1969), the court applied this rule to hold that if A had issue, the property was taxable in her estate at death.

22. 2 W. Blackstone, *Commentaries* *360 (1765).

23. *Restatement, Second, of Property (Donative Transfers)* § 30.1, Statutory note par. 7 (1987).

the heirs of her body" gave her by statute a fee simple, defeasible if she died without issue.[24]

Since the phrase "heirs of her body" is subject to several possible constructions, drafters should avoid it.

*The Rule in Shelley's Case*    A settlor created a trust for his grandson for life, "and upon his death to the heirs of his body." The court held these words gave the grandson a fee tail under the notorious Rule in Shelley's Case. "Where a freehold is limited to one for life, and, by the same instrument, the inheritance is limited * * * to his heirs, or to the heirs of his body, the first taker takes the whole estate, either in fee simple or in fee tail; and the words "heirs," or "heirs of his body" are words of limitation, and not words of purchase."[25] The Rule was created to prevent evasions of the medieval equivalent of the estate tax,[26] and has been invoked in modern times by the Internal Revenue Service for the same reason,[27] but skilled drafters can easily avoid the Rule, so it operates as a trap for clients of unskilled drafters.

The Rule promotes alienability, but it is arbitrary. A devise "to my son for life, remainder to his heirs," imposes no greater restriction on alienability than a devise "to my son for life, remainder to his issue." But the Rule in Shelley's Case does not apply to the latter because it only covers remainders to "heirs."[28]

The Rule in Shelley's Case has been abolished in most states by statute, and, according to the second Restatement of Property, "should be abolished prospectively by judicial decision" if a statute has not already done so.[29]

Most rules of construction apply both to land and to personal property, but the Rule in Shelley's Case applies only to land.[30] It applies both to wills and deeds, and to legal interests as well as trusts.

*Doctrine of Worthier Title*    The Doctrine of Worthier Title, like the Rule in Shelley's Case, holds that the word "heirs" is not a word of purchase, thereby preserving the feudal incidents which

**24.** Russell v. Russell, 399 S.E.2d 415 (N.C.App.1991). In some states these words would give the daughter a life estate with a remainder to her issue. Williams v. Kimes, 949 S.W.2d 899 (Mo. 1997)

**25.** Society Nat. Bank v. Jacobson, 560 N.E.2d 217, 221 (Ohio 1990).

**26.** 2 W. Blackstone, *Commentaries* \*242 (1765); *Restatement, Second, of Property (Donative Transfers)* § 30.1, comm. a (1987).

**27.** Estate of Forrest, TC Memo 1990–464.

**28.** *Restatement, Second, of Property (Donative Transfers)* § 30.1, comm. g (1987); Estate of Forrest, TC Memo 1990–464.

**29.** *Restatement, Second, of Property (Donative Transfers)* § 30.1 (1987).

**30.** *Restatement, Second, of Property (Donative Transfers)* § 30.1(3) (1987). *But see* Society Nat. Bank v. Jacobson, 560 N.E.2d 217 (Ohio 1990) (local version of rule covers personal property as well).

accrued when land passed by descent rather than purchase.[31] (Acquisition by descent was considered a "worthier title"). Both rules promote alienability, and may permit early termination of trusts by eliminating any interest in the heirs of a living person.[32]

Whereas the Rule in Shelley's Case applies to remainders to the "heirs" of a life tenant, the Doctrine of Worthier Title applies to the "heirs" of the grantor in a deed or the settlor of a living trust. The Doctrine of Worthier Title has been extended to personal property whereas the Rule in Shelley's Case generally applied only to *land*.[33]

The Rule in Shelley's Case overrides the donor's intention but the Doctrine of Worthier Title (where it still exists) is only a rule of construction which gives way to an indication of contrary intent.[34] The Uniform Probate Code abolishes the doctrine "both as a rule of law and as a rule of construction."[35] Its principal role in modern cases has been to allow settlors to terminate trusts which purport to give an interest to their "heirs." New York has abolished the Doctrine but allows settlors to revoke a trust regardless of any interest given to their heirs.[36]

The Doctrine of Worthier Title does not apply to gifts to the settlor's "issue" as distinguished from "heirs." Modern substitutes for the Doctrine make the same distinction. The New York statute abolishing the Doctrine was held inapplicable to a remainder to the settlor's "issue."[37]

## § 10.3   Rule of Convenience; Rule in Wild's Case

The primary concern of this chapter has been remaindermen who die too soon, *i.e.*, before the preceding interest terminates. The present section deals with persons who are born too late to be included in a class gift even though they literally fall within its terms. For example, a will created a trust for "the children of Ralph." The trustee was to distribute a share to each child at age 25. When the testator died Ralph had five children, but he later adopted another. The 6th child was allowed to share in the trust. "If a testamentary gift is to a class in general terms * * *, the death of the testator will, as a general rule, fix the time for distribution, and close the class.[1] * * * However, if the gift is * * *

---

**31.** Both rules may cause property to be subject to death taxes today. McGovern, *Facts and Rules in the Construction of Wills*, 26 UCLA L.Rev. 285, 304 (1978).

**32.** *Restatement, Second, of Property (Donative Transfers)* § 30.2, comm. a (1987).

**33.** *Id.*, § 30.2.

**34.** *Ibid.*

**35.** Uniform Probate Code § 2–710. *See also* Cal.Prob.Code § 21108.

**36.** N.Y. EPTL §§ 6–5.9, 7–1.9(b).

**37.** In re Dodge's Trust, 250 N.E.2d 849 (N.Y.1969).

**§ 10.3**

**1.** Thus if there had been a simple devise to "the children of Ralph," the after-born 6th child would have been

to be distributed at a later determinable date, the class members who are in being at the testator's death take a vested interest in the fund then, subject to the addition of members of the class who are born after the testator's death but before the time of distribution."[2] Ralph's 6th child was adopted before Ralph's oldest child reached 25. Any child born or adopted thereafter would be excluded.[3]

The rule excluding after-born class members is called the "rule of convenience" because it avoids "the otherwise necessary complex safeguards in favor of possible but not as yet conceived or adopted takers."[4] Most class gifts are to groups which close naturally at the time of distribution, e.g. a devise "to my children." In an outright devise "to my grandchildren," on the other hand, if the testator is survived by children, grandchildren may be born after the testator dies, but they would be excluded by the rule of convenience.

The rule turns on the time when distribution is made. In some instruments the time of distribution is unclear, *e.g.* "when my youngest grandchild reaches [or when all of my grandchildren have reached] age 21." Has this time arrived when all of the transferor's *living* grandchildren have reached twenty-one? If children of the transferor are still alive a later grandchild may turn out to be the "youngest," but the quoted language is generally read to call for distribution when there is no living grandchild under 21.[5] Although this interpretation cuts off any grandchild born thereafter, these are not likely to appear, since few parents have children after their youngest child reaches 21.

In a direction to distribute "when the youngest grandchild reaches 21" what happens if the youngest grandchild dies before reaching 21; does the trust terminate then, or only when the grandchild *would have* reached 21, or when the *next* youngest grandchild reaches 21? The last is the most sensible solution,[6] since the testator's probable purpose was to avoid distribution to persons under 21.

If an interest preceding the class gift is disclaimed, many courts hold that the disclaimer "accelerates" the remainder and closes the class.[7]

excluded. *Restatement, Second, of Property (Donative Transfers) §* 26.1 (1987).

**2.** Central Trust Co. v. Smith, 553 N.E.2d 265, 271 (Ohio 1990).

**3.** *Restatement, Second, of Property (Donative Transfers) §* 26.2, comm. m (1987).

**4.** *Id.,* § 26.1, comm. a.

**5.** South Carolina Nat. Bank v. Johnson, 197 S.E.2d 668 (S.C.1973). The

idea can be expressed by the phrase "when no living grandchild is under the age of 21." See Uniform Statutory Will Act § 8(b).

**6.** *Restatement, Second, of Property (Donative Transfers)* § 26.2, comm. o (1987).

**7.** Pate v. Ford, 376 S.E.2d 775 (S.C. 1989); *Restatement, Second, of Property*

---

*Income* Many trusts provide for the distribution of income to or among a class. A distribution of an income installment does not close the class because "there is no * * * real inconvenience in allowing the class to remain open to those children born after the distribution of income begins. * * * Each distribution of income can be made to the children * * * living at that time."[8]

*Posthumous and Adopted Children* When a class "closes" under the rule of convenience, any child who has been *conceived* is included. This may delay the fixing of shares for a few months, but this is not a significant inconvenience. Similarly intestacy statutes include as heirs persons who were conceived before but born after the decedent's death.[9] A recent decision even allowed children born over 18 months after their father's death to inherit from him.[10] However, another court in a similar case said that "the mere genetic tie of the decedent to any posthumously conceived child" is not enough "without evidence that the deceased intestate parent affirmatively consented to (1) the posthumous reproduction and (2) to support any resulting child."[11]

If a person enters a class by adoption, the crucial date is the adoption, not birth, *i.e.*, any child adopted after the class closed is excluded regardless of the date of birth.[12]

*Exceptions to the Rule of Convenience* The rule of convenience does not apply if "a contrary intent of the donor is found from additional language or circumstances."[13] Courts rarely find such a "contrary intent." A court applied the rule of convenience even to a trust for "all" of the settlor's children who attained the age of 21 "whether now living, or hereafter to be born." The quoted words were held to refer only to children born after the trust was executed but before the date of distribution.[14]

To avoid rendering a gift totally ineffective, courts do not apply the rule of convenience if no class member is alive at the time of distribution. In such cases all class members get a share whenever born.[15]

---

(*Donative Transfers*) § 26.1, comm. j (1987).

**8.** Hamilton Nat. Bank v. Hutcheson, 357 F.Supp. 114, 119–20 (E.D.Tenn. 1973).

**9.** Uniform Probate Code § 2–108.

**10.** In re Estate of Kolacy, 753 A.2d 1257, 1262 (N.J.Super.A.D.2000).

**11.** Woodward v. Commissioner of Social Security, 760 N.E.2d 257, 270 (Mass. 2002).

**12.** In re Silberman's Will, 242 N.E.2d 736, 742 (N.Y.1968). As to the right of adoptees generally to inherit or take under a class gift see Section 2.10.

**13.** *Restatement, Second, of Property* (*Donative Transfers*) § 26.1 (1987).

**14.** In re Wernher's Settlement Trusts, [1961] 1 All E.R. 184, 189–90 (Ch. 1960).

**15.** *Restatement, Second, of Property* (*Donative Transfers*) §§ 26.1(2), 26.2(2).

*Intent to Limit the Class* An instrument may limit a class more narrowly than the rule of convenience. When a will divided the estate "equally between my three grandchildren Francis, Manley, and Willie," a fourth grandchild was not allowed a share even though he was born prior to distribution, because the use of names and the number "three" showed that the testator did not intend a class gift.[16]

Even a class gift may be restricted by its terms, e.g. a trust provided for distribution when the youngest grandchild reached 21 "to such of my grandchildren as may be living at the time of my death." Two grandchildren were born after the testator died but before the youngest reached 21. They would not have been barred by the rule of convenience, but the court excluded them as a matter of interpretation.[17]

*Wild's Case: "To Charles and His Children"* A devise "to Charles and his children" invokes Wild's Case, a 16th-century decision almost as celebrated as Shelley's Case. The *dicta* in Wild's Case included two resolutions. First, "if A devises his land[18] to [Charles] and to his children or issues, and [Charles] hath not any issue at the time of the devise,"[19] Charles gets a fee tail. Second, if Charles *does* have issue at the time of the devise, they take together with Charles, cutting out any after-born children.

These resolutions reflect the tension between the "manifest intent" that Charles' children take, and the inconvenience of giving an interest to unborn children. The first resolution, if applied today in states where a fee tail is turned into a fee simple,[20] would give the children no interest.[21] Charles' children could be given an interest by interpreting the words as giving Charles a life estate with a remainder to his children. The Restatement of Property adopts this solution.[22]

The second resolution in Wild's Case, which gives Charles and his children (if he has any) immediate interests, is still widely followed,[23] but the Restatement adopts the life-estate-remainder construction here too.[24] This postpones alienability during Charles

---

**16.** Platt v. Romesburg, 348 S.E.2d 536 (S.C.App.1986).

**17.** Estate of Houston, 421 A.2d 166 (Pa.1980).

**18.** Although these resolutions apply by their terms only to *devises* of *land*, they have also been applied to deeds and to gifts of personal property. Link, *The Rule in Wild's Case in North Carolina*, 55 N.C.L.Rev. 751, 773, 783 (1977).

**19.** Modern American cases apply this test at the time of the testator's

death rather than when the will was executed. Link, note 18 *supra*, at 771.

**20.** See Section 10.2.

**21.** Estate of Murphy, 580 P.2d 1078 (Or.App.1978).

**22.** *Restatement, Second, of Property (Donative Transfers)* § 28.3 (1987).

**23.** In re Parant's Will, 240 N.Y.S.2d 558, 564 (Surr.1963).

**24.** *Restatement, Second, of Property (Donative Transfers)* § 28.3 (1987). *See*

lifetime, but it allows later-born children to share, only a theoretical advantage if Charles is unlikely to have more children when the gift takes effect.[25]

*Planning* The rule of convenience and Wild's case may not provide the best solution in a particular situation. Suppose land is devised to "the children of Charles" or "to Charles and his children," and Charles has one child, but plans to have more. Why should his later children be excluded? Conversely, suppose that Charles is fifty, and a bachelor who has no intention of marrying. Why should the title to the land be kept in abeyance for his lifetime to protect children who are not likely to materialize?

Gifts "to Charles and his children" raise additional problems. In what proportions should they share? If Charles or one of his children dies, is this a class gift? a joint tenancy? A life estate in Charles, followed by a remainder to his children avoids these problems but raises others. A trust for Charles with remainder to his "issue" who survive him is preferable.[26]

## § 10.4   Powers of Appointment

*Definitions* If John's will gives Mary a power of appointment, John is the "donor" of the power and Mary is the "donee," even if she cannot benefit from exercise of the power. If a power is reserved, the donor and the donee are the same person.

A trustee who has discretion in distributing income or principal has another kind of power of appointment,[1] but the donee of a power, unlike a trustee, is not a fiduciary and can be "dictated by considerations other than the welfare" of the possible appointees in making appointments,[2] whereas trustees should not be motivated by self-interest. Trustees' decisions are subject to court control whereas formally valid appointments made under a power are not reviewable.

Powers of appointment are of two types: "general" and "special."[3] A donee who can appoint to herself or to her estate has a general power. If she can appoint to anyone in the world *except*

*also* Neb.Rev.Stat. § 76–113; Kan.Stat. § 58–505.

**25.** *Restatement, Second, of Property (Donative Transfers)* § 26.1, comm. a (1987).

**26.** For the advantages of a bypass trust over a legal life estate see Section 9.3.

**2.** *Id.* § 20.2, comm. h.

**3.** Cal.Prob.Code § 611; N.Y. EPTL § 10–3.2. The Restatement prefers the term "non-general" to special. *Restatement, Second, of Property (Donative Transfers)* § 11.4 (1984).

### § 10.4

**1.** *Restatement, Second, of Property (Donative Transfers)* § 11.1, comm. d (1984).

herself, her estate or her creditors, her power is special. Special powers are usually more limited, *e.g.*, to appoint among her issue.

A power is "testamentary" if the donee can appoint only by a will. If powers are "presently exercisable," the donee can make an appointment by deed.

*Relation Back* The exercise of a power of appointment generally "relates back" to the donor, so that the appointee takes directly from the donor. The donee of the power is viewed as an agent who "fills in the blanks" in the donor's will or trust, and not as the owner of the appointed assets. Courts invoke relation back, but they do not apply the idea in all situations.

*Taxes* Before 1942, powers were distinguished from property under the federal estate tax. Appointive assets were not taxed in the donee's estate unless the power was exercised. Today, however, appointive assets are taxed in the donee's estate, whether or not the power is exercised, if the power is general and was created after 1942. Special powers, on the other hand, are not taxed even if they are exercised.[4]

Powers are treated as equivalent to ownership for some income tax purposes. A person with "a power exercisable solely by himself to vest the corpus or the income" of a trust in himself is taxed on the trust income even if it is accumulated or paid to someone else.[5] Even special powers, if reserved by the settlor, may cause the settlor to be taxed on the trust income.[6]

*Rights of Creditors* State laws vary as to the rights of creditors of the donee of a power. Some courts do not allow creditors to reach a debtor's right to withdraw money from a trust,[7] but many states have changed the rule by statute.[8] If a donee of a presently exercisable general power goes bankrupt, the donee's trustee in bankruptcy can reach the trust assets. But if a power is only testamentary, creditors cannot reach the trust assets while the donee is alive even under the Bankruptcy Code.[9]

Even states which allow creditors of the donee of a general power to reach the appointive assets do not apply the same rule to

---

**4.** See Section 15.3. However, appointive assets are not always subject to *state inheritance tax* when the donee dies even if the power is general. In re Estate of Nelson, 571 N.W.2d 269 (Neb. 1997).

**5.** Internal Revenue Code § 678.

**6.** *Id.* § 674.

**7.** University Nat. Bank v. Rhoadarmer, 827 P.2d 561, 562 (Colo.App.

1991); *Restatement, Second, of Property (Donative Transfers)* § 13.2 (1984).

**8.** N.Y. EPTL § 10–7.2. *See also Restatement, Second, of Property (Donative Transfers)* § 13.2, Statutory Note (1984).

**9.** *Id.* § 13.6. *See also* Bynum v. Campbell, 419 So.2d 1370 (Ala.1982).

special powers; even in bankruptcy creditors of the donee of such a power cannot reach the appointive assets.[10]

*Spouse's Rights*   The relation back concept has been held to prevent a donee's spouse from including appointive assets in the elective share,[11] but the Uniform Probate Code makes subject to the elective share (1) property over which the decedent spouse "held a presently exercisable general power of appointment" regardless who created it, and (2) property transferred during the marriage in which the decedent reserved a general power, including a testamentary power.[12]

*Capacity*   A donee can make an effective appointment "if the donee has capacity to make an effective transfer of similar owned property."[13] The tendency to set a lower standard for capacity for wills than for inter-vivos gifts applies to powers as well.[14]

When the donee of a presently exercisable power is under conservatorship, a conservator can exercise the power on the donee's behalf, although this generally requires court approval.[15] Testamentary powers are more problematic since many states deny conservators the power to make a will for the conservatee.

*Formalities*   The instrument granting a power usually says that it shall be exercised "by will" or "by deed." This means a will or deed which complies with the legal requirements prescribed for such instruments,[16] but substantial compliance may suffice.[17] The Restatement, however, distinguishes between requirements imposed by the donor and those imposed by law: as to the latter, "approximation is never sufficient."[18]

*Contracts to Exercise Powers*   A promise by the donee of a testamentary power to exercise the power in a particular way is unenforceable. The Restatement justifies this rule on the ground

---

**10.** *Restatement, Second, of Property (Donative Transfers)* § 13.1 (1984); 11 U.S.C § 541(b)(1).

**11.** *Restatement, Second, of Property (Donative Transfers)* § 13.7 (1984), followed in Bongaards v. Millen, 793 N.E.2d 335, 341 (Mass.2003).

**12.** Uniform Probate Code § 2–205. In Matter of Reynolds, 664 N.E.2d 1209 (N.Y.1996), a similar statute was construed to allow a widower to reach a trust created by his wife in which she had reserved a broad special power.

**13.** *Restatement, Second, of Property (Donative Transfers)* § 18.1 (1984).

**14.** In re Wood's Estate, 108 Cal. Rptr. 522, 534 (App.1973).

**15.** Cal.Prob.Code § 2580(b)(3); Uniform Probate Code § 5–411(a)(3); Re-

statement, Second, of Property (Donative Transfers) § 18.1(2) (1984).

**16.** *Id.,* § 18.2, comm. b, d. Thus a codicil not executed in conformity with the statutory requirements for wills was ineffective to exercise a testamentary power. In re Estate of Scott, 77 P.3d 906 (Colo.App.2003).

**17.** Estate of McNeill, 463 A.2d 782, 784 (Me.1983).

**18.** *Restatement, Second, of Property (Donative Transfers)* § 18.3, comm. b (1984). *See also* In re Estate of Kouba, 116 Cal.Rptr.2d 319 (App.2002) (testamentary power not effectively exercised by instrument where witnesses signed after donee died).

that a testamentary power indicates "an intent that the selection of the appointees be made in the light of the circumstances" existing when the donee dies.[19] But the Restatement allows donees to *release* a testamentary power by deed.[20]

*Intent to Exercise* The question whether or not a donee intended to exercise a power often arises. For example, the will of a donee of a general power left "all the residue of my estate of every kind and nature to a trust." The court held that the power was not exercised, following a presumption of non-exercise in the Uniform Probate Code.[21] The Restatement adopts the same presumption,[22] but some statutes presume the opposite.[23]

Many instruments conferring powers require the donee to specifically refer to the power. Such provisions have been variously construed. A will which devised all the donee's property "including all property over which I may have a power of appointment" was held a sufficient exercise, even though it did not identify the power.[24] Other courts on similar facts have held the power was not exercised.[25] The Uniform Probate Code presumes that such provisions are designed only "to prevent an inadvertent exercise," and are satisfied by general language "if the donee had knowledge of and intended to exercise the power."[26]

According to the Restatement "direct declarations by the donee as to whether the donee intended a will to exercise the power may not be considered,"[27] but the Uniform Probate Code seems to be contrary on this point.[28]

The Restatement does allow evidence of "circumstances existing at the time of the execution of the donee's deed or will" to show the donee's intent.[29] These include the adverse tax consequences of

**19.** *Restatement, Second, of Property (Donative Transfers)* § 16.2, comm. a (1984). *See also* In re Brown's Estate, 306 N.E.2d 781 (N.Y.1973) (promise in divorce settlement to exercise testamentary power in favor of a son unenforceable).

**20.** *Restatement, Second, of Property (Donative Transfers)* § 14.1, comm. a, § 16.2, comm. a (1984). *See also* Cal. Prob.Code § 661.

**21.** Matter of Estate of Allen, 772 P.2d 297, 299 (Mont.1989).

**22.** *Restatement, Second, of Property (Donative Transfers)* § 17.3, comm. a (1984).

**23.** First Union Nat. Bank v. Ingold, 523 S.E.2d 725 (N.C.App.1999) (based on a N.C. statute).

**24.** McKelvy v. Terry, 346 N.E.2d 912 (Mass.1976).

**25.** Matter of Smith's Estate, 585 P.2d 319, 321 (Colo.App.1978).

**26.** Uniform Probate Code § 2–704 and Comment thereto.

**27.** *Restatement, Second, of Property (Donative Transfers)* § 17.5, comm. a (1984).

**28.** Kurtz, *Powers of Appointment under the 1990 Uniform Probate Code,* 55 Alb.L.Rev. 1151, 1167 (1992). For a general discussion of the use of extrinsic evidence in construing ambiguous wills see Section 6.1.

**29.** *Restatement, Second, of Property (Donative Transfers)* § 17.5 (1984).

exercising the power, "an extremely close and affectionate relationship" between the donor, donee and the beneficiary of the donee's will,[30] and the donee's own property, e.g. a donee must have intended to exercise a power by a will which made pecuniary devises totaling $90,000 and left the residue to five individuals, since the pecuniary devises alone would have exhausted the donee's own assets.[31] An intent *not* to exercise a special power may be inferred if a devise includes persons who are not permissible appointees.[32]

The fact that the donee's will was executed before the power was created is not determinative, e.g., when a woman executed a will, and two years later her mother died with a will giving her a power of appointment, the daughter's will was held to have exercised the power.[33]

*Lapse*  If the donee appoints to a person who predeceases her, the appointment lapses, but an anti-lapse statute may apply. A testator gave his wife a special power of appointment, which she exercised to appoint to the donor's brother. The appointment failed because the brother predeceased the donee; he had survived the testator, but (despite the relation back theory) an appointee must survive the donee as well as the donor in order to take.[34] The brother's children claimed the property under an anti-lapse statute, but the statute applied only if a devisee who was "a relative of the testator" and the brother was not related to the donee.[35] Also, the brother's children were not permissible appointees, since the donee was only authorized to appoint to the brother. The Uniform Probate Code and the second Restatement of Property would remove both these difficulties. The anti-lapse statute applies if the appointee is related to "either the testator or the donor" of the power, and, unless the power expressly provides otherwise, "a surviving descendant of a deceased appointee * * * can be substituted for the appointee * * * whether or not the descendant is an object of the power."[36]

*Limitations on Special Powers*  Special powers often restrict appointments to a relatively small group such as "children." Courts interpret such words the same way they would construe a gift to

---

**30.**  Bank of New York v. Black, 139 A.2d 393, 400 (N.J.1958).

**31.**  Little Red Schoolhouse v. Citizens & Southern Nat. Bank, 197 S.E.2d 342 (Ga.1973).

**32.**  MacLean v. Citizens Fidelity Bank & Trust Co., 437 S.W.2d 766 (Ky. 1969).

**33.**  In re Buck Trust, 277 A.2d 717 (Del.1971). See also *Restatement, Second, of Property (Donative Transfers)* § 17.6 (1984). However, the terms of the power may preclude exercise by an earlier instrument. *Id.* comm. c.

**34.**  *Restatement, Second, of Property (Donative Transfers)* § 18.5 (1984).

**35.**  Dow v. Atwood, 260 A.2d 437, 441 (Me.1969).

**36.**  Uniform Probate Code § 2–603(b); *Restatement, Second, of Property (Donative Transfers)* § 18.6 (1984).

the same class. A power given to the testator's son to appoint to "one or more of my descendants" was held not to include an adult whom the son had adopted.[37] Most courts would not permit appointment to a grandchild if the power says "children."[38]

Appointments in trust, or the creation of further powers of appointment, are sometimes held invalid, e.g., when a will directed the trustee to pay the assets "free from trust, to and among [the] children and issue [of the testator's daughter] as she may appoint," the daughter was not permitted to appoint to a trust for her children.[39] The Restatement, however, presumes that a donee was intended to have "the same breadth of discretion in appointment to objects that he has in the disposition of his owned property."[40]

If a special power is "non-exclusive" the donee must include every object of the power in an appointment. The Restatement and some statutes provide that powers are "exclusive" unless the donor specifies a minimum share which each object must receive,[41] and most recent cases have construed questionable powers as exclusive.[42]

An appointment to a permissible appointee may be upset if the donee's motive was to benefit a non-object of the power. Thus if a donee has a power to appoint among her issue, her appointment to a child who has agreed to give part of the property to the donee's sister may be disallowed as a "fraud on the power."[43] But the donee's exercise of the power need not be totally disinterested. Appointment to a child "because of the attention and kindness she has always shown to me" is permitted even if the power is special.[44]

If a donee wishes to benefit a non-object of the power, she can use her own property (if she has some) to accomplish this. Courts sometimes validate the exercise of a power by "marshalling" after the donee has died, using the donee's own property to fulfill objects not authorized by the power.[45]

*Failure to Effectively Appoint* A well-drafted power should include a gift in default of appointment. Even if it does not, if the power is special, a gift in default of appointment to the objects of

**37.** Cross v. Cross, 532 N.E.2d 486 (Ill.App.1988). For the inclusion of adoptees in class gifts generally see Section 2.10.

**38.** Equitable Trust Co. v. Foulke, 40 A.2d 713 (Del.Ch.1945); *Restatement, Second, of Property (Donative Transfers)* § 20.1, illus. 4 (1984).

**39.** Loring v. Karri–Davies, 357 N.E.2d 11 (Mass.1976).

**40.** *Restatement, Second, of Property (Donative Transfers)* § 19.3, comm a, illus 4 (1984).

**41.** *Id.,* § 21.1.

**42.** Ferrell–French v. Ferrell, 691 So.2d 500 (Fla.App.1997).

**43.** *Restatement, Second, of Property (Donative Transfers)* § 20.2 (1984).

**44.** *Id.* , comm. h, illus. 16 (1984).

**45.** Dollar Savings & Trust Co. v. First Nat. Bank, 285 N.E.2d 768, 772 (Ohio Com.Pl.1972).

the power is often implied, but not if the class of permissible appointees is very large.[46]

If the donee of a general power fails to exercise it and no gift in default of appointment is expressed, the appointive assets revert to the donor's estate. But an *ineffective appointment* by the donee (as contrasted with failure to exercise) may "capture" the assets and even override a gift in default of appointment. A man gave his wife a general testamentary power with a gift in default of appointment to his son. The wife's will left her property, including the appointive assets, to devisees who all predeceased her so the appointment lapsed. The son's estate claimed the property under the gift in default of appointment, but the court awarded it to the donee's heirs instead. "When the donee of a general power of appointment makes an ineffective appointment * * * the appointive property passes to the donee or his estate if the instrument of appointment manifests an intent to assume control of the property for all purposes."[47]

*Choice of Law*    Since the rules governing powers vary choice of law may be crucial. The logic of the relation back theory suggests that the law of the donor's domicile should control, and many cases so hold,[48] but recent cases have applied the law of the donee's domicile.[49]

Choice of law can also be an issue when the law has changed. A husband gave his wife a general testamentary power of appointment at a time when a statute presumed that a devise of all the testator's property exercised a power. Prior to the wife's death the statute was altered to reverse the presumption. The wife's will did not mention the power. The court held that she had not exercised it, saying "the law in effect at the time of the exercise of a power of appointment controls its exercise."[50]

*Powers and Planning*    Powers of appointment provide flexibility to deal with changing conditions. If a husband gives his wife a power, she can adjust their estate plan to account for circumstances which arise after his death. "For example, it may appear best that the children not share equally. * * * Perhaps the interest of one descendant should be sheltered by a continuing trust."[51] The argu-

---

**46.** Schroeder v. Herbert C. Coe Trust, 437 N.W.2d 178, 182 (S.D.1989); *Restatement, Second, of Property (Donative Transfers § 24.2),* comm. c (1984).

**47.** Estate of Eddy, 176 Cal.Rptr. 598, 610–11 (App.1981). *See also* Hochberg v. Proctor, 805 N.E.2d 979, 991 (Mass.2004); *Restatement, Second, of Property (Donative Transfers)* § 23.2 (1984).

**48.** Beals v. State Street Bank & Trust Co., 326 N.E.2d 896, 899–900 (Mass.1975).

**49.** White v. United States, 680 F.2d 1156, 1159 (7th Cir.1982). *See also Restatement, Second, of Property (Donative Transfers)* § 18.6, comm. d (1984).

**50.** Hund v. Holmes, 235 N.W.2d 331, 334 (Mich.1975).

**51.** Bolich, *The Power of Appointment: Tool of Estate Planning and Drafting,* [1964] Duke L.J. 32, 39–40.

ments for including powers for appointment in a trust are stronger the longer the period the trust is expected to last.

Ownership also provides flexibility, but powers have some advantages over ownership. If the husband wishes to keep property out of his wife's taxable estate *and* allow her to alter the disposition at her death, he can give her a *special* power. A donor may also wish to limit the donee's choices for non-tax reasons, *e.g.,* allow her to provide for their issue but not her other relatives or a second husband.

Even if a donor is unconcerned with avoiding taxation in the donee's estate, the donor may prefer to put property in trust (1) to free the donee from the burden of managing it and (2) to avoid passing assets through the donee's probate estate. In *this* situation a presently exercisable general power may be appropriate, since it would allow the donee to take the property out of trust if the trustee is not doing a good job.

If the children are given *general* powers, the assets will be taxable in their estates. This is not necessarily a disadvantage; without any power the property may be subject to a generation-skipping tax which is higher than the estate tax.[52] On the other hand, the donor may wish to give the children only special powers in order to keep the property in the family.

Many testamentary powers require that the donee refer to the power specifically in their wills in order to exercise it. Otherwise, a donee may exercise the power inadvertently. The donor may also wish to require that any instrument exercising the power be filed with the trustee so the trustee will know whether the power has been exercised and can distribute the assets immediately after the donee dies.

*Dealing with Powers* The *donee* of a power of appointment must decide whether or not to exercise it. A key factor in this decision is the gift in default of appointment. The donee may prefer to leave the property to someone else, or to put assets into a trust which would otherwise pass outright. If there is no gift in default of appointment, exercising the power may avoid uncertainty after the donor dies.

Exercising a power can put the assets in the donee's taxable estate or subject them to an otherwise avoidable state inheritance tax, or to claims of the donee's creditors. These adverse consequences of exercise do not often apply, since exercise of a power has the same effect as nonexercise in many situations.[53]

---

**52.** See Schwab, *General Powers of Appointment May Cause Unexpected Tax,* 19 Est.Plan. 75, 80 (1992). As to the generation-skipping tax, see Section 15.4.

**53.** The federal estate tax is the most important or only death tax in

If donee wishes to exercise a testamentary power, the will should specifically refer to it. The drafter should ascertain the limits of the power, and also beware of violating the Rule against Perpetuities.[54]

most estates, and exercise or nonexercise is relevant for this purpose only for general powers created before 1942, rarely encountered today.

**54.** As to the application of the Rule to powers of appointment see Section 11.5.

# Chapter 11

# THE RULE AGAINST
# PERPETUITIES

## § 11.1   History and Policy of the Rule

*The Fee Tail*   The first "perpetuity" so-called in the law was created by the Statute de Donis of 1285 which provided that if land was conveyed "to *A* and the heirs of his body," *A* could not alienate it. After courts began to allow fee tails to be barred,[1] landowners looked for new ways to keep land in their families. One method was to attach a proviso to a fee tail that any attempt to bar it would cause a forfeiture. Courts refused to give effect to such provisos, calling them "perpetuities."

*Destructibility of Contingent Remainders*   Landowners also used contingent remainders to keep land in the family, but this was frustrated by the destructibility of contingent remainders. For example, a testator devised land to his son Robert "for his life, and afterwards to the next heir male of Robert." When Robert conveyed the land to a stranger, this destroyed the remainder in his heir, since contingent remainders had to vest when (or before) the preceding estate ended. Robert's conveyance put an immediate end

§ 11.1
1.   See Section 10.2.

to his life estate, and Robert's "next heir male" could not be ascertained until Robert died.[2]

The destructibility of contingent remainders did not apply to trusts, and a trust to preserve contingent remainders arose in the 17th century.[3] Destructibility thus placed a premium on the drafting skills of lawyers who knew how to avoid it. The destructibility of contingent remainders has been abolished by statute in many states, and some courts have rejected it even without a statute as "a relic of the feudal past."[4]

*Executory Interests*  Lawyers came up with another way to avoid the destructibility of contingent remainders, the executory interest. A father with two sons, William and Thomas, devised land "to Thomas and his heirs," with a proviso that if Thomas died without issue, the land should pass to William. Thomas suffered a common recovery (the traditional device for breaking a fee tail), but this was held ineffective because Thomas had a fee *simple*. Furthermore, William's interest was not a *remainder*, because "one fee cannot be in remainder after another," but rather an "executory devise," which was not destructible.[5]

Later a trust for the Duke of Norfolk came before Chancellor Nottingham. The basic plan again was a gift to a younger son if his elder brother died without issue. The common-law judges, whom Nottingham consulted, advised him that the limitation was void[6] but Nottingham did not want to frustrate the father's intent. He and the judges agreed that the same rule should apply in law and in Equity. This distinguishes the Rule against Perpetuities from the destructibility of contingent remainders. Nottingham also agreed with the judges that "perpetuities" were undesirable, but as to where the line should be drawn, the Chancellor rejected the technical distinctions which the common law had drawn, saying "I will stop wherever any visible Inconvenience doth appear."

*Lives in Being, Plus 21 Years*  The Duke of Norfolk's case held only that "where it is within the Compass of one Life, that the Contingency is to happen, there is no Danger of a Perpetuity." The "one Life" was later expanded to many lives in being on the ground that this did not greatly expand the restraint.[7] The persons used as measuring lives did not have to be beneficiaries of the interest,

---

**2.** Archer's Case, 76 Eng.Rep. 146 (1597).

**3.** 2 W. Blackstone, *Commentaries* *171–72 (1765).

**4.** Abo Petroleum Corp. v. Amstutz, 600 P.2d 278, 281 (N.M.1979).

**5.** Pells v. Brown, 78 Eng.Rep. 504 (1620); 2 W. Blackstone, *Commentaries* *173–74 (1765).

**6.** 22 Eng.Rep. 931, 940 (1685).

**7.** Scatterwood v. Edge, 91 Eng.Rep. 203 (1699).

because the "length of time will not be greater or less, whether the lives taken have any interest or have not."[8]

Twenty one years was added to the period of the Rule in a case involving a devise to the "eldest son of my daughter Mary who attains the age of twenty one years." This did not restrain "the power of alienation * * * longer than the law would restrain it" viz. during the infancy of Mary's son, who could not make a conveyance so long as he was a minor.[9] This reasoning suggests that a postponement of vesting beyond lives in being must be connected with the minority of a beneficiary, but the law soon came to permit an absolute term of 21 years.[10]

The Rule against Perpetuities thus moved from Nottingham's general idea of "stopping when any visible inconvenience doth appear" to a more precise rule which can be concisely expressed as follows: "No interest in property shall be valid unless it must vest, if at all, not later than twenty-one years after one or more lives in being at the creation of the estate and any period of gestation involved."[11] The Rule is more comprehensive than the destructibility of contingent remainders: it applies to trusts and legal interests, real and personal property, and executory interests as well as remainders. But it has the same unfortunate quality of constituting a trap which only skilled drafters can avoid.

*Policy Behind the Rule: Alienability*   Many opinions attribute the Rule to the public interest in keeping property alienable, or "in commerce." Perpetuities were defined as limitations which make "an estate unalienable, though all mankind join in the conveyance."[12] Even persons who question whether the operations of a free market foster society's best interests should support the Rule, because it favors "free marketability versus restrictions imposed by an erratic testator; not free enterprise versus governmental regulation."[13]

A New York statute invalidates any suspension of the power of alienation which lasts longer than lives in being plus 21 years. The power of alienation is "suspended" within the meaning of this statute "when there are no persons in being by whom an absolute fee * * * can be conveyed."[14] Similar statutes in some states replace the Rule against Perpetuities,[15] but in New York interests may be invalid under the Rule against Perpetuities even though

---

**8.** Thellusson v. Woodford, 32 Eng. Rep. 1030, 1040–41 (H.L. 1805).

**9.** Stephens v. Stephens, 25 Eng.Rep. 751, 752 (1736).

**10.** *Restatement, Second, of Property (Donative Transfers)* § 1.1, comm. a (1981).

**11.** N.Y. EPTL § 9–1.1(b).

**12.** Scatterwood v. Edge, 91 Eng. Rep. 203 (1699).

**13.** L. Simes, *Public Policy and the Dead Hand* 38 (1955).

**14.** N.Y. EPTL § 9–1.1(a).

**15.** Idaho Code § 55–111; Wis. Stat.§ 700.16.

they do not suspend the power of alienation, e.g., a perpetual option which does not suspend the power of alienation, since the optionor and optionee can join to convey the land.[16] A sale of property is theoretically possible when all interests in property are held by living, identifiable persons, but the owners of contingent interests are not likely to join in a sale because they will not be able to agree on how to allocate the sales proceeds.[17]

*Trusts*  Concerns about alienability are reduced when property is held in trust where the trustee has a power of sale. Some states do not apply the Rule to trusts if the trustee can sell the trust assets.[18] In most states, however, a trustee's power to sell property does not take the case out of the Rule against Perpetuities.

*Wealth Concentration*  Morris and Leach asserted that the Rule against Perpetuities prevented "enormous concentrations of land in the hands of a very few and thereby brought it about that England never suffered unbearably from those conditions which elsewhere have produced violent social revolution."[19] The Rule, by freeing up property, allows the rich to dissipate their wealth. But the role of the Rule in preventing undue concentration of wealth is small.

The estate tax depends to some extent on the Rule. If persons had unlimited freedom, they might create by-pass trusts for their children, grand-children, great-grandchildren, etc., and so avoid the estate tax for centuries. But tax law does really not need the Rule. Today the generation-skipping tax reaches successive interests even before the period allowed by the Rule runs out.[20]

*Fair Balance Between Generations*  The most persuasive argument for the Rule today is that it "strikes a fair balance between the desires of members of the present generation, and similar desires of succeeding generations to control the property."[21] If parents could tie up their property in perpetuity, their descendants would have no power over it, and their claim to control property is as strong as that of their forbears. Furthermore, long-term arrangements for controlling property often become inappropriate as conditions change.

**16.** Buffalo Seminary v. McCarthy, 451 N.Y.S.2d 457 (App.Div.1982).

**17.** Simes, *supra* note 13, at 37–38. *See also* J. Morris & W. Leach, *The Rule Against Perpetuities* 14 (1962).

**18.** Wis.Stat. § 700.16(3); *cf.* Del. Stat. tit. 25, § 503 (Rule not applicable to trusts but they must terminate after 110 years). Other states have recently moved in this direction in order to at-tract trust business. See Fox & Huft, *Asset Protection and Dynasty Trusts*, 37 Real Property, Prob. and T.J. 287, 309–20 (2002).

**19.** Morris & Leach, *supra* note 17, at 11–12.

**20.** For the generation-skipping tax see Section 15.4.

**21.** Simes, *supra* note 16, at 58.

Arguably the Rule is too lax. Is it really a "fair balance" between generations when parents can tie up property so that their descendants who are lives in being have no power over it?[22] Professor Waggoner agrees that the Rule is "overpermissive" in allowing "donors in some cases to extend control through or into generations completely unknown and unseen by them," but he adds that there is almost "no enthusiasm" among knowledgeable persons to make the Rule coincide more precisely with its rationale.[23] This would be difficult and not worth the effort, since few testators today seek to exert dead hand control to the extent allowed by the Rule; most use the Rule's permissiveness simply as a "safety valve" to secure reasonable estate plans.

John Chapman Grey, who wrote an often-cited treatise on the Rule at the end of the nineteenth century, delighted in the Rule's precision. "If a decision agrees with [the Rule] it is right; if it does not agree with it, it is wrong. * * * If the answer to a problem does not square with the multiplication table one may call it wrong."[24] The mathematical precision had an unfortunate effect on the Rule as an instrument of policy. It caused many trusts to fail, even though they did not violate the policy behind the Rule, while skilled drafters can violate its spirit while complying with the letter.

## § 11.2  Operation of the Rule

*Starting Point*  In testing an instrument for a Rule violation one should first determine when the period begins to run. For wills this is the time of the testator's death, regardless of when the will was executed. For irrevocable trusts or deeds, it is the time of execution of the instrument (or delivery if required).[1] Some perpetuities violations occur because the drafter overlooked the difference between wills and inter-vivos transfers, e.g., an irrevocable trust was to last "until the death of the last surviving grandchild of the Grantor who shall be living *at the time of his death.*" This would have been all right had this been a will or a revocable trust, but not in an irrevocable trust because a grandchild born after its execution could not serve as a measuring life.[2]

After determining the starting date, one must determine whether there is any possibility that the trust in question[3] will

**22.** Wiedenbeck, *Missouri's Repeal of the Claflin Doctrine—New View of the Policy Against Perpetuities* 50 Mo.L.Rev. 805, 828 (1985).

**23.** Waggoner, *The Uniform Statutory Rule Against Perpetuities,* 21 Real Prop.Prob. and Trust L.J. 569, 586–89 (1987).

**24.** J. Gray, *The Rule Against Perpetuities* xi (4th ed. 1942).

**§ 11.2**

**1.** See Restatement, Second, of Property (Donative Transfers) § 1.2 (1983).

**2.** Ryan v. Ward, 64 A.2d 258 (Md. 1949).

**3.** The Rule applies also to legal interests, but most modern cases involve trusts so it is convenient to use them as examples.

continue beyond lives in being at the starting date plus 21 years. If
not, there is no problem, but any possibility, however remote, that
the trust may continue beyond lives in being plus 21 years raises
the specter of a Rule infraction.[4] Five types of cases occur with
some frequency.

*(1) Period in Gross*  A testamentary trust which was to continue
for twenty-five years after the testator's death violated the Rule
because there was the possibility of vesting after a life in being plus
twenty-one years.[5] This shows how the letter and the spirit of the
Rule often diverge. A valid trust can be drafted in which the drafter
designates a group of lives in being and provides that 21 years after
the death of the survivor of them the trust will terminate. Such a
trust will probably endure for a century, and will not violate the
Rule, but one which is certain to last for 25 years does.

*(2) Age Contingencies*  A testamentary trust was to terminate
"when the youngest living child of my son has reached age of
twenty-five years." Since it was possible that the son might have a
child born after the testator's death who would not reach 25 until
more than 21 years after every life in being at the testator's death
had died, the Rule was violated.[6] Infractions like this are not
unusual, since many testators do not want grandchildren to receive
property as soon as they reach 21, believing that they will not be
ready to handle property at that age.

*(3) Two-generation Trust*  Many Rule violations arise from trusts
which are designed to last for two generations, *e.g.*, the lives of the
testator's children and grandchildren. Such trusts may infringe the
Rule even if the testator has no grandchildren born after his death
because some might have been born. "At the time of his death the
testator was survived by three children and five grandchildren.
* * * There remained the possibility that another grandchild would
be born. * * * The law looks forward from the time the limitation
is made to see what may be, not backward to see what has been."[7]
However, if the testator's children all predecease him, such a trust
does not violate the Rule since the possibility of an after born
grandchild is eliminated.[8]

Sometimes a trust is saved by construing it to exclude after-
born class members, e.g., when a trust was to terminate "upon the
death of my last surviving grandchild" the court construed this to
mean only those grandchildren whom the testator had named

**4.** This has been changed today in
many states by the adoption of "wait
and see." *See* Section 11.4.

**5.** However, the court saved the
trust by reducing the term to 21 years.
Berry v. Union Nat. Bank, 262 S.E.2d
766 (W.Va.1980). See Section 11.4.

**6.** Hagemann v. National Bank and
Trust Co., 237 S.E.2d 388 (Va.1977).

**7.** Connecticut Bank & Trust Co. v.
Brody, 392 A.2d 445, 450 (Conn.1978).

**8.** *Restatement of Property* § 374,
comm. j, § 384, illus. 3 (1944).

previously in the will, so the Rule was not violated.[9] However, this construction is rejected in most cases of class gift language; if the testator had meant only grandchildren then living wouldn't the will have named them instead of referring generally to grandchildren?

*(4) Unborn Widow*   A will provided an income interest "to the wife of my son," followed by a contingent remainder at her death. Since the son might marry a woman who was unborn when the testator died, the trust violated the Rule.[10] Some courts avoid this by construing the will to refer only to the spouse at the time the will took effect,[11] but this construction is subject to the objection that if the testator meant that, the will would have said so or named the wife instead of using the general term "widow."

*(5) Administrative Contingencies*   A trust provided for termination five years after the testator's estate was distributed. The heirs claimed that the Rule was violated because the distribution might be delayed too long.[12] Some courts find that the Rule is not violated by such a provision because the law requires administration to proceed expeditiously, so it cannot possibly last for more than 21 years. Others reject this reasoning on the ground that the Rule requires "absolute certainty," and distribution of a decedent's estate is subject to many possible delays.[13]

### Are the Interests Vested?

Even if a trust may continue beyond lives in being, the Rule is still not violated if all the interests vest in time. A trust for the testator's daughters and their children was to last "until each of said grandchildren shall reach the age of 25," but this did not violate the Rule, because "the will can be construed to intend vesting in each grandchild immediately at birth, with only distribution delayed until age 25."[14]

A similar trust included a further provision that if any grandchild died before reaching 25, the share should go to his or her descendants. This gift over violated the Rule, but the preceding clause, providing for distribution to the grandchildren at age 25, was upheld; the invalidity of the divestiture clause left the grandchildren with an indefeasibly vested remainder.[15]

---

**9.** Southern Bank & Trust Co. v. Brown, 246 S.E.2d 598 (S.C.1978).

**10.** Pound v. Shorter, 377 S.E.2d 854, 856 (Ga.1989).

**11.** Matter of Chemical Bank, 395 N.Y.S.2d 917 (Surr.1977) (irrevocable trust for settlor's "widow" meant his present wife so Rule not violated).

**12.** Lucas v. Hamm, 364 P.2d 685 (Cal.1961).

**13.** Prime v. Hyne, 67 Cal.Rptr. 170, 173 (App.1968).

**14.** Foley v. Evans, 570 N.E.2d 179, 181 (Mass.App.Ct.1991).

**15.** Thornhill v. Riegg, 383 S.E.2d 447, 452 (N.C.App.1989). As to the distinction between contingent and vested subject to divestment, see Section 10.1.

*Class Closing* A class gift is not "vested" for purposes of the Rule so long as more persons can become members of the class.[16] A gift to the grandchildren (or more remote issue) of living persons risks violation of the Rule, but may be saved by the rule of convenience. A devise to the testator's daughter for life, remainder to his great grandchildren was upheld, because the rule of convenience would close the class when the daughter died.[17] Usually a class remains open until the time for distribution under the rule of convenience, but courts may construe gifts more narrowly in order to avoid perpetuities violations, e.g., the devise of an annuity to the "issue of *N*" was construed to mean only *N*'s issue living at testator's death.[18]

*Effect of the Rule on Construction* The question whether the Rule was violated often turns on constructional questions, such as when a class closes, or whether there was a condition of survival. If the Rule is violated under one construction but not under another, should this affect the way a court resolves the construction question? According to John Chipman Grey, "every provision in a will or settlement is to be construed as if the Rule did not exist and then to the provision so construed the Rule is to be remorselessly applied,"[19] but many modern courts say "a document should be interpreted if feasible to avoid the conclusion that it violates the rule against perpetuities."[20]

*Effect of Rule Violation* Infractions of the Rule usually appear in the residuary clause of a will and result in property passing intestate, so claims that the Rule was violated are typically raised by heirs who hope to get property outright which was left in trust. This effort may fail because normally a Rule violation does not invalidate the income interests of the trust but only remainder interests.[21] However, courts sometimes use "infectious invalidity" to strike down valid interests in order to better effectuate the testator's intent. For example, a will created trusts for the testator's three children. The termination provision for two of them violated the Rule. The one for the third child's trust did not but the court struck it down also. "Even if the provisions for Walter be

---

**16.** Abram v. Wilson, 220 N.E.2d 739 (Ohio Prob.1966). As to when a class closes, see Section 10.3.

**17.** In re Greenwood's Will, 268 A.2d 867 (Del.1970).

**18.** In re Trust of Criss, 329 N.W.2d 842 (Neb.1983). Normally such periodic payments do not close the class under the rule of convenience. Section 10.3.

**19.** Quoted in Hagemann v. National Bank and Trust Co., 237 S.E.2d 388, 393 (Va.1977).

**20.** Estate of Grove, 138 Cal.Rptr. 684, 688 (1977).

**21.** White v. Fleet Bank of Maine, 739 A.2d 373, 378 (Me.1999). Some statutes provide that a Rule violation results in "vesting the fee in the last taker under the legal limitations;" this gives the person designated as life beneficiary the remainder as well. Pound v. Shorter, 377 S.E.2d 854 (Ga.1989).

valid, \* \* \* they cannot be permitted to stand alone, because such would result in significant distortion or defeat of the Testator's underlying objectives. \* \* \* The underlying plan of the Testator was for his three children to have equal shares."[22] When a remainder violates the Rule, preceding income interests may also be stricken as "inextricably intertwined" with them.[23] If the trust was created in order to bypass the estates of the testator's children, and if the Rule violation causes the remainder to fall to the children as intestate property, why should the trusts be established at all?[24]

When application of the Rule produces an intestacy, this may not seriously disrupt the testator's estate plans when the wills creates a trust for the testator's heirs. But when the beneficiaries of the challenged will are not the testator's heirs, the distortion of the testator's wishes when a Rule violation is found can be extreme.

*Separability of Class Gifts*  Most infractions of the Rule involve class gifts. Courts generally refuse to sever them to hold the interests of some members valid. For example, a will left property to the testator's grandchildren who attained the age of 25. He had five grandchildren when he died and three more were born thereafter. The interests of the grandchildren who were alive when the testator died were certain to vest, if at all, in time because they were lives in being. The interest of the after-born grandchildren might vest too late. The court refused to distinguish between the two groups.[25]

Gifts to "sub-classes" are treated differently. A trust provided for the testator's daughter and grandchildren, with a remainder to remoter issue upon the death of each grandchild. When one grandchild died, the court invoked "the doctrine of vertical separability" under which the remainder to the issue of any grandchild who was alive at the testator's death was separable from the remainder to the issue of an after-born grandchild.[26] But in a similar case, the court refused to separate the remainders because the will did "not indicate any intention that each of his grandchildren should have a separate share.\* \* \* Rather the entire corpus of the trust \* \* \* was to be held for the benefit of his grandchildren as a class."[27]

---

**22.** Merrill v. Wimmer, 481 N.E.2d 1294, 1299–1300 (Ind.1985).

**23.** Connecticut Bank & Trust Co. v. Brody, 392 A.2d 445, 451 (Conn.1978).

**24.** But a court declined to void the life estate when a spendthrift provision in the trust showed that "the testator's obvious purpose was to protect the [grandson] against his own improvidence," and this would be frustrated by

an outright distribution to him. In re Estate of Davis, 297 A.2d 451, 455 (Pa. 1972).

**25.** Leake v. Robinson, 35 Eng.Rep. 979, 989 (1817).

**26.** In re Estate of Weaver, 572 A.2d 1249, 1256 (Pa.Super.1990).

**27.** Connecticut Bank and Trust Co. v. Brody, 392 A.2d 445, 452 (Conn.1978).

Separability is an appealing way to avoid the Rule if no after born beneficiaries are born, since no one loses thereby. But when after-born grandchildren actually appear, courts are reluctant to treat subclasses differently, and so they adopt an "all or nothing" approach.[28]

## § 11.3  Planning to Avoid the Rule

*Bad Ways to Avoid the Rule*  Many lawyers unnecessarily distort sensible estate plans in order to avoid Rule violations. Some suggested "prescriptions for avoiding violation of the Rule"[1] are questionable. For example:

1.  "Beware of gifts to grandchildren." Such gifts may be desirable if settlors do not want property to pass outright to their children, for tax or other reasons.

2.  "Describe beneficiaries by name rather than by class designation." This may exclude after-born grandchildren, a result most testators would want to avoid.

3.  "Beware of gifts contingent upon the taker attaining an age over twenty-one." A distribution at age 21 may be premature. How many fortunes have been dissipated after they were distributed to beneficiaries at age 21 in order to avoid the Rule?

*Savings Clauses*  A savings clause can avoid Rule violations without producing such undesirable side effects. For example, a trust for the testator's daughter and her children provided that each child's share vested at age 30. The trial court reduced the age to 21 in order to avoid violating the Rule, but the appellate court reversed, because this change "creates possibilities that the trust property could pass out of the decedent's family * * * earlier than was intended by the decedent." A savings clause in the trust, providing "that all trusts created by the will are to terminate on the date limited by the applicable Rule against Perpetuities" made the change unnecessary.[2]

Savings clauses have two parts: a termination provision, and a direction for distribution. The termination clause in the foregoing case failed to make clear what "the date limited" by the Rule was. Lives in being plus 21 years, of course, but *what* lives? The court found the relevant measuring life was the testator's daughter, so the trust would have to end 21 years after she died. But a well-drafted savings clause can specify a *reasonable number* of measur-

---

**28.**  In re Morton's Estate, 312 A.2d 26, 27 (Pa.1973).

**2.**  In re Estate of Burrough, 521 F.2d 277, 280 (D.C.Cir.1975).

**§ 11.3**

**1.**  Link, *The Rule against Perpetuities in North Carolina*, 57 N.C.L.Rev. 727, 817 (1979).

ing lives, e.g. "unless sooner terminated in accordance with its provisions, this trust shall terminate 21 years after the death of the last survivor of my spouse and my issue who are living at the time of my death." An unmarried testator could designate "the issue of my parents who are living at the time of my death" (or some other comparable group) instead. An irrevocable trust should refer to "issue now living," or name the measuring lives.

If the trust terminates under the savings clause, to whom should distribution be made? If this is not made clear, the clause may be ineffective.[3] Many savings clauses provide that upon termination the assets should be "distributed to the persons then entitled to the income." In most situations this makes sense, but if the income beneficiary at the time of termination under the savings clause is an "unborn widow," giving the trust assets to her outright may frustrate a settlor's wish to keep property in the family.

*Duration of Trusts* Although the Rule allows trusts to continue beyond lives in being plus 21 years if all the interests are vested, knowledgeable estate planners advise against keeping trusts going so long.[4] If the trust gives the trustee discretion to accumulate income, invade principal, or sprinkle income, the beneficiaries' interests are contingent upon the trustee's discretion, and so invalid if the trust continues beyond the period of the Rule.[5] A savings clause, therefore, ought to terminate any trust which is still operating when the period of the Rule ends. This will be unfortunate if a beneficiary is then a minor, but in most cases the trust will actually terminate not under the savings clause but at a time when all the distributees are mature.

*Perpetual Trusts* The foregoing suggestions for avoiding the Rule will not satisfy those who (for whatever reason) want to create perpetual (or very long-terms) trusts. Today several states offer a haven for such trusts, seeking a "comparative advantage in attracting trust business and capital."[6]

## § 11.4 Modern Reforms

*Wait and See* Professor Leach was a zealous crusader for reforming the Rule. He attacked its focus on possibilities rather than the actual facts. "The public interest is not damaged by a tying up of property that *might have* exceeded the period of

---

**3.** Hagemann v. National Bank & Trust Co., 237 S.E.2d 388, 392 (Va. 1977).

**4.** Link, *supra* note 1, at 818.

**5.** Arrowsmith v. Mercantile–Safe Deposit, 545 A.2d 674, 677 (Md.1988); *Restatement, Second, of Trusts* § 62, comm. q (1959). This is ironic, since such flexible trusts are less subject to the objection of dead hand control. Hirsch & Wang, *A Qualitative Theory of the Dead Hand*, 68 Ind.L.J. 1 (1992).

**6.** Dukeminier & Krier, *The Rise of the Perpetual Trust*, 50 UCLA L.Rev. 1303, 1315–16 (2003).

perpetuities," so courts should "wait and see" whether the contingency happens within the period of the Rule.[1] This idea had already been adopted in a Pennsylvania statute and has since been accepted in some judicial decisions.[2]

The court in this cases did not actually *wait* to see what would happen; by the time the litigation arose it had become clear that the trust would not last beyond twenty one years plus lives in being. Often no one raises the perpetuities question until after the relevant facts have become clear.

*Who Are the Measuring Lives?* Many courts have rejected "wait and see."[3] The great difficulty with the concept is determining the appropriate measuring lives. Consider a devise "to my descendants living 120 years after my death." At the end of 120 years should a court uphold the devise if it discovers *any person* in the world who was alive at the testator's death who died at age 100?[4]

The "possibilities" approach of the common-law Rule avoids this dilemma. Even a *25–year* postponement of vesting (without a savings clause) violates the common-law Rule because *whoever* is picked as a measuring life in advance *may* die within 4 years. Taking advantage of hindsight under "wait and see" substantially lengthens the time during which property can be tied up even though the period of the Rule remains nominally the same.

A Uniform Statutory Rule Against Perpetuities, promulgated in 1986 and now adopted in about half the states, accepts wait and see but rejects the use of measuring-lives because of the difficulty of defining them. Instead USRAP validates any interest which "either vests or terminates within 90 years after its creation."[5] The 90–year period was selected as "a reasonable approximation of * * * the period of time that would on average, be produced through the use of a set of actual measuring lives identified by statute and then adding the 21 year tack-on period after the death of the survivor."[6]

*Cy Pres* Leach also espoused a second reform of the Rule, often called cy pres by analogy to the doctrine which allows courts to modify charitable trusts to meet changing circumstances.[7] Cy pres extends the idea that ambiguous instruments should be *construed*

---

**§ 11.4**

**1.** Leach, *Perpetuities in Perspective: Ending the Rule's Reign of Terror,* 65 Harv.L.Rev. 721, 729–30 (1952) (emphasis added).

**2.** 20 Pa.Stat. § 6104(b); Matter of Estate of Anderson, 541 So.2d 423, 433 (Miss.1989).

**3.** Pound v. Shorter, 377 S.E.2d 854, 856 (Ga.1989).

**4.** Simes, *Is the Rule against Perpetuities Doomed?,* 52 Mich.L.Rev. 179, 187 (1953).

**5.** Uniform Statutory Rule Against Perpetuities § 1(a)(2).

**6.** *Id.* Prefatory Note.

**7.** Leach, *supra* note 1, at 734–35.

to avoid violating the Rule; it allows unambiguous terms to be reformed, *e.g.,* changing "age 40" to "age 21." A New York statute providing for this result saved a trust for the testator's grandchildren by reducing the age of distribution from 35 to 21.[8]

Some statutes give courts a more general authorization to reform instruments, not limited to reducing a designated age to 21.[9] The Uniform Statutory Rule combines cy pres with wait and see.[10] Wait and see is applied first. In most cases, this renders alteration in the instrument unnecessary, but not always, e.g. a will which created a "perpetual" trust for scholarships "to any blood heirs of my husband or myself."[11] The trust was reformed to direct that any remaining principal be distributed "twenty one years after the death of the last heir of the testator or her husband who was living at the time of the testator's death."

Some courts have reformed wills to avoid a Rule violation even without statutory authority, but others have refused to do so.[12] Some criticize the idea as too vague. For instance, in a case involving an age contingency over 21, a court might reduce the specified age to 21, or confine the relevant class to persons born before the testator's death, or leave the specified distribution date and class intact but make the interests vest prior to the trust termination.[13] Professor Browder suggested that the best way to reform wills was to insert a perpetuities savings clause.[14] This would allow any reasonable estate plan to be carried out unchanged. When cy pres is implemented by inserting a savings clause, the result is virtually the same as wait and see.

The Uniform Statutory Rule is only prospective with respect to wait and see, but it provides for reformation even of existing instruments.[15] A case arose under the statute involving a devise of land to the testator's son and his children for their lives with a remainder to the testator's great grandchildren. The son had no further children after the testator died, but the wait and see provisions of USRAP did not apply to this 1915 will. The court

---

**8.** Matter of Estate of Kreuzer, 674 N.Y.S.2d 505, 508 (App.Div.1998).

**9.** Mo.Stat. § 442.555(2); Tex.Prop. Code art. 5.043.

**10.** Uniform Statutory Rule Against Perpetuities § 3.

**11.** Matter of Estate of Keenan, 519 N.W.2d 373, 375 (Iowa 1994). Because of the limitation to relatives, the trust could not qualify as charitable. See Section 9.7.

**12.** *Compare* Berry v. Union Nat. Bank, 262 S.E.2d 766, 771 (W.Va.1980) (25 year trust reduced to 21 years) *with* Hagemann v. National Bank and Trust Co., 237 S.E.2d 388, 392n (Va.1977).

**13.** Foley v. Evans, 570 N.E.2d 179, 181 (Mass.App.Ct.1991).

**14.** Browder, *Construction, Reformation, and the Rule Against Perpetuities*, 62 Mich.L.Rev. 1, 6 (1962).

**15.** Uniform Statutory Rule Against Perpetuities § 5.

reformed the will, however, to restrict the grandchildren to those "who are alive at the time of my death."[16]

## § 11.5   Powers and the Rule

*Exercise of Power—Starting Point*   In determining the validity of interests created by the exercise of a power of appointment, general powers which are presently exercisable are differentiated from other types. For example, when a trust gave the settlor's son a testamentary power of appointment which he exercised by creating a trust for his children for their lives, the period of the rule was calculated from the date of the trust creating the power and not from date of exercise of the power by the son's will.[1] This premise made the appointment invalid, since the son's children were born after the trust which conferred the power was created. The Uniform Statutory Rule agrees that an interest created by the exercise of a power is deemed to have been created at the time the power was created, unless the power allows the donee "to become the unqualified beneficial owner."[2] The exception for presently exercisable general powers applies also at common law. Thus when the donee of a power exercised it to create trusts which were to terminate 21 years after "the death of the survivor of her issue in being at the time of her death," the trusts were valid because the donee also had power to withdraw the assets from the trust during her lifetime, even though she had made little use of this power.[3]

As to interests created by exercise of special powers, almost all states agree that the period of the Rule starts when the power was created.[4] In Delaware, however, interests created by exercise of any power were "deemed to have been created at the time of the exercise and not at the time of the creation of such power of appointment."[5] The Delaware rule inspired a special provision of the Internal Revenue Code to deal with the tax-evasion possibilities it presented.[6]

*Second Look*   All jurisdictions allow a "second-look" when a power of any kind is exercised. Even though the starting period for the Rule is the date on which the power was created, circumstances existing on the date the power was exercised are taken into account

---

**16.** Abrams v. Templeton, 465 S.E.2d 117 (S.C.App.1995).

### § 11.5

**1.** Arrowsmith v. Mercantile–Safe Deposit, 545 A.2d 674, 678 (Md.1988). See also *Restatement, Second, of Property (Donative Transfers)* § 1.2, comm. d (1983). There is some contrary authority. Industrial Nat. Bank v. Barrett, 220 A.2d 517 (R.I.1966).

**2.** Uniform Statutory Rule § 2.

**3.** Matter of Moore, 493 N.Y.S.2d 924, 928 (Surr.1985).

**4.** United Cal. Bank v. Bottler, 94 Cal.Rptr. 227 (App.1971); *Restatement, Second, of Property (Donative Transfers)* § 1.2, illus. 11 (1983).

**5.** Del.Code tit. 25, § 501. Now modified by id. § 504.

**6.** Int.Rev.Code § 2041(a)(3).

in determining the validity of the interests created by the exercise.[7] If, for example, a donee exercises a power given by a parent by creating trusts for the lives of the donee's children, the second look will validate the trusts if the children were born before the power was created. The second look is a limited form of "wait and see," but even opponents of wait and see favor the second look.[8]

Second look does not go as far as wait and see. The second look does no good if a donee exercises a power to create trusts in which persons born after the power was created are measuring lives,[9] whereas under wait and see such a trust would be valid if the after-born persons happened to die within 21 years after the death of the last to die of the lives in being when the power was created (or within 90 years under the Uniform Statutory Rule).[10]

*Capture*   When an appointment violates the Rule, the property may pass under a gift in default of appointment in the instrument which created the power, but some courts invoke "capture," i.e., replace the invalid remainders by a gift to the donee's heirs.[11] Capture applies only to general powers. If a special power is invalidly exercised, the property passes to the takers in default of appointment.[12]

*Choice of Law*   The law in effect at the date a power is exercised determines the validity of the exercise, so some courts have used modern reform statutes to avoid or soften the consequences of a Rule violation.[13]

*Planning*   What can the creator of a power do to prevent the donee from violating the Rule? A requirement that the donee specifically refer to the power may help, since some violations of the Rule arise from an inadvertent exercise. The donor should also consider giving the donee a presently exercisable general power, so that the Rule will not begin to run until the donee's death, but not if the donor fears that the donee might use a presently exercisable power to squander the trust assets.

In drafting a will for the donee of a power (other than a presently exercisable general power), the perpetuities savings

**7.**   N.Y. EPTL § 10–8.3.

**8.**   5A R. Powell, *Real Property* § 788(3). Professor Powell opposed wait and see.

**9.**   Second Nat. Bank v. Harris Trust and Savings Bank, 283 A.2d 226 (Conn. Sup.1971).

**10.**   *Restatement, Second, of Property (Donative Transfers)* § 1.4, comm. *l* (1983).

**11.**   Amerige v. Attorney General, 88 N.E.2d 126, 131 (Mass.1949). *See also Restatement, Second, of Property (Donative Transfers)* § 23.2 (1983). For other examples of "capture," see Section 10.4.

**12.**   United California Bank v. Bottler, 94 Cal.Rptr. 227, 232 (App.1971).

**13.**   Dollar Savings & Trust Co. v. First Nat. Bank, 285 N.E.2d 768 (Ohio Com.Pl.1972).

clause must refer to lives in being when the power was created rather than persons living at the testator-donee's death.

## § 11.6   Gifts to Charity; Reversionary Interests

*Duration of Trusts*   Charitable trusts can be perpetual, because courts can utilize their cy pres power to modify terms which become obsolete.[1] Nevertheless, the Rule can frustrate charitable gifts or provisions connected with them.

*Vesting*   Gifts to charity must vest within the period prescribed by the Rule.[2] If the charity's interest "vests" in time, it need not actually receive the gift within the period of the Rule. The same rule applies to private trusts, but courts are especially prone to treat charitable gifts as "vested." A trust for the lives of the testator's grandchildren and their children, provided a gift at their death to Mt. Zion Methodist Church and "to an orphan or childrens home or homes selected" by the trustee. The charitable remainders were held to have vested at the testator's death, although it is hard to see how homes to be selected by the trustee had "vested" interests.[3]

*Executory Interests Following Charitable Gift*   Gifts over to an individual if a charity ceases to use the property are subject to the Rule. A testator who died in 1931 left money for a hospital; if the hospital ceased to operate, the funds were to go to George Green. When the hospital ceased to operate in 1975, the provision for George Green was held invalid.[4] Under the Uniform Statutory Rule, since the gift to George Green actually vested within 90 years, it would have been valid.[5] However, under the Uniform Trust Code a provision in a charitable trust for distribution to a noncharitable beneficiary can only be given effect "if fewer than 21 years have elapsed" since the trust was created.[6] The comment notes that most charitable trusts are designed to get a tax deduction and so the application of the limitation will be rare, since any gift over to an individual may cause the deduction to be lost.

If the gift over in this case had been to another charity instead of an individual, it would be valid under a special exception to the

### § 11.6

**1.**   See Sections 9.7 as to cy pres and the time limits on trusts for non-charitable purposes ("honorary" trusts).

**2.**   *Restatement (Second) of Property (Donative Transfers)* § 1.6 (1983).

**3.**   Burt v. Commercial Bank & Trust Co., 260 S.E.2d 306, 310 (Ga.1979). *Compare* Arrowsmith v. Mercantile–Safe Deposit and Trust Co., 545 A.2d 674, 677 (Md.1988) (income interests in indi-

viduals not vested because distributions were discretionary).

**4.**   Nelson v. Kring, 592 P.2d 438, 442 (Kan.1979). *Accord, Restatement (Second) of Property (Donative Transfers)* § 1.6, comm. c (1983).

**5.**   In Harrison v. Marcus, 486 N.E.2d 710, 715 (Mass.1985) the court used wait and see to avoid a similar perpetuities problem.

**6.**   Unif.Trust Code § 412.

Rule.[7] Some commentators have questioned this exception, since it applies even if an event unrelated to charity causes the shift from one charity to another, *e.g.,* a gift for UCLA, but if it should neglect to keep the testator's grave in repair, the property should go to USC.

*Effect of Invalid Executory Interest*    If the gift to an individual following a charitable gift is invalid, what happens to the property? Some cases have allowed the charitable donee to keep the property free of the restriction on the theory that when a divesting condition is invalid under the Rule, the prior interest becomes absolute.[8]

In some cases courts simply order the trustee to comply with the terms of the charitable trust. A trust "for the relief of aged needy and deserving women and couples" provided that if the funds were not used for this purpose, they should go to named individuals. When the trust ceased to operate, the gift to the individuals was held invalid, and the court appointed new trustees to carry out the testator's charitable intent.[9] Where compliance with the terms of a gift is impossible, *e.g.* land given for a park is taken to build a highway, the court may apply the proceeds to a related purpose under *cy pres*.[10]

*Possibility of Reverter*    The invalidity of the gift to a third person sometimes causes property to revert to the donor/testator or his or her successors.[11] This does not violate the Rule because future interests reserved by the grantor or testator, as distinguished from those given to third persons, are not subject to the Rule.[12] The desire to support charity may explain this, since reversionary interests are often linked to charitable gifts.[13] Also, the Rule period of lives in being plus 21 years is not appropriate for such interests, as distinguished from trusts for children and grandchildren or other individuals.[14]

---

**7.** *Restatement, Second, of Property (Donative Transfers)* § 1.6 (1983); Uniform Statutory Rule Against Perpetuities § 4(5).

**8.** Standard Knitting Mills, Inc. v. Allen, 424 S.W.2d 796, 800 (Tenn.1967); *Restatement, Second, of Property (Donative Transfers)* § 1.5, comm. b (1983). Compare cases holding that the invalidity of a divestiture clause makes the preceding interest indefeasibly vested. Section 11.2

**9.** Davenport v. Attorney General, 280 N.E.2d 193, 198 (Mass.1972).

**10.** State v. Rand, 366 A.2d 183 (Me. 1976). This requires a finding that the testator had a "broader charitable intent" beyond the specified purpose. Nelson v. Kring, 592 P.2d 438, 444 (Kan. 1979); Section 9.7.

**11.** *Restatement, Second, of Trusts* § 401, comm. d (1959).

**12.** Howson v. Crombie St. Congregational Church, 590 N.E.2d 687, 689 (Mass.1992).

**13.** Some statutes which restrict possibilities of reverter make an exception for conveyances to charity. Fla.Stat. § 689.18(5); Mich.Comp.Laws § 554.64(c).

**14.** Leach, *Perpetuities in Perspective: Ending the Rule's Reign of Terror,* 65 Harv.L.Rev. 721, 745 (1952).

*Reverter Statutes*  An Illinois statute provides that possibilities of reverter and rights of entry for breach of a condition shall be valid for only 40 years.[15] The statute applies to interests previously created. Some courts have held such retroactive statutes amount to an unconstitutional taking from persons who owned such reversionary interests when the statute was enacted,[16] but the Illinois Supreme Court upheld its statute on the theory that possibilities of reverter were not property but only "an expectation."[17] Other statutes extend to existing interests unless the owner records a reservation of rights within a brief period after the statute is passed. Many owners, being unaware of such statutes, have failed to record their claims and thus lost them. Courts have upheld such statutes.[18]

*Transfers of Possibilities and Rights of Entry*  The common law distinction between executory interests (subject to the Rule) and reversionary interests (exempt from the Rule) becomes absurd when a grantor transfers a reversionary interest. A woman conveyed land to a church for use as a parsonage; if the church ceased to use the land for religious purposes, it was to "revert to me, or if I should be deceased, then to the persons who at such time would be entitled to the residue of my estate."[19] The successors to the grantor's residuary devisees recovered the land after it ceased to be used for religious purposes. Their interest did not violate the Rule because they took as devisees of the grantor's right of entry, which was valid as an interest reserved by the grantor and passed under the residuary clause of her will. In other words, although the Rule invalidated the executory interest in the deed, the same persons took as devisees of the grantor.

This result hinges on the transferability of reversionary interests. In the 15th century, rights of entry could not be assigned. If the grantor attempted to do so, they were destroyed, on the theory that the assignee could not enforce them (because they were nonassignable) and neither could the grantor because he had given the interest away.[20] The first Restatement of Property distinguished between rights of entry, which were not assignable, and possibilities

---

**15.** 765 ILCS § 330/4. A similar Massachusetts statute allows 30 years for both reversionary and executory interests, thus eliminating the common law's disparate treatment of the two.

**16.** Biltmore Village v. Royal Biltmore Village, 71 So.2d 727 (Fla.1954). Followed in Board of Education v. Miles, 207 N.E.2d 181 (N.Y.1965).

**17.** Trustees of Schools of Township No. 1 v. Batdorf, 130 N.E.2d 111, 114–15 (Ill.1955). *See also* Hiddleston v. Nebraska Jewish Education Soc'y., 186 N.W.2d 904 (Neb.1971).

**18.** Kilpatrick v. Snow Mountain Pine Co., 805 P.2d 137 (Or.App.1991).

**19.** Howson v. Crombie St. Congregational Church, 590 N.E.2d 687, 688 (Mass.1992).

**20.** T. Littleton, *Tenures* § 347.

of reverter which were.[21] This distinction raises difficult questions of classification because many deeds use language which does not neatly fit into either category.[22] Many modern statutes make rights of entry alienable in keeping with the trend to allow transfer of all interests.[23]

## § 11.7  Commercial Transactions

The Rule against Perpetuities was not applied to commercial transactions until late in its history. In recent years, however, cases involving the Rule in commercial transactions have outnumbered those in donative transfers,[1] perhaps because lawyers who handle commercial transactions are less familiar with the Rule and the ways to avoid it.

*Options*  The Rule applies only to property, not to contracts to pay money. Options to buy land or unique goods, on the other hand, because they give the optionee a right to specific performance even against third persons, create property interests and are subject to the Rule. An option is invalid if it might be exercised beyond the period of the Rule.[2] This includes options to repurchase given to a seller, despite the general exemption from the Rule for interests reserved by a grantor.[3]

Options are denied enforcement even if the optionee seeks to exercise it only a few years after the option was created. Some courts have applied "wait and see" to make the option enforceable,[4] but others have refused to do so.[5] Other theories have been used to validate options. One is to imply a time limit for their exercise.[6] But some courts refuse to do this on the ground that if the parties had

**21.** *Restatement of Property* §§ 159–60 (1936).

**22.** Fennell v. Foskey, 225 S.E.2d 231, 233 (Ga.1976) (deed interpreted to create an alienable possibility of reverter rather than an inalienable right of entry).

**23.** Cal.Civ.Code § 1046; Oak's Oil Serv., Inc. v. Massachusetts Bay Transp. Auth., 447 N.E.2d 27 (Mass.App.Ct. 1983). But some statutes makes *both* possibilities of reverter and rights of entry *inalienable*. 765 ILCS § 330/1; Neb. Rev.Stat. § 76–299.

**§ 11.7**

**1.** Bloom, *Perpetuities Refinement: There Is an Alternative,* 62 Wash.L.Rev. 23, 76 (1987).

**2.** Symphony Space v. Pergola Properties, 669 N.E.2d 799 (N.Y.1996); Low

v. Spellman, 629 A.2d 57 (Me.1993) (right of repurchase).

**3.** As to the exemption of reserved interests see Section 11.6.

**4.** Colby v. Colby, 596 A.2d 901 (Vt. 1990). As to "wait and see" see Section 11.4.

**5.** Symphony Space v. Pergola Properties, 669 N.E.2d 799, 808 (N.Y.1996) (no wait and see statute); Low v. Spellman, 629 A.2d 57 (Me.1993) (conveyance was prior to wait and see statute).

**6.** Peterson v. Tremain, 621 N.E.2d 385, 387 (Mass.App.Ct.1993). This argument can backfire; if the optionee has waited more than a reasonable time to enforce it, enforcement will be denied for that reason. Lawson v. Redmoor Corp., 679 P.2d 972 (Wash.App.1984).

intended a time limit they would have specified one in the contract.[7]

Options can be saved by finding that they were "personal" to the optionor or optionee, so they will expire within a life in being, e.g. the optionee's death.[8]

*Leases and Covenants*  Long term leases which give the lessee an option to purchase have been held not to infringe the Rule. Whereas options unconnected with a lease deter "the free marketability of the real estate and the possibility of its development," an option in a lease gives the lessee an incentive to develop the property fully. To hold it invalid under the Rule "could very well have a reverse effect."[9] By similar reasoning perpetual options to renew a lease do not violate the Rule.[10] but an option to buy additional land *is* subject to the Rule.[11]

Restrictive covenants limiting the use of land are also exempt from the Rule.[12] The policy against dead-hand control is here effectuated by refusing to enforce covenants which have become out of date.[13]

*Policy Analysis; USRAP*  Some have questioned whether the Rule is appropriate in commercial cases. It is troubling to let a party use the Rule to get out of a bargain for which he received valuable consideration.[14] If the consideration paid for an option was clearly identifiable it could be recovered to avoid unjust enrichment, but it is usually an inseparable part of a larger transaction.

The Rule may be necessary to limit foolish dispositions by a testator, but when two parties with conflicting interests make a contract, their self-interest should protect against unreasonable restrictions.[15] The Uniform Statutory Rule Against Perpetuities exempts interests "arising out of a nondonative transfer" on the ground that the period of the Rule is "not suitable" for them.[16] One court invoked USRAP in upholding a contract provision challenged

**7.** Shaffer v. Reed, 437 So.2d 98 (Ala. 1983); Buffalo Seminary v. McCarthy, 451 N.Y.S.2d 457 (App.Div.1982).

**8.** Stratman v. Sheetz, 573 N.E.2d 776, 779 (Ohio App.1989). *But see* Buck v. Banks, 668 N.E.2d 1259 (Ind.App. 1996).

**9.** St. Regis Paper Co. v. Brown, 276 S.E.2d 24, 25 (Ga.1981).

**10.** Camerlo v. Howard Johnson Co., 710 F.2d 987 (3d Cir.1983).

**11.** Crossroads Shopping Center v. Montgomery Ward & Co., Inc., 646 P.2d 330 (Colo.1981).

**12.** Lowry v. Norris Lake Shores Development Corp., 203 S.E.2d 171 (Ga. 1974).

**13.** Nutis v. Schottenstein Trustees, 534 N.E.2d 380, 385 (Ohio App.1987) (residence restriction no longer enforceable because of change in character of neighborhood).

**14.** Morris & Leach, *The Rule Against Perpetuities* 224 (2d ed. 1962).

**15.** *Ibid.*

**16.** The drafters suggested that they could be controlled by a special statute like the Illinois 40 year limit on options. Uniform Statutory Rule Against Perpetuities § 4(1), Comment; Section 11.6.

under the Rule, but another struck down an option on the theory that the USRAP exemption left the transaction subject to the common-law Rule. [17]

## § 11.8  Restraints on Alienation

*History and Rationale* Closely related to the Rule against Perpetuities is a much older rule against restraints on alienation which appeared in the 15th century. "If a feoffment is made on condition that the feoffee not alienate the property to anyone, the condition is void, for when a man is enfeoffed of lands or tenements, he has power to alienate them to anyone by law [so] if this condition were good, the condition would take away the power which the law gives him, which would be against reason."[1] The rule is often stated in the same conclusory terms today,[2] but this "rationale" begs the question why the power of alienation is "necessarily incident to" a fee simple.

It is commonly said that the rule is designed to keep property alienable in order to allow "the utilization of land in the most effective manner."[3] This policy also underlies the Rule against Perpetuities, and courts sometimes examine a provision under both rules,[4] but the conclusion is not always the same. A provision in a deed requiring the grantor's consent to sell the land was held not to violate the Rule under a "wait and see" statute, but the provision was nevertheless invalid as an unreasonable restraint.[5] Conversely, a provision may violate the Rule but not constitute an invalid restraint.

*Reasonableness* The Restatement of Property says that in general a restraint is valid if "under the circumstances of the case, [it] is found to be reasonable."[6] Two factors determine whether a restraint is reasonable. First, does it serve a purpose which the court finds worthy? One court found an restraint invalid because it served "no worthwhile purpose * * * other than to allow [the grantor] to 'keep property in the family,'"[7] while another court upheld a provision which was "reasonably designed to attain or

**17.** *Compare* Juliano & Sons v. Chevron, U.S.A., 593 A.2d 814, 819 (N.J.Super.A.D.1991) *with* Buck v. Banks, 668 N.E.2d 1259 (Ind.App.1996).

**§ 11.8**

**1.** T. Littleton, *Tenures* § 360.

**2.** Hankins v. Mathews, 425 S.W.2d 608, 610 (Tenn.1968). *See also* Cal.Civ. Code § 711 (conditions restraining alienation are void "when repugnant to the interest created").

**3.** 6 *Amer. Law of Prop.* § 26.3.

**4.** Colby v. Colby, 596 A.2d 901 (Vt. 1990) (repurchase option valid under both analyses); Low v. Spellman, 629 A.2d 57 (Me.1993) (repurchase option invalid under both analyses).

**5.** Gartley v. Ricketts, 760 P.2d 143 (N.M.1988).

**6.** *Restatement, Second, of Property (Donative Transfers)* § 4.2(3) (1981).

**7.** Gartley v. Ricketts, 760 P.2d 143, 146 (N.M.1988).

encourage accepted social or economic ends."[8] A second factor is how substantial a bar to alienability the restraint imposes.

(1) *Partial Restraints*   Restraints which simply forbid alienation to one person, or a small group, are valid.[9] But a restraint is not valid simply because it allows the land to be transferred to a small group, such as the testator's descendants.[10] If the prohibited group contains the probable purchasers of the land, even though a small number, the restraint is invalid, and the converse is also true.[11]

(2) *Restraints on Use*   Courts distinguish between restraints on alienation and restrictions on use.[12] The latter are exempt because they cease to be enforceable when they become obsolete. [13]

(3) *Life Estates*   A restraint is not valid just because it is limited in time,[14] but restraints on alienation of a *limited interest* such as a life estate are permitted.[15] Life estates differ from a fee simple because they are hard to sell anyway—few purchasers want to buy an interest which will end when the seller dies.[16]

The Restatement distinguishes between forfeiture and disabling restraints in this connection. A provision that simply says "the grantee shall not alienate the land" is a disabling restraint; a forfeiture restraint is one which says the grantee shall lose the land if he tries to alienate it. As to a fee simple, both types of restraint are invalid. As to life estates, forfeiture restraints are permitted, but disabling restraints are not.[17] Some courts obliterate the distinction by *implying* a forfeiture provision whenever a will restrains alienation by a life tenant.[18] Spendthrift trusts are disabling restraints on equitable interests, and are permitted in nearly all states.[19]

---

**8.**   Kerley v. Nu–West, Inc., 762 P.2d 631, 635 (Ariz.App.1988).

**9.**   Pritchett v. Turner, 437 So.2d 104 (Ala.1983) (forfeiture if devisees convey land to testator's ex-wife); *Restatement, Second, of Property (Donative Transfers)* § 4.2, illus. 3 (1983).

**10.**   Williams v. Williams, 73 S.W.3d 376 (Tex.App. 2002).

**11.**   *Restatement, Second, of Property (Donative Transfers)* § 4.2, comm. r (1983).

**12.**   *Id.* § 3.4.

**13.**   Cast v. National Bank of Commerce, 183 N.W.2d 485 (Neb.1971); *Restatement, Second, of Property (Donative Transfers)* § 3.4, illus. 4 (1983).

**14.**   Williams v. Williams, 73 S.W.3d 376 (Tex.App. 2002) (restraint for lifetimes of testator's children); *Imery's*

Marble Co. v. J.M. Huber Co., 577 S.E.2d 555 (Ga.2003) (same).

**15.**   Wise v. Poston, 316 S.E.2d 412 (S.C.App.1984).

**16.**   *Restatement, Second, of Property (Donative Transfers)* § 4.2, comm. c (1983).

**17.**   *Id.,* § 4.1 (disabling restraints), § 4.2 (forfeiture restraint).

**18.**   Atkinson v. Kish, 420 S.W.2d 104, 109 (Ky.1967); *cf. Restatement of Property* § 419 (1944) (ambiguous restraint construed not to be disabling).

**19.**   See Section 13.1. "Protective trusts" operate as forfeiture restraints, and are allowed even where spendthrift provisions are not. *Id.*

(4) *Future Interests*   Restraints on the alienation of future interests are often upheld, because "a future interest from its very nature is not as marketable as a present interest."[20] Also, the restraint serves a useful purpose, viz. protecting against improvident dispositions, since future interests are often sold at a large discount.

(5) *Contract for Deed; Lease*   Contracts to sell land which allow the buyer to take possession and pay the price in installments usually prohibit the buyer from transferring his interest without the seller's consent. These provisions are upheld, because of the seller's legitimate concern with possible waste committed by an unreliable assignee while the price remains unpaid.[21] The law allows restraints on assignment by a lessee for years for similar reasons, but many courts hold that a lessor may not "unreasonably" withhold consent to an attempted assignment.[22]

(6).  *Transfer with Consent*   The second Restatement allows restraints which allow alienation with another's consent if they are reasonable. If a father gives property to his son and requires consent by a family friend to any transfer until the son reaches 40, this restraint is considered to serve a reasonable purpose and is allowed.[23]

(7) *Preemptive Rights*   Options are sometimes held invalid as unreasonable restraints on alienation,[24] but preemptive provisions giving "a right of first refusal" if property is offered for sale, are not regarded as restraints if their terms are reasonable as to price and other conditions.[25] Some courts say "a repurchase option at market or appraised value" is permissible, but a "fixed price" option is not because it "discourages any improvements of the land by the existing property owner."[26] However, some courts have upheld even fixed-price options, while others have invalidated preemptive rights which were based on current value.[27]

---

**20.** *Restatement, Second, of Property (Donative Transfers)* § 4.2, comm. u (1983).

**21.** Carey v. Lincoln Loan Co., 998 P.2d 724, 732 (Or.App.2000).

**22.** *Restatement, Second, of Property (Landlord and Tenant)* § 15.2(2) (1976); *cf.* Carey v. Lincoln Loan Co., 998 P.2d 724, 732 (Or.App.2000) (seller's right to refuse to consent to assignment is "tempered by the duty of good faith").

**23.** *Restatement, Second, of Property (Donative Transfers)* § 4.1, illus. 11 (1983).

**24.** Low v. Spellman, 629 A.2d 57 (Me.1993). They may also be held to violate the Rule against Perpetuities. See Section 11.7.

**25.** *Restatement, Second, of Property (Donative Transfers)* § 4.4 (1981).

**26.** Iglehart v. Phillips, 383 So.2d 610, 615 (Fla.1980). *See also Restatement, Second, of Property (Donative Transfers)* § 4.4, illus. 4 (1981).

**27.** *Compare* McDonald v. Moore, 790 P.2d 213 (Wash.App.1990) *with* Atchison v. City of Englewood, 463 P.2d 297 (Colo.1969).

(8) *Trusts* Reasonable restraints against the alienation of trust property by the trustee are valid,[28] but they may be overridden, if "the purpose of the trust would be defeated or substantially impaired unless the property is sold."[29]

Courts do not as a general rule cut down unreasonable restraints to make them reasonable.[30]

*Planning* Since restraints on alienation are upheld where "reasonable," mechanical applications of the rule are infrequent and the trend to soften the Rule against Perpetuities has not gone nearly so far with regard to restraints on alienation. Nevertheless, the rule against restraints may frustrate a reasonable plan if the drafter is not sophisticated. When a restraint on alienation is held invalid, often the objective could have been accomplished by use of a trust, as to which the limits are more generous.[31]

# § 11.9   Accumulations

*Thelluson v. Woodford,*[1] the leading case on the legality of accumulations of income, involved a trust which directed that the income be accumulated for nine lives. The House of Lords upheld the trust. Some have objected that accumulations of income may allow huge fortunes to be amassed contrary to the law's policy against extreme inequality of wealth. However, as with the Rule against Perpetuities itself, this problem can be dealt with by tax law. Present law discourages accumulating income in a trust by taxing it at higher rates than those imposed on income distributed to beneficiaries.[2]

Even before the House of Lords rendered its decision upholding the Thelluson trust, Parliament passed a statute which prospectively imposed stringent time limits on accumulations. Some American states followed suit, but nearly all these statutes have since been repealed. Commentators have generally condemned them.[3]

Today virtually all states allow trusts to accumulate income for the period of the Rule against Perpetuities but no longer. Any income released by the invalidity of the direction to accumulate is to be applied cy pres to effectuate the settlor's intent to the extent possible.[4] But a recent case held that the direction to accumulate was void ab initio, and the income should pass intestate.[5]

---

**28.** Ohio Society for Crippled Children & Adults, Inc. v. McElroy, 191 N.E.2d 543 (Ohio 1963); *Restatement, Second, of Trusts* § 190 (1959).

**29.** *Id.* § 190, comm. f. *See also* Section 9.6.

**30.** But see In re Kelly's Estate, 193 So.2d 575 (Miss.1967).

**31.** Baskin v. Commerce Union Bank, 715 S.W.2d 350, 352 (Tenn.App. 1986).

**§ 11.9**

**1.** 32 Eng.Rep. 1030 (1805).

**2.** Section 15.5.

**3.** L. Simes, *Public Policy and the Dead Hand* 100 (1955).

**4.** *Restatement, Second, of Property (Donative Transfers)* § 2.2 (1983).

**5.** White v. Fleet Bank of Maine, 739 A.2d 373 (Me.1999).

*Presumption Against Accumulation*   Hostility to accumulation of income may affect construction of a trust. A court construed an ambiguous trust as authorizing the trustee to distribute income rather than accumulating it because of "the general policy against accumulations."[6] Nevertheless, courts often find an implied direction to accumulate trust income.[7]

*Charitable Trusts*   An accumulation in a charitable trust can continue beyond the period of the Rule against Perpetuities,[8] but courts will not allow "unreasonable" accumulations. A settlor created a trust to accumulate income for 500 years; in the year 2444 the principal and accumulated income was to go to the state of Pennsylvania. This was held to be "unreasonable, contrary to public policy, and void."[9] Other courts have simply whittled down directions for excessive accumulation.[10] Views of what is reasonable may alter as conditions change. When "continued accumulation no longer furthers the purpose of the trust" courts may order it to cease.[11]

**6.**   Matter of Trust Estate of Daoang, 953 P.2d 959, 968 (Haw.App.1998).

**7.**   Godfrey v. Chandley, 811 P.2d 1248 (Kan.1991); Jones v. Heritage Pullman Bank & Trust Co., 518 N.E.2d 178 (Ill.App.1987) (income in excess of annuity).

**8.**   *Restatement, Second, of Property (Donative Transfers)* § 2.2(2) (1983).

**9.**   Trusts of Holdeen, 403 A.2d 978 (Pa.1979).

**10.**   Matter of Booker, 682 P.2d 320 (Wash.App.1984).

**11.**   Mercantile Trust Co. Nat. Ass'n v. Shriners' Hosp., 551 S.W.2d 864, 868 (Mo.App.1977).

# Chapter 12

# PROBATE AND ADMINISTRATION

## § 12.1  Probate

The court which hears challenges to wills in most states is called the probate court, but the general trend is to unify the various courts in a state.[1]

*Necessity for Probate*  Until a will is admitted to probate, it has no legal effect. "Without probate, no determination of testamentary capacity, freedom from undue influence, or due execution have been made."[2] The notion that only a specialized "probate" court can determine the validity of a will goes back to a time when ecclesiastical courts had jurisdiction over wills of personal property. Probate had no effect on devises of land in the will; an heir could assert that the will was invalid even though it had been probated.

Having two courts pass on the validity of the same will made no sense. In keeping with the modern trend to assimilate the rules for land and personal property, a statute of 1857 made the probate of a will, or a decree that a will was invalid, binding as to all the

---

§ 12.1
1. Cal.Prob.Code § 7050 and Law Revision Commission Comment.

2. Matter of Guardianship and Conservatorship of Slemp, 717 P.2d 519, 521 (Kan.App.1986).

testator's property.[3] The assimilation of land and personal property might have been accomplished by abolishing probate, and having the validity of wills tried in any court whenever it became relevant in a proceeding. Other forms of transfer are handled in this way: if person conveys a home by deed, no probate of the deed is necessary. But requiring probate of wills may promote efficiency, since wills often affect many persons and so might give rise to many lawsuits between heirs and devisees, whereas a single probate proceeding binds them all.

*Multi-State Probate* Because probate is an *in rem* proceeding, a decree admitting a will to probate binds persons who live in other states, assuming the court has jurisdiction. A will can be probated either (a) in the state where the testator was domiciled at death or (b) where assets of the testator are located.[4]

Even though probate operates in rem, proceedings in two states may be necessary, and may reach different outcomes. The heirs of a woman whose will had been probated in Florida were allowed to contest the will in Kentucky where the testator owned land.[5] The result might have been different if the dispute had involved personal property, or if the contestants had been served in the Florida proceedings.[6] Some states recognize foreign probate decrees even as to local land,[7] but only if the other probate was in the state of the decedent's domicile,[8] and all interested persons were given notice and an opportunity to contest the will.[9]

*Notice of Probate* Historically, there were two forms of probate, "common" in which no notice to the testator's heirs was given, and "solemn" which did require notice. The Uniform Probate Code provides similar options, but uses the terms "informal" and "formal."[10] Orders in formal proceedings are "final as to all persons,"[11] whereas wills which have been informally probated may be contested for 12 months thereafter or up to 3 years after the decedent's death, whichever is later.[12] Even if a will is informally

---

**3.** Statute, 1857, 20 & 21 Vict. c. 77, § 62.

**4.** *Restatement, Second, of Conflict of Laws* § 314 (1971); Uniform Probate Code § 3–201(a).

**5.** Marr v. Hendrix, 952 S.W.2d 693, 695 (Ky.1997).

**6.** Estate of Waitzman, 507 So.2d 24 (Miss.1987) (contest of will probated in Florida not permitted because personal property involved); *Restatement, Second, of Conflict of Laws* § 317 (1971).

**7.** Uniform Prob.Code § 3–408; Cal. Prob.Code §§ 12522–23.

**8.** In re Estate of Stein, 896 P.2d 740 (Wash.App.1995) (Oregon probate bind-ing only as to assets in Oregon, since decedent was domiciled in Washington).

**9.** In re Estate of Farley, 397 N.W.2d 409 (Minn.App.1986) (Texas probate decree not binding when only "posted courthouse notice given").

**10.** Uniform Prob.Code §§ 3–301, 3–401.

**11.** *Id.*, § 3–412; Matter of Estate of Gaines, 830 P.2d 569 (N.M.App.1992) (proponent bound by order in formal proceeding finding will invalid).

**12.** Uniform Probate Code § 3–108(a)(3); Vieira v. Estate of Cantu, 940 P.2d 190 (N.M.App.1997) (informally

probated, the personal representative, after being appointed, must notify the heirs.[13]

Some state courts have held that any probate of a will without notice to the heirs which limits their right to contest the will is an unconstitutional denial of due process.[14] Other courts have held that heirs have a "mere expectancy" which is "not entitled to constitutional protection,"[15] at least when the statute allowed a probated will to be contested for 5 months thereafter. A statute which purported to make a probate decree immediately binding without prior notice to ascertainable heirs would probably be held invalid.

Informal probate has legal consequences beyond triggering a limitation period on contest. One who deals with the executor under an informally probated will in good faith, e.g. purchases property of the estate, is protected even if the probate of the will is later set aside.[16] The drafters of the Uniform Probate Code retained informal probate, fearing that people would avoid probate altogether if it was made "more awkward than non-probate alternatives" such as joint tenancy.[17] In order to deter "misuse [of] the no-notice feature of informal proceedings," applicants are required to file a verified statement that they believe that the will was validly executed and was the decedent's last will.[18] The rules of professional conduct provide a sanction against abuse by lawyers. [19]

*Will Contests* Some states allow wills to be contested even after they have been probated with notice to the heirs.[20] This may reflect lack of confidence in probate judges, who in some states are lay persons, whereas will contests take place in a court of general jurisdiction. Under the Uniform Probate Code informal probate is handled by a Registrar, who is not necessarily a judge,[21] whereas formal proceedings are heard by a judge with "the same qualifications as a judge of the court of general jurisdiction."[22]

Most courts hold that constitutional provisions preserving the right to jury trial do not apply to will contests,[23] but many state

probated will may be challenged as being made under undue influence).

**13.** Uniform Probate Code § 3–705.

**14.** Estate of Beck v. Engene, 557 N.W.2d 270 (Iowa 1996).

**15.** Matter of Estate of Wilson, 610 N.E.2d 851, 858 (Ind.App.1993).

**16.** Ky.R.S. § 395.330; Cal.Prob. Code § 8272(b).

**17.** Wellman, *The Uniform Probate Code: Blueprint for Reform in the 70's,* 2 Conn.L.Rev. 453, 497–99 (1970).

**18.** Uniform Probate Code § 3–301, comment.

**19.** In re Conduct of Hedrick, 822 P.2d 1187, 1190 (Or.1991) (lawyer suspended for filing for probate a will which was not the testator's last).

**20.** Ohio Rev.Code §§ 2107.71, 2107.76.

**21.** Uniform Prob.Code §§ 1–307, 3–301.

**22.** *Id.* §§ 1–309, 3–401.

**23.** In re Estate of Johnson, 820 A.2d 535 (D.C.2003).

statutes provide for it.[24] Some commentators suggest that juries in will contests are "more disposed to work equity for the disinherited" than to follow the law.[25] This is sometimes advanced as a reason for using will substitutes like a revocable trust in place of a will.

*Time Limits on Contest*  The time limits for contest of a probated will are typically quite short, *e.g.* three months from the date of probate.[26] These short limitations provide a counter argument to the common advice to avoid probate. "If circumstances suggest the possibilities of such a contest, the commencement of probate proceedings is advisable to bar the right of contest."[27] Some statutes provide comparable short limits to contests of living trusts.[28]

Courts may allow an untimely contest in cases of fraud, e.g., the proponent of a will sent a notice of probate to the testator's heirs, but told their mother that "the boys' interests were well represented," neglecting to tell her that the will gave him most of the estate. The court set aside the probate because of the proponent's "extrinsic fraud," defined as fraud which prevents a party "from presenting all of his case to the court."[29] The Uniform Probate Code allows relief "whenever fraud has been perpetrated in connection with any proceeding" under the Code, if proceedings are brought within 2 years of discovery of the fraud.[30]

Some courts give contestants relief on a tort or constructive trust theory after the time for a will contest is over,[31] but others hold that such claims are precluded by a probate decree, or have rejected them on the ground that a will contest provides an adequate remedy for the plaintiff's claim.[32]

**24.** Mo.Rev.Stat. § 473.083(7); Matter of Estate of Ruther, 631 P.2d 1330, 1332 (N.M.App.1981).

**25.** Langbein, *Living Probate: The Conservatorship Model,* 77 Mich.L.Rev. 63, 65 (1978). An empirical study suggested that jury trials "appear to improve materially the [contestants'] chances for success." Schoenblum, *Will Contests: An Empirical Study,* 22 Real Prop. Prob. and Trust J. 607, 614 (1987).

**26.** Ohio Rev.Code § 2107.76. If a contest is timely filed, an heir who was not originally a party may join the proceeding after the time for filing has expired. Estate of Helms v. Helms–Hawkins, 804 N.E.2d 1260, 1264 (Ind.App. 2004).

**27.** Parks, *Varied Duties Face the Successor Trustee of a Revocable Trust,* 19 Est.Plann. 203, 206 (1992).

**28.** Unif.Trust Code § 604(a)(2). *See also* Cal.Prob.Code § 16061.8.

**29.** Estate of Sanders, 710 P.2d 232 (Cal.1985). *But cf.* Young v. Thompson, 794 N.E.2d 446 (Ind.App.2003) (heirs had no right to rely on erroneous statement of attorney for the estate as to time within which they could contest will).

**30.** Uniform Probate Code § 1–106.

**31.** Barone v. Barone, 294 S.E.2d 260 (W.Va.1982). A tort suit can be based on undue influence, but not on the testator's incapacity. Griffin v. Baucom, 328 S.E.2d 38 (N.C.App.1985).

**32.** Hadley v. Cowan, 804 P.2d 1271, 1276 (Wash.App.1991); Minton v. Sackett, 671 N.E.2d 160 (Ind.App.1996).

Expiration of the time limit on will contests does not bar raising questions of will construction, or even claims that a will provision is invalid on policy grounds.[33] A claim that a devise to the testator's spouse was revoked by divorce was not barred by the limit on contests.[34]

Courts are divided as to whether attempting to probate a later-discovered will after an earlier one has been probated amounts to a "contest" subject to the time limit.[35] The Uniform Probate Code allows even formal testacy orders to be modified if proponents of a later will show that "they were unaware of its existence at the time of the earlier proceeding."[36]

*Ante-Mortem Probate* Courts generally refuse to determine the validity of a will while the testator is alive.[37] Many have argued that such determinations should be permitted so that the testator's capacity can be better evaluated by the fact finder, and a few states have enacted statutes allowing ante-mortem probate.[38]

Despite its potential advantages, ante-mortem probate raises many problems. Many testators do not want to disclose the contents of their will during their lifetime, but a proceeding to approve a will would be unfair unless the contents were revealed since they may constitute relevant evidence. Use of ante-mortem probate even in states that allow it is not common.

*Binding Effect on Persons not Sui Juris* Heirs under disability often get additional time to file a contest.[39] This may leave the disposition of an estate in doubt for a considerable time. The Uniform Probate Code circumvents this problem by allowing parties non sui juris to be bound by representation. Orders against a trustee in probate proceedings bind the trust beneficiaries "to the extent that there is no conflict of interest between them."[40] Court approval of the settlement of a will contest is binding even on persons "unborn, unascertained or who could not be located" if the court finds that its effect on persons "represented by fiduciaries or other representatives is just and reasonable."[41]

**33.** Matter of Estate of Worsham, 859 P.2d 1134 (Okl.App.1993); Hall v. Eaton, 631 N.E.2d 805, 807 (Ill.App. 1994).

**34.** In re Marriage of Duke, 549 N.E.2d 1096, 1101 (Ind.App.1990). *But see* Martin v. Kenworthy, 759 P.2d 335 (Or.App.1988) (claim that marriage revoked will barred).

**35.** *Compare* Coussee v. Estate of Efston, 633 N.E.2d 815 (Ill.App.1994) *with* In re Will of Fields, 570 So.2d 1202 (Miss.1990).

**36.** Uniform Prob.Code § 3–412(a)(1); *cf.* Cal.Prob.Code § 8226(b).

**37.** Burcham v. Burcham, 1 P.3d 756 (Colo.App.2000).

**38.** N.D. Code § 30.1–08.1–01; Ohio Rev.Code § 2107.081; Ark.Code § 28–40–201.

**39.** Ohio Rev.Code § 2107.76; 58 Okl.Stat. § 67; N.C.Gen.Stat. § 31–32.

**40.** Uniform Probate Code § 1–403(2).

**41.** *Id.,* §§ 1–1101–1102. *See also* Hunter v. Newsom, 468 S.E.2d 802, 807

*Time Limits on Probate*   Many states limit the time within which a will must be probate, e.g. within three years of the testator's death under the Uniform Probate Code.[42] Some states allow wills to be probated at any time.[43] Since delay in probating a will may mislead third parties, many statutes protect bona fide purchasers or mortgagees from an heir if a will is not probated or recorded within a specified time.[44] The Uniform Probate Code bars probate of a will after a court enters a decree of distribution to the heirs.[45]

*Standing*   In order to discourage "strike" suits seeking to extract money by threatening costly litigation, courts allow wills to be contested only by persons with a financial interest, e.g., a contest by the testator's grandchild was dismissed on the ground that she was not an heir, since the testator's children had survived him.[46] A devisee under an earlier will has standing to contest a later one.[47] The testator's heirs may have standing, even if the testator left more than one will disinheriting them.[48] The state can contest the will of a testator who died without relatives in order to claim an escheat.[49] Courts are split on the question whether an heir's creditors can contest a will if the heir does not.[50] An heir's right to contest a will survives and passes to his heirs or devisees.[51]

Fiduciaries have been permitted to contest wills in some cases. Personal representatives can contest a will on behalf of the heirs or beneficiaries of an earlier will,[52] but a trustee was not allowed to contest a codicil, which did not affect any beneficial interest; the

(N.C.App.1996) (denying approval to settlement as "unfair to the remainder interests of the unborn and unknown heir").

**42.** Unif.Probate Code § 3–108. *But cf.* Matter of Estate of McGrew, 906 S.W.2d 53 (Tex.App.1995) (5 year limit on probate not applicable when proponent not "in default" for not offering it earlier).

**43.** Mitchell v. Cloyes, 620 P.2d 398 (Okl.1980).

**44.** N.C.Stat. § 31–39; Ohio Rev. Code § 2107.47; Kan.Stat. § 59–618.

**45.** Matter of Estate of Chasel, 725 P.2d 1345 (Utah 1986), based on Uniform Prob.Code § 3–412(3)(i). This is not true in all states. Matter of Estate of Cornelius, 465 N.E.2d 1033 (Ill.App. 1984).

**46.** Martone v. Martone, 509 S.E.2d 302, 306 (Va.1999).

**47.** Spicer v. Estate of Spicer, 935 S.W.2d 576 (Ark.App.1996).

**48.** Power v. Scott, 837 So.2d 202, 206·(Miss.App.2002).

**49.** Matter of Estate of Barnhart, 339 N.W.2d 28 (Mich.App.1983).

**50.** Hirsch, *The Problem of the Insolvent Heir*, 74 Cornell L.Rev. 587, 645–51 (1989).

**51.** Sheldone v. Marino, 501 N.E.2d 504 (Mass.1986). *But see* In re Estate of Davis, 467 N.E.2d 402 (Ill.App.1984) (right to contest is not assignable intervivos); Matter of Will of Calhoun, 267 S.E.2d 385 (N.C.App.1980) (legatee of legatee cannot contest later will).

**52.** Toon v. Gerth, 735 N.E.2d 314, 320 (Ind.App.2000) (executor of earlier will).

wish to manage the trust and receive trustee's fees did not confer standing.[53]

*Attorney's Fees* Successful contestants of a will may recover attorneys' fees from the estate. Normally in the United States the prevailing party in a lawsuit does not recover attorney fees, but if attorney fees were not paid from the estate, distributees who benefited from the contest without participating in it would be unjustly enriched.[54]

The Uniform Probate Code allows personal representatives reimbursement for attorney fees from the estate for any proceeding prosecuted or defended "in good faith" regardless of the outcome.[55] This may allow executors under two wills both to be reimbursed for their expenses in a contest as to which will should be probated.[56] Some courts deny fees for attorneys hired by beneficiaries as distinguished from a personal representative,[57] but the fact that an executor was also a beneficiary did not preclude his recovering fees.[58]

*Forfeiture Clauses* Many testators seek to forestall will contests by providing in the will that a devisee who contests the will loses any interest. Under the Uniform Probate Code such provisions are unenforceable "if probable cause exists for instituting proceedings."[59] Many cases apply a similar test, but some courts enforce the clause even if the contestant had probable cause.[60] (If the will is held invalid, the forfeiture clause fails along with the rest of the will.) Conversely in some states forfeiture clauses are ineffective in all cases.[61]

The question what acts are covered by a forfeiture provision is not always clear. A claim to assets in the testator's estate, *e.g.* that land was held in joint tenancy and so did not pass under the will, does not constitute a contest of the will.[62] Nor is a suit to construe a

**53.** Matter of Estate of Getty, 149 Cal.Rptr. 656 (App.1978). *But see* In re Estate of Milward, 73 P.3d 155, 158 (Kan.App.2003) (executor has standing to challenge a codicil naming another executor).

**54.** Matter of Estate of Foster, 699 P.2d 638 (N.M.App.1985).

**55.** Uniform Probate Code § 3–720; *cf.* In re Estate of Herbert, 979 P.2d 1133, 1136 (Haw.1999) (fees denied to executor for attempting to probate will rejected for undue influence, since this "imported bad faith")

**56.** Enders v. Parker, 66 P.3d 11 (Alaska 2003).

**57.** In re Estate of Zonas, 536 N.E.2d 642 (Ohio 1989).

**58.** Matter of Estate of Killen, 937 P.2d 1375 (Ariz.App.1996).

**59.** Uniform Probate Code § 3–905; In re Estate of Mumby, 982 P.2d 1219 (Wash.App.1999) (clause effective where bad faith found).

**60.** Larson v. Naslund, 700 P.2d 276 (Or.App.1985). Under Cal.Prob.Code §§ 21303, 21306 "probable cause" prevents a forfeiture under a clause only if the contest is based on certain grounds, but not, for example, a claim that the testator was incapacitated.

**61.** Ind.Code § 29–1–6–2; Fla.Stat. § 732.517.

**62.** Jacobs–Zorne v. Superior Court (Swonetz), 54 Cal.Rptr.2d 385 (App. 1996).

will a "contest" within the meaning of a forfeiture clause.[63] Although forfeiture provisions are narrowly construed, a broadly drafted one will be given effect. An extremely broad clause "prohibiting not only a 'contest' of the trust" but also "seeking 'otherwise' to ... nullify * * * its provisions" was held to cover a claim that property characterized in a trust as separate was actually community property.[64]

Some clauses simply charge a contestant with the expenses of a proceeding instead of voiding the contestant's devise altogether.[65] Some courts have charged expenses caused by frivolous claims against the claimant even without a provision for this in the will.[66]

## § 12.2   Necessity for Administration

*Probate and Administration*   Probate and administration are closely connected. When a will is admitted to probate, the court appoints an executor to administer the estate. But probate of a will usually takes little time (absent a contest) whereas administration of an estate typically lasts for many months or even years. Thus the widespread desire to "avoid probate" is more appropriately directed at administration.

The connection between probate and administration is not inevitable. "The fact that the latter is customarily carried on * * * at the same time, and in the same court, is likely to lead to the conclusion that the two constitute a single proceeding. Historically and functionally, however, they are separate. * * * A will may be probated without being followed by administration."[1]

Administration is necessary even if there is no will to probate. The person appointed to administer an intestate estate is called an administrator. Administrators and executors have similar functions, except that executors carry out ("execute") a will, whereas administrators' distribution of an estate is controlled by the intestacy statute. The term "personal representative" includes both executors and administrators.

*History and Comparative Law*   Administration of estates is designed to assure that claims against the decedent are paid before the assets are distributed to the heirs or devisees. Originally only

---

**63.**   Reed v. Reed, 569 S.W.2d 645 (Tex.Civ.App.1978).

**64.**   Estate of Pittman, 73 Cal. Rptr.2d 622, 631 (App.1998).

**65.**   Feldman, *Reviewing Wills and Trusts: What Planners Should Look For,* 29 Est.Plann. 299, 302 (2002) (recommending such a provision).

**66.**   Matter of Estate of Leslie, 886 P.2d 284 (Colo.App.1994). *See also* Cal. Prob.Code §§ 8906(e), 11003 (costs of

bad faith contest of an account or attempt to remove executor).

**§ 12.2**

**1.**   Basye, *Dispensing with Administration,* 44 Mich.L.Rev. 329, 424 (1945); *cf.* Uniform Prob.Code § 3–401 (petition for probate "may, but need not, involve a request for appointment of a personal representative").

personal property went to the executor; land passed directly to the devisees or heirs without administration. But just as England extended probate to devises of land, administration was extended to land in 1897 by a statute which provided that land as well as chattels should pass to the decedent's personal representative. Some American states preserve vestiges of the old distinction between land and personal property, but the practical effects are not much different from the English system: "title" to land may pass directly to the decedent's heirs or devisees but this is "a mere empty shell" because of the extensive powers over land which modern statutes confer on personal representatives.[2]

Administration is not the only possible way to assure that a decedent's creditors are paid. Creditors could be allowed to sue the debtor's heirs or devisees,[3] but such suits give rise to problems. If an intestate has several heirs, must creditors seek a proportionate amount from each, or can they collect the whole from any heir? If the decedent died insolvent, his heirs and devisees should not be personally liable for his debts. Conversely, if the estate is solvent but the heirs and devisees are not, creditors of the estate would be prejudiced if they were remitted to claims against the latter. Creditors should share the decedent's assets in a rational order; certain claims have priority, and creditors in the same class should get the same share. Devises abate in a prescribed order in order to pay claims against a testator. Without administration this might require a series of lawsuits. Multiple litigation can be avoided in administration in which the personal representative, like a trustee in bankruptcy, carries out the prescribed order of abatement among devisees and follows the prescribed order in distributing the assets of an insolvent estate to creditors.

In such situations, administration helps to handle the payment of claims in a fair way. In the great majority of cases, however, the decedent is not insolvent, and administration is a needless expense. The civil law system of continental Europe usually dispenses with administration.[4] Louisiana follows the civil law system and "probably has the least expensive system in the nation" for succession.[5] Heirs may seek administration in order to avoid personal liability when the decedent was insolvent, but this is infrequent. If creditors fear that lack of administration will jeopardize their rights, they

---

**2.** 3 *Amer.Law of Prop.* § 14.7, at 578; *cf.* 84 Okl.Stat. § 212 (real and personal property passes to heirs, "subject to the possession of any administrator ... for the purpose of administration")

**3.** As they once were. 2 W. Blackstone, *Commentaries* *243–44, 340, 378 (1765).

**4.** Rheinstein, *The Model Probate Code: A Critique,* 48 Colum.L.Rev. 534, 538 (1948).

**5.** Sarpy, *Probate Economy and Celerity in Louisiana,* 34 La.L.Rev. 523, 524 (1974). The low cost is attributable to the absence of an executor's fee and a reduction in attorney's fees. *Id.* at 528.

can apply for appointment of an executor or administrator, but this also rarely happens. Creditors in other states have shown a similar lack of concern about will substitutes which avoid administration.

*Practical Problems in Avoiding Administration*   Usually the heirs or devisees can enjoy a decedent's tangible personal property without bothering to have the estate administered, but they cannot collect choses in action like a bank account or securities registered in the decedent's name. "The executor or administrator of a decedent's estate has standing to file suit on behalf of a decedent, but the legatees, heirs, and devisees have no such standing," because the court cannot be sure that they are the sole claimants to the estate.[6] Persons who owe money to a decedent sometimes voluntarily pay the decedent's successors without administration, but they run the risk that an administrator will later sue them on the same obligation. Payment to the decedent's heirs is no defense to such a suit.[7]

Heirs or devisees may be able to take possession of the decedent's land without having the estate administered, but if they want to sell or mortgage it, third persons are reluctant to deal with them, for good reason, e.g., a mortgage executed by an heir was later held subject to a claim by a creditor of the decedent.[8]

*Small Estates*   The expense of administration is particularly burdensome for small estates because the cost represents a larger percentage of the estate, and the beneficiaries are usually needier. If an estate is smaller than the statutory exemptions,[9] the rationale for administration—protection of creditors—does not apply. Therefore, many states exempt small estates from administration. The provisions are of two types, "collection by affidavit" and "summary distribution."

Collection by affidavit requires no court action.[10] Suppose a man's will leaves his entire estate to his wife. When he dies he had a small bank account in his own name[11] and a claim for unpaid wages. The widow would have to wait thirty days after the husband

---

**6.**  McGill v. Lazzaro, 416 N.E.2d 29, 31 (Ill.App.1980); Inlow v. Ernst & Young, LLP, 771 N.E.2d 1174, 1183 (Ind.App. 2002) (heirs cannot sue accountant for the estate). In Louisiana, on the other hand, heirs can sue on a decedent creditor's obligation if they establish their right to inherit. Taboni ex rel. Taboni v. Estate of Longo, 810 So.2d 1142 (La. 2002).

**7.**  Bayse, supra note 1, at 334.

**8.**  Janes v. Commerce Federal Savings & Loan Ass'n, 639 S.W.2d 490 (Tex. App.1982).

**9.**  See Section 3.4.

**10.**  Sections 3–1201 and 3–1202 of the Uniform Probate Code allow this. They have influenced legislation in states which have not adopted the whole Code. Johnson, *Wills, Trusts & Estates*, 68 Va.L.Rev. 521, 529 (1982).

**11.**  If the account was a joint account with the wife, she could collect it as a surviving party.

died; then she can execute an affidavit stating that she is entitled to payment and that the estate is less than $5,000. If the bank and employer pay the widow when she produces the affidavits, they are discharged from liability, even if the facts asserted in the affidavit turn out to be untrue.[12] If they refuse to pay the widow she can sue them.[13] If a creditor of the decedent later initiates proceedings to have the estate administered, the widow must account for the money she received.

In some states the ceiling on "small estates" for which this procedure is available is much higher than $5,000; California allows an estate of up to $100,000 to be collected in this way.[14] On the other hand, some statutes cover only particular kinds of property, such as bank accounts, for no apparent reason except that they were promoted by banks so they could "clear their books."[15] The Uniform Probate Code covers all assets, other than land, and can be used by any successor, whereas in some states only the decedent's spouse and children can collect by affidavit.[16]

The Uniform Probate Code also allows summary distribution after administration has begun. Suppose a widow has the decedent's will probated, is appointed executor, and files an inventory of the estate which shows that it is so small that nothing would be left for ordinary creditors after paying the family allowance and other exemptions and preferred claims like funeral expenses. On these facts she can distribute the estate immediately.[17]

*Larger Estates*   Some states allow even large estates to escape administration. If an estate consists entirely of community property which passes to the surviving spouse, in several states no administration is necessary.[18] In California, even separate property need not be administered if the spouse gets it outright.[19] A spouse who receives property without administration, like heirs under the civil law system, becomes personally liable for the decedent's obligations to the extent of the property received.[20] In order to avoid such personal liability, the spouse can elect to have the property administered.[21]

---

**12.** Uniform Prob.Code § 3–1202; Clark v. Unknown Heirs of Osborn, 782 P.2d 1384 (Okl.1989).

**13.** Uniform Prob.Code § 3–1202. Some statutes only *allow* the debtor to pay without administration. Basye, *supra* note 1, at 402.

**14.** Calif.Prob.Code § 13100.

**15.** Basye, *supra* note 1, at 401.

**16.** Uniform Probate Code § 3–1201, comment; 20 Pa.Stat. § 3101 (spouse, child, parents, or siblings); Ohio Rev.

Code § 2113.04 (wages up to $2,500 to spouse, adult children, or parents).

**17.** Uniform Probate Code § 3–1203.

**18.** Basye, *supra* note 1, at 382–84.

**19.** Calif.Prob.Code § 13500.

**20.** *Id.* §§ 13550–51; cf. BGB (German Civil Code) § 1967(I) (heir liable for decedent's debts), § 1975 (liability limited when estate is insolvent).

**21.** Cal.Prob.Code § 13502.

## § 12.3  Ancillary Administration

Even if a will leaves the entire estate to the testator's wife, for example, she may be unable to collect her husband's assets without a court appointment certified by "letters testamentary" that she is his executor. (If she is acting as administrator, the letters would be called "letters of administration.") The problem is further complicated if the decedent owned assets in several states. Suppose he was a resident of Maryland, but owned land in Georgia, a bank account in Virginia, stock in a Pennsylvania corporation, and had a tort claim against a resident of Illinois. If a Maryland court appoints the wife executor of the will, she may be unable to collect assets in other states without ancillary administration because personal representatives are "clothed with authority to administer only such assets as are within the jurisdiction of the court" which appoints them.[1]

*Rationale*  This limitation on the powers of personal representatives is usually explained by the need to protect local creditors of the decedent who should not be forced to go to the decedent's domicile to collect their claims.[2] But many have questioned whether this is enough to justify the burden of ancillary administration. Professor Basye called ancillary administration "a wasteful expenditure of time, effort and expense."[3] Often there are no local creditors in the state of ancillary administration, or they are quickly paid and need no protection.[4]

The Uniform Probate Code avoids the need for ancillary administration by giving personal representatives appointed in the state of the decedent's domicile standing to sue in the courts of other jurisdiction.[5] by filing a copy of their appointment.[6] By doing this she becomes subject tò suit by local creditors.[7]

*Particular Assets*  In practice, the need for ancillary administration depends upon (1) the type of asset, and (2) the state where it is located.

1.  *The Stock of a Pennsylvania Corporation.*  If the decedent's interest is represented by a stock certificate in the executor's possession, even if it is registered in the decedent's name, the executor can have it transferred without ancillary administration. The Restatement of Conflicts allows corporations to transfer shares

### § 12.3

1.  Eikel v. Burton, 530 S.W.2d 907, 908 (Tex.Civ.App.1975).

2.  *Restatement, Second, of Conflict of Laws* § 354, comm. a (1971).

3.  Basye, *Dispensing With Administration*, 44 Mich.L.Rev. 329, 409 (1945). *See also* E. Scoles & P. Hay, *Conflict of Laws* § 22.14 (2d ed. 1992).

4.  Atkinson, *The Uniform Ancillary Administration and Probate Acts*, 67 Harv.L.Rev. 619, 623 (1954).

5.  Uniform Probate Code § 3–703(c).

6.  This applies only if no local administration is pending. Uniform Probate Code § 4–204.

7.  Uniform Prob.Code § 4–301. *See also Restatement, Second, of Conflict of Laws* § 358, comm. g (1971).

"to any executor or administrator of the decedent who surrenders [the] share certificate" and allows an executor or administrator to sue a corporation which refuses to transfer the shares.[8]

2. *Virginia Bank-account.* An ordinary bank account is not represented by a significant document like a stock certificate, so the executor will not possess anything apart from her Maryland appointment to show her right to the account. If the bank pays the money to her voluntarily, a Virginia ancillary administrator might later force it to pay again. The Restatement says such payment discharges the debtor "in the absence of knowledge of the appointment of a local executor or administrator,"[9] but not all cases agree.[10] Under the Uniform Probate Code the bank could safely pay the executor if it waited 60 days after the testator died and got an affidavit from the executor that no local administration was pending.[11]

3. *Georgia Land.* The executor may be able to take possession of the land without dealing with a third party, but if she tries to sell it, prospective purchasers might question her title.[12] However, a Georgia statute now allows foreign executors to sell land in the state if no ancillary administration is pending.[13]

4. *Illinois Tort Claim.* The executor may seek to be appointed ancillary administrator in Illinois to pursue the claim on the theory that the decedent had property in Illinois.[14] A "cause of action" against an Illinois resident may constitute an asset of an estate for this purpose.[15]

*Identity of Ancillary Administrator* If ancillary administration is necessary, the burden is reduced if the domiciliary representative also acts as the ancillary administrator. The Uniform Probate Code gives an executor appointed by the decedent's domicile priority in being appointed ancillary representative[16] but some states require that administrators be residents of the appointing state.[17]

*Claims Against a Decedent* Suppose that a resident of Michigan has a claim against a person who died domiciled in Maryland. She could file her claim in Maryland, but she might prefer to sue in

---

8. *Id.,* § 324, comm. c.

9. *Id.,* § 329.

10. Atkinson, *supra* note 4, at 620.

11. Uniform Probate Code § 4–201.

12. Allen v. Amoco Production Co. 833 P.2d 1199 (N.M.App.1992) (deed by Colorado executor ineffective as to New Mexico land).

13. Ga.Code Ann. §§ 53–5–42.

14. Either domicile or property in a state are the bases of probate jurisdiction. Section 12.1.

15. In re Estate of Hoffman, 286 N.E.2d 103, 104 (Ill.App.1972).

16. Uniform Prob.Code §§ 3–203(g), 3–611(b); In re Estate of Kuralt, 30 P.3d 345 (Mont. 2001) (error not to appoint domiciliary executors to administer Montana property).

17. As to non-resident personal representatives generally see Section 12.4.

Michigan. As a creditor of the decedent, she could begin ancillary administration in Michigan if the decedent owned property there.[18] But if decedent does not have enough assets in Michigan to satisfy the claim, a Michigan judgment may be worthless in other states. "A judgment against one executor or administrator does not make the facts found by the court in the action res judicata in an action against another executor or administrator of the same decedent."[19] This rule has been much criticized and is changed by the Uniform Probate Code.[20]

*Suit Against Foreign Representative*   Claimants can not sue a personal representative of a decedent outside the state which appointed the representative unless a statute provides otherwise.[21] Statutes in many jurisdictions change this rule. The Uniform Probate Code allows domiciliary personal representatives to be sued in any state in which the decedent could have been sued at death.[22]

*Distribution of Ancillary Assets*   If a decedent had assets in another state and an ancillary administrator collects them, the administrator after paying local creditors remits the balance to the domiciliary executor for distribution there under the Uniform Probate Code with certain exceptions, *e.g.* if the decedent's successors "are identified pursuant to the local law of" the state of ancillary administration.[23]

*Planning*   The inconvenience of ancillary administration is sometimes advanced as an argument for using will substitutes, since trustees of living trusts are not normally appointed by a court, and even a trustee who is so appointed can sue outside the state of appointment.[24] However, this is not a problem in every estate. Ancillary administration may be no great inconvenience, or not necessary at all even for assets passing through probate if the relevant states have statutes like the Uniform Probate Code. In any event, estate planning attorneys should ascertain the location of the client's assets, since this may be hard to do after the client dies.

## § 12.4   Choice of Fiduciary

A fiduciary is a person who is entrusted with another's property; the word comes from the Latin *fiducia,* trust. This chapter is

---

**18.**   Sheahan v. Rodriguez, 753 N.Y.S.2d 664, 668 (Surr.2002).

**19.**   *Restatement, Second, of Conflict of Laws* § 356, comm. b (1971).

**20.**   Uniform Probate Code § 4–401. *See also* Beacham v. Palmer, 523 N.E.2d 1007 (Ill.App.1988) (dismissal of suit against ancillary administrator bars suit against domiciliary).

**21.**   State ex rel. Mercantile Nat. Bank v. Rooney, 402 S.W.2d 354 (Mo.

1966);, *Restatement, Second, of Conflict of Laws* § 358, comm. b (1971).

**22.**   Uniform Probate Code § 3–703(c).

**23.**   *Id.,* § 3–816. *But cf.* Estate of Miller v. Miller, 768 P.2d 373, 377 (Okl. App.1988) (ancillary assets distributed to widow of decedent).

**24.**   4 A. Scott, *Trusts* § 280.6 (4th ed. 1987).

primarily concerned with personal representatives of a decedent (executors and administrators) and trustees, but agents under a power of attorney, custodians under the Uniform Transfers to Minors Act, and conservators similar perform functions and are subject to similar rules.

*Court Appointment* Personal representatives and conservators acquire their powers by court appointment,[1] but trustees under a living trust, agents under a power of attorney and custodians under the Transfers to Minors Act need no court appointment. Even where a court is not involved in the initial designation of a fiduciary, court proceedings may be necessary to designate a successor when the original fiduciary is unable or unwilling to continue to serve, for example, a trustee dies. Usually the death of a trustee does not cause a trust to terminate, so a court may need to appoint a successor, but not if the trust instrument designates a successor, or provides a procedure for doing so. Because court proceedings are time consuming and expensive, many wills and trusts provide such a procedure.[2] The Uniform Transfers to Minors Act allows custodians to designate a successor by a written instrument,[3] but personal representatives and trustees cannot designate their successors unless the governing instrument authorizes this.[4]

Another possibility is to empower the beneficiaries to designate a new fiduciary. Absent authorization in the instrument beneficiaries are not entitled to do this,[5] although courts in selecting a fiduciary give weight to the beneficiaries' wishes.[6] Often some beneficiaries of a trust or estate are minors or unascertained persons, so California allows vacancies in the office of trustee to be filled by "agreement of all adult beneficiaries who are receiving * * * income under the trust or [would be entitled] to receive a distribution of principal if the trust were terminated at the time."[7]

*Administrators and Executors* State statutes provide priorities for the choice of an administrator when someone dies intestate. The Uniform Probate Code first designates the decedent's spouse, but courts can depart from the statute and appoint "any suitable person."[8] Under a similar statute, a court chose the decedent's

---

**§ 12.4**

**1.** *E.g.,* Uniform Prob.Code § 3–103, 5–104.

**2.** Uniform Statutory Will Act § 12(c).

**3.** Uniform Transfers to Minors Act § 18(b).

**4.** Cal.Prob.Code § 8422 (executor cannot designate a successor unless the will so provides).

**5.** *Restatement, Third, of Trusts* § 34, comm. c(1) (2001). But under Uniform Transfers to Minors Act § 18(d) a minor who has attained age 14 can designate a successor custodian.

**6.** *Restatement, Third, of Trusts* § 34, comm. f(1) (2001); Cal.Prob.Code § 15660(d).

**7.** Cal.Prob.Code § 15660(c). *See also* Unif.Trust Code § 704(c)(2); Uniform Statutory Will Act § 12(d).

**8.** Persons eligible for appointment may instead nominate another. Uniform Probate Code § 3–203(b). A similar (but

brother instead of his widow because her claim to certain property in the estate "created a conflict of interest that rendered her unfit."[9]

When a will fails to designate an executor, or the designated executor cannot or will not serve, the court appoints an administrator "with will annexed" (sometimes designated in Latin: *cum testamento annexo* or simply *cta*). Under the Uniform Probate Code devisees under the will have priority over heirs in seeking appointment, or in nominating an administrator with will annexed.[10]

Executors are by definition nominated in a will to carry out its terms. They must be appointed by a court, but courts normally appoint the person named in the will unless the nominee is disqualified. Under the Uniform Probate Code, for example, courts can refuse to appoint a nominated executor who is "unsuitable," e.g. because of a conflict of interest.[11]

*Conflicts of Interest*  A conflict does not always disqualify a fiduciary, especially if it was obvious to the testator or settlor who nominated the fiduciary. When a will designated the testator's child by a prior marriage as a trustee as well as remainderman, the court held it was an error not to appoint the child.[12] A conflict which was "unknown to the settlor at the time of the designation, or that came into being at a later time" presents a stronger case for removal or refusal to appoint.[13]

A conflict of interest can be removed without completely disqualifying the fiduciary, *e.g.* by restricting the fiduciary's powers. A Wisconsin statute bars trustees from making discretionary distributions to themselves unless the trust instrument provides otherwise.[14]

Even if a testator or settlor believes that a family member is sufficiently fair-minded to overlook his or her selfish interests, putting them in a position of conflict of interest may present tax problems. Under Internal Revenue Code Section 678, anyone who has "a power solely exercisable by [herself] to vest the corpus or the income" of a trust in herself is taxed on income even if it was distributed to others or accumulated in the trust. Use of a family

---

not identical) list of priorities for the appointment of conservators appears in *id.* § 5–413.

**9.** Ayala v. Martinez, 883 S.W.2d 270, 272 (Tex.App.1994).

**10.** Uniform Probate Code § 3–203(a); *cf.* Calif.Prob.Code § 8441.

**11.** Uniform Probate Code § 3–203(f)(2); In re Estate of Fogleman, 3 P.3d 1172 (Ariz.App.2000).

**12.** Lovett v. Peavy, 316 S.E.2d 754, 757 (Ga.1984). *See also Restatement, Third, of Trusts* § 37, comm. f (2001).

**13.** *Id.,* comm. f(1) (2001); Estate of Hammer, 24 Cal.Rptr.2d 190 (App.1993) (husband of devisee later involved in acrimonious divorce with her).

**14.** Wisc.Stat. § 701.19(10). *See also* First Union Nat. Bank v. Cisa, 361 S.E.2d 615 (S.C.1987) (beneficiary trustee cannot participate in decisions to distribute to herself).

member as trustee can also have adverse estate tax consequences. The objective of a bypass trust will be defeated if as trustee or otherwise the beneficiary can distribute corpus to herself unless the power is limited "by an ascertainable standard relating to [the beneficiary's] health, education, support or maintenance."[15]

*Other Grounds for Removal or Refusal to Appoint* Another ground for removing or not appointing a designated executor or trustee is hostility between the fiduciary and the beneficiaries, e.g., a court refused to appoint the executor designated in a will who had acted so abrasively toward the testator's wife and children that "there was no way" they could get along with him.[16] If a trustee has broad discretion in making distributions, hostility between the trustee and a particular beneficiary may make the trustee unsuitable.[17] But hostility between a trustee and beneficiaries is not always grounds for removal. Trial courts have wide discretion on this issue.

A change of circumstances after a will or trust is executed may throw in question the suitability of the designated fiduciary. In most states, when a testator marries or has a child after executing a will, the new spouse or child get a share of the estate despite the will, but the named executor is still appointed.[18] If the testator divorces a spouse who is designated as a fiduciary in an instrument, however, the divorce revokes the designation under the Uniform Probate Code.[19]

If an executor or trustee becomes insolvent, the risk that assets of the estate or trust will become confused with those of the fiduciary often leads courts to remove the fiduciary.[20] Trustees and executors can also be removed for misconduct in office. The Restatement of Trusts speaks of "repeated or flagrant failure or delay in providing accountings or information to the beneficiaries, gross or continued under performance of investments," and "unwarranted preference" toward certain beneficiaries or "a pattern of indifference" toward others.[21] Courts do not remove fiduciaries who have been guilty of only minor wrongs.

**15.** Internal Revenue Code § 2041(b).

**16.** Matter of Petty's Estate, 608 P.2d 987, 995 (Kan.1980).

**17.** Shear v. Gabovitch, 685 N.E.2d 1168, 1193 (Mass.App.Ct.1997).

**18.** Matter of Bowman's Estate, 609 P.2d 663, 666 (Idaho 1980) (error to appoint testator's husband whom she married after will executed when will named another executor).

**19.** Uniform Probate Code § 2–804(b). Homicide also negates the killer's nomination as fiduciary. *Id.*, § 2–803(c)(1); Cal.Prob.Code § 250(b)(3). Uniform Trust Code § 706(b)(4) has a more general provision for replacement of trustees when "there has been a substantial change of circumstances."

**20.** *Restatement, Third, of Trusts* § 37, comm. e (2001); Calif.Prob.Code § 15642(b)(2).

**21.** *Restatement, Third, of Trusts* § 37, comm. e (2001); McNeil v. McNeil, 798 A.2d 503, 513 (Del. 2002) (removal of trustee who failed to keep beneficiary informed).

Some trusts give designated beneficiaries the right to remove a trustee with whom they are dissatisfied. In this case no ground for the removal is necessary.[22] There are risks that the power will be improperly used, e.g., as a threat in order to receive larger distributions, so it may be desirable to limit the pool of candidates for trustee to institutions likely to have the desired experience and objectivity.[23]

A fiduciary who has become incompetent, e.g. by senility, can be removed. In order to avoid court proceedings, some trusts provide that the certificate of designated individuals shall be conclusive that the trustee is no longer qualified to serve.[24]

*Nonresidents* Some wills designate a person residing in another state as fiduciary. Usually nonresidence is not disqualifying, but under a few statutes it is. Some states have reciprocity provisions; a foreign bank can be appointed only if its home state would do the same in the converse situation.[25] Others condition the appointment of a nonresident on naming a resident co-fiduciary.[26] A fiduciary ought to be subject to process in the state of appointment, but this can be accomplished simply by requiring out-of-state fiduciaries to consent to local jurisdiction.[27]

Distance between the fiduciary and the beneficiaries or the property which the fiduciary administers may make a fiduciary unsuitable. A New York court approved a transfer of the situs of a trust to California after the beneficiaries had moved to that state.[28] The Uniform Probate Code provides for such transfers, which may involve "removal of the trustee and appointment of a trustee in another state."[29] The Restatement of Trusts lists "geographic inconvenience" as a possible ground of removal of a trustee.[30]

*Corporations* A corporation, usually a bank, is often appointed fiduciary. Many states impose special regulations on corporate fiduciaries. In California a corporation cannot engage in the trust

**22.** *Restatement, Third, of Trusts* § 37, comm. c (2001); First Nat. Bank v. State, Office of Public Advoc., 902 P.2d 330, 334 (Alaska 1995) (guardian acting on behalf of incompetent settlor with power of removal).

**23.** Moore, *Trustees Under a Microscope,* 142 Trusts & Estates (July 2003) pp. 44. In Rock Springs Land and Timber, Inc. v. Lore, 75 P.3d 614, 624 (Wyo. 2003), an attempt by beneficiaries to replace a corporate trustee with a beneficiary failed because of such a limitation.

**24.** Buchanan & Buchanan, *Strategies for Clients Residing in Nursing Homes,* 20 Est. Plann. 27, 30 (1993).

**25.** Ohio Rev. Code § 2109.21B.

**26.** Estate of White, 509 N.Y.S.2d 252 (Surr.1986) (nondomiciliary alien can act as trustee only if a N.Y. resident also serves).

**27.** Uniform Probate Code § 3–602; Md. Estates and Trusts Code § 5–105(b)(6).

**28.** In re Weinberger's Trust, 250 N.Y.S.2d 887 (App.Div.1964).

**29.** Uniform Probate Code § 7–305. *See also* Unif.Trust Code § 108(c).

**30.** *Restatement, Third, of Trusts* § 37, comm. e (2001)

business unless it obtains a certificate of authority and deposits security with the state treasurer.[31] National banks engaging in trust business are regulated by the Comptroller of Currency.

Whereas individual fiduciaries may die or become incompetent before the job is over, this is not a problem with corporations, so instruments often name a bank as successor fiduciary if a designated individual(s) cannot or can no longer act.

Banks charge for their services, whereas individual family members often do not. This may push toward the choice of an individual. But executors' and trustees' fees are deductible for tax purposes, so part of the cost is actually borne by the government. In small estates, however, this tax deduction is worth little and a professional's fee may be prohibitive. The cost-saving in using a family member may be offset by the need for professional advice. If an individual fiduciary has to hire an investment counselor, the cost may be equivalent to that of a professional trustee who provides investment expertise as part of the job.[32]

If a corporate fiduciary mismanages a trust or estate, it usually can pay for any damages imposed on it. An individual is more likely to be judgment-proof. This risk can be avoided by having the individual give a bond with sureties, but the cost of such a bond reduces the cost-advantage of an individual fiduciary.

Professional fiduciaries are expected to be experts in making investments and are held to higher standards than individuals.[33] But if the trust is to operate a business, an individual familiar with the business may be a better choice for trustee than a bank.[34]

One may want to avoid the conflicts of interest and related tax problems which arise when a beneficiary is named trustee by naming a corporation, but "by using proper precautions in planning, coupled with precise drafting, the estate planner may feel safe in employing whomever is best suited for a particular circumstance."[35]

*Multiple Fiduciaries* Multiple fiduciaries allow the particular skills of various persons to be utilized. A corporate trustee may be best suited to handle records and perform routine administration while a business associate may have desirable investment skills and a family friend or relative may be the best person to exercise discretion over distributions.

**31.** Cal.Financial Code § 1500.

**32.** Bromberg & Fortson, *Selection of a Trustee: Tax and Other Considerations*, 19 Sw.L.J. 523, 530 (1965).

**33.** See Section 12.7.

**34.** Bromberg & Fortson, *supra* note 32, at 532.

**35.** Pennell, *Estate Planning Considerations in Employing Individual Trustees*, 60 N.C.L.Rev. 799, 820 (1982).

Multiple fiduciaries also have disadvantages. Unless they serve without compensation, the total fees may be higher. If the co-fiduciaries disagree, court proceedings may be needed to resolve the deadlock.[36] The chance of a deadlock can be reduced by designating an uneven number of fiduciaries and providing that the majority's decision will control. Absent such a provision, according to the second Restatement of Trusts all of the trustees must agree to exercise their powers,[37] but the third Restatement and many statutes provide for majority rule.[38] The Uniform Probate Code provides that all personal representatives must concur in an action unless the will provides otherwise.[39] This can impede efficient administration even if there is no actual disagreement among the fiduciaries, but this can be reduced by authorizing fiduciaries to delegate routine matters to a co-fiduciary.[40]

If a will or trust names more than one fiduciary, if one ceases to act the others can usually continue without any need to appoint a successor.[41]

*Resignation* A person will not be appointed executor or trustee over his or her objection, but a fiduciary who has accepted the office needs court approval to resign unless the trust instrument provides otherwise or all the beneficiaries consent.[42] Court proceedings are wasteful since requests to resign are usually approved, but a court may refuse to allow a trustee to resign when no suitable successor has been found.[43]

*Successor's Powers* The powers conferred by an instrument on a fiduciary are usually not construed as personal to the original trustee or executor, *i.e.*, a successor can also exercise them. The Uniform Probate Code gives successor personal representatives the same powers as the original except for any power "expressly made personal to the executor named in the will."[44] The Restatement of Trusts is similar, but a restrictive intent can be inferred from the circumstances, e.g., the relationship between the settlor and the

---

**36.** *Restatement, Third, of Trusts* § 39, comm. e (2001).

**37.** *Restatement, Second, of Trusts* § 194, comm. a (1959). For charitable trusts, majority rules. *Id.*, § 383.

**38.** Unif.Trust Code § 703(a); *Restatement, Third, of Trusts* § 39 (2001).

**39.** Uniform Probate Code § 3–717.

**40.** *See Restatement, Third, of Trusts* § 39, comm. c, d (2001).

**41.** Uniform Probate Code § 3–718; *Restatement, Third, of Trusts* § 34, comm. d (2001).

**42.** *Id.*, § 36. *But cf.* Uniform Transfers to Minors Act § 18(c) (custodian can resign by giving notice); Unif.Trust Code § 705(a)(1)(trustee may resign by giving 30 day notice to "qualified beneficiaries").

**43.** Matter of Sherman B. Smith Family Trust, 482 N.W.2d 118, 119 (Wis. App.1992); *cf.* Uniform Probate Code § 3–610 (c) (personal representative can resign by giving written notice, but this is effective only upon appointment of a successor).

**44.** Uniform Probate Code § 3–716.

named trustee may show "an intention to place confidence in him and only in him."[45]

*Attorneys' Role*  Testators and settlors often ask attorneys for advice as to who should be named as executor or trustee. A designation of the attorney who drafted the will as a fiduciary is sometimes challenged for undue influence or as a violation of the rules of professional conduct.[46]

Knowledgeable estate attorneys disagree about the propriety of attorneys serving as executors. Stein suggests that it is "usually more efficient than the ordinary division of labor" between the personal representative and the estate's attorney; the attorney-representative is in a position to act quickly because it is unnecessary to wait for a lay representative to be informed and to participate. On the other hand, many time-consuming tasks of a personal representative require no legal expertise,[47] while others require skills which many lawyers lack. An attorney who becomes a fiduciary must become financially sophisticated with investments.

Even lawyers who do not serve as fiduciaries profit from being chosen as attorneys for the executor or trustee. A provision in a will directing the executor to hire a particular attorney is usually held unenforceable on the ground that the executor should have "unfettered discretion to select an attorney,"[48] but executors typically hire the attorney who drafted the will to handle administration This practice has been criticized,[49] but a court refused to remove an executor which had hired the drafter of the will as attorney for the estate, saying it was reasonable to select a lawyer familiar with the testator's property.[50]

## § 12.5  Fees

An important factor in choosing a fiduciary is cost. This section deals with the fees of personal representatives, trustees, their attorneys, and related costs, such as bond and appraisal fees. The rules are not the same for all fiduciaries. In California the fees of personal representatives and their attorneys are based on a percentage of the estate, whereas trustees, custodians and conservators are allowed "reasonable" compensation.[1]

**45.** *Restatement, Second, of Trusts* § 196 (1959).

**46.** McGovern, *Undue Influence and Professional Responsibility*, 28 Real Prop.Prob. and T.J. 643, 670 (1994).

**47.** Stein & Fierstein, *The Role of the Attorney in the Administration of the Estate*, 68 Minn.L Rev. 1107, 1164 (1984).

**48.** In re Estate of Deardoff, 461 N.E.2d 1292, 1293 (Ohio 1984).

**49.** C. Wolfram, *Modern Legal Ethics* § 8.12.4 (1986).

**50.** Matter of Estate of Effron, 173 Cal.Rptr. 93, 102 (App.1981).

### § 12.5

**1.** Cal.Prob.Code §§ 10800, 10810 (personal representatives and their attorneys), 15681 (trustee), 3915(b) (custodian), 2640 (guardian and conservator).

*Size of the Estate* In many states fiduciary fees are based on the size of the estate or trust. New York allows personal representatives commissions on a sliding scale, starting at 5% of the first $100,000 down to 2% of property in excess of $5,000,000.[2] Trustees are entitled to annual fees of $10.50 per $1,000 of principal up to $400,000, $4.50 per $1,000 for the next $600,000, and $3 per $1,000 for the rest.[3] Thus fees for larger trusts are higher in amount, but smaller in proportion to the trust assets.

The fees of personal representatives are typically based on the size of the probate estate.[4] The Uniform Probate Code, however, provides for "reasonable compensation,"[5] and the Restatement of Trusts and Uniform Trust Code use the same language for trustees. But some states have fee schedules for trustees based on the income and principal of the trust.[6]

Is there a practical difference between a "reasonable fee" and a percentage of the estate (or income)? Most percentage fee provisions allow "further compensation" for "any extraordinary services" provided by the fiduciary,[7] while some are expressed as a maximum.[8]

"Reasonable compensation" takes custom into account,[9] and professional trustees customarily base their fees on a percentage of the income and principal of the trust. A termination fee of 2% of the trust assets was upheld under a "reasonable compensation" statute, since most other trust institutions in the state charged such a fee.[10]

State and local bar associations used to issue fee schedules which based lawyers' fees on the size of the estate until the Supreme Court held that such fee schedules violated the antitrust laws.[11] This decision contributed to a trend to base fees on factors

---

**2.** N.Y.Surr.Ct.Proc. Act § 2307.

**3.** Id., § 2309. In addition trustees receive 1% for all principal paid out.

**4.** In re Estate of Preston, 560 A.2d 160, 164 (Pa.Super.1989) (error to include assets held in joint tenancy in computing executor's fee).

**5.** Uniform Probate Code § 3–719 (personal representatives), § 5–413 (conservators).

**6.** Md. Estates and Trusts Code § 14–103. In Hawaii the legislature distinguished between trusts and estates, finding that a statutory fee schedule was appropriate only for the former. In re Trust Dated Nov. 15, 1917, 88 P.3d 202, 206 (Haw.2004).

**7.** Wis.Stat. § 857.05(2); Matter of Estate of Barber, 779 P.2d 477, 488

(Mont.1989) (additional fees for extraordinary services of attorney).

**8.** Ark.Code § 28–48–108(a); Estate of Stone, 768 P.2d 334 (Mont.1989) (fee claim based on statutory maximum disallowed).

**9.** *Restatement, Third, of Trusts* § 38, comm. c(1) (2001); Unif.Trust Code § 708, comment; In re Estate of Berthot, 59 P.3d 1080, 1087 (Mont.2002) (fees "consistent with the fees generally charged by corporate fiduciaries" upheld).

**10.** Matter of Trusts Under Will of Dwan, 371 N.W.2d 641, 642–43 (Minn. App.1985).

**11.** Goldfarb v. Virginia State Bar, 421 U.S. 773 (1975).

other than the size of the estate,[12] but a California court upheld that state's statutory percentage fee system. The anti-trust laws did not apply because the statute constituted state action. The legislature after studying the issue had concluded that its system was "both cost effective and fair," because it saved judicial time which would otherwise be spent establishing reasonable fees,[13] favored small estates, and encouraged the efficient use of time.

The Restatement of Trusts lists the "amount and character of the trust property" as a factor in determining a reasonable fee along with the "responsibility and risk assumed in administering the trust."[14] But holding a block of stock in a big company may involve little effort compared to managing a small business.[15] A court reversed a fee award based on a percentage of the estate which "contained liquid assets of a readily ascertainable value."[16]

Basing trustee's fees on the value of the trust principal rewards trustees who make shrewd investments, just as the compensation of mutual fund managers is often based on the value of the fund. But percentage formulas also create perverse incentives. Lawyers whose fees are based on the size of the probate estate have an incentive not to advise clients to avoid probate.[17]

Robert Stein has observed, "folklore in some legal communities suggests * * * that attorneys price estate planning services cheaply in the expectation that they will later be retained to provide the more profitable estate administration services." But Stein's study found that "whatever the historical pattern, * * * estate planning services are now priced similarly to estate administration and other legal services performed by the attorney." The study also found that fees in California based on a percentage of the estate were comparable to fees charged in states with a reasonable compensation system.[18]

*Other Factors* Factors other than the size of the estate are relevant in determining a reasonable fee. The Restatement of Trusts mentions "the time devoted to trust duties."[19] The ABA

**12.** In re Estate of Secoy, 484 N.E.2d 160, 164 (Ohio App.1984).

**13.** Estate of Effron, 173 Cal.Rptr. 93, 99 (App.1981).

**14.** *Restatement, Third, of Trusts* § 38, comm. c(1) (2001). *See also* Unif. Trust Code § 708, comment.

**15.** Matter of Trusts Under Will of Dwan, 371 N.W.2d 641, 643–44 (Minn. App.1985) (dissent); Adams, *Professional Fees: The Consumer's Perspective*, 141 Trusts & Estates, No. 5, p. 64 (2002) (trustee fees should be adjusted for type of property in trust, and be reduced for

"self-directed" trust where trustee has no investment responsibility).

**16.** In re Estate of Secoy, 484 N.E.2d 160, 164 (Ohio App.1984).

**17.** In Matter of Tobin, 628 N.E.2d 1268 (Mass.1994) a lawyer was suspended inter alia for advising probate of an estate where all the assets were held in joint tenancy.

**18.** Stein & Fierstein, *The Role of the Attorney in Estate Administration*, 68 Minn.L.Rev. 1107, 1193 (1984).

**19.** *Restatement, Third, of Trusts* § 38, comm. c(1) (2001).

Model Rules of Professional Conduct also make "the time and labor required" a factor in determining a reasonable lawyer's fee.[20] A fee claimed by a personal representative was rejected when "there was no evidence of the time spent in performing the claimed services."[21] On the other hand, fees exceeding the assets remaining in an estate were allowed where "an inordinate amount of time was spent by the attorneys for the estate, the time spent was reasonable and necessary" under the circumstances.[22] However, no statute fixes fees on a per hour basis, and courts have also resisted this notion. A claim for attorneys' fees based on 364.5 hours of work in administering an estate was rejected because "a number of routine matters had occupied an inordinate amount" of time.[23] Moreover, "an attorney is not entitled to fees at professional legal rates for tasks that should be performed by staff, such as depositing checks in a bank." This is a common theme in cases in which the attorney also serves as executor, or the executor is a family member who lets the lawyer do all the work.[24]

A reasonable compensation standard also takes into account "the trustee's skill, experience and facilities."[25] For attorney fees, "the experience, reputation, and ability of the lawyer" are relevant.[26]

Poor performance may cause a reduction or even total loss of fees. An executor was denied all compensation because of unjustified delays in closing an estate.[27] The fees of a trustee which had improperly left cash in a checking account were reduced by 10% in addition to surcharging the trustee for the loss suffered by the trust.[28] But fiduciaries who acted in good faith and performed valuable services may receive a fee despite a breach of duty.[29]

**20.** Rule 1.5(a)(1). *See also* Matter of Tobin, 628 N.E.2d 1268, 1269–70 (Mass. 1994) (lawyer suspended for unreasonable fee based on former fee schedule "and not on time spent" of which he kept no records).

**21.** Noble v. McNerney, 419 N.W.2d 424, 430 (Mich.App.1988). *But see* In re Estate of Salus, 617 A.2d 737, 743 (Pa.Super.1992) (trustee awarded fee despite lack of time records).

**22.** In re Estate of Schaffer, 656 N.E.2d 368, 372 (Ohio App.1995).

**23.** Matter of Estate of Larson, 694 P.2d 1051, 1055–59 (Wash.1985).

**24.** Estate of Coughlin, 633 N.Y.S.2d 610 (App.Div.1995).

**25.** *Restatement, Third, of Trusts* § 38, comm. c(1) (2001). *See also* Shear v. Gabovitch, 685 N.E.2d 1168, 1192 (Mass.App.Ct.1997) (proper to disallow claim by individual trustee to fees based on a corporate fiduciary fee schedule).

**26.** ABA Model Rule 1.5. *See also* Code of Prof.Resp. DR 2–106.

**27.** Estate of Heller, 9 Cal.Rptr.2d 274 (App.1992).

**28.** Maryland Nat'l Bank v. Cummins, 588 A.2d 1205, 1219–20 (Md. 1991).

**29.** In re Saxton, 712 N.Y.S.2d 225, 233 (App.2000) (abuse of discretion to deny compensation to a trustee who was surcharged but without a "finding of self-dealing or fraud").

*Contract* A provision in an instrument stating what a fiduciary or lawyer is to receive provision may preclude a claim for more.[30] The Restatement of Trusts, however, says that although a trustee's compensation is "ordinarily governed" by such a provision, if the amount specified "is or becomes unreasonably high or unreasonably low, the court may allow a smaller or higher compensation."[31] Such relief is denied if a trustee has agreed with the settlor to act for a certain compensation, and such an agreement is normally inferred when a trustee accepts a trust which contains such a provision, but even in this case a "substantial and unanticipated change" in the circumstances may warrant ignoring it.[32]

Under the Uniform Probate Code "if a will provides for compensation of the personal representative and there is no contract regarding compensation, he may renounce the provision before qualifying and be entitled to reasonable compensation."[33] A personal representative "may renounce his right to all or any part of the compensation."[34] A trustee who distributes assets without deducting a fee may be deemed to have waived any claim to one.[35]

A provision for an unreasonably *high* fee for a fiduciary may be valid as a devise or gift,[36] but is subject to attack for undue influence. An attorney who drafted a will that named him as executor with a designated fee was limited to reasonable compensation because of the "fiduciary relationship" between lawyer and client.[37]

The classification of such provisions has tax consequences; for devises there is no deduction to the estate and no income to the recipient, whereas fees are deductible to the estate but taxable income to the recipient.[38] It may be advantageous for a family member to take a fee, since the deduction under the estate tax may be larger than the income tax to the recipient.

---

**30.** Lehman v. Irving Trust Co., 432 N.E.2d 769 (N.Y.1982). *See also* Estate of Scheid, 657 N.E.2d 311 (Ohio App. 1995) (executor bound by will provision that she was to get no compensation).

**31.** *Restatement, Third, of Trusts* § 38, comm. e (2001). *See also* Unif. Trust Code § 708(b).

**32.** Compare other cases of deviations from the terms of a trust when circumstances change. Section 9.6.

**33.** Uniform Probate Code § 3–719. However, a comment to the Code says that "if a will provision is framed as a condition on the nomination, it could not be renounced."

**34.** Uniform Probate Code § 3–719.

**35.** Rutanen v. Ballard, 678 N.E.2d 133, 142 (Mass.1997).

**36.** If the will is ambiguous on the point, the Restatement presumes that a devise to a person who is also designated as a fiduciary is in addition to compensation, and is not conditioned on the devisee's acceptance of the trusteeship. *Restatement, Third, of Trusts* § 38, comm. e (2001).

**37.** Andrews v. Gorby, 675 A.2d 449, 454 (Conn.1996); *cf.* Matter of Bales, 608 N.E.2d 987 (Ind.1993) (lawyer reprimanded for drafting a will providing high compensation for her services as executor and attorney).

**38.** Treas.Reg. § 20.2053–3(b)(2).

Fiduciaries and attorneys sometimes contract with the beneficiaries of an estate for a higher than normal fee. The Restatement allows trustees to contract for an enlarged fee from the trust beneficiaries if they "disclose all the relevant circumstances" and the agreement is not "unfair."[39]

*Compensation of Agents* Fiduciaries often seek reimbursement for the cost of hiring others to assist them. A trustee's right to reimbursement depends on "how the advisor's employment relates to the responsibilities reasonably expected of" the trustee.[40] Thus the fees of an accountant were charged against an executor's commission rather than the estate on the theory that "if one hires a professional to assist in carrying out one of the ordinary duties of being a personal representative," the latter's fees should be adjusted accordingly.[41]

*Attorneys' Fees* Trustees and personal representatives can be indemnified for reasonable attorneys fees, but only if the services benefited the trust or estate rather than the fiduciary personally. The line between the two is sometimes fuzzy. An executor who was also a principal beneficiary of a contested will, was denied reimbursement for her attorney fees in an appeal from a decree rejecting the will because "the appeal promoted only the [executor's] personal interests."[42] But a trustee who successfully resisted an attempt to remove and surcharge it was awarded attorney fees.[43] The Uniform Probate Code, allows personal representatives reasonable attorney fees when they "defend or prosecute any proceeding in good faith, whether successful or not."[44]

Some courts deny attorney fees incurred in litigation over the amount of the fiduciary's compensation,[45] but others reason that if fiduciaries are not reimbursed for such expenses, "their compensation for the underlying services may be effectively diluted."[46]

Courts also award attorneys' fees from an estate to beneficiaries who are not fiduciaries. The attorneys for two heirs recovered fees from the estate on the theory there would otherwise be "an unfair advantage to the other [heirs] who * * * should bear their

---

**39.** *Restatement, Third, of Trusts* § 38, comm. f (2001). *But see* Haw.Rev. Stat. § 607–18(c) (agreement for higher compensation for trustee is void).

**40.** *Restatement, Third, of Trusts* § 38, illus. 1 (2001). *See also* Unif. Prud.Inv.Act § 9, Comment.

**41.** In re Estate of Billings, 278 Cal. Rptr. 439, 442 (App.1991).

**42.** Matter of Estate of Jones, 492 N.W.2d 723, 727 (Iowa App.1992). *But*

*see* Shepherd v. Mazzetti, 545 A.2d 621, 623–4 (Del.1988) (executor-devisee entitled to attorney fees in unsuccessfully resisting claim against the estate).

**43.** Matter of Trust Created by Hill, 499 N.W.2d 475, 494 (Minn.App.1993).

**44.** Uniform Probate Code § 3–720.

**45.** Matter of Trust of Grover, 710 P.2d 597, 602 (Idaho 1985).

**46.** In re Estate of Trynin, 782 P.2d 232, 238 (Cal.1989).

share of the burden of the recovery."[47] Fees to attorneys for both sides in a will construction have been allowed on the basis that resolution of an ambiguity in the will benefited the estate.[48] The cases on attorney fees are hard to reconcile, because trial courts have much discretion on the question.[49]

Attorney fees are sometimes charged against persons who raise frivolous claims.[50] Fees of attorneys for beneficiaries who successfully sued a fiduciary have been charged to the fiduciary on the theory that they were a loss to the estate resulting from the fiduciary's breach.[51] The Uniform Trust Code allows courts to award attorney fees "to any party, to be paid by another party or from the trust * * * as justice and equity may require."[52]

*Attorney as Executor or Trustee* Can an executor or trustee who is a lawyer receive compensation both as fiduciary and as attorney? English courts refuse to compensate trustees for any legal services they render to the trust on the ground that this involves self-dealing,[53] but some courts allow dual compensation, citing the efficiencies involved in having the same individual act in both capacities.[54] The Uniform Probate Code allows personal representatives to employ attorneys "even if they are associated with the personal representative."[55] The Restatement of Trusts is more guarded; trustees can be compensated for services to the trust as an attorney "when it is advantageous that the trustee rather than another perform those services."[56] A claim for compensation by a conservator's spouse as attorney was rejected for failure to satisfy this test.[57]

A similar problem arises when an estate or trust owns a company which employs the fiduciary. A will named Chambers as co-executor and trustee. Chambers became the president of a company owned by the trust and received salary increases, for which he

---

**47.** In re Keller, 584 N.E.2d 1312, 1317 (Ohio App.1989).

**48.** Landmark Trust Co. v. Aitken, 587 N.E.2d 1076, 1086 (Ill.App.1992). *But see* Matter of Estate of Greatsinger, 492 N.E.2d 751 (N.Y.1986) (unsuccessful contender in will construction denied counsel fees because acting in his own interest).

**49.** Matter of Estate of Mathwig, 843 P.2d 1112, 1115 (Wash.App.1993) (statute allows court "in its discretion" to award attorney fees).

**50.** Matter of Estate of Barber, 779 P.2d 477, 489 (Mont.1989); Cal.Prob. Code § 11003 (bad faith contest or opposition to contest of account by personal representative).

**51.** In re Estate of Stowell, 595 A.2d 1022, 1026 (Me.1991).

**52.** Unif.Trust Code § 1004.

**53.** Hallgring, *The Uniform Trustees' Powers Act and the Basic Principles of Fiduciary Responsibility*, 41 Wash. L.Rev. 801, 819 (1966). As to self-dealing in sales and investment see Section 12.9.

**54.** In re Estate of Duffy, 774 N.E.2d 344 (Ohio App.2002).

**55.** Uniform Probate Code § 3–715(21).

**56.** *Restatement, Third, of Trusts* § 38, comm. d (2001).

**57.** Conservatorship of Bryant, 52 Cal.Rptr.2d 755, 759 (App.1996).

was later surcharged.[58] The Restatement, however, allows a trustee to receive a salary as an officer of a company controlled by the trust so long as the trustee "performs necessary services * * * and receives no more than proper compensation."[59]

*Multiple Fiduciaries*  When a will or trust names more than one executor or trustee, does each collect a full fee or do they divide a single fee? The answer varies in different states. In California, if there are two or more personal representatives, the compensation is apportioned among them,[60] but in Missouri the ordinary fee of the personal representative can be doubled if two or more serve, and in New York the fee can be tripled.[61] The Restatement of Trusts says that the aggregate fees for several trustees may reasonably exceed those of a single trustee because the "normal duty of each trustee to participate in all aspects of administration" may "result in some duplication of effort."[62]

When one fiduciary is an individual and the other is corporate, the latter usually gets a larger share,[63] but not where "the individual co-trustee has the lion's share of the responsibilities of management."[64]

Many people use living trusts to avoid the cost of executor's fees based on the probate estate, but some trust companies impose a special charge "for services performed by the bank which are similar to those usually performed by an Executor."[65] Fees can often be saved by designating the same person as executor and trustee, since many corporate trustees do not charge an acceptance fee if they also serve as executor.

*Court Review*  In most states prior court approval is required before fees can be paid to personal representatives or their attorneys.[66] The Uniform Trustees' Powers Act, on the other hand, allows trustees to pay themselves without court authorization,[67] and this is the prevailing practice in living trusts which are freer of court supervision than decedent's estates, but courts have jurisdic-

---

**58.** Schmidt v. Chambers, 288 A.2d 356, 370–71 (Md.1972).

**59.** *Restatement, Second, of Trusts* § 170, comm. o (1959). *See also* Harper v. Harper, 491 So.2d 189 (Miss.1986) (salary "commensurate with prior amounts" paid).

**60.** Calif.Prob.Code § 10805. A similar rule applies to trustees *Id.*, § 15683.

**61.** Mo.Stat. § 473.153(2); N.Y.Surr. Ct.Proc.Act § 2307(5).

**62.** *Restatement, Third, of Trusts* § 38, comm. i (2001). *See also* Unif. Trust Code § 708, comment.

**63.** Fred Hutchinson Cancer Research Center v. Holman, 732 P.2d 974, 978–79 (Wash.1987).

**64.** Estate of Ingram v. Ashcroft, 709 S.W.2d 956, 959 (Mo.App.1986).

**65.** Quoted in G. Bogert, *The Law of Trusts and Trustees* § 975, at 26 (2d rev. ed. 1983).

**66.** In re Altstatt, 897 P.2d 1164, 1169 (Or.1995) (lawyer suspended for taking fee without court approval).

**67.** Uniform Trustees' Powers Act § 3(a), (c)(20). *See also* N.J.Stat. § 3B: 18–17 (can take annual allowance without court action).

tion to review the reasonableness of a trustee's compensation.[68] The Uniform Probate Code follows this model even for decedent's estates, permitting personal representatives to "fix their own fees and those of estate attorneys," but "any interested person can get judicial review of fees."[69] Lawyers who charge excessive fees for representing an estate are subject to discipline.[70]

When fee questions come before courts, appellate courts affirm trial courts' determinations unless they find an "abuse of discretion." Some lower court decisions, however, are reversed on appeal.[71]

*Bond*    Another expense in many estates is caused by the requirement that the personal representatives file a bond. The amount of the bond is generally based on the value of the personal property of the estate, because real estate is not subject to administration, but if land is sold the bond is increased.[72] The bond must have sureties, so if the executor or administrator is unable to pay a surcharge imposed for mismanagement, the sureties are liable to the extent of the bond, with a right of reimbursement against the fiduciary.[73] The sureties naturally charge a fee for this, the cost of which is born by the estate.[74] No bond is required when a corporation is the fiduciary, since corporations must have substantial assets in order to act as fiduciaries.[75]

A will can waive bond, but even if it does, a court may "for good cause" require one.[76] The testator's confidence in the designated executor may prove to be mistaken, or the fiduciary designated in the instrument may not actually serve.[77] Also, executors have duties to the testator's creditors as well as to the devisees, and testators cannot "waive" protection to which their creditors are entitled.

---

**68.** Cal.Prob.Code §§ 17200(b)(9), 17209.

**69.** Uniform Probate Code § 3–721, comment. *See also id*. § 7–205 (review of fees of trustee); Vogt v. Seattle–First Nat. Bank, 817 P.2d 1364 (Wash.1991) (trustee to refund excessive fees with interest).

**70.** Matter of Tuley, 907 P.2d 844 (Kan.1995) (lawyer censured for charging a fee amounting to 8% of estate where normal fee was 5%).

**71.** Matter of Estate of Anderson, 432 N.W.2d 923, 928 (Wis.App.1988). *See also* Duggan v. Keto, 554 A.2d 1126, 1142 (D.C.App.1989) (remand for an explanation of fee award).

**72.** Calif.Prob.Code § 8482.

**73.** *Id.* § 8488; Uniform Probate Code § 3–606.

**74.** Calif.Prob.Code § 8486.

**75.** Id., § 301; Unif.Trust Code § 702(c).

**76.** Calif.Prob.Code § 8481 (personal representatives), § 15602(a)(2) (waiver of bond for trustee is ineffective if a bond is "necessary to protect the beneficiaries").

**77.** Id., § 15602(a)(3) (waiver of bond ineffective as to "a trustee not named in the instrument").

Most estate planners believe a bond is usually not worth the expense. The Uniform Statutory Will Act waives it.[78] The Uniform Probate Code allows courts to dispense with a bond if it is not necessary, even if the will does not waive it. [79]

Bond requirements are more relaxed for trustees. In California executors must give a bond unless the will waives it whereas trustees do not have to give a bond unless the trust instrument requires one.[80] Trustees of living trusts do not usually give bonds, nor do custodians under the Uniform Transfers to Minors Act.[81] For conservators, on the other hand, bond requirements "are somewhat more strict than those for personal representatives;" here the beneficiary of the arrangement (the conservatee) is incapable of waiving the requirement.[82]

*Appraisal* Personal representatives usually must file with the court an inventory listing the assets in the estate soon after they are appointed.[83] The Uniform Probate Code requires an inventory, but the personal representative can simply mail it to the interested parties rather than file it in court so that the information does not become public.[84]

In California the assets in the estate must be appraised by a court-appointed "probate referee" unless a court waives this requirement "for good cause."[85] Referees get a fee of one tenth of one percent of the total value of the assets appraised.[86] Appraisal has been attacked as "a needless and expensive formality which rarely serves any useful purpose."[87] Many assets do not require a professional appraisal.[88] The Uniform Probate Code makes use of an appraiser optional with the personal representative.[89]

*Conclusion* The desire to avoid probate is motivated to a large extent by the costs of administration, which often reflect payment for unnecessary services or overcompensation of the persons who provide them. The Uniform Probate Code has diminished the cost advantages of avoiding probate, but not eliminated them completely.

**78.** Uniform Statutory Will Act § 14.

**79.** Uniform Probate Code § 3–603, comment.

**80.** Calif.Prob.Code § 15602.

**81.** Uniform Transfers to Minors Act § 15(c).

**82.** Uniform Probate Code § 5–415, comment.

**83.** *E.g.*, Cal.Prob.Code § 8800.

**84.** Uniform Probate Code § 3–706.

**85.** Calif.Prob.Code § 8902–03.

**86.** Calif.Prob.Code § 8961.

**87.** Smith, *Appraisers and Appraisements Under the Texas Probate Code*, 45 Texas L.Rev. 842 (1967). Under present Texas law appraisers are appointed only if deemed necessary by the court or requested by an interested person. Texas Prob.Code § 248.

**88.** California exempts certain items, such as bank accounts, from appraisal by the referee. Calif.Prob.Code § 8901.

**89.** Uniform Probate Code § 3–707; Matter of Estate of Wagley, 760 P.2d 316, 319 (Utah 1988) (error to order appraisal by court's own appraiser).

# § 12.6   Sales by Fiduciaries

*Power of Sale*[1] Can an executor or administrator or trustee sell assets of the estate or trust or must they be preserved for distribution in kind to the beneficiaries when the estate is closed or the trust terminated? Historically, the powers granted to trustees were "typically few, since the trustees' job was simply to hold and then to convey to the remainderpersons."[2] Most wills and trusts today, however, confer broad powers of sale on the executor or trustee. Knowledgeable estate planners so recommend.[3] Some instruments are silent on this question, however, and for conservatorships, there is no governing instrument to serve as a source of powers. A statute may then give the answer. The Uniform Probate Code allows personal representatives, unless restricted by will, to "dispose of an asset, including land" so long as they act "reasonably for the benefit of the interested persons."[4] Similar powers are conferred on conservators.[5] The Uniform Trust Code has similar provisions for trustees.[6] Many statutes are more restrictive. In Illinois trustees have broad powers of sale, but personal representatives can sell property only "by leave of court and upon such terms as the court directs" unless the will gives a power of sale.[7]

The Third Restatement of Trusts[8] implies a somewhat broader power of sale for the Second Restatement which allowed a sale when it was "necessary or appropriate to carry out the purposes of the trust." Operating under the earlier version a court invalidated a deed by a trustee on the ground that no power of sale was conferred in the trust instrument, "nor was any evidence adduced to indicate that the sale was necessary or appropriate to carry out the purpose of the trust."[9]

Courts are reluctant to allow personal representatives to sell property which the will specifically devised, even when a will confers a power of sale in general terms.[10] The statutory power given to personal representatives in many states allows a sale only

**§ 12.6**

**1.** The question whether a fiduciary has a "power of sale" can be misleading. A sale may be effective to transfer title to a bona-fide purchaser for value, even if the fiduciary was not authorized to make it. Section 12.8. But such a sale may make the trustee liable for damages.

**2.** Langbein, *The Contractarian Basis of the Law of Trusts*, 105 Yale L.J. 625, 640 (1995).

**3.** Uniform Statutory Will Act § 13(a)(4), (b).

**4.** Uniform Probate Code § 3–715.

**5.** *Id.* § 5–425(b)(7).

**6.** Unif.Trust Code § 816. *See also* Uniform Trustees' Power Act § 3(a)(7).

**7.** 755 ILCS §§ 5/20–4(a), 5/20–15 (personal representatives); 760 ILCS § 5/4.01(trustees)

**8.** *Restatement, Third, of Trusts* § 190 (1990).

**9.** Schaneman v. Wright, 470 N.W.2d 566, 576 (Neb.1991).

**10.** Diana v. Bentsen, 677 So.2d 1374 (Fla.App.1996) (error to order sale of specifically devised stock where not needed to pay debts).

when needed to raise money to pay debts.[11] The Uniform Probate Code is not so restricted, but it provides that "the distributable assets of a decedent's estate shall be distributed in kind to the extent possible."[12] Similarly under the Restatement of Trusts, the beneficiaries can compel the trustee to transfer the trust property in kind to them when the trust terminates even if the trust instrument authorizes or even directs the trustee to sell it and distribute the proceeds.[13]

Courts may find various justification for a sale. An executor may be authorized to sell property in order to pay administration expenses.[14] An asset may be a bad investment. An executor's sale of stock was upheld despite the absence of claims against the estate on the ground that the stock "was subject to rapid fluctuation in value, * * * and the return on the stock was not sufficient" to warrant its retention.[15] Similarly trustees have a power (as well as a duty) to sell trust assets in order to carry out an appropriate investment program.[16]

A sale may be necessary to effectuate distribution when an estate or trust terminates. A court allowed an executor to sell a residence, since it could not be divided among the devisees and the estate was not large enough to allow the residence to be assigned to one beneficiary and the remaining assets to the others so as to effect an equal distribution as the will required.[17]

Courts' willingness to infer a power to sell may depend on the type of property involved. The Restatement distinguishes between land occupied as a residence and land purchased as an investment, and between securities in general and stock in a family corporation.[18] A court refused to authorize a transfer of a ward's home by her guardian, saying that "transfers of a ward's real property should be disfavored."[19]

The concept of prudence, to be discussed in more detail in the next section, governs sales as well as investments. The powers conferred on personal representatives by the Uniform Probate Code

---

**11.** In re Bettis' Estate, 340 A.2d 57 (Vt.1975) (sale of land by administrator voided because not necessary to pay debts).

**12.** Uniform Probate Code § 3–906.

**13.** *Restatement, Second, of Trusts* § 347, comm. o (1959).

**14.** Estate of Henry v. St. Peter's Evan. Church, 785 N.E.2d 1049 (Ill.App. 2003).

**15.** McInnis v. Corpus Christi Nat. Bank, 621 S.W.2d 451, 453 (Tex.Civ. App.1981).

**16.** *Restatement, Third, of Trusts* § 190, comm. d (1990). As to investments by trustees see Section 12.7.

**17.** Estate of Barthelmess, 243 Cal. Rptr. 832, 834 (App.1988). *See also* Lloyds Bank v. Duker, [1987] 3 All E.R. 193 (Ch. 1987) (stock sold to avoid disadvantage to devisees who would be minority shareholders).

**18.** *Restatement, Third, of Trusts* § 190, comm. d (1990).

**19.** In re Guardianship of Mabry, 666 N.E.2d 16, 21–22 (Ill.App.1996).

are coupled with the duty of "acting reasonably for the benefit of the interested persons."[20] A sale may be imprudent because of its collateral consequences. A guardian was surcharged for selling the ward's residence when the sale "resulted in unnecessary dissipation of estate assets" because the proceeds rendered her ineligible for public welfare.[21]

Some wills and trusts prohibit sale. Such restrictions are valid, but courts may overrule them when the circumstances have changed.[22]

Normally fiduciaries do not have to notify or get the consent of beneficiaries before selling property, but such a requirement may be found in the terms of an instrument.[23] Certainly it is good policy for fiduciaries to consult the beneficiaries about the sale of a major asset.

*Leases and Options*    The Uniform Probate Code allows personal representatives to lease property of the estate, and the Uniform Trustees' Powers Act gives a similar power to trustees.[24] Some statutes are more restrictive, on the theory that the beneficiaries should not be saddled with a lease which extends beyond the closing of the estate or trust.[25] The Restatement of Trusts allows leases for a term which will not extend "beyond the probable period of the trust," but under proper circumstances courts can approve longer leases.[26]

Fiduciaries may lack power to grant an option. "A fiduciary's authority to sell real estate does not normally include authority to grant an option to purchase it" unless "inclusion of an option agreement in a lease is clearly necessary to make the most advantageous arrangement."[27] Other courts, however, have assumed that a power to sell or lease included a power to grant options.[28] The Uniform Trustees' Powers Act authorizes trustees to grant options, in connection with a lease or otherwise,[29] but some statutes are more restrictive.[30]

---

**20.** Uniform Probate Code § 3–715. Section 5–425 uses similar language for conservators. As to custodians see Uniform Transfers to Minors Act § 12(b).

**21.** Matter of Guardianship of Connor, 525 N.E.2d 214, 216 (Ill.App.1988). See also In re Estate of Anderson, 196 Cal.Rptr. 782, 793 (App.1983) (adverse tax consequences from a sale).

**22.** See Section 9.6.

**23.** Taylor v. Crocker National Bank, 252 Cal.Rptr. 388, 395 (App.1988) (ordered not to be officially published).

**24.** Uniform Probate Code § 3–715(23); Uniform Trustees' Powers Act § 3(c)(10); Unif.Trust Code § 816(9).

**25.** 20 Pa.Stat. § 7142 (trustee may grant leases for up to 5 years, more with court approval).

**26.** *Restatement, Second, of Trusts* § 189, comm. c, d (1959).

**27.** Nelson v. Maiorana, 478 N.E.2d 945, 948 (Mass.1985).

**28.** Jost v. Burr, 590 N.E.2d 828, 832 (Ohio App.1990).

**29.** Uniform Trustees' Powers Act § 3(c)(10), (12). *See also* Unif.Trust Code § 816(10).

**30.** N.Y. EPTL § 11–1.1(b)(7) (fiduciaries can grant options for up to 6 months).

*Terms of Sale*  A power of sale does not necessarily permit sale on credit. Although a will authorized trustees to sell stock, their contract to sell it for a price payable in installments over eight years was enjoined.[31] The Third Restatement of Trusts, on the other hand, says "it is proper and not unusual for a trustee to sell property partly for cash and partly for a secured promissory note of investment quality."[32] Many statutes expressly authorize executors and trustees to sell on credit,[33] but some impose special requirements for this.[34]

Sales can be challenged because the price is too low. A trustee who had sold an asset of the trust to a private purchaser was surcharged.[35] Another was surcharged for leasing property at less than its rental value.[36] But courts do not use hindsight in evaluating sales; an administrator who sold an apartment in 1997 for $775,000 was not surcharged even though an appraisal in 2000 put its value at $1 million.[37] Executors have also been surcharged for delaying a sale by asking too high a price.[38]

Prudence does not always require a public sale.[39] Nor is it always necessary for a fiduciary to accept the highest offer. A court upheld a trustee's rejection in a timber sale of a higher offer by an "inexperienced operator [who] * * could not ensure compliance with the strict environmental and other land and water protections."[40] But whether fiduciaries can in general take "social considerations" into account in choosing a buyer is more problematic.[41]

It may be prudent for a trustee to abandon property. The Uniform Trust Code allows trustees to abandon or disclaim property which is "of insufficient value to justify its * * * continued

---

**31.** In re Gould's Will, 234 N.Y.S.2d 825, 827 (App.Div.1962).

**32.** *Restatement, Third, of Trusts* § 190, comm. j (1990).

**33.** Uniform Probate Code § 3–715(23); Uniform Trustees' Powers Act § 3(c)(7); Unif.Trust Code § 816(2).

**34.** Cal.Prob.Code §§ 10257–28 (on credit sale of personal property buyer must pay 25% down, but court may waive this if to the advantage of the estate), § 10315 (on credit sale of land, buyer's note must be secured by mortgage on the property).

**35.** Allard v. Pacific Nat. Bank, 663 P.2d 104, 111 (Wash.1983). *See also* Es-tate of Blouin, 490 A.2d 1212 (Me.1985) (executor surcharged for sale at inadequate price).

**36.** Mest v. Dugan, 790 P.2d 38 (Or. App.1990).

**37.** In re Estate of Vale, 739 'N.Y.S.2d 21 (App.Div.2002).

**38.** Sims v. Heath, 577 S.E.2d 789, 791 (Ga.App.2002).

**39.** Bourne v. Lloyd, 642 A.2d 270 (Md.App.1994).

**40.** Aloha Lumber Corp. v. University of Alaska, 994 P.2d 991, 1000 (Alaska 1999).

**41.** Section 12.9.

administration" or because it "may have environmental liability attached to it."[42]

A fiduciary may be bound to accept a below-market price set by the terms of the will, or by an option given by the testator while living.[43]

*Court Approval*   Many states require sales by personal representatives to be confirmed by a court.[44] Sometimes fiduciaries contract to sell property, and before the sale is confirmed another buyer offers a higher price. Some courts refuse to confirm the sale when this occurs,[45] but others hold that if the sale was for a "reasonable value" it should be confirmed despite the later offer.[46]

Whether court proceedings perform a useful function in avoiding sales for an inadequate price is questionable. The Uniform Probate Code allows personal representatives to "proceed without adjudication, order or direction of the Court," although they may invoke the Court's jurisdiction "to resolve questions."[47] This is also true of trustees in most states.[48] Several states provide for "independent administration" of decedent's estates, which allows sales without court approval provided that prior notice is given to affected parties.[49]

## § 12.7   Investments

Fiduciaries have a power and a duty to invest. They can be surcharged or removed for failure to invest and for making improper investments. This Section will discuss the basic rules pertaining to investing. The remedies against fiduciaries who have acted improperly will be treated in the following Section.

*Different Fiduciaries*   The rules which govern trustees, personal representatives, conservators, custodians under the Uniform Transfers to Minors Act, and directors of charitable corporations[1]

**42.** Unif.Trust Code § 816(12)(13); *cf Restatement, Second, of Trusts* § 192, comm. c (1959) (abandonment of claims).

**43.** McPherson v. Dauenhauer, 69 P.3d 733 (Or.App.2003) (will); Colorado Nat. v. Bank Friedman, 846 P.2d 159 (Colo.1993) (partnership agreement).

**44.** Matter of Estate of Ostrander, 910 P.2d 865 (Kan.App.1996) (sale of trailer without court approval set aside); Calif.Prob.Code § 10309. Trustees, however, can sell without court approval. *Id.* § 16200.

**45.** Kapur v. Scientific Gas Products, Inc., 454 N.E.2d 1294 (Mass.App.Ct. 1983).

**46.** In re Estate of Hughes, 538 A.2d 470 (Pa.1988) (sale for $42,000 approved despite later offer of $60,000).

**47.** Uniform Probate Code § 3–704. As to the extent to which a fiduciary who gets court approval of a transaction is protected thereby see Section 12.8.

**48.** Uniform Trustees' Powers Act § 3(a); Unif.Trust Code §§ 201, 815.

**49.** Cal.Prob.Code § 10503. Washington has a similar provision for "nonintervention" administration when authorized by a will, but courts can nevertheless intervene when the executor mismanages the estate. In re Estate of Jones, 93 P.3d 147 (Wash.2004).

**§ 12.7**

**1.** See *Restatement, Second, of Trusts* § 389, comm. b (1959). Today charitable trusts are in most states governed by the Uniform Management of Institution-

are similar but not identical. The "investment authority and responsibilities" of personal representatives are generally "more limited than those of trustees."[2] The Uniform Prudent Investor Act covers only trustees, but the drafters suggest that states may adapt it to "other fiduciary regimes, taking account of such changed circumstances as the relatively short duration of most executorships."[3] California has adopted the Act, but has a more restricted rule for investments by personal representatives which limits them (with exceptions) to "short term fixed income obligations."[4] However, many wills give the same investment powers to the executor and the trustee.

*Terms of the Instrument*  The will or trust instrument is a primary source of the rules controlling investments. The Uniform Prudent Investor Act provides "a default rule, [which] may be expanded, restricted eliminated or otherwise altered by the provisions of a trust."[5] The Restatement of Trusts requires trustees to "conform to the terms of the trust directing or restricting investments,"[6] and a term in the instrument may justify what would otherwise be an improper investment.[7] However, courts may authorize trustees to ignore such terms when circumstances have changed, and trustees may even have a duty to seek such authorization.[8]

*Court Approval*  Prior court approval for investments by trustees is not usually required. Such a requirement for conservators is common,[9] but the Uniform Probate Code allows them "without Court authorization or confirmation [to] invest and reinvest funds of the estate as would a trustee."[10]

The need for court approval may turn on the type of investment. The Uniform Probate Code generally allows personal representatives to invest without court order, but court approval is needed to continue operating an unincorporated business for more than four months.[11] Conversely, even conservators can make certain kinds of investment without prior court approval.[12]

al Funds Act. Agents are also fiduciaries, but they generally must follow the instructions of the principal.

**2.**  *Restatement, Third, of Trusts* § 5, comm. c (2001).

**3.**  Unif.Prud.Inv.Act,      Prefatory Note.

**4.**  Cal.Prob.Code § 9730.

**5.**  Unif.Prud.Inv.Act § 2(b). *See also* Unif.Man.Inst.Funds Act § 4.

**6.**  *Restatement, Third, of Trusts* § 228(b) (1990). *See also* Dardaganis v. Grace Capital Inc., 889 F.2d 1237, 1240 (2d Cir.1989) (pension fund trustees lia-

ble for exceeding the limit on equity investments in agreement).

**7.**  Hoffman v. First Virginia Bank, 263 S.E.2d 402, 407 (Va.1980).

**8.**  *Restatement, Third, of Trusts* § 228, comm. e (1990); Section 9.6.

**9.**  Cal.Prob.Code §§ 2570 (conservator may invest "after authorization by court"), 17209 (administration of trusts "free of judicial intervention").

**10.**  Uniform Probate Code § 5–425(b).

**11.**  *Id.* § 3–715(24). *See also* Calif.Prob.Code § 16222.

**12.**  Cal.Prob.Code § 2574 (government bonds, listed securities).

Even when it is not required, fiduciaries may seek court approval for a questionable investment decision. Courts will instruct trustees in doubtful questions,[13] but excessive resort to courts is discouraged. A trustee can get instructions only "if there is a reasonable doubt as to the extent of his powers or duties," and courts "will not instruct him how to exercise his discretion."[14]

*Legal List v. "Prudent Man (Person)"* Historically the law has followed two approaches to controlling investments, the legal list and the "prudent man (person)" rule. Legal lists tend to be conservative. Only in 1961 was the English statute amended to allow trustees to invest in equities subject to a ceiling of half the trust fund.[15] In America the predominant view appeared in the second Restatement of Trusts: absent a statute or trust terms providing otherwise, trustee could "make such investments as a prudent man would make of his own property having in view the preservation of the estate and the amount and regularity of the income to be derived."[16] This formula has been adapted with variations in many statutes, such as the Uniform Transfers to Minors Act, where the "prudent man" dealing with "his own property" became "a prudent person dealing with the property of another."[17]

Studies have showed that the return on trust investments in "prudent man/person" states, which generally allow investment in common stocks, was almost double those controlled by legal lists. As a result, most states have abandoned legal lists, at least for trustees.[18]

*Fiduciary's Expertise* The "prudent person" standard is used in many contexts. The Uniform Trust Code requires trustees to "administer the trust as a prudent person would," and the Uniform Probate Code uses a similar formula for personal representatives. [19]

---

**13.** *Id.,* § 17200, 17209.

**14.** *Restatement, Second, of Trusts* § 259 (1959).

**15.** Langbein, *The Uniform Prudent Investor Act and the Future of Trust Investing,* 81 Iowa L.Rev. 641, 643 (1996). For a similar American statute see Ohio Rev.Code § 2109.37.

**16.** *Restatement, Second, of Trusts* § 227(a) (1959).

**17.** Uniform Transfers to Minors Act § 12(b). The Uniform Prudent Investor Act, on the other hand, rejects any distinction between a person "investing for another and investing on his or her own account." Unif.Prud.Inv.Act § 2, Comment.

**18.** Begleiter, *Does the Prudent Investor Really Need the Uniform Prudent Investor Act—An Empirical Study of trust Investment Practices,* 51 Me.L.Rev. 27, 32 (1999). The dichotomy between "legal lists" and "prudent person" states is somewhat misleading, since some legal lists allow a broad range of investments, and conversely, "prudence" can be narrowly interpreted.

**19.** Unif.Trust Code § 804; Uniform Probate Code § 3–703, referring to § 7–302. *See also* 29 U.S.C. § 1104(a)(1)(B) (ERISA).

The standard is objective. A family member who served as trustee without compensation was surcharged for failing to invest funds despite her "good faith."[20] The Restatement justifies this rule by emphasizing "the importance of obtaining competent guidance and assistance sufficient to meet the standards."[21]

A higher standard is imposed on professional fiduciaries. The Uniform Probate Code and Uniform Prudent Investor Act agree that "if the trustee has special skills or is named trustee on the basis of representations of special skills or expertise, he is under a duty to use those skills."[22]

*Speculation* Although prudent persons make often make speculative investments if the possible rewards outweigh the risk, fiduciaries were not supposed to do this. The second Restatement of Trusts barred "purchase of securities for speculation" and "in new and untried enterprises."[23] A court surcharged fiduciaries for buying real estate investment trusts (REITs) because they had existed "for only a short period" and so "there was no solid history of a productive return." REITs "were subject to substantial risks," whereas "the primary objective of a trustee should be preservation of the trust."[24]

Fiduciaries who followed the crowd were considered prudent: trustees could invest in stocks which "prudent men in the community are accustomed to invest in."[25]

This aversion to "speculation" and penchant for sticking to well-trodden paths has disappeared in the Third Restatement which expressly approves speculative and "unconventional" investments.[26] A Uniform Prudent Investor Act, promulgated in 1994 and widely adopted, "disavows the emphasis in older law on avoiding 'speculative' or 'risky' investments."[27]

*Diversification* The Act's answer to risk is not to avoid "speculative" investments but to diversify.[28] One of the central findings

---

**20.** Witmer v. Blair, 588 S.W.2d 222 (Mo.App.1979). *See also* Cal.Prob.Code § 16041 (standard of care not affected by lack of compensation).

**21.** *Restatement, Third, of Trusts* § 77, comm. b (Prel.Dft.2003). In Vento v. Colorado Nat. Bank–Pueblo, 907 P.2d 642 (Colo.App.1995), a trustee was surcharged for failing to consult coal mining experts during the negotiations for a mineral lease which resulted in terms unfavorable to the trust.

**22.** Uniform Probate Code § 7–302; Uniform Prud.Inv.Act § 2(f). *See also* Unif.Trust Code § 806.

**23.** *Restatement, Second, of Trusts* § 227, comm. f (1959).

**24.** Matter of Newhoff's Will, 435 N.Y.S.2d 632, 636 (Surr.1980). *See also* Matter of Goldstick, 581 N.Y.S.2d 165, 171 (App.Div.1992) (investment in company with no earnings history).

**25.** *Restatement, Second, of Trusts* § 227, comm. m (1959).*See also* Chase v. Pevear, 419 N.E.2d 1358, 1368–69 (Mass.1981)

**26.** *Restatement, Third, of Trusts* § 227, comm. e (1990).

**27.** Unif.Prud.Inv.Act § 2(e) and Comment thereto.

**28.** *Id.* § 3.

of Modern Portfolio Theory is that there are huge and essentially costless gains to diversifying the portfolio thoroughly.[29] A requirement of diversification was already present in earlier law, so it remains to be seen what effect the increased emphasis on diversification will have. A court in 1997 refused to surcharge a trustee who had failed to dispose of real property which made up the bulk of a trust's assets because the land "was placed in the trust by the settlor and comprised a majority of the trust, thus indicating the settlor's intent that the land remain the primary asset of the trust."[30] But another court surcharged executors who delayed selling a block of Kodak stock which made up 71% of the portfolio, because risk "is significantly exacerbated when a portfolio is heavily concentrated in one such growth stock.[31]

Even the Prudent Investor Act does not require diversification if "the trustee reasonably determines that, because of special circumstances the purposes of the trust would be better served without diversifying." The Comment suggests as a possible special circumstance the tax costs of selling low-basis stock in order to diversify.[32] A court refused to surcharge trustees for failure to sell realty in an undiversified portfolio when the absence of a strong market meant that a sale would have been at a sacrifice.[33]

Many statutes and judicial opinions apply different standards to new investments and retention of received asset.[34] The second Restatement of Trusts required trustees to dispose of assets which would be improper investments "within a reasonable time," but an authorization in the trust instrument to retain property (a common provision) could be construed to abrogate the requirement of diversification.[35] The third Restatement and the Uniform Prudent Investor Act are less approving of fiduciaries who maintain the status quo; trustees must "within a reasonable time" review the portfolio and bring it into compliance with the Act.[36] A general authorization to retain investments "does not ordinarily abrogate the trustee's duty with respect to diversification," and even an authorization to

---

**29.** Langbein, *supra* note 15, at 647.

**30.** Matter of Estate of Maxedon, 946 P.2d 104, 109 (Kan.App.1997). *See also* Atwood v. Atwood, 25 P.3d 936, 944 (Okl.Civ.App.2001) (authorization to retain investments justified trustee's failure to diversify).

**31.** Matter of Estate of Janes, 681 N.E.2d 332, 338 (N.Y.1997).

**32.** Unif.Prud.Inv.Act § 3 and Comment. See also *Restatement, Third, of Trusts* § 229, comm. a (1990).

**33.** In re Estate of Cavin, 728 A.2d 92, 100 (D.C.App.1999).

**34.** Gardner v. Cox, 843 P.2d 469, 471–72 (Or.App.1992) (distinguishing between buying and retaining a "speculative" investment).

**35.** *Restatement, Second, of Trusts* § 230, comm. j (1959).

**36.** Unif.Prud.Inv.Act § 4.

retain a specific investment ("my XYZ stock") does not control "if retention would otherwise be imprudent."[37]

A Restatement illustration approves a portfolio of 20 carefully selected stocks, noting that diversification "is not simply a matter of numbers." But it also touts the advantages of index funds which match the performance of the market as a whole.[38] "Studies have found that professionally managed institutional portfolios as a group actually underperformed the broad stock market averages such as the Standard and Poor's 500 stock index." Since everything knowable about a publicly traded security is already reflected in its price,[39] research in attempting to pick the "best" stocks is a waste of money.

Since a small portfolio is hard to diversify, many banks have established "common trust funds" which pool the assets of many small trusts to facilitate diversification. Mutual funds provide another way to diversify. The objection that this investment delegates the trustee's responsibility to the manager of the mutual fund is "of relatively trivial importance compared to the virtues which may be gained by" such funds.[40] The Prudent Investor Act and the third Restatement reject the idea that delegation is improper.[41]

*Adapting Investments to the Circumstances*    The situations of beneficiaries differ widely. Some persons are more risk averse than others. Prudence requires fiduciaries to consider *inter alia* a beneficiary's "ability to absorb losses in the event an investment is unsuccessful."[42] A trust "to support an elderly widow of modest means will have a lower risk tolerance than a trust to accumulate for a young scion of great wealth."[43]

The goal of investing, according to the second Restatement, was "preservation of the estate and the amount and regularity of the income."[44] This remains true in the third Restatement only for those trusts in which one or more beneficiary's rights depend on income.[45] Many beneficiaries are more concerned about protecting against inflation than about regular income, and prefer non-dividend-paying growth stocks to high-yield bonds. Investments of this type were not allowed by the second Restatement, which only

---

**37.** *Restatement, Third, of Trusts* § 229, comm. d (1990).

**38.** *Id.,* § 227, illus. 14, comm. b.

**39.** Langbein, *supra* note 15, at 655, 657.

**40.** Farr & Wright, *An Estate Planner's Handbook* 208 (4th ed. 1979).

**41.** Unif.Prud.Inv. Act § 9; *Restatement, Third, of Trusts* § 227, comm. j (1990).

**42.** Erlich v. First Nat'l Bank, 505 A.2d 220, 235 (N.J.Super.A.D.1984) (imprudent to invest in a single stock for a person who had little income and few assets apart from investment).

**43.** Unif.Prud.Inv.Act § 2, Comment.

**44.** *Restatement, Second, of Trusts* § 227 (1959).

**45.** *Restatement, Third, of Trusts* § 79(2) (Prel.Dft.2003)

permitted trustees to invest in stock which paid "regular dividends."[46]

The third Restatement notes that in many trusts distributions do not depend on the trust's income and so the trustee should be free "to disregard income productivity in managing investments."[47] Moreover, it is the trust estate as a whole, not any particular investment that must be productive. The Prudent Investor Act requires that individual investments "be evaluated not in isolation but in the context of the trust portfolio as a whole,"[48] so trustees can hold some non-income-producing investments if the portfolio as a whole produces a reasonable income.

Investments which are expected to appreciate even if they produce no income are justifiable, but not failure to invest at all, *e.g.* leaving money in a checking account. Many fiduciaries, even executors, have been surcharged for this.[49] But liquidity can be a legitimate concern for fiduciaries. California allows trustees to keep amounts "reasonably necessary for the orderly administration of the trust" in a checking account.[50]

The beneficiaries of a trust often have conflicting interests with respect to investments, *e.g.* income beneficiaries who wish the trust to produce more income and remaindermen who are concerned only with the principal. Trustees are supposed to be "impartial" in such conflicts.[51] A trustee was surcharged for investing 87% of the assets in bonds because "the prudent investor standard requires that the trustee maintain a balance between the rights of the income beneficiaries with those of the remainderman."[52]

The Prudent Investor Act directs trustees to consider the "tax consequences of investment decisions," e.g., "it may be prudent for the trust to buy lower-yielding tax-exempt securities for high tax-bracket taxpayers."[53] In some cases tensions between beneficiaries in different tax situations can be reduced by dividing trusts.[54]

**46.** *Restatement, Second, of Trusts* § 227, comm. m (1959). *See also* Perfect Union Lodge v. Interfirst Bank, 748 S.W.2d 218 (Tex.1988) (order to sell land which produced less than 1% of its value in income).

**47.** *Restatement, Third, of Trusts* § 227, comm. i (1990);. See also Shear v. Gabovitch, 685 N.E.2d 1168, 1185 (Mass.App.Ct.1997) (proper for trustee to hold stock paying no dividends since settlor implicitly authorized this); Unif. Man.Inst.Funds Act, Prefatory Note, § 4(1) (allowing investment in property "whether or not it produces a current return")

**48.** Unif.Prud.Inv.Act § 2(b).

**49.** Maryland Nat'l Bank v. Cummins, 588 A.2d 1205, 1210–12 (Md.

1991); Whitaker v. Estate of Whitaker, 663 N.E.2d 681, 686 (Ohio App.1995).

**50.** Cal.Prob.Code § 16225(e).

**51.** *Restatement, Third, of Trusts* § 227, comm. c (1990); Unif. Prud.Inv.Act § 6. The duty of impartiality is not limited to investments. Unif. Trust Code § 803.

**52.** Matter of Estate of Cooper, 913 P.2d 393, 398 (Wash.App.1996).

**53.** Unif.Prud.Inv.Act § 2(c)(3), and Comment; *cf.* In re Estate of Feinstein, 527 A.2d 1034, 1038 (Pa.Super.1987) (upholding trustee's investment in tax-free bonds over objection of charitable remaindermen).

**54.** Matter of Will of Kaskel, 549 N.Y.S.2d 587, 590 (Surr.1989).

Under the second Restatement "preservation of the estate" (along with production of income) was the goal of trust investment, but the third Restatement describes the goal as preservation of the "real value" of the trust property, *i.e.* "seeking to avoid the loss of the trust estate's purchasing power as a result of inflation."[55] A court surcharged a trustee under whose management a portfolio had increased by $226,000 because due to inflation the purchasing power of the trust assets had decreased by 4 percent a year.[56]

*Family Business* "A personal representative breaches his trust if he continues to operate a trade or business on behalf of an estate in the absence of testamentary direction."[57] Since the success of such a business often depends on the ability of its manager, it may be imprudent to continue the business after he or she dies.[58] Some courts apply this rule only to *unincorporated* businesses because their unlimited liability may deplete the whole estate. The Uniform Probate Code requires court approval to continue an unincorporated business for more than 4 months, but an incorporated business can be operated "throughout the period of administration" if no potential distributee objects.[59]

A sale of the business may be the best solution, but a mere authorization (or direction) to sell may be hard to carry out after the client dies, so the client may need to negotiate a "buy-out" agreement with others associated with the business.

*Evaluating Performance.* Older decisions surcharging fiduciaries for speculative investments are obsolete under the new rules. Older decisions said that the fact that a portfolio showed substantial overall increase in value did "not insulate the trustee from responsibility for imprudence with respect to individual investments."[60] Such statements cannot be squared with the Prudent Investor Act's instruction that trustees' decisions "must be evaluated not in isolation, but in the context of the trust portfolio as a whole."[61] The Act also says that a trustee's actions must not be judged "by hindsight;" the fact that a portfolio has gone down in

**55.** *Restatement, Third, of Trusts* § 227, comm. e (1990).

**56.** Matter of Estate of Cooper, 913 P.2d 393, 397–98 (Wash.App.1996). *See also* Dennis v. Rhode Island Hosp. Trust Nat. Bank, 744 F.2d 893, 899 (1st Cir. 1984) (surcharge based on consumer price index because proper investments would have "preserved the real value" of the principal).

**57.** In re Kurkowski's Estate, 409 A.2d 357, 361 (Pa.1979).

**58.** Fortune v. First Union Nat. Bank, 359 S.E.2d 801, 805 (N.C.App. 1987).

**59.** Uniform Probate Code § 3–715(24).

**60.** In re Bank of New York, 323 N.E.2d 700, 703 (N.Y.1974).

**61.** Unif.Prud.Inv.Act § 2(b). *See also Restatement, Third, of Trusts* § 227(a) (1990).

value does not *ipso facto* mean that the trustee has been imprudent.[62] How then is a fiduciary's prudence to be assessed? Langbein noted that the cases "give great weight to the trustee's internal procedures for investing and monitoring investments; * * * the courts have sometimes been willing to treat this paper trail as presumptive evidence of prudence," but under the Prudent Investor Act a "paper trail" cannot excuse a seriously underdiversified portfolio, and trustees who "persistently underperform" comparable funds may be found imprudent.[63] Is this consistent with the command not to use "hindsight" in evaluating trustees? The Act requires trustees to have "an overall investment strategy,"[64] but presumably the absence of a defensible strategy will not cause a trustee whose investment performance was above average to be surcharged. It is not clear what effect the Act will have on surcharges of trustees but it will change the investment practices of trustees by opening up a broader range of investments.

## § 12.8 Remedies

*Jurisdiction* The court which appoints a fiduciary may have exclusive jurisdiction over claims against the fiduciary. Beneficiaries of a will probated in Ohio were not allowed to sue the executor in federal court for "irregularities" in her administration, since federal courts have no probate jurisdiction, and can entertain actions to redress wrongs in the administration of an estate only if the state allows such actions to be pursued in courts of general jurisdiction, and Ohio gave exclusive jurisdiction of probate matters to its probate court.[1]

A state continues to have jurisdiction over fiduciaries who move to another state.[2] But if the *beneficiaries* of a trust move to another state, their new residence may not have jurisdiction over a trustee whose only contact with the state had been sending accounts and distributions to the beneficiaries at their new residence.[3]

A court which has jurisdiction may decline to proceed if another court offers a more convenient forum.[4]

**62.** Unif.Prud.Inv.Act § 8. *See also Restatement, Third, of Trusts* § 227, comm. b (1990).

**63.** Langbein, *supra* note 15, at 662.

**64.** Unif.Prud.Inv.Act § 2(b)

**§ 12.8**

**1.** Bedo v. McGuire, 767 F.2d 305 (6th Cir.1985). But another federal court upheld a similar suit arising from Illinois, because Illinois did *not* give its probate court exclusive jurisdiction of such cases. Hamilton v. Nielsen, 678 F.2d 709 (7th Cir.1982).

**2.** Norton v. Bridges, 712 F.2d 1156, 1162 (7th Cir.1983).

**3.** Rose v. Firstar Bank, 819 A.2d 1247 (R.I.2003). *But cf.* Guardianship and Conservatorship of Miles, 660 N.W.2d 233, 242 (S.D.2003) (California trustee had sufficient contacts with S.D. to give court jurisdiction over him).

**4.** Bartlett v. Dumaine, 523 A.2d 1, 15 (N.H.1986).

*Form of Trial*   Since historically trusts were enforced in equity, there is usually no right to trial by jury in suits for breach of trust, or against a conservator or personal representative,[5] but the historical distinction between courts of law and equity does not bar states from extending jury trial to trust cases.[6] Also, a trustee can be sued at law for money which is presently due to the claimant as distinguished from one to compel the trustee to put money into the trust.[7]

*Equitable Remedies*   Courts can enjoin an improper investment or sale, or order a sale.[8] An improper sale which has already taken place can be vacated.[9] A trustee who has wrongfully sold property to a bona fide purchaser can be compelled to buy a replacement if this is reasonably possible.[10]

The beneficiaries can elect to affirm a wrongful purchase if the property later rises in value, or may affirm an improper sale if the property declines in value.[11] This right of election allows beneficiaries to speculate at the fiduciary's expense, but if they delay too long, their remedy may be barred by laches.

*Damages*   Sometimes damages are the only appropriate remedy. These may be based on profits arising to the fiduciary from a breach. When a trustee used trust assets to secure a loan with which he made a profitable purchase for himself, the court awarded damages even though the trust had suffered no loss.[12] Any profits claimed against a fiduciary must be shown with reasonable certainty. However, a court held a trustee accountable for profits it had made with excessive fees. "[I]n the regular course of business, the banks put the overcharges to work. * * * [T]raceability * * * is not required."[13]

**5.** Matter of Trust Created by Hill, 499 N.W.2d 475, 490 (Minn.App.1993); Estate of Grove v. Selken, 820 P.2d 895, 900 (Or.App.1991).

**6.** First Union Nat. Bank v. Turney, 839 So.2d 774, 776 (Fla.App.2003) (affirming jury award of damages in suit for breach of trust).

**7.** Jefferson Nat. Bank v. Central Nat. Bank, 700 F.2d 1143 (7th Cir.1983). *See also Restatement, Second, of Trusts* § 198 (1959).

**8.** Donovan v. Bierwirth, 680 F.2d 263 (2d Cir.1982) (injunction against trustees of pension fund); Matter of Estate of Rolczynski, 349 N.W.2d 394 (N.D.1984) (executor ordered to sell land); Unif.Trust Code § 1001(b).

**9.** Matter of Estate of Ostrander, 910 P.2d 865 (Kan.App.1996) (unauthorized sale by administrator set aside).

But not if the buyer is a bona fide purchaser. Jarrett v. U.S. National Bank, 725 P.2d 384, 388 (Or.App.1986).

**10.** Application of Kettle, 423 N.Y.S.2d 701 (App.Div.1979); *Restatement, Third, of Trusts* § 208 (1990).

**11.** *Restatement, Third, of Trusts* § 208 (election to affirm a sale), § 210(b) (election to affirm an improper investment) (1990).

**12.** Coster v. Crookham, 468 N.W.2d 802, 806–07 (Iowa 1991). *See also* 29 U.S.C. § 1109(a) (ERISA); Unif.Trust Code § 1002(a)(2).

**13.** Nickel v. Bank of American Nat. Trust and Sav. Ass'n, 290 F.3d 1134 (9th Cir.2002).

Even if a fiduciary makes no profit from a breach, damages may be recovered for any loss suffered by the trust. If a sale was proper but the price was too low, damages are based on the difference between what the trustee received and what the buyer should have paid.[14] But when a trustee sells an asset which should have been retained, the damages are based on the present value of the asset.[15] Dividends paid on stock after it was improperly sold (reduced by interest received on the sales proceeds) are also awarded.[16]

Trustees may also be surcharged for failing to sell assets which are improper investments.[17] An executor who unduly delayed selling stock while its value dropped was charged the value of the stock on the date it should have been sold less "the proceeds from the sale of the stock [when sold] or, if the stock is still retained, the value of the stock at the time" of trial.[18]

The court added to the damages so computed prejudgment interest at the legal rate, compounded from the date when the sale should have occurred.[19] However, the third Restatement of Trusts in place of interest speaks of "an appropriate additional amount to compensate for the loss of return" on the amount lost which can be "based on total return experience (positive or negative) for other investments of the trust," or "portfolios of other trusts having comparable objectives and circumstances."[20] A bank which invested solely for the benefit of the income beneficiaries without regard to the growth of corpus had to pay damages based on the rate of appreciation realized by its common equity funds.[21] On the other hand, a court awarded prejudgment interest but not "investment potential" on estate funds wrongfully used by an executor, on the theory that "while a trustee has a duty to invest * * *, an executor has a duty to conserve estate assets."[22]

Courts refuse to impose a surcharge if they find no causal link between the breach of trust and the loss. A trustee which was authorized to invest in bonds with AAA or AA ratings bought some

---

**14.** *Restatement, Third, of Trusts* § 205, comm. d (1990). Conversely when a fiduciary pays too much for a proper investment, damages are based on the excess payment. Id., comm. e.

**15.** *Id.*, § 208.

**16.** Matter of Donald E. Bradford Trust, 538 So.2d 263, 268 (La.1989).

**17.** Rutanen v. Ballard, 678 N.E.2d 133, 137 (Mass.1997).

**18.** Matter of Estate of Janes, 681 N.E.2d 332, 339 (N.Y.1997).

**19.** *See also* Jarrett v. U.S. National Bank, 768 P.2d 936, 938 (Or.App.1989)

(proper to charge trustee with interest on damages).

**20.** *Restatement, Third, of Trusts* §§ 209(1), 205, comment a (1990). *See also* Estate of Wilde, 708 A.2d 273, 275 (Me.1998) (damages based on the value of trust assets "had they been managed by a prudent trustee").

**21.** Noggle v. Bank of America, 82 Cal.Rptr.2d 829, 836 (App.1999).

**22.** NC Illinois Trust v. First Illini Bancorp, 752 N.E.2d 1167, 1180 (Ill.App. 2001).

with only an A rating. They declined in value but the decline in higher rated bonds was even greater. The court refused to surcharge the trustee because the loss would have occurred in the absence of the breach.[23] But a trustee who buys an asset from himself which declines in value is surcharged even though the same decline would have occurred if he had bought the asset from someone else,[24] since the trustee might not have bought the asset at all without the conflict of interest.

Fiduciaries are not liable for losses to property which occur without their fault. But the general duty of prudence may require them to take out insurance against such eventualities.[25]

*Punishment* Historically it was not a crime for trustees to misappropriate property, but this is no longer true.[26] Attorneys have been disbarred for stealing money from a trust of which they were the trustee.[27]

Traditionally, equity courts did not award punitive damages,[28] but more recent cases have imposed them on trustees who acted in "bad faith or conscious indifference to the rights of the beneficiaries."[29]

Courts may also use contempt procedures against recalcitrant fiduciaries. However, an order to imprison a guardian until he turned over funds which he had dissipated was reversed. "The court's inherent power to impose sanctions for civil contempt [applies only for] * * * the omission or refusal to perform an act which is yet in the power of a defendant to perform."[30]

Beneficiaries of a trust have an advantage over ordinary creditors of a debtor who becomes insolvent; the beneficiaries "retain their equitable interests in the trust property if it can be identified, or in its product if it can be traced into the product."[31] Also, claims arising out of "fraud or defalcation while acting in a fiduciary capacity" are not dischargeable in bankruptcy.[32]

**23.** Fort Myers Mem. Gardens v. Barnett Banks, 474 So.2d 1215, 1218 (Fla.App.1985).

**24.** Matter of Guardianship of Eisenberg, 719 P.2d 187, 191 (Wash.App. 1986).

**25.** *Restatement, Second, of Trusts* § 176, illus. 3 (1959).

**26.** Commonwealth v. Garrity, 682 N.E.2d 937 (Mass.App.Ct.1997) (executor convicted of embezzlement from an estate).

**27.** Matter of Stern, 682 N.E.2d 867 (Mass.1997); People v. Rouse, 817 P.2d 967 (Colo.1991).

**28.** Kohler v. Fletcher, 442 N.W.2d 169 (Minn.App.1989).

**29.** Cartee v. Lesley, 350 S.E.2d 388, 390 (S.C.1986). *See also* NC Illinois Trust v. First Illini Bancorp, 752 N.E.2d 1167 (Ill.App. 2001) ($1.3 million punitive damages against an executor).

**30.** Matter of Elder, 763 P.2d 219, 221–22 (Alaska 1988).

**31.** *Restatement, Third, of Trusts* § 5, comm. k (2001).

**32.** 11 U.S.C. § 523(a)(4).

*Defenses: Standing*   We shall now turn to possible defenses of a fiduciary. A suit may be dismissed for lack of standing. A testator's children were not allowed to challenge the fees paid to his personal representative because they had no interest since the will had disinherited them.[33] Even a beneficiary has no standing to challenge actions which do not affect his interest; e.g., remaindermen were not permitted to question a loan made by the trustee at an interest below the market rate, because any increased income would not go to them but to the income beneficiary.[34] On the other hand, the fact that a trust beneficiary's interest is contingent does not deprive the beneficiary of standing to sue,[35] since the recovery goes to the trust itself for eventual distribution under its terms.

Courts are liberal about standing when incapacitated persons are involved. An attorney was allowed to challenge a conservator's accounts, since "any person may petition the court as the next friend of the children to bring the conservator's conflict of interest to the court's attention."[36]

Co-trustees have standing to sue fellow trustees,[37] and successor trustees can sue the predecessor (or the personal representative of the estate in the case of a testamentary trust) for breaches by the latter.[38] However, a settlor who has reserved no interest in the trust has no standing.[39] Courts sometimes raise questions about a fiduciary's conduct on their own motion.[40]

*Good Faith*   Occasionally courts refuse to impose liability on a trustee who has committed a breach of trust in good faith, e.g. sums disbursed "grounded on a good faith, albeit erroneous, interpretation of the trust document."[41] But a trustee who makes a mistake in interpreting the law or the instrument is not immune from liability "merely because he acts in good faith," because in doubtful cases "he can protect himself by obtaining instruction from the court."[42]

---

**33.**  Estate of Miles v. Miles, 994 P.2d 1139, 1145 (Mont.2000).

**34.**  Regan v. Uebelhor, 690 N.E.2d 1222, 1226 (Ind.App.1998).

**35.**  Gaynor v. Payne, 804 A.2d 170, 176 (Conn. 2002).

**36.**  Matter of Conservatorship of L.M.S., 755 P.2d 22, 25 (Kan.App.1988). *See also Restatement, Second, of Trusts* § 214, comm. a (1959); Uniform Probate Code § 5–414.

**37.**  Cal.Prob.Code § 16013(b); Unif. Trust Code § 703(g).

**38.**  *Id.*, § 812. A good faith determination by successor trustees not to pursue a possible claim against a former trustee bars the beneficiaries from doing so. Axelrod v. Giambalvo, 472 N.E.2d 840, 846 (Ill.App.1984).

**39.**  *Restatement, Second, of Trusts* § 200 (1959).

**40.**  Estate of Kerns v. Western Surety Co., 802 P.2d 1298 (Okl.1990).

**41.**  Griffin v. Griffin, 463 So.2d 569, 574 (Fla.App.1985). *See also* Cal.Prob. Code § 16440(c).

**42.**  *Restatement, Second, of Trusts* § 201, comm. b, § 226, comm. b (1959).

*Exculpatory Clauses* Clauses which exculpate a fiduciary from liability are sometimes effective. When a trust provided that the trustee "shall not be liable if [the trust powers] are exercised in good faith," a judgment surcharging the trustee for imprudent transactions was reversed.[43] However, a trustee was held liable for a wrongful distribution despite a clause holding the trustee harmless for actions taken "except in the case of fraud." Although the trustee's actions were not "wanton or malicious" it had "acted with reckless indifference" and hence was liable for compensatory damages.[44] Courts are particularly hostile when such clauses are invoked by professional fiduciaries.[45] For a lawyer to attempt to limit liability for malpractice by an exculpatory clause may violate the rules of professional conduct.[46]

An exculpatory clause will be disregarded if it was "improperly inserted" in the instrument, *e.g.* when a lawyer who drafted a trust in which he was named trustee failed to bring the clause to the settlor's attention and explain its implications.[47]

*Throwing the Blame on Others* Fiduciaries sometimes try to shift the responsibility for a breach to others. A court surcharged a personal representative for penalties incurred by the estate for a late tax return despite her claim that "she reasonably relied on the advice of her accountant." She was not justified in leaving "all tax matters to the accountant."[48] On the other hand, an executor who had relied on the advice of the lawyer in filing an improper estate tax return was exonerated. "The Bank had a right to * * * rely on the attorney's advice, unless the Bank knowingly chose incompetent counsel or had some reason to know that the advice given was not sound."[49]

The second Restatement of Trusts said that trustees had a duty "not to delegate to others the doing of acts which the trustee can reasonably be required to perform personally."[50] The third Restatement reflects a more favorable attitude toward delegation; indeed trustees may now be deemed imprudent for *failure* to

---

**43.** Kerper v. Kerper, 780 P.2d 923, 930–31 (Wyo.1989).

**44.** Feibelman v. Worthen Nat. Bank, N.A., 20 F.3d 835, 836 (8th Cir. 1994), following *Restatement, Second, of Trusts* § 222(2) (1959). *See also* Unif. Trust Code § 1008(a)(1).

**45.** Erlich v. First Nat'l Bank, 505 A.2d 220, 233 (N.J.Super.A.D.1984).

**46.** ABA Model Code of Prof.Resp. DR 6–102; ABA Model Rules of Prof. Cond. 1.8(h).

**47.** Rutanen v. Ballard, 678 N.E.2d 133, 141 (Mass.1997). *But cf.* Marsman

v. Nasca, 573 N.E.2d 1025, 1032–33 (Mass.App.Ct.1991).

**48.** Gudschinsky v. Hartill, 815 P.2d 851, 855 (Alaska 1991).

**49.** Jewish Hospital v. Boatmen's Nat. Bank, 633 N.E.2d 1267, 1281 (Ill. App.1994). *But see* NC Illinois Trust v. First Illini Bancorp, 752 N.E.2d 1167 (Ill.App. 2001) in which the court found a bank was unreasonable in relying on the advice of counsel.

**50.** *Restatement, Second, of Trusts* § 171 (1959).

delegate in some situations.[51] The Uniform Prudent Investor Act "reverses the much-criticized rule that forbad trustees to delegate investment and management functions." Trustees must exercise reasonable skill in selecting the agent and "periodically reviewing the agent's actions."[52] If they do, they are not liable for the agent's actions.[53]

*Multiple Fiduciaries and Advisors* A similar problem arises when there are multiple fiduciaries and one takes a leading role. An attempt by a co-trustee to escape liability for the failure to sell a trust asset was rejected because "a cotrustee must 'participate in the administration of the trust and use reasonable care to prevent a co-trustee from committing a breach of trust.' "[54]

Each fiduciary is jointly liable for the whole loss, but has a right of contribution against the other(s) if the beneficiary sues only one of them.[55] A fiduciary who is substantially more at fault than the other(s) is not entitled to contribution and other fiduciaries can get full indemnity from the one primarily at fault.[56]

The more liberal attitude of the third Restatement of Trusts toward delegation by trustees apparently encompasses delegation to a co-trustee, at least when authorized by the terms of the trust,[57] but the Uniform Trust Code distinguishes the two situations, at least where "the settlor reasonably expected the trustees to perform jointly."[58]

Some trust instruments allow a person other than the trustee to control investments. If the power is for the sole benefit of its holder, the trustee's only obligation is to follow directions, but if the holder is "subject to fiduciary obligations" the trustee may be liable for complying with improper directions, just as if the power holder were a co-trustee.[59]

**51.** *Restatement, Third, of Trusts* § 171, comm. a (1990). *See also id.,* comm. g (trustee may "be virtually compelled by considerations of efficiency" to delegate)j.

**52.** *Cf.* Whitfield v. Cohen, 682 F.Supp. 188 (S.D.N.Y.1988) (ERISA trustee liable for failure to exercise care in selecting investment advisor and monitoring its performance).

**53.** Unif.Prud.Inv.Act § 9. *See also* Unif.Trust Code § 807.

**54.** Rutanen v. Ballard, 678 N.E.2d 133, 140 (Mass.1997) (quoting *Restatement, Second, of Trusts* § 184 (1959)). The same principles apply to co-executors. Matter of Estate of Donner, 626 N.E.2d 922, 926 (N.Y.1993).

**55.** In re Estate of Chrisman, 746 S.W.2d 131, 134–35 (Mo.App.1988).

**56.** *Restatement, Second, of Trusts* § 258 (1959). For a discussion of relevant factors in giving or denying contribution see Unif.Trust Code § 1002, Comment.

**57.** *Restatement, Third, of Trusts* § 171, comm. i (1990).

**58.** Unif.Trust Code § 703(e). Contrast *id.* § 807 as to delegation to agents. Uniform Prudent Investor Act § 9 only speaks of delegation to an agent.

**59.** *Restatement, Second, of Trusts* § 185, comms. d, e (1959); Steiner v. Hawaiian Trust Co., 393 P.2d 96, 107 (Haw.1964). The Uniform Trust Code is similar, but it presumes that the holder of a directive power is a fiduciary. Unif. Trust Code § 808(d).

*Res judicata*   Fiduciaries frequently claim they are protected by a prior judgment. A trustee who gets court instructions as to the propriety of an action should be protected for actions taken in compliance with them.[60] However, this does not preclude relief from a judgment under the general rules of civil procedure. A judgment approving fees was set aside for "excusable neglect" by devisee who had "no prior experience with the probate system * * * and no idea what an estate attorney's fees should have been."[61] Nor does res judicata extend to questions not covered by the decree. An order approving a executor's sale of property at a specified price did not bar a later claim that the executor had "mishandled the business in such a manner that the value [of the property had] decreased significantly."[62]

What effect does court approval of a fiduciary's accounts have? After trustees filed annual accounts for several years, beneficiaries claimed that they had wrongfully retained an under-productive asset. The court gave summary judgment to the trustees. "A judicial settlement of a trustee's accounts * * * bars subsequent litigation seeking to raise defaults or defects with the matters shown or disclosed in the accountings. * * * The beneficiaries are barred from questioning later matters which are disclosed by the accounting, but *not* those *not* disclosed."[63] The approval of an administrator's final account, on the other hand, has been held a "bar not only to issues which were actually raised but to causes of action which could have been litigated," at least where the devisees "were aware of the facts giving rise to their collateral attack."[64] But even approval of a final accounts may leave certain issues open. When a woman left property in trust to her husband, approval of his final account as executor did not preclude a later claim by the remainderman under the trust. "The approval of the final report in the probate proceedings did not determine the capacity in which the assets, which should have been in the trust, were received" or relieve the husband of his fiduciary duties as trustee.[65]

Sometimes court approval is not binding because the court was not informed of a relevant fact.[66] When an administrator sold land to his step-daughter, a court approved the sale without being aware

**60.**  Harper v. Harper, 491 So.2d 189, 199 (Miss.1986) (challenge to action which court had approved rejected).

**61.**  Johnson v. Doris, 933 P.2d 1139, 1143 (Alaska 1997).

**62.**  First of America Trust v. First Illini Bancorp, 685 N.E.2d 351, 358 (Ill. App.1997).

**63.**  Fraser v. Southeast First Bank, 417 So.2d 707, 710–12 (Fla.App.1982).

*See also Restatement, Second, of Trusts* § 220, comm. a (1959).

**64.**  Goldberg v. Frye, 266 Cal.Rptr. 483, 486 (App.1990).

**65.**  Kemper v. Kemper, 532 N.E.2d 1126, 1128 (Ill.App.1989).

**66.**  *Restatement, Second, of Trusts* § 220, comm. a (1959).

of the relationship; the approval was later revoked.[67] The Uniform Probate Code protects personal representatives from claims not brought within 6 months after filing of a "closing statement," but not if there was "fraud, misrepresentation, or inadequate disclosure."[68] Not all claims of "fraud" are sufficient to avoid res judicata. A claim that a bank "fraudulently misrepresented its skill" as an investor was not enough to allow an account to be reopened, since "it had no effect on [the ward's] ability to attend the hearing of which she received notice and to litigate * * * her claims of wrongdoing by Bank."[69]

The court which renders a judgment must have jurisdiction in order for it to have res judicata effect. An Oklahoma court rejected a guardian's attempt to rely on a Michigan judgment approving withdrawals from an estate, because "the Michigan court never acquired jurisdiction over the guardianship assets."[70] An approved account binds beneficiaries who live outside the jurisdiction of the court only if they are given notice and an opportunity to appear. Notice by publication is sufficient for beneficiaries whose interests or addresses were unknown to the trustee, but as to those whose addresses were on the trustee's books "a serious effort to inform them personally of the accounting at least by ordinary mail to the record addresses" is constitutionally required.[71]

Court orders do not bind incompetent beneficiaries unless they are adequately represented. An order authorizing a conservator to use assets to pay a claim was not binding because no guardian ad litem had been appointed.[72] Appointing a guardian ad litem for incompetent beneficiaries is costly because they are entitled to compensation from the estate. The Uniform Probate Code requires appointment of a GAL only where "representation of the interest would otherwise be inadequate;"[73] it allows, for example, parents to represent their minor children when there is no conflict of interest between them. After a sale by personal representatives was approved, the court rejected an attack by remaindermen under a testamentary trust, saying that they had been adequately represented by the trustee named in the will.[74]

**67.** Satti v. Rago, 441 A.2d 615 (Conn.1982).

**68.** Uniform Probate Code § 3–1005.

**69.** Bank of America Nat. Trust v. Superior Court, 226 Cal.Rptr. 685, 690 (App.1986).

**70.** In re Estate of LaRose, 1 P.3d 1018, 1023 (Okl.Civ.App.1999).

**71.** Mullane v. Central Hanover Bank & Trust Co., 339 U.S. 306, 313 (1950). *See also* Unif.Trust Code § 202(b).

**72.** Matter of Conservatorship of L.M.S., 755 P.2d 22, 25 (Kan.App.1988). Even when a guardian was appointed, the judgment may not be binding when the guardian "failed to … defend the action with due diligence." *Restatement, Second, of Judgments* § 72 (1982).

**73.** Uniform Probate Code § 1–403. *See also* Unif.Trust Code § 305.

**74.** Matter of Estate of Jones, 770 P.2d 1100 (Wyo.1989). *See also* Uniform Probate Code § 1–403(2)(ii) (orders binding a trustee bind beneficiaries of

Requiring court approval of transactions may not be an adequate safeguard against abuses because often "the proceeding is not adversary", and court scrutiny of fiduciary accounts tends to be superficial.[75] Therefore the Uniform Probate Code allows personal representatives and trustees to dispense with it; they are protected from claims for breach of fiduciary duty 6 months after they file a closing statement which adequately discloses their handling of the estate.[76]

*Laches and Statutes of Limitations* According to the second Restatement of Trusts most states have "no Statute of Limitations applicable to equitable claims" but they may be barred by "laches of the claimant." Laches depends on a variety of factors in addition to the mere lapse of time, such as the reason (if any) for the plaintiff's delay in bringing suit, and the extent of hardship to the defendant if relief were given despite the delay.[77] A complaint that a bank trustee committed a breach of trust in selling stock was barred by laches when the beneficiary "had or should have had knowledge * * * of the trustee's conduct for nearly nineteen years before filing suit," and "the trustee was prejudiced by the delay. * * * Various records were misplaced or destroyed. * * * More importantly, * * * the ability of the trustee to reverse its actions by repurchasing the stock became more difficult."[78] On the other hand, a court rejected the laches defense asserted against two beneficiaries, one of whom was a minor. "Laches cannot be imputed to a person during his or her minority." As to the other beneficiary, when "a fiduciary has a duty to disclose certain facts to the plaintiff but fraudulently fails to do so, the plaintiff's failure to discover the facts is excused and the time begins to run when the fraud is actually discovered."[79]

In most recent cases, the defense is a statute of limitations rather than laches. Such statutes provide a fixed period rather than leaving it to the court's discretion,[80] but the statutes also may involve a "balancing test to weigh the hardship imposed on the claimant by the application of the statute of limitations against any

the trust in proceedings to probate a will).

**75.** Fratcher, *Trustees' Powers Legislation*, 37 NYU L.Rev. 627, 662 (1962); Wellman, *Recent Developments in the Struggle for Probate Reform,* 79 Mich. L.Rev. 501, 516 (1981).

**76.** Uniform Probate Code § 3–1005. Id., § 7–307 is similar as to trustees.

**77.** *Restatement, Second, of Trusts* § 219, comm. a (1959).

**78.** Stevens v. National City Bank, 544 N.E.2d 612, 621 (Ohio 1989); *cf.*

First Ala. Bank v. Martin, 425 So.2d 415, 424 (Ala.1982) (laches defense rejected because no showing of prejudice to the defendant).

**79.** Kurtz v. Solomon, 656 N.E.2d 184, 192 (Ill.App.1995).

**80.** *E.g.*, McDonald v. U.S. National Bank, 830 P.2d 618 (Or.App.1992) (trustee protected by 2 year statute); Beall v. Beall, 577 S.E.2d 356, 360 (N.C.App. 2003) (custodian protected by three year statute).

prejudice to the defendant resulting from the passage of time."[81] The Uniform Trust Code allows beneficiaries only one year to bring suit if the trustee sent them "a report that adequately disclosed the existence of a potential claim for breach of trust."[82]

*Consent* Beneficiaries' consent may prevent them from challenging a fiduciary's action. An attempt to surcharge trustees for "an aggressive, risky investment policy" failed because the beneficiaries had signed a form by which they "acknowledge the high degree of economic risk associated with these investments" and nevertheless approved them.[83] Writing is not necessary.[84] The Restatement says that mere failure to object does not amount to consent,[85] but there are many cases to the contrary.[86] Consent and laches sometimes overlap. Beneficiaries who sought to upset an executor's sale of mineral interests were held to have "ratified" the sale by accepting checks arising therefrom. Furthermore, because of the "violent fluctuations of value" in mineral interests, "there is no class of cases in which the doctrine of laches has been more relentlessly enforced."[87]

When one beneficiary has consented but others have not, courts will give a remedy to the nonconsenting beneficiaries.[88] But some trusts provide that children are bound by their parents' consent.[89] Consent by the holder of a general power of appointment may bar relief for the persons designated to take in default of appointment.[90] Consent to a breach by the settlor of a revocable trust bars claims by all the beneficiaries.[91]

A spendthrift trust beneficiary can effectively consent but not an incapacitated beneficiary, or one of "limited understanding,"[92] e.g. "an elderly woman whose schooling had ended at age 10."[93] But

**81.** Snow v. Rudd, 998 P.2d 262, 266 (Utah 2000).

**82.** Unif.Trust Code § 1005(a).

**83.** Beyer v. First Nat. Bank, 843 P.2d 53, 56 (Colo.App.1992). *See also* In re Estate of Gleeson, 655 N.W.2d 69, 74 (N.D.2002) (sale by executor at below market value not a breach when devisees consented).

**84.** *Restatement, Second, of Trusts* § 216 (1959).

**85.** *Id.,* comm. (a).

**86.** In re Estate of Winograd, 582 N.E.2d 1047, 1050 (Ohio App.1989). *See also* Matter of Trusts Under Will of Dwan, 371 N.W.2d 641, 643 (Minn.App. 1985) (failure to object for years "constituted a waiver").

**87.** Jackson v. Braden, 717 S.W.2d 206, 208 (Ark.1986).

**88.** Gaynor v. Payne, 804 A.2d 170, 176 (Conn. 2002) (release by income beneficiaries did not bar their children who had remainder interests).

**89.** In re McGuire Marital Trust, 660 N.W.2d 308, 316 (Wis.App.2003) (trust provision making income beneficiaries' approval of accounts binding).

**90.** *Restatement, Second, of Trusts* § 216, comm. h (1959). *See also* Uniform Prob.Code § 1–108.

**91.** Head v. Wachovia Bank of Georgia, N.A., 88 S.W.3d 180 (Tenn.App. 2002); Cal.Prob.Code § 16462.

**92.** *Restatement, Second, of Trusts* § 216, comm. e, m (1959).

**93.** Stephan v. Equitable Savings and Loan Ass'n, 522 P.2d 478, 489 (Or. 1974).

trustees who reasonably believed that a beneficiary was capable of consenting may be protected. When the settlor authorized withdrawals from a revocable trust, a claim that she was incompetent was irrelevant if "the trustee did not know or have any reason to believe" this.[94]

Consent given by a beneficiary who did not know relevant facts is ineffective, e.g., a beneficiary who consented to a trustee's buying land from the trust for $40,000 without knowing that the property had been appraised at $500,000.[95]

*Remedies Against Third Parties* Beneficiaries of an estate or trust may also have remedies against persons other than the fiduciary. Trust beneficiaries were allowed to sue accountants hired by the trustees; a beneficiary "has the right that third persons shall not knowingly join with the trustee in a breach of trust. * * * Mere knowledge by a third person that a breach of trust is in process, coupled with a failure to notify the beneficiary or to interfere with the action of the trustee does not amount to participation in a breach * * * On the other hand if the third party by any act whatsoever assists the trustee in wrongfully transferring the benefits of the trust property * * * liability can be [imposed]."[96] A court upheld a claim against a lawyer who had established a guardianship without having the guardian post a bond as required by law, saying that an "action for breach against the guardian is likely to be an empty remedy absent a bond."[97] But another court rejected a claim by beneficiaries of an estate against the attorney for the personal representative, saying that imposing duties on lawyers "to a nonclient creates a risk of divided loyalties because of a conflicting interest."[98]

Officers of a corporate trustee who cause the trustee to commit a breach of trust have been held liable for the resulting loss.[99] The Uniform Prudent Investor Act imposes on agents exercising a delegated function a duty of reasonable care to the trust.[100] A person who has power by the terms of a trust to control the trustee's actions may be deemed a fiduciary and "liable for any loss

**94.** Cloud v. United States Nat. Bank, 570 P.2d 350, 355 (Or.1977). Under *Restatement, Second, of Trusts* § 216(2) (1959) and Cal.Prob.Code § 16463(b), however, a trustee's reasonable belief is relevant as to the beneficiary's knowledge of material facts, but not as to the beneficiary's capacity.

**95.** Ford City Bank v. Ford City Bank, 441 N.E.2d 1192, 1195 (Ill.App. 1982).

**96.** Gillespie v. Seymour, 796 P.2d 1060, 1065 (Kan.App.1990). *See also Re-*statement, Second, of Trusts § 326 (1959).

**97.** In re Guardianship of Karan, 38 P.3d 396, 400–01 (Wash.App. 2002).

**98.** Trask v. Butler, 872 P.2d 1080, 1085 (Wash. 1994).

**99.** Seven G Ranching Co. v. Stewart Title, 627 P.2d 1088, 1091 (Ariz.App. 1981).

**100.** Unif.Prud.Inv.Act § 9(b).

resulting to the trust estate from a breach of his duty as fiduciary."[101]

Normally actions against third persons who injure trust property must be brought by the trustee, but a beneficiary can sue when "the beneficiary's interests are hostile to those of the trustee,"[102] *e.g.* when the third party and trustee have participated in a breach of trust. A fiduciary who has been surcharged for an improper distribution may claim indemnification from the recipient.[103]

*Banks* Banks according to the Restatement are liable for permitting a withdrawal of trust funds from an account "with notice of a breach of trust,"[104] but if they had no actual knowledge, they are usually protected by a statute.[105]

Banks have been held liable for paying a depositor's money to an "agent" under a forged power of attorney.[106] But in order to encourage banks to deal with agents under durable powers, many statutes protect third persons who deal with an agent "in good faith" despite defects in the agent's power, e.g., a savings and loan association which had allowed an agent to withdraw over $135,000 from the principal's account. "Where an agent draws checks on his principal's bank account, payable to himself, and deposits them to his own account, the mere form of the transaction * * * is not sufficient to put the depositing bank on notice of the agent's fraud."[107]

The second Restatement of Trusts imposed liability on corporations who registered transfers of securities "with notice" that the transfer was a breach of trust, but added that "experience indicates" that this rule "has not been very effective" in preventing breaches of trust, and should be abolished.[108] This was accomplished by a widely adopted Uniform Act for the Simplification of Fiduciary Security Transfers.

*Bona–Fide Purchase* When property of a trust has been transferred to a bona-fide purchaser for value, the latter is protected even if the fiduciary was acting improperly. Uniform Probate Code

**101.** *Restatement, Second, of Trusts* § 185, comm. h (1959).

**102.** Anderson v. Dean Witter Reynolds, Inc., 841 P.2d 742, 745 (Utah App. 1992); *cf. Restatement, Second, of Trusts* § 282(2) (1959) (beneficiary can sue when trustee improperly neglects to sue).

**103.** *Id.,*§ 254; Section 12.10.

**104.** *Restatement, Second, of Trusts* § 324 (1959).

**105.** Heilig Trust and Benef. v. First Interstate, 969 P.2d 1082, 1085 (Wash. App.1998).

**106.** In re Estate of Davis, 632 N.E.2d 64 (Ill.App.1994).

**107.** Bank IV, Olathe v. Capitol Federal S & L, 828 P.2d 355, 357–58, 363 (Kan.1992). See also Johnson v. Edwardsville Nat. Bank & Trust Co., 594 N.E.2d 342, 345 (Ill.App.1992) (bank protected where principal incompetent when power executed).

**108.** *Restatement, Second, of Trusts* § 325 (1959).

§ 3–714 similarly protects persons who deal with a personal representative "in good faith for value."[109]

Persons claiming to be bona-fide purchasers often flounder on the issue of good faith. One who knows *or should know* of the breach of trust does not qualify.[110] A guarantee given to a bank by only one of two trustees was ineffective because a bank officer had read the trust instrument and someone who "has actual knowledge of what a trust says is charged with actual knowledge of what it means."[111]

Traditionally purchasers could rarely be in "good faith" if they knew they were dealing with a fiduciary. This in turn depended on how title to the property was held. If land was conveyed "to *X*" in trust, but without designating *X* as trustee in the deed, *X* might be treated as the outright owner as to persons "dealing with *[X]* in good faith and for a valuable consideration."[112] Transactions in securities could be facilitated if title was registered in a way which did not reveal that the registered owner was a trustee. At common law trustees were supposed "to see that trust property is designated as property of the trust," but modern trusts often expressly allow trustees to hold property in the name of a nominee rather than "as trustee."[113] Modern statutes, such as the Uniform Trustees' Powers Act, also permit this.[114]

Historically, the liability of third parties was often needed to make the beneficiaries whole, since their remedies against a defaulting trustee might be of little value. Today fiduciaries are usually solvent (or bonded), and so modern law tends to protect purchasers in order not to deter them from dealing with fiduciaries. In order to "facilitate prompt and economic administration of estates" third parties should "be able to deal with personal representatives without concern for [their] authority or duty to the beneficiaries .* * * The beneficiaries' remedy is not to void the transaction but to seek damages for the personal representative's breach of his fiduciary duty."[115]

Under the Restatement purchasers from a trustee had "to inquire as to the terms of the trust,"[116] but the Uniform Probate

---

**109.** The same principle applies to other persons dealing with fiduciaries. *Restatement, Second, of Trusts* § 284 (1959); Uniform Trust Code § 1012(a).

**110.** *Restatement, Second, of Trusts* § 297 (1959).

**111.** Farmers State Bank of Yuma v. Harmon, 778 F.2d 543, 547 (10th Cir. 1985). *See also Restatement, Second, of Trusts* § 297, comm. j (1959) (one who knows the terms of a trust "is chargeable with notice of the legal effect of those terms").

**112.** Cal.Prob.Code § 18103.

**113.** *Restatement, Second, of Trusts* § 179 (1959).

**114.** Unif.Trust Code § 816(7)(B); N.Y. EPTL § 11.1–1(b)(10); Wisc.Stat. § 701.19(6).

**115.** Wittick v. Miles, 545 P.2d 121, 126 (Or.1976).

**116.** *Restatement, Second, of Trusts* § 297, comm. f (1959).

Code relieves third parties who deal with personal representatives from any such duty.[117] These provisions facilitate transfers and protect the privacy of the trust beneficiaries. Under the Uniform Trust Code third persons who do inquire into the terms of a trust must be content with a certification of the facts relevant to them, e.g., the powers of the trustee, without seeing the dispositive terms of the trust.[118]

*Creditors and Donees*    Creditors of a trustee sometimes seek to reach trust property claiming they had no notice that it was held in trust. A court rejected such a claim, not; since the creditors had not relied on the trustee's apparent ownership of the property in lending him money.[119]

A donee is not a bona fide purchaser for value even if he had no inkling that the transfer was improper.[120] But a donee who has "so changed his position that it would be inequitable to compel him to restore" the property is protected.[121]

# § 12.9   Duty of Loyalty

Trustees must "administer the trust solely in the interest of the beneficiary."[1] This "duty of loyalty" also applies to other fiduciaries, such as agents[2] and fiduciaries of pension plans.[3] It applies most often to situations in which the fiduciary's personal interests conflict with those of the beneficiaries, e.g. when a trustee sells the trustee's own property to the trust or buys an asset of the trust. A trustee-executor was removed because he sold an asset of the estate to his son, even though the land was sold at a public auction for a fair price.[4]

The Uniform Probate Code makes voidable "any transaction which is affected by a substantial conflict of interest on the part of the personal representative."[5] Since self-dealing transactions are

**117.** Uniform Probate Code § 3–714. *See also* Unif.Trust Code § 1012(c).

**118.** Unif.Trust Code § 1013, based on Calif.Prob.Code § 18100.5.

**119.** Lagae v. Lackner, 996 P.2d 1281 (Colo.2000).

**120.** Kampschroeder v. Kampschroeder, 887 P.2d 1152, 1158 (Kan.App. 1995); *Restatement, Second, of Trusts* § 289 (1959).

**121.** *Id.* § 292(1).

**§ 12.9**

**1.** *Restatement, Second, of Trusts* § 170(1) (1959). *See also* Unif.Trust Code § 802(a).

**2.** First Nat. Bank v. Cooper, 312 S.E.2d 607 (Ga.1984) (agent cannot use

principal's property to secure loan to agent).

**3.** 29 U.S.C. § 1104(a)(1).

**4.** Matter of Estate of Hawley, 538 N.E.2d 1220, 1222 (Ill.App.1989). *But see* In re Estate of Howser, 639 N.W.2d 485, 490 (N.D. 2002) (refusing to remove an executor who purchased a car from the estate at a fair price).

**5.** Uniform Probate Code § 3–713. *See also* Williamson v. Williamson, 714 N.E.2d 1270 (Ind.App.1999) (sale by executor to himself set aside).

only "voidable," the beneficiaries can affirm them. It does not matter that a disinterested co-fiduciary approved a self-dealing transaction.[6]

Although the basic duty of loyalty is well settled, there is some uncertainty around the edges. A court refused to void an executor's sale to his daughter, saying that the ban applied to sales to the fiduciary or the fiduciary's spouse but not "to other persons who bear a close family relationship."[7] The Uniform Trusts Act, however, bars purchases and sales "from or to a relative" which is defined to include a spouse, ancestor, descendant or sibling.[8]

The duty of loyalty also applies when a fiduciary has ties to a company which deals with the estate or trust. An executor's sale of stock to a company of which he was an officer and director was set aside under a statute barring executors from buying estate property "directly or indirectly."[9] However, some conflicts of interest are deemed insubstantial; a court vacated a sale of stock by a corporate trustee to its president but not a sale to a stockholder of the trustee.[10]

Lawyers who represent a family with a business may also encounter conflicts of interest. A lawyer who represented an estate was held liable for a below-market-value sale made by the estate to a client of the lawyer; the lawyer had recommended the sale without disclosing the conflict of interest.[11] Lawyers involved in self dealing while acting as fiduciaries are subject to discipline under the rules of professional conduct.[12]

*Exceptions: Court Approval*   The duty of loyalty is qualified by exceptions. Otherwise, it would pose difficulties for estates or trusts which need to sell property for which there is an inadequate market, like a family corporation, where the fiduciary may be the most likely buyer.[13]

---

**6.** Stegemeier v. Magness, 728 A.2d 557 (Del.1999) (sale by estate to company owned by an administrator is voidable although approved by a disinterested administrator). In this respect trustees differ from directors of corporations. Oberly v. Kirby, 592 A.2d 445, 466–67 (Del. 1991).

**7.** In re Estate of Hughes, 641 N.E.2d 248, 251 (Ohio App.1994). *But see* note 4 supra.

**8.** Uniform Trusts Act §§ 1(3), 5. *See also Restatement, Third, of Trusts* § 78, comm. e (PrelDft.2003) which is stricter than *Restatement, Second, of Trusts* § 170, comm. e (1959).

**9.** In re Estate of Martin, 86 Cal. Rptr.2d 37 (App.1999). *See also* Unif.

Trust Code § 802(c)(4) (sale to or investment in a company in which the trustee has a significant interest).

**10.** Steiner v. Hawaiian Trust Co., 393 P.2d 96, 104 (Haw.1964).

**11.** Kelly v. Foster, 813 P.2d 598 (Wash.App.1991).

**12.** Office of Disciplinary Counsel v. Kurtz, 693 N.E.2d 1080 (Ohio 1998) (lawyer-trustee suspended for lending trust funds to self); In re Cohen, 8 P.3d 429 (Colo.1999) (lawyer suspended for loan of trust funds to company which lawyer represented).

**13.** Wellman, *Punitive Surcharges Against Disloyal Fiduciaries*, 77 Mich. L.Rev. 95, 114 (1978). "ERISA's duty of

The Uniform Probate Code allows self-dealing if "the transaction is approved by the Court after notice to interested persons."[14] Courts approve such transactions only when the advantages are clear, *e.g.* if "there are no other available purchasers willing to pay the same price the trustee is willing to pay."[15] Approval need not precede the transaction. A conservator's sale of a house to his daughter, though not approved at the time, was not subject to challenge because of orders approving his annual accountings.[16]

*Authorization in Instrument*  Self dealing is proper if it is authorized by the will or trust,[17] but even a broadly drafted power does not necessarily permit self-dealing. A court set aside sales by an executor to himself even thought the will allowed the executor to sell to "any purchaser."[18] Even explicit authorization for self dealing does not permit a trustee to "act in bad faith."[19] Although a trust allowed the trustees to lease trust property to their automobile dealership, they were surcharged for making the lease without any "determination whether the rental rates were reasonable in the current market."[20] But sales which are personally advantageous to the fiduciary may be authorized, *e.g.,* when the will or a contract gave an executor an option to buy property at a favorable price.[21]

Authorization for self-dealing can be inferred from the circumstances. A court upheld a sale by trustees of stock to a company of which a trustee was officer and director. The settlor was aware of his brother's interest in the closely-held family corporations and yet chose to "name his brother * * * as Co–Trustee of trusts whose primary assets were stock in those same corporations. * * * The settlor must have understood that his Co–Trustee would take into consideration the interests of the corporation as well as the interest of the beneficiary in making any decisions concerning the family corporations' stock held by the Trusts."[22]

loyalty is buttressed by the so-called 'prohibited transactions rules' which are so sweeping that they require an elaborate set of exemptions to rescue innocent transactions." Langbein, *What ERISA Means by "Equitable": The Supreme Court's Trail of Error in Russell, Mertens, and Great West*, 103 Colum.L.Rev. 1317, 1325n (2003).

**14.**  Uniform Probate Code § 3–713. *See also* Unif.Trust Code § 802(b)(2).

**15.**  Wachovia Bank and Trust Co. v. Johnston, 153 S.E.2d 449, 460 (N.C. 1967).

**16.**  Matter of Conservatorship of Holman, 849 P.2d 140, 142 (Kan.App. 1993).

**17.**  Uniform Probate Code § 3–713; Unif.Trust Code § 802(b)(1).

**18.**  Powell v. Thorsen, 322 S.E.2d 261, 263 (Ga.1984).

**19.**  *Restatement, Second, of Trusts* § 170, comm. t (1959).

**20.**  Mest v. Dugan, 790 P.2d 38, 41 (Or.App.1990).

**21.**  McPherson v. Dauenhauer, 69 P.3d 733 (Or.App.2003).

**22.**  Huntington Nat'l Bank v. Wolfe, 651 N.E.2d 458, 464 (Ohio App.1994). Although Unif.Trust Code § 802(b)(1) speaks of the duty of loyalty being overridden "by the terms of the trust," the comment says that such an override can sometimes be "implied."

*Statutory Exceptions*    The Uniform Trustees' Powers Act and many state statutes allow banks serving as trustee to deposit trust funds in their own banking department.[23] Nevertheless, a bank trustee was surcharged for keeping excessive sums on self-deposit. "A bank-trustee does not commit a per se breach of trust by depositing with itself * * * cash which it holds as trustee," but it should not leave cash unproductive except for overriding liquidity needs.[24]

A corporate trustee holding its own stock in the trust also raises conflict of interest problems; the trustee may hold on to the stock in order to avoid depressing its value, or to bar a take-over by a purchaser who plans to install a new management.[25] The Restatement does not allow corporate trustees to purchase their own shares for the trust or even to "retain shares of its own stock which it has received from the settlor * * * unless such retention is expressly or impliedly authorized by the terms of the trust or by statute,"[26] but many statutes allow corporate trustees to retain, but not to purchase their own shares.[27]

*Self-Hiring*    Many statutes authorize corporate fiduciaries to invest in mutual funds which they manage for a fee.[28] A comment to the Uniform Trust Code justifies this exception by the advantages of investing in mutual funds, and suggests that such investments "may be taken into account" in setting the trustee's compensation.[29]

*Fiduciaries Acting in Two Capacities*    Often the same fiduciary acts in two capacities for the same beneficiaries, *e.g.* as executor and trustee, or as trustee of several trusts for the same family. Can the ABC Bank as trustee of an insurance trust buy assets from itself as the executor of the insured's probate estate? Such a transaction can provide a market for hard to sell assets, and the potential conflict of interest is attenuated since the Bank has no personal interest in the matter. The California Probate Code allows sales and exchanges between two trusts where the same trustee administers both if the transaction is "fair and reasonable with respect to the beneficiaries of both trusts" and the beneficiaries are

---

**23.** Uniform Trustees' Powers Act § 3(c)(6); Unif.Trust Code § 802(h)(4); Cal.Prob.Code (§ 16225).

**24.** Maryland Nat'l Bank v. Cummins, 588 A.2d 1205, 1213 (Md.1991).

**25.** Donovan v. Bierwirth, 754 F.2d 1049 (2d Cir.1985) (trustee used pension fund to buy stock to block a takeover).

**26.** *Restatement, Second, of Trusts* § 170, comm. n (1959); First Ala. Bank v. Spragins, 515 So.2d 962 (Ala.1987) (trustee surcharged for retaining its own

stock). *Contra,* Elmhurst Nat. Bank v. Glos, 241 N.E.2d 121 (Ill.App.1968).

**27.** Tex.Prop.Code § 113.055; Ky. Rev.Stat. § 386.025; Mo.Stat. § 362.550(5).

**28.** *E.g.,* Estate of Vail v. First of America Trust, 722 N.E.2d 248, 252 (Ill. App.1999) (upholding such an investment as authorized by statute); Unif. Trust Code § 802(f).

**29.** Unif.Trust Code § 803, comment.

notified.[30] The Uniform Trustees' Powers Act, however, requires court approval regardless whether a conflict involves the trustee's "individual interest or his interest as trustee of another trust."[31]

*Contracts Between Fiduciary and Beneficiary* In any dealings between a fiduciary and a competent beneficiary, the beneficiary can protect his or her own interests and so such contracts are not *ipso facto* voidable.[32] But often the parties do not deal on equal terms, *e.g.* the very reason why the settlor put property in trust was the beneficiary's lack of business acumen. Therefore the Restatement of Trusts requires trustees who contract with a beneficiary "on the trustee's own account" to "deal fairly" and communicate to the beneficiary all material facts in connection with the transaction.[33] An agreement between an executor and his siblings that he should receive $56,000 in settlement of his claims against the estate was set aside because the executor had failed to advise his siblings, over whom he enjoyed "total domination," that his claims were barred because they had not been filed in time.[34] These restrictions only apply to contracts which are "within the scope of the fiduciary relationship," a line which is not easy to draw.

*Social Investing* Scott argued that in choosing investments trustees could avoid securities of corporations whose actions were "contrary to fundamental and generally accepted ethical principles. They may consider such matters as pollution, race discrimination, fair employment and consumer responsibility."[35] Langbein and Posner on the other hand argue that any consideration of social objectives is inconsistent with the trustees' duty "to administer the trust *solely* in the interest of the beneficiary."[36] They particularly objected to pension funds divesting their holdings in companies which did business in South Africa during the era of apartheid. Nevertheless, Scott's view was approved by a court in upholding a city ordinance that required pension trustees to divest their South Africa holdings.[37]

The third Restatement of Trusts, accepts the Langbein/Posner view: a trustee's investment decisions "must not be motivated by a purpose of advancing or expressing the trustee's personal views

**30.** Cal.Prob.Code § 16002. *See also* Unif.Trust Code § 802(h)(3).

**31.** Uniform Trustees' Powers Act § 5(b).

**32.** Matter of Winslow's Estate, 636 P.2d 505 (Wash.App.1981).

**33.** *Restatement, Second, of Trusts* § 170(2) (1959). *See also* Unif. Trust Code § 802(d).

**34.** Matter of Hamilton, 637 P.2d 542, 545 (N.M.1981). *See also* delaVergne v. delaVergne, 514 So.2d 186 (La.

App.1987) (executor's purchase of property from devisee voided).

**35.** 3 A. Scott, *Trusts* § 227.17 (4th ed. Fratcher 1987).

**36.** Langbein & Posner, *Social Investing and the Law of Trusts*, 79 Mich. L.Rev. 71, 85, 96–98 (1979).

**37.** Board of Trustees v. City of Baltimore, 562 A.2d 720, 727, 737 (Md. 1989).

concerning social or political issues."[38] Discussion on this issue has focused primarily on pension funds, perhaps because of their vast size. Most pension funds are governed by ERISA which, like trust law, requires fiduciaries to act "solely in the interests of the participants and beneficiaries."[39]

Charitable trusts differ from private trusts because social benefits *are* their objective and they have no private beneficiaries. However, money which is given for one charitable purpose cannot be diverted to another, and any investing decision must be justified "on grounds of advancing" one of the trust purposes.[40]

## § 12.10    Accounting and Distribution

*Accounting to Beneficiaries* Fiduciaries have a duty to keep the beneficiaries informed about the property they are managing for them and the terms of the governing instrument.[1] Trustees must also "keep and render clear and accurate accounts with respect to the administration of the trust."[2] A beneficiary can compel a trustee to account without alleging any wrongdoing by the trustee. Even contingent beneficiaries and persons to whom the trustee is authorized but not required to make distributions can demand an accounting.[3] But the beneficiaries of a revocable trust are not entitled to one so long as the settlor is still alive and has capacity.[4]

Provisions in a trust relieving the trustee from any duty to account have been held invalid, assuming that a true trust was intended rather than a gift to the "trustee."[5] A "settlor who attempts to create a trust without any accountability in the trustee is contradicting himself."[6]

*Accounting in Court* Accounting to the beneficiaries must be distinguished from accounting in court. Guardians/conservators must file accounts periodically in court.[7] Many states require court

---

**38.** *Restatement, Third, of Trusts* § 227, comm. c (1990).

**39.** 29 U.S.C. § 1104(a)(1).

**40.** *Restatement, Third, of Trusts* § 227, comm. c (1990).

### § 12.10

**1.** *Restatement, Second, of Trusts* § 173 (1959); Unif.Trust Code § 813(a); McNeil v. McNeil, 798 A.2d 503, 510 (Del. 2002) (trustees properly surcharged for failure to tell beneficiary that he was one).

**2.** *Restatement, Second, of Trusts* § 172 (1959). *See also* Uniform Probate Code § 7–303(c). Uniform Trust Code § 813 uses the term "reports" instead of

"accounting" so as to "negate any inference that the report must be prepared in any particular format." Comment.

**3.** Goodpasteur v. Fried, 539 N.E.2d 207 (Ill.App.1989).

**4.** Cal.Prob.Code § 16064(b); Unif. Trust Code § 603; In re Malasky, 736 N.Y.S.2d 151 (A.D. 2002).

**5.** McNeil v. McNeil, 798 A.2d 503, 509 (Del. 2002); *Restatement, Second, of Trusts* § 172, comm. d (1959); Unif. Trust Code § 105(b)(9) (duty to inform beneficiaries prevails over trust terms).

**6.** Raak v. Raak, 428 N.W.2d 778, 780 (Mich.App.1988).

**7.** Cal.Prob.Code § 2620.

accountings for personal representatives,[8] but under the Uniform Probate Code, however, if administration is not "supervised," the personal representative can close an estate simply by filing a statement that he has given an account to the distributees, although the personal representative or any interested person can ask for court review of an account.[9] A direction for supervised administration in the will may be ignored if "circumstances bearing on the need for supervised administration" changed after the will was signed. Conversely, a direction for unsupervised administration is not binding if supervision is found to be necessary to protect interested persons.[10] Cautious fiduciaries may seek the "greater protection" afforded by court approval of accounts even when it is not required.[11]

Many states also require court accounting by testamentary trustees.[12] Court supervision of testamentary trusts has come under attack. Some trustees charge higher fees for testamentary trusts because of the cost of court accountings, which also focus "unwanted publicity" on the beneficiaries' financial affairs. These disadvantages are not justified by the protection they afford.[13] Also, it is hard to justify the distinction between living and testamentary trusts.[14] Many states have reduced or eliminated periodic judicial review of trustees' accounts. The Uniform Probate Code makes trust administration "free of judicial intervention."[15] Courts have jurisdiction, however, when it is "invoked by interested parties" to "review and settle interim or final accounts."[16]

Even states which require court accountings allow the interested parties to waive them,[17] but beneficiaries who are unborn, unascertained, or minors cannot approve or waive accounts. The fee of a guardian ad litem to represent such beneficiaries is often a significant cost which can be avoided by a provision in the trust instrument allowing one or more adult beneficiaries to approve accounts.[18] Under the Uniform Probate Code guardians ad litem are

**8.** In California, this includes even "independent" executors and administrators *Id.*, § 10501(a)(3).

**9.** Uniform Probate Code §§ 3–1001, 3–1003(a).

**10.** *Id.* § 3–502.

**11.** *Id.* § 3–1005, comment..

**12.** 12 Del.Code Ann. § 3521. This is one of the reasons for avoiding probate by a revocable living trust. See Section 9.1.

**13.** Westfall, *Nonjudicial Settlement of Trustees Accounts,* 71 Harv.L.Rev. 40, 49–50 (1958).

**14.** Uniform Probate Code, Article VII, comment.

**15.** *Id.,* § 7–201(b).

**16.** *Id.,* § 7–201. *See also* Cal.Prob. Code § 17200(a)(5).

**17.** *Id.,* § 10954 (waiver of account by personal representative).

**18.** Approval by such a designated beneficiary discharges the trustee only if it is given "in good faith." *Restatement, Second, of Trusts* § 172, comm. d (1959).

appointed only if "representation of the interest otherwise would be inadequate."[19]

*Decree of Distribution* Normally when a court approves a final account it also enters a decree of distribution. The Uniform Probate Code allows personal representatives to distribute assets of the estate without court authorization.[20] No court order is generally required for distributions by trustees, but a beneficiary can get a court order if a distribution is improperly made or withheld and trustees in doubt as to a distribution can seek instructions from the court.

A decree of distribution may supersede the terms of a will or trust,[21] but decrees made without proper notice to interested parties do not bind them.[22] A notice of a hearing is insufficient if it does not "provide sufficient information that will allow the [recipient] intelligently to ascertain the issue the hearing will address"[23]

A decree can also be attacked on the ground that it purported to determine title to property which did not belong to the decedent. "A probate court may only determine who takes property owned by the decedent,"[24] but the Uniform Probate Code allows the probate court "to determine title to property alleged to belong to the estate."[25]

Some courts ignore a mistaken decree if the court which rendered it failed to focus on the relevant issue. Collateral attack on a judgment is barred if "the court had actually construed a will, albeit erroneously" but not if the court "made an obvious mistake."[26] Finally, a decree of distribution has been set aside for "extrinsic fraud" when the applicant for an estate failed to reveal the existence of a closer heir of the decedent.[27]

*Liability for Improper Distribution* Fiduciaries can be held liable for making distributions to the wrong person.[28] The Restatement of Trusts exonerates trustees "for a misdelivery resulting from a reasonable, good faith reliance" on the terms of the trust,

**19.** Uniform Probate Code § 1–403(4). As to "virtual representation" see Section 12.8.

**20.** Unless the administration is "supervised." Uniform Probate Code §§ 3–504, 3–704.

**21.** First Hawaiian Bank v. Weeks, 772 P.2d 1187, 1191 (Haw.1989).

**22.** Matter of Estate of Hoffas, 422 N.W.2d 391, 395 (N.D.1988).

**23.** Booth v. McKnight, 70 P.3d 855, 865 (Okl.2003).

**24.** Apple v. Kile, 457 N.E.2d 254, 258 (Ind.App.1983).

**25.** Uniform Probate Code § 3–105.

**26.** Loberg v. Alford, 372 N.W.2d 912, 918 (N.D.1985). *See also* Harvey v. Harvey, 524 P.2d 1187, 1192 (Kan.1974) (invalidity of restraint on alienation can be asserted because issue "was not raised in the probate court").

**27.** Estate of McGuigan, 99 Cal. Rptr.2d 887 (App.2000).

**28.** Deluca v. Jordan, 781 N.E.2d 849 (Mass.App.2003) (administrator surcharged for erroneous distribution based on heir's forged signature).

but if the trust terms are ambiguous, the trustee must apply to a court for instructions.[29] The Restatement also protects trustees who make payments under a trust which is later held invalid or revoked unless they knew had reason to suspect the true situation.[30] Similarly, the Uniform Probate Code exonerates personal representatives for distributions which were "authorized at the time" *e.g.,* a distribution of apparently intestate assets to the heirs when a will is later probated.

A person who receives an erroneous distribution is liable under the Uniform Probate Code unless the distribution can "no longer can be questioned because of adjudication, estoppel, or limitation."[31] Thus a personal representative who was forced to pay estate taxes personally was allowed reimbursement from a distributee; the defendant's claim of laches was rejected because he was not substantially prejudiced by the delay.[32] The Restatement of Trusts has a similar provision for trustees.[33]

*Retainer* When a devisee or heir owes money to the decedent, personal representatives can normally set off this debt against any distribution to which the debtor is entitled. But under the Uniform Probate Code, they cannot thereby indirectly collect an unenforceable debt, since the debtor "has the benefit of any defense which would be available to him in a direct proceeding for recovery of the debt," such as a statute of limitations or a discharge in bankruptcy.[34]

*Distributions to Incompetents* Fiduciaries who distribute to persons who are legally incapacitated risk having to pay again. A trustee was surcharged for permitting an incompetent settlor to withdraw funds from a revocable trust when the trustee should have known of her incompetency.[35] To be safe, executors and administrators usually must distribute shares of a minor heir or devisee to a guardian or conservator, but many states have "facility of payment" statutes for small amounts. The Uniform Probate Code allows "a person required to transfer money or property to a minor" to do so "as to an amount or value not exceeding $5,000 a year, by transferring it to (1) a person who has the care and custody of the minor with whom the minor resides." The recipient

**29.** *Restatement, Third, of Trusts* § 76, comm. f (Prel.Dft.2003)

**30.** *Ibid. See also Restatement, Second, of Trusts* § 226A (1959); *cf.* Unif. Trust Code § 604(b).

**31.** Uniform Probate Code § 3–909.

**32.** Quintana v. Quintana, 802 P.2d 488, 491 (Idaho App.1990).

**33.** *Restatement, Second, of Trusts* § 254 (1959). *See also* Unif. Trust Code § 604(c); In re Estate of Berger, 520 N.E.2d 690 (Ill.App.1987) (conservator's surety).

**34.** Uniform Probate Code § 3–903; Matter of Will of Cargill, 420 N.W.2d 268 (Minn.App. 1988) (trustee cannot withhold income to satisfy claim against beneficiary which was discharged in bankruptcy).

**35.** Cloud v. United States Nat. Bank, 570 P.2d 350, 355–56 (Or.1977).

must apply the money for the minor's support and turn over any balance to the minor at majority.[36]

Even without a statute, trustees can apply income for the benefit of an incapacitated beneficiary instead of paying it to the beneficiary. "If the trustee has good-faith doubt concerning a beneficiary's practical or legal capacity to handle funds, distributions to which the beneficiary is entitled may be retained and managed by the trustee. * * * Thus, it will ordinarily be unnecessary for a personal fiduciary (guardian, conservator, or the like) to be appointed for the beneficiary."[37]

Many trusts and wills confer broad powers to deal with this problem, e.g. authorizing the executor to deliver any sum due to a minor "to the then living parents of such minor, without bond."[38]

*Distribution in Kind* Distributions are sometimes made in cash, sometimes in kind. Distributions in kind to satisfy pecuniary devises raise the problem of valuation. If a will leaves $10,000 to the testator's sister and the executor proposes to satisfy this by distributing XYZ stock, the stock must be valued for this purpose at the date of distribution.[39] Thus if the assets of an estate appreciate or depreciate during administration, the benefit or burden of the change falls on the residuary and specific devisees, not pecuniary devisees.

When heirs or residuary devisees are entitled to fractional shares, can a fiduciary make non-prorata distributions, *e.g.,* all the XYZ stock to one, and other assets of comparable value to the others? The California Probate Code authorizes trustees to make such non-pro-rata distributions,[40] but the Uniform Probate Code gives each residuary beneficiary a right "to his proportionate share of each asset constituting the residue."[41] Non-pro-rata distributions can avoid divided ownership, but they too raise valuation problems.

*Delay in Distribution* One of the most common complaints about lawyers and the legal system arises from delay in distribution of assets in administration. This is a commonly cited reason for the widespread popular desire to avoid probate. Some states penalize personal representative who unduly delay distribution.[42] However, courts defer to reasonable decisions by fiduciaries, e.g., they can

**36.** Unif.Prob.Code § 5–104.

**37.** *Restatement, Third, of Trusts* § 49, comm. c(2) (2001).

**38.** In re Estate of Tate, 543 S.W.2d 588, 590 (Tenn.1976). *See also* Uniform Statutory Will Act § 9.

**39.** Uniform Probate Code § 3–906(a)(2)(ii); Van Schaack v. AmSouth Bank, NA, 530 So.2d 740, 744 (Ala. 1988).

**40.** Calif.Prob.Code § 16246. *See also* Unif.Trust Code § 816(22).

**41.** Uniform Probate Code § 3–906, comment.

**42.** 755 ILCS 5/24–10; Cal.Prob.Code § 12205.

withhold property to the extent reasonably needed to cover potential liability for taxes.[43]

**43.** Unif.Trust Code § 817, comment.

# Chapter 13

# RIGHTS OF CREDITORS

*Table of Sections*

## § 13.1   Creditors' Remedies Against Trusts

Generally speaking, creditors of a trustee have no rights against the trust property, which in equity belongs to the beneficiaries.[1] Other creditors' rights to reach interests in a trust can be divided into two categories: creditors of the settlor, and creditors of beneficiaries.

*Creditors of Settlor* Creditors can only reach property which belongs to their debtor. If *S* creates a trust which requires the trustee to pay the income and principal to others, *S*'s creditors have no right to reach the trust, unless the creation of a trust involved a fraudulent conveyance. Creditors of a man were allowed to reach an irrevocable trust which he had created for his children on the basis of a statute providing that "every conveyance made * * * by a person who is, or will thereby be rendered, insolvent is fraudulent as to creditors" if the conveyance was made without "fair consideration."[2] Most states have similar statutes which cover all gratuitous transfers, including the creation of trusts.[3]

---

**§ 13.1**

1.  Unif.Trust Code § 507. According to the comment to this section even a creditor who was unaware of the trust cannot claim the rights of a bona-fide purchaser from a trustee. Compare Sections 12.8 and 6.4.

2.  Territorial Sav. & Loan Ass'n v. Baird, 781 P.2d 452 (Utah App.1989).

3.  *Restatement, Second, of Property (Donative Transfers)* § 34.3, Statutory Note (1990).

Even when the creation of a trust was not fraudulent, if the settlor reserves the right to revoke the trust, most states allow the settlor's creditors to reach the trust assets, either by virtue of a statute or by case law.[4] Even after the settlor has died and the power to revoke has expired, many authorities allow the settlor's creditors to reach the trust assets, at least if the settlor's probate estate is insufficient to satisfy claims.[5]

Even if a trust is irrevocable, creditors of the settlor can reach any interest which the settlor has reserved, e.g. if a trust provides that the trustee shall pay the income to the settlor for her life, remainder to her children, her creditors can reach her income interest. They can also reach the principal if the trustee has discretion to distribute it to the settlor.[6] If several persons contribute property to a trust, each is treated as the settlor of a portion reflecting his or her contributions.[7]

*Beneficiaries Other Than the Settlor* Creditors of beneficiaries other than the settlor traditionally had to resort to "equitable" remedies. In accordance with the traditions of equity, courts have discretion in deciding how to use the beneficiary's interest to satisfy claims.[8] Where the debtor-beneficiary is entitled to the trust income "the court will normally direct the trustee to make the payments to the creditor until the claim * * * is satisfied," but it may award less than all the income to the creditor, leaving some for the basic needs of the beneficiary. The court may alternatively order a sale of the beneficiary's interest, particularly when it is a future interest which produces no current income. But if "the uncertainty or remoteness of the interest [is] such that its forced sale would produce little relative to its value to the beneficiary," the court may simply give creditors "a lien on the beneficiary's interest, to be realized if and when it falls into possession."[9]

If the trustee has discretion to pay principal or income to a debtor other than the settlor, the creditor's rights are limited because a beneficiary "does not have 'property' or any 'right to property' in nondistributed trust property before the trustees have exercised their discretionary powers of distribution."[10] But creditors can get an order directing the trustee to pay them rather than the

---

**4.** Calif.Prob.Code § 18200; Unif. Trust Code § 505(a)(1); Markham v. Fay, 74 F.3d 1347, 1359 (1st Cir.1996) (Mass. law); *Restatement, Third, of Trusts* § 25, comm. e (2001).

**5.** Uniform Probate Code § 6–102 (1998); Matter of Estate of Nagel, 580 N.W.2d 810 (Iowa 1998).

**6.** *Restatement, Third, of Trusts* § 60, comm. f (2001). See also Unif. Trust Code § 505(a)(2).

**7.** Matter of Shurley, 115 F.3d 333 (5th Cir.1997).

**8.** Unif.Trust Code § 501.

**9.** *Restatement, Third, of Trusts* § 56, comm. e (2001).

**10.** United States v. O'Shaugnessy, 517 N.W.2d 574, 578 (Minn.1994).

beneficiary if the trustee decides to exercise the discretion in the beneficiary's favor.[11] The Third Restatement of Trusts also gives creditors "judicial protection from abuse of discretion by the trustee."[12] The Uniform Trust Code, on the other hand, does not allow creditors to compel a trustee to make a discretionary distribution even if the trustee "has abused the discretion" unless the claim is for support by a child, spouse or former spouse of the beneficiary.[13] In any event, courts are unlikely to find that a trustee has abused discretion when the issue is raised by a beneficiary's creditors.

The Restatement gives creditors more rights when the debtor by the terms of the trust has authority, as trustee or otherwise, "to determine his or her own benefits" even if this authority is restricted by a standard. In this situation the beneficiary's creditors, like the creditors of the settlor, can reach "the maximum amount" which the beneficiary can properly take.[14] Case support this rule is thin.[15]

*Spendthrift Provisions* Most states do not allow most creditors to reach a beneficiary's interest in a trust if it contains a spendthrift clause. Such clauses rarely contain the word "spendthrift." A typical provision says "Every beneficiary hereof is hereby restrained from anticipating, assigning, selling or otherwise disposing of his or her interest in the Trust, and none of the interests of the beneficiaries hereunder shall be subject to the claims of creditors or other persons."

Some state statutes make all trusts spendthrift unless the debtor created the trust.[16] In most states, however, unless the trust instrument contains a spendthrift provision, beneficiaries' interests which are not dependent on the trustee's discretion are subject to claims.

England does not give effect to spendthrift provisions,[17] but most American states do.[18] In states which recognize them, spendthrift provisions are effective even in bankruptcy.[19]

**11.** Wilcox v. Gentry, 867 P.2d 281 (Kan.1994); *Restatement, Third, of Trusts* § 60, comm. c (2001).

**12.** *Restatement, Third, of Trusts* § 60, comm. e (2001).

**13.** Unif.Trust Code § 504(c)(2).

**14.** *Restatement, Third, of Trusts* § 60, comm. g.

**15.** *Compare* Morrison v. Doyle, 582 N.W.2d 237 (Minn.1998) (beneficiary's powers do not allow his creditors to reach his interest) *with* In re Baldwin, 142 B.R. 210 (Bktcy.S.D.Ohio 1992)

(spendthrift provision ineffective when beneficiary had power to replace the trustee and control investments).

**16.** Rev.Code Wash. § 6.32.250. These provisions go back to a New York statute of 1828.

**17.** Brandon v. Robinson, 34 Eng. Rep. 379 (1811).

**18.** Scott v. Bank One Trust Co., 577 N.E.2d 1077 (Ohio 1991); *Restatement, Third, of Trusts* § 58 (2001).

**19.** Matter of Shurley, 115 F.3d 333 (5th Cir.1997); 11 U.S.C. § 541(c)(2).

A New York statute which has been copied in several states allows creditors to reach trust income in a spendthrift trust if it exceeds the amount necessary for the beneficiary's support.[20] This statute has been construed to exempt large amounts of income on the ground that they were necessary to support the beneficiary's "station-in-life."[21]

Spendthrift trusts have been justified by analogy to the protection which the law confers on minors and incapacitated adults.[22] But "spendthrift protection is not limited to beneficiaries who are legally incompetent or who, as a practical matter, lack the ability to manage their finances in a responsible manner."[23]

It is often said that creditors have no reason to complain about spendthrift provisions because they have notice of them. This argument has been challenged on the ground that inter vivos trusts of personal property are not matters of public record, but the paucity of legislation restricting spendthrift trusts suggests that creditors, who are not generally slow to seek favorable legislation, do not regard them as a serious problem.

Income or principal from a spendthrift trust that has actually been distributed to a beneficiary becomes subject to creditors' claims.[24] Even if no distribution has yet taken place, but the beneficiary has the right to demand it—*e.g.* she has reached the age specified in the trust instrument for distribution, the beneficiary's creditors can reach it despite the spendthrift provision.[25] Thus *eventually* the money in a spendthrift trust becomes subject to claims against the beneficiary, so the objections to (or benefits of, depending on your viewpoint) a spendthrift provision are limited. But it may be hard for creditors to collect money after it reaches the beneficiary's hands, particularly if the beneficiary is really a spendthrift.

*Protective Trusts* Jurisdictions which do not allow spendthrift provisions permit "protective" trusts, which provide that if a creditor seeks to reach a beneficiary's interest it is forfeited, or it becomes discretionary with the trustee whether to pay the beneficiary.[26] Opponents of spendthrift trusts object that they allow debtors not to pay creditors and still retain their property. This is

**20.** N.Y.EPTL § 7–3.4. *See also* Calif.Prob.Code § 15307. Most states have no such limits.

**21.** Powell, *The Rule Against Perpetuities and Spendthrift Trusts in New York*, 71 Colum.L.Rev. 688, 699 (1971); *cf.* Section 9.5.

**22.** Nichols v. Eaton, 91 U.S. at 727.

**23.** *Restatement, Third, of Trusts* § 58, comm. a (2001).

**24.** *Ibid.*, comm. d.

**25.** Unif.Trust Code § 506; Brent v. State Cent. Collection Unit, 537 A.2d 227 (Md.1988).

**26.** *Restatement, Third, of Trusts* § 57 (2001); N.C.Stat § 36A–115(b)(3). As to the distinction between "forfeiture" and "disabling" restraints see Section 11.8.

not true of protective trusts, but the distinction makes little practical difference to creditors.

*Special Claims* Some claims override spendthrift provisions. Creditors who supply necessaries to a beneficiary can reach the beneficiary's interest despite a spendthrift clause.[27] Both the settlor and society have an interest in having beneficiaries provided with necessaries. Similar reasoning underlies an exception for persons who have rendered services to protect the beneficiary's interest in the trust, e.g. an attorney who represented a beneficiary in a suit to surcharge the trustee.[28]

The Restatement, as well as many cases and statutes, allow claims for alimony and child support to be asserted against spendthrift trusts.[29] Some say that a spouse and children "are in quite a different position from ordinary creditors who have voluntary extended credit." Furthermore, "unless the interest of the beneficiary can be reached, the state may be called upon for their support."[30] The *beneficiary* may also become dependent on state support if the spendthrift trust is dissipated, but alimony and child support are based upon the extent of the beneficiary's resources, so they will not leave the beneficiary destitute. Support claims can be satisfied from a spendthrift trust only after taking account of "the beneficiary's actual need for some part of the distributions."[31]

The question whether tort claims should be subject to a spendthrift provision has been discussed in the literature, but there is little case law, perhaps because of the prevalence of liability insurance. In a recent case in which the beneficiary of a spendthrift trust had seriously injured a man by drunken driving, the court held that the spendthrift provision did not immunize his interest.[32] The Restatement approves the result in this case, but the Reporter's Note suggests that it was overturned by later legislation allowing spendthrift provisions with an exception only for self-settled trusts.[33] A recurring problem in interpreting statutes is whether the statement of *some* exceptions to spendthrift protection preclude courts from creating others.[34] The exceptions listed in the Restate-

**27.** Sisters of Mercy Health v. First Bank, 624 N.E.2d 520 (Ind.App.1993); *Restatement, Third, of Trusts* § 59(b) (2001). This exception is rejected in the Uniform Trust Code § 503, comment.

**28.** Schreiber v. Kellogg, 50 F.3d 264 (3d Cir.1995).

**29.** *Restatement, Third, of Trusts* § 59(a) (2001); Cal.Prob.Code § 15305; Unif.Trust Code § 503(a).

**30.** Council v. Owens, 770 S.W.2d 193, 197 (Ark.App.1989).

**31.** *Restatement, Third, of Trusts* § 59, comment b (2001).

**32.** Sligh v. First Nat. Bank, 704 So.2d 1020 (Miss.1997).

**33.** *Restatement, Third, of Trusts* § 59, comm. a, Reporter's Note (2001), citing Miss.Code § 91–5–903.

**34.** Scheffel v. Krueger, 782 A.2d 410 (N.H. 2001) (tort claim not covered by statutory exceptions and so spendthrift provision governs).

ment for spendthrift trusts are expressly stated to be "not exclusive."[35]

Liens for unpaid federal taxes are held generally to override a spendthrift or protective provision.[36]

*Self–Settled Trusts* Creditors can reach any interest of the settlor of a trust notwithstanding a spendthrift provision. This is well-settled by case law, and many statutes so provide.[37] The reasons generally advanced for not allowing them—*e.g.* a debtor should not be allowed to "have his cake and eat it too"[38]—apply to *all* spendthrift trusts, so the special status of self-settled trusts is puzzling, particularly since the ERISA's immunity of pension plans from creditors includes plans built up by contributions of the employee-beneficiary.[39]

The special rule for self-settled trusts occasionally raises the question "who *was* the settlor of the trust?" Form is not determinative. An employee who had been injured in an accident settled his claim with an insurance company which gave him an unassignable annuity. When the employee later went into bankruptcy, the annuity was held to be part of his bankruptcy estate on the ground that the employee "was the settlor of the trust."[40] But this reasoning has not been extended to spouses who accept a spendthrift trust created by the other spouse's will instead of taking an elective share of the testator's estate.[41] Nor does the fact that a beneficiary asked the settlor to put the property into a spendthrift trust for him make the beneficiary the settlor.

The general refusal to allow self-settled spendthrift trusts is not world wide. "More than a half-dozen nations compete for foreign investment by * * * providing havens for judgment debtors from their foreign creditors ... by validating self-settled spendthrift trusts." According to one estimate "this offshore trust industry already administers a trillion dollars in assets."[42] In recent

**35.** *Restatement, Third, of Trusts* § 59, comm. a(2) (2001). The exceptions in the Uniform Trust Code appear to be exclusive, however. Section 502(c)

**36.** United States v. Grimm, 865 F.Supp. 1303 (N.D.Ind.1994); Bank One Ohio Trust Co., N.A. v. United States, 80 F.3d 173 (6th Cir.1996).

**37.** *Restatement, Third, of Trusts* § 58(2) (2001); Calif.Prob.Code § 15304.

**38.** Matter of Shurley, 115 F.3d 333, 337 (5th Cir.1997).

**39.** Patterson v. Shumate, 504 U.S. 753 (1992) (exemption under ERISA does not depend on plan qualifying as spendthrift trust under state law); Ga.

Code Ann. § 53–12–28(d) (spendthrift provision in a *pension* trust is valid "even if the beneficiary is also the settlor of the trust").

**40.** In re Jordan, 914 F.2d 197, 198–99 (9th Cir.1990). *See also* Speed v. Speed, 430 S.E.2d 348 (Ga.1993).

**41.** American Security and Trust Co. v. Utley, 382 F.2d 451 (D.C.Cir.1967). *Restatement, Third, of Trusts* § 58, comm. f agrees, but suggests that in community property states the result may be different, and that an heir may be deemed the settlor of a spendthrift trust created to settle a will contest.

**42.** LoPucki, *The Death of Liability,* 106 Yale L.J. 1, 33 (1996).

years a few American states have followed the lead of these foreign jurisdictions by allowing self-settled spendthrift trusts in an effort to attract trust business which would otherwise go abroad.[43] However, because of the full faith and credit clause of the American constitution, trusts set up in an American jurisdiction may not offer debtors as much protection against judgments in other states as an "offshore" trust.

*Voluntary Transfers* Interests in trusts are normally transferable, but a spendthrift provision typically bars transfers by the beneficiary as well as claims of creditors. According to the Restatement, a spendthrift restraint that seeks only to prevent creditors from reaching the beneficiary's interests, while allowing the beneficiary to transfer the interest, is invalid,[44] but the beneficiaries of spendthrift trusts can *disclaim* or *release* their interest.[45]

A spendthrift restraint may prevent a beneficiary who gets into a high tax bracket from giving away her interest to reduce income taxes.[46] New York, however, allows beneficiaries, despite a spendthrift clause, to assign income in excess of $10,000 a year to a spouse or relatives.[47]

*Planning* Many lawyers routinely insert spendthrift provisions in all trusts. This is a questionable practice, because it may prevent a desirable transfer of income by a beneficiary in a high income tax bracket. On the other hand, a spendthrift clause can prevent improvident transfers and unwise use of credit. It is difficult to resolve these competing considerations, since settlors often cannot know whether the beneficiaries—*e.g.,* young children or others still unborn—will turn out to be spendthrifts.

A discretionary trust may better achieve the settlor's goals than a fixed income spendthrift trust. Discretionary trusts may be effective against claims like alimony which prevail over a spendthrift provision. They also avoid the problem of an unassignable income interest held by a beneficiary in a high tax bracket.

*Insurance and Pensions* The common law generally held that provisions barring alienation of property were against public policy. Spendthrift trusts are (in America) considered distinguishable be-

**43.** These statutes are discussed and criticized in Boxx, *Gray's Ghost—A Conversation About the Onshore Trust,* 85 Iowa L. Rev. 1195 (2000).

**44.** *Restatement, Third, of Trusts* § 58, comm. b (1999). *See also* Unif. Trust Code § 502(a). *But see* Bank of New England v. Strandlund, 529 N.E.2d 394 (Mass.1988).

**45.** *Restatement, Third, of Trusts* § 58, comm. c (2001). *See also* Uniform Probate Code § 2–801(a).

**46.** Howard v. Chapman, 241 N.E.2d 492 (Ill.App.1968) (refusing to allow the beneficiary of a spendthrift trust with an income of over $200,000 to assign her interest).

**47.** N.Y.EPTL § 7–1.5(b)(1). *See also* 12 Del.Code § 3536(b).

cause the trustee normally has a power of sale and so the property in the trust is not kept out of commerce.[48]

Benefits paid in installments under insurance policies are not technically trusts but they have similar characteristics and purposes, and so "a restraint on the interest of the interest of the beneficiary of an insurance policy may be valid."[49]

Of particular importance, in view of the vast number of persons entitled to pension benefits, is the federal Employee Retirement Income Security Act of 1974 (ERISA) which covers most pension plans and requires that benefits under the plan be unassignable.[50] The limitations on spendthrift trusts as to claims for alimony and child support have counterparts with respect to pensions; spouses can garnish pension benefits in order to collect a maintenance obligation.[51] However, the ineffectiveness of spendthrift provisions in self-settled trusts is not matched by a like restriction on pension plans to which a beneficiary has contributed.

## § 13.2  Joint Tenancy and Insurance

*Joint Tenancy* Traditionally, property in joint tenancy can not be reached by creditors of a tenant after he or she dies,[1] even if the decedent had mortgaged or pledged the property,[2] although this rule has been changed by statute in some states.[3] If a lien is foreclosed by sale before the joint tenant dies, this severs the joint tenancy so the creditor prevails.[4]

Sophisticated creditors can protect themselves by getting all joint tenants to sign a note when they extend credit. Although "will substitutes impair the mechanism by which probate protects creditors, * * * modern creditors * * * have acquiesced without a struggle" in the movement to avoid probate because "the data processing revolution has virtually eliminated the problem toward which much of the debt-resolving phase of probate procedure has been oriented."[5] Nevertheless, the limits on creditor rights in joint

---

**48.** *Restatement, Second, of Property (Donative Transfers)* Introductory Note to Chapter 4 (1983). For further discussion of restraints on alienation see Section 11.8, on a trustee's power of sale, Section 12.6.

**49.** *Restatement, Second, of Trusts* § 12, comm. k (1959). In Drewes v. Schonteich, 31 F.3d 674 (8th Cir.1994), a nonassignable annuity was held to be a "trust" and thus excludable from the annuitant's bankruptcy estate.

**50.** 29 U.S.C. § 1056(d).

**51.** 29 U.S.C. § 1056(d)(3); Hogle v. Hogle, 732 N.E.2d 1278 (Ind.App.2000).

**§ 13.2**

**1.** Irvin L. Young Foundation, Inc. v. Damrell, 511 A.2d 1069 (Me.1986).

**2.** Kalk v. Security Pacific Bank Washington, 894 P.2d 559 (Wash.1995). *Contra*, Heffernan v. Wollaston Credit Union, 567 N.E.2d 933, 939 (Mass.App. Ct.1991).

**3.** Wis.Stat. § 700.24; Conn.Gen. Stat. § 47–14e.

**4.** Jolley v. Corry, 671 P.2d 139 (Utah 1983).

**5.** Langbein, *The Nonprobate Revolution and the Future of the Law of Succession*, 97 Harv.L.Rev. 1108, 1124–

tenancy are unjust to tort claimants who have no chance to protect themselves by getting security. The original Uniform Probate Code subjected joint bank accounts to claims if the decedent debtor's probate estate was insufficient to satisfy them.[6] This was not extended to securities registered in TOD form when the Code authorized this form of transfer in 1989,[7] but 1998 Section 6–102 was added which subjects beneficiaries of nonprobate transfers to liability if the debtor's probate estate is insufficient. The protection of creditors is not as extensive as that for disinherited spouses because "creditors are better able to fend for themselves."[8] Survivorship interests in joint tenancy in real estate are expressly excluded from the reach of creditors of a deceased joint tenant.

Subjecting nonprobate transfers to creditors' claims can have unpleasant consequences for transferees, e.g. if the surviving party to a joint bank account spends the funds without knowing that the decedent died insolvent. Therefore, the UPC imposes a limit of one year from the decedent's death on enforcement of claims against non-probate transferees.[9]

*During Lifetime* Claims of creditors to assets held in joint tenancy can also arise while all the parties are still living. Under the Uniform Probate Code a joint account belongs to the parties "in proportion to the net contributions by each to the sums on deposit, unless there is clear and convincing evidence of a different intent."[10] Therefore creditors of a non-contributing party have no claim to the account while the depositor is living any more than creditors of a devisee under the will of a living testator. Most courts have reached this result without a statute,[11] but the result is not always clear.[12]

25 (1984). *See also* Prefatory Note to Uniform Probate Code § 6–102 (1998) ("commercial creditors . . . have demonstrated lack of interest in probate law protections").

**6.** Uniform Prob.Code § 6–107. Section 6–215 of the 1989 version is similar.

**7.** McGovern, *Nonprobate Transfers under the Revised Uniform Probate Code*, 55 Alb.L.Rev. 1329, 1347 (1992); Estate of Reed, 681 A.2d 460 (Me.1996) (UPC does not allow creditors to reach funds in decedent's brokerage account).

**8.** Uniform Probate Code § 6–102, Comment. As to the augmented estate for the spouse's elective share under the UPC see Section 3.7.

**9.** Uniform Probate Code § 6–102(h). Cal.Prob.Code § 19100 allows

the trustee of a revocable trust to cut off claims after 30 days by appropriate notice to creditors, by analogy to the nonclaim statutes governing claims in probate. See the next section.

**10.** Uniform Prob.Code § 6–211(b). This provision has been widely copied in states which have not enacted the UPC as a whole.

**11.** General Motors Acceptance Corp. v. Deskins, 474 N.E.2d 1207 (Ohio App.1984).

**12.** United States v. National Bank of Commerce, 472 U.S. 713 (1985); Tierney v. Department of Human Services, 793 A.2d 210 (R.I. 2002) (funds in joint account render party ineligible for Medicaid; because she had access to them she is presumed to own the funds).

In community property states, use of the joint tenancy form may create a presumption that the property is community and thus available to any creditor of the community.[13] The Uniform Probate Code presumes that when parties are married, their contributions to the account were equal,[14] but lays down no presumption when the parties are not married.

The creation of a joint tenancy in land is viewed as a present gift to a tenant who does not contribute to the cost of acquisition. Thus when a mother bought land and put title in the names of herself and her sons, a creditor of a son was able to execute on his interest.[15]

*Tenancy By the Entirety* In some states when land is held jointly by two spouses as tenants by the entirety, creditors of one spouse cannot reach it.[16] The immunity applies to "proceeds from the sale of property so held, as long as they are left intact * * * although normally there can be no tenancy by the entirety in personalty."[17] Some states no longer recognize tenancy by the entirety.[18] It is recognized, if at all, only between spouses.[19] Even where tenancy by the entirety is recognized, federal tax liens against one spouse can be enforced.[20]

*Insurance* The Uniform Probate Code provision allowing creditors to reach nonprobate transfers is subject to any statutory exemptions for insurance.[21] Many statutes exempt insurance in whole or in part from claims of the insured's creditors. If I buy insurance on my life, even though I retain the right to alter the policy, my creditors are restricted in reaching the cash surrender value during my life[22] or the proceeds at my death in many states.[23] These exemptions vary. In California the loan value of unmatured life insurance policies is exempt only up to $8,000, and the proceeds of matured policies only "to the extent reasonably necessary for the

---

**13.** Swink v. Fingado, 850 P.2d 978 (N.M.1993). *See also* Cal.Prob.Code § 5305 (when parties to a joint account are married, the account is presumed to be community property).

**14.** Uniform Probate Code § 6–211(b).

**15.** Remax of Blue Springs v. Vajda & Co., Inc., 708 S.W.2d 804, 806 (Mo. App.1986).

**16.** Central Nat. Bank v. Fitzwilliam, 465 N.E.2d 408 (Ohio 1984); Danforth, *Rethinking the Law of Creditors' Rights in Trusts*, 53 Hastings L.J. 287, 333–37 (2002).

**17.** Matter of Agnew, 818 F.2d 1284 (7th Cir.1987). *But see* Diss v. Agri Business Intern., Inc., 670 N.E.2d 97, 99

(Ind.App.1996) (half of rental income from entirety property is subject to claims of a spouse's creditors).

**18.** Lurie v. Sheriff of Gallatin County, 999 P.2d 342 (Mont.2000).

**19.** Traders Travel Intern., Inc. v. Howser, 753 P.2d 244, 247 (Haw.1988).

**20.** United States v. Craft, 535 U.S. 274 (2002).

**21.** Uniform Probate Code § 6–102(b) and comment, par. 2.

**22.** In re Marriage of Gedgaudas, 978 P.2d 677 (Colo.App.1999) (cash surrender value of insurance exempt up to $25,000).

**23.** In re Estate of Grigg, 545 N.E.2d 160, 161 (Ill.App.1989).

support of the judgment debtor and the spouse and dependents of the judgment debtor."[24]

*Promises Made at Divorce* Frequently at the time of a divorce *H* promises to designate *W* or his children or both as beneficiary(ies) of an insurance policy on his life to assure their continued support if he dies. He later remarries and, in violation of his agreement, changes the beneficiary of the policy to a new wife, who tries to bar the contractual claim of the first family on the basis of an exemption of insurance from creditors. Courts usually get around the exemption by imposing a constructive trust on the proceeds.[25]

The constructive trust rationale presents difficulties if the agreement does not refer to a specific policy, or if the promisor simply lets the designated policy lapse, since a trust requires an identifiable *res*.[26] But many courts are not meticulous about this.[27]

What happens if the insurance proceeds exceed the insured's support obligation? When an agreement required a father to name his daughter as beneficiary "for the purpose of insuring her education," the court held that any funds not needed for this purpose would pass to the beneficiary whom the father later designated.[28] But an agreement that the husband should maintain "at all times" an insurance policy for his daughter was held to be enforceable even though the daughter was 32 when her father died.[29]

The constructive trust rationale used in these cases may be trumped by federal law if the insured was a federal employee. A serviceman's former wife and children could not enforce a promise to give them the proceeds of a policy because "Congress has insulated the proceeds of SGILA insurance from attack or seizure by any claimant other than the beneficiary designated by the insured."[30] This reasoning has been extended to policies of civilian employees of the federal government.[31]

## § 13.3  Probate Estate

*Priorities* A primary duty of a personal representative is to pay claims against the estate. If its assets are insufficient to pay all

**24.** Cal.Code Civ.Proc. § 704.100; *Cf.* 11 U.S.C. § 522(d)(8) (federal exemption in bankruptcy of loan value of unmatured policy up to $4,000).

**25.** Bailey v. Prudential Ins. Co. of America, 705 N.E.2d 389, 392–93 (Ohio App.1997).

**26.** Oregon Pacific State Ins. Co. v. Jackson, 986 P.2d 650 (Or.App.1999).

**27.** Zobrist v. Bennison, 486 S.E.2d 815 (Ga.1997).

**28.** Aetna Life Ins. Co. v. Hussey, 590 N.E.2d 724, 728 (Ohio 1992).

**29.** Miller v. Partridge, 734 N.E.2d 1061, 1065 (Ind.App.2000).

**30.** Ridgway v. Ridgway, 454 U.S. 46, 63 (1981).

**31.** Dean v. Johnson, 881 F.2d 948 (10th Cir.1989). *But cf.* Rollins v. Metropolitan Life Ins. Co., 912 F.2d 911 (7th Cir.1990) (constructive trust prevails when new spouse not specifically named as beneficiary of FEGLI policy).

claims, the law establishes priorities. Section 3–805 of the Uniform Probate Code requires payment in the following order: (1) expenses of administration, (2) funeral expenses, (3) debts and taxes preferred under federal law, (4) medical expenses of the decedent's last illness, (5) claims preferred under other state laws, (6) other claims. Mortgages and other liens come ahead of even administration expenses.[1]

Claims in the same class receive an equal pro-rata share.[2] When a decedent was in bankruptcy at the time of death, the bankruptcy court retains jurisdiction over the assets and applies bankruptcy rules which differ somewhat from those governing insolvent decedent estates by state law.[3]

Normally neither the heirs and devisees nor the personal representative are personally liable for claims against the estate, but a personal representative may incur such liability by neglecting the specified priorities.[4] The distributees of an insolvent estate may be held liable to the extent of the property they received in the distribution.[5]

*Non–Claim Statutes* Personal representatives need to know the extent of the claims against an estate; otherwise they may pay a claim in full or distribute to an heir or devisee and later discover that there are not enough assets to satisfy all claims. "Non-claim" statutes serve to prevent this from happening. The Uniform Probate Code, for example, allows personal representatives to publish a notice to creditors to present their claims within four months "or be forever barred."[6] The Supreme Court in Tulsa Professional Collection Services, Inc. v. Pope,[7] held a similar statute unconstitutional because it barred claims without giving adequate notice to creditors who are unlikely to see "an advertisement in small type inserted in the back pages of a newspaper." Such notice by publication is sufficient only for creditors who are not "reasonably ascertainable;" the personal representative must make "a good-faith search of decedent's personal and business financial records * * * in attempting to discover claims."[8] Some unnotified claimants have been barred on the ground that they were not reasonably ascertainable.[9] Other late claims have been rejected because the claimant,

§ 13.3
1. Uniform Probate Code § 3–812; Lundgren v. Gaudiane, 782 P.2d 285, 288 (Alaska 1989).
2. Uniform Probate Code § 3–805(b).
3. Fed.R.Bank.Proc. 1015.
4. Uniform Probate Code § 3–807(b). *See also* In re Robinson ex rel Snell, 754 N.Y.S.2d 525 (Surr.2003) (executor liable to claimant with statutory priority for using estate funds to pay another creditor).
5. Uniform Probate Code § 3–909.
6. *Id.*, § 3–801(a).
7. 485 U.S. 478 (1988).
8. Matter of Estate of Anderson, 615 N.E.2d 1197, 1206 (Ill.App.1993).
9. Matter of Estate of Ragsdale, 879 P.2d 1145 (Kan.App.1994).

although not given notice, had actual knowledge of the administration proceedings.[10]

The drafters of the Uniform Probate Code responded to the *Tulsa* decision by making the traditional publication of notice to creditors optional, on the ground that it "is useless except as to bar unknown creditors." It provides for notice "by mail or other delivery" to creditors who are barred 60 days 'thereafter.' To avoid the bar a creditor must deliver or mail to the personal representative "a written statement of the claim, indicating its basis."[11] The UPC also bars all claims, whether or not notice was given, which are not filed within one year after the decedent's death.[12]

There are several exceptions to the non-claim bar.

1. *Suit Pending.* A claimant who had a suit pending at the time of the decedent's death need not present the claim in the estate proceedings under the Uniform Probate Code.[13] If a claimant files suit during the non-claim period, service of process on the personal representative may satisfy the statute.[14]

2. *Claims arising after death.* Claims which arise after the decedent's death are governed by a special rule. Under the Uniform Probate Code they can be presented within 4 months after performance is due (contracts) or the claim arises (other claims).[15]

Claims which are only potential at the time of the decedent's death are troublesome. A court allowed a claim on a guaranty after the non-claim period had run, saying: "the filing of a contingent claim * * * is not required. * * * To reserve against such contingencies may greatly impede the full distribution of an estate."[16] But many non-claim statutes expressly include claims "whether due, or to become due, absolute or contingent."[17] This means contingent claims must be *presented,* but they are not necessarily *paid* during administration because it is difficult to ascertain the amount due. Under the Uniform Probate Code the claimant may accept the present value of the claim "taking any uncertainty into account,"

**10.** Venturi v. Taylor, 41 Cal.Rptr.2d 272, 276 (App.1995).

**11.** Uniform Probate Code § 3–801, Comment, 3–804.

**12.** *Id.,* § 3–803(a). Courts have upheld statutes cutting off claims one year after death without regard to notice. Estate of Kruzynski, 744 A.2d 1054 (Me. 2000).

**13.** Uniform Probate Code § 3–804(2); Reese v. Reese, 637 P.2d 1183 (Mont.1981). *Contra,* In re Worrell's Estate, 442 N.E.2d 211 (Ill.1982).

**14.** Mathe v. Fowler, 469 N.E.2d 89 (Ohio App.1983). *But see* Dodson v. Charter Behav. Health System, 983 S.W.2d 98, 106 (Ark.1998).

**15.** Uniform Probate Code § 3–803(b).

**16.** Security S & L v. Estate of Kite, 857 P.2d 430, 433 (Colo.App.1992). *See also* Priestman v. Elder, 646 N.E.2d 234, 237 (Ohio App.1994) (contingent claims need not be presented until they accrue).

**17.** Uniform Probate Code § 3–803(a).

or can insist on an arrangement for future payment, such as a bond from the distributees of the estate.[18]

3. *Governmental Claims.* The Uniform Probate Code non-claim provision expressly includes claims by the state or its agencies, but some states treat them as exceptions.[19] The federal government is not subject to state non-claim statutes, but the Internal Revenue Code contains comparable provisions discharging personal representatives from liability for unpaid taxes of which they are not notified within nine months after a request.[20]

4. *Recoupment.* If an estate sues on a claim, many courts allow the defendant to assert by recoupment a claim against the estate even if the period allowed by the non-claim statute has expired, but there is also contrary authority. [21]

5. *Insurance.* Most non-claim statutes apply to tort as well as contract claims, but if the tort is covered by liability insurance, "a failure to file within the statutory period bars only the right to enforce any liability of the estate beyond the limits of the insurance policy."[22]

6. *Devises.* Devisees do not have to file claims. The line between creditors and devisees is sometimes fuzzy. A claim against an estate for services rendered during the testator's last illness was rejected as untimely even though the will directed the executor "to pay the expenses of my last sickness * * * and all of my other just debts."[23] On the other hand, a direction in a will that any "property in my name and that of another as joint tenants" pass to the survivor was held to constitute a devise not subject to the non-claim statute.[24]

7. *Property.* If an executor erroneously inventories property which did not belong to the testator, the owner need not file a claim protect her property.[25] Also, persons holding mortgages and other security interests in estate assets are not required to present their claims unless their security is insufficient and they wish to collect the deficiency from the decedent's other assets.[26]

---

**18.** *Id.*, § 3–810(b); *cf.* Cohen v. Cronin, 346 N.E.2d 524 (N.Y.1976) (fund to pay contingent claim retained when balance of estate distributed).

**19.** *Compare* Uniform Probate Code § 3–803(a) *with* Ohio Dept. of Human Services v. Eastman, 763 N.E.2d 193 (Ohio App.2001); Cal.Prob.Code §§ 9200 et seq. (special time periods prescribed for claims by various "public entities").

**20.** Internal Revenue Code §§ 2204, 6905.

**21.** *Compare* Estate of Ruehl v. Ruehl, 623 N.E.2d 741 (Ohio Mun.1993)

*with* In re Estate of Kremer, 546 N.E.2d 1047, 1052 (Ill.App.1989).

**22.** Corlett v. Smith, 763 P.2d 1172, 1174–75 (N.M.App.1988).

**23.** Matter of Bachand's Estate, 307 N.W.2d 140 (S.D.1981).

**24.** Matter of Estate of Powers, 552 N.W.2d 785, 787 (N.D.1996).

**25.** In re Estate of Kolbinger, 529 N.E.2d 823, 827 (Ill.App.1988).

**26.** Uniform Probate Code § 3–803(c)(1).

8. *Estoppel* Sometimes a personal representative is held to be "estopped" to raise the non-claim bar, *e.g.* "where an estate * * * makes representations to the claimant which lead the claimant to believe that it is not necessary to protect his claim by filing a creditor's claim."[27] But the Uniform Probate Code does not allow personal representatives to "waive any defense of limitations available to the estate" except "with the consent of all whose interests would be affected."[28]

*Statute of Limitations* Non-claim statutes resemble statutes of limitations but they have different purposes and each operates independently. A claim which is presented within the limits of a non-claim statute may be dismissed because the statute of limitations has run and vice-versa. If a claim is not yet due—*e.g.,* a note payable in 2007, the non-claim period may expire before the statute of limitations starts to run.[29]

Since a decedent's creditor has no one to sue until administration of the debtor's estate begins, the Uniform Probate Code suspends the running of any statute of limitations for 4 months following the decedent's death. The statute of limitations stops running when a claim is presented.[30] But if the personal representative "disallows" a claim which has been timely presented, the claimant must bring suit within 60 days.[31]

*Court Approval* In some states courts closely supervise the payment of claims by personal representatives, like other aspects of administration. For example, in Mississippi claims against an estate must be "registered, probated, and allowed" in court.[32] But the Uniform Probate Code allows personal representatives to "pay any just claim which has not been barred, with or without presentation."[33] Some states make special provisions for claims which a personal representative has against the estate because of the conflict of interest. In Ohio such claims must be "proved to and allowed by the probate court" after notice to the decedent's heirs and devisees.[34]

Personal representatives may be surcharged for paying invalid

**27.** Boyer v. Sparboe, 867 P.2d 1116, 1119–20 (Mont.1994).

**28.** Uniform Probate Code § 3–802(a).

**29.** State v. Goldfarb, 278 A.2d 818, 821 (Conn.1971).

**30.** Uniform Probate Code § 3–802.

**31.** *Id.,* § 3–806.

**32.** Miss.Code §§ 91–7–151, 91–7–155; Harper v. Harper, 491 So.2d 189 (Miss.1986).

**33.** Uniform Probate Code § 3–807(b). However, they risk being personally liable if they pay before the non-claim period expires and the estate is insolvent.

**34.** Ohio Rev.Code §§ 2117.01, 21107.02. Compare the need for court authorization for other types of self-dealing. Section 12.9.

claims,[35] but the Code allows them to "satisfy written charitable pledges of the decedent" even if they are not binding obligations or properly presented "if in the judgment of the personal representative the decedent would have wanted the pledges completed."[36]

## § 13.4  Claims Arising During Administration

*Contracts* A personal representative who makes a contract on behalf of the estate may be personally liable on it.[1] Trustees are also personally liable on contracts they make in administering a trust, even though in making the contract they were properly performing their duties.[2] They can avoid such personal liability by an express provision in the contract, but simply signing the contract "as trustee" is not enough, nor the fact that the trust instrument provides that the trustee shall not be personally liable on such a contract.[3] Trustees and executors can get reimbursement from the trust or estate for their liability if the contract was properly made, but if the estate is insufficient to cover their liability they may be left "holding the bag."[4]

If a trustee is personally insolvent, the claimant will want to reach the assets of the trust. The Restatement allows them to do so "to the extent to which the trustee is entitled to exoneration out of the trust estate."[5] This limitation bars relief to claimants if the trustee is liable to the trust in an amount which exceeds the trustee's right of exoneration. Professor Scott criticized this rule. "Where the trustee acted within his powers * * * it seems unjust to the creditor to deny him a recovery out of the trust estate merely because in some other matter the trustee has committed a breach of trust subjecting him to a surcharge."[6]

The modern trend is to treat trustees like agents. Agents are not liable on contracts which they make for a principal, but they subject the principal to liability if they act within the scope of their authority.[7] Under the Uniform Probate Code "a trustee is not

---

**35.** Estate of Sturm, 246 Cal.Rptr. 852 (App.1988) (claims paid which were time-barred); Estate of Stellwag v. Kennedy, 817 S.W.2d 466 (Mo.App.1990) (same).

**36.** Uniform Probate Code § 3–715(4).

### § 13.4

**1.** Sanni, Inc. v. Fiocchi, 443 N.E.2d 1108, 1111 (Ill.App.1982).

**2.** *Restatement, Second, of Trusts* § 262 (1959); First Eastern Bank, N.A. v. Jones, 602 N.E.2d 211, 216 (Mass. 1992).

**3.** *Restatement, Second, of Trusts* § 263 (1959).

**4.** *Id.,* § 246, comm. a, § 262, comm. b (1959).

**5.** *Id.* § 268.

**6.** 3A A. Scott, *Trusts* § 268.2, at 478 (4th ed. (Fratcher) 1988).

**7.** *Restatement, Second, of Trusts* § 271A, comm. a (1959). Sometimes it is not clear whether a person in a transaction was acting as agent or as trustee. Botwood Investments Ltd v. Johnson, 36 O.R.2d 443 (1982) (defendant liable if Field was acting as agent rather than as trustee for him)

personally liable on contracts properly entered into in his fiduciary capacity * * * unless he fails to reveal his representative capacity and identify the trust estate in the contract."[8] This is restricted to "contracts properly entered;" a trustee who makes an *unauthorized* contract incurs personal liability.[9] Similar provisions apply to personal representatives and conservators, and to custodians under the Uniform Transfers to Minors Act. [10]

When creditors try to reach trust assets both they and the trustee have an incentive to argue that the contract was within the trustee's powers since this (a) allows the creditor to reach the trust assets, and (b) negates any personal liability of the trustee. This creates a conflict of interest between the trustee and the beneficiaries, so the Uniform Probate Code allows the latter to intervene in any litigation against the trustee.[11]

*Tort Claims* Similar rules govern tort claims. A trustee is personally liable for torts committed by an agent or employee in the course of the administration of the trust.[12] This rule is harsh if the trust estate is insufficient to indemnify the trustee, but trustees can protect themselves by buying liability insurance and paying the premiums from the trust.[13] Since they are in a better position than a tort victim to get insurance, they should bear the "risk of insolvency of the trust estate."[14]

The Uniform Probate Code treats trustees and personal representatives as if they were agents of the trust or estate for purposes of tort as well as contract liability. They are not liable for torts committed in the course of administration of the estate unless they are "personally at fault."[15] The tort victim can reach the assets of the estate or trust if the tort was "committed in the course of administration of the estate."[16]

A type of liability of great concern to fiduciaries today can arise out of land ownership. When a bank as trustee succeeded to ownership of a landfill which it later sold to a city, the city sued the

**8.** Uniform Probate Code § 7–306; *cf.* Unif.Trust Code § 1010(a) which requires only that the trustee "disclosed the fiduciary capacity" in the contract.

**9.** *Restatement, Second, Trusts* § 263(2) (1959).

**10.** Uniform Probate Code §§ 3–808, 5–430; Uniform Transfers to Minors Act § 17.

**11.** Uniform Probate Code § 7–306, comment.

**12.** *Restatement, Second, of Trusts* § 264 (1959); Uniform Trusts Act § 14(4); Evans v. Johnson, 347 N.W.2d 198 (Mich.App.1984) (executor).

**13.** Unif.Trust Code § 816(11), According to *Restatement, Second, of Trusts* § 247, comm. e (1959) the trustee has a *duty* to obtain liability insurance and loses the right to exoneration if she fails to do so.

**14.** Cook v. Holland, 575 S.W.2d 468, 472 (Ky.App.1978).

**15.** Uniform Probate Code §§ 3–808(b), 7–306(b). *See also* Unif.Trust Code § 1010(b).

**16.** Uniform Probate Code §§ 3–808(c), 5–430(c), 7–306(c).

bank under CERCLA (Comprehensive Environmental Response, Compensation and Liability Act) to recover costs it had incurred in cleaning up hazardous substances deposited on the land while it was in the trust. The court held that if the trustee "had the power to control the use of the property at the time it was contaminated," it would be personally liable "regardless of the trust's ability to indemnify him."[17] Presumably the result would be the same under the Uniform Probate Code which imposes personal liability on a trustee "for obligations arising out of the ownership or control of property of the trust estate * * * if he is personally at fault."[18]

Trust beneficiaries are not usually liable for torts committed by the trustee in administering the trust.[19]

**17.** City of Phoenix v. Garbage Services Co., 827 F.Supp. 600, 604–5 (D.Ariz.1993) (citing *Restatement, Second, of Trusts* § 264).

**18.** Uniform Probate Code § 7–306(b). *See also* Unif.Trust Code § 1010(b).

**19.** *Restatement, Second, of Trusts* § 276 (1959). This is also true of con-

tractual liability, *id.* § 275, but not if the trustee acts under the control of the beneficiaries as their agent. Kessler, Merci, and Lochner, Inc. v. Pioneer Bank & Trust Co., 428 N.E.2d 608, 611 (Ill.App.1981).

# Chapter 14

# LIVING WILLS AND DURABLE
# HEALTH CARE POWERS
# OF ATTORNEY

*Table of Sections*

## § 14.1  Introduction

"Every human being of adult years and sound mind has a right to determine what shall be done with his own body."[1] These oft-quoted words of Judge (later Justice) Benjamin Cardozo have become the foundation for the law of "informed consent." Under the doctrine of informed consent an adult competent patient, at least in a non-emergent situation, has the right to have the risks and benefits of proposed medical treatment explained to her before that treatment is provided, and the right to either refuse or accept medical treatment. The right to refuse or accept medical treatment can be grounded in either the common law, statute or state constitutions, and, in *Cruzan v. Director, Missouri Department of Health*[2] all of the Justices of the United States Supreme Court, excepting Justice Scalia, either stated or strongly implied that the right of a

§ 14.1

1. Scholendorff v. Society of New York Hospital, 105 N.E. 92, 93 (1914).

2. 497 U.S. 261, 278 (1990) (hereinafter cited as "Cruzan"). See, Cruzan at 287 (O'Connor concurring); Cruzan at 304–05 (Brennan, Marshall and Blackmun dissenting); Cruzan at 331 (Stevens dissenting).

competent adult patient to refuse medical treatment was a constitutionally protected "liberty" interest.

The ethical and moral dilemmas surrounding the right to refuse medical treatment, whatever its source, were not severely tested until medical technologies made it possible to physically sustain the life of a person in a persistent (or permanent) vegetative state.

The dilemmas were first publicly sharpened in the oft-cited case of *In the Matter of Karen Quinlan*.[3] Karen Ann Quinlan, age 22, stopped breathing for at least two 15 minute periods. As a result, the flow of blood to her brain ceased, destroying her cortex but not her brain stem. She was diagnosed as being in a persistent vegetative state "with the capacity to maintain the vegetative parts of neurological function but"[4] no longer having any cognitive function. Karen was connected to a respirator to assist her in breathing and to feeding tubes to provide her with food and hydration. Karen's doctors believed that she had no reasonable hope of recovery and, in all likelihood, would die if she were removed from the respirator.[5] Her father sought to be appointed her legal guardian for the purpose, among other things, of directing her health care providers to remove her from the respirator. The New Jersey court found that Karen had a constitutionally protected right of privacy which would have permitted her, had she been competent, to demand that the life-sustaining procedures be withdrawn even if withdrawal would result in her death. Because, in the court's view, this right of privacy is not extinguished because Karen became incompetent, it could be exercised on her behalf by her father, who was her legally appointed guardian.[6] The court did not engage in any extended discussion of the standards to be used by her guardian in determining whether the respirator should be removed. Rather, the court concluded that the guardian had the right to require the removal of the respirator if Karen's attending physicians, with the consent of an appropriate ethics committee, were of the view that there was "no reasonable possibility of Karen's ever emerging from her present comatose condition to a cognitive, sapient state."[7]

Later cases from New Jersey and many other states have attempted to develop standards to guide decision makers. In addition, Quinlan sparked a national interest in both living wills and durable health care powers of attorney (sometimes called "advance directives") which has ultimately led to the adoption of statutes

---

**3.** 355 A.2d 647 (1976).

**4.** Id. at 24, 355 A.2d at 654.

**5.** Karen's father did seek the removal of the feeding tubes.

**6.** In some jurisdictions, a conservator rather than a guardian would be appointed to represent the patient.

**7.** Id. at 55, 355 A.2d at 671.

throughout the country designed to empower patients to have health care decisions made on their behalf consistent with their wishes.

When patients are unable to express their own health care decisions, those decisions may be expressed by a so-called "surrogate" or "agent."[8] For example, in *Quinlan* the surrogate was Karen's guardian. Generally, surrogate's make decisions by complying with either the substituted judgement or the best interest standard.

Under the "substituted judgment" standard, the surrogate is expected to make that decision the patient would have made if the patient had decision making capacity. To do this, the surrogate should take into account the patient's previously expressed preferences, if any, as well as the patient's known values and interests.[9] The substituted judgement standard presumes that the patient had once been competent to express his or her preferences and values.

A surrogate's decision might be challenged on the grounds that the patient's preferences cannot be ascertained. This was the core of the dispute in *Cruzan v. Director, Missouri Department of Health*.[10] Nancy Cruzan was in a persistent vegetative state unable to breath or be nourished without the use of a respirator and feeding tube. Her parents, after some considerable period of time, asked that the feeding tube be withdrawn, knowing that, if it were withdrawn, Nancy would die. The employees at the state hospital where Nancy resided refused to honor that request. Her parents then sued in state court.

The *Cruzan* trial court found that Nancy had a "fundamental right" under state and federal law to "refuse or direct the withdrawal of 'death prolonging procedures.' " It also found that in at least one conversation Nancy had with a friend she evidenced her intent not to be maintained on life sustaining technologies. This, in the trial court's view, was sufficient to permit her parents to exercise substituted judgement.

On appeal from an order in the parents' favor, the Missouri Supreme Court reversed. It held that any decision to withdraw life support from Nancy must be based upon clear and convincing evidence that withdrawal would be consistent with Nancy's intent.

**8.** As used in this chapter, a "surrogate" could be either a family member to whom by custom health care providers look to for guidance in making medical decisions for a patient lacking decision making capacity or a person authorized by statute, the courts or under a durable health care power to make decisions on behalf of a patient.

**9.** See generally, In re Fiori, 543 Pa. 592, 673 A.2d 905 (1996); Barry R. Furrow, Thomas L. Greaney, Sandra H. Johnson, Timothy Stoltzfus Jost & Robert Schwartz, Health Law, vol. 2, § 17–18 (1995) (hereinafter "Furrow").

**10.** 497 U.S. 261 (1990).

The parents appealed that decision to the United States Supreme Court which held that the Constitution did not proscribe the Missouri Supreme Court from imposing the heightened "clear and convincing" standard to the facts. Said the Court: "[w]e believe that Missouri may permissibly place an increased risk of an erroneous decision on those seeking to terminate an incompetent individual's life-sustaining treatment. An erroneous decision not to terminate results in a maintenance of the status quo; the possibility of subsequent developments such as advancements in medical science, the discovery of new evidence regarding the patient's intent, changes in the law, or simply the unexpected death of the patient despite the administration of life-sustaining treatment, at least create the potential that a wrong decision will eventually be corrected or its impact mitigated. An erroneous decision to withdraw life-sustaining treatment, however, is not susceptible of correction."[11]

While the Court did not decide whether a person had a constitutional right to die or a right to direct the withholding or withdrawal of life-sustaining treatment, it stated in dicta that "for purposes of this case, we assume that the United States Constitution would grant a competent person a constitutionally protected right to refuse lifesaving hydration and nutrition."[12] On the other hand, state courts have held that such protection can be found or grounded either in state constitutions or state statutes.

*Cruzan* is important because it emphasizes the importance of planning for end-of-life decisions making. *Cruzan* implicitly supports the need for persons to clearly express their end-of-life decisions through the execution of either living wills or durable health care powers.[13]

Both *Quinlan* and *Cruzan* focused on the substituted judgement standard. Use of the substituted standard may be illogical and thus inappropriate in cases where the patient *never* had decision making capacity. This, for example, could be true in the case of infants, young minors, or severely retarded persons. The substituted judgement standard may also be inappropriate to use where

---

**11.** Id. at 263.

**12.** Id. at 278.

**13.** Justice O'Connor opined that states might be required to respect the decisions of duly-designated surrogate decision makers. She stated: "In my view, such a duty may well be constitutionally required to protect the patient's liberty interest in refusing medical treatment. Few individuals provide explicit oral or written instructions regarding their intent to refuse medical treatment should they become incompetent.

States which decline to consider any evidence other than such instructions may frequently fail to honor a patient's intent." Such failures might be avoided if the State considered an equally probative source of evidence: the patient's appointment of a proxy to make health care decisions on her behalf. Delegating the authority to make medical decisions to a family member or friend is becoming a common method of planning for the future. Id. at 289.

there is little or no evidence that a patient who once had decision making capacity had any preferences, values or interest that would inform the decision to be made. For such patients the best interest standard is more appropriate.

The best interest standard seeks what is best for the patient. However, some courts find the use of a best interest test inappropriate because "it lets another make a determination of the patient's quality of life, thereby undermining the foundation of self-determination and inviolability of the person upon which the right to refuse medical treatment stands."[14]

Because of the respect and deference given to a once-competent patient's expressed wishes respecting medical procedures and treatment, lawyers are keenly aware of the importance of having their clients communicate their wishes and desires respecting the health care they receive when they no longer are able to communicate themselves, particularly in the context of what has come to be called "end-of-life decision making." Lawyers also know that state statutes frequently give adults the power to designate agents or surrogates to make health care decisions on their behalf when they are no longer capable of making their own decisions. Thus, lawyers, and particularly lawyers who practice in the area of estate planning, invariably discuss with their clients both living wills and durable health care powers and prepare appropriate legal documents reflecting their clients' wishes. The statutory law surrounding these documents is rapidly evolving. While the following sections rely on the available uniform acts,[15] most of the issues raised in the discussion can be resolved in each state by resort to the local statutes.

## § 14.2  End-of-life Decision Making for the Competent Patient[1]

State case law or statutes or state constitutions generally recognize the right of competent persons to accept or reject medical treatment, including treatment that may be life-sustaining. The right to refuse medical treatment is closely aligned with the law of battery which recognizes the right of persons to be free of any unwanted touching.[2] *Bouvia v. Superior Court*[3] is illustrative. Eliza-

---

**14.** Mack v. Mack, 329 Md. 188, 218, 618 A.2d 744, 758 (1993) quoting from In re Estate of Longeway, 133 Ill.2d 33, 549 N.E.2d 292, 299 (1989)

**15.** The two principal acts are the Uniform Health–Care Decisions Act, and the Uniform Rights of the Terminally Ill Act of 1989. See also, Uniform Rights of the Terminally Act of 1985.

**§ 14.2**

**1.** The use of the phrase "competent patient" is misleading. The notion here

is that the patient has decision making capacity, however that might be generally determined in interactions between the patient and the patient's health care providers.

**2.** See generally, Scholendorff v. Society of New York Hospital, 105 N.E. 92, 93 (N.Y.1914).

**3.** 225 Cal.Rptr. 297 (1986).

beth, a 28–year–old woman, was a quadriplegic who suffered from severe cerebral palsy. She was completely bed-ridden, essentially immobile, constantly in pain and totally dependent on others to assist her with her all of her activities of daily living. Elizabeth had to be spoon fed. Elizabeth, who was fully mentally competent, refused to eat because she wanted to starve herself to death, primarily because she believed her life to be intolerable. To keep her alive, therefor, the health care providers at the publicly owned hospital inserted a feeding tube into her body against her will. With the feeding tube, Elizabeth had a life expectancy of 15–20 years. Elizabeth sued to have the tube removed.

The court held that Elizabeth had the right to refuse medical treatment, including medical treatment needed to sustain her life. The question for the court was whether the state had any countervailing interests that would trump Elizabeth's right to refuse life-sustaining treatment. The court noted that the state might assert up to four countervailing interests. These were the state's interest in (1) preserving life, (2) preventing suicide, (3) protecting the interest of third parties, and (4) maintaining the integrity and ethical standards of the medical profession.[4] But the court found that none of these interests trumped Elizabeth's right, as an exercise of her personal autonomy, to determine whether to receive medical treatment. The exercise of her personal rights are not dependent on her motives, even if those motives include a desire to die. Said the court: "it certainly is not illegal or immoral to prefer a natural, albeit sooner, death than a drugged life attached to a mechanical device."[5]

In so holding, the court relied on its earlier holding that a competent terminally-ill man had a right to require the removal of life-sustaining medical treatment even over the objections of the pro-life hospital where he was a patient.[6]

The court further stated that even though the removal of the feeding tube was opposed by the public hospital which no longer wanted to participate in her care, because, as a public hospital it was required to accept her as a patient, it could not deny her relief from pain and suffering while she starved to death.[7] However, in *Brophy v. New England Sinai Hospital, Inc.*[8] the Massachusetts

**4.** See also, Superintendent of Belchertown State School v. Saikewicz, 370 N.E.2d 417 (1977).

**5.** Bouvia, *supra* note 3 at 1145, 225 Cal.Rptr. at 1145.

**6.** Bartling v. Superior Court, 209 Cal.Rptr. 220 (1984).

**7.** But see, Conservatorship of Morrison, 253 Cal.Rptr. 530 (Ct. App. 1st Dist.

1988) (where hospital staff had a moral objection to removing life support, was willing to transfer patient to a facility which would and conservator failed to show no physician would remove tube, hospital could refuse to remove life support system)

**8.** 497 N.E.2d 626 (1986).

court, while upholding the right of a family to have a feeding tube removed from a patient in a persistent vegetative state, also held that, where the hospital had an ethical objection to doing so, the patient's family could be required to remove the patient to a facility more receptive to the family's request. Thus, courts are divided over whether the health care provider's objections to a decision to remove life-sustaining have to be accommodated. It may be, however, that greater accommodation may be required when the hospital is a private rather than a public hospital.

## § 14.3    End-of-life Decision Making for the Adult Incompetent Patient[1]

With respect to incompetent patients, distinctions are drawn between those patients who were never legally competent, such as minors, and those patients who were once competent but no longer are. Additionally, distinctions are drawn between those once competent patients who have signed living wills, advanced directives, or durable health care powers and those who have not.

For adult patients who were never competent, surrogate decision makers are expected to apply what is called the "best interest" test rather than the "substituted judgement" test. For such patients, application of the "substituted judgement" test where the decision maker would, in theory, make that decision the patient would have made if the patient could make a decision, is logically impossible. Under the "best interest" test, the decision maker makes whatever decision he believes is in the patient's best interest. Account is not taken, in theory, of what choice the patient might have made because the patient had never been able to make a rationale choice. However, this makes the most sense only for infants and young minors and for persons with profound mental retardation. But for mature minors and persons with less severe mental retardation, it is quite possible that they could rationalize a health care decision and, thus, it would be entirely appropriate to take their views into account using a substituted judgement approach. Furthermore, at least one influential court has held that even for adult patients who had never been competent, health care decisions made on their behalf must take their wants into account. Joseph Saikewicz[2] was an adult mental retardate with the mental

---

**1.** The use of the phrase "incompetent patient" is misleading. The notion is that the patient lacks decision making capacity as determined by the health care provider, not that the patient has been judicially declared incompetent. Of course, minors and judicially declared incompetents as a matter of law cannot make legally binding medical decisions. Even so, health care providers will often respect the decisions of "mature minors."

**2.** *Superintendent of Belchertown State School v. Saikewicz*, 370 N.E.2d 417 (Mass. 1977).

age of a 2 year, 8–month–old infant who suffered from leukemia. Leukemia aside, he was generally in good health. He could not communicate verbally but would resort to gestures and grunts to communicate his wishes. His disease was invariably fatal. His guardian ad litem refused to consent to Joseph receiving chemotherapy because that would cause significant adverse side effects and discomfort and would cause Joseph, who was incapable of understanding the purpose of the treatment, fear and pain. The guardian concluded that the limited benefits of the treatment did not outweigh the burdens of treatment. The trial judge agreed with that assessment. The appellate court heard the appeal even though Joseph died in the interim because of the importance of the issue for future patients.

Although the court recognized that Joseph could never have made a rationale decision, use of a best interest standard to determine whether he'd receive chemotherapy, in the court's view, was not appropriate. Rather the guardian should "ascertain the incompetent person's actual interests and preferences . . . and the decision . . . should be that which would be made by the incompetent person, if that person were competent, but taking into account the present and future incompetency of the individual as one of the factors which would necessarily enter in the decision-making process of the competent person."[3] This standard, in the court's view, recognizes that the autonomy interest of the incompetent is as deserving of protection as the autonomy interest of competent persons.

Other courts, however, have been less concerned about protecting the autonomy interests of adult persons who are profoundly disabled and believe it is only appropriate to apply a best interest standard to such persons. For example John Storar[4] was a 52–year–old profoundly mental retardate. He had terminal bladder cancer which his doctors wanted to treat with radiation therapy at a local hospital. After a period of time, John's mother, his guardian, withdrew her permission to treat John because he found the treatments disagreeable, distressful and painful. The treatment center then brought an action to compel treatment arguing that without treatment he would die within a few weeks. The court ordered the treatments stating that while a parent or guardian ordinarily has the right to consent to the ward's medical treatment, "the parent . . . may not deprive a child of life saving treatment, however well intentioned."[5] As the court saw it, sustained life is always in the ward's best interest—life is better than death. It appears that it was for this belief that the *Storar's* court approach

3.  370 N.E.2d at 431.

4.  *In re Storar*, 420 N.E.2d 64 (N.Y. 1981).

5.  Id at 73.,

was rejected in *Saikewicz*. The *Saikewicz* court expressed concern that a best interest standard mandates "an unvarying responsibility by the courts to order necessary medical treatment for an incompetent person facing an immediate and sever danger to life."[6]

For an adult incompetent who were once competent, almost all courts adopt the substituted judgement standard as the appropriate standard to protect the patient's autonomy interest. What judgement the patient would have made may be ascertained from any oral or written instructions communicated by the patient through a living will, durable health care power, or otherwise, such as direct communication with a physician or family members. If a surrogate's decision using substituted judgement is based on the patient's statements, the decision is more likely to be upheld, if challenged, if the court finds that the patient's statements were made (1) consistently, (2) on serious occasions, (3) by a mature person with an understanding of the consequences of the decision, (4) shortly before the treatment, and (4) with some specificity in relation to the patient's actual condition.[7] While courts do not require all four conditions, the more of these conditions that are met the more likely the court will respect the decision. Courts also look to see if the statements attributed to the patient are consistent with other known values of the patient.[8] Courts will consider other evidence of a patient's intent including the patient's religious convictions, value structure, attitude generally about health care, prior interactions with the health-care system, reaction generally to illness, reaction to disease in others, and relationship to friends and family.[9]

The New Jersey courts have assumed a leadership role in this area. Consider the case of Claire Conroy.[10] Claire was a 84-year-old woman with serious and irreversible physical and mental impairments who had been declared mentally incompetent. She resided in a nursing home where her life was maintained by the artificial administration of food and hydration because of her inability to swallow sufficient amounts of these nutrients. All doctors agreed that if her tubes were removed she would die of dehydration within one week. The evidence was inconclusive regarding whether she was experiencing pain. She was not in a coma. Her nephew sought the removal of her feeding tubes. The trial court granted his request finding that Claire's "intellectual functioning had been permanently reduced to a very primitive level, that her life had become impossibly and permanently burdensome, and that removal

---

**6.** Superintendent of Belchertown State School v. Saikewicz, § 14.2 *supra* note 4 at 427.

**7.** Furrow, § 14.2, *supra*, note 10, vol. 2, at § 17.25 at 369–370.

**8.** Id. at 370.

**9.** Id. at 371.

**10.** *In re Matter of Conroy* 486 A.2d 1209 (N.J. 1985).

of the feeding tube should ... be permitted."[11] The intermediate appellate court reversed believing that the withdrawal of the tubes "would be tantamount to killing [Claire]—not simply letting her die—and that such active euthanasia was ethically impermissible." The New Jersey Supreme Court reversed.

The New Jersey court developed a series of rules to be applied to determine under what circumstances life sustaining treatment could be withdrawn from incompetent patients incapable of making medical decisions. First, and in recognition of the patient's autonomy rights, the court stated that life-sustaining treatment could be withdrawn or withheld "when it is clear that the particular patient would have refused the treatment under the circumstances involved."[12] The patient's intent may be evidenced by a living will, oral declarations, a durable health care power, the patient's reactions to the medical treatment others received or deduced from the patient's religious beliefs or from other decisions the patient might have made with respect to his or medical treatment. The probative value of the evidence could vary depending upon a number of factors, including, the "remoteness, consistency, and thoughtfulness of the prior statements or actions and the maturity of the person at the time of the statements or acts."[13] For persons who had never clearly expressed their wishes but who are suffering a prolonged and painful death, the court adopted two additional tests—the limited objective best interest test and the pure objective best interest test.

Under the limited objective best interest test, life support may be withheld or withdrawn where "there is some trustworthy evidence that the patient would have refused the treatment, and the decision-maker is satisfied that it is clear that the burdens of the patient's continued life with the treatment outweigh the benefits of that life for him."[14] This test allows for the termination of treatment when the patient's intent expressed before he or she became incompetent is ambiguous but it is clear that the life sustaining treatment would merely prolong the patient's suffering.

Absent any trustworthy evidence of the patient's intent or any evidence of the patient's intent, the decision maker employs the pure objective test. Here again there is a balance between the net burdens of treatment and the benefits. If the burdens outweigh the benefits, treatment can be withdrawn if "the recurring, unavoidable and severe pain of the patient's life with the treatment ... [are such] that the effect of administering the life-sustaining treatment would be inhumane."[15]

11. Id. at 1209.
12. Id. at 1229.
13. Id. at 1230.

14. Id. at 1231.
15. Id. at 1232.

In a subsequent case, the New Jersey court backed away from this test in the case of patient's in a persistent vegetative state who are incapable of feeling pain. For such patient the court held that the decision of close and caring family members or a close friend should control and their right to decide is not circumscribed by any balancing of benefits and burdens.[16]

## § 14.4 End-of-life Decision Making for Minors

As a general proposition, the right to make health care decisions for minors, including decisions to withhold or withdraw life support, are made by the minor's parents. However, the right of a parent to make health care decisions for a minor child is not absolute. Parental authority may be limited in at least three cases: (1) where the parents are in violation of child abuse laws, (2) where the minor is a "mature minor," and (3) the parents disagree.

Child abuse and neglect statutes prohibit parents from, among other things, depriving their children of necessary medical care. When parents deprive their children of appropriate medical care, the state may step in, take custody of the child, and direct medical decisions for the child. In the context of end-of-life decision making, the issue is whether the parents judgement to withhold or withdraw treatment is neglect or abuse. While some courts have held that a parental decision to withhold or withdraw life support is neglect *per se*, many courts have used a balancing test to make that determination.

Colin Newmark was a three years old with terminal cancer. His parents were Christian Scientists who wanted to reject a proposed radical form of chemotherapy with a 40% chance of success, preferring to rely on prayer and spiritual aid as the means to cure Colin. The trial court held that the parents' decision constituted neglect. The Delaware Supreme Court[1] held that whether the parents approach to treatment was neglect depended on a balancing of factors. Factors to be taken into account included: (1) family primacy in medical decision making for minor children, (2) the state's parens patriae power exercisable to protect the health and safety of children, (3)the child's best interests taking into account the prognosis with or without treatment, the risks of the treatment, the invasiveness of the treatment, the burdens of the treatment and the chances of success.

Where the prognosis is good but parents refuse treatment, courts are more likely to step in to overrule a parent's decision to withhold treatment. Where the prognosis is grim or less certain and

**16.** In re Jobes, 529 A.2d 434 (1987).

**§ 14.4**
**1.** Newmark v. Williams, 588 A.2d 1108 (1991).

the child is likely to experience much pain and discomfort, courts are less prone to overrule a decision to withhold treatment.

Often courts are asked to overturn parents' decisions where those decisions are based upon the parents' religious views. This is typical with Jehovah's Witnesses and Christian Scientists. The extent of respect accorded parental decisions motivated by their religious views varies. For example, religiously-based decisions to withhold blood transfusions that would save a child's life are typically not respected by the courts. As noted in *Prince v. Massachusetts*,[2] "parents may be free to become martyrs themselves. But it does not follow they are free, in identical circumstances, to make martyrs of their children before they have reached the age of full and legal discretion when they can make that choice for themselves."[3]

In the case of mature minors, wider latitude is given to permit the minor to participate in his or her own health care decisions although if push comes to shove health care providers are most unlikely to follow a minor's directive when it conflicts with that of the minor's parents.

## § 14.5   Living Wills and Durable Powers

Almost all states now have statutes permitting persons over the age of 18 to execute both living wills (sometimes called "advance directives" or "advance health-care directive") and durable health care powers (sometimes called "power of attorney for health care"). The formalities necessary to execute these instruments also vary widely. Typically, these documents must be evidenced by a writing, but the Uniform Health–Care Decisions Act (unlike most statutes) permits an advance directive to be oral.[1] While the Uniform Health–Care Decisions Act does not expressly require that any directive or durable power be witnessed or notarized, most states impose at least one of these requirements. It is often common for the state statute to prohibit certain health care professionals from being a witness to a living will.

Some states also provide that a living will validly executed in another state is valid in the state where the patient is currently residing.

The living will typically becomes effective when it is executed, although the Uniform Rights of the Terminally Act provides that the living will becomes operative after it is communicated to the attending physician and the declarant is determined to have a

---

**2.**  321 U.S. 158 (1944).

**3.**  Id. at 170

§ 14.5

**1.**  Unif. Health–Care Decisions Act (hereafter UHDA) § 2(a) & (b).

terminal condition and no longer capable of making decisions regarding the use of life-sustaining procedures.[2] It is not uncommon, however, for a state law to suspend the operation of a living will during the declarant's pregnancy.

Living wills usually are easy to revoke. They can be revoked orally or by a writing and often without regard to the declarant's mental or physical condition. However, to protect health care providers, it is generally provided that a revocation is effective "upon its communication to the attending physician or other health-care provider by the declarant or a witness to revocation."[3]

While state laws differ, a typical living will usually provides that, if the maker has an "incurable and irreversible" condition that will result in death within "a relatively short time"[4] or, as some states add, if the maker becomes "unconscious and, to a reasonable degree of medical certainty ... will not regain consciousness,"[5] then life-sustaining or life-prolonging procedures be withheld or withdrawn.[6] The quoted phrases are fraught with ambiguity, although there is little case law to suggest that they have become the subject of much litigation. The language of living will statutes necessarily clothes the physician with a lot of authority to determine whether the declarant has a medical condition described in the living will.

Once the living will becomes operative, life-sustaining treatment can be withheld or withdrawn. State laws differ regarding whether artificial nutrition and hydration are included within the concept of life-sustaining or life-prolonging procedures.

Interestingly, the typical living will is at best precatory although some states provide that they shall govern decisions regarding the administration of life-sustaining procedures. Where merely precatory, physicians and other health care providers are not required to honor them. On the other hand, the typical statute provides that if the living will is honored and the patient dies as a result of the withdrawal or withholding of life support, the patient's death is not treated as a suicide or homicide.

A 1997 study published in the Journal of the American Medical Association found a high incidence of physicians' failing to abide by patients' living wills. This study appears to confirm anecdotal information that lawyers often hear and underlies, as well, the movement to enable persons to sign durable health care powers.

**2.** Unif. Rights of the Terminally Ill Act, § 3.

**3.** Id. at § 4.

**4.** Unif. Health Care Decisions Act § 4; Unif. Rights of the Terminally Ill Act § 2. In some jurisdictions the living will becomes operative if death is likely to occur within 6 months.

**5.** Id. § 4.

**6.** Id.

The durable power is conceptually broader in scope than the living will in that it permits an agent designated by the principal to make any health-care decision for the principal whenever the principal is unable to make a health care decision for himself.[7] Durable powers generally become operative whenever the principal is incapable of making a health-care decision. They are not limited to cases where the principal has a terminal condition.

Generally, the agent can be any competent adult although there are often prohibitions on the principal's physician or an employee of the physician being designated as an agent.

Whether the principal is capable of making a health-care decision is determined by the principal's primary physician.[8]

Under UHDA, the decision of the agent should comport with the principal's expressed instructions or other wishes to the extent known, or, if there are none, then in accordance with the agent's judgement of the principal's best interest.[9] Given that the agent's first duty is to make a decision consistent with the principal's wishes, it is important that the durable power adequately reflect the desires of the principal, or that those desires be communicated to the principal by some other means. The agent's powers can be limited in most any way by the terms of the durable power, although often a principal will want the agent to act in all cases where the principal is unable to act to the fullest extent possible.

Lawyers who prepare these health care documents for their clients often combine the living will and health care power. A combination document provides a written expression of the principal's intent, particular when end-of-life decision making is required, that not only guides the agent but also helps assuage possible psychological concerns that an agent might have in making a decision that could end the principal's life.

## § 14.6   Family Consent Laws

Because most patients have not executed either living wills or durable health care powers, physicians and other health care providers must often look to family members as alternative decision makers. In the absence of express statutory authority empowering family members to make health care decisions for a loved one, there is a concern whether physicians expose themselves to risk by relying on the family member's decisions. These concerns are eliminated in jurisdictions that have adopted some form of family consent rules.[1] Some of these statutes apply only to end-of-life

---

**7.**  Id.at §§ 2(b) & 4

**8.**  Id. at §§ 2(c) & 4.

**9.**  Id. at § 2(e).

**§ 14.6**

**1.**  See, e.g., Iowa Code § 144A.7.

decision making, while others apply to all health care decisions. The typical statute provides that, absent an effective living will or durable power, health care decisions can be made on behalf of a patient who the attending physician has determined is incapable of making a health-care decision by a designated family member or family members. The typical priority among family members is spouse, then adult child, or if more than one, a majority of them, parents, adult siblings or a majority of them. Often, these statutes permit close friends to make decisions where family members are unavailable. If the patient had designated a surrogate decision maker or had a judicially appointed guardian, the surrogate or guardian, typically in that order, would be empowered to make the decision.

# Chapter 15

# OVERVIEW OF THE FEDERAL TAX LAWS RELATING TO ESTATES AND TRUSTS

## Table of Sections

## § 15.1   Income Taxation of Gifts and Bequests and Basis of Gifted and Inherited Property

Section 102 of the Internal Revenue Code excludes from gross income for income tax purposes the amount of property received by a donee or beneficiary as either a lifetime gift or a testamentary bequest.[1] This exclusion does not apply, however, to income on gifts or bequests.[2]

Section 102 fails to define the meaning of a gift or bequest. Thus, the definition of a gift or bequest is largely left to state law. Likewise section 102 does not delineate how a gift or bequest excluded from gross income should be distinguished from the income on a gift or bequest which should be included in gross income. For outright gifts or bequests, this is also left to state law, For gifts or bequests in trust, however, the delineation is essentially provided by the rules of Subchapter J.

**§ 15.1**

1. Likewise, section 101 excludes from gross income the proceeds of any life insurance payable by reason of an insured's death from the beneficiary's gross income.

2. I.R.C. § 102(b).

For outright gifts or bequests the operation of section 102 is fairly straight forward. For example, if Oscar gives Sally 100 shares of X Corporation, common stock, the value of the stock on the date of the gift is excluded from Sally's gross income. On the other hand, all dividends paid by X Corporation to Sally after the date of the gift are included in Sally's gross income.

The making of a gift is not a taxable event for income tax purposes. Thus, if a donor gives appreciated stock to a donee, the donor realizes no capital gain as a result of the gift. On the other hand, the basis of gifted property in the donee's hands is the donor's adjusted basis[3] increased by the gift tax paid, if any, on the difference between the donor's basis and the property's fair market value on the date of the gift.[4] If no gift tax was paid with respect to the gift, then the donee's basis equals the donor's basis. The adjustment for gift taxes paid is determined by multiplying the gift tax paid by a fraction. The numerator of the fraction is the difference between the property's fair market value and the donor's adjusted basis immediately before the gift; the denominator is the value of the gift.[5] For example, suppose Orville gives Harry property valued at $10. In Orville's hands, the property had an adjusted basis of $2. Orville pays a gift tax of $4 on the transfer. The basis of the property in Harry's hands is $2 plus 80% of the $4 gift tax, or $5.20.

If the donor's adjusted basis in gifted property is greater than the property's fair market value at the time of the gift, then for purposes of determining loss on a sale or exchange of the property, its basis equals its fair market value on the date of the gift.[6]

This "transferred basis" rule means that any appreciation on gifted property is taxed in the donee's hands, not the donor's hands, and, of course, only when the donee disposes of the gifted property during the donee's life. For example, suppose Anna gives John 100 shares of Y Corporation, common stock having a value of $1,000 on the date of the gift. Suppose further that Anna paid $100 for this stock. Anna realizes no gain on this gift even though at the time of the gift the stock had appreciated by $900 over what Anna had paid for it. If two years later, John sells the stock for $1,500, John realizes a capital gain of $1,400. This amount is the difference between the amount he realized and the transferred basis of $100.

For property acquired by bequest or inheritance, the basis of the property in the beneficiary's hands is the property's estate tax value in the case of property that was included in a decedent's

---

**3.** Ordinarily the donor's adjusted basis in the gift property equals the donor's cost. I.R.C. § 1012. In certain cases, the donor's cost basis will have to be adjusted. See, *e.g.*, I.R.C. § 1016.

**4.** I.R.C. § 1015(a), (d)(6).

**5.** *Id.*

**6.** I.R.C. § 1015(a).

estate tax return.[7] The property's estate tax value is its fair market value as of decedent's death or its fair market value determined under the alternate valuation method.[8] Because the basis of inherited property, is "stepped up" to its estate tax value, to the extent that value exceeds decedent's basis in the property[9], such excess avoids being taxed for income tax purposes. The "stepped up" basis rule provides a powerful incentive to hold property until death rather than sell the property during life and incur a potential tax on capital gains, or gift the property to a donee who, under section 1015, would acquire the donor's basis in the property.[10] For example, Alice buys Blackacre for $50,000. It is worth $450,000 when she dies. Under her will she bequeaths Blackacre to Chris. In Chris' hands the basis of Blackacre is $450,000 which means that if Chris immediately sells Blackacre for $450,000 Chris realizes no gain on the sale because his basis in Blackacre is $450,000. Thus, the $400,000 of appreciation occurring during Alice's lifetime wholly escapes the income tax.[11]

As noted the stepped up basis rule applies to property acquired by bequest or inheritance. It also applies to property otherwise included in a decedent's gross estate that is acquired by the donee by means other than a bequest or inheritance. For example, if Bob transferred stock into a revocable trust which Bob acquired for $5,000, the basis of the stock in the trustee's hand is $5,000 under section 1015. When Bob later dies, the trust assets will be included in Bob's gross estate because of his retained power of revocation and subject to the federal estate tax.[12] If, at Bob's death, the stock is worth $50,000 and it then becomes distributable to Jim, the remainder person of the trust, Jim's basis in the property will be $50,000. Likewise, suppose Nancy purchases Blackacre for $5,000 and takes title in the name of herself and Drew as joint tenants with right of survivorship. At Nancy's death, Blackacre will be

---

**7.** I.R.C. § 1014.

**8.** See, § 15.3, infra. If decedent's estate was not required to file an estate tax return, then the property's basis is its fair market value on the date of the decedent's death.

**9.** Decedent's basis usually equals the cost of the asset in the decedent's hand. See generally, I.R.C. § 1012.

**10.** Proposals to eliminate the estate tax also include repeal of the stepped up basis rule, at least for larger estates, in favor of a transferred or carryover basis which would cause the inherited property's basis in the beneficiary's hands to be determined by reference to the decedent's basis. A proposal to this effect was adopted by Congress in 2000 but vetoed by President Clinton. To some extent Democrats also support repeal or modification of the transfer tax laws and with the election of President Bush it is expected that some significant changes will occur in the tax.

**11.** See also, § 15.3, and notes 11 et. seq. and accompanying text.

**12.** I.R.C. § 2038. The step up in basis is available even if Bob's estate is too small to warrant the filing of an estate tax return, although in such case the property tax basis will equal its fair market value on Bob's death, not its estate tax value. See generally, I.R.C. § 1014.

included in her gross estate for federal estate tax purposes.[13] At her death Blackacre is worth $150,000. The basis of Blackacre in Drew's hands is $150,000.

## § 15.2  Gift Tax

Federal law imposes a transfer tax upon the privilege of transferring property by gift, bequest or inheritance. This transfer tax takes the form of a gift tax in the case of completed lifetime gifts[1] and an estate tax in the case of property owned by the decedent at the time of death, certain lifetime transfers, annuities, joint tenancy property, property over which decedent had, exercised or released a general power of appointment, life insurance and certain qualified terminable interest property.[2]

Generally, gifted property is not included in the donor's gross estate but this is not always the case. However, where gifted property is included in the donor's estate, available credits assure that only the increase in value of the gifted property between the date of the gift and the date of the donor's death is effectively subject to the estate tax. For example, suppose Helen transfers property with a gift tax value of $500,000 to a trust and retains the income for life with a remainder to her children. This property is worth $750,000 when Helen dies and is included in her gross estate because of her retained life estate.[3] While at face value it might appear that at least $500,000 of the property's value is subject to both the gift and estate tax, in fact and because of the gift tax credit against the estate tax, only the property's $500,000 value is subject to the gift tax; the balance of $250,000 is subject to the estate tax.

Gift and estate taxes are computed on the progressive unified rate schedule set forth in Section 2001 of the Internal Revenue Code. The tentative tax computed under that section is reduced by a number of credits. The two more important of these are the unified credit and the state death tax credit which is applicable only to the estate tax. The unified credit when fully phased in by 2009[4] will exempt estates valued at $3,500,000 or less from the estate tax.

The state death tax credit equals the lesser of the actual amount of state death taxes payable by reason of the decedent's death or the scheduled credit in Section 2011.

The rates of tax are applied against cumulative lifetime and death time transfers. The cumulative nature of the gift and estate

**13.** I.R.C. § 2040.

**§ 15.2**

**1.** See notes 34 *infra* and accompanying text.

**2.** See § 15.3, *infra.*

**3.** I.R.C. § 2036.

**4.** I.R.C. § 2010.

taxes is assured by adding to taxable gifts in the current year, or to a decedent's taxable estate, all prior taxable gifts and reducing the tentative tax on this tax base by the gift tax on all prior gifts.

*The Meaning of Taxable Gift:* A federal gift tax is imposed on the value of lifetime gifts. For gift tax purposes a gift is defined as the transfer of property for less than adequate and full consideration in money or money's worth, other than a transfer in the "ordinary course of business."[5]

Most transfers that meet the common law definition of a gift also are gifts for gift tax purposes but certain lifetime transfers may not be gifts for state property law purposes that nonetheless are gifts for gift tax purposes. This can result from the fact that the consideration necessary to support a contract under state law may not be sufficient to avoid a gift under federal tax law.

For gift tax purposes, consideration that cannot be expressed in money or money's worth is ignored. Thus, if the consideration received does not replace the value of the donor's personal wealth that has been transferred to another, then, for gift tax purposes, the transfer was not for adequate consideration in money or money's worth. For example, if John transfers Blackacre, valued at $100,000, to his daughter, Mary, for cash in the amount of $100,000, John receives adequate and full consideration in money or money's worth. Both before and after the transfer John's personal wealth is valued at least at $100,000. On the other hand, suppose John promises to pay Mary $20,000 if Mary does not smoke for a year. Mary stops smoking for one year and John pays her $20,000. John makes a gift to Mary of $20,000 of which, after the annual exclusion unadjusted, only $10,000 is taxed. While Mary's performance may be sufficient consideration under state law to support the enforcement of John's promise, it is not consideration in money or money's worth because it does not replenish the value of John's personal estate which has been depleted by $20,000.

A transfer in consideration for the donee's release of dower or curtesy or a statutory right in lieu thereof is not consideration in money or money's worth.[6] On the other hand, a transfer to a spouse in consideration for the spouse's release of a support obligation is a

---

**5.** A transfer is in the "ordinary course of business" if it is a bona fide arms' length transaction free of any donative intent. For example, when a department store has a sale and sells goods at a price that is less than the marked price, no gift results because of the ordinary business transaction exception.

**6.** Merrill v. Fahs, 324 U.S. 308, 65 S.Ct. 655, 89 L.Ed. 963 (1945), rehearing denied 324 U.S. 888, 65 S.Ct. 863, 89 L.Ed. 1436 (1945); I.R.C. § 2043. *But see* I.R.C. § 2516 and note 80 *infra* and accompanying text.

transfer for adequate and full consideration in money or money's worth.[7]

According to the Treasury Regulations "the terms 'taxable gifts' means the 'total amount of gifts' made by the donor during the 'calendar period' * * * less the deductions" allowable under Sections 2522 and 2523 for certain charitable and interspousal transfers. The term "total amount of gifts" means the sum of the values of gifts during the calendar period less any available annual exclusion.

The annual exclusion equals the value of present interest[8] gifts to any donee each year up to the amount of $10,000.[9] To illustrate, suppose Mary gave Alice $100,000 in cash. With respect to this gift both the "total amount of gift" and the "taxable gift" is $90,000. On the other hand, suppose the gift had been made to Mary's husband, George. In this case the "total amount of gift" is $90,000 but the "taxable gift" is $0 because of the availability of the gift tax marital deduction.[10]

The amount of a donor's taxable gift is also affected by the so-called "split gift" rule,[11] under which a married donor's gifts can be treated for gift tax purposes as having been made half by the donor and half by the donor's spouse if the donor and the donor's spouse so elect. Thus, if Mary gives Alice $20,000 and Mary and her husband, George, elect to split the gift for gift tax purposes, then for purposes of computing the taxable gifts of Mary and George, each of them is deemed to have given Alice $10,000. Since each of them is entitled to an annual exclusion for present interest gifts up to $10,000, each of them makes a taxable gift of $0 to Alice. The split gift rules permit electing married couples to double up on their annual exclusions and unified credits. Thus, between them they can make gifts of $20,000 annually to any donee gift tax free, and gifts in excess of that amount can be shielded from transfer tax by the use of their individual unified credits.

*Valuation of Gifted Property:* Gifted property is valued at its fair market value on the date of the gift.[12] Fair market value is the "price at which [gifted] * * * property would change hands between a willing buyer and a willing seller, neither being under any

---

**7.** See, *e.g.*, Glen v. Comm'r, 45 T.C. 323 (1966).

**8.** See notes 13, 14 & 27 *infra* and accompanying text (relating to present and future interests).

**9.** For gifts made after 1998, the amount of the $10,000 annual exclusion is subject to increase for an inflation adjustment in multiples of $1,000. See I.R.C. § 2503(b)(2). In the text, the annual exclusion will continue to be referred to as $10,000.

**10.** See notes 74–76 *infra* and accompanying text.

**11.** I.R.C. § 2513. The split gift option is designed to equalize the treatment of gifts for married persons whether they live in common law property states or community property states.

**12.** A gift is deemed made when the gift is complete. See notes 34–61, *infra* and accompanying text.

compulsion to buy or to sell, and both having reasonable knowledge of relevant facts."[13]

Where the gifted property is an annuity, life estate or remainder or reversion, the value of the property from which the annuity, life estate, remainder or reversion is carved must first be valued under the willing seller-willing buyer test. This value is then multiplied by the appropriate factor set forth in the Treasury regulations[14] taking account of the age of the relevant beneficiary or the term for which the interest is payable. To illustrate, suppose Mary transfers Blackacre to Alice for life, remainder to Bernie. In order to value the gifts to Alice and Bernie Blackacre first must be valued. Assume that under the willing seller-willing buyer test, Blackacre is valued at $100,000. Alice's interest, under the appropriate valuation table, is valued at $98,198; Bernie's interest is valued at $1,934. In computing the amount of Mary's gift tax liability, Mary is deemed to have made a gift of $98,198 to Alice and a transfer of $1,934 to Bernie. However, the gift to Alice is a present interest[15] and qualifies for a $10,000 annual exclusion but the gift to Bernie is a future interest[16] and does not qualify for the annual exclusion.

If the donor retains an interest in gifted property, then the value of the gift must be reduced by the value of the donor's retained interest. However, under section 2702 in most cases where the donor transfers property in trust for the benefit of a family member and retains any interest in the trust, the value of the donor's retained interest will be deemed to be zero. This results in the transferred property's entire value being subject to the gift tax notwithstanding that under state law the donor has retained an interest in the transferred property. For example, suppose Oscar transfers $100,000 to T in trust to pay the income to Oscar for life, remainder to Oscar's daughter. Under the appropriate valuation tables, Oscar's retained interest is worth $62,000 and the daughter's remainder interest is worth $38,000. Nonetheless, section 2702 provides that Oscar's retained interest is to be valued at zero Since Oscar's taxable gift equals the difference between the amount transferred and the value of his retained interest and under section 2702 Oscar's retained interest is valued at zero, he makes a taxable gift of $100,000. Section 2702 does not apply to otherwise complet-

---

**13.** Treas.Reg. § 25.2512–1.

**14.** Treas.Reg. § 25.2512–5.

**15.** A present interest for gift tax purposes is an "unrestricted right to the immediate use, possession, or enjoyment of property or the income from property." Treas.Reg. § 25.2503–3(b).

**16.** A future interest for gift tax purposes is "a legal term, and includes reversions, remainders, and other interests or estates, whether vested or contingent, and whether or not supported by a particular interest or estate, which are limited to commence in use, possession, or enjoyment at some future date or time." Treas.Reg. § 25.2503–3(a).

ed gifts if the donor's retained interest is in the form of a (a) guaranteed annuity (pay Oscar $8,000 per year), (b) a unitrust interest (pay Oscar an annual payment equal to 6% of the value of the trust principal valued on the first day of each calendar year), or (c) a remainder interest in a trust in which another has either an annuity or unitrust interest. Section 2702 also is inapplicable to trusts of a qualified personal residence. Under this exception it remains possible to transfer the remainder interest in a personal residence and have the value of the donor's retained life estate reduce the amount of the gift. However any transfer tax savings would be lost as the entire residence would be included in the donor's gross estate under section 2036. On the other hand, if the donor retained only a term interest in the residence, the value of the donor's retained interest reduces the amount of the gift and, if the donor outlives the term, the residence would not be included in the donor's gross estate and thus future appreciation would have escaped transfer taxes.

Even if section 2702 is inapplicable, if the donor's retained interest cannot be valued by recognized actuarial methods, then its value is presumed to be zero.[17]

The gift tax payable on gifts made during a calendar year is payable on or before April 15 following the close of the calendar year.[18]

*Identity of the Donee:* Since the gift tax is imposed on the value of property transferred by a donor, rather than upon the value of property received by a donee, ordinarily the identity of a donee is not important to the assessment of the gift tax. In certain cases, however, the identity of the donee or the nature of the interest received by the donee rather than the nature of the interest transferred by the donor may be important.

If the donee is a charity, gifts to the donee can qualify for a gift tax charitable deduction.[19] If the donee is the donor's spouse, the gift can qualify for a gift tax marital deduction.[20] If the interest passing to the donee is a "present interest," the value thereof qualifies for the annual exclusion. Lastly, if transfers are made in trust, the donee is the person or persons entitled to the beneficial interests in the trust, not the trustee. This can be important in determining not only the availability of a charitable or marital deduction but also the value of the donated interest from the valuation tables published in the Treasury Regulations[21] and the amount, if any, that qualifies for the annual exclusion.

**17.** Robinette v. Helvering, 318 U.S. 184, 63 S.Ct. 540, 87 L.Ed. 700 (1943).

**18.** I.R.C. §§ 6075(b); 6151.

**19.** See notes 70–73, *infra* and accompanying text.

**20.** See notes 74–77, *infra* and accompanying text.

**21.** Treas.Reg. § 25.2512–5(f).

*The Annual Exclusion and Medical and Tuition Payment Exclusion:* Section 2503(b) provides an annual exclusion not to exceed $10,000 (adjusted for inflation) for gifts of a present interest to any donee in each calendar year.[22] Gifts of a future interest do not qualify for the exclusion.[23] An unrestricted right to the use, possession or enjoyment of property or the income therefrom is a gift of a present interest.[24] Gifts of discretionary income interests even if limited by a standard do not qualify for the annual exclusion. Similarly, gifts of reversions and remainders do not qualify for the annual exclusion as they are gifts of a future interest.

Use of the annual exclusion to avoid gift taxes on annual transfers can result in a significant shift of wealth from one generation to another without any transfer tax cost. For example, if $10,000 is given annually to a child for 20 years, $200,000 of tax free gifts can be made to that child over a 20 year period. For married couples utilizing the split gift rules, annual gifts to any donee of $20,000 can be made gift tax free. Gifts shielded from tax by the annual exclusion do not result in any further use of the donor's unified credit. For large families the potential to shift wealth from one generation to another at little or no transfer tax cost using only the annual exclusion to fully shield gifts from tax can be significant.

A transfer to a minor that does not meet the ordinary definition of a present interest can qualify for the annual exclusion if the transfer qualifies as a present interest under Section 2503(c). Under Section 2503(c) no part of a gift is considered to be a gift of a future interest if the gift is made to a person under age 21 and if the gifted property and the income therefrom may be paid to, or applied towards the benefit of, the donee prior to the donee attaining age 21, and such property and the income will pass to the donee when the donee attains age 21 or, if the donee dies prior to attaining age 21, such property and the income is payable to either the donee's estate or as the donee may appoint pursuant to a general power of appointment.

This statute has led to the creation of so-called Section 2503(c) trusts under the terms of which income in the trustee's discretion may be paid to the donee prior to the donee attaining age 21 or accumulated for distribution to the donee when the donee attains age 21. These Section 2503(c) trusts must also provide that (1) when the donee attains age 21, the principal and any accumulated income shall be paid to the donee, or (2) if the donee dies under age 21, the principal and any accumulated income will be paid to his

---

**22.** For 2004, the annual exclusion, adjusted for inflation, is $11,000.

**23.** I.R.C. § 2503(b).

**24.** Treas.Reg. § 25.2503–3(b).

estate.[25] Many donors prefer to provide that if the donee dies under age 21 the principal and accumulated income will be paid to such persons as the donee appoints pursuant to a general testamentary power of appointment and then designate takers in default of appointment in the event (which is quite likely) the donee's general power is unexercised. If the trustee's power to pay income to the donee is substantially restricted, the gift will not qualify as a present interest under Section 2503(c).[26] A trustee's discretion is not substantially restricted if payments are limited to providing for the donee's "support," "care," or "education."[27]

Gifts to minors under Uniform Gifts (Transfers) to Minors Act qualify for the annual exclusion under the Section 2503(b) exception.[28]

In lieu of a Section 2503(c) trust donors may qualify transfers in trust for the annual exclusion even though the donee's interest is not described in Section 2503(c) by the use of so-called "Crummey" powers.[29] A Crummey power is a species of a general power that enables the donee of the power to appoint the property subject to the power to himself for a limited period of time, at the end of which, the power lapses if, in fact, it is not exercised. Since the donee has a general power, albeit, for a limited period, it qualifies as a present interest and the property over which the power is exercisable qualifies for the annual exclusion. To illustrate, suppose Bob transfers $10,000 in trust to pay the income to Sandy, or, in the trustee's discretion, to accumulate the trust income. The trust will terminate when Sandy dies or attains age 40 when the trust principal is payable to Sandy, if living, or otherwise to Sandy's issue. Sandy is age 17. On its face the trust does not qualify for the annual exclusion under Section 2503(c). If Bob also granted Sandy a Crummey power exercisable only for the first three months after the contribution to the trust, then the annual exclusion would be allowable because the Crummey power vests Sandy with a present interest in the trust. It is irrelevant that Sandy lets the power lapse. Crummey powers work so long as (i) the donee receives notice of the contribution and a reasonable opportunity to exercise the power,[30] and (ii) in the Service's but not the courts' view, the

**25.** It is possible to qualify the value of the under age 21 income interest as a present interest even if the trust corpus is not payable to the donee when the donee attains age 21. See Herr v. Comm'r, 35 T.C. 732 (1961), affirmed 303 F.2d 780 (3d Cir.1962); Estate of Levine v. Comm'r, 63 T.C. 136 (1974), reversed 526 F.2d 717 (2d Cir.1975).

**26.** Treas.Reg. § 25.2503–4(b)(1).

**27.** See Rev. Rul. 67–270, 1967–2 C.B. 349.

**28.** Rev. Rul. 59–357, 1959–2 C.B. 212. See generally, § 9.2, note 5 et. seq. for a discussion of these acts.

**29.** Crummey v. Comm'r, 397 F.2d 82 (9th Cir.1968).

**30.** See Rev. Rul. 81–7, 1981–1 C.B. 474.

holder of the power has either a current income interest or a vested remainder.[31]

Payments made on behalf of a person's tuition at an educational institution or for such person's medical care are not taxable gifts. This exclusion is not available if the payments are made to the intended donee who then pays the tuition or medical expense.[32] The wording of the statute places a premium on direct payments to the educational institution as payments through the student do not qualify for the exclusion.

*Complete and Incomplete Gifts:* The gift tax is imposed only upon so-called completed gifts. A transfer for less than adequate and full consideration in money or money's worth is a completed gift for gift tax purposes only if the enjoyment of the transferred property is placed beyond the donor's dominion and control. The dominion and control test is explained as follows:[33]

> As to any property, or part thereof or interest therein, of which the donor has so parted with dominion and control as to leave in him no power to change its disposition, whether for his own benefit or for the benefit of another, the gift is complete. But if upon the transfer of property (whether in trust or otherwise) the donor reserves any power over its disposition, the gift may be partially complete and partially incomplete, depending upon all the facts in the particular case.

If the donor transfers property outright and the transferred property is beyond the donor's dominion and control, the gift is complete for gift tax purposes. Alternatively, if the donor retains any power to regain possession or ownership of the property or retains the power to determine who shall enjoy the benefits of the property, the gift is incomplete[34] and no taxable gift is made until the donor's dominion and control terminates over the transferred property. In many cases, however, the donor's dominion and control will not terminate in the donor's lifetime. In this case, more likely than not, the property will be included in the donor's gross estate for estate tax purposes[35] and not be included in the donor's gift tax base. For

---

**31.** See Tech. Adv. Mem. 96–28–004 (7/12/96). Crummey power granted to persons with no underlying interest in the trust are called "naked powers." The Tax Court rejects the Service's view. See, e.g, Kohlsaat v. Comm'r, 73 T.C.M (CCH) ¶ 2732 (1992); Cristofani v. Comm'r, 97 T.C. 74 (1991).

**32.** I.R.C. § 2503(e).

**33.** Treas.Reg. § 25.2511(b).

**34.** An apparent exception is found in Treas.Reg. § 25.2511–2(d) where it is provided that if the donor retains the power only to affect the time and manner of enjoyment of property, the gift is complete for gift tax purposes. For example, if the donor transfers property to T in trust to pay the income to A until A attains age 21 when the trust terminates and the corpus is distributable to A, the gift is complete even though the donor retains the power to direct trust income be accumulated until A attains age 21 and distributed to A at that time.

**35.** See § 15.3, *infra* notes 49 et. seq. and accompanying text.

example, if Mary transfers property into a revocable trust, no gift occurs when the trust is created because Mary retains dominion and control over the transferred property. If two years later Mary releases the power of revocation, a gift occurs at that time since after the release Mary no longer has dominion and control.[36] If Mary fails to release the power during her life and dies in possession of the power, the property in the trust is included in Mary's gross estate.[37]

Mary is deemed to retain dominion and control even though the power she retains cannot be exercised for her pecuniary benefit. For example, suppose Mary transfers property in trust to pay the income to such of Alice, Bob and Charlie as Mary from time to time directs. Upon Mary's death the trust terminates and the principal is distributable to Alice, Bob and Charlie. In this case, Mary retains dominion and control over the income interest[38] but no dominion and control over the value of the remainder interest. Thus, the gift of the income interest is incomplete; the gift of the remainder interest is complete. In other words, in measuring whether there is a completed gift, each interest in the trust is considered separately. In this case, the trust property will also be included in Mary's gross estate because Mary retained a power to control the beneficial enjoyment of the income interest.[39] When the estate tax is computed on Mary's estate, however, appropriate credit will be allowed for the gift tax paid on the value of the completed gift of the remainder interest.

An incomplete gift may become complete for gift tax purposes because the property that is the subject of the gift is distributed to a beneficiary free of a donor's retained power. For example, suppose John creates a revocable trust for the primary benefit of Alice and transfers $100,000 to the trustee. This transfer is not a completed gift because of John's retained dominion and control. The following year the trustee distributes the trust's entire income for that year to Alice. In Alice's hands the income is no longer subject to John's power of revocation. The distribution of income to Alice results in John making a taxable gift of that income to Alice even though with respect to the trust the gift continues to be incomplete.[40]

Whether a gift is complete or incomplete for gift tax purposes does not determine whether the gifted property is included or

**36.** Treas.Reg. § 25.2511–2(f).

**37.** I.R.C. § 2038.

**38.** Treas.Reg. § 25.2511–2(c).

**39.** See I.R.C. § 2036.

**40.** Treas.Reg. § 25.2511–2(f). To the extent the amount of income payable to Alice is less than the available annual exclusion, it is not a taxable gift.

Under I.R.C. § 676 John will include the income paid to Alice in his gross income. Section 676 treats John as the owner of any portion of a trust with respect to which John has a power of revocation. When the income is distributed to Alice, she receives it income tax free. I.R.C. § 101.

excluded from the donor's gross estate. The taxability of any transfer is separately determined under rules governing each tax. In those cases where a gift is incomplete for gift tax purposes the entire gift or some portion thereof will be included in the donor's gross estate. Counter intuitively, however, gifts that are wholly complete for gift tax purposes may also be included in the donor's gross estate. One example is where property is transferred in trust to pay the income to Alice until she attains age 21 when any accumulated income and principal is to be paid to her. John, the grantor, retains the power to direct the trustee to accumulate the income rather than pay it to Alice. This gift is complete for gift tax purposes[41] but the entire trust also is included in John's gross estate if John dies before Alice reaches age 21.[42]

A more common example occurs where a donor retains a power over transferred property that is exercisable only with the consent of an adverse person. Under the gift tax, if a donor retains a power over transferred property that is exercisable only with the consent of an adverse person, the gift of the interest in which there is adversity is complete. For example, if Doris transfers property in trust to pay the income to Lauren for life, remainder to Arthur, and Doris retains the power to accumulate the income for ultimate distribution to Arthur, for gift tax purposes the gift of the income interest is incomplete because of Doris' retained power; the gift of the remainder, however, is complete.[43] Furthermore, the entire trust is included in Doris' gross estate under Section 2036 because of her retained power. If, however, Doris' power to accumulate income was exercisable only with Lauren's consent, the gift of the income and remainder interests would be complete.[44] The gift of the remainder interest is complete because Doris retains no dominion and control over that interest; the gift of the income interest is complete because Doris' power is exercisable only with Lauren's consent and Lauren has an interest that would be adversely affected if Doris exercised the power. Nonetheless, the entire trust is included in Doris' gross estate under Section 2036 because of her co-held power to accumulate the income.[45]

A substantial adverse interest exists only if there is a substantial economic interest that could be prejudiced or destroyed if the power over the interest was exercised. No adverse interest exists in

---

**41.** Treas.Reg. § 25.2511–2(d).

**42.** I.R.C. § 2036. This is precisely what happens when the donor acts as custodian under either the Uniform Gifts or Transfers to Minors Acts.

**43.** Doris' power to increase to value of the remainder interest by directing an accumulation of income is effectively a power to make additions, not a power to alter Arthur's initial interest in the trust.

**44.** Treas.Reg. § 25.2511–2(e).

**45.** In computing the estate tax liability on Doris' estate credit will be allowed for any gift tax paid on this transfer.

a property interest in which the co-holder of power has no economic benefits. For example, suppose Mary creates a revocable trust under which income is payable to Allan and the remainder is distributable to Betty. Mary retains the power to revoke the trust but only with Allan's consent. In this case there is a completed gift only of the income interest. Allan has no economic interest in the remainder interest distributable to Betty when he dies. Admittedly, if Allan joined with Mary in terminating the trust in favor of Mary, Allan's income interest would terminate. However he could be persuaded to join with Mary in revoking the trust by an agreement that Mary pay him the present value of his income interest.

If a donor declares himself trustee, or transfers property to himself and another as trustees, retains no beneficial interest in the property but retains a fiduciary power the exercise of which is limited by an ascertainable standard which would permit him to change beneficiaries, the gift is complete for gift tax purposes.[46] For example, if Bob creates a trust to pay so much of the income to Pat and Jenny as they need for their support and upon the death of Bob to distribute the corpus to Emily, the gift of the income interest is complete even though Bob is a trustee.[47] The retention of a power limited by an ascertainable standard is not the equivalent of a discretionary power and does not amount to the retention of dominion and control such that the gift is incomplete.

*Subject Matter of A Gift:* The gift tax is assessed against transfers of property. Property includes real and personal property, tangible and intangible property.[48] The tax applies whether a legal or equitable interest in property is transferred.[49] A gift can be made of a present or a future interest, a vested or a contingent interest.[50] An income interest can be the subject of a gift. Thus, if John creates a trust under which Alice is entitled to the income for life and subsequently Alice transfers her income interest to Bob, Alice makes a gift to Bob equal to the value of her income interest at the time of the transfer measured by reference to her life expectancy.[51]

A gift of a check is complete when the donee cashes the check[52] because until the check is cashed the donor can revoke the transfer.

Property applied towards the benefit of another rather than paid to him can constitute a gift. Thus, if Don owes Arnie $5,000

---

**46.**  Treas.Reg. § 25.2511–2(g).

**47.**  See the discussion of the ascertainable standard exception under the estate tax law at § 15.3, *infra*, notes 65 & 97, and accompanying text.

**48.**  I.R.C. § 2511(a).

**49.**  Treas.Reg. § 25.2511–1(g)(1).

**50.**  Goodwin  v.  McGowan,  47 F.Supp. 798 (W.D.N.Y.1942).

**51.**  See, *e.g.,* Lockard v. Comm'r, 166 F.2d 409 (1st Cir.1948).

**52.**  Rev. Rul. 67–396, 1967–2 C.B. 351. If the donor dies before the donee cashes the check, the value of the checks is included in the donor's gross estate. See McCarthy v. United States, 806 F.2d 129 (7th Cir.1986); § 4.5, supra, note 36.

and Oscar gratuitously pays Don's debt to Arnie, Oscar makes a gift to Don, not Arnie. This fact may be important for purposes of the $10,000 annual exclusion.

The forgiveness of a debt is a gift.[53]

Life insurance can be the subject matter of a gift although the value of the gift, if the insured is living, is necessarily less than the face value of the policy.[54] A gift of a life insurance policy can be made by its irrevocable assignment to another.[55] However, the designation of someone as the beneficiary of a life insurance policy is not a gift if the owner retains the right to change the beneficiary as is usually the case. Likewise an irrevocable beneficiary designation would not result in the making of a gift under the dominion and control test if the owner retained the power to cancel the policy or surrender the policy for its cash surrender value. The proceeds of gifted life insurance are included in the insured's gross estate if the insured dies within three years of the gift.[56]

The gift tax does not apply to a gift of personal services by the donor regardless of value.[57] If the donor pays a third person to perform a personal service for another, the amount paid is a gift.[58] Thus, if Scott pays Nancy $15,000 to perform a medical procedure on Tom, Scott makes a gift to Tom of $15,000.

*Powers of Appointment:* Section 2514 governs the gift taxation of general powers of appointment that have been exercised or released during the donee's lifetime.[59] For gift tax purposes a general power of appointment is a power under which the donee can appoint to himself, "his estate, his creditors, or the creditors of his estate."[60] Under Section 2514 if a donee of a general power exercises or releases the power, the donee is deemed to have made a transfer. Whether this transfer results in the making of a taxable gift further depends upon whether, as a result of the exercise or

53. Treas.Reg. § 25.2511–1(a).

54. See Treas.Reg. § 25.2511–6 for the valuation of gifted life insurance policies.

55. Treas.Reg. § 25.2511–1(h)(8).

56. I.R.C. § 2035. Gifts of life insurance can be an effective way to transfer significant wealth at little or no transfer tax cost. See § 15.3, *infra,* and note 143, and accompanying text.

57. *See generally,* Comm'r v. Hogle, 165 F.2d 352 (10th Cir.1947); Rev.Rul. 64–225, 1964–2 C.B. 15, Rev.Rul. 66–167, 1966–1 C.B. 20, Rev.Rul. 70–237, 1970–1 C.B. 13.

58. Regs. § 25.2511–1(h)(3).

59. Section 2514 distinguishes between general powers created on or before October 21, 1942 (so-called "pre–42 powers") and powers created after October 21, 1942 (so-called "post–42 powers".) The discussion in the text is limited to post–42 powers. See also, § 10.4, note 6 for a discussion of powers.

60. I.R.C. § 2514(c). This broad definition of a general power is subject to a number of refinements. These are discussed in § 15.3 *infra.* The distinction is similar to the one drawn between general and special powers of appointment for non-tax purposes. See § 10.4, *supra,* note 6.

release, the donee has surrendered dominion and control over the property that was subject to the power.

Suppose Olive transfers property in trust to pay the income to Cecil for life, remainder to Cecil's surviving issue. Olive grants Cecil a general inter vivos power to appoint the property to himself or anyone else. Two years later Cecil exercises the power and appoints the entire trust principal to Jack. The exercise of the power results in a transfer of the trust property from Cecil to Jack. Since Cecil retains no dominion and control over the transferred property, the exercise of the power also results in his making a taxable gift.

Similarly, suppose that Cecil exercises the power by directing that the trustee hold the property in trust to pay the income to Jack for life, remainder to Jack's children. In this case Cecil also makes a transfer under Section 2514 and a gift because he retains no dominion and control. But, suppose that when exercising this power, Cecil provided that he could revoke the appointment in trust for the benefit of Jack and Jack's children. In this case Cecil makes a transfer under Section 2514 because he exercised the power. However, no gift results from the exercise of the power in this manner because Cecil retained dominion and control by retaining a power of revocation.

If Cecil does not exercise the power but rather releases the power, Cecil also makes a transfer of the property subject to the power under Section 2514. Of course, since a person cannot make a gift to himself, this release/transfer results in a gift of the remainder interest only. This gift would not qualify for any annual exclusion because it is a gift of a future interest. Cecil's release of the general power does not result in the termination of his income interest.[61]

The lapse of a general power is considered to be a release of a power.[62] A lapse of a power occurs when the donee fails to exercise the power within a time period specified in the instrument creating the power. Thus, if Oscar grants Felix a general inter vivos power exercisable prior to January 1, 1990 and Felix fails to exercise the power by that date, on January 1, 1990 when the power lapses Felix is deemed to have released the power. This "lapse equals a release" rule is tempered by a special provision that the lapse of a power during any calendar year is treated as a release of a power in that year "only to the extent that the property which could have been appointed by exercise of such lapsed powers exceeds in value the greater of '$5,000 or 5% of the aggregate value of the assets out

---

**61.** While Cecil's makes a gift only of the remainder interest, the value of that interest will equal the value of trust

corpus since the value of Cecil's retained interest is zero under section 2702.

**62.** I.R.C. § 2514(e).

of which', or the proceeds of which, the exercise of the lapsed powers could be satisfied."[63] This so-called "5 and 5" rule has lead to the development of an important estate planning tool.

Under the "5 and 5 rule" a donee may be granted a general power, exercisable annually, to withdraw from the principal of a trust an amount equal to the greater of $5,000 or 5% of trust principal valued annually. If the donee exercises the power there is no gift because a person cannot make a gift to herself. If the donee permits the power to lapse, no release (and therefore no transfer) occurs because of the 5 and 5 rule. This type of power is attractive because it permits the donee to withdraw trust principal to the dollar limits of the power for any reason whatsoever and without the approval of any other person.[64]

If a donee is given an annual withdrawal power measured by a fixed dollar amount which exceeds the 5 and 5 limits, the lapse of the power results in a release of the power *only to the extent of the excess*. For example, suppose Dolly has an annual withdrawal power exercisable in the amount of $15,000 with respect to a trust that at all times is valued at $150,000. In any year Dolly exercises the power in full, there is no gift tax consequence. (Remember, Dolly can't make a gift to herself). In any year in which there is a lapse of the power in an amount of $7,500 or less, there is no gift tax consequence because the lapsed power is valued under the 5 and 5 limits. However, in any year there is a lapse of the power in excess of $7,500, the excess is deemed to have been transferred by Dolly and subject to gift tax unless she retains dominion and control over the property. For example, suppose Dolly, in addition to having a $15,000 withdrawal power, possessed a testamentary special power to appoint the property among her children. A lapse of the power results in a transfer of $7,500 ($15,000 a $7,500) but no gift because Dolly retains dominion and control over the property subject to the lapsed power because of her testamentary special power. If, on the other hand, Dolly did not have the testamentary special power, the lapse of the power would result in a gift of the remainder interest in $7,500, assuming Dolly was the income beneficiary of the trust. This would be a gift of a future interest and would not qualify for the annual exclusion.[65] Any tax on the remainder interest, however, could be avoided by the use of Dolly's unified credit.

---

**63.** I.R.C. § 2514(e).

**64.** See also § 15.32, *infra*, notes 128–132 and accompanying text.

**65.** *See also* notes 24–33, *supra* and accompanying text. The fact that the 5 & 5 rule is not coextensive with the $10,000 annual exclusion can result in possible adverse tax consequence if the donee of a Crummey power permits it to lapse. See, notes 43–49, *supra* and accompanying text.

*Transfers Pursuant to a Property Settlement Agreement:* Section 2516 sets forth special rules relating to the gift tax consequences of property transfers made pursuant to the terms of a property settlement agreement. If a married couple executes a written agreement relating to their marital and property rights and the parties are divorced within a three year period beginning on a date that is one year prior to when the agreement is made, transfers of property or interests in property pursuant to the terms of the agreement to either spouse in settlement of the spouse's marital or property rights or to provide a reasonable allowance for the support of the issue of the marriage during minority are deemed to be transfers for adequate and full consideration in money or money's worth.[66] Section 2516 applies even though the agreement is not approved by the divorce decree.

*Qualifying Income Interest for Life:* If a person transfers a qualifying income interest for life in any property, the transferor is deemed to have made a transfer of the remainder interest as well.[67] A more thorough discussion of this provision is contained in the section on qualified terminable interest property.[68]

*Gifts to Charity or to the Donor's Spouse:* Gifts to qualified[69] charitable organizations qualify for an unlimited charitable deduction.[70] Special rules apply when gifts are made in trust for the benefit of both charities and private individuals.[71] These special rules are more fully discussed in the section on the estate tax charitable deduction.[72]

A gift to the donor's spouse qualifies for an unlimited marital deduction[73] so long as the gift is not disqualified for the deduction under the nondeductible terminable interest rule.[74] The marital deduction rules are more fully discussed in the section on the estate tax marital deduction.[75]

## § 15.3  Estate Tax

A federal estate tax, in common with the federal gift tax, is a tax on the right of transferring property at death.[1] The tax is

**66.** I.R.C. § 2516.

**67.** I.R.C. § 2519.

**68.** See § 15.3, *infra,* notes 174–178 and accompanying text.

**69.** I.R.C. § 2522(a). The definition of "charitable" for tax purposes, while similar, is not identical to its definition for "trust law" purposes. See § 9.7, *supra,* note 5 et. seq.; § 15.3, *infra.*

**70.** I.R.C. § 2522.

**71.** I.R.C. § 2522(c).

**72.** See § 15.3 *infra,* notes 153–161, and accompanying text.

**73.** I.R.C. § 2523.

**74.** I.R.C. § 2523(b).

**75.** See § 15.3, *infra,* notes 162–180 and accompanying text.

**§ 15.3**

**1.** See, Irving v. Hodel, 481 U.S. 704 (1987)(holding that the complete abolition of both the devise and descent of property can be an unconstitutional taking).

measured against a tax base that includes not only the assets of decedent's probate estate[2] but also certain gifts by the decedent during life that are deemed to be the equivalent of testamentary transfers because decedent retained either an interest or power over the gift. Items included in a decedent's gross estate are reduced by other items to calculate decedent's taxable estate.

The gross estate is computed by taking into account the following:

1. Property owned at death.[3]

2. Certain property transferred within three years of death.[4]

3. Lifetime transfers in which decedent retained an interest for life.[5]

4. Certain lifetime transfers taking effect at the decedent's death.[6]

5. Revocable transfers.[7]

6. Annuities.[8]

7. Joint tenancy property.[9]

8. General powers of appointment.[10]

9. Life insurance.[11]

10. Qualified Terminable Interest Property.[12]

The deductions available to compute the decedent's taxable estate are:

1. Debts, expenses and taxes.[13]

2. Losses.[14]

3. Charitable deduction.[15]

4. Marital deduction.[16]

In order to assure that cumulative lifetime and testamentary transfers are taxed in accordance with the progressive unified rate schedule, the estate tax base also includes the value of decedent's

---

**2.** Probate estate property is limited to property capable of passing by a decedent's will or under the laws of intestate succession. Thus, it excludes such property as joint tenancy property, life insurance and annuities payable to a named beneficiary. For possible, non-tax advantages to keeping property out of the probate estate, see § 9.1, *supra*.

**3.** I.R.C. § 2033.

**4.** I.R.C. § 2035.

**5.** I.R.C. § 2036.

**6.** I.R.C. § 2037.

**7.** I.R.C. § 2038.

**8.** I.R.C. § 2039.

**9.** I.R.C. § 2040.

**10.** I.R.C. § 2041.

**11.** I.R.C. § 2042.

**12.** I.R.C. § 2044.

**13.** I.R.C. § 2053.

**14.** I.R.C. § 2054.

**15.** I.R.C. § 2055.

**16.** I.R.C. § 2056.

adjusted taxable gifts.[17] A tentative estate tax is then computed against this base which is then reduced by the gift taxes payable on adjusted taxable gifts. The resulting tax is then reduced by a unified credit as well as credits for state and foreign death taxes and certain gift taxes.

*Valuation and Income Tax Basis: Due Date of the Return:* Two separate questions must be kept clearly in mind when calculating the value of the gross estate. The first is whether a particular asset is included in the gross estate; the second is what is the included asset's value. An included asset's value is determined under one of three sections of the estate tax law.

Section 2031 provides that assets included in the gross estate are valued at the "fair market value" on the date of the decedent's death. In common with the gift tax, fair market value is determined under the willing seller-willing buyer test.[18]

In lieu of the date of death valuation method, the executor may elect on the estate tax return[19] to value all[20] of the estate assets under the alternate valuation method. This valuation method is available only if as a result of the election (1) the value of the gross estate will be less than its value based upon date of death values and (2) the amount of the estate tax will be less than it would be if estate tax values were determined on decedent's date of death.[21] This provision prevents the use of the alternate valuation method merely for the purpose of obtaining higher estate tax values and therefor a higher income tax basis where there would be no estate tax cost. This might occur where the estate qualified for an unlimited marital deduction.

Under the alternate valuation method gross estate assets are valued on the sixth month anniversary of the decedent's date of death or, if any asset is sold, distributed, exchanged or otherwise disposed of between the date of decedent's death and the sixth months anniversary thereof, on the date of its sale, distribution, exchange or other disposition.

To illustrate if Harry owned Asset A valued at $100 at his death and $50 on the sixth month anniversary of his death, Asset A would be valued at $100 if date of death values were used or at $50

**17.** Adjusted taxable gifts are gifts made after December 31, 1976 that are not included in the decedent's gross estate. I.R.C. § 2001(b). While "adjusted taxable gifts" are added to the taxable estate to assure progressivity in the calculation of the estate tax, that should not suggest there is not benefit in the making of lifetime gifts. That is because, once a lifetime gift is made subsequent appreciation on that gift is excluded

from both the donor's gift and estate tax base.

**18.** Treas.Reg. § 20.2031–1(b).

**19.** Ordinarily the estate tax return is due on or before the ninth month anniversary of the decedent's death. *But see,* I.R.C. § 2032(d).

**20.** Treas.Reg. § 20.2032–1(b)(2).

**21.** I.R.C. § 2032(c).

if the alternate valuation method was used. If between Harry's death and the sixth month anniversary thereof Asset A were sold for $65 and Harry's estate was valued under the alternate valuation method, Asset A would be valued at $65.

Under Section 2032A, certain qualifying real estate can be valued under the so-called "special use" valuation method.[22] Under this method, value is not determined by reference to the property's highest and best use but at its actual value taking account of its farming or business use. Section 2032A is exceptionally complicated by rules designed to assure that the statutory benefits are available only to committed, long-time farm and small-business owners.

The income tax basis of inherited property equals its estate tax value determined as of date of death or under the alternate or special use valuation methods.[23] Thus, decedent's income tax basis in the property is ignored in favor of a basis that is "stepped up" (or "stepped down") to the property's estate tax value.

This rule applies even though decedent's estate was too small to require the filing of an estate tax return. In such case, however, the property's fair market value on the date of decedent's death controls since the alternate valuation method is only available for estates for which an estate tax return must be filed.[24] Section 1014 applies with respect to all property included in the gross estate.[25]

The effect of Section 1014 is to assure that increases in the value of property between the time decedent acquired the property and the time the decedent dies escapes income tax. Similarly, losses in value between those dates go unrecognized.

The federal estate tax return, and any tax payable thereon, is due nine months after the date of the decedent's death[26] unless the time has been extended.

*Property Owned at Death:*    The gross estate includes the value of all interests in property owned by the decedent at the time of death,[27] including real property, tangible and intangible personal property, such as stocks, bonds, notes and cash. The decedent's property interest must have been a beneficial interest.[28] Thus if decedent owned property merely as a trustee at the time of his death, the property is not included in the decedent's gross estate.[29]

**22.** I.R.C. § 2032A.

**23.** I.R.C. § 1014. See also § 15.1, *supra*, notes 7–13 and accompanying text.

**24.** See Rev.Rul. 56–60, 1956–1 C.B. 443; Treas.Reg. § 20.2032–1(b)(1).

**25.** An important exception to this rule is Section 1014(c) providing that the general basis rule of Section 1014 does not apply to income in respect of a decedent. *See also* I.R.C. § 691.

**26.** I.R.C. §§ 6075(a); 6151.

**27.** I.R.C. § 2033.

**28.** See, *e.g.* Reed v. Comm'r, 36 F.2d 867 (5th Cir.1930).

**29.** *Id.*

Decedent's property interest can be a future interest.[30] While literally read property owned at death would include property interests which simultaneously expired with the decedent's death, such as a life estate measured by decedent's life, a contingent remainder, or a joint tenancy, only those interests capable of passing from the decedent by the laws of intestate succession or by decedent's will are included in the decedent's gross estate under the provision relating to property owned at death.[31] Thus if decedent's life estate terminates at decedent's death it is not included in the decedent's gross estate.[32]

Generally, whether decedent has a property interest is determined under state law[33] but a state law characterization of an interest may not control for federal estate tax purposes. This fact is well illustrated by the case of *Commissioner v. Bosch's Estate.*[34] After Mr. Bosch died his estate claimed a marital deduction for property passing to Mrs. Bosch under the terms of a revocable trust that was included in Mr. Bosch's gross estate. The availability of that deduction depended upon whether Mrs. Bosch possessed a general power of appointment over the trust.[35] While the case was pending in the Tax Court the executor of Mr. Bosch's estate initiated a state court proceeding for the settlement of certain accounts. In that proceeding, to which the federal government was not a party, it was held that Mrs. Bosch had a general power. The Tax Court accepted that judgement as controlling and a divided Court of Appeals affirmed. The Service contended that the federal courts did not have to accept the correctness of the state court determination since the government had not been a party to the state court proceeding. The Supreme Court, in reversing the lower court decisions, held that the federal courts were required only to give the state court determination "proper regard;" a state trial court decision should be given some weight; its intermediate appellate court decision should be given greater weight and its highest court's decision should be followed.

Property owned at death includes property that under state law is distributable to the decedent's spouse as dower, curtesy or a

---

**30.** Adriance v. Higgins, 113 F.2d 1013 (2d Cir.1940).

**31.** *But see* I.R.C. § 2040 relating to joint tenancies.

**32.** In some cases not all of the income due the decedent was paid to the decedent prior to his death. Any accrued or undistributed income due the decedent would be included in the decedent's probate and gross estates. See, *e.g.*, Corbett v. Comm'r, 12 T.C. 163 (1949); § 9.4, *supra*, note 61. While property may not be included in the income bene-

ficiary's estate, the property may be subject to the generation skipping transfer tax at the income beneficiary's death.

**33.** Blair v. Comm'r, 81 L.Ed. 465 (1937).

**34.** 387 U.S. 456, 87 S.Ct. 1776, 18 L.Ed.2d 886 (1967), on remand 382 F.2d 295 (2d Cir.1967).

**35.** I.R.C. § 2056(b)(5). *See also* notes 119–127, *infra* and accompanying text.

statutory right in lieu thereof.[36] It does not include the surviving spouse's share of community property, if applicable. If the spouse's interest qualifies for the estate tax marital deduction,[37] it is excluded from the decedent's taxable estate.

*Transfers Within Three Years of Death:* The gross estate includes the value of all life insurance policies transferred by the decedent within three years of the decedent's death for less than adequate and full consideration in money or money's worth.[38] For example, if Mary gratuitously transfers to Andy a life insurance policy having a cash value on the date of transfer of $5,000 and a face value of $100,000 and dies within three years of the transfer, $100,000 is included in Mary's gross estate. If, on the other hand, Andy paid Mary $5,000 for the transfer, the policy is excluded from Mary's gross estate because the lifetime transfer was for adequate and full consideration in money or money's worth.

The gross estate also includes the amount of any gift taxes paid by the decedent or the decedent's estate on gifts made by the decedent or the decedent's spouse after December 31, 1976 and within the three year period immediately preceding the decedent's death.[39] Inclusion of such gift tax in the decedent's gross estate is not dependent upon the gift subject to that tax being included in the decedent's gross estate. This section prevents the making of substantial gifts within three years of death with the effect (intended or not) of removing the gift tax thereon from the donor's estate tax base. The estate tax is a so-called "gross up" tax meaning that the estate tax base includes funds that will be used to pay the estate tax. The gift tax, on the other hand, is not grossed up. The gift tax is computed on the value of the gift, not the value of the gift increased by the amount of gift tax thereon. However, gifts within three years of death cannot be used to avoid the "gross up" effect of the estate tax with respect to gifts within the three year period.[40]

Lastly, the gross estate includes the value of any interest in property transferred by the decedent within three years of death or the value of any property over which the decedent relinquished a power within three years of death if the value of such property would have been included in the decedent's gross estate under section 2036 (relating to retained life estates), 2037 (relating to transfers taking effect at death) and 2038 (relating to revocable transfers) had the transfer or relinquishment not occurred.[41] However, this rule does not apply to distributions from, or powers

---

**36.** I.R.C. § 2034.

**37.** I.R.C. § 2056.

**38.** I.R.C. § 2035(a)(2).

**39.** I.R.C. § 2035(b).

**40.** I.R.C. § 2035(c).

**41.** I.R.C. § 2035(a).

relinquished over, trusts if the trust was revocable and the grantor was treated as the owner of the trust under section 676 for income tax purposes.[42] For example, suppose Gary creates a revocable trust and two years before he died he exercised his power of revocation and directs the trustee to distribute $50,000 of trust principal of Anita. For gift tax purposes, Gary makes a taxable gift of $40,000 after taking account of the annual exclusion. The $50,000 is not included in his gross estate. If Gary's power was exercisable only with the consent of persons having an adverse interest, then for purposes of section 676 Gary is not treated as the owner of the trust. In this case, the $50,000 would be included in his gross estate since section 2038 applies without regard to whether the grantor had a power of revocation exercisable only with the consent of another.

*Transfers with a Retained Life Estate:* The gross estate includes the value of all property to the extent of the decedent's interest therein transferred by the decedent during life, in trust or otherwise, for less than adequate and full consideration in money or money's worth[43] under which the decedent retained (1) for his life, (2) for any period not ascertainable without reference to decedent's death,[44] or (3) for any period that does not in fact end before the decedent's death,[45] either (1) the possession or enjoyment of, or the right to receive the income from, the transferred property, or (2) the right to designate the persons who shall enjoy the transferred property or the income therefrom.

The most common example of a retained life estate transfer that is included in the decedent's gross estate occurs where a decedent transferred property in trust and retained the income interest in the trust for life.[46] Similarly, if decedent transferred real property and retained a legal life estate in the property, then at death the real estate would be included in the decedent's gross estate.[47]

---

**42.**   I.R.C. § 2035 (e).

**43.**   If decedent received partial consideration for the transfer, then the amount that would otherwise be included in the decedent's gross estate under Section 2036 is reduced by the amount of the partial consideration received. *See generally,* I.R.C. § 2043.

**44.**   For example, if decedent retained the income for a period that would end three months before his death, Section 2036 applies because the period of time for which decedent retained the income cannot be determined without reference to his death.

**45.**   For example, suppose decedent retained the income from the property transferred in trust for 10 years and decedent died three years after the transfer was made. Decedent retained an interest that did not in fact end before his death. If decedent outlived the 10 years period, Section 2036 is inapplicable.

Unless otherwise stated and for convenience purposes, all three time periods are simply referred to as "retained for life."

**46.**   I.R.C. § 2036(a)(1).

**47.**   See, *e.g.,* Tubbs v. United States, 348 F.Supp. 1404 (N.D.Tex.1972), judgment affirmed 472 F.2d 166 (5th Cir. 1973), cert. denied 411 U.S. 983, 93

A transfer with a retained life estate also occurs where the decedent retained the right to have the income used to discharge decedent's legal obligations, such as the support of the decedent's dependents.[48]

There has been much litigation focusing on whether decedent's right must be expressly retained or whether it is sufficient that decedent's right arises from an implied understanding. Where payments to the decedent are wholly discretionary and there has been no implied understanding to make payments to the decedent, Section 2036 may not apply.[49] Where, however, payments to the decedent were to be wholly discretionary but there had been actual payments of income to the decedent during his life, receipt may give rise to an inference of an implied understanding. It would seem that the more regularized the "discretionary" income payments are, the greater the inference.[50]

Decedent is deemed to have retained the use or enjoyment or the right to income from transferred property if decedent retained the right to vote share of controlled corporation stock[51] even though decedent retained no right to the dividends paid on the stock.

S.Ct. 2274, 36 L.Ed.2d 959 (1973). But see, Gutchess v. Comm'r, 46 T.C. 554 (1966), acq. 1967–1 C.B. 2 (Section 2036 inapplicable to case where husband transfers family home to wife and continues to live in home as incident of the marital relationship.)

**48.** See Comm'r v. Douglass' Estate, 143 F.2d 961 (3d Cir.1944), acq. 1971–1 C.B. 2; Estate of Chrysler v. Comm'r, 44 T.C. 55 (1965), reversed 361 F.2d 508 (2d Cir.1966), acq. in result only, 1970–2 C.B. xix; National Bank of Commerce in Memphis v. Henslee, 179 F.Supp. 346 (M.D.Tenn.1959); Exchange Bank of Fla. v. United States, 694 F.2d 1261 (1982).

In those cases where decedent's right to income is limited to either decedent's support or the support of a dependent, it may be relevant for valuation purposes to consider the level of support due the decedent or decedent's dependent. See Pardee's Estate v. Comm'r, 49 T.C. 140, 148 (1967).

**49.** See Skinner's Estate v. United States, 316 F.2d 517 (3d Cir.1963). See also McNichol's Estate v. Comm'r, 265 F.2d 667 (3d Cir.1959), cert. denied,361 U.S. 829, 80 S.Ct. 78, 4 L.Ed.2d 71 (1959). See also Estate of German v. United States, 55 AFTR2d 85–1577 (Ct. Cl. 1985). But see, Estate of Uhl v. Commissioner, 25 T.C. 22 (1955), rev'd,

241 F.2d 867 (7th Cir.1957) (in dicta concluding that if under local law the creditors of the grantor of a wholly discretionary trust could reach the trust assets, trust included in gross estate because grantor could reach trust assets merely by incurring debt). Cf., Outwin v. Commissoner, 76 T.C. 153 (1981)(grantor of discretionary trust makes incomplete gift where, under state law, grantor's creditors could reach the trust assets to satisfy grantor's debts accruing after trust created.)

**50.** See generally, Lowndes, Kramer & McCord, Federal Estate and Gift Taxes, 3rd Ed. § 9.12.

**51.** I.R.C. § 2036(b). A corporation is a controlled corporation if at any time after the transfer of the corporation's stock and within three years of the decedent's death the decedent owned (using family attribution rules under Section 318) or had the right to vote alone or in conjunction with another stock possessing 20% or more of the total combined voting power of all classes of the corporation's stock.

This statutory section legislatively overturns the holding in United States v. Byrum, 408 U.S. 125, 92 S.Ct. 2382, 33 L.Ed.2d 238 (1972) rehearing denied 409 U.S. 898, 93 S.Ct. 94, 34 L.Ed.2d 157 (1972).

Transfers with a retained life estate also include transfers in which decedent did not retain any economic benefits but retained the power, exercisable alone or in conjunction with any other person, to designate the persons who shall possess or enjoy the transferred property or the income therefrom.[52] Thus, if John creates a trust for the primary benefit of Alice, Bob and Charlie and retains the power to determine their respective shares of the income for his life, the trust is included in John's gross estate.

The statute also applies where there is one or more income beneficiaries and the decedent retained the power to direct that income be accumulated for ultimate distribution to the remainderman of the trust.[53] For example, if Mary creates a trust to pay the income to John, remainder to John's children and retains the power to accumulate and capitalize the income, the trust is included in Mary's gross estate because her retained power permits her to shift the enjoyment of the income from John to his children.

There is some disagreement, however, whether a power to accumulate income is a power to designate under Section 2036 where there is only one income beneficiary who will ultimately receive the accumulated income at the termination of the trust. Suppose John created a trust for the primary benefit of Alice to terminate when Alice dies or reaches age 25, whichever first occurs. Upon the termination of the trust the corpus and any accumulated income would be paid to Alice or her estate. John retained a power exercisable prior to Alice attaining age 25 to pay the income to Alice or accumulate the income for ultimate distribution to her. If John dies before Alice attains age 25, is the trust included in his gross estate under Section 2036?[54] Arguably Section 2036(a)(2) is inapplicable because it requires a power to designate among "persons" and in this case there is only one beneficiary, namely, Alice.[55] Therefore, the decedent's power is only a power that affects Alice's time of enjoyment of the trust income, not who shall enjoy the income.[56]

Section 2036(a)(2) is inapplicable if decedent retained only managerial powers over the transferred property, such as the power to allocate receipt and disbursements between income and principal

**52.** I.R.C. § 2036(a)(2).

**53.** Cf., United States v. O'Malley, 383 U.S. 627, 86 S.Ct. 1123, 16 L.Ed.2d 145 (1966).

**54.** The value of Alice's income interest would be included in the decedent's gross estate under Section 2038. See Treas.Reg. § 20.2038–1.

**55.** *But see* Struthers v. Kelm, 218 F.2d 810 (8th Cir.1955) holding to the

contrary apparently on the belief that Lober v. United States, 346 U.S. 335, 74 S.Ct. 98, 98 L.Ed. 15 (1953), decided under the predecessor to Section 2038, controlled.

**56.** Walter v. United States, 341 F.2d 182 (6th Cir.1965). *See also* Lowndes, Kramer & McCord, *Federal Estate and Gift Taxes,* 3rd ed. § 8.13; § 16.8, infra.

or the power to make investments.[57] Furthermore, the statute is inapplicable if the power to designate is controlled by an ascertainable standard and the beneficiaries are not dependents of the decedent.[58] An ascertainable standard is a standard relating to health, education, or support. It does not include a power to pay for mere comfort or happiness.[59]

Section 2036(a)(2) applies even though decedent's power is exercisable only in conjunction with a person having a substantial adverse interest in its exercise.[60] Thus, even though the gift of the interest is complete for gift tax purposes, the transferred property is still in the donor-decedent's gross estate. Of course, since a gift tax credit is allowable in computing the federal estate tax on the donor-decedent's estate, effectively only the value of the appreciation, if any, between the time of the gift and the donor-decedent's date of death is subject to estate tax.

Section 2036(a)(2) applies even if the decedent retained the power to designate who shall enjoy the income from the transferred property in a fiduciary capacity. Furthermore, even if the decedent did not retain the power directly but granted it exclusively to a third party trustee, if the decedent retained the power to fire the trustee and appoint a successor trustee, including himself, Section 2036 applies.[61] The statute also applies if decedent could name himself trustee only if the independent trustee resigned, died or was removed from office.[62]

Section 2036 can apply even though the decedent was not the formal creator of the trust. For example, suppose John creates a trust to pay the income to Mary for life, remainder to their children. Mary also creates a trust to pay the income to John for life, remainder to their children. Formally, neither John nor Mary is the creator of the trust of which he or she is the income beneficiary. Nonetheless, Section 2036 could apply causing the trust formally created by John of which Mary is the income beneficiary to be included in Mary's gross estate (and the trust formally created by Mary of which John is the income beneficiary to be included in John's gross estate) if a court concluded that the trusts were reciprocal.[63] The basic notion underlying the reciprocal trust doc-

---

**57.** See, *e.g.*, Old Colony Trust Co. v. United States, 423 F.2d 601 (1st Cir. 1970).

**58.** See, *e.g.*, Jennings v. Smith, 161 F.2d 74 (2d Cir.1947); Leopold v. United States, 510 F.2d 617 (9th Cir.1975).

**59.** See Old Colony Trust Co. v. United States, *supra* note 63. *See also* Estate of Cutter v. Comm'r, 62 T.C. 351 (1974).

**60.** Treas.Reg. § 20.2036–1(b)(3).

**61.** Treas.Reg. § 20.2036–1(b)(3).

**62.** Estate of Farrel v. United States, 213 Ct.Cl. 622, 553 F.2d 637 (1977). The statute also applies if the original trustee was a corporate trustee and decedent could fire the corporate trustee and appoint only another corporate trustee. See Rev. Rul. 79–353, 1979–2 C.B. 325.

**63.** The reciprocal trust doctrine can also apply to Section 2037 and Section 2038 transfers. See also § 13.1, note 77

trine, as originally formulated,[64] was that if two trusts were created in consideration of each other, the grantors of each trust would be switched for estate tax purposes to the effect that each would be deemed to be the substantive grantor of the trust formally created by the other. This initial test was based upon subjective intent. In *United States v. Grace's Estate*[65] the Court held that application of the reciprocal trust doctrine did not depend upon a finding that the trusts were created in consideration of each other. Rather, "the application of the * * * doctrine requires only that the trusts be interrelated, and that the arrangement, to the extent of mutual value, leaves the settlors in approximately the same economic position as they would have been in had they created trusts naming themselves as life beneficiaries."[66]

If Section 2036 applies then the entire trust, not merely the value of the decedent's retained interest, generally is included in the decedent's gross estate.[67] However, if decedent retained only a portion of the income interest or the right to designate only a portion of the income, then only a like portion would be included in the decedent's gross estate under Section 2036. For example, if decedent created a trust and retained only one-half of the income, then only one-half of the trust would be included in the decedent's gross estate.[68]

Also, if decedent created an interest in property preceding decedent's retained interest, the value of that interest is excluded from the decedent's gross estate. For example, suppose George created a trust to pay the income to Ann for life, then to George for life, remainder to Barney, and George dies survived by Ann and Barney. The value of Ann's income interest is excluded from George's gross estate.[69] Apparently, only the value of the preceding

---

(application of self-settled spendthrift trust rules to cases where formal designation of settlor is not always controlling).

**64.** See Lehman v. Comm'r, 109 F.2d 99 (2d Cir.1940), cert. denied 310 U.S. 637, 60 S.Ct. 1080, 84 L.Ed. 1406 (1940).

**65.** 395 U.S. 316, 89 S.Ct. 1730, 23 L.Ed.2d 332 (1969), rehearing denied 396 U.S. 881, 90 S.Ct. 147, 24 L.Ed.2d 141 (1969).

**66.** United States v. Grace's Estate, 395 U.S. 316, 324, 89 S.Ct. 1730, 23 L.Ed.2d 332 (1969), rehearing denied 396 U.S. 881, 90 S.Ct. 147, 24 L.Ed.2d 141 (1969). See also § 14.4 *supra*, note 93. For a further discussion of *Grace* see, Lowndes, Kramer & McCord, Federal Estate and Gift Taxes, 3d ed. § 9.8.

**67.** Treas.Reg. § 20.2036–1. *Cf.* I.R.C. § 2038 where only interests sub-

ject to a power to revoke, alter, amend or terminate are included in the decedent's gross estate. This would also include any income accumulated as a result of the decedent's lifetime directions. See United States v. O'Malley, *supra* note 59.

**68.** Treas.Reg. § 20.2036–1(a). If the decedent retained the right to a specific dollar amount of income, then only such percentile of the trust necessary to produce that amount of income is included in the decedent's gross estate. See United States National Bank v. United States, 188 F.Supp. 332 (D.C.Or.1960). *Cf.*, Industrial Trust Co. v. Comm'r, 165 F.2d 142 (1st Cir.1947).

**69.** See Marks v. Higgins, 213 F.2d 884 (2d Cir.1954). *See also,* Treas.Reg. § 20.2036–1(a).

estate being enjoyed at George's death is excluded from his gross estate. Thus, if George transferred property in trust to pay the income to Ann for life, then to Barney for life, then to George for life and then to Don, and George died survived by both Ann and Barney, only the value of Ann's life estate would be excluded from George's gross estate.

*Transfers Taking Effect at Death:* Section 2037 provides that the gross estate includes the value of all property transferred by the decedent during life for less than adequate and full consideration in money or money's worth if (1) possession or enjoyment of the property transferred by the decedent can only be obtained by the transferee surviving the decedent *and* (2) immediately before the decedent's death, decedent had a reversionary interest retained at the time of transfer valued at more than 5% of the transferred property.[70] However, Section 2037 will not apply if possession or enjoyment could have been obtained by a beneficiary during the decedent's life through the exercise of a general power of appointment that was exercisable immediately before the decedent's death.[71]

The statute applies only if both the survivorship test and the reversionary interest test are satisfied. If the decedent has a reversion in the property but Section 2037 is inapplicable, the value of the reversion is included in decedent's gross estate under Section 2033.[72]

The survivorship test relates to whether a beneficiary can obtain possession or enjoyment of the transferred property *only* by surviving the decedent. If John transfers property to Amy for life, remainder to Amy's children who survive her, Section 2037 is inapplicable even though John has a reversionary interest because neither Amy nor her children must survive John to obtain possession or enjoyment of their interest. On the other hand, if John transfers property to Amy for life, remainder to such of Amy's children as survive John, Section 2037's survivorship test is met and, if John's reversion exceeds 5% of the value of the trust immediately before his death, the value of the remainder is included in his gross estate.

The survivorship test relates to the possession or enjoyment of the property not the vesting of a property interest. For example, suppose Arnold creates a trust to pay the income to Agnes for life, remainder to Dick, or if Dick predeceases Agnes then to Arnold, or

---

**70.** If decedent received partial consideration for the transfer, then the amount otherwise included under Section 2037 is reduced by the amount of partial consideration received. *See generally,* I.R.C. § 2043.

**71.** I.R.C. § 2037(b).

**72.** See Graham v. Comm'r, 46 T.C. 415 (1966).

if he is not then living to Zelda or Zelda's estate. Zelda cannot obtain personal possession and enjoyment of the property without surviving Arnold even though her interest vests (for property law purposes) if Dick and Arnold predecease Agnes.[73] Thus Section 2037 applies even though Zelda's interest can vest without Zelda surviving Arnold. It applies because Zelda cannot personally obtain possession or enjoyment without surviving Arnold.

The survivorship test applies if a beneficiary can obtain possession or enjoyment only by surviving the decedent *and* another event. According to the regulations, it also applies if the beneficiary can obtain possession by surviving the decedent *or* some other event if the other event is unreal and, in fact, the decedent dies before the other event occurs.[74] For example, suppose Arthur creates a trust to accumulate the income for 12 years or until Arthur dies, if earlier, at the end of which time all accumulated income and principal shall be paid to Andrea. Five years later Arthur dies. Andrea's possession and enjoyment was dependent upon either the running of 12 years or Arthur's death. If at the time of transfer Arthur had a life expectancy of more than 12 years and was then in good health, Andrea is considered able to possess or enjoy the property without having to survive Arthur. On the other hand, if at the time of transfer Arthur's life expectancy was less than 12 years or he was terminally ill, Andrea is not considered able to possess or enjoy the property without surviving Arthur.[75] If Andrea could obtain possession at the later of 12 years or Arthur's death, Section 2037 applies since possession and enjoyment can only be obtained by surviving both events.

Under the reversionary test, decedent must have retained a reversionary interest valued at more than 5% immediately before death using the appropriate valuation methods and tables. A reversionary interest includes any possibility that the transferred property will return to the decedent or to the decedent's estate or that the property will be subject to decedent's power of disposition.[76] A power of disposition need not be a general power.[77] It is irrelevant whether the reversionary interest arises under the express terms of the governing instrument or by operation of law.[78] Therefore, Section 2037 can apply if Herb transfers property to Beverly for

---

**73.** *See also* Treas.Reg. § 20.2037–1(e) ex. 4.

**74.** Treas.Reg. § 20.2037–1(e) ex. 5.

**75.** *Id.*

**76.** A power of disposition does not include the possibility that the income from the property alone will be subject to the power. I.R.C. § 2037(b). If decedent had such a power either Section 2036 or 2038 would apply.

The possibility the decedent might receive back the property by inheritance through the estate of another person is not a reversionary interest. Treas.Reg. § 20.2037–1(c)(2).

**77.** See Costin v. Cripe, 235 F.2d 162 (7th Cir.1956).

**78.** *But see* Treas.Reg. § 20.2037–1(f).

life, remainder to Beverly's children who survive Herb, or if none, then to Herb (express reservation of a reversion) as well as where Herb transfers property to Beverly for life, remainder to her children who survive Herb (Herb's reversion arises by operation of law).

The value of the reversionary interest must exceed 5%. In determining whether the more than 5% test is met, the reversionary interest is valued immediately before the decedent's death on the assumption that the estate assets are valued under the date of death valuation method only.[79] The value of the reversionary interest is compared to the value of the entire property not merely the value of the interest dependent upon survivorship.[80] For example, suppose Elaine created a trust valued at $100,000 immediately before her death which provided that the income should be paid to Peter for life, then to his children who survive Elaine. Peter's life estate is valued at $60,000; his children's remainder is valued at $40,000. If Elaine's reversion is valued at $5,000 or under, Section 2037 is inapplicable even though were it valued at anywhere between $2,000 and $5,000, it would be valued at more than 5% of the value of the children's remainder interest. If Elaine's reversion is valued at more than $5,000, Section 2037 applies and the value of the remainder interest is included in her gross estate.

Even if both the reversionary interest and survivorship tests are met Section 2037 is inapplicable if possession or enjoyment of the property could be obtained by a beneficiary during decedent's life through exercise of a general power of appointment.[81] Suppose Sam creates a trust to pay the income to Betsy for life, remainder to her children who survive Sam. Sam grants Betsy a general inter vivos power to appoint the property to anyone. In this case even though Sam's reversionary interest meets the more than 5% test, Section 2037 is inapplicable because Betsy has a general power.[82]

If Section 2037 applies the amount included in the decedent's gross estate is the value of the interest whose possession or enjoyment is dependent upon surviving the decedent. Thus, if Section 2037 applies to John's transfer to Alice for life, remainder to Alice's children who survive John, only the children's interest is included in John's gross estate. If both the income interest and remainder interest are dependent upon surviving the decedent, then the entire property is included in the decedent's gross estate. For example,

---

**79.** Treas.Reg. § 20.2037–1(c)(3). For Section 2037 purposes, the valuation tables should be used exclusively. The actual circumstances surrounding the decedent's death should be ignored. See Roy's Estate v. Comm'r, 54 T.C. 1317 (1970). *Contra,* Hall v. United States, 353 F.2d 500 (7th Cir.1965).

**80.** Treas.Reg. § 20.2037–1(c)(4).

**81.** I.R.C. § 2037(b).

**82.** See notes 119–127, *infra* for a discussion of a general power.

suppose Ginny transfers property in trust to accumulate the income during her life and at her death to distribute the accumulated income and principal to Walter if he survives Ginny, or if he predeceases her, to her estate. In this case, the entire trust is included in Ginny's gross estate.

*Revocable Transfers:* The gross estate includes the value of all interests in property transferred by the decedent during life for less than adequate and full consideration in money or money's worth which at the time of the decedent's death are subject to a power, exercisable by the decedent alone or in conjunction with any other person, to alter, amend, revoke or terminate.[83] If decedent had a power of revocation that was relinquished within three years of decedent's death, the property interest subject to such power also is included in the decedent's gross estate.[84]

In order for Section 2038 to apply the decedent must have been possessed of the power of revocation at the time of death or relinquished the power within three years of death. It is irrelevant whether the decedent's power was exercisable in a fiduciary capacity. If the power of revocation was only exercisable by someone other than the decedent, Section 2038 is inapplicable. However, if the decedent possessed the power to fire the trustee and hire himself as trustee, all the trustee's powers are attributable to the decedent and, if the trustee possessed a power of revocation, decedent will be deemed to possess it as well.[85]

Section 2038 applies even though decedent had only a co-held power and even though the co-holder of the power has a substantial adverse interest in the exercise of the power.[86] Thus if Jim creates a trust to pay the income to Priscilla for life, remainder to Bonny and Jim reserves a power exercisable only with Priscilla's consent to revoke the trust, the trust is included in Jim's gross estate even though Priscilla must join in the exercise of the power. Suppose, however, the trust provides that Jim can revoke the trust only with the consent of both Priscilla and Bonny. In *Helvering v. Helmholz*[87] the Court held that a trust that could be revoked only with the consent of all beneficiaries of the trust was not a revocable trust

---

**83.** I.R.C. § 2038. If decedent received partial consideration for the transfer, the entire value less the amount of partial consideration received would be included in the gross estate. See I.R.C. § 2043. In most states, inter vivos trusts are irrevocable unless the grantor expressly retains a power of revocation. However, in some states, the opposite rule applies. In those states it is essential to expressly provide in the trust instrument that the trust is irrevocable to avoid section 2038.

**84.** I.R.C. § 2038(a)(1). *See also* I.R.C. § 2035(d)(2).

**85.** Treas.Reg. § 20.2038–1(a)(3). *See also* notes 64–65, supra and accompanying text.

**86.** Helvering v. City Bank Farmers Trust Co., 296 U.S. 85, 56 S.Ct. 70, 80 L.Ed. 62 (1935).

**87.** 296 U.S. 93, 56 S.Ct. 68, 80 L.Ed. 76 (1935).

because even in the absence of the revocation clause they could, under state law, revoke the trust in any event. Therefore, the clause did not enhance the rights of the grantor.[88]

Section 2038 applies even though the deceased transferor did not retain the power at the time of the transfer. This conclusion is based upon the statutory parenthetical directing that the source of the power is irrelevant.[89] For example, suppose John creates a trust that a trustee is empowered to alter or amend and names Mary as trustee. Ten years later Mary resigns and the court having jurisdiction of the trust appoints John as successor trustee. John dies in possession of the power to alter or amend. The trust is included in John's gross estate.

In order for Section 2038 to apply decedent must have possessed a power to alter, amend, revoke or terminate. The distinction between a power to revoke and a power to terminate is unclear. Both appear to address a power permitting the decedent, through exercise of the power, to regain title or possession of the trust property. A power to alter or amend contemplates a power that affects the enjoyment of the trust property or some interest therein without revoking or terminating the trust. It does not include powers to administer or manage the trust property, such as a power to control investments or allocate receipts between income and principal.[90] If the power to alter or amend is limited by an ascertainable standard relating to health, support, education or maintenance (sometimes called nondiscretionary powers), it is not a power to alter or amend for Section 2038 purposes unless the exercise of the power would permit the deceased transferor to enjoy the economic benefits of the trust.[91]

Section 2038 applies only if the deceased transferor possessed a power of revocation at death or the power was relinquished within three years of death.[92] If the decedent's power was subject to a contingency beyond the decedent's control such that it was not exercisable at the time of the decedent's death then Section 2038 is inapplicable if the contingency had not occurred prior to the decedent's death.[93] For example, if John transfers property subject to

---

**88.** Accord, Treas.Reg. § 20.2038–1(a)(2). *See also* § 9.6, *supra*, note 74.

**89.** The statutory language overturns the Supreme Court decision in White v. Poor, 296 U.S. 98, 56 S.Ct. 66, 80 L.Ed. 80 (1935).

**90.** See also, note 63–65, *supra* and accompanying text.

**91.** See Jennings v. Smith, *supra* note 58. There has been much litigation concerning whether the language attached to a power limiting its exercise

causes the power to be limited by an ascertainable standard. *See generally,* Lowndes, Kramer & McCord, *Federal Estate and Gift Taxes,* 3rd ed. § 8.9.

**92.** But see I.R.C. § 2035(e)(three-year rule inapplicable to transfers from a revocable trust where grantor was the owner of the trust under I.R.C. § 676.)

**93.** Treas.Reg. § 20.2038–1(b). On the other hand, the contingent power may be taxable under Section 2036 if the power is a right to designate who shall

his power to revoke the trust if Alice survives Bob and at the time of John's death both Alice and Bob are living, the trust is not included in John's gross estate because the power was not in existence at his death. A power is deemed to be in existence when decedent dies even though the decedent was incompetent to exercise the power.[94]

If the exercise of the power is subject to a precedent giving of notice that was not given at the time of the decedent's death, the power is deemed to be in existence at the time of the decedent's death although proper adjustment "shall be made representing the interests which would have been excluded from the power if the decedent had lived, and for such purpose, if the notice has not been given or the power has not been exercised on or before the date of his death, such notice shall be considered to have been given, or the power exercised, on the date of his death."[95] For example, suppose Ron creates a trust revocable only upon the giving of one year's notice. Ron dies without having given such notice. The trust is included in Ron's gross estate but the amount included in the gross estate is reduced by a one year term certain to take account of the fact that if Ron had given the notice on the date of his death, he could not have received the economic benefit of next year's income.

Only the value of the interest subject to the power of revocation is included in the gross estate under Section 2038. If decedent possessed the power to revoke the entire trust, then the value of the entire trust is included in the gross estate. If decedent only possessed to power to revoke the income interest, then only the value of that interest is included in the gross estate under Section 2038 although, since the power to revoke is also a right to designate who shall enjoy the income, the whole trust is included in the gross estate under Section 2036. If the power to revoke affects only the remainder interest, then only the value of that interest is included in the gross estate under Section 2038. For example, suppose Ron creates a trust to pay the income to Nancy for life, remainder to Bob. If Ron reserves the power to direct payment of income to Sue rather than Nancy, then under Section 2038 the value of the income interest is included in Ron's gross estate although under Section 2036(a)(2) the entire trust is included in Ron's gross estate. If Ron reserves no power over the income but reserves a special testamentary power to designate a remainderman other than Bob, then the value of the remainder interest only is included in Ron's

possess or enjoy the property or the income therefrom. See Treas.Reg. § 20.2036–1(b)(3)(iii).

**94.** Hurd v. Comm'r, 160 F.2d 610 (1st Cir.1947). As to whether a conserva-

tor can exercise a power to revoke when the settlor is incompetent, see § 7.2, *supra*, notes 35–36.

**95.** I.R.C. § 2038(b).

gross estate under Section 2038 and Section 2036 is inapplicable.[96] Suppose Ron only possessed the power to invade the trust principal on behalf of Nancy. Clearly, the value of the remainder interest is included in Ron's gross estate since the invasion power is a power to shift the enjoyment of the remainder interest from Bob to Nancy. Would this power also cause the income interest to be included in Ron's gross estate? The answer should be no.[97]

As suggested by the preceding discussion there are some cases in which either Section 2038 or Section 2036(a)(2) or both could apply to decedent's lifetime transfer. Most transfers that are taxable under one of those provisions are taxable under the other, but there are important exceptions. Furthermore, the amount that is included in the gross estate can differ depending upon which of the statutes governs. For example, if decedent possesses a power at death that she retained at the time of the transfer to alter the interests of two or more beneficiaries in trust income, both sections apply. However, under Section 2036(a)(2) the entire trust is included in the gross estate whereas under Section 2038 only the income interest subject to the power would be included in the gross estate. If decedent did not retain the power at the time of the transfer but acquired the power thereafter, Section 2036 could not apply; Section 2038 would. Contingent powers are taxable under Section 2036 but not under Section 2038.

*Annuities:*  Under Section 2039 annuities with survivorship benefits can be included in a decedent's gross estate. More particularly, Section 2039(a) provides that the value of decedent's gross estate includes the value of an annuity or other payment (other than life insurance)[98] that is receivable by any beneficiary by reason of surviving the decedent under the terms of a contract or agreement[99] if, under the terms of the same contract or agreement, an annuity or other payment had been payable to the decedent at the time of death or the decedent had the right to receive an annuity or other payment,[100] alone or in conjunction with another person, for life or for a period not ascertainable without reference to decedent's

---

**96.**  See, *e.g.,* Comm'r v. Bridgeport City Trust Co., 124 F.2d 48 (2d Cir. 1941), cert. denied 316 U.S. 672, 62 S.Ct. 1042, 86 L.Ed. 1747 (1942).

**97.**  See Walter v. United States, 341 F.2d 182 (6th Cir.1965); Rev. Rul. 70–513, 1970–2 C.B. 194. *But see* In re Inman's Estate v. Comm'r, 203 F.2d 679 (2d Cir.1953).

**98.**  This phrase refers to one or more payments that extend over a period of time whether the payments are equal or unequal, conditional or uncon-ditional, periodic or sporadic. Treas.Reg. § 20.2039–1(b).

**99.**  A contract or agreement includes any arrangement, understanding or plan, or any combination thereof, written or oral. Treas.Reg. § 20.2039–1(b).

**100.**  This language contemplates the case where decedent had a right to receive an annuity in the future without regard to whether decedent was receiving payments at the time of his death. Treas.Reg. § 20.2039–1(b)(1).

death or for a period that did not in fact end before the decedent's death.

Section 2039 cannot apply to a single life annuity payable to the decedent that terminates at the decedent's death but it does apply to a common commercial annuity contract providing benefits to the decedent and then to another upon the decedent's death. It is irrelevant if the beneficiary was also entitled to benefits while the decedent was living. It also applies to annuity arrangements between employers and employees, such as deferred compensation agreements.

The value of the survivor's interest is determined under Treasury Regulation § 20.2031–8 which provides that value equals the cost of a comparable annuity purchased from the annuity company on the life of the survivor with benefits equal to those payable to the survivor under the contract. Replacement cost, however, is unavailable if the survivor's interest is not payable under the terms of a commercially available contract. For such contracts, the annuity tables[101] apply. If decedent did not contribute the entire purchase price for the annuity, the amount included in the gross estate equals replacement cost or value under the tables, whichever is applicable, multiplied by a fraction. The numerator of the fraction equals decedent's contribution; the denominator is the total purchase price. For example, suppose Harry purchases a joint and survivor annuity contract for himself and his wife, Dorothy, at a cost of $100. At Harry's death the entire value of Dorothy's survivorship interest is included in Harry's gross estate. If, however, Dorothy predeceases Harry, nothing is included in her gross estate.

If decedent's employer made contributions towards the contract or other agreement, they are deemed to have been made by the decedent if they were made "by reason of [decedent's] employment."[102]

Section 2039 also applies to many common pension and profit sharing arrangements and IRAs to which contributions during the decedent's life were deductible for income tax purposes. These tax deferred plans are not only included in the decedent's gross estate but also the recipient-beneficiary's gross income as income in respect of a decedent under Section 691. Thus the aggregate income and estate tax liabilities associated with these assets are quite significant. The impact of assessing both an income and estate tax on "income in respect of a decedent" is ameliorated to some extent by allowing the person including income in respect of a decedent in

**101.** Treas.Reg. § 20.2031–5.
**102.** I.R.C. § 2039(b).

her gross income to claim a deduction for the estate tax attributable to such income.[103]

*Marital Joint Tenancies:* If husband and wife own property as joint tenants with right of survivorship or as tenants by the entirety, then upon the death of the first of them to die, one-half of the property's estate tax value is included in the decedent's gross estate.[104] The entire value of the property is included in the survivor's estate under Section 2033 unless transferred or consumed during the survivor's lifetime. Section 2040 is inapplicable to tenancies in common. With respect to a tenancy in common, each co-tenants undivided interest is included in his or her gross estate under Section 2033. Since only one-half of the property is included in the gross estate of the first spouse to die, only that half receives a step-up in basis for income tax purposes. For example, John and Mary purchase Blackacre for $50,000 as joint tenants with right of survivorship. John dies ten years later when Blackacre is worth $150,000. One-half of Blackacre's value is included in John's gross estate such that in Mary's hands Blackacre has a basis of $100,000 ($75,000 attributable to the half included in John's gross estate and $25,000 attributable to Mary's one-half cost basis in the property).[105] If John and Mary owned Blackacre as community property, only one-half of its value would be included in John's gross estate but both John and Mary's community halves would get a step-up in basis by virtue of a special rule in section 1014 inapplicable to marital joint tenancies.

*Other Joint Tenancies:* Under Section 2040(a) a decedent's gross estate includes the entire value of all non-marital joint tenancy property in which the decedent had an interest at the time of his death, except to the extent the surviving joint tenant can prove that he contributed part of the property or consideration for the property. If the decedent and the survivor acquired the joint tenancy property by gift, bequest or inheritance, the value of the property included in the gross estate of the first joint tenant to die is determined by multiplying that value by the number of joint tenants.

To illustrate, suppose Andrea and Becky own Blackacre as joint tenants. Andrea dies survived by Becky. Blackacre's entire value is included in Andrea's gross estate unless Becky can prove that she contributed towards the acquisition of Blackacre or that they acquired Blackacre by gift, bequest or inheritance. In that case, none or less than all of Blackacre's value is included in Andrea's gross estate.

**103.** I.R.C. § 691(c).          **105.** See I.R.C. § 1014(b)(6).
**104.** I.R.C. § 2040(b).

If Becky can establish that she contributed towards the acquisition of Blackacre, then a proportionate part of Blackacre's value is excluded from Andrea's gross estate. For example suppose they acquire Blackacre as joint tenants. Of the $5,000 purchase price, Andrea contributed $2,000 and Becky contributed $3,000. At Andrea's death, 40% of the value of Blackacre is includible in her gross estate; if Becky predeceases Andrea, then 60% of Blackacre's value is included in Becky's gross estate.[106] Section 2040(c) applies even though the joint tenants who make unequal contributions towards the acquisition and maintenance of the property have agreed to equal ownership.

The survivor's contribution must not have been acquired from the decedent for less than adequate and full consideration in money or money's worth. For example, suppose Andrea gives Blackacre to Becky. Thereafter Becky reconveys Blackacre to Andrea and herself as joint tenants. Andrea dies survived by Becky. The entire value of Blackacre is included in Andrea's gross estate.[107] On the other hand, joint tenancy property acquired by the survivor with the income from property the survivor received from the decedent is deemed to be the survivor's contribution.[108] Therefore, if Becky, in the preceding example, retained the title to Blackacre in her own name but deposited the rents from Blackacre into a joint bank account in the name of Andrea and herself, at Andrea's death survived by Becky, no portion of that bank account would be included in Andrea's gross estate.[109] The survivor's contribution towards the joint tenancy property can take the form of the assumption of liability on a mortgage. For example, in *Bremer v. Luff*.[110] Louis and Emma acquired Blackacre as joint tenants. Each assumed joint and several liability on the purchase money mortgage. The court held that each

---

**106.** *But see,* Peter's Estate v. Comm'r, 386 F.2d 404 (4th Cir.1967). In *Peters* the surviving joint tenant did not contribute to the acquisition of joint tenancy property. Rather the survivor contributed towards an improvement to the property. The court held that the value of the joint tenancy property less the amount of the contribution towards the improvement was included in the decedent's estate. No appreciation in the value of the property subsequent to the improvement was credited to the survivor's contributions. See also § 6.4, *supra*, note 66.

**107.** Treas.Reg. § 20.2040–1(c) ex. 4. *See also* Dimock v. Corwin, 305 U.S. 593, 59 S.Ct. 357, 83 L.Ed. 375 (1939).

**108.** Treas.Reg. § 20.2040–1(c)(5).

**109.** *See also* Harvey v. United States, 185 F.2d 463 (7th Cir.1950);

Swartz v. United States, 182 F.Supp. 540 (D.Mass.1960) (gain from sale of property acquired by survivor from decedent; the survivor's contribution equals the gain attributable to appreciation in value of property between time survivor acquired property from decedent and time of decedent's death).

If the survivor contributes stock dividends on stock acquired from the decedent in a joint tenancy, the courts are divided whether the contribution falls within the income exception. *Compare* McGehee v. Comm'r, 260 F.2d 818 (5th Cir.1958) with In re Schlosser's Estate, 277 F.2d 268 (3d Cir.1960), cert. denied 364 U.S. 819, 81 S.Ct. 53, 5 L.Ed.2d 49 (1959).

**110.** 7 F.Supp. 148 (N.D.N.Y.1933).

was deemed to have contributed one half of the mortgage liability towards acquisition of the property.[111] Their percentage contributions remain unchanged if the mortgage is discharged with income from the joint tenancy property. However, if either Louis or Emma uses personal funds to discharge the mortgage debt, their respective contributions on account of the mortgage must be readjusted.[112]

*Powers of Appointment:*  The gross estate includes the value of all property over which the decedent:

    1.  Possessed at the time of his death a general power of appointment,[113] or

    2.  During life exercised or released a general power of appointment[114] if, as a result of such exercise or release, decedent retained the income from the property subject to the exercised or released power or the right to designate who would possess or enjoy the income therefrom or decedent retained the power to alter, amend, revoke or terminate any interest resulting from the exercise or release.[115]

For example, if Ruth held a general power of appointment over the principal of a trust created by another and later exercised her general power by directing the trustee to hold the trust assets in a revocable trust for the primary benefit of Andy, this trust is included in Ruth's gross estate if Ruth retained the power to revoke the trust at the time of her death or released such power within the three year period ending with her death.[116] On the other hand, if during life Ruth exercised a general power by appointing the property outright to Andy and Ruth retained no interest in, or power over, the appointive assets, then the property would not be included in her gross estate, although the exercise would be a transfer for gift tax purposes.[117]

---

**111.**  Accord, Rev. Rul. 79–302, 1979–2 C.B. 328, Rev. Rul. 81–183, 1981–2 C.B. 180, Rev. Rul. 81–184, 1981–2 C.B. 181.

**112.**  See Awrey v. Comm'r, 5 T.C. 222 (1945).

**113.**  I.R.C. § 2041.

**114.**  The textual discussion relates only to general powers created after October 21, 1942. Property subject to a general powers created on or before that date is included in the decedent's gross estate only if the decedent exercised the power by will or in a disposition that if made by the decedent with his own property would cause that disposition to be included in the decedent's gross estate under Sections 2036, 2037 or 2038.

**115.**  I.R.C. § 2041(a)(2). Additionally, the gross estate includes property over which decedent exercised or released a general power in such manner that if the property subject the power had been transferred by the decedent it would have been included in his gross estate under Section 2037 relating to transfers taking effect at death.

**116.**  *Cf.* I.R.C. § 2038.

**117.**  I.R.C. § 2514. Even if the decedent exercised or released the power in a manner that would cause the property to be included in the decedent's gross estate, decedent's exercise or release could result in a transfer for gift tax purposes. *Id.* In such case, credit for gift taxes paid as a result of the exercise or release would be available in computing the estate tax on the decedent's estate.

A general power of appointment is a power that enables the donee of the power to appoint the assets subject to the power to the donee, the donee's estate, the donee's creditors *or* the creditors of the donee's estate.[118] It does not include a power to consume, invade or appropriate property for the donee if the donee's power is limited by an ascertainable standard relating to the donee's health, education, support or maintenance.[119] Special rules apply if decedent could exercise the general power only with the consent of another. These rules are:

1.   If the donee could only exercise the general power with the consent of the donor of the power, the power is not a general power for estate or gift tax purposes.[120]

2.   If the donee could only exercise the general power with the consent of another person who has a substantial interest in the property subject to the power adverse to the donee's exercise of the power, the donee's power is not a general power.[121] For this purpose if the co-holder of the power would have a general power to appoint the property to himself after the donee's death, such person is deemed to have a substantial adverse interest. For example, suppose Frank creates a trust to pay the income to Eleanor for life, remainder to Ruth for life, remainder to Charles. Frank grants Eleanor a general power to appoint the property to herself which is exercisable only with Ruth's consent. Since Ruth has a substantial adverse interest in the exercise of the power, no portion of this trust is included in Eleanor's gross estate. If Eleanor's power was exercisable only with the consent of Dan who had no interest in the trust except that he could appoint the property to himself after Eleanor died, the trust would not be included in Eleanor's gross estate because Dan has a substantial adverse interest.

3.   If the donee of the general power can exercise the power with the consent of another in whose favor the power can also be exercised, then the power is deemed to be a general power only with respect to a fractional part of the property. The fraction is determined by dividing the property's value by the number of persons who must join in the exercise and in whose favor the power can be exercised. Thus, if John transfers property in trust to pay the income to Alice for life, remainder to Benny, and John grants Alice a general power to appoint the property to anyone exercisable only with Larry's consent, Alice has a general power but only one-half of the value of the property subject to the power is included in her gross estate.

---

**118.**   I.R.C. § 2041(b)(1).

**119.**   I.R.C.   § 2041(b)(1)(A).   See § 9.5, *supra* (standard on a trustee's exercise of a discretionary power to distribute trust assets).

**120.**   I.R.C. § 2041(b)(1)(C)(i).

**121.**   I.R.C. § 2041(b)(1)(C)(ii).

The lapse of a power is treated as the release of a power.[122] A lapse of a power occurs when the right to exercise the power terminates upon the passage of time or the happening of an event, other than the donee's death. Thus, if Jerry grants Betty a general power exercisable on or before January 1, 1990 and Betty fails to exercise the power by that date, then on that date the power lapses and Betty is deemed to have released the power. However, during any calendar year the lapse of a power is a release of a power "only to the extent that the property, which could have been appointed by exercise of such lapsed power, exceeded in value, at the time of such lapse, the greater of" $5,000 or 5% of the aggregate value at the time of the lapse of the property, or the proceeds of the property, out of which the power could have been satisfied."[123] Thus, if the donee possessed an annual noncumulative power to draw down from the principal of a trust an amount limited to the greater of $5,000 or 5%, the annual lapse of the power would not result in a release. Even if the donee's power exceeded the 5 and 5 standard, only annual lapses valued *in excess of the greater of $5,000 or 5%* are taxable releases. For example, suppose Mary had the power to withdraw up to $25,000 annually from a $200,000 trust. If in any year she exercised the power and drew down $25,000, there is no lapse.[124] If Mary permitted the power to lapse in any calendar year, there would be a release of only $15,000, the difference between $25,000 and 5% of $200,000. If Mary exercised the power and drew down $10,000, there would be a lapse of $15,000 but a release of only $5,000, being $15,000 less 5% of $200,000.

Where a lapse results in a taxable release, the amount that is included in the donee's gross estate because of the release is determined by computing what percentage of the trust the donee is deemed to own because of the release and applying that percentage to the value of the trust as determined for estate tax purposes. In the preceding example Mary withdrew $10,000 from the trust and let her power lapse over $15,000. She made a taxable release of $5,000. This represents 1/40 of a $200,000 trust. Assuming no further releases, then 1/40 of the trust is included in Mary's gross estate valued at Mary's death. If there had been releases in more than one calendar year, Mary's percentage ownership interest in the trust for each year is aggregated for the purpose of computing the amount included in the donee's gross estate. Thus, if in the second year Mary released an additional $5,000, her percentage interest would increase from 1/40 to 2/40.[125]

---

**122.** I.R.C. § 2041(b)(2).

**123.** I.R.C. § 2041(b)(2)(A) & (B).

**124.** Of course the withdrawn funds could find their way into the donee's gross estate under Section 2033 if, for example, the donee deposited the funds into her personal bank account.

**125.** See Treas.Reg. § 20.2041–3(d)(5).

The 5 and 5 rule applies only to calendar years in which the power lapsed and the donee survived. If the donee dies during any calendar year without having exercised the power and prior to the lapse of the power, the entire amount the donee could have withdrawn that year is included in the donee's gross estate because with respect to such amounts the donee died in possession of a general power.[126]

*Life Insurance:*   The gross estate includes the value of all life insurance payable to the insured's estate.[127]

The gross estate also includes the value of all life insurance on the decedent's life payable to a named beneficiary if, at the time of the insured's death, the insured possessed any incidents of ownership with respect to the life insurance exercisable alone or in conjunction with any other person.[128]

The phrase "incidents of ownership" is not limited to ownership in the strict sense. Rather it refers to the ability of the insured to affect who shall enjoy any of the economic benefits of the policy. Thus, incidents of ownership include, among other things, the right to change the beneficiary, the right to cancel the policy or borrow against it, and the right to pledge the policy as security for a loan.[129] The term "incident of ownership" also includes certain reversionary interests the decedent might have in a life insurance policy.[130]

Under certain circumstances the incidents of ownership held by a corporation may be attributed to the insured. If the deceased insured was the sole or controlling shareholder of a corporation, the corporation's incidents of ownership are deemed possessed by the insured unless the insurance proceeds are payable to, or for the benefit of, the corporation.[131] If policy proceeds are not payable to, or for the benefit of, the corporation and thus are ignored in valuing the corporation for estate tax purposes, the corporation's incidents of ownership are attributable to the deceased insured.[132] The decedent is a controlling shareholder if decedent owned stock possessing more than 50% of the total combined voting power of the corporation.[133]

There has been much litigation concerning whether Section 2042 applies where the insured possessed incidents of ownership over policies on the insured's life that were exercisable by the insured only in a fiduciary capacity. Some courts hold the capacity

**126.**  Treas.Reg. § 20.2041–3(d)(3).

**127.**  I.R.C. § 2042(1). Insurance payable to the estate would include insurance payable to the insured's creditors in discharge of the decedent's debts. Treas.Reg. § 20.2042–1(b)–1.

**128.**  I.R.C. § 2042(2).

**129.**  Treas.Reg. § 20.2042–1(c)(2).

**130.**  I.R.C. § 2042(2); Treas.Reg. § 20.2042–1(c)(3).

**131.**  Treas.Reg. § 20.2042–1(c)(6).

**132.**  *Id.*

**133.**  *Id.*

in which the incidents of ownership are exercisable is irrelevant;[134] other courts hold that Section 2042 applies only if the insured fiduciary could exercise the incidents of ownership for his own economic benefit.[135] The Internal Revenue Service has adopted the latter position.[136]

Insurance on the insured's life transferred by the insured within three years of death is included in the insured's gross estate even though the insured possessed no incidents of ownership over the policy at the time of this death.[137] Insurance transferred by the insured more than three years before death is excluded from the insured's gross estate if the insured retained no incidents of ownership and the proceeds were not payable to the insured's estate. These rules have resulted in a popular estate planning device—the irrevocable life insurance trust. Abe transfers a $1,000,000 term life insurance policy to a trust for his wife, Mary, remainder to their children. At the time of this transfer the policy has no value and therefore is not subject to gift tax. If Abe dies within three years the insurance is in his gross estate. If Abe survives three years, the policy is not included in his gross estate. In either case the proceeds are not included in Mary's gross estate and thus pass to the children transfer tax free at her death. If the proceeds are also excluded from Abe's gross estate then ultimately the children have received $1,000,000 transfer tax free. It is also possible to create a life insurance trust that is excluded from the gross estate even though the insurance proceeds payable to the trustee at the insured's death can be used for the payment of the debts, expenses, and taxes of the insured's estate. This can occur so long as the use of the insurance proceeds for such purposes is wholly discretionary with the trustee of the insurance trust. However, if the trustee is required to use the insurance proceeds for such purposes, then to that extent the proceeds are included in the insured's gross estate under section 2033 even though the they would have been excluded under both sections 2042 and 2035.

*Qualified Terminable Interest Property:* The gross estate includes the value of all property in which the decedent possessed a qualified income interest for life at the time the decedent died so long as Section 2519 did not apply to such property as a result of a disposition made by the decedent during life. The rules relating to such property are discussed in a subsequent section of this chapter.[138]

**134.** See, *e.g.*, Rose v. United States, 511 F.2d 259 (5th Cir.1975).

**135.** See, *e.g.*, Estate of Skifter v. Comm'r, 468 F.2d 699 (2d Cir.1972).

**136.** See Rev. Rul. 84–179, 1984–2 C.B. 195.

**137.** I.R.C. § 2035(a)(2).

**138.** See notes 174–178, *infra,* and accompanying text.

*The Taxable Estate*: The federal estate tax is computed against an estate tax base equal to the sum of the taxable estate and decedent's adjusted taxable gifts. Adjusted taxable gifts are taxable gifts[139] made by the decedent after December 31, 1976, other than gifts that are included in the decedent's gross estate. The taxable estate equals the value of the gross estate less the deductions allowed under Section 2053 for debts, expenses and taxes, Section 2054 for losses, Section 2055 for transfers to charity, Section 2056 for transfers to the surviving spouse and Section 2056 for family-owned business interests.

*Deductible Debts, Expenses and Taxes:* In computing the value of the taxable estate a deduction is allowed against the gross estate for decedent's funeral expenses, expenses incurred in the administration of the estate,[140] claims against the estate,[141] and unpaid mortgages and other indebtedness against property where decedent's interest therein is included in the gross estate at a value that does not take the mortgage or other indebtedness into account.[142]

Additionally, a deduction is allowed for expenses incurred in administering "property not subject to claims" that is included in the gross estate[143] to the extent such expenses would be deductible if such property had been subject to claims if such expenses are paid before the running of the statute of limitations on the decedent's estate tax return.[144]

The deduction under Section 2053 for claims, unpaid mortgages or any other indebtedness founded upon a promise or agreement are limited to the extent that they were incurred bona fide and for adequate and full consideration in money or money's worth.[145] Thus, if John promised to pay Mary $50,000 if she stopped smoking and John owed Mary this amount when he died, no deduction is allowed for this claim because it was not a promise for adequate and full consideration in money or money's worth.

---

**139.** See note 18, *supra* and accompanying text.

**140.** This would include attorneys' fees and executors' fees. See generally, Treas.Reg. § 20.2053–3.

**141.** Claims would include decedent's unpaid federal and state income, gift and property taxes. It would not include the federal estate tax payable on the decedent's estate. *See generally*, Treas.Reg. § 20.2053–6.

**142.** I.R.C. § 2053(a).

**143.** This would include property transferred during the decedent's life that is included in the decedent's gross estate which under state law is immune from claims against the decedent's estate. *See generally*, Treas.Reg. § 20.2053–8. See also, § 13.2 (joint tenancy and insurance) and § 13.1, *supra*, note 4 et. seq. (revocable trust) regarding the extent to which non-probate property is exempt from the claims of the decedent's creditors.

**144.** I.R.C. § 2053(b).

**145.** I.R.C. § 2053(c).

*Losses:* Losses incurred during the administration of the estate arising from fire, storm, shipwreck, or other casualty or from theft that are not compensated for by insurance or otherwise are deductible in computing the value of the taxable estate.[146]

*Swing Deduction Rule:* Section 642(h) provides that administration expenses and losses allowable as deductions in computing the value of decedent's taxable estate can not be allowed as a deduction for income tax purposes or as offsets for the purpose of computing gain or loss on sales for income tax purposes, unless the right to have such expenses, losses or offsets allowed as an estate tax deduction is waived.

Ordinarily the executor will claim such items as deductions (or offsets) on whichever return results in the greatest tax savings. For example, if the estate is in the marginal estate tax bracket of 38% but the marginal income tax bracket of 28%, it would ordinarily be most beneficial to claim these "swing deductions" as an estate tax deduction since overall estate and income taxes will be reduced by an additional 10%. Of course, if the estate is not subject to any estate tax liability, it would be advisable to claim swing deductions as an income tax deduction or offset.[147]

*Charitable Transfers:* In computing the value of the decedent's taxable estate an unlimited deduction is allowable for outright transfers to charity. For purposes of both the gift and estate tax laws, charities include the federal and state governments and subdivisions thereof and most organizations engaged in religious, charitable, scientific, literary, or educational activities

If decedent bequeaths her entire estate to charity, decedent's taxable estate would be zero. The amount of the charitable deduction cannot exceed the value of the property transferred to charity that is included in the decedent's gross estate. Property passing to charity as a result of the decedent's death that is not included in the decedent's gross estate cannot qualify for a charitable deduction.

For purposes of Section 2055 transfers include property passing to charity as a result of a bequest, legacy, devise and inter vivos dispositions that are included in the decedent's gross estate.[148] For example, if decedent created a revocable inter vivos trust providing that upon her death the remainder would be paid to charity, the property passing to charity at decedent's death qualifies for the estate tax charitable deduction because the revocable trust is in-

**146.** I.R.C. § 2054.

**147.** See also § 15.5, *supra*, note 73.

**148.** It has been held that property passing to a state because decedent died intestate does not qualify for the deduction because it does not pass to charity as the result of decedent's transfer. See Senft v. United States, 319 F.2d 642 (3d Cir.1963).

cluded in the decedent's gross estate. On the other hand, if George grants Martha a special testamentary power of appointment enabling Martha to appoint the trust property to her issue and to charity, property Martha appoints to charity does not qualify for the estate tax charitable deduction because it is not included in Martha's gross estate.

To the extent that the property passing to charity is subject to the payment of any death tax, the charitable deduction must be reduced by the amount of that tax.[149]

If property passes in a form that benefits both individuals and charity, special and complex rules apply to the allowance of the charitable deduction for charity's interest in the transfer. If the transfer is in the form of a trust in which the remainder interest passes to charity, no deduction is allowed for the charitable remainder interest unless the trust qualifies as either a charitable remainder annuity trust or a charitable remainder unitrust.[150]

Generally, a charitable remainder annuity trust is a trust providing that an annuity in an amount at least equal to 5% of the initial value of the trust principal shall be paid to the individual beneficiary or beneficiaries for their lives or for a term of years not in excess of 20 years, from which no amount, other than the annuity, can be paid to the noncharitable beneficiaries, and upon the termination of which the remainder will pass to charity.[151]

A charitable remainder unitrust is a trust providing that a fixed percentage, not less than 5% of the value of the trust assets determined annually and no other amounts,[152] be paid to the noncharitable beneficiary for life or for a term of years not to exceed 20 years and that upon the termination of the trust the remainder shall pass to charity.[153]

Under the unitrust, the amount paid to the noncharitable beneficiary varies each year and rises or falls as the value of the trust principal rises or falls over the life of the trust. With an annuity trust, the amount the noncharitable beneficiary receives remains constant.

A charitable deduction is also available for so-called charitable "lead" trusts which provide for payment of an annuity or unitrust amount to charity for a term certain or a term measured by the life of an individual and a remainder to a noncharitable beneficiary.[154]

---

**149.** Reg. § 20.2055–3(a).

**150.** I.R.C. § 2055(d)(2)(A). See § 9.4, *supra*, note 73 (non-tax reasons for using an annuity or unitrust)

**151.** See I.R.C. § 664(d)(1).

**152.** An income pay out exception is available for the unitrust. See I.R.C. § 664(d)(3).

**153.** I.R.C. § 664(d)(2).

**154.** I.R.C. § 2055(d)(2)(B).

Similar rules apply in the case of the unlimited gift tax charitable deduction.[155]

The split-interest charitable trust provides some significant estate planning opportunities for many taxpayers by generating some large charitable deductions while preserving substantial assets for family members. These trusts have become common estate and financial planning tools not only for their potential to avoid or reduce transfer taxes but also to minimize the donor's income taxes to the extent these trusts qualify for an income tax deduction under section 170 of the Code.

*Marital Deduction:* An unlimited deduction is allowed in computing the value of the taxable estate for the value of all property included in the decedent's gross estate passing[156] from the decedent to the decedent's surviving spouse. This is the most important deduction available to married couples wishing to minimize the transfer taxes on their property. This deduction reflects a strongly held policy that it is inappropriate to assess transfer taxes on transfers of property between spouses.

The marital deduction is available only for a deductible interest passing from the decedent to the surviving spouse. A deductible interest is a property interest passing to the spouse that is not made nondeductible by the so-called "nondeductible terminable interest rule."[157] Under the nondeductible terminable interest rule, a property interest passing from the decedent to the surviving spouse is not deductible if, upon the happening of an event or contingency or upon the lapse of time, the spouse's interest will terminate, and upon such termination the interest or the property from which the interest is carved passes to someone other than the spouse for less than adequate and full consideration in money or money's worth.[158] For example, if John bequeaths $100,000 in trust to pay the income to Abagail for 20 years, remainder to John, Jr., Abagail's term interest is nondeductible because (1) it will terminate upon the lapse of 20 years, and (2) upon the termination of that interest the trust will pass to John, Jr. for less than adequate and full consideration in money or money's worth. On the other hand, if John bequeaths Abagail his remaining term interest in a copyright, the interest passing to Abagail qualifies for the marital deduction. While Abagail's interest terminates at the end of the copyright term, upon the termination of her interest no interest passes to any other person for less than adequate and full consideration in money or money's worth.

---

**155.** See I.R.C. § 2522.

**156.** See I.R.C. § 2056(c) (broadly defining passing to include all interests included in the decedent's gross estate whether or not the interest was included in the decedent's probate estate.)

**157.** I.R.C. § 2056(b).

**158.** I.R.C. § 2056(b)(1).

The nondeductible terminable interest rule essentially assures that property passing from one spouse to another escapes tax only if such property is transferred in such a way that it will be included in the surviving spouse's gift or estate tax base unless consumed by the surviving spouse during the spouse's lifetime.

The nondeductible terminable interest rule is subject to a number of important exceptions. First, if the spouse's interest will terminate because the gift to the spouse is conditioned upon the spouse surviving the decedent by six months or less, or upon the spouse and the decedent not dying as the result of a common accident or disaster, and in fact the spouse's interest does not terminate, the property passing to the spouse qualifies for the marital deduction.[159]

Second, if the property passing from the decedent passes in form such that (1) the spouse is entitled to all of the income[160] from the property, or a specific portion thereof,[161] for life payable at least annually, (2) the spouse has a power to appoint the property either to herself or to her estate[162] which is exercisable alone and in all events[163] and (3) no person, except the spouse, has a power to appoint the property to any person other than the spouse, the property passing from the decedent qualifies for the marital deduction.[164] To illustrate, suppose Dolly creates a $100,000 trust to pay the income to her husband, James, for life, remainder to such persons, including James' estate, as he appoints by will and in default of appointment to Allan. Dolly's estate is entitled to a marital deduction in the amount of $100,000. The same marital deduction would be allowable even though James had a special inter vivos power of appointment exercisable in favor of his issue, in addition to his testamentary general power. Likewise, the trust would qualify for a $100,000 marital deduction even if the trustee of the trust could invade the trust corpus for James. However, if the trustee could invade the corpus for the benefit of another

**159.** I.R.C. § 2056(b)(3). The six-months clause obviously is consistent with the 120 hours survivorship rules under the Uniform Probate Code. For the problem of simultaneous death and the planning considerations relevant thereto, see § 8.3, *supra*, note 85 et. seq.

**160.** Treas.Reg. § 20.2056(b)–5(f).

**161.** The specific portion can be either a specific portion of the income from the entire trust, or all of the income from a specific portion of the trust. *See generally*, Treas.Reg. § 20.2056(b)–5(a)(1).

**162.** Treas.Reg. § 20.2056(b)–5(g). The terms of this general power are not coterminous with the definition of a general power in Section 2041. Under Section 2041 a general power includes a power to appoint to the donee, the donee's estate, the donee's creditors or the creditors of the donee's estate.

**163.** *Id.* Thus, co-held powers do not qualify for the Section 2056(b)(5) exception and a general power that is not exercisable from the date of the decedent's death until the date of the surviving spouse's death either as an inter vivos power or a testamentary power does not qualify under Section 2056(b)(5).

**164.** I.R.C. § 2056(b)(5).

person, other than James' dependent and in satisfaction of his legal obligation of support, the trust would not qualify for the marital deduction.

Property qualifying for the marital deduction under the life estate/power of appointment exception is included in the surviving spouse's transfer tax base either because the spouse exercises or releases the general power during life[165] or possessed the general power at the time of his death.[166]

Third, property transferred to the spouse for life, remainder to the spouse's estate qualifies for the marital deduction even if the spouse is not entitled to the income for life or the income may be paid to the spouse or accumulated. This transfer is not disqualified by the nondeductible terminable interest rule because no one but the spouse's alter ego—her estate—is entitled to the property at the termination of the spouse's life interest.[167]

Fourth, under Section 2056(b)(7) qualified terminable interest property passing from the decedent to the surviving spouse qualifies for the marital deduction. Qualified terminable interest property ("QTIP") is property in, or with respect to, which (1) the spouse is entitled to all of the income for life payable at least annually,[168] (2) no person, including the spouse, has the power to appoint any of the property to someone other than the spouse during the spouse's lifetime[169] and (3) the executor has made an election that the property should qualify for the marital deduction. To illustrate, a transfer from Helen in trust to pay the income to her husband, William, for life, remainder to Helen's issue qualifies as QTIP if the executor of Helen's estate elects to treat the property as QTIP so long as no one can appoint the property to someone other than William during his life. This type of devise is often used by spouses who have children from a prior marriage and who do not wish to risk the loss of property for their children by the other spouse's exercise of a power of appointment.

Since the negative power rule applies only to powers exercisable during the spouse's life, the surviving spouse can be granted a special testamentary power of appointment.

To assure that QTIP enters into the surviving spouse's transfer tax base either under the gift or the estate tax law, Section 2519

---

**165.** I.R.C. §§ 2514; 2041.

**166.** I.R.C. § 2041. Although it does not matter for tax purposes, whether the spouse exercised the power is a question frequently litigated when the takers in default of appointment differ from the beneficiaries named in the spouse's will. See, § 10.4, *supra*, note 45 et. seq.

**167.** Treas.Reg. § 20–2056(e)–2(b).

**168.** QTIP also includes property in which the spouse has a usufruct interest for life. I.R.C. § 2056(b)(7)(B)(ii).

An annuity can be treated as an income interest. I.R.C. § 2056(b)(7)(B).

**169.** *Cf.* I.R.C. § 2056(b)(5) discussed *supra* at notes 169–171, and accompanying text.

and Section 2044 were enacted. If a person with a qualifying income interest for life in QTIP transfers[170] that income interest to another, the person is deemed to also have transferred the remainder interest.[171] If the transfer of the income interest is for less than adequate and full consideration in money or money's worth, the transfer results in the making of a taxable gift of that income interest.[172] Whether or not the transfer of the income interest is a transfer for less than adequate and full consideration in money or money's worth, a transfer of that interest also results in a transfer of the remainder under Section 2519. Of course, whether there is a gift of the remainder interest depends upon whether the transferor surrendered dominion and control over that remainder. Thus, suppose Grace transfers $100,000 in trust to pay the income to her husband, Cal, for life, remainder to Jim. Grace elects to treat the $100,000 as QTIP and the transfer qualifies for the gift tax marital deduction. Five years later when Cal's life estate is worth $40,000, he transfers it to Bert who therefore acquires a life estate in the property measured by Cal's life. Whether the transfer of the life estate results in a taxable gift is determined under general gift tax principles. The transfer of the life estate also results in Cal making a transfer of the $60,000 remainder interest under Section 2519. This transfer is a gift unless Cal received adequate and full consideration for the transfer of the remainder (an unlikely event) or retained dominion and control over the remainder interest. For example, if Cal had a special testamentary power over the remainder interest deemed transferred under Section 2519, there would be no gift of that interest but it would be included in his gross estate.

When the spouse who possesses a qualifying income interest in QTIP dies, the QTIP is included in the spouse's gross estate under Section 2044 unless during the spouse's life a Section 2519 transfer occurred. Thus, in the preceding example, if Cal died never having transferred the income interest, the trust is included in his gross estate under Section 2044. Any estate tax attributable to the inclusion of QTIP in Cal's gross estate is payable from the trust unless the trust instrument or Cal's will otherwise provides. If Cal made a Section 2519 disposition with respect to that trust, nothing would be included in his gross estate under Section 2044.

Fifth, section 2056(b)(8) creates an additional exception to the nondeductible terminable interest rule for charitable remainder trusts[173] in which the surviving spouse has an annuity or unitrust interest. This exception is necessary to qualify the spouse's interest for the marital deduction because, of necessity, the spouse's inter-

---

**170.** A transfer may be by sale, gift or otherwise.

**171.** I.R.C. § 2519.

**172.** See I.R.C. § 2511.

**173.** See notes 155–159, *supra* and accompanying text.

est is not otherwise deductible under Section 2056(b)(5) or Section 2056(b)(7) since such trusts do not give the spouse all of the income for life. If the decedent's surviving spouse is the only noncharitable beneficiary of a charitable remainder trust, the spouse's interest qualifies for the marital deduction and the remainder interest qualifies for the charitable deduction. Thus, the entire value of the property passing into the charitable remainder trust is excluded from decedent's taxable estate. The utility of this exception is questionable because similar tax consequences can result through the use of a QTIP trust of which charity is the remainderman which, unlike the charitable remainder trust, could permit the trustee to invade the corpus for the benefit of the spouse.

Section 2523 contains comparable provisions for the gift tax marital deduction, including a gift tax nondeductible terminable interest rule,[174] a life estate power of appointment[175] and a QTIP[176] exception to that rule and a special rule for gifts to a charitable remainder trust.[177]

*Marital Deduction Planning:* Use of the unlimited marital deduction may result in higher aggregate transfer taxes on the estates of both spouses than might otherwise be payable. This can result from the first spouse to die failing to take full advantage of the unified credit. Mary has a personal estate of $2,000,000 which she is prepared to leave to John, her husband, in the full expectation that he will bequeath it to their children. If Mary dies in 2002 bequeathing all of this to John who has no property of his own, no estate taxes are payable on her estate because of the unlimited marital deduction. When John dies in 2003, however, $551,000 in estate taxes are payable on the $2,000,000 bequeathed to the children. Alternatively, if Mary created a $700,000 trust for John with a remainder to their children and the remaining $1,300,000 outright to John, then no estate taxes would be payable on her taxable estate of $700,000 but only $239,000 of estate taxes would be payable on his taxable estate of $1,300,000. If Mary divides her estate in that way $312,000 of estate taxes are saved. The difference in result arises because through proper planning Mary utilized her unified credit and did not avoid its tax saving potential by avoiding all estate taxes on her estate by the use of an unlimited marital deduction. Even if Mary and John lived in a community property state such that only $1,000,000 was included in Mary's estate, it would continue to be advisable for her to maximize the use of the unified credit by sheltering $700,000 from John's estate such that only $1,300,000 ($300,000 from Mary and $1,000,000 of his community share) is included in his gross estate at his death.

---

174.  I.R.C. § 2523(b).          176.  I.R.C. § 2523(f).
175.  I.R.C. § 2523(e).          177.  I.R.C. § 2523(g).

The terms of the trust for John that bypasses his estate when he dies can be as broad or restrictive as Mary wishes so long as John does not have a general power which would cause the trust to be included in his gross estate when he died. Similarly, Mary's estate can claim the $1,400,000 marital deduction not only for an outright bequest to John but also for a life estate/power of appointment or QTIP trust created for John's benefit. Which of those transfers Mary prefers depends, among other things, on how well John manages money and how much power Mary wishes to give John to determine the ultimate takers of the property.

In determining how much Mary should bequeath to John to take optimum advantage of both the unified credit and the marital deduction, she could use a marital deduction formula clause. These clauses are used because changes in the value and composition of Mary's assets, how much debt she owes to others, and the amount of the available unified credit can change between the time the will is executed and the time she dies.[178] Under these clauses the exact amount passing to or for the benefit of the surviving spouse is not determined until the deceased spouse's death when the precise value of the decedent's assets, as well as the amount of debts and expenses and the allowable unified credit, is known.

Proper marital deduction planning should also take into account the advisability of lifetime interspousal gifts. If Mary failed to make gifts to John and John predeceased Mary, then Mary's estate would not benefit from the marital deduction and the $2,000,000 she bequeathed to her children would be subject to a tax of $588,000.

*Family-owned Business Interest:* Prior to 2004, if the decedent's estate included a so-called "qualified family-owned business interest," the estate was entitled to a deduction in an amount equal to the lesser of the adjusted value of such interest or $675,000.[179] However, if an estate was entitled to this deduction, the amount of the unified credit to which it would otherwise have been entitled was reduced. If the family-owned business interest deduction was $675,000, the unified credit would have been limited to $202,050.[180] If the deduction was less than $675,000, the unified credit was increased by an amount provided in the statute.

The definition of a qualified family-owned business interest is quite complex and to some extent parallels the rules relating to

**178.** *See generally,* Kurtz, *The Impact of the Revenue Act of 1978 and the 1976 Tax Reform Act on Estate Tax Marital Deduction Formulas,* 64 Iowa L.Rev. 739 (1979); Kurtz, *Marital Deduction Estate Planning Under the Economic Recovery Tax Act of 1981: Opportunities Exist, But Watch the Pitfalls,* 34 Rutgers L.Rev. 591 (1982). Such formula gifts should make clear whether the spouse shares in appreciation and depreciation on estate assets.

**179.** I.R.C. § 2057.

**180.** I.R.C. § 2057(a)(3).

"special use" valuation.[181] The section applied if the value of the business exceeded 50% of the value of the adjusted gross estate[182] and the executor made an appropriate election.[183]

*Disclaimers:* Under Section 2518(a), if a person makes a qualified disclaimer which satisfies the provision of Section 2518(b) with respect to any interest in property, the estate tax is computed as if the disclaimed interest had not been transferred to the disclaimant. For example, if T bequeaths $100,000 to spouse S who disclaims the bequest in the statutory manner, and by reason of the disclaimer the bequest passes to friend F, the legacy is treated as not passing from T to S and does not qualify for the estate tax marital deduction. Likewise, it would not be treated as a taxable gift from S to F.[184] Alternatively, if T bequeaths $100,000 to Child A who timely disclaims and as a result of the disclaimer the property passing to T's spouse who is the residuary legatee, the property is deemed to pass from T to the spouse and qualifies for the marital deduction.

Under Section 2518(b), a qualified disclaimer is an irrevocable and unqualified refusal by a disclaimant to accept an interest in property if:

1.　The refusal is in writing;[185]

2.　The writing is received by the transferor of the disclaimed interest, by his legal representative or by the holder of the legal title to the property from which the disclaimed interest is carved, not later than nine months after the day on which the transfer creating the interest is made.[186] However, in no event will the period for making the disclaimer expire until nine months after the day on which the disclaimant attains age twenty-one.[187] Accordingly, if T bequeaths $10,000 to child A who is twenty years and nine months old at T's death, A may disclaim the interest one year after T's death and not nine months after T's death because A may in all events timely disclaim within nine months after A attains age twenty-one. Similarly, if T establishes a testamentary trust to pay the income to A for life and upon A's death to pay the corpus to A's children, A's children would have at least until nine months after

**181.** I.R.C. § 2032A.

**182.** The "adjusted gross estate" is the value of the gross estate less deductions only for debts and expenses. I.R.C. § 2057(c).

**183.** I.R.C. § 2057(b).

**184.** I.R.C. § 2518.

**185.** I.R.C. 2518(b)(1).

**186.** I.R.C. § 2518(b)(2)(A). See also § 2.8, *supra,* note 30 (relating to longer times allowed to make disclaimers for future interests under the Uniform Probate Code and other state laws)

**187.** The possibility of a child disclaiming several years later after the child reaches age 21 may present problems if one seeks to disclaim in order to increase the marital deduction. With respect to the possibility of a guardian disclaiming on behalf of the child, see § 2.8, *supra,* note 52 et. seq.

they attained age twenty-one to disclaim the interest. If this event occurs prior to A's death, they must disclaim before A dies and not after.[188] If decedent dies testate, it appears that a transfer is made as of decedent's death and that no qualified disclaimer is possible if the will is probated and an interest is disclaimed more than nine months after decedent's death;

3. The disclaimant has not accepted the interest or any of its benefits prior to the disclaimer;[189] and

4. The disclaimed interest must pass as a result of the disclaimer and without any direction on the part of the disclaimant to either the decedent's spouse or to a person, other than the disclaimant.[190] Thus, a decedent's spouse may effectively disclaim an interest passing to the spouse under the decedent's will even though the disclaimed interest would then pass into a trust of which the spouse is the income beneficiary.

In order to assure uniformity for the treatment of disclaimers under federal law which might not otherwise be possible because of Section 2518(b)(4)'s requirements effectively incorporating various state laws in the federal statute, Section 2518(c)(3) provides that a written transfer of the transferor's entire interest in property within the time limits provided in Section 2518 and before the transferor accepts any benefits in the transferred property is treated as a qualified disclaimer if the transferee is a person who would have received the property had the transferor made a qualified disclaimer.

A disclaimer of an undivided portion of an interest is treated as a qualified disclaimer of the portion of the interest if the disclaimer otherwise satisfies the foregoing four requirements.[191]

## § 15.4  Generation Skipping Transfer Tax

The federal estate tax does not apply to property passing as the result of the termination of an interest of a beneficiary in a trust having beneficiaries of different generations unless the beneficiary whose interest terminates has a general power of appointment.[1] Transfer taxes on property passing into a trust providing benefits to beneficiaries of different generations generally are payable only when the trust is created. This permits persons of substantial wealth to avoid transfer taxes at each generation level through the use of so-called generation skipping trusts. To illustrate, suppose

**188.** I.R.C. § 2518(b)(2)(B).
**189.** I.R.C. § 2518(b)(3).
**190.** I.R.C. § 2518(b)(4). As to what happens to disclaimed property under state law, see § 2.8, *supra*, note 52 et. seq.

**191.** I.R.C. § 2518(c)(1).

**§ 15.4**

1. I.R.C. §§ 2041; 2514.

John bequeaths his personal estate of $5,000,000 to daughter Carol who, in turn, bequeaths her entire estate that she inherited from John to her daughter, June. Upon John's death in 1985, $2,083,000 of estate taxes were paid, and Carol received $2,917,000. Upon Carol's death in 1995 an additional $1,041,500 of estate taxes were paid and June inherited $1,875,500. Thus a total of $3,124,500 of estate taxes are paid as John's property wound its way down to June who received only $1,875,500. On the other hand, if John had created a trust to pay the income to Carol for life, remainder to June, only $2,083,000 of estate taxes would have been paid and June would ultimately receive $2,917,000.

In 1976 Congress enacted Chapter 13 of the Internal Revenue Code for the purpose of minimizing the opportunities to avoid transfer taxes through the use of such trusts. The initial provisions of Chapter 13 were, however, retroactively repealed by the Internal Revenue Code of 1986 and in lieu thereof the provisions of Chapter 13 discussed below were enacted.

*Critical Definitions: Transferor* With one exception[2] the transferor, in the case of a transfer that is included in the transferor's gross estate under chapter 11 of the Code is the decedent.[3] In the case of a transfer that is included in the transferor's gift tax base under chapter 12, the transferor is the donor.[4] Two special rules relate to the determination of who is the transferor. First, if one spouse makes a lifetime transfer to someone, other than the other spouse, and the spouses elect, under Section 2513 to split this gift for gift tax purposes,[5] then for purposes of Chapter 13 each spouse is deemed the transferor of one-half of the gift even though under state property law rules only one of the spouses was in fact the donor.[6]

Second, if a donor spouse or a deceased spouse transfers property to the other spouse in a form that qualifies for the estate or gift tax marital deduction as qualified terminable interest property,[7] the donor spouse or the estate of the deceased spouse may

---

**2.** I.R.C. § 2653(a).

**3.** I.R.C. § 2652(a)(1)(A).

**4.** I.R.C. § 2652(a)(1)(B).

**5.** Under Section 2513 if spouses elect to split a gift made by one spouse to a third person, then for gift tax purposes, each spouse is deemed the donor of one half of the gift. For example, if Wife gives $100,000 to Child A and Wife and Husband elect to split this gift for gift tax purposes, then Wife and Husband, for gift tax purposes, are each treated as having made a $50,000 gift to A. In calculating the amount of gift tax payable on this transfer, both Wife and Husband are entitled to claim the $10,000 annual exclusion against the gift each of them is deemed to have made to A. I.R.C. § 2503(b). Additionally, each of them is fully entitled to claim his or her remaining unified credit against any tentative gift tax computed on the taxable gift of $40,000 each is deemed to have made to A. I.R.C. § 2505.

**6.** I.R.C. § 2652(a)(2).

**7.** I.R.C. §§ 2056(b)(7); 2523(f). *See also* § 15.3, notes 174–177, *supra*.

elect, for purposes of Chapter 13, not to treat such property as qualified terminable interest property.[8] If no such election is made, then the donee spouse of qualified terminable interest property is treated as the transferor of such property.[9] If an election is made, then the deceased spouse or the donor spouse is treated as the transferor for Chapter 13 purposes even though the property is later included in the transfer tax base of the donee spouse.[10] This election assists married persons in assuring that each spouse can be a transferor under Chapter 13 and possibly claim the benefits of available deductions and exclusions.

*Interest:* Under Chapter 13 it may be important at certain times to determine whether a person has an interest in a trust. Ordinarily the time a determination is to be made is when some other person's interest has terminated.[11] A person has an interest in a trust if the person has a present right to receive the income or corpus of the trust[12] or is a permissible *current* recipient of either the income or corpus of the trust.[13] However, the person with this permissible interest cannot be a charity[14] unless the trust[15] is either a charitable remainder trust[16] or a pooled income fund.[17] A charitable beneficiary of a charitable remainder trust or a pooled income fund has an interest even though the interest is only a future interest. An interest which is created primarily to avoid the Chapter 13 tax is disregarded.[18]

*Skip Person and Non-skip Person:* A "skip person" is a person who is assigned to a generation that is at least two generations below the transferor's generation.[19] A trust can be a skip person if (i) all present interests in the trusts are held by skip persons or (ii) no person holds a present interest in the trust and after the

---

**8.** I.R.C. § 2652(a)(3).

**9.** See Id.

**10.** No similar election is available for property qualifying the marital deduction under the life estate/power of appointment exceptions in I.R.C. §§ 2056(b)(5) and 2523(e).

**11.** See I.R.C. § 2612(a). *See also* notes 42–53, 293, *infra* and accompanying text.

**12.** I.R.C. § 2652(c)(1)(A). A trust includes a legal life estate followed by a remainder and similar trust equivalents. I.R.C. § 2652(b)(1).

**13.** *Id.* Presumably the "current" requirement means that a person who will only be a permissible recipient in the future has no interest in the trust.

**14.** For this purpose a charity is an organization described in I.R.C. § 2055(a).

**15.** I.R.C. § 2652(c)(1)(C).

**16.** I.R.C. § 664.

**17.** I.R.C. § 642(c)(5).

**18.** I.R.C. § 2652(c)(2).

**19.** I.R.C. § 2613(a)(1). See notes 25–41, *infra* and accompanying text for a discussion of the generation assignment rules. Under prior law such a person was called a "younger generation beneficiary." Former I.R.C. § 2613(c). However, under prior law a younger generation beneficiary also could include a person assigned to the first generation below the grantor's generation.

transfer no distribution, including terminating distributions, can be made to a non-skip person from the trust.[20]

A non-skip person is a person who is *not* a skip person.[21] To illustrate suppose Amy creates a trust to pay the income to her son, Bernie, for life, remainder to his children (grandchildren of Amy). This trust is *not* a skip person because Bernie, who is assigned to the first generation below Amy and therefore is not a skip person, has the present interest in trust. Bernie's children, however, are skip persons.[22] But if Amy transfers property in trust to pay the income to her grandchildren for their lives remainder to her great-grandchildren the trust is a skip person.[23] Suppose this trust also provided that if none of Amy's great-grandchildren survived Amy's grandchildren, then upon the death of the survivor of them, the corpus would be distributed to Amy's nieces and nephews. The nieces and nephew are in the first generation below the grantor's generation and thus are non-skip persons. Nonetheless, the trust is a skip person because all present interests (which by definition excludes future interests)[24] are held by skip persons.

*Assignment of Generations:* Chapter 13 sets forth detailed rules to determine a person's generation assignment.[25] These rules fall into three categories: rules relating to the generational assignments of lineal descendants of the transferor,[26] rules relating to the generational assignment of persons related to the transferor by marriage,[27] and rules relating to the generational assignment of persons who are not related to the transferor.[28] These rules are:

1. The transferor's children are assigned to the first generation below the transferor,[29] the transferor's grandchildren are assigned to the second generation below the transferor, the transferor's great-grandchildren are assigned to the third generation below the transferor and so forth. The transferor's siblings are assigned to the transferor's generation; nieces and nephews are assigned to the first generation below the transferor, grandnieces and grandnephews are assigned to the second generation below the transferor and so forth.

---

**20.** I.R.C. § 2613(a)(2). An example of this trust would be a transfer to T in trust to accumulate the income for 15 years and at the end of the term to distribute the corpus and accumulated income to the grantor's then living grandchildren and more remote descendants.

**21.** I.R.C. § 2613(b).

**22.** The fact that a trust is not a skip person does not mean it or its beneficiaries are not subject to the generation skipping transfer tax.

**23.** I.R.C. § 2613(a)(2).

**24.** I.R.C. § 2652(c).

**25.** I.R.C. § 2651.

**26.** I.R.C. § 2651(b).

**27.** I.R.C. § 2651(c).

**28.** I.R.C. § 2651(d).

**29.** Determined by subtracting the number of generations between the transferor and his grandparents (2) from the number of generations the transferor's children are removed from the transferor's grandparents(3).

2.  A lineal descendant of the grandparents of the transferor's spouse, other than the transferor's spouse who is always assigned to the same generation as the transferor,[30] is assigned to the generation resulting from comparing the number of generations between the lineal descendant and the grandparent and the number of generations between the grandparent and the transferor's spouse.[31]

3.  In determining the generation assignments of lineal descendants of the grandparents of the transferor or the transferor's spouse, relationships created by adoption are treated as relationships by blood[32] and relationships by half-blood are treated as relationships by whole blood.[33]

4.  A person who at any time was married to the transferor is assigned to the transferor's generation.[34] A person who at any time was married to a lineal descendant of the grandparents of either the transferor or the transferor's spouse is assigned to the same generation as that lineal descendant.[35]

5.  If none of the foregoing rules apply, a person born no more than 12½ years after the transferor is assigned to the transferor's generation, a person born more than 12½ years after the birth of the transferor but not more than 37½ years after the transferor is assigned to the first generation below the transferor and every person in the next successive 25 year period is assigned to the next younger generation.[36]

6.  If, in applying the foregoing rules, a person could be assigned to more than one generation, such person shall be assigned to the youngest such generation.[37] For example, suppose Harry adopts his grandchild, Allan, who but for the adoption would be assigned to the second generation below Harry. Under the general rule relating to the generation assignment of adopted persons, Allan would be in the first generation below Harry. However, under the rule of Section 2652(e)(1) Harry is assigned to the second generation.[38]

---

**30.** I.R.C. § 2651(c)(1).

**31.** I.R.C. § 2651(b)(2). There was no comparable provision under prior law.

**32.** I.R.C. § 2651(b)(3)(A).

**33.** I.R.C. § 2651(b)(3)(B). Half-bloods unlike whole bloods are related to each other only through one common ancestor. For example, if H and W have Child A, H dies and W remarries H–2 with whom she has Child B, Child A and Child B are half bloods. Only W is the parent they have in common. See also § 2.2, *supra* note 54.

**34.** I.R.C. § 2651(c)(1).

**35.** I.R.C. § 2651(c)(2).

**36.** I.R.C. § 2651(d). This is identical to the provisions under prior law. Former I.R.C. § 2611(c)(5).

**37.** I.R.C. § 2651(e)(1). This provision is identical to Former I.R.C. § 2611(b)(6). The Service is authorized to adopt exceptions to this rule by regulation.

**38.** Under the proposed regulations to former chapter 13 it was provided that the rule relating to the person who

7. If the transferee is a lineal descendant of the parent of the transferor (or the transferor's spouse or former spouse) and (i) the transferee's parent is dead at the time of the transfer from which the transferee's interest is either established or derived, (ii) such transfer was subject to the estate or gift tax upon the transferor or his estate, then the generation assignment of the transferee shall be either 1 generation below that of the transferor, or, if lower, that generation assignment of the transferee's youngest living ancestor who is also a descendant of the transferor's parent (or the parent of the transferor's spouse or former spouse).[39] However, this provision shall not apply to a person who is a collateral relative of the transferor if at the time of the transfer the transferor had any living relatives.[40]

8. If an entity[41] has an interest in property, every person having a beneficial interest in that entity is treated as having an interest in the property.[42] Each such person is then assigned to a generation under the foregoing rules.[43]

*Generation Skipping Transfers and Multiple Skips:* There are three types of generation skipping transfers. They are taxable terminations, taxable distributions and direct skips.

*Taxable Termination:* A taxable termination means "the termination (by death, lapse of time, release of power, or otherwise) of an interest in property held in a trust *unless*—

(A) immediately after such termination, a non-skip person has an interest in such property, or

might be assigned to two different generations "does not apply to the adoption of an unrelated person by the grantor or any beneficiary, or the marriage of an unrelated person to the grantor or any beneficiary." In these cases the * * * [rules relating to the generation assignment of lineal descendants] apply. Prop. Treas.Reg. § 26.2611–3(c).

**39.** I.R.C. § 2651(e)(1).

**40.** I.R.C. § 2651(e)(2).

**41.** An entity includes an estate, trust, partnership, corporation or other entity. I.R.C. § 2651(f)(2).

**42.** I.R.C. § 2651(f)(2).

**43.** Proposed regulations under the prior statute provided that (i) a person was a beneficiary of a trust if that person had an interest in either an estate or trust that was the beneficiary of the trust, (ii) both general and limited partners of partnerships interested in a trust were treated as beneficiaries of the trust, (iii) and shareholders of corporations having interests in trusts were treated as beneficiaries of the trust. Prop.Treas.Reg. § 26.2611–3(e). This proposal seems overly broad. For example, suppose O transfers property to T in trust to pay the income to D for ten years, remainder to X. D dies five year later leaving an estate of $500,000. Under the terms of D's will D leaves $10,000 to A and the residue of his estate to B. Under the proposed regulations both A and B are beneficiaries of the trust and that appears to be so even though A's interest in D's estate is limited to $10,000 and D's estate is more than adequate to fully fund that bequest.

Organizations described in Section 511(a)(2) and charitable trusts described in Section 511(b)(2) are assigned to the transferor's generation. I.R.C. § 2651(e)(3). This provision incorporates prior law. See Former I.R.C. § 2611(c)(7).

(B) at no time after such termination may a distribution (including distributions on termination) be made from such trust to a skip person."[44]

The amount taxed generally equals the value of property with respect to which the taxable termination has occurred.[45] The tax is payable by the trustee of the trust.[46]

For example, suppose Bess creates a trust to pay the income to her husband, Harry, for life, remainder to their surviving children, or to the survivors or survivor of them,[47] for their lives and upon the death of the survivor of them to distribute the corpus equally to their surviving grandchildren. Harry is assigned to Bess's generation and is a non-skip person, their children are assigned to the first generation below Bess. They are also non-skip persons. The grandchildren are assigned to the second generation below Bess and are skip persons. Harry dies survived by two children, Ann and Billy. No taxable termination then occurs, even though Harry's interest terminates because immediately after this termination non-skip persons, Ann and Billy, have interests in the trust. Likewise if Ann dies survived by Billy, no taxable termination then occurs because Billy, who has the continuing present interest, is a non-skip person. When Billy dies survived by Bess's grandchildren, a taxable termination occurs.[48] If, at Bess' death, all of her children had predeceased her, then no taxable termination would occur at Harry's death even though the principal then became distributable to her grandchildren, because, under Section 2651(e)(1) such grandchildren would have been assigned to generation #1 and would not be skip persons. On the other hand, if Bess' children survived her, then died in Harry's lifetime, the distribution to the grandchildren at Harry's death would be a taxable termination because Section 2651(e)(1) would not apply and the grandchildren would be assigned to generation #2 and, therefore, be skip persons.

Suppose Rhoda creates a trust to pay the income to her child Andy for life, remainder to Andy's surviving children. Andy is assigned to the first generation below Rhoda; his children are assigned to the second generation. Andy, accordingly, is a non-skip person; his children are skip persons. Since Andy is entitled to the trust income he has an interest in the trust.[49] This interest termi-

**44.** I.R.C. § 2612(a) (emphasis added). This is essentially similar to the definition of a taxable termination under prior law. I.R.C. § 2613(b).

**45.** I.R.C. § 2621.

**46.** I.R.C. § 2603(a)(2).

**47.** See § 10.1, *supra* note 141 et. seq. (discussion of cross remainders).

**48.** This definition of a taxable termination represents a significant simplification of the prior definitions and eliminates the need for the numerous provisions under prior law deferring the time at which a taxable termination is deemed to occur. *See generally,* Former I.R.C. § 2613(b).

**49.** I.R.C. § 2652(c)(1)(A).

nates by reason of Andy's death. Since immediately after the termination of Andy's interest no non-skip person has an interest in the trust and distributions from the trust can be made to a skip person (Andy's children), a taxable termination occurs at Andy's death.[50] If Andy had a special power to appoint the property during his life among his children, his children would have interests in the trust because they are permissible recipients of current income should Andy exercise the power. If Andy exercises the power during his life by appointing the corpus outright to his child Bernie, Andy's interest terminates and a taxable termination occurs.[51] If Andy exercises the power and appoints only the remainder interest in the trust to Bernie, no taxable termination occurs because immediately after the exercise of the power, Andy, a non skip person, has an interest in the trust.[52] Lastly, if Andy releases the special power terminating the interest of his children as permissible recipients of current income or corpus, no taxable termination occurs. While the children's interest (as objects of Andy's special power) terminates, immediately thereafter Andy, a non skip person, continues to have an interest in the trust.

*Taxable Distribution:* A taxable distribution means any distribution, including distributions of income from a trust to a skip person (other than a taxable termination).[53] In the case of a taxable distribution, the taxable amount is generally the value of the property received by the transferee.[54] The tax on a taxable distribution is paid by the transferee.[55] To illustrate, suppose Martha creates a trust to pay the income among her children and grandchildren and their spouses living at Martha's death in such shares as the trustee deems advisable. Upon the death the survivor of them, the corpus is distributable to Martha's surviving issue per stripes. The children and their spouses are assigned to the first generation below Martha and, therefore, they are non skip persons. The grandchildren and their spouses and Martha's more remote descendants are assigned to the second and lower generations. Only the children, grandchildren and their spouses, however, have an interest in the trust.[56] Distributions of income or corpus to Mar-

---

**50.** The fact that a taxable termination occurs, however, does not mean a generation skipping transfer tax is payable. As will be discussed below there are a number of reasons why this taxable termination may not actually result in the payment of a tax. See notes 61–71, *infra* and accompanying text.

**51.** A taxable termination occurs not because the exercise of the power terminates the power; rather it occurs because Andy's income interest has terminated.

**52.** This is true even though the exercise of the power to appoint the remainder interest is deemed to be a termination of the interest of Andy's children as permissible objects of the power.

**53.** I.R.C. § 2612(b).

**54.** I.R.C. § 2622.

**55.** I.R.C. § 2603(a)(1).

**56.** I.R.C. § 2652(c).

tha's children and their spouses are not taxable distributions because the children are non skip persons. Discretionary distributions of income or principal to the grandchildren or their spouses are taxable distributions because they are skip persons.

*Direct Skip:* A "direct skip" is a transfer to a skip person that is subject to the estate or gift tax.[57] In the case of a direct skip the taxable amount is the value of the property received by the transferee.[58] In the case of a direct skip, other than a direct skip from a trust, the generation skipping tax is paid by the transferor.[59] In the case of a direct skip from a trust, the tax is paid by the trustee.[60]

For purposes of determining whether a transfer is a direct skip, if the transfer is to the grandchild of either the transferor or the transferor's present or former spouse and the parent of such grandchild is not living, the grandchild is treated as if she was a child of the transferor or the transferor's spouse.[61] The issue of such grandchild (great-grandchildren of the transferor or the transferor's spouse) are treated as if they were grandchildren of the transferor or the transferor's spouse.[62] The most obvious example of a direct skip is an outright gift from grandparent to a grandchild whose parent who is the donor's child is living. If the grandchild's parent is not living at the time of the transfer, the transfer is not a direct skip.

*Multiple Skip:* A special rule applies in the case of so-called multiple skips to assure that the generation skipping tax is assessed only once at each generation. If immediately after a generation skipping transfer the property is held in trust, for purposes of applying Chapter 13 (except the rules relating to the assignment of generation) to subsequent transfers from the portion of the trust representing a generation skipping transfer, the trust will be treated as if the transferor was assigned to the first generation above the highest generation of any beneficiary having an interest in the trust immediately after the transfer.[63] Two illustrations are helpful to illustrate the operation of this provision.

Suppose Oscar creates a discretionary trust to pay income and corpus among his daughter, Dolly, his grandson, Felix and his great-granddaughter, Greta. The trust will terminate upon the death of the survivor of them at which time the corpus and any accumulated income is payable to Greta's surviving issue. If Dolly

**57.** I.R.C. § 2612(c). A direct skip would not include aggregate gifts to any donee in any year less than the amount of the annual exclusion.

**58.** I.R.C. § 2623.

**59.** I.R.C. § 2603(a)(3).

**60.** I.R.C. § 2603(a)(2).

**61.** I.R.C. § 2612(c)(2). See also I.R.C. § 2652(f)(2).

**62.** *Id.* A similar increase in generational levels applies to descendants more remote than great-grandchildren.

**63.** I.R.C. § 2653.

dies survived by Felix and Greta a taxable termination occurs. Since following the termination of Dolly's interest, the property continues to be held in trust, Section 2653 applies. Felix is the person with an interest in the trust assigned to the highest generation; therefore the transferor is presumed to be assigned to Dolly's generation. Accordingly any distribution of income or corpus to Felix, who is now a non-skip person, is not a taxable distribution although distributions to Greta, who continues to be a skip person, would be taxable distributions. Furthermore, upon Felix's death, another taxable termination would occur.

Suppose Allen transfers property to a trust to pay the income to grandchild, George, for life, remainder to George's surviving issue. At the time of the transfer George's parents are living. The transfer to the trust is a direct skip. George is assigned to the highest generation level and therefore after the direct skip someone in George's parent's generation is deemed to be the transferor and George is a non-skip person. Thus, distributions to George during the term of the trust are not taxable distributions. At George's death, however, a taxable termination occurs. If the trust provided that upon George's death the corpus should be paid to his sibling, John, no taxable termination would occur at George's death since John is also a non-skip person.

*The $1,000,000 Exemption:*  Every person is allowed an aggregate $1,000,000 so-called "GST exemption."[64] If married persons elect to split their gifts, each spouse is entitled to a GST exemption of $1,000,000 and may allocate the exemption to any property with respect to which the person is deemed to be the transferor.[65] Generally, lifetime allocations are made on a timely filed gift tax return;[66] allocations on behalf of a decedent are made by the executors on the decedent's estate tax return.[67]

If the entire exemption is allocated to a $1,000,000 transfer, then the entire transfer is exempt from the Chapter 13 tax for all times even though at a later time the property's value exceeds $1,000,000. For example, suppose Oscar transfers $1,000,000 in trust to pay the income to son, Sam, for life, remainder to grandchild, Eddie, for life, remainder to Eddie's surviving issue. Oscar allocates his entire GST exemption to this transfer. When Sam dies the trust property is worth $10,000,000. It is worth $15,000,000 when Eddie dies. No generation skipping transfers occur upon the deaths of Sam or Eddie. On the other hand, if only $400,000 of

---

**64.**  I.R.C. § 2631. For persons dying or gifts made after 1997, the $1,000,000 exemption is subject to an inflation adjustment in multiples of $10,000. See I.R.C. § 2631(c).

**65.**  *Id.* See I.R.C. § 2632 for special rules relating to the allocation of the GST exemption.

**66.**  I.R.C. §§ 2632(a); 2642(b)(1) & (b)(3).

**67.**  I.R.C. § 2632(a).

Oscar's GST exemption had been allocated to the transfer, 40% of the property is exempt from the Chapter 13 tax and upon the deaths of Sam and then Eddie, 40% of the trust's value at that time would be subject to the Chapter 13 tax. It is advisable to allocate the exemption to transferred assets that are expected to increase significantly in value, such as a life insurance trust or closely held corporate stock.

*Exemption Planning with the Marital Deduction:*  For wealthy persons, integrating the marital deduction with the generation skipping transfer tax exclusion is extremely important. For example, if the decedent's basic plan also includes creating a trust to take advantage of the unified credit, it often is advisable to create a bypass trust along with two separate shares set aside in some manner to qualify for the marital deduction. For example, suppose Charlie has an estate of $5,000,000. If Charlie dies in 2003, he can set aside $1,000,000 into a bypass trust, and the balance could be disposed of in a manner that qualified for the marital deduction. The tax on the $1,000,000 would be zero because of the available unified credit. While Charlie could leave the remaining $4,000,000 outright or in trust for this spouse Lise in a manner that qualifies for the marital deduction, and, if left in trust, even allocate his $1,000,000 to that trust such that 1/4 of it would not be subject to the generation skipping transfer tax, Charlie might be better advised to create two separate funds that qualify for the marital deduction. For example, he could bequeath $3,000,000 directly to Lise or into a QTIP trust for her benefit, and the other $1,000,000 to a separate trust for her benefit that also qualifies for the marital deduction. If Charlie were to then allocate his entire $1,000,000 GST exemption to this latter trust, it would never be subject to the generation skipping transfer tax. Putting the marital deduction qualifying property into two separate trusts may have administrative and investment advantages.

*Computation of the Tax:*  The Chapter 13 tax on a transfer equals the "taxable amount" multiplied by the "applicable rate."[68] The taxable amount in the case of taxable distribution is generally the value of property received by the transferee;[69] in the case of a taxable termination, it is generally the value of the property with respect to which a taxable termination occurs;[70] with respect to a direct skip it is the value of property received by the transferee.[71] Generally, values are determined at the time the generation skipping transfer occurs and in certain cases an alternate valuation method is available.[72]

**68.**  I.R.C. § 2602.
**69.**  I.R.C. § 2621.
**70.**  I.R.C. § 2632.

**71.**  I.R.C. § 2623.
**72.**  See I.R.C. § 2624.

The "applicable rate" equals the maximum federal estate tax rate times the inclusion ratio.[73] The inclusion ratio equals 1 minus the "applicable fraction."[74] The applicable fraction is determined as follows: The numerator of this fraction is the amount of the GST exemption allocated to the trust or to the direct skip; the denominator is generally the value of the property transferred to the trust or involved in the direct skip.[75]

To illustrate, in 1994 suppose John transfers $5,000,000 in trust to pay the income to daughter, Sally, for life, remainder to Sally's daughter, Roz, for life, remainder to Roz's issue. No portion of John's GST exemption is allocated to this trust. Therefore the applicable fraction is zero and the inclusion ratio is 1 (1–0). With respect to the generation skipping transfers occurring at the death of Sally and then Roz, the applicable rate applied to the value of the property at the time the transfers occurs would be 48%. Thus, if the $5,000,000 value remains unchanged, then at Sally's death, the Chapter 13 tax is $2,400,000; at Roz's death it is at most $1,248,000.

Suppose, however, that John allocated $500,000 of his GST exemption to this trust. In this case the applicable fraction for this trust is $500,000/$5,000,000 or 10%; the inclusion ratio is 90% (1B.10) and the applicable rate would be 43.2% (48% times 90%).[76] At the termination of the trust the amount of the generation skipping transfer valued at that time is taxed at most at the rate of 43.2%.

*Other Exemptions:*   Chapter 13 is inapplicable to transfers from a trust that if made by an individual would not be subject to gift tax because of the exclusion for payments of tuition or medical expenses.[77] For example, if Mary creates a trust to apply the income towards the medical expenses of her children and grandchildren, such payments are not generation skipping transfers.

Transfers to or for the benefit of an individual that are exempt from the gift tax because of the annual exclusion or the exclusion for certain tuition and medical payments also are exempt from the Chapter 13 tax.

## § 15.5  Income Taxation of Estates and Trusts

*The Subchapter J Estate:*   Both estates and trusts are separate entities for income tax purposes, just as corporations and partner-

---

**73.** I.R.C. § 2641.

**74.** I.R.C. § 2642(a).

**75.** I.R.C. § 2642(a)(2). This value is reduced by the sum of federal and state death tax attributable to the property and recovered from the trust and any gift or estate tax charitable deduction with respect to the property. *Id.*

**76.** *But see* I.R.C. § 2653(b) directing an adjustment of the inclusion ratio in the case of multiple skips.

**77.** I.R.C. § 2611(b). *See also,* I.R.C. § 2503(e).

ships are entities for income tax purposes. The income taxation of estates and trusts is governed by the provisions of Subchapter J of the Internal Revenue Code and particularly the provisions of sections 641 through 663.

The so-called Subchapter J estate (the property subject to taxation under Subchapter J) is not co-extensive with the property of a decedent subject to the federal estate tax. The estate tax reaches property in a decedent's probate estate as well as certain lifetime-transferred property, joint tenancy property and life insurance.[1] In the case of a decedent, however, the Subchapter J estate is limited to the decedent's probate estate. For income tax purposes, the Subchapter J estate terminates when the decedent's estate terminates.

With respect to lifetime or testamentary trusts, the Subchapter J estate includes the value of the trust property in the hands of the trustee and lasts so long as the trust is in existence.

At one time there was a significant income tax advantage in creating a trust, not distributing all of the trust's income, and having undistributed income taxed in the hands of the trust for ultimate income-tax free distributions to the trust beneficiaries. This advantage has largely dissipated because of the current income tax rates for estates and trusts which escalate from 15% for taxable income up to $1,500 to 39.6% once taxable income reaches $7,500.[2] Under current law it is often advisable to have the trust's income taxed in the hands of the beneficiaries rather than the hands of the trust because the rate of tax on the income in the beneficiary's hands is significantly lower.

*The Purpose of Subchapter J:* The primary purpose of Subchapter J is to provide a vehicle by which it can be determined whether the estate or its beneficiaries, or a trust or its beneficiaries, is taxable on the entities' income for any particular taxable year. Subchapter J is designed to assure that either the entity or its beneficiaries, but not both, are taxed on the entity's income in each year. Estates and trusts are taxed differently than corporations and partnerships. Net income of a corporation is taxed at both the corporate and shareholder level because the corporation is not entitled to any deduction for dividends paid to shareholders. Partnerships don't pay taxes; all partnership income is deemed distributed to the partners and taxed to them even if the income is actually retained by the partnership.

**§ 15.5**

1. See § 15.3, *supra.*

2. I.R.C. § 1(e). For unmarried individuals the 39.6% rates kicks in once taxable income reaches $79,772 and for married taxpayers $250,000.

*The Distributions Deduction and the Beneficiary Gross Income Inclusion:* The starting point in the analysis is that the gross income of an entity is determined in the same manner as an individual's gross income is determined. For entities, this generally means that gross income includes dividends, interests, rents and capital gains. Entities are also entitled to certain deductions in calculating their taxable income. One of these deductions, unavailable to individuals, is the "distributions deduction."[3]

The distribution deduction equals the amount during the taxable year that is actually distributed to, or set aside for the benefit of, the beneficiaries. Amounts distributed include both cash and property distributed in kind, such as securities. If property in kind is distributed, it is valued, for purposes of computing the distributions deduction, at its fair market value on the date of distribution.[4] The flip side of this deduction is that the beneficiaries must include in their gross income amounts that the entity claimed as a distribution deduction.[5]

It is the combination of the entity's distribution deduction and the beneficiaries' gross income inclusion that assures that the income received by the entity is taxed to the entity or to the beneficiary but not both. Needless to say, there are many nuances that complicate how the taxable income of the entity and its beneficiaries is calculated but these nuances do not substantially change the above picture.

*Specific Bequest Rule:* For estates, and to a limited extent for trusts, certain distributions can be made which do not generate either a distributions deduction for the estate or a gross income inclusion for the beneficiary. These distributions are described in section 663 and generally are referred to as specific bequests. Specific bequests include both specific bequests as defined by state law[6] as well as general legacies, typically of a specific sum of money. They do not include distributions to residuary legatees.

For example, if, in the year 2000, the estate has gross income of $20,000 and pays $5,000 to John in satisfaction of a general legacy the estate is not entitled to any deduction in computing its taxable income for the amount of the distribution to John and none

**3.**  I.R.C. §§ 651; 661.

**4.**  Treas. Reg. § 1.661(a)–2(f)(2). If property is distributed in kind to a residuary legatee or remainderman, no gain or loss is realized by the entity as a result of this distribution even though the fair market value of the distributed property differs from the property's income tax basis. On the other hand, if property is distributed in kind in satisfaction of a right to receive a specific

dollar amount, gain or loss can result to the entity from the distribution. Treas. Reg. § 1.661(a)–2(f)(1).

**5.**  I.R.C. §§ 652; 662.

**6.**  Typically, these are bequests of specific, identifiable property. The distinction discussed in § 8.1, *supra*, note 9 et. seq. between specific and general devises for ademption purposes is not determinative in interpreting section 663.

of the $5,000 is included in John's gross income. On the other hand, if the $5,000 had been distributed to a residuary legatee, the estate would have been entitled to a distributions deduction of $5,000 and $5,000 would have been included in the gross income of the residuary beneficiary. Thus, of the estate's $20,000 of income, $15,000 is taxed to the estate and $5,000 to the residuary legatee.

*Distributable Net Income:* Unlike trusts, an estate is rarely required to make distributions to beneficiaries until it terminates. As a result, estate distributions, except in the year of the estate's termination, are essentially discretionary. Trusts, on the other hand, are often required to make distributions, and, like estates, are required to make distributions to the beneficiaries when they terminate. Also, trustees often are permitted to make discretionary distributions.[7] It is not uncommon, for example, for a trust to mandate required distributions and authorize discretionary distributions. To illustrate, suppose Rhonda transfers property to Bank in trust. The trust instrument directs Bank to distribute all of the trust's income to Able and authorizes Bank to invade corpus in its discretion for the benefit of Able and Able's children. Here, there are both required and possible discretionary distributions.

Under Subchapter J, all required and discretionary distributions, other that distributions in payment of a specific bequest, most likely will, but may not necessarily, generate a distributions deduction for the entity as well as a gross income inclusion for the beneficiary. To sort out the possibilities, Congress created the concept of distributable net income (DNI), which has no counterpart in the income taxation of corporations, partnerships, or individuals.

Essentially, DNI[8] equals the entity's gross income plus the entity's tax exempt income,[9] if any, less net gains included in its gross income, deductions, other than the distributions deduction, and the entity's personal exemption.[10] For example, assume the entity has $20,000 of rents, $5,000 of capital gains, and $8,000 of tax-exempt municipal bond interest. It paid $4,000 in state income taxes last year. Its DNI equals $24,000, which includes the rents and the municipal bond interest less the state income taxes. DNI excludes the capital gains.[11]

---

7. These distinctions are reflected in the fact the sections 651 and 652 apply exclusively to trusts required to distribute all of their income currently whereas sections 661 and 662 apply to all other trusts as well as estates.

8. I.R.C. § 643.

9. I.R.C. § 103 (tax-exempt interest is interest payable on state and municipal bonds).

10. An estate is entitled to a $600 personal exemption; trusts are entitled to either a $100 or a $300 exemption. See I.R.C. § 642(b).

11. Capital gains are included in DNI if they are required to be distribut-

In the income taxation scheme for estates and trusts, DNI serves both a qualitative and quantitative function. Qualitatively, DNI preserves the characterization of items included in DNI as either rents, dividends, interests, tax exempt income and, when applicable, capital gains. This assures that to the extent such items are entitled to any special tax benefits, the benefits are achieved regardless of whether they are ultimately taxed at the entity or beneficiary level.

Quantitatively, DNI is the uppermost ceiling on the entity's distributions deduction and the amount that can be included in a beneficiary's gross income because of a distribution from the entity. Amounts distributed to beneficiaries that exceed DNI do not qualify for a distributions deduction and are not included in the beneficiary's gross income. They are effectively income-tax free gifts and inheritances.

To the extent DNI is characterized as including amounts of tax-exempt income, no deduction is allowable to the estate for that item and no amount of that item is included in the beneficiary's gross income.[12] If the amounts distributed are less than DNI, then it is these amounts that serve as the ceiling on the distributions deduction and beneficiary gross income inclusion. However, in that case, the distribution that is less than DNI also must be characterized in proportion to DNI to assure that no deduction is allowable for and no gross income inclusions result for amounts deemed to be tax-exempt income.

For example, suppose the entity has $20,000 of rents, $5,000 of capital gains, and $8,000 of tax-exempt municipal bond interest. DNI equals $28,000.[13] If more than $28,000 is actually distributed to the beneficiary, then the entity is entitled to a distributions deduction of $20,000 and that amount, characterized as rents, is included in the beneficiary's gross income. On the other hand, suppose only $7,000 actually is distributed to the beneficiary. This distribution is deemed to include a portion of rents and a portion of tax-exempt income. The portion is determined by reference to DNI. Since 5/7th of DNI was rents and 2/7th was tax exempt, so too, 5/7th or $5,000 of the $7,000 distribution is characterized as rents and 2/7th or $2,000 is characterized as tax exempt income. The estate gets a distributions deduction of $5,000 which amount also in included in the beneficiary's gross income.

---

ed. I.R.C. § 643(a)(3). Usually this only occurs in the taxable year the entity terminates when all of its income is required to be distributed as capital gains are not treated as income for trust ac-

counting purposes. See § 9.4, *supra*, note 11.

**12.**  I.R.C. §§ 651; 661.

**13.**  Capital gains are excluded from DNI.

*The Tier Structure:* For purposes of Subchapter J a distinction is made between distributions of income which by state law are required to be distributed in the current taxable year and all other distributions, whether discretionary income distributions or principal distributions. While the entity is entitled to an income tax deduction for the smaller of the amount of DNI or the sum of distributions of both income required to be distributed and discretionary distributions,[14] subject to characterization to exclude tax exempt income, the distributees of income required to be distributed[15] include DNI, to the extent of the required income distribution in their gross income but subject to characterization in the event tax exempt income is included in DNI. Only if there is an excess of DNI, do the distributees of the other distributions include any amounts in their gross income.

For example, suppose a trustee is required to distribute $500 of income to A and also makes a $4,000 distribution of principal to B. DNI equals $2,000 and is wholly characterized as rents. A includes $500 in A's gross income; B includes $1,500 in B's gross income (thus exhausting DNI) and B receives the balance income tax free. If the trustee had been required to distribute $2,000 of income to A, then $2,000 of income would be included in A's gross income and nothing would be included in B's gross income.

The tier structure places the beneficiaries of discretionary distributions in a favored position over beneficiaries of income required to be distributed because beneficiaries of discretionary distributions only include amounts distributed to them in their gross income to the extent the beneficiaries of income required to be distributed have not exhausted DNI. For estates, however, this is of little consequence because, for years prior to termination there are rarely, if ever, beneficiaries to whom income is required to be distributed, and for the year of termination all of the residuary legatees are beneficiaries of income and other amounts required to be distributed. Thus, they include the distributions in their gross income to the extent of their proportionate share of DNI.

*Terminating Distributions–Excess Deductions:* In the year in which an entity terminates, if the entity has deductions, other than a distributions deduction and personal exemption, that exceed its gross income, the excess deduction is allowable as a deduction on the personal tax returns of the persons succeeding to the entities property.[16] For example, Alice's estate is about to terminate. In the

---

**14.** Excluding items characterized as tax-exempt income.

**15.** Income required to be distributed is also called "state law income" and means that amount of income to which a beneficiary is entitled under state law.

Typically, the amount of such income is determined by reference to applicable income and principal statutes. See, e.g., Unif. Inc. & Prin. Act.

**16.** I.R.C. § 642(h).

year of termination it has gross income of $12,000 and pays the deductible attorney fee of $15,000. The $3,000 excess can be claimed as a deduction on the residuary legatee's personal income tax return. The deduction is allowable only in computing taxable income, not adjusted gross income, and, thus, is unavailable to beneficiaries claiming the standard deduction.[17]

*Charitable Deduction for Entity:*    Estates and trusts, like individuals, are entitled to a charitable deduction but the deduction available to estates and trusts differs in a two important respects from that available to an individual. First, the deduction is unlimited.[18] It is not subject to a percentage limitation as it is with individuals. Thus, if all of the estate or trust's income is paid to charity, all of it qualifies for the charitable deduction. Second, only estate or trust income distributable or set aside for charity pursuant to the terms of the governing instrument qualify for the charitable deduction.[19] Thus, no deduction is available to intestate estates which escheat as there is no governing instrument.

## § 15.6    Income Taxation of Grantor Trusts

Sections 671 through 677 set forth a series of rule under which a grantor of an inter vivos trust may be required to include in her gross income either the trust's ordinary income or capital gains or both. Generally, these rules apply whenever the grantor has retained an economic interest or "too much power over" either the income interest or the remainder interest or both. The most important of the provisions are as follows:

*Grantor Retains a Reversionary Interest:*    The grantor is treated as the owner of any portion of a trust (that is the income interest or the remainder) in which the grantor has a reversionary interest if the value of the grantor's reversionary interest exceeds 5% of the value of such portion.[1] Harry creates a trust to pay the income to Able for life, and when Able dies, to pay the trust corpus to distribute the corpus to Harry. Harry's owns the entire reversion in this trust. Thus all of the trust's capital gains are included in Harry's gross income under section 673. Section 673 does not apply to the grantor's reversion in a trust in which any lineal descendant has a present interest, such as the right to receive the income, if the grantor's reversion would take affect solely because the lineal descendant were to die under age 21.[2] Thus, if grantor has a reversion in a section 2503(c) trust[3] which would become possessory

---

**17.**   Treas. Reg. § 1.642(h)–2(a).

**18.**   I.R.C. § 642(c).

**19.**   Id.

**§ 15.6**

**1.**   I.R.C. § 673(a).

**2.**   I.R.C. § 673(b).

**3.**   See § 15.2, note 39 and accompanying text.

should the grantor's lineal descendant die under age 21, the trust's capital gains would not be included in the grantor's gross income.

*Power to Control Beneficiary Enjoyment or Retains Administrative Control:* Section 674 and 675 apply when the grantor, whether or not in the capacity of trustee, *or a nonadverse party* retains the power to control the beneficial enjoyment of the trust power or retains certain administrative powers over the trust. It bears emphasis that section 674 and 675 can apply even if the grantor has no retained power and the only "tainted" power is held by a nonadverse party.

In particular, section 674 treats the grantor as the owner of the portion of any trust over which the grantor or a nonadverse party has a "power of disposition." A power of disposition is a power "to dispose of the beneficial enjoyment of the corpus or income unless the power"[4] is specifically excepted under the provisions of either section 674(b), (c) or (d). The exceptions to the general rule of section 674, all of which are highly nuanced and thus capable of being inapplicable absent careful planning and drafting relate to the following: (1) power to apply income to support a dependent, (2) power exercisable only the occurrence of an event, (3) testamentary power, (4) power affecting charities, (5) power to distribute corpus, (6) power to withhold income temporarily, (7) power to withhold income during the beneficiary's disability, (8) powers exercisable by certain independent trustees and (9) powers limited by an ascertainable standard.

Section 675 applies to powers held by the grantor or a nonadverse party without the consent of an adverse party (1) permitting the grantor or any other person to deal with the trust assets for less and adequate and full consideration, (2) enabling the grantor to borrow trust assets without adequate interest or security, (3) permitting the exercise of certain powers of administration.

Because the rules of section 674 and 675 are highly nuanced and not easily committed to memory, whenever an attorney prepares an inter vivos trust in which the grantor has any retained power, the attorney would be well-advised to carefully scrutinize sections 674 and 675 to assure that the power held by the grantor or a nonadverse party will not result in any adverse income tax consequences to the grantor.

*Revocable Trust:* Under section 676 the grantor is treated as the owner of any portion of a trust where the title to the portion can be revested in the grantor by a power exercisable by the grantor or a nonadverse power. The typical trust to which section 676 applies is the revocable trust. Thus, is Ralph transfers property

**4.** Treas. Reg. § 1.674(a)–1(b).

into a revocable trust to pay the income to Sally for life, remainder to Don and Ralph retains the power to revoke the trust, or the trust on its face is irrevocable but the trustee-bank can distribute income or corpus to Ralph, all of the trusts ordinary income and capital gains will be included in Ralph's gross income.

*Trust's Whose Income Payable to Grantor:*  With some limited exceptions, the grantor is treated as the owner of any portion of a trust the income from which is, or may be, distributed to the grantor or the grantor's spouse or held or accumulated for future distribution to the grantor or the grantor's spouse.[5] In addition, the grantor is treated as the owner of any portion of a trust the income from which is, or may be applied, applied towards to payment of premiums on life insurance policies on the grantor or grantor spouse's life.[6]

The typical section 677 trust includes the trust where either the grantor or the grantor's spouse is entitled to the income for life. But it also includes trusts where the trustee has discretion to distribute income or corpus to the grantor or the grantor's spouse. Thus, if Carrie creates a trust to pay the income to Mary for life, remainder to Jo and empowers the trustee to distribute the corpus to the grantor, all of the ordinary income and capital gains will be included in the grantor's gross income even if the trust income in the particular taxable year is actually distributed to Mary and all of the gains are retained by the trustee as part of the principal of the trust. Carrie includes these in gross income because the trustee could have distributed them to her. It is irrelevant that the trustee did not do so.

In common with the fact that not all completed gifts in trust are necessarily excluded from the grantor's gross estate, not all completed gifts in trust necessarily result in the income from the gifted property being excluded from the grantor's gross income. For example, suppose George creates a $100,000 trust to pay the income to Donna for life, remainder to Sam. The trustee decides to purchase a life insurance policy on George's life either in the trustee's exercise of its discretion to make trust investments or because the trust instrument expressly directed that such invest-ment be made. The trustee anticipates paying the insurance premi-ums with trust income and deducting those premiums from the amount of income otherwise payable to Donna. While the gift of the $100,000 is a completed gift for gift tax purposes, to the extent trust income can be used to purchase the life insurance policy once acquired on George's life, it is includible in his gross income. Because of this rule, it is not uncommon for life insurance trusts to

**5.**  I.R.C. § 677(a).
**6.**  Id.

be unfunded such that the trust has no income that could be included in the grantor's gross income. Of course, this necessitates other ways for the trustee to acquire funds to pay premiums, such as subsequent year gifts from the grantor.

*Income Taxation of Beneficiary's With a General Power of Appointment:* Among the grantor trust provisions of the Code is a provision treating the holder of a general power of appointment exercisable during the donee's life (as distinguished from solely by the donee's will) as the owner of the portion of the trust over which the lifetime general power is exercisable.[7] Thus, suppose Patricia creates a trust to pay the income to Don for life, remainder to Alice. The trustee is granted the discretion to accumulate income rather than pay it to Don. However, Don is granted a lifetime general power to distribute the trust corpus to himself. Under section 678 all of the trust income and gains are included in Don's gross income even though none of the income or gains are actually distributed to Don. Because of section 678, persons creating marital deduction qualifying trusts by coupling the spouse's income interest with a general power of appointment often prefer to grant the spouse a general testamentary, rather than a general inter vivos, power of appointment.

**7.** I.R.C. § 678.

## CHART I

## Computation of Federal Estate Tax Due For Decedents Dying After December 31, 1981

GROSS ESTATE

    § 2031(a) (valuation at date of death).

    § 2032 (alternate valuation method).

    § 2032A (special use valuation method).

    § 2033 Property interests owned at death including under § 2034 the

MINUS    surviving spouse's dower or curtesy interest or an estate in lieu thereof.

    § 2035 Transfers within 3 years of death.

    § 2036 Transfers with retained life estates.

    § 2037 Transfers conditioned on surviving decedent.

    § 2038 Revocable Transfers.

    § 2039 Annuities.

    § 2040 Jointly-owned property.

    § 2041 Property subject to general power of appointment.

    § 2042 Life insurance on decedent's life.

    § 2044 Qualified Terminable Interest Property.

    § 2046 Disclaimers.

DEDUCTIONS FROM GROSS ESTATE

    § 2053 Funeral, debts, expenses and taxes.

    § 2054 Losses incurred during administration.

    § 2055 Unlimited charitable deduction.

EQUALS    § 2056 Unlimited marital deduction.

    § 2058 State Death Taxes (for persons dying after 2004).

TAXABLE ESTATE    Defined § 2051.

PLUS

ADJUSTED TAXABLE GIFTS    (post-1976 gifts in excess of annual exclusion, other than those gifts includible in gross estate.)

EQUALS

TAX BASE

APPLY TAX RATES
(§ 2001)

TENTATIVE TAX BEFORE CREDITS

MINUS

GIFT TAX PAYABLE ON POST-1976 GIFTS    § 2001(b)(2).

    § 2010 Unified Credit.

MINUS    § 2011 State death tax credit (for decedent's dying before 2005).

OTHER CREDITS    § 2012 Gift tax credit on pre-1977 gifts.

    § 2013 Credit for tax on prior transfers.

EQUALS    § 2014 Foreign death tax credit.

    § 2015 Credit for death tax on remainder.

FEDERAL ESTATE TAX DUE BEFORE SURCHARGE

PLUS    § 2001(c)(2) Phaseout of graduated rates and unified credit.

FEDERAL ESTATE TAX DUE

(M., K. & W.) Wills, Trusts & Est. HB—26

# CHART II

## Computation of Federal Gift Tax
## Due on post–1981 transfers

GIFTS DURING CALENDAR    § 2511 Defined generally.
  YEAR
                        § 2512 Valuation of gifts.
    MINUS               § 2513 Gifts attributable from spouse.
                        § 2514 Powers of appointment.
                        § 2516 Property settlement agreements.
                        § 2517 Annuities.
                        § 2518 Disclaimers.
                        § 2519 Qualifying income interest for life.

GIFTS ATTRIBUTABLE TO    § 2513 Gift by husband or wife to third party.
  SPOUSE

    EQUALS

GIFTS DURING CALENDAR
  YEAR BEFORE DEDUC-
  TIONS AND EXCLUSIONS

    MINUS

DEDUCTIONS AND EXCLU-    § 2503(b), (c) & (e) Annual exclusion of $10,000 per donee for present interests.
  SIONS
    EQUALS               (Must be claimed first); gifts of certain educational and medical expenses.
                        § 2522 Unlimited charitable deduction.
                        § 2523 Unlimited marital deduction.

TAXABLE GIFTS FOR CAL-   § 2503(a) Defined.
  ENDAR YEAR

    PLUS

TAXABLE GIFTS FOR PRIOR   § 2504 Defined.
  YEARS

    APPLY TAX RATES
      (§ 2502)

TAX ON TOTAL GIFTS

    MINUS

TAX ON GIFTS FOR PRIOR
  PERIODS

    EQUALS

TAX BEFORE UNIFIED
  CREDIT

    MINUS

UNIFIED CREDIT           § 2505 Defined.

    EQUALS

GIFT TAX DUE BEFORE SURCHARGE

    PLUS                 § 2001(c)(2) Phaseout of graduated rates and unified credit.

    FEDERAL GIFT TAX DUE

# Table of Cases

## A

A. v. B., 158 N.J. 51, 726 A.2d 924 (N.J.1999)—§ **7.4, n. 6.**

Ablin v. Richard O'Brien Plastering Co., 885 P.2d 289 (Colo.App.1994)—§ **2.5, n. 2.**

Abney v. Western Res. Mut. Cas. Co., 76 Ohio App.3d 424, 602 N.E.2d 348 (Ohio App. 12 Dist.1991)—§ **4.5, n. 15.**

Abo Petroleum Corp. v. Amstutz, 93 N.M. 332, 600 P.2d 278 (N.M.1979)—§ **11.1, n. 4.**

Abram v. Wilson, 220 N.E.2d 739 (Ohio Prob.1966)—§ **11.2, n. 16.**

Abrams v. Templeton, 320 S.C. 325, 465 S.E.2d 117 (S.C.App.1995)—§ **10.1, n. 21; § 11.4, n. 16.**

Ackel v. Ackel, 595 So.2d 739 (La.App. 5 Cir.1992)—§ **3.8, n. 34.**

Adams v. Jankouskas, 452 A.2d 148 (Del.Supr.1982)—§ **2.11, n. 40.**

Adams v. Vidal, 60 So.2d 545 (Fla. 1952)—§ **10.1, n. 36.**

Adkins v. Oppio, 105 Nev. 34, 769 P.2d 62 (Nev.1989)—§ **4.9, n. 1.**

Adriance v. Higgins, 113 F.2d 1013 (2nd Cir.1940)—§ **15.3, n. 30.**

Aetna Life Ins. Co. v. Boober, 56 Wash. App. 567, 784 P.2d 186 (Wash.App. Div. 1 1990)—§ **3.8, n. 35.**

Aetna Life Ins. Co. v. Hussey, 63 Ohio St.3d 640, 590 N.E.2d 724 (Ohio 1992)—§ **13.2, n. 28.**

Agans, In re Estate of, 196 Ariz. 367, 998 P.2d 449 (Ariz.App. Div. 1 1999)—§ **3.4, n. 14.**

Agnew, Matter of, 818 F.2d 1284 (7th Cir.1987)—§ **13.2, n. 17.**

Akers v. Hodel, 871 F.2d 924 (10th Cir. 1989)—§ **7.1, n. 6.**

Albro v. Allen, 434 Mich. 271, 454 N.W.2d 85 (Mich.1990)—§ **5.5, n. 25.**

Alexander, In re Estate of, 445 So.2d 836 (Miss.1984)—§ **2.11, n. 36.**

Alexander v. Alexander, 537 N.E.2d 1310 (Ohio Prob.1988)—§ **2.9, n. 6.**

Alexander v. Georgia Baptist Foundation Inc., 245 Ga. 545, 266 S.E.2d 165 (Ga.1980)—§ **9.7, n. 51.**

Allard v. Pacific Nat. Bank, 99 Wash.2d 394, 663 P.2d 104 (Wash.1983)—§ **12.6, n. 35.**

Allen, Matter of Estate of, 237 Mont. 114, 772 P.2d 297 (Mont.1989)—§ **10.4, n. 21.**

Allen v. Amoco Production Co., 114 N.M. 18, 833 P.2d 1199 (N.M.App. 1992)—§ **12.3, n. 12.**

Allen v. Dalk, 826 So.2d 245 (Fla. 2002)—§ **4.1, n. 18.**

Allen v. Hall, 328 Or. 276, 974 P.2d 199 (Or.1999)—§ **7.3, n. 3.**

Allen v. Storer, 235 Ill.App.3d 5, 175 Ill.Dec. 805, 600 N.E.2d 1263 (Ill. App. 4 Dist.1992)—§ **1.2, n. 21.**

Aloha Lumber Corp. v. University of Alaska, 994 P.2d 991 (Alaska 1999)—§ **12.6, n. 40.**

Alsenz v. Alsenz, 101 S.W.3d 648 (Tex. App.-Hous. (1 Dist.) 2003)—§ **3.8, n. 15.**

Altazan, Succession of, 682 So.2d 1320 (La.App. 1 Cir.1996)—§ **5.2, n. 14.**

Altstatt, In re, 321 Or. 324, 897 P.2d 1164 (Or.1995)—§ **12.5, n. 66.**

Amcore Bank, N.A. v. Hahnaman–Albrecht, Inc., 326 Ill.App.3d 126, 259 Ill.Dec. 694, 759 N.E.2d 174 (Ill.App. 2 Dist.2001)—§ **9.2, n. 22, 26.**

American Cancer Soc., St. Louis Division v. Hammerstein, 631 S.W.2d 858 (Mo.App. E.D.1981)—§ **9.5, n. 7.**

American Nat. Bank and Trust Co. of Chicago v. Vinson, 273 Ill.App.3d 541, 210 Ill.Dec. 426, 653 N.E.2d 13 (Ill.App. 1 Dist.1995)—§ **6.4, n. 45, 55.**

American Nat. Bank of Cheyenne, Wyo. v. Miller, 899 P.2d 1337 (Wyo. 1995)—§ **9.6, n. 37.**

American Sec. & Trust Co. v. Utley, 382 F.2d 451, 127 U.S.App.D.C. 235 (D.C.Cir.1967)—§ **13.1, n. 41.**

American Western Life Ins. Co. v. Hooker, 622 P.2d 775 (Utah 1980)—§ **5.5, n. 15.**

# B

Byrum, United States v., 408 U.S. 125, 92 S.Ct. 2382, 33 L.Ed.2d 238 (1972)—§ **15.3, n. 51.**

# C

Caffrey, Matter of Estate of, 120 Ill. App.3d 917, 76 Ill.Dec. 493, 458 N.E.2d 1147 (Ill.App. 1 Dist.1983)— § **3.4, n. 6.**

Calcutt, Estate of v. Calcutt, 576 N.E.2d 1288 (Ind.App. 5 Dist.1991)—§ **3.9, n. 13, 34.**

Calden, Estate of, 712 A.2d 522 (Me. 1998)—§ **2.4, n. 7; § 8.3, n. 23.**

Caldwell v. Walraven, 268 Ga. 444, 490 S.E.2d 384 (Ga.1997)—§ **9.3, n. 17.**

Calhoun v. Higgins, 103 Or.App. 414, 797 P.2d 404 (Or.App.1990)—§ **4.5, n. 9.**

Calhoun's Will, Matter of, 47 N.C.App. 472, 267 S.E.2d 385 (N.C.App. 1980)—§ **12.1, n. 51.**

Califano v. Boles, 443 U.S. 282, 99 S.Ct. 2767, 61 L.Ed.2d 541 (1979)—§ **2.11, n. 32.**

Came, In re Estate of, 129 N.H. 544, 529 A.2d 962 (N.H.1987)—§ **3.5, n. 14.**

Camerlo v. Howard Johnson Co., 710 F.2d 987 (3rd Cir.1983)—§ **11.7, n. 10.**

Camin's Estate, In re, 212 Neb. 490, 323 N.W.2d 827 (Neb.1982)—§ **7.1, n. 15.**

Canoy v. Canoy, 135 N.C.App. 326, 520 S.E.2d 128 (N.C.App.1999)—§ **10.1, n. 34.**

Cappetta, In re Estate of, 315 Ill.App.3d 414, 247 Ill.Dec. 962, 733 N.E.2d 426 (Ill.App. 2 Dist.2000)—§ **9.7, n. 30.**

Carey v. Lincoln Loan Co., 165 Or.App. 657, 998 P.2d 724 (Or.App.2000)— § **11.8, n. 21, 22.**

Cargill, Matter of Will of, 420 N.W.2d 268 (Minn.App.1988)—§ **12.10, n. 34.**

Carlson v. Carlson, 113 Cal.Rptr. 722, 521 P.2d 1114 (Cal.1974)—§ **3.8, n. 52.**

Carr v. Carr, 120 N.J. 336, 576 A.2d 872 (N.J.1990)—§ **2.11, n. 19.**

Cartee v. Lesley, 290 S.C. 333, 350 S.E.2d 388 (S.C.1986)—§ **12.8, n. 29.**

Carter v. Carter, 526 So.2d 141 (Fla. App. 3 Dist.1988)—§ **7.3, n. 11.**

Carter v. First United Methodist Church of Albany, 246 Ga. 352, 271 S.E.2d 493 (Ga.1980)—§ **5.3, n. 1.**

Casey, In re Estate of, 222 Ill.App.3d 12, 164 Ill.Dec. 529, 583 N.E.2d 83 (Ill. App. 1 Dist.1991)—§ **4.9, n. 14.**

Cason v. Taylor, 51 S.W.3d 397 (Tex. App.-Waco 2001)—§ **5.1, n. 4.**

Cast v. National Bank of Commerce Trust & Sav. Ass'n of Lincoln, 186 Neb. 385, 183 N.W.2d 485 (Neb. 1971)—§ **11.8, n. 13.**

Cavenaugh, Estate of v. Commissioner, 51 F.3d 597 (5th Cir.1995)—§ **3.8, n. 3.**

Cavin, In re Estate of, 728 A.2d 92 (D.C. 1999)—§ **12.7, n. 33.**

Central Nat. Bank of Cleveland v. Fitzwilliam, 12 Ohio St.3d 51, 465 N.E.2d 408 (Ohio 1984)—§ **13.2, n. 16.**

Central Trust Co. of Northern Ohio, N.A. v. Smith, 50 Ohio St.3d 133, 553 N.E.2d 265 (Ohio 1990)—§ **10.3, n. 2.**

Certain Scholarship Funds, In re, 133 N.H. 227, 575 A.2d 1325 (N.H. 1990)—§ **9.7, n. 20.**

Chandler v. Central Oil Corp., Inc., 253 Kan. 50, 853 P.2d 649 (Kan.1993)— § **2.11, n. 7.**

Chandler, United States v., 410 U.S. 257, 93 S.Ct. 880, 35 L.Ed.2d 247 (1973)—§ **4.5, n. 14.**

Chapman v. Chapman, 577 A.2d 775 (Me.1990)—§ **8.1, n. 18.**

Charleston Nat. Bank v. Thru the Bible Radio Network, 203 W.Va. 345, 507 S.E.2d 708 (W.Va.1998)—§ **4.4, n. 6.**

Chase v. Pevear, 383 Mass. 350, 419 N.E.2d 1358 (Mass.1981)—§ **12.7, n. 25.**

Chasel, Matter of Estate of, 725 P.2d 1345 (Utah 1986)—§ **12.1, n. 45.**

Chemical Bank, Matter of, 90 Misc.2d 727, 395 N.Y.S.2d 917 (N.Y.Sup. 1977)—§ **11.2, n. 11.**

Cheuvront v. Haley, 444 S.W.2d 734 (Ky.1969)—§ **2.4, n. 9; § 10.2, n. 19.**

Chicago Title and Trust Co. v. Steinitz, 288 Ill.App.3d 926, 224 Ill.Dec. 354, 681 N.E.2d 669 (Ill.App. 1 Dist. 1997)—§ **1.3, n. 9.**

Chiesi, Estate of v. First Citizens Bank, N.A., 613 N.E.2d 14 (Ind.1993)— § **2.7, n. 32.**

Chlebos, In re Estate of, 194 Ill.App.3d 46, 141 Ill.Dec. 23, 550 N.E.2d 1069 (Ill.App. 1 Dist.1990)—§ **7.1, n. 9.**

Choyce, Succession of, 183 So.2d 457 (La.App. 2 Cir.1966)—§ **2.11, n. 10.**

Chrisman, In re Estate of, 746 S.W.2d 131 (Mo.App. E.D.1988)—§ **12.8, n. 55.**

Chrysler v. Commissioner, 44 T.C. 55 (Tax Ct.1965)—§ **15.3, n. 48.**

## D

# F

# I

Murdock, Matter of Estate of, 20 Kan. App.2d 170, 884 P.2d 749 (Kan.App. 1994)—§ **9.6, n. 8; § 9.7, n. 64.**

Murphy, Estate of, 35 Or.App. 225, 580 P.2d 1078 (Or.App.1978)—§ **10.3, n. 21.**

Murphy v. Glenn, 964 P.2d 581 (Colo. App.1998)—§ **4.9, n. 11.**

Musselman v. Mitchell, 46 Or.App. 299, 611 P.2d 675 (Or.App.1980)—§ **4.9, n. 24.**

Myers v. Maxey, 915 P.2d 940 (Okla. App. Div. 1 1995)—§ **7.2, n. 2.**

Myers v. Weems, 128 Or.App. 444, 876 P.2d 861 (Or.App.1994)—§ **6.4, n. 2.**

# N

Nable v. Godfrey's Estate, 403 So.2d 1038 (Fla.App. 5 Dist.1981)—§ **2.7, n. 6.**

Nagel, Matter of Estate of, 580 N.W.2d 810 (Iowa 1998)—§ **13.1, n. 5.**

Nahar v. Nahar, 656 So.2d 225 (Fla.App. 3 Dist.1995)—§ **3.2, n. 18.**

National Bank of Commerce, United States v., 472 U.S. 713, 105 S.Ct. 2919, 86 L.Ed.2d 565 (1985)—§ **13.2, n. 12.**

National Bank of Commerce in Memphis v. Henslee, 179 F.Supp. 346 (M.D.Tenn.1959)—§ **15.3, n. 48.**

National City Bank of Cleveland v. Ford, 299 N.E.2d 310 (Ohio Com.Pl. 1973)—§ **10.2, n. 16.**

National Home Life Assur. Co. v. Patterson, 746 P.2d 696 (Okla.App. Div. 3 1987)—§ **2.10, n. 38.**

NationsBank of Virginia, N.A. v. Estate of Grandy, 248 Va. 557, 450 S.E.2d 140 (Va.1994)—§ **9.5, n. 3.**

Natl. City Bank v. Beyer, 89 Ohio St.3d 152, 729 N.E.2d 711 (Ohio 2000)— § **10.1, n. 4, 14.**

Naumoff, In re Estate of, 301 A.D.2d 802, 754 N.Y.S.2d 70 (N.Y.A.D. 3 Dept.2003)—§ **7.2, n. 26.**

NC Illinois Trust Co. v. First Illini Bancorp, Inc., 323 Ill.App.3d 254, 256 Ill.Dec. 925, 752 N.E.2d 1167 (Ill. App. 3 Dist.2001)—§ **12.8, n. 22, 29, 49.**

Nelson, In re Estate of, 253 Neb. 414, 571 N.W.2d 269 (Neb.1997)—§ **10.4, n. 4.**

Nelson, Matter of Estate of, 419 N.W.2d 915 (N.D.1988)—§ **6.2, n. 16.**

Nelson v. Kring, 225 Kan. 499, 592 P.2d 438 (Kan.1979)—§ **11.6, n. 4, 10.**

Nelson v. Maiorana, 395 Mass. 87, 478 N.E.2d 945 (Mass.1985)—§ **12.6, n. 27.**

Nelson v. McGoldrick, 127 Wash.2d 124, 896 P.2d 1258 (Wash.1995)—§ **2.8, n. 36.**

Neumann v. Rogstad, 232 Mont. 24, 757 P.2d 761 (Mont.1988)—§ **2.11, n. 39.**

Newhoff's Will, Matter of, 107 Misc.2d 589, 435 N.Y.S.2d 632 (N.Y.Sur. 1980)—§ **12.7, n. 24.**

Newick v. Mason, 581 A.2d 1269 (Me. 1990)—§ **9.5, n. 36.**

Newmark v. Williams, 588 A.2d 1108 (Del.Supr.1991)—§ **14.4, n. 1.**

Nichols Hills Bank v. McCool, 104 Wash.2d 78, 701 P.2d 1114 (Wash. 1985)—§ **3.8, n. 5.**

Nickel v. Bank of America Nat. Trust and Sav. Ass'n, 290 F.3d 1134 (9th Cir.2002)—§ **12.8, n. 13.**

Nielson, Estate of, 105 Cal.App.3d 796, 165 Cal.Rptr. 319 (Cal.App. 4 Dist. 1980)—§ **5.1, n. 6.**

Nile v. Nile, 432 Mass. 390, 734 N.E.2d 1153 (Mass.2000)—§ **1.2, n. 23.**

Noble v. McNerney, 165 Mich.App. 586, 419 N.W.2d 424 (Mich.App.1988)— § **12.5, n. 21.**

Noggle v. Bank of America, 82 Cal. Rptr.2d 829 (Cal.App. 2 Dist.1999)— § **12.8, n. 21.**

Norton, Matter of Estate of, 330 N.C. 378, 410 S.E.2d 484 (N.C.1991)— § **6.2, n. 2.**

Norton v. Bridges, 712 F.2d 1156 (7th Cir.1983)—§ **12.8, n. 2.**

Norton v. Hinson, 337 Ark. 487, 989 S.W.2d 535 (Ark.1999)—§ **4.3, n. 4.**

Norwood, Estate of, 178 Mich.App. 345, 443 N.W.2d 798 (Mich.App.1989)— § **8.1, n. 7.**

Nunnally v. Trust Co. Bank, 244 Ga. 697, 261 S.E.2d 621 (Ga.1979)— § **2.10, n. 2.**

Nutis v. Schottenstein Trustees, 41 Ohio App.3d 63, 534 N.E.2d 380 (Ohio App. 10 Dist.1987)—§ **11.7, n. 13.**

Nwabara v. Willacy, 135 Ohio App.3d 120, 733 N.E.2d 267 (Ohio App. 8 Dist.1999)—§ **2.9, n. 6.**

# O

Oak's Oil Service, Inc. v. Massachusetts Bay Transp. Authority, 15 Mass.App. Ct. 593, 447 N.E.2d 27 (Mass.App.Ct. 1983)—§ **11.6, n. 23.**

Oberly v. Kirby, 592 A.2d 445 (Del. Supr.1991)—§ **12.9, n. 6.**

# S

N.E.2d 799 (N.Y.1996)—§ **11.7, n. 2, 5.**

Syracuse University, Application of, 171 N.Y.S.2d 545, 148 N.E.2d 671 (N.Y. 1958)—§ **9.7, n. 61.**

# T

Taboni ex rel. Taboni v. Estate of Longo, 810 So.2d 1142 (La.2002)—§ **12.2, n. 6.**

Taliaferro v. Taliaferro, 260 Kan. 573, 921 P.2d 803 (Kan.1996)—§ **4.6, n. 3.**

Tannler v. DHSS, 211 Wis.2d 179, 564 N.W.2d 735 (Wis.1997)—§ **3.7, n. 46.**

Tate's Estate, In re, 543 S.W.2d 588 (Tenn.1976)—§ **12.10, n. 38.**

Taylor, Matter of, 693 N.E.2d 526 (Ind. 1998)—§ **3.9, n. 24.**

Taylor v. Abernethy, 149 N.C.App. 263, 560 S.E.2d 233 (N.C.App.2002)— § **4.9, n. 33.**

Taylor v. Crocker Nat. Bank, 205 Cal. App.3d 459, 252 Cal.Rptr. 388 (Cal. App. 4 Dist.1988)—§ **12.6, n. 23.**

Taylor v. Hutchinson, 17 Ariz.App. 301, 497 P.2d 527 (Ariz.App. Div. 1 1972)—§ **9.6, n. 2.**

Temple Beth Israel v. Feiss, 167 Or.App. 113, 2 P.3d 388 (Or.App.2000)— § **10.1, n. 6, 19.**

Territorial Sav. & Loan Ass'n v. Baird, 781 P.2d 452 (Utah App.1989)— § **13.1, n. 2.**

Thellusson v. Woodford, 1805 WL 1031 (Unknown Court 1805)—§ **11.1, n. 8;** § **11.9;** § **11.9, n. 1.**

Thomann, In re Estate of, 649 N.W.2d 1 (Iowa 2002)—§ **2.7, n. 4.**

Thomas, In re, (1984) 1 W.L.R. 237 (1983)—§ **3.10, n. 6.**

Thomas v. Reid, 94 N.M. 241, 608 P.2d 1123 (N.M.1980)—§ **6.4, n. 12.**

Thomas v. Sullivan, 922 F.2d 132 (2nd Cir.1990)—§ **2.11, n. 32.**

Thompson, In re, [1934] 1 Ch. 342— § **9.7, n. 23.**

Thompson v. Nesheim, 280 Minn. 407, 159 N.W.2d 910 (Minn.1968)—§ **6.4, n. 25.**

Thor v. McDearmid, 63 Wash.App. 193, 817 P.2d 1380 (Wash.App. Div. 3 1991)—§ **6.4, n. 31.**

Thornhill v. Riegg, 95 N.C.App. 532, 383 S.E.2d 447 (N.C.App.1989)—§ **11.2, n. 15.**

Thornton, Matter of, 192 Mich.App. 709, 481 N.W.2d 828 (Mich.App.1992)— § **2.5, n. 10.**

Tierce v. Macedonia United Methodist Church of Northport, 519 So.2d 451 (Ala.1987)—§ **6.2, n. 7.**

Tierney v. Department of Human Services, 793 A.2d 210 (R.I.2002)— § **13.2, n. 12.**

Tobin, Matter of, 417 Mass. 81, 628 N.E.2d 1268 (Mass.1994)—§ **12.5, n. 17, 20.**

Todd v. Cartwright, 684 S.W.2d 154 (Tex.App.-Hous. (14 Dist.) 1984)— § **4.9, n. 4.**

Tomlinson v. Tomlinson, 960 S.W.2d 337 (Tex.App.-Corpus Christi 1997)—§ **4.6, n. 18.**

Tomlinson's Estate, In re, 65 Ill.2d 382, 3 Ill.Dec. 699, 359 N.E.2d 109 (Ill. 1976)—§ **9.7, n. 50.**

Toon v. Gerth, 735 N.E.2d 314 (Ind.App. 2000)—§ **12.1, n. 52.**

Totten, In re, 179 N.Y. 112, 71 N.E. 748 (N.Y.1904)—§ **4.6, n. 17.**

Trabits v. First Nat. Bank of Mobile, 345 So.2d 1347 (Ala.1977)—§ **9.6, n. 24.**

Traders Travel Intern., Inc. v. Howser, 69 Haw. 609, 753 P.2d 244 (Hawai'i 1988)—§ **13.2, n. 19.**

Trammell v. Elliott, 230 Ga. 841, 199 S.E.2d 194 (Ga.1973)—§ **9.7, n. 15.**

Transamerica Occidental Life Ins. Co. v. Burke, 179 W.Va. 331, 368 S.E.2d 301 (W.Va.1988)—§ **6.1, n. 19.**

Trask v. Butler, 123 Wash.2d 835, 872 P.2d 1080 (Wash.1994)—§ **12.8, n. 98.**

Trim v. Daniels, 862 S.W.2d 8 (Tex. App.-Hous. (1 Dist.) 1992)—§ **4.2, n. 2.**

Trimble v. Gordon, 430 U.S. 762, 97 S.Ct. 1459, 52 L.Ed.2d 31 (1977)— § **2.9, n. 5.**

Trout v. Parker, 72 Ohio App.3d 720, 595 N.E.2d 1015 (Ohio App. 4 Dist. 1991)—§ **5.5, n. 6.**

Troy v. Hart, 116 Md.App. 468, 697 A.2d 113 (Md.App.1997)—§ **2.8, n. 10.**

Trust Agreement of Westervelt v. First Interstate Bank of Northern Indiana, 551 N.E.2d 1180 (Ind.App. 4 Dist. 1990)—§ **10.1, n. 52.**

Trust Created by Belgard, Matter of, 829 P.2d 457 (Colo.App.1991)— § **2.10, n. 21.**

Trust Created by Hill, Matter of, 499 N.W.2d 475 (Minn.App.1993)— § **12.5, n. 43;** § **12.8, n. 5.**

Trust Created Under Will Dated Nov. 15, 1917 of Cunha, In re, 88 P.3d 202 (Hawai'i 2004)—§ **12.5, n. 6.**

Trustees of Schools of Tp. No. 1 v. Batdorf, 6 Ill.2d 486, 130 N.E.2d 111 (Ill.1955)—§ **11.6, n. 17.**

# W

# Y

# Z

*

# Table of Uniform Probate Code Sections

# Table of Restatement References

# Index

References are to Pages

**499**

**ATTESTATION CLAUSE**
See Witnesses

**ATTORNEYS FEES**
See also Legal Profession
Award to beneficiaries, 300
Bar fee schedules, 296
Estate planning services, 297
Fiduciary-attorney, 301
Indemnification of fiduciaries for, 300
Litigant charged with, 301
Time spent, 298

**BANKS**
Liability for dealing with agent, 329
Participating in breach of trust, 329
Self-deposit, 334

**BASIS**
Generally, 375
Gift tax, 376
Estate tax, 376, 394

**BENEFICIARIES**
Indefinite, 208
Powers of appointment, 209

**BONA FIDE PURCHASER**
Defense to claim for reformation or resulting trust, 290
Donees, 331
Duty to inquire, 330
Gifts by incapacitated person, 298
Protection against unrecorded deed, 203
Registration of title, 330
Wrongful transfer by fiduciary, 329

**BOND**
Personal representatives, 303
Trustees, 304
Waiver, 303

**CAPACITY**
See Incapacity

**CHANGE IN THE LAW**
Date of death, 21
Date of execution of instrument, 20
Determination of heirs, 234
Elective share, 157
Fiduciary administration, 22
Future interests, 22
Powers of appointment, 247
Procedural changes, 23
Prospective overruling, 19
Retrospective application of statutes, 19
Reverter statutes, 267
Rule against perpetuities, 262
Unconstitutional laws, 21
Vested interests, 22

**CHARGE**
See Trusts

**CHARITABLE TRUSTS**
See also Cy Pres
Accumulations, 274
Attorney general, 218
Comparison with corporations, 223
Construction of restrictions, 219–20
Definition of charitable, 215
Gender restrictions, 217
Honorary trusts, 217
Maintenance of tombs, 216, 218
Narrow group of recipients, 216
Peculiarities of, 215
Promoting change in the law, 215
Racial restrictions, 216
Religious restrictions, 217
Restricted gift to charitable entity, 219
Settlor's right to enforce, 219
Social investing, 336
Special interests, 219
Standing to enforce, 218
Tax definition, 215

**CHILDREN BORN OUT OF WEDLOCK**
Construction of wills, 53
History and policy, 49
Inheritance by parents, 53
Inheritance from father, 50
Inheritance from mother, 50
Planning, 54
Presumption of paternity, 51
Proof of paternity, 49
Social security, 53

**CLAIMS AGAINST ESTATE**
Arising after death, 354
Contingent, 354
Court approval of payment, 356
Covered by insurance, 355
Devises, 355
Estoppel, 356
Governmental, 355
Liability of personal representatives, 356
Non-claim statutes, 353
Notice to claimants, 353
Priorities, 352
Property, 355
Recoupment, 355
Statutes of limitation, 356
Suit pending, 354

**CLASS GIFTS**
See also Rule of Convenience, Rule Against Perpetuities
Adoption, 56
Anti-lapse statutes, 332
Children born out of wedlock, 53
Computation of shares, 29
Joint tenancy distinguished, 333
Step-children, 58
What constitutes a, 334

**CLEAN HANDS**
Defense to claim for equitable relief, 160

**CLEAR AND CONVINCING EVIDENCE**
Contracts to make wills, 127
Requirement for proof of gift, 117
Reformation, 159

**CODE OF PROFESSIONAL RESPONSIBILITY**
See Legal Profession

**CODICIL**
Republication of will, 151

**COMMUNITY PROPERTY**
Agreement, 92
Choice of law, 94
Classification of property, 90
Differences between community and elective share, 93
Election, 93
Federal law preemption, 95
History and rationale, 89
Income from and appreciation of separate property, 90
Life insurance, 91
Managerial powers, 93
Non-probate transfers, 92
Presumption, 92
Quasi-community property, 94
Separation, 91
Significance of classification, 88
Survival of right to, 93
Tax treatment, 89
Third persons, 92

**CONDITIONS**
Contrast with trust, 123
Charitable gifts, 220
Relating to divorce, 101
Relating to marriage, 100

**CONFIDENTIAL RELATIONSHIP**
See Undue Influence, Constructive Trust

**CONFLICT OF LAWS**
See also Domicile
Community property, 94
Designation by transferor, 14
Drafting, 18
Elective share, 88
Favoring validity, 18
Interest analysis, 18
Law of forum, 17
Powers of appointment, 247
Renvoi, 15
Situs, 15

**CONSENT**
By one of several beneficiaries, 327
Contract between fiduciary and beneficiary, 335

**CONSENT**—Cont'd
Defense to breach of trust, 327
Incapacitated beneficiary, 327
Knowledge of facts, 335

**CONSERVATOR**
Capacity of conservatee to make a gift, 164
Capacity of conservatee to make a will, 164
Comparison with trust, 191
Gifts by conservator, 166
Power to revoke a trust, 166
Standard for appointment, 164
Standing to challenge acts of, 321

**CONSTRUCTIVE TRUST**
Confidential relationship, 157
Deeds, 157
Fraud, 157
Ineffective revocation of a will, 133
Preventing change of will, 149
Promise by devisee or heir, 149
Promise to maintain insurance beneficiary, 352
Remedy for homicide, 40
Semi-secret trusts, 150
Third parties, 161
Will substitutes, 154

**CONTRACTS TO MAKE WILLS**
Clear and convincing evidence, 127
Effect on third parties, 128
Executory contracts, 127
Fairness, 127
Inter-vivos transfers, 128
Joint and mutual wills, 126
Part performance, 127
Planning, 129
Remedies, 129
Writing requirement, 126

**CORPORATIONS**
Liability for transfer of securities, 329
Trustee holding own stock, 334

**COTRUSTEES**
Contribution and indemnification, 323
Duty to participate, 323
Standing to sue, 321

**CREDITORS**
See also Spendthrift Trusts
Bankruptcy of trustee, 291
Contingent future interests, 343
Discretionary trusts, 343
Fraudulent conveyance, 342
Insurance, 351
Joint tenancy, 349
Nonprobate transfers, 350
Of trust beneficiaries, 343
Of donee of power of appointment, 242
Of settlor of discretionary trust, 343

**GENERATION SKIPPING TRANSFER TAX**—Cont'd
Transferor, 429

**GIFT TAX**
See also Estate tax
Annual exclusion amount, 383
Charitable deduction, 392
Completed gifts, 385
Consideration in money or money's worth, 379
Crummey power, 384
Disclaimers, 427
Donee, identity, 382
Dower and curtesy, release as consideration, 379
Five and Five power, 390
Incomplete gifts, 385
Marital deduction, 392
Medical payments, 383
Minors,
    Gifts (or Transfers) to Minors Act, 383
    Section 2503(c) trust, 383
    Transfer to, 383
Powers of appointment, 389
Property settlements, 392
Qualifying income interest for life, 392
Retained powers, 386
Split gifts for married persons, 380
Substantial adverse interest, 387
Taxable gift, defined, 379
Tuition payments, 383
Valuation of gifts,
    Generally, 380
    Retained interest of donor, 381

**GIFTS**
Causa mortis, 137
Checks, 116
Clear and convincing evidence, 117
Delivery, 116
Expectancies, 118
History of formal requirements, 113
Implied conditions, 140
Intangible property, 115
Power to revoke, 137
Promises, 118
Recording statutes, 114
Tangible personal property, 115
Testamentary transfers, 117

**GRANTOR TRUSTS**
Income interest retained, 447
Power of appointment, beneficiary with, 448
Power to control beneficial enjoyment, 446
Reversionary interest retained, 445
Revocable trusts, 446

**GUARDIAN**
See Conservator

**GUARDIAN AD LITEM**
See also Representation
Approval of accounts, 325
Consent to trust modification, 212

**HEIR**
Change in the law, 234
Choice of law, 35
Distinguished from devisees, 34
Doctrine of Worthier Title, 236
Equivalent words, 34
Fee tail, 235
Immediate devise to "heirs of A," 234
Incongruity when heir has life interest, 233
Rule in Shelley's Case, 236
Spouse as "heir", 35
Termination of trusts, 237
"Then," 234
Time of determination, 232
Use of word in drafting, 36, 232
Word of limitation, 234

**HOLOGRAPHIC WILLS**
Date, 111
Desirability of, 112
Printed matter, 111
Testamentary intent, 112

**HOMESTEAD**
See Limits on Testamentary Power

**HOMICIDE**
Alternate takers, 43
Avoiding forfeiture, 42
Degree of crime, 41
History, 40
Insurance, 43
Joint tenancy, 42–3
Other misconduct, 44
Proof of crime, 42
Protection of third parties, 44
Statutes, 41

**HONORARY TRUSTS**
See Charitable Trusts

**INCAPACITY**
Age requirements, 162
Bona-fide purchasers, 165
Changes as evidence of, 167
Evidence of subscribing witnesses, 163
Insane delusion, 163
Medical evidence, 163
Mental capacity, 162
Naturalness of will, 163
Powers of appointment, 243
Revocation of trust, 165
Standard for gifts, 165

†